INQUISITION

INQUISITION

THE PERSECUTION AND
PROSECUTION OF THE
REVEREND SUN MYUNG MOON

CARLTON SHERWOOD

REGNERY GATEWAY

WASHINGTON, D.C.

Library of Congress Cataloging-In-Publication Data

Sherwood, Carlton.
Inquisition : the persecution and prosecution of the Reverend Sun Myung Moon / Carlton Sherwood.
p.   cm.
Includes bibliographical references and index.
ISBN 0-89526-532-X
1. Moon, Sun Myung—Trials, litigation, etc.   2. Trials (Tax evasion)—New York (N.Y.)   3. Trials (Conspiracy)—New York (N.Y.)
4. Malicious prosecution—United States.   5. Persecution—United States.   6. Unification Church.   I. Title.
KF224.M59S54   1991
345.73'0233—dc20
[347.305233]   91-2896
                                                                   CIP

Published in the United States by
Regnery Gateway
1130 17th Street, NW
Washington, DC 20036

Distributed to the trade by
National Book Network
4720-A Boston Way
Lanham, MD 20706

1991 printing
Printed on acid free paper
Manufactured in the United States of America

My special thanks goes to Stephen Comiskey, my agent, lawyer and friend, for his patience, tenacity and wisdom. Also my deepest appreciation to the editors, Patricia Bozell and Tony Dolan, both first-class pros, and to my publishers, Regnery Gateway, Inc. for their diligence and grace under deadline pressures.

This book is dedicated to the many men and women at the Justice Department and U.S. Attorneys offices around the country who adhere passionately to the fundamental principles of equal justice under the law and continue to resist those who would corrupt and manipulate the legal process to further their own ambitions. To these individuals, courageous women and men who quietly rage against racism, bigotry and prejudice, we all owe a debt of gratitude.

PUBLISHER'S PREFACE

THIS is a book about religious and racial bigotry. It tells a story that should not have happened, particularly in America, particularly in the 1980s. It is a book about a boring tax case that was appealed to the U.S. Supreme Court, and a book about an unpopular religious leader who was sent to prison.

You may, or may not, like the Reverend Sun Myung Moon. You may, or may not, like the Unification Church, or the "Moonies," as they are often called. Frankly, I don't know much about them. But that is not the point, and that is not what *Inquisition* is all about.

Many people in our country believe that if the government wants to get you badly enough, it will. What most people don't know, or at least don't like to admit, is that people in the government will get you if they don't like your religion or what you stand for. *Inquisition* demonstrates, I am sorry to say, that government can, and indeed will, do just that.

Moon had plenty of people to help him fight the government. His trial lawyers were highly competent, and the best money could buy. In his appeal he was represented by Laurence Tribe, one of the best skilled constitutional lawyers in the country, professor at Harvard Law School, known to every judge, legal scholar and lawyer in America.

Moon had the support, as well, of the ACLU and dozens of religious people and organizations, from Jerry Falwell, to the Southern Christian Leadership Conference, to the Catholic Church. Former Senator and presidential candidate Eugene Mc-

Carthy, at least three states, and countless foundations and public interest groups all filed briefs on his behalf. But against the U.S. government, even that was not enough to beat a trumped-up charge.

We find it telling that somebody of the stature of Carlton Sherwood wrote this book. Sherwood is a hard-hitting and totally professional investigative reporter who has worked for some of the country's most powerful news organizations. He is the only reporter to have ever won both a Pulitzer Prize and a Peabody Award. He has broken many major stories. In *Inquisition* he breaks another. Most interestingly, he set out to break *the* story of the Unification Church and the Reverend Moon. Instead, he found a bigger story, a story of religious and racial bigotry, and a story of our tax and justice systems gone awry.

Moon went to federal prison for 18 months. The offense? The IRS and Justice Department called it criminal tax evasion. But what it amounted to was the acknowledged use of church money for everyday living expenses. Not an unusual phenomenon in virtually every mainline Protestant and Catholic Church in America. And the amount of taxes involved? Less than $8,000. The IRS and the Justice Department, and the politicians who liked Moon even less, got what they wanted. The federal court system went along. So did the press, who found Moon to be an easy target.

We have been publishing hard-hitting books, often by unpopular authors or about unpopular people, since 1947. As publishers, we are a conduit of information to the public, and when we see information that we think needs to be exposed, we expose it. That is exactly what we are doing in *Inquisition*.

The *Moon* tax case goes to the essence of the First Amendment. We hope this book will stand as an example of its fragility, and serve as a reminder to those who might otherwise take our constitutional freedoms for granted, that they do so at their peril.

Alfred S. Regnery
Publisher, Regnery Gateway, Inc.
March 1991

CONTENTS

INQUISITION

CHAPTER I

THE SECRET TAPES

Conscience is the inner voice which warns us that someone may be looking.

H.L. MENCKEN

THE Reverend Sun Myung Moon and Takeru Kamiyama were found guilty on the afternoon of May 18, 1982, on charges of tax evasion and conspiracy. After the defendants were convicted and the jury dismissed, defense counsel filed post-trial motions; they were argued and denied between July 5 and 14. Two days later, Moon and Kamiyama were sentenced and fined, although they remained free on bail pending appeal.

These highly structured events all took place in the open. They were orderly, neat, and normal, even dull, except to the defendants. Underneath all that coming and going, however, something else was taking place that was about to send the *Moon* case into the far reaches of legal outer space.

It was a random series of events, which began with a telephone call in June 1982, only weeks after the conclusion of the celebrated trial. The call involved a Moon juror and her longtime friend, a down-and-out handyman. Virginia Steward was officially designated Juror No. 3, and she was an upstate New York housewife with serious marital problems. She had also been somewhat un-

3

willingly recruited into jury duty in the federal courthouse of the
U.S. District Court, Southern District of New York.

Virginia Steward's chief virtue in the court's eyes was that she
apparently knew nothing about the Reverend Moon or the Unification Church. She later admitted that when people talked
about "the Moonies" all she could think of was her cousin Tom
Mooney because she had never heard of the Reverend Sun Myung
Moon.

With such ignorance, Mrs. Steward became an ideal juror for the
case, one of a rare few who had no preconceptions about Moon's
guilt or innocence—at least not until she was placed on the jury.

At the other end of the telephone line was John Curry, calling
long distance from Brooklyn. They had been friends—they both
stated later—for twenty-six years. Curry described their friendship as a brother-sister relationship. It made sense. Virginia had
been closer to Curry's wife. After Mrs. Curry's death the year
before, Steward and Curry had remained in touch.

For his part, John Curry was one of nature's congenital losers.
He lived in Brooklyn with four of his children and four of his
grandchildren. "I have," he later told the court, "a lot of pressures
on me."[1]

Indeed, he did. His wife was dead. His finances were in such
poor shape that his phone was disconnected during the Labor Day
weekend of 1982.

Curry did odd jobs for a very uncertain living: painting and
decorating for his son-in-law's company—and surveillance work.
What was an unsuccessful handyman doing playing detective?

Curry wasn't a licensed investigator or licensed anything. Although it is sometimes difficult for Americans who have always
lived in the quiet, predictable certainty of middle-class life to
understand, some ne'er-do-wells will work at just about anything
for a few bucks. And so John Curry did leg work for a couple of
detective agencies. Freelance surveillance work doesn't require
talent, just an ability to handle boredom and stay awake. That's
why it doesn't pay very well. Curry did even simpler stuff, like
taking statements on accident cases. As one associate described
John Curry, he wasn't "the forward type."

Another curious character in this curious drama was Curry's
boss, Bruce Romanoff.

Romanoff was fifty-five at the time, working as a security consultant because he had lost his P.I. ticket almost ten years before. In the course of a nearly twenty-year career as a dime store Philip Marlowe, Romanoff had been convicted of illegal wiretapping and invasion of privacy in 1966—both rather standard offenses in the real and dreary world of private detectives.

Seven years later it would get serious for Romanoff. This time, he was charged and convicted of trying to sell $8.4 million of stolen and forged cashier's checks. After serving his sentence, he was arrested again in 1979 on witness tampering charges in which it was claimed that Romanoff offered a $5,000 bribe to a rape victim if she would drop charges against his client. She didn't. Undeterred, Romanoff turned around and testified against the client. The court let him off with three years' probation ending in March 1982.[2]

Undaunted by life's reverses, Bruce Romanoff returned to his old profession, private investigation, albeit unlicensed—a rather common practice for the down-and-out shamus.

One of Bruce Romanoff's operatives was John Curry. Doing surveillance work for Romanoff netted John a couple thousand dollars over several years. In 1982 both were broke and in all kinds of trouble. Neither was especially bright, particularly Curry.

Curry was aware, however, that his friend Virginia Steward—Romanoff thought she was Curry's cousin—was on the Moon jury and he talked to her twice during the trial, according to Curry's post-trial testimony.[3]

Nothing remarkable about that. But after the trial, Virginia Steward gave an interview to her old neighborhood Brooklyn newspaper, the *Prospect Press*, which she wasn't supposed to do. Since she never received a copy of the edition with her interview in it, her friend Curry promised to get one. Bruce Romanoff obtained a copy of the interview as well, although Curry professed not to know how Romanoff got hold of it.

The Steward interview was a curious one. She was questioned a few days after the trial's conclusion on May 18, and the story was printed on May 27. The lapse in time was caused by the cautious Mrs. Steward who demanded the right to review the transcript before it was printed.

As the government pointed out, Virginia Steward expressed little doubt in that interview about the fairness of the Moon trial.

Had personal exposure to the Reverend Sun Myung Moon's followers affected her judgment? Answer: no.

Could she separate the religious question from the matter at hand, tax evasion? Of course: "[W]e never once talked about anything outside of the taxes."

How about Judge Gerard Goettel who heard the case in federal district court? "The judge was very fair. He gave equal opportunity to both sides."

What about the defendant? Steward felt a natural sympathy for him, but in conclusion she observed, "[N]o matter how much money you have, once you do something wrong you're going to get caught one way or another. Crime doesn't pay."[4]

Perhaps that pious sentiment set off second thoughts within Mrs. Steward. Maybe it was something else. But something did. The farther Virginia Steward moved away from the authority of the court, the more it seemed she began to wonder if justice had really been done to Sun Myung Moon.

Mrs. Steward's doubts about the outcome of the case were expressed to John Curry, the old friend. Why not? Curry was no reporter. Just an old friend. Besides, Virginia was godmother to one of Curry's children. How often and exactly when she talked to Curry about the Moon case is not clear. The participants' memories on these and other points would prove conveniently obscure.[5]

Curry's recollection was that the first substantive conversation about the case occurred shortly after June 19, but, in fact, it took place the following day, June 20. That conversation he taped without Virginia Steward's knowledge.[6]

It was at this point, according to Curry, that he went to Romanoff with the tape. Unfortunately, there wouldn't be any more from Curry on this matter—or any other—because Judge Goettel, in conducting a post-trial inquiry on the tape, suddenly interrupted his testimony. Curry's somewhat hazy, but not blatantly inaccurate, account made the judge uneasy. Perhaps Curry was only stupid; if not, he was approaching perjury.

[T]his Court has reason to believe that certain of the answers that you have given here today are inaccurate in material respects. I can't tell whether the inaccuracy of your answers comes from a failure of recollection or whether you are intentionally attempting to mislead the Court.[7]

Then followed the solemn warning about the costs and consequences of perjury and the suggestion that John Curry suspend further testimony until he had acquired an attorney. Curry agreed instantly.

Thanks to this untimely interruption of the court, under what circumstances the second tape was made on July 26, or whether other conversations took place between Curry and Steward on the Moon case, became unclear.

So we are left with Bruce Romanoff to explain what happened next.

Romanoff was even less clear than Curry had been. Romanoff, however, was more cagey than Curry; the answers to questions put to him are obviously more self-serving and self-protective. They did not invite the same degree of court suspicion. Romanoff, for example, admitted that he told Curry to tape any conversations with Mrs. Steward, but was careful not to suggest any illegality. In fact, taping phone conversations without permission is legal in New York.

A few days later, Romanoff's would-be operative handed him the first tape of Virginia Steward.

Subsequently, Romanoff, not the sort to miss a main chance, and aware the tape could be valuable to Moon's well-financed legal efforts, contacted David Hager, an attorney and a member of the Unification Church. A few days later, probably in early July, Romanoff played the tape for Hager.

Hager was not impressed. The tape quality was poor and the brief conversation on it was all but inaudible.[8]

Romanoff went back to Curry, suggesting that this time he get a better and longer recording of Mrs. Steward expressing her doubts about the Moon trial.

A month later, Curry had the second tape in hand. After the two men played it in Romanoff's office, Romanoff took the second tape to David Hager. That was on August 4. This recording proved more satisfactory than the first. The two tapes were turned over to Moon's lawyers and they formed the basis of the lawyers' motion with a supporting affidavit requesting a post-trial inquiry into the question of whether there had been irregularities in the jury process—in short, whether the jury had been tainted and whether there was cause for a new trial.[9]

So much for background. Although the government tried to impugn the motives of Curry, Romanoff, and Steward, not to mention defense counsel, the heart of the matter is what Virginia Steward actually said on that vital second tape recorded on July 26, more than two months after she and her fellow jurors had been dismissed with thanks by Judge Goettel.

The transcript of the tape was also sealed—at least, until now. Although it has been chewed over *in camera* by the court and its officers, the transcript still provides a shock to the first-time reader.

After John Curry asked Virginia Steward whether she had gotten her copy of the *Prospect Press* interview, the Moon juror gave this unprompted reply:

> You know, the more I read that [the interview] the more I wonder if I did the right thing.[10]

Again, uncoached, she continued:

> I was there and I was hesitant on some of, you know, the things he was charged with, you know, and they kept talking to me and talking to me, you know, I was there—was me and this other fellow John [fellow juror John McGrath], I didn't believe on Count 13, like you know, that he was guilty but kept asking, asking, alright [sic] you know, there was only one more left and I said alright [sic] guilty then, you know, but I'm really sorry in a way that I said it now because I'm not sure whether he was guilty on all counts.[11]

Remorse and sympathy for the defendant after conviction are hardly novel psychological reactions. But here the guilt feelings are quite specifically linked to the heavy pressure Steward admitted that she had been placed under by her fellow jurors. Peer group pressure, as any beginning student of small group dynamics knows, is hardly new in jury trials; such pressure does form the dark side of the American jury system. In this case, it is evident that peer pressure played a large part in persuading Steward to vote guilty on at least one count about which she had major reservations.[12]

But that was hardly the end of the tape.

Steward then told her friend that until the trial, she had known nothing of the Reverend Sun Myung Moon and his church. She was soon educated, however, principally by the jury's "fore-lady," Mary Nimmo.

Indeed, Mrs. Nimmo played a major role in this drama. According to the trial and post-trial transcripts, Nimmo appears as the strongest juror with the firmest opinions. The wife of a New York policeman and a staunch Roman Catholic, her views carried weight with the rest of the jury. As foreman, Nimmo was the major internal influence on the other eleven jurors, as is often the case.

Virginia Steward's taped recollection underlines the point:

[Y]ou know, Mary the fore-lady, she kept saying you know who he is, he's the one, he takes these kids' minds and he twists them, he brainwashes them, he doesn't want them with their family, and everything else, you know oh you know him, they want to deport him and everything else so.[13]

At this point Steward made clear (after prompting from Curry) that Nimmo's statements had been made right before the trial began. She added that one juror (John McGrath) had reminded Nimmo (apparently repeatedly) of her prejudice, and the latter's reply was simply, "he's guilty, he's guilty, that's it."[14]

Virginia Steward was not quite finished. After a long soliloquy on Moon's possible guilt, and prompted by Curry, she stated her belief that there were other doubters on the jury. Four, all told.

Then in a fascinating *non sequitur*, Virginia Steward related the trials and tribulations of Esperanza Torres who had confessed her fear that someone, possibly the "Moonies," was harassing her by, first, firing a BB gun through her window, and, second, rear-ending her car.[15]

But it was Mary Nimmo that kept popping up in the conversation between Steward and Curry. Steward, for example, recounted that the fore-lady had also had some strong ideas about the Reverend Sun Myung Moon and his family. According to Steward:

[T]his woman Mary she's saying yes, she said one of [Moon's] kids was going to the day schools that's right near my house, the day school you know, one of those younger ones and the kid was a troublemaker and all this stuff, hey, his kid ain't honest, why bring up his family.[16]

Why indeed?

The "fore-lady," Mary Nimmo, in Steward's opinion also wouldn't let up because she was tired of the whole business and "wanted to get this trial over with."[17]

There was one last ugly revelation from Mrs. Steward regarding the jury's deliberations. Later the government took pride in the claim that the jury had taken four whole days to deliberate on the charges against Moon and Kamiyama.[18]

But that is not exactly how it happened, according to Virginia Steward. Thursday and Friday were given over to actual deliberation, and on the weekend the jury went home.

By Monday, she said:

[W]e would have given it to them . . . only they said no, it would look bad coming right back in with it right away, you know, but that's why, I asked to see some of the papers because, especially the one dealing with Kamiyama, they turned around and they had that thing with the half done . . . and I said anyone can put somebody's name on a paper and put figures on a paper, that doesn't mean a person is guilty of it.[19]

Once again, Mrs. Steward expressed a feeling that the wrong decision had been made. And that was that.

So there it was. Allegations of a jury foreman seriously and actively prejudiced against a defendant; another juror who felt she and her family were threatened by that defendant; two other jurors who complained of undue pressure from their peers; a lengthy delay by the jury in announcing its decision done solely for the theatrical purpose of not appearing to be prejudiced.

Surely enough to raise serious questions about the jury's conduct and the fairness of its verdict.

Surely enough to result in an exhaustive post-trial hearing to explore the possibility of a tainted jury.

Or so it seemed; so it seemed.

CHAPTER II

THE STORY UNFOLDS

Facts do not cease to exist because they are ignored.

ALDOUS HUXLEY

ONE spring afternoon in 1985, shortly after I had left the newsroom at the *Washington Times* where I was working as an investigative reporter, I ran into a couple of lawyer friends in a Washington bar off K Street. I had met both of them a few years earlier when I was doing a story about the Civil Rights Division of the Justice Department for CNN where I worked before the *Times*. At that time they worked in separate criminal divisions of Justice in Washington, and through our mutual interests in my piece, we got to know each other fairly well and developed a friendly but professional relationship.

When we met in 1985, one man was still at the Justice Department but the other had recently gone into private practice. We chatted over drinks and swapped a few stories and eventually the topic turned to what I had been up to for the last three years. I filled them in on my decision to leave television news and then told them about the year at the *Washington Times* and how while there I had made a vigorous but failed attempt at digging up some dirt on the Unification Church which owned the paper.

Both men looked at me slack-jawed and then began to laugh. In

11

short order, they informed me that the Justice Department and virtually every federal law enforcement agency in the country had spent nearly ten years and untold millions in taxpayers' money trying to get the Unification Church and they had come up empty handed, too.

What about the tax evasion and conspiracy case against Moon? I asked. Then they dropped the bomb.

"That was a bad case," one of the lawyers said.

"We never had a case," the other corrected. "All of the seniors in Tax [career, senior prosecutors in the Criminal Tax Division of the Justice Department] are still bitching about the prosecution which was forced down their throats. The place is still in chaos. There's a lot of very unhappy people there."

That was for openers. For the next couple of hours my two prosecutor friends spun out one amazing story after another concerning the details of the case against Moon and how the Justice Department, after years of receiving complaints and huge amounts of political pressure all aimed at running the Reverend Sun Myung Moon out of the country, had ended up being coerced into prosecuting, over the repeated oral and written objections of the department's most experienced criminal attorneys.

Neither of my informants had worked in the tax division but, they said, they didn't have to in order to know about the case—the internal dispute at the Justice Department had been so bitter and the discontent so widespread.

I didn't need to hear any more. Within hours I was pulling boxes of documents back out of the closet and reexamining records, particularly court files I had only given a glance to previously. To my utter astonishment and embarrassment, there they were, memos and letters authored by the Justice Department's own prosecutors, explaining in great detail why the government had no case against Moon or any of his followers.

In fact, the Justice Department's own chief of criminal tax prosecution not only argued strenuously against indictment but warned that if Moon was brought to trial on trumped-up tax evasion charges, the government might find itself in the embarrassing position of owing him a tax refund.

That was unprecedented—the senior government prosecutors sounded more like defense lawyers for Moon.

It proved a turning point for me, but in the months and years that followed I would read and see far more startling, truly amazing records, all documenting what has to be one of the most egregious examples of raw, vengeful abuse of government power. A government assault that before it was over would bring to the defense of the Reverend Moon different activists as disparate as Eugene McCarthy and Senator Orrin Hatch, Harvard law professor Laurence Tribe and Clare Booth Luce; journalists, like liberals William Raspbery and Colman McCarthy, and conservative James Jackson Kilpatrick. As well as organizations and people like the National Council of Churches, the American Civil Liberties Union, the Catholic bishops, the Marxist Spartacist League, and the attorney generals of the states of Hawaii, Oregon, and Rhode Island.

For me, the story began in the early spring of 1984. At the time I was working for Ted Turner's Cable News Network in Washington, D.C., as an investigative reporter in CNN's special Assignment Unit. I was putting the finishing touches on a series of reports probing the suspicious deaths of dozens of newborn infants at an Oklahoma City hospital, a particularly exhausting, controversial, and nasty investigation which wound up capturing the attention of President Reagan himself and spawning a string of federal investigations, House and Senate hearings, lawsuits before the U.S. Supreme Court, and a battery of new federal laws protecting newborns from medical experimentation.

I had worked as an on-air television reporter less than three years and although I had been fortunate enough to win the George Foster Peabody Award, considered television's highest journalistic honor, I began yearning for the relative sanity and stability of a daily newspaper, my journalistic roots of some fourteen years.

As luck would have it, I began receiving unsolicited job offers from several publications in February of 1984. Among those calling was Woodie West, managing editor of the *Washington Times.*

Even under normal circumstances, the *Washington Times* would have been the last publication I would have considered working for, if I had thought of the *Times* at all. For one thing, at the time it was only two years old and published just five days a week, with a circulation of less than 100,000 and a staff of around two hundred.

For another, its direct competition was the only other daily newspaper in the District of Columbia, the mighty *Washington Post*, which had eight times the circulation and three times the staff. So, the *Post* had a virtual lock on the region's advertising dollar, to say nothing of a monopoly on D.C.'s political power elite—the two most cherished and necessary elements in a town where power and money or, nearer to the truth, the perceptions of influence and the aura of big bucks, were the keys to success.

But despite its David and Goliath match-up with the *Post*, my biggest concern about signing on with the *Times* involved the newspaper's ownership. It was common knowledge then, as it is now, that the *Times* is owned by a holding company whose majority stockholders are members of the Reverend Sun Myung Moon's Unification Church. Furthermore, the *Washington Times'* operations were and continue to be financed by the Unification Church: at last count, according to *Time* magazine, to the tune of $25 million per year.

It was one thing to work for a new, struggling daily; quite another to be part of a news organization whose owner is a recently convicted felon and a religious zealot to boot.

Eventually, after weeks of waffling, I decided to take the leap, though at the time I made it clear that I would only work as the *Times* chief investigative reporter for a year.

In the end, I had two basic reasons for making such a decision.

The first was personal. To be perfectly honest, I was flattered by who did the asking. Woodie West and most of the editors at the *Washington Times* were old newsmen who had formerly worked for some of the most respected, but now defunct, big-city newspapers in the country.

Woodie and many of the other editors and senior reporters— people like Smith Hempstone, the *Times* editor-in-chief, Jerry O'Leary, the *Times* White House correspondent, Coit Henley, the assistant managing editor, and Miles Cunningham, the chief political reporter—had spent long and colorful careers at various other large-circulation dailies like Washington's *Evening Star* which had folded during the dark days of the early 1980s.

Cunningham and Henley had worked for the *Philadelphia Evening Bulletin*, which shut down its presses in 1980. West, Hempstone, and O'Leary were formerly career staffers at the venerable and respected *Evening Star*, which closed its doors after finishing second and last in a circulation war with the aforementioned, well-financed *Post*.

Like most newspapermen—we used to call ourselves that and not journalists—I, too, lamented that Washington, D.C., like too many large cities, had become a one-newspaper town. I regretted the passing of the old *Washington Star*, but not so much for the lofty reasons often mouthed by professional media mourners.

Sure, it was a shame that a city so alive with news, truly internationally significant news, would have only one print voice. But for us newspapermen it was far worse because it signaled the passing of an era, perhaps an entire profession. The *Star* was one of the last real city newspapers, an unpretentious, smoke-filled, coffee-stained news room populated by the likes of West, Hempstone, and O'Leary: men who, for the most part, never took a course in journalism, much less earned degrees from Ivy League colleges. These were the last of a breed that knew that paying your dues meant spending years as copy boys, rewrite men, and cub reporters.

Learning the trade, earning the title of reporter, required years of working the streets and many, many long nights on trains, planes, and in bus depots, or huddled in a phone booth dictating a story. When they sat down to report, they weren't liberal or conservative and they would have slugged anyone stupid enough to call them intellectuals.

These were the men who covered the wars in the mud and from the foxholes, not from airconditioned briefing rooms safely behind the lines or from the bar of the Hilton Hotel. These were the men who wrote what they saw and experienced themselves—the misery and cruelty of war as well as the valor and self-sacrifice. Indeed, most of these old newspapermen distinguished themselves in battle—in World War II and Korea—sometimes interrupting their own successful careers to serve as volunteers in the armed services. That, too, was considered part of paying your dues.

I had war in common with them. In Vietnam, I did not report the war, but I fought in it. As a Marine NCO stuck in the DMZ, I Corps, I went through a hitch of dangerous and scary work in places like Khe Sanh and Con Thien. I was wounded three times and saw too many friends turned into hamburger. But I don't regret the experience for a moment. And it made me neither a flagwaver nor a flagburner.

I had come out of the Marines, spent time as a reporter with the Gannett newspapers, won some awards including a Pulitzer for an investigation of religious corruption, and then gone on to CNN.

But I was weary of TV news and sound bit journalism and longed for a return to the print game. In short, I was honored and flattered that these newspapermen, the genuine article and probably the last of their kind, would find a pup like myself worthy of their company, much less consider me a colleague—a newspaperman.

My second reason for taking the job at the *Times* was far less noble. I saw this as a once-only chance to get an inside track on one of the most controversial religious organizations in the United States. With luck and persistence, I hoped to accomplish what until then no reporter had been able to do: to penetrate the organizational and financial structure of the Unification Church.

My reason for deciding to tackle this subject dealt mainly with what I can best describe as professional curiosity. Over the last twenty-one years or so spent mostly as a newspaper investigative reporter, I had come across more than my share of religious scandals. In fact, many of the national awards I'd picked up along the way, including that 1980 Pulitzer Prize Gold Medal and a couple of other nominations for the prize, were the results of successful investigations into church-related scandals of one kind or another.

The 1970s and early 1980s were of course boom years for press investigations into church scandals. I spent several years putting together ironclad cases against what I regarded as some of the most despicable characters in America, so-called holy men who used their positions in their churches and the good faith of their followers to lie, cheat, and steal. These were for me truly the worst! Scoundrels, scumbuckets.

Yet for all their misdeeds—many illegal, all immoral—not one of them ever spent so much as an hour behind bars. In fact, none was even defrocked by his church.

Each of those stories involved money—huge sums of cash— greed, fraud, deceit, and, of course, power. Some were laced with healthy doses of sex, organized crime figures, drugs, and even murder.

So, for me, the question was, What had the Reverend Sun

Myung Moon done to warrant being—until that time—the only religious leader in this century to be imprisoned?

My first experience, for example, with a newspaper investigation into a church-related scandal occurred in 1973 and centered on the LaSalette Fathers, a small Roman Catholic missionary order. A handful of LaSalette priests concocted an ambitious get-rich-quick scheme which centered on selling worthless shares in an electronic computer company. When the bottom fell out of the deal, the LaSalette priests were forced into bankruptcy, the first time anything like that had happened in the United States.

Although a plethora of state and federal racketeering and securities laws had been broken, no action was taken against any of those involved.

My second encounter with church crime occurred about a year later. The Pallotine Fathers, another Catholic religious order, headquartered in Baltimore, Maryland, developed what was then the most sophisticated mass mailing operation in the country; over the years they raised hundreds of millions of dollars, ostensibly to feed starving children through their overseas missions. As it turned out, only a small fraction of those funds ever got to the missions. Instead, the Pallotines used their amassed wealth for business and real estate investments which included partnerships in race tracks and loans to political figures and even $54,000 in cash to help then-governor of Maryland Marvin Mandel with his divorce settlement.

Although the Pallotines were eventually charged with more than sixty counts of fraud, racketeering, and conspiracy, not one of the priests ever spent a day in jail. Governor Mandel and several of his aides weren't so lucky. They all did long stretches in prison in part, at least, as a result of their deals with the Pallotines.

The Pauline Fathers, a small order of monks whose monastery is located just outside of Doylestown, Pennsylvania, had a similar scam going in 1979. But instead of raising money for starving children they never intended to feed, the Paulines created a nationwide collection for a shrine they never planned to complete. Elderly, retired couples were the main targets of this flim-flam operation, and many of these unfortunates lost their entire life's savings—in all, more than $21 million. Most of those funds went to underwrite the Paulines' lavish lifestyles: such things as cars, clothes, expensive vacations, and girlfriends. To make matters worse, when the Vatican and several U.S. bishops discovered the Pauline fraud, they made no attempt to pay back the ill-gotten money or even discipline the guilty monks. Instead, they launched a massive cover-up operation, paying hush money to those involved and hiring a gaggle of lawyers to fend off any attempts by former donors to collect their money.

Once more law enforcement officials turned a blind eye to the matter and not even the Paulines' lawyer—a known organized crime figure previously jailed on federal racketeering charges— was ever indicted, much less prosecuted.

Finally, in 1980, I was assigned to look into the financial mal- practices of the aged John Cardinal Cody, archbishop of Chicago and the single most powerful Catholic figure in America. Another national scandal.

And now, in 1984, I decided to spend a year or so at the *Washington Times* to discover what I could about another so-called holy man, the Reverend Sun Myung Moon.

Working within an organization to probe its benefactor's records may seem a bit unethical or opportunistic to some. I'll plead guilty to the latter, but working inside an organization for the purpose of exposing corruption, criminal activities, or wrongdoing of any kind is a time-honored journalistic practice. Some of my best stories—those which received the most accolades from the jour- nalistic community—were the result of long months and even years of undercover work.

But if I was never fated to produce a newspaper exposé on the Reverend Sun Myung Moon, it wasn't for lack of trying. I launched my own investigation into the Unification Church long after he had been convicted of income tax evasion and sentenced to eigh- teen months in federal prison. For more than two years I scoured internal church financial records, government files, and court testimony and interviewed dozens of people directly involved with church financial operations.

Why go to all this trouble after Moon had been convicted of income tax evasion? There are a couple of reasons.

First, despite all the press coverage involving the so-called "Moonies"—clippings which go back to the early 1970s when I first took an interest in church scandals—there was a noticeable absence of any professional, in-depth newspaper account of the organization's financial practices. To be sure, there were many speculative articles, as there are even today about the Unification Church's wealth and activities; news stories that vary widely, sometimes in the same publication, about the church's finances and influence. But even as this is written, no publication—newspaper or magazine—has ever produced a documented series dealing specifically with the Unification Church's financial operations, much less with any improper or illegal use of funds.

There are rules, of course, which should be followed when working inside an organization as a journalist. Duplicity is out. I never joined the Unification Church or even came close to doing so, and though I might have walked a thin line obtaining internal records—the laws in many states, for example, draw a fine distinction on whether documents are stolen when copies are made and delivered by a third party—I tried in every way to keep my investigation clean of illegalities and improprieties.

I should admit that ethically I wasn't simon-pure when it came to biases, prejudices, and preconceptions. I took the job at the *Times* believing the Unification Church, its leaders, and at least some of its members were up to no good. And, like many people even today, I assumed Sun Myung Moon and his co-defendant, Takeru Kamiyama, were guilty as hell and deserved exactly what they got. I also believed much, if not all, of the horror stories I heard and read concerning the "Moonies" and their bizarre cult practices. I bought the whole line, from "love bombing," to "heavenly deception," "zombies," "brainwashing," "kidnapping," etc., etc.

Within a few months of settling in with the routine of working on a daily newspaper again, I achieved my initial goal of making contact with some members of the Unification Church and developing a casual relationship. Contrary to popular belief—just one of many press fictions—there weren't many Unification Church members working at the *Times*. In all, about a dozen or so occupied mid- or low-level editorial or administrative positions with neither hiring, firing, nor decision-making authority. All were well-educated American men and women in their early to late thirties.

Within six months of taking the job at the *Washington Times* I had finagled introductions to some of the highest-ranking American church members and managed to insert myself in many of their social activities: lunches, dinners, occasional card games, even a couple of fishing trips.

For the most part, these were men who had joined the church in the late 1960s, fresh out of college, and now headed the Unification Church's various corporations and foundations. All had been participants in the church's early U.S. formation and most had been directly involved in the public controversies and criminal prosecution of Sun Myung Moon. One had even prepared the 1974 tax return which was used to convict and jail Moon nearly a decade later. Others had been threatened with indictment and prosecution; and another had been literally pulled from his sickbed in Virginia by federal marshals and dragged across five states to testify in federal court.

Though I had developed a comfortable relationship with key Unification Church leaders, my objective remained to get inside the church organizations themselves and to uncover wrongdoing, to find where the bodies were buried. Once I had gained the trust of church officials, it was relatively easy to cultivate contacts with others—clerks, secretaries, assistants—most of whom were not members of the Unification Church. Within eight months I had built up a small network of sources who were furnishing me almost daily with sensitive papers, internal papers, financial records, correspondence, memos, corporate documents, real estate transactions, even court records and letters from attorneys and accountants.

By the end of the year, I had amassed a virtual mountain of documents, literally thousands of pages of internal records, and I had spent at least a couple of hundred hours listening to church officials and their employees. And what did I learn?

Well, for one thing, the Unification Church is scrupulous about its bookkeeping and management and spends huge sums of money, far too much in the view perhaps of some, on lawyers, accountants, and an army of professional experts and consultants.

The church owns large parcels of real estate in New York City, Washington, D.C., and a few other cities, but compared to the holdings of, say, the Roman Catholic archdioceses of those cities or other smaller denominations, the Unification Church real estate portfolio is minuscule. On top of that, the Unification Church, unlike all other denominations, pays taxes on its land and buildings. Heavy taxes.

On the same subjects of money and taxes, I was flabbergasted to learn just how much money the church pumps into the United States: easily $100 million or more a year, mostly from Korea and Japan, and that money is also taxed.

I also learned from its records that the Unification Church owns and operates several businesses in the U.S., the largest of which involve publishing companies and fishing and processing operations. The church's publishing companies, which include the *Washington Times*, a couple of magazines, and a book publishing firm, are consistently in the red and rely almost entirely on overseas church funding. The church fishing operations are profitable but the proceeds from those businesses—all fully taxed—remain in the United States to support the Unification Church's own charitable activities.

And what are those charitable works?

Again, I was amazed to learn that the Unification Church has given away millions to a number of inner city churches: poor, black, ghetto churches. And if the private, internal correspondence is to be believed, there were and are no strings attached to the donations, no attempts made at recruitment or even acknowledgement that the funds came from Moon.

The Unification Church has also spent millions more underwriting the activities of national black leaders, men like the late Reverend Ralph Abernathy, and has supplied large-scale research funding for organizations and individuals involved with the study of First Amendment rights, constitutional law, racial discrimination, ethics, the sciences, politics, the arts, and culture.

All of these contributions, literally tens of millions of dollars, were donated without fanfare—no press releases, pictures of people holding checks, or other PR gimmicks—and, once more, without any indication of any quid pro quo, implied or otherwise.

If the Unification Church was trying to buy influence, there was no evidence of it in even the most sensitive, internal documents, and never even the remotest hint of proselytizing. Likewise, if these activities were merely ploys, albeit expensive ones, to gain public respect, then the church and its leaders would have been

wise to advertise their philanthropic activities rather than keeping
them quiet.

All this was mildly interesting, but pretty tame and hardly the
stuff of an exposé. So once more I went over my notes and asked
myself the big questions.

Where were the secret blue-chip, multi-million-dollar stock
portfolios? Just about every church had one. The Unification
Church had none.

What about offshore banks or hidden Swiss bank accounts?
Again, the Unification Church came up clean.

How about all those breathless newspaper and magazine reports
about how the Unification Church had secretly infiltrated our
legislatures and planned to take over America and form a theocracy? Well, every state house in the Union, every office of every
governor, senator, and congressman is besieged almost daily by
legions of high-powered lobbyists representing virtually every
mainstream religion and church in this country. And these men do
influence legislation, everything from our taxes and schools to
communications laws, and even how much and where our tax
dollars are spent on military defense.

None, however—not one—represents the Unification Church.
Furthermore, if a poll were taken of the religion of every elected
official in this country, it's a near certainty all religious beliefs
would be represented, from dyed-in-the-wool atheists to Christian
Scientists, and maybe even Zen Buddhists, for all I know. All but
one religion—the Unification Church.

So stories about Moon's overthrowing the government of the
United States were nonsense. How about a nice juicy sex scandal?
A Jim Bakker or Jimmy Swaggart clone running around loose
somewhere? Zero again. I learned that if there's anything the
Unification Church won't tolerate it's sex out of marriage. Pre-
marital and extramarital sex are strictly forbidden.

Then what about the stories written and rumored about the
church: kids brainwashed and forced to disavow and hate their
parents, kidnapped, forced to labor for little or no pay? In a word:
bunk. First, none of those who joined the church were "kids." All
were legally adult and a vast majority were college graduates in
their twenties, and some in their thirties. In every case I studied—
and I looked into more than one hundred—those whose families

initially objected to their joining the church have all reconciled their differences. And any kidnappings which took place, and there were quite a few, were conducted by well-paid professionals, many with criminal records, who snatched church members off the street and spent days attempting to coerce and brainwash them, not the other way around. As for charges of forced labor, most church members are educated professionals with middle- to upper-middle-class incomes. Like many people, they occasionally do volunteer work for the church for little or no pay. They are not required to do so.

My acquaintance with top American church leaders proved no more successful at producing a viable exposé than a search of the records, not that the time spent with them was wasted.

I did learn, for example, what it's like to have to hide your religious beliefs closely from everyone around you, your neighbors, friends, business associates, even the mailman. I also experienced, first-hand, what it's like for people, seemingly normal families, to live in daily fear of a knock on the door or a phone call or a certified letter informing them that once again they were the targets of an investigation by this or that government agency. I saw men cry in frustration and anger because their country, a nation supposedly founded on the principle of religious tolerance, had made them and their families outcasts and turned their everyday existences into a nightmare. And I remember feeling as if I had been kicked in the gut as I overheard a father gently explain to his six-year-old daughter before her first day of school why she should never talk about her religion with her classmates because some bad people might hear and hurt her.

This was America—white, affluent, suburban, and cosmopolitan America in the enlightened 1980s. Yet, many times when I was with these men it was as though I had been strapped in a time machine and shot back to Nero's Rome, or seventeenth-century New England or Hitler's Germany.

To be sure, we don't feed people with odd religious beliefs to the lions or burn them at the stake or gas them in concentration camps. After all, we're civilized Americans, good and decent Christians, not barbarians. No, we don't do that to people who worship differently. We just harass, intimidate, and ridicule them and their families and occasionally throw their leaders in jail. And if that fails to break their spirits or run them out of town, we look the other way while a few are killed, beaten, or raped. Think I'm being a bit melodramatic? Just ask a Jehovah's Witness or a Mormon about American religious tolerance. Better yet, talk to an Orthodox Jew.

But in the end, although I had learned much that was fascinating, particularly for a journalist, it was not what I had been looking for and it certainly wasn't material for a book-length scandal, at least not a religious scandal.

So, for me the question was, What had the Reverend Sun Myung Moon done to warrant being—until that time—the only religious leader in this century to be imprisoned?

Did he use church money to buy a house in Florida for a lady friend as Cardinal Cody did?

Did he build condo high rises with millions of dollars which were supposed to save thousands of African children from starving to death as the Pallotines had?

Did he bilk old and infirm widows out of their last pennies so he could buy a fleet of new cars and take European vacations like the Pauline monks?

Or, did he squander millions in charitable donations, hire mob lawyers, pay off politicians, keep secret bank accounts, or attempt to cover up criminal activities as so many respected members of the Roman Catholic hierarchy had done?

The answer, I would find, was *no*. Moon did none of these things or anything approaching the kind of unconscionable practices all too often found in mainstream American churches. In fact, I discovered that by just about any standard the Reverend Sun Myung Moon and his followers had done nothing wrong, certainly nothing worthy of criminal prosecution. Indeed, after years of plowing through mounds of church corporate and government papers it became painfully evident that even much of what's been written or rumored about Moon's "vast financial empire" is fiction or, at best, gross exaggeration.

The truth, I found, was quite simple: the Unification Church, its leaders and followers were and continue to be the victims of the worst kind of religious prejudice and racial bigotry this country has witnessed in over a century. Moreover, virtually every institution we as Americans hold sacred—the Congress, the courts, law enforcement agencies, the press, even the U.S. Constitution itself—was prostituted in a malicious, oftentimes brutal manner, as part of a determined effort to wipe out this small but expanding religious movement.

So perhaps the best way to describe my own part in this story and the reason for this book is to relate an old news room chestnut, retold with variations that every cub reporter hears a hundred times, about a fictional reporter assigned to cover a gubernatorial press conference at the city airport.

The reporter returned to the news room later that day, his assignment apparently completed. But rather than churning out a piece on the governor's remarks, he sauntered back to his desk and, with feet propped up, began thumbing through a magazine.

The deadline neared, but still the reporter showed no signs of filing a story. Finally, the city editor, who had been monitoring the young man's peculiar behavior, marched over and asked what was holding up the copy.

"Sorry, I thought you knew," the reporter said. "The press conference was cancelled—no story."

Seemingly satisfied, the editor turned to leave but paused momentarily to ask if any reason had been given for the cancellation.

"Oh, sure," the reporter said, eyes glued on the magazine. "The governor's plane crashed."

On more than one occasion over the last few years I've had cause to remember that timeworn tale. For like the hapless reporter, too lazy or too dimwitted to recognize a much bigger story than the one he set out to cover, I too had developed a one-track mindset while conducting an in-depth financial investigation of Moon and his church. In the process, I came close to ignoring a far more important and historically significant story—one which had little to do with money but dealt instead with the corrupting effects that ignorance, hatred, and ambition can have on a free and democratic society.

After speaking to my two friends from the Justice Department and digging into the files of the department's own prosecutors of the Unification Church, I realized that I, like the cub reporter, had completely missed the story. Put another way, I was so intent on covering the governor's press conference, that I had failed to notice when his plane crashed right under my investigative reporter's nose.

And now, what I do expect, what I hope, is that my findings, contained in the following pages, will be taken in the spirit in which they are intended. Not as an attack on society or American institutions, but as a warning: a warning that we, as a people, have not come as far as we think in two hundred or even two thousand years. A warning that bigotry is always with us. A warning that we can't always depend on our systems—whether it's the government, the congress, the courts, or the press—to keep the darker side of our nature in check. And, finally, a warning that our institutions are man made, run by men and women who share all of our own weaknesses and prejudices.

If we fail to understand this, remember it and remain ever vigilant against it, then surely in the future others will also be crushed under the weight of fear, ignorance, hatred, and bigotry. And next time it may be you and I, my friend, who are the victims.

CHAPTER III

WITCH HUNT

Hating people is like burning down your own house to get rid of a rat.

HARRY EMERSON FOSDICK

THE Reverend Sun Myung Moon and his Unification Church surely have one distinction overriding all others. And it's not the size, wealth, or power of the movement. As a religion the church doesn't even come close, in any of these categories, to the established denominations and sects that populate America.

But the Reverend Sun Myung Moon does have one characteristic no other contemporary religious figure can come close to matching: he and his followers have been more thoroughly investigated in the past by more government agencies than just about anyone else. Only a select few serial killers, members of the legendary *cosa nostra*, and perhaps the U.S. Communist party have received anything approaching the tender, loving care with which Sun Myung Moon has been treated over the years.

Ordinarily, religious groups are spared intense government scrutiny for First Amendment reasons, a barrier peculiar to the American system. But with the Unification Church that barrier simply broke down, especially after 1976.

There are a number of reasons for this, but for the moment just

27

absorb this one simple fact: records show that, at one time or another, the Central Intelligence Agency, the Federal Bureau of Investigation, the Internal Revenue Service, the Department of Justice, the Immigration and Naturalization Service, the Department of State, the Federal Trade Commission, the Securities and Exchange Commission, the Comptroller of the Currency, the Department of Labor, the U.S. Postal Service, the U.S. Customs Service, the National Security Agency, the Defense Intelligence Agency, and the Drug Enforcement Agency, plus several dozen Senate, congressional, and state investigative committees and hundreds of federal and local law enforcement officials, have all poked, prodded, probed, pried, bugged, and generally kept books on Moon and the Unification Church.

American probes go back at least to the early 1960s judging from the bulky government files that have been released under the Freedom of Information Act, or FOIA (pronounced "foy'-a"). How much more stuff lies moldering in the federal records warehouses in Suitland, Maryland, is anyone's guess.

It's more than a bit odd. For a relatively obscure church from Korea with followers in the United States numbering just a few thousand, why the investigative overkill? Why devote tens of thousands of man hours and squander millions upon millions in tax dollars for the kind of ferocious full-court press not even reserved for such distinguished citizens as the murderous Gambino crime family?

Put another way, how and why was it decided that Moon was Public Enemy Number One?

There is really no answer, but there are many reasons, both extraordinary and convoluted. But here a little context might be useful.

By the mid-1970s, the IRS and a veritable alphabet soup of federal and state law enforcement agencies were hot on Moon's trail. By any standard it was a dogged chase that eventually led to the Korean reverend's going to jail for thirteen months. But that's history.

Let's fast-forward more than ten years and what do we find in a family newspaper?

It is an announcement in the *Washington Post* that the IRS is beginning a high-priority investigation of high-rolling American television evangelists like Pat Robertson, Oral Roberts, and Jerry Falwell.

How come it took the feds so much time to get around to doing that, long after they had drawn and quartered the relatively unknown Moon?

Moreover, the IRS zeal for investigating TV's biggest preachers—whose followers number in the tens of millions—was fired up only after the numerous scandals of Jim and Tammy Faye Bakker's truly weird PTL show business ministry. The IRS investigation of Jim and Tammy began—and timidly at that—a full quarter century after the first known U.S. government probe of Sun Myung Moon.[1]

So how come the First Amendment shielded that pair—and all the rest—far, far longer than it did the Reverend Sun Myung Moon and his relatively small band of believers?

The IRS has been widely criticized, of course, for not acting earlier on ministerial malfeasance. But what really moved it this time was the heat it was getting from Congress.

In this case, the Oversight Subcommittee of the House of Representatives' Ways and Means Committee and its chairman, the Texas Democrat J.J. Pickle.

After Pickle's November 1987 hearings on the teleministries, he concluded that new legislation was not needed. Instead, the Internal Revenue Service had failed to do its duty. Since this House subcommittee had a lot to do with the IRS's funding, its top officers got the message. And, as a result, more than one television preacher—First Amendment or not—went scurrying in search of high-priced legal talent.

It has become a very familiar pattern. But the questions remain. How is it that Moon, who had no television ministry, became the first religious leader in this century to be imprisoned? Why was he singled out when others of the cloth lived far more lavishly, publicly flaunting their multi-million-dollar rectories, gold-plated plumbing, and air-conditioned dog houses? And why did so many get into the Unification Church investigating act long before the PTL temple came crashing down on its founders? The same First Amendment that had so thoroughly protected the nation's Elmer

Gantrys had been swept aside by U.S. government agents madly pursuing one Korean reverend and his tiny band of American followers. Why?

Mrs. Alma Clark of Chattahoochee, Florida, was worried. She had been fretting for months. But now she was going to do something about her twenty-one-year-old son. Mrs. Clark wrote a letter in a neat, cursive longhand to the FBI. And she sent it to the bureau's director, Clarence M. Kelley.

What bothered Clark was her son's work for New Education Development, Inc., located in Berkeley, California. The NEDI was one of many Bay area organizations associated with the Unification Church at the time. That was January 1975, when stories of the "Moonies" and their supposed doings were filling America's newspapers and magazines, not to mention the television networks.

Mrs. Clark told Director Kelley that her boy was a gardener and sold flowers for the church—all without pay. It also annoyed her that the boy had no idea whether or not he was covered by medical insurance and Social Security benefits.

That didn't seem right to Mrs. Clark, a law-abiding citizen. Moreover, her boy, she told Kelley, was idealistic and "easily duped." What bothered her even more was that her son had been selected by the Unification Church to participate in a three-month swing through the Far East.

What she wanted to know from the FBI was this: Where did the Unification Church get the money to pay for the trip and what did it expect in return? Could the church legally hire people for no pay? And was the organization communist or subversive in any way? And what about our embassies? Do they ever check out these groups and their leaders?

Director Kelley's reply to Mrs. Clark of course was boilerplate.

The FBI, he wrote Mrs. Clark, is "strictly an investigative agency of the Federal Government and, as such, neither makes evaluations nor draws conclusions as to the character or integrity of any organization, publication or individual."[2]

And, just to be on the safe side, Kelley added: "I hope you will not infer either that we do or do not have material in our files relating to the groups you mentioned."[3]

In an attached note to the Kelley letter to Clark, an FBI clerk informs the reader that the bureau's files ("Bufiles") contain nothing about the correspondent, Mrs. Clark, but that the bureau had received one other letter complaining about New Education Development, Inc. As for Moon's teachings, the clerk's note said, they "extend Judeo-Christianity to replace Oriental concepts of God and man."[4]

Whatever that means—but then the FBI was not set up to engage in theological hairsplitting. And in 1975 the bureau was not that interested in investigating Moon and his movement either. But the lady from Chattahoochee was not the only one to write the FBI about the church in the early and mid-1970s. In fact, the bureau was peppered with letters from Americans worried about the mysterious oriental church. Many suspected a communist plot. Others wrote their congressmen, who in turn directed their concerns to the FBI.

Some allegations were downright strange.

A lady in Albany, New York, claimed the "Moonies" were after her, burgling her apartment for the information she was compiling on them for the FBI. She had evidence, she said, that the church was targeting "Senator Carl Albert" [sic] and Senator Edward Kennedy with good-looking young women in miniskirts. "Moonies" were going to take over the government through mind control. There were Unification Church ties to Squeakie Fromme (one of the original Charles Manson family members who later was imprisoned for an attempted assassination of President Gerald Ford). The lady in Albany dropped the name of "deprogrammer" Ted Patrick. The lady in Albany seemed confused and spoke in a rambling manner, according to the FBI Special Agent who took all this down and forwarded it to Washington, D.C.[5]

What all the inquiries and complaints got, of course, was a polite listen and a stock response about the bureau's being an investigative arm of the federal government and not some kind of temple police.

Congressmen fared little better with the bureau. And Kelley wasn't exactly lying either when he told the same thing to Senators Walter Mondale of Minnesota, Robert Byrd of West Virginia, Strom Thurmond of South Carolina, and Phillip Hart of Michigan or to Congressmen Hamilton Fish of New York, Robert Kastenmeier of Wisconsin, and Charles Whalen, Jr., of Ohio after they all had routed their constituents' concerns about the Unification Church to the bureau.

The men from Capitol Hill were Democrats and Republicans, conservatives and liberals, but the answer they got was still the same: "the FBI is strictly an investigative agency of the Federal Government, and as such, neither makes evaluations nor draws conclusions as to the character or integrity of any organization, publication or individual."[6]

That particular response was sent to Fritz Mondale, but in no way was it different from the others. For his part, Mondale simply wanted to find out more (because a voter wanted to know) about a church-sponsored organization: CARP, or the Collegiate Association for the Research of Principles. Fritz never found out anything—at least not from the FBI. Mondale, like most of his colleagues in Congress, did not pursue the matter after making the first inquiry.[7]

Of course, the FBI form replies did leave out a few things. For example, attached to the letters to Senator Hart and Congressman Fish is a note for internal use that said the church had sponsored an anti-Vietnam war rally at the University of Arkansas in 1972, a bad piece of intelligence since the Unification Church supported the U.S. military effort in Southeast Asia. The note also stated that "[w]e have investigated the Rev. Sun Myung Moon and the Unification Church on a bribery charge in the past which was not verified."[8]

Kelley also omitted mentioning that the FBI files were full of raw reports on the church. In many cases, technically, the FBI had conducted no active investigation of Moon and his church, but its agents at home and abroad did file reports. Which was their job. Even former FBI Special Agents (SAs) could get into the act.

An internal memo dated September 17, 1973, from the FBI's Washington Field Office (WFO) to the director said that a former SA (name deleted), a staff member of the Subcommittee on Internal Security of the Senate Judiciary Committee, had furnished this tidbit to the bureau's Intelligence Division.

According to the ex-SA's source (identity also deleted) who had been traveling to the United States on a church-sponsored trip, "the Unification Church has plans to penetrate the offices of U.S.

Senators by placing female members, referred to as 'Eves,' therein."⁹

The informant also said he intended to return to the United States and apply for admission to an American university in order to infiltrate the Unification Church and learn more about its activities. That report, pretty typical of raw reporting anywhere, seemed far-fetched and obviously self-serving. Not surprisingly, the bureau didn't seem much impressed by the information, but the WFO passed it on to the U.S. Capitol Hill police anyway. In any case, the Judiciary Committee's then-Chairman James O. Eastland of Mississippi wasn't buying it either. Eastland refused to make any further inquiries for First Amendment reasons.¹⁰

Sometimes, former FBI agents take direct action, leaving the bureau scrambling to catch up.

Here's one story.

James Sheeran was from the old-school FBI. Good was good and bad was real bad, and the latter would always be in trouble if Special Agent Sheeran were on the case. He had been retired from the bureau for a few years, but deep in his heart he had never left. Just as there are no ex-Marines, there are no former Special Agents.

James Sheeran was also, at the time, one of the most powerful figures in New Jersey politics. He had served as one of the state's top Republican party leaders and become then-Governor William Cahill's insurance commissioner and closest political confidant. The New Jersey press corps, which is often given to colorful descriptives, affectionately labeled those in the Cahill administration the "Irish Catholic Mafia." This was due in no small part to Sheeran, who seemed to have only three passions: Catholicism, hard-ball Republican politics, and family, particularly his three daughters of whom it can be said he was fiercely protective.

When all three of his girls—first Jamie, then Vicki, and finally Josette—joined the Unification Church, Sheeran went ballistic. D-Day came on August 28, 1975, and the bureau would record Sheeran's every move.

According to the FBI's own files, Sheeran, then 52, in the company of his wife, Sarah, 51, and his son James, Jr., 14, entered the Unification Church training center in Tarrytown, New York. It was August 28 but the time was a bit unusual: it was five o'clock in the morning.[11]

The previous evening Sheeran had called the church's Tarrytown Training Center and demanded to speak with his daughters. Since they were not there, the ex-SA did not get his wish. But that did not stop Sheeran. Convinced that he was being lied to by the church members, he planned his pre-dawn assault for the next morning. Forcing his way past the gatekeeper ... but the FBI report speaks for itself:

> He then entered the main building in the area where [Joe] Tully was sleeping and started going up and down the halls shouting for his daughters. Tully told him to stop and he continued. Tully then forced him to the floor, and with assistance from others, held him there. The State Police were called. Sheeran continued to keep shouting and a towel was obtained and stuffed over his mouth. Sheeran's wife and son were kicking at the persons holding Sheeran down. When the State Police arrived he was released and was taken to the hospital.[12]

After this choice scene from contemporary American life was concluded, charges, quite naturally, were pressed. Sheeran filed a third-degree assault charge against Tully alleging his "limbs had been twisted and contorted and he had been gagged." Also his wife and son had been bruised in the encounter.

Tully, in turn, signed a complaint against Sheeran accusing him of second-degree trespass and third-degree assault.[13]

The Dutchess County district attorney, reviewing the record, decided not to begin grand jury proceedings against anyone— giving everyone time to cool off. Which is exactly what happened. A month later, the parties to the Tarrytown brawl met with the county district attorney and the local magistrate. Each was persuaded to drop the charges.

Was that the end of it? No, not quite. The Dutchess County prosecutor took the opportunity to run down a number of other complaints that local residents had filed about the Tarrytown Training Center. And what did he find?

I quote the words of the FBI memo:

> No specific evidence of a criminal violation of the laws of the State of New York have been obtained to date. Investigation has included

examination of hospital records, interviews of members of the Church as well as former members. No illegal or criminal violation has been established.[14]

And even that was not quite the end of it. In a memorandum written for the FBI director in early January 1976, Richard Thornburgh, then assistant attorney general, chronicled the further adventures of James Sheeran. According to Thornburgh, Sheeran had after the Tarrytown incident given an interview to *People* magazine which featured his charge that his daughters had been brainwashed and he, himself, had been assaulted by a band of "half-crazed Moonies."

As a result, Thornburgh suggested to the director that the bureau contact the local authorities and determine "the scope and status" of any investigation into the Unification Church in Dutchess County.[15]

No wonder congressmen got letters. But even before worried Americans were writing their congressmen about the "Moonie" menace, the FBI was getting reports from its "legal attachés" posted in American embassies around the world.

The LEGATs were all that remained of J. Edgar Hoover's ambitious plans for a world-wide intelligence empire. At the brink of the Second World War, Hoover wanted no less than to turn his beloved FBI into a super intelligence system that would combine internal U.S. security and crime fighting with an overseas intelligence collection and operational capability. Franklin Roosevelt, sensing trouble if too much power were to rest in one man's hands (other than his own), said no and created instead the Office of Strategic Services, the OSS, for foreign cloak and dagger.

Still, Hoover was no bureaucratic creampuff. He continued the fight and managed to secure the entire Western Hemisphere for FBI operations during the war. Only after yet another bitter turf conflict was the newly created Central Intelligence Agency given charge of all overseas intelligence activities in 1947. What was left of the FBI's glory days in foreign operations were the bureau's legal attachés still scattered around the world.

In the case of the church, the industrious LEGATs had been collecting information as early as the 1960s. One example illustrates the kind of thing that was being reported by them. In

February 1967, the FBI's legal attaché in the American Embassy in Tokyo (LEGAT, TOKYO) relayed to Washington, D.C., information from a deleted source that the Unification Church was a possible subversive threat.

According to the attaché, in a highly censored (by the FBI) cable that was classified Secret:

> In late 1964 [deletion] the Unification Church had components in every neutral country throughout the world where there are Koreans resident, and that all these components were "infiltrated or controlled by communists." [Deletion] the KCFF was a forerunner to a branch of the church located in Washington, D.C., instrumental in whose establishment was PAK Po-hui. [Deletion] KIM Chong-pil, former Director of ROK CIA, had been "using" the Korean Unification Church and the KCFF since 1961. [Deletion] KIM Chong-pil had organized the church while he was ROK CIA Director and had used the church as a political tool.[16]

Unfortunately, the next two paragraphs of this report are blacked out, but LEGAT Tokyo's concluding recommendation is not. The FBI's man in Tokyo suggested that the Washington Field Office (WFO) "discreetly" check out Unification Church and KCFF activities in the United States in order "to determine if they warrant investigation under the Registration Act or Nationalistic Tendency classification."[17]

The question is: Did the bureau's Washington Field Office take up the recommendation from Tokyo? The answer seems to be yes, but the released documents are so heavily airbrushed by the bureau that it is difficult to tell with precision what happened next.

The released documents show that, in March 1967, the WFO relayed information similar to LEGAT Tokyo's to its special agent in charge (SAC) in Newark, New Jersey, to check up on "subject's" Immigration and Naturalization Service file. The subject is most likely Colonel Bo Hi Pak, mentioned in the Tokyo LEGAT's cable.[18]

The Washington Field Office then proceeded to check the bureau's files concerning the Korean Cultural and Freedom Foundation. In a memo circulated in May 1967 to interested parties, including LEGAT Tokyo, the WFO reported that the KCFF was extensively investigated by WFO during 1964 to 1966 at the request of the Internal Security Division [U.S. Department of Justice]. . . . it was concluded that no additional investigation was warranted.[19]

That, too, was the conclusion of Mrs. Ulda Poland of the Justice Department's Division of Internal Security who, it appears, through the heavy curtain of censorship, did not believe the Reverend Sun Myung Moon or the church were agents belonging to the Korean CIA.[20]

That early FBI probe should have put to rest any notion that the Unification Church was in any way a front for the KCIA. Nonetheless, more than a decade later other intelligence agencies, congressmen and their staffs, along with anti-cult zealots, would resurrect and continue to float that particular piece of mythology. Even today, nearly twenty-five years after the FBI investigation, the Moon-KCIA connection remains a favorite piece of "background" when even reputable newspapers, such as the *Washington Post* and the *New York Times*, publish stories concerning the Unification Church. It's pure bunk but not the only myth exploded by careful scrutiny of federal records.

By December 1967, the bureau had compiled a summary on the Unification Church and Moon based on its files and those of the U.S. Army's G-2 for the edification of LEGAT Tokyo, among others. It appears to be a cobbled-together memorandum based on everyone's raw files. No attempt at analysis or evaluation of the sources seems to have been made.

Some of the material is merely reproduced from Embassy Tokyo's original report. Other portions include the familiar facts of Moon's biography. Curiously, the memorandum is available in two editions. One is highly censored, and virtually nothing of this three-page, single-spaced report remains intact. The second version, however, is only lightly airbrushed, leaving little to the reader's imagination to fill in. Unlike most classified government documents, this one tells a salty tale, especially about the early years of the Unification Church.

True, it does start slow and dull. The Reverend Sun Myung Moon, we are told, was a graduate of Pyongyang Medical College, graduation date unknown, but never practiced medicine. His wife reportedly was a licensed pharmacist working in a drug store in Seoul.

Now for the good part. According to the FBI/G-2 sources, Unification Church doctrine is based on the belief that heaven on earth is possible through the pursuit of physical and material pleasures. And that gets us to the good stuff. The memorandum then states:

> The precepts of the Church include [the report discloses] complete sexual permissiveness, based on the sexual desire of Adam, and the "baptism" of female members was done by MUN himself.[21]

It gets better.

> [The baptism] consisted of having nude women in a darkened room with MUN while he recited a long prayer and caressed their bodies.... At these meetings MUN prepared special food and drink, and gathered his nude congregation into a darkened room, where they all prayed for 24 hours.[22]

As a consequence, Moon was arrested in 1957 for "corrupting the public morals and adultery." But, the report goes on, he was acquitted when it was discovered that none of the allegations including those recounted above had any basis in fact. (Indeed, as it turned out, all of the sexual fantasies, it seems, were manufactured by a few jealous boyfriends and husbands who feared their mates were devoting too much time and attention to the church and not enough to them.[23])

But the stories of rampant sex in the Unification Church were far too titillating to be forgotten, never mind the dry dull facts. And like the intriguing but totally false church-KCIA scenario, they would take on a life of their own and continue to be part of the church mythology.

As for church membership, the 1968 FBI/G-2 estimate was 40,000 to 50,000 members in Korea, with 2,000 in Japan—the main body being Korean residents. Sixty percent of those, it alleged, came from the "communist General Federation of Koreans Residing In Japan (*Chosen Soren*)."[24]

And last, the report indicated that the Unification Church had no "overt" political affiliation or backing. Unfortunately, the next five or six lines of text have been airbrushed—a deletion that may well have detailed allegations about suspected "covert" political ties.[25]

So, in short, Director Kelley was not being entirely candid about the FBI's interest in Moon and the Unification Church before 1975. But the FBI was hardly alone. America's other foreign intelligence agencies were also busy trying to unravel the mysteries of the Unification Church.

At about the same time that the FBI took an interest in the Unification Church, so did the Pentagon's Defense Intelligence Agency, which was created in 1961 by President Kennedy after the Bay of Pigs fiasco. It was supposed to have combined the various service intelligence arms like the Army's G-2 and the Navy's Office of Naval Intelligence.

But another reason for the DIA's creation was to give the CIA a little competition. The Kennedy brothers, John and Robert, had largely blamed that feeble failure to oust Fidel Castro on the CIA. So had many others in the pro-Kennedy press. (And yes, Virginia, the American media were not always so adversarial.)

In any case, the military brass, who had no love for the civilian-run CIA or its predecessor, the Office of Strategic Services, were glad to have a joint intelligence agency of their own, although they too had little regard for Kennedy's handling of the Bay of Pigs operation.

The brand-new DIA was an aggressive pup and, in the early years especially, collected from whatever, whenever, and from whomever it could. Not surprisingly, the military's answer to the CIA was initially off the mark when it came to snooping about the still largely Korean-bound Unification Church.

The DIA's information from the field came in the form of Defense Department "intelligence information reports." Later would come the Central Intelligence Agency "intelligence information cables" and internal memoranda.

The DIA field cables, like the CIA's (which are better known as TDs), are considered raw intelligence: information gathered from a variety of sources, often untested, as the caveats on present-day TDs now state. At best, they provide "the consumer" information on subjects of importance to the policymaker. Often they are hardly more than gossip passed along from the field. At worst, the sources, for whatever reasons, are supplying completely fabricated information, even disinformation.

Dispatched from Seoul, the first military intelligence cables, all marked Confidential, came in a somewhat steady stream from late 1967 through the spring of 1968.

They appear to be based on a single source labelled by the reporter as a "casual informant" with grade C-6 information. He was using the intelligence community's system of rating reliability (now discarded), which ran from A through F; 1 to 10. A "C-6" is the equivalent of a C- and like the school grade it may be passing, but only barely.[26]

And what the DIA obtained, especially in the first reports, was precisely that.

One dated November 29, 1967, outlines the familiar early history of the Unification Church, including Moon's July 1955 indictment by South Korean authorities and its subsequent dismissal three months later. It also notes that Unification Church membership at that time was some three thousand in South Korea divided among forty chapter offices scattered throughout the republic.[27]

The report also noted Unification Church difficulties with Korea's Christian churches—difficulties, the DIA believed, that had led to the movement's stagnating in Korea, which forced it to expand elsewhere, chiefly in Japan.[28]

Two days later, another DIA report from Seoul spelled out in greater detail the structure of the Unification Church and its leader "Son-myong Mun." Inexplicably, the DIA also reported that the size of the church was 150,890 persons, in stark contrast to its earlier reported estimate. Even more interesting is the first American-reported information on the sources of Unification Church funding.

According to the DIA:

> The total property of the UC consists of the church building and the site where it is built. The necessary funds required for the UC operation are mainly contributed by UC members.[29]

The cable then noted the Unification Church's unconventional method of collecting funds. It was an eerie antecedent of what would later truly fascinate a bundle of American government departments, bureaus, and agencies about the Unification Church. It read:

> Contrary to the general methods of contribution being employed by other Christian churches, the UC is allegedly resorting to extraordinary ones. In accordance with one of the methods, UC members are directed to contribute funds by saving rice which was accumulated by skipping their meals.[30]

Even more ominous, however, is the report's seventh and concluding paragraph, dealing with "Links to Communists Socialists." It noted cryptically:

> There is a possibility that the UC may attempt to establish links with hostile countries through its overseas propaganda efforts.[31]

What precisely the reporter or his informant had in mind about possible ties with hostile countries or which hostile countries they had in mind was left unexplained.

I might add that, in contrast to later intelligence cables, these early raw reports have not been "sanitized"—intelligence community jargon for censoring out sensitive information.

A companion DIA report of the same date gives the by now familiar organizational details of Moon's church, but estimates church membership in Korea at between 40,000 and 50,000.

More intriguing, however, is the DIA's perception of Moon's recruiting practices. According to this report:

> Directly under Founder/Sect Leader MUN, are his six main disciples, all females, who are called "Marys" in the UC. In spreading the religion, each of the "Marys" first recruited three males, each of them was then required to recruit three females, repeating this cycle. Under this Triangular Organizational Method, each group of three persons constitutes a basic unit; four Units, a Team; and three Teams, a Group.[32]

But the DIA cable has even more interesting things to disclose. Under this triangular system, it suggests, "immoral acts involving illicit sexual relationships are being allegedly perpetuated be-

tween the female and male members." The DIA also reported that
Unification Church dogma insisted that true marriages could only
take place between church members. If one partner refused membership, the DIA report said, divorce would be encouraged by the
Unification Church. Mass marriages were also part of the religion's practice, even then. According to the DIA:

> On 15 May 1961, in accordance with a directive made by MUN, 36
> married UC couples held a combined marriage ceremony in
> SEOUL, creating a sensation among the general public. It was
> learned that staff officials of the UC involving MUN were either
> divorced or married again based on the dogma.[33]

On the Reverend Sun Myung Moon's theology, the same intelligence report observed that church dogma contained "unique
interpretations" of creation and Christ's Second Coming. At the
same time, it noted, the Unification Church and its leader had
been accused of "swindling" their followers.

But the charges did not stick, according to the 1967 DIA cable,
because church members, the alleged victims, "were reluctant to
cooperate with the court."

This particular report concludes: "Founder MUN fancies himself to be the inheritor of Christ. There have been no reports of
subversive activities involving the UC as of this date."[34]

Another DIA report from Seoul, dated December 4, 1967, concentrated on church membership in Korea. This time the figure is
50,000 souls, with 600 in the Seoul area while the rest were distributed in some 1,000 "chapters" across the country. But the DIA did
enter one caveat on membership. "The churches in the ROK," it
stated, "tend to exaggerate their membership in an effort to boost
their prestige when they make an annual report to the Ministry of
Education."[35]

The Unification Church, it also noted, is no exception to this
Korean rule.

The DIA also reported that the three principal beliefs of the
Unification Church are: the unification of the world "dedicated to
God, the Creator"; the creation of a paradise on earth; and finally,
"opposition to dialectic materialism." It was the first mention of
Moon's anti-communism in a U.S. intelligence document.[36]

As for Unification Church activities, the December 4 report states that the church was increasing its membership by forming alliances "with athletic organizations and by holding revival meetings . . . in rural areas and fishing villages." It also reports for the first time church missionary work in Japan and the United States.[37]

And finally, the DIA report, once again, ends on a cryptic note. In contrast to the earlier cable, the informant reports that the Unification Church is now considered "an ordinary church," although before the 1960 collapse of Syngman Rhee's government it was "regarded as a quasi-religious group"—whatever that meant.[38]

No attempt, by the way, was ever made to explain that observation.

Another DIA report from Seoul dated December 21 detailed Unification Church activity in the Pusan area which at the time placed emphasis on anti-communist propaganda activity.[39]

Finally, there was an April 1968 DIA intelligence report dispatched from Seoul which said that a Unification Church effort to conduct an anti-communist campaign among Korean students in Japan had proved a failure: a failure in part caused by Japan's Christian churches, which found Moon no more to their taste than was the case for many of their brothers in Korea.[40]

The natural question arises: Why did the DIA gather intelligence on a subject which seems so safely removed from the normal concerns of military intelligence?

In fact, raw reporting from the field does not follow neat and tight lines of inquiry. Anything and everything can be sucked up and is normally passed on to the Pentagon and subsequently the whole intelligence community. Thus, only later is that information combined with other reporting from other services, then turned into finished intelligence—but only when it is deemed necessary.

DIA reporters, in particular, are noted for their industry if not their high degree of discrimination, sophistication, or accuracy, as any CIA analyst can tell you.

The DIA reporting on the church had about it a rather odd air. For one thing, the information was internally contradictory. For another, it still seemed far removed from any conceivable subject of interest to the military.

Defense intelligence is supposed to concentrate on reporting that is at least tangentially military in nature. If a policymaker needs to know the specs of a new Bulgarian machinegun, chances are the DIA will tell him more than he ever wanted to know. So intelligence on a seemingly obscure Korean quasi-Christian sect strikes even a well-read member of the intelligence community as somewhat strange.

CIA reporting, on the other hand, makes a certain amount of sense, especially that done in the mid-1970s. Unfortunately, in contrast to the DIA cables, the agency's FOIA released intelligence cables and internal memoranda are severely censored. In some cases, almost nothing is left of the reporting. Still, with a little judicious reading between the lines and help from friends of mine who have read by now several million pages of agency cables, something can be made of the material.

One CIA memo—the date tag removed, but apparently written in 1973—recounts, amid the many security deletions, the familiar early history of Moon while also noting the Korean's visits to the United States in 1961 and 1964. It also reported the Unification Church's subsidizing of Radio Free Asia.

On the touchy question of financing, the CIA memo expresses a certain puzzlement:

> It is not clear where MUN gets all of his money. However, more than a small amount comes from street collections and large private donations from religious followers. He claims that some funds also derive from his private business interests in South Korea. His ... estimated fortune has been valued at between $10–15 million although no one has had access to his personal books.[41]

In another internal CIA memorandum written sometime in mid- or late 1976 (and also heavily censored), the agency made it clear that it—the agency—had no ties with Moon and the Unification Church, and that it had already made a recent review of the record on that subject owing to the publication of a *New York Times* story alleging these ties.[42]

A CIA Outgoing Message—in effect a cable from headquarters to the field—dated September 1975 reviews the by-now-familiar Moon biography. And, despite its numerous deletions, the key "FYI" paragraph remains.

It says in its clipped, telegraphic style: "Mun extremely wealthy and owns numerous businesses and properties in South Korea and U.S. It certainly believed he has sources of funds other than the Unification Church."[43]

And the TD adds: "[Deletion] source claims MUN in part supported by ROKCIA for selected activities."[44]

In June 1976, an unusually long ten-page agency cable provided the most complete CIA run-down of Moon and his church that has yet to appear under the FOIA. Unfortunately, most of the summary and much of the report have been airbrushed by Langley censors.[45]

About six pages of it have been blacked out and all tags including the source or sources and their reliability have been removed. Still, the cable—and cables of this kind are routinely stamped Secret—does tell us a thing or two.

From what remains, it can be seen that the June 10, 1976, cable evaluates the influence of the Unification Church and its founder within South Korea. For example, one surviving sentence, set in a lengthy but blacked-out paragraph, says: "The church has a significant following in all sectors of ROK society."[46]

In the following paragraph, the CIA cable explains:

The poor image created for the ROK by the Unification Church in the U.S. since mid-1975 [deletion] Mun and his group have been careful not to break any ROK laws. Thus, the government is almost powerless to influence the group's activities. Within the ROK the Unification has been careful to comply with all ROK laws.[47]

What then follows is a lengthy portion of censored material which, in turn, is followed by this passage:

Many Koreans have been attracted to the Unification Church because of its financial power. When Mun held an event in the Chosun Hotel in Seoul some time ago, many important government officials, business and social leaders were invited and most attended.[48]

The cable then mentions "Mun's" staunchly anti-communist beliefs, which in Korea are equated with national survival since militantly communist, heavily armed North Korean forces remain a forty-five-minute cab ride from the South's capital, Seoul.[49]

The agency report next details Moon's contribution to South
Korea's defense build-up:

> Mun is also involved in contributing to the defense of the ROK
> through church ownership of a plant complex in Changwoi which
> manufactures the Vulcan-20 gun [deletion] These points unfor-
> tunately give the impression that Mun and his church have official
> ties to the ROK government but that impression is incorrect.[50]

Then follows a lengthy and lightly censored account of Moon's
defense plant holdings. The CIA reports that the Tong-Il (the
word means unification) Industrial Corporation by the mid-1970s
had become the main producer favored by the South Korean
government because "of its ability to finance its own capital expan-
sion projects and material requisitions from Unification Church
coffers."[51]

Another reason for Tong-Il's popularity? Since 1973, the cable
reported, the church firm's production standards and productivity
were considered to be among the best in the whole South Korean
defense manufacturing sector. As a result, Tong-Il was selected to
assemble the M-167 Vulcan air defense system—a crucial selection since South Korea, especially at that time, was heavily depen-
dent on the United States for protection against the North's
overwhelmingly superior air power.[52]

Finally, in the only other remaining uncensored paragraph, the
agency's intelligence cable reports that Korean officials traveling
abroad are said to be amazed at "the excellent contacts the church
has developed in other nations."[53]

And finally, the CIA produced a classified one-page biography
of Moon shortly after the June 10 agency cable. The date can be
inferred since such bios—usually stamped Secret—are compiled
from all intelligence sources. The June TD is the last classified
source to be listed.

The Reverend Sun Myung Moon's classified biography is also
heavily censored. The entire middle part, in fact, has been removed. However, here is what is left. The church, it says, was
"reportedly organized" in 1961 in South Korea by "Kim Chong-
p'il" while he was director of Korea's KCIA. Sources, it reports,
have said that Kim has used the Unification Church repeatedly as

a political tool. As proof, the CIA bio states that Kim helped found the Korean Cultural and Freedom Foundation as a propaganda tool for the church (and indirectly, it is assumed) the Seoul regime.

Unfortunately, further explanatory material on this charge has been wiped out by agency censors. The remaining paragraph dwells on Moon's ties to the Korean defense industry, no more than a rehash of the June 10 Agency TD.[54]

And that's it. What we have seen is the available record from America's intelligence agencies on Moon and his movement through the mid-1970s.

What can be said about it?

First, it is very much a mixed record. The reporting itself is relatively scanty, as perhaps befits a rather small Korean religious movement. But the reporting varies considerably in what is said as well as in its quality. It should be said, or rather repeated, that all field reporting is considered raw and by itself unreliable and incomplete. It is simply assumed that such reporting is virtually indiscriminate—like a vacuum cleaner picking up anything it can—ready for testing and checking from all other sources. If there ever are any. Raw intelligence can rest unused for years or even decades before anything can legitimately be made of it. Most times, the stuff is of no use whatever.

When it is, it only becomes so after all the bits and pieces are put together. Only then does a more-or-less finished piece of intelligence analysis emerge. In and of itself, however, the individual field report is not reliable or meaningful (nor is it meant to be) even when the sources themselves are considered high quality. And in the case of the DIA Moon reports, the sources were labeled casual and of mediocre reliability.

It is not surprising, then, that the raw reports could be wildly contradictory on such elementary questions as church membership. Perceptions of Moon and his movement also varied, depending, obviously, on the sources. In the intelligence reporting already looked at, the image of Moon and the Unification Church varies radically from one of basic normality to the bizarre. The same can be said about Moon's alleged ties with the Korean CIA.

In short, when dealing with raw intelligence the reader is often presented with a smorgasbord from which to pick and choose as he pleases.

The system, when improperly used, is also open to an enormous amount of abuse. And at least one House subcommittee and its chairman did just that by selecting some raw intelligence files to make their preconceived point. That subcommitee, dealing with international organizations and led by Congressman Donald Fraser of Minnesota, attempted during hearings held in the fall of 1977 to portray falsely the Reverend Sun Myung Moon and his church as a major threat to American institutions. The hearings were made more buoyant by the seemingly related Koreagate scandal in which congressmen were taking payoffs from the South Korean government thanks to that industrious man about town, Tongsun Park.

In particular, Fraser and his staffers zeroed in on the old, previously disproven allegation that the Unification Church might be a tool of the Korean CIA. Fraser and his staff carefully selected the outdated CIA field report but left out, of course, other reports refuting the connection. In addition, his staffers leaked to the *Chicago Tribune* a then-decade-old raw DIA field report—which we have discussed—on the alleged sexual practices of church members including the founder, the Reverend Sun Myung Moon.

Staffers who did so knew perfectly well that the report was not finished intelligence, but rather low-level reporting from a casual informant. They also knew the charges had been proven false. But reporters, ignorant of intelligence methods, did not, and therefore greedily gulped it down raw, thus producing a hard-hitting story based on "intelligence sources" whose very authority was designed to appear beyond question.

Before he was finished, Fraser had not only worked the press into an anti-church frenzy but had managed to persuade the normally benign Federal Trade Commission, the Securities and Exchange Commission, the Comptroller of Currency, and the U.S. Customs Service into using their full investigative powers to uncover church wrong-doing.

Naturally, all those efforts were for naught, but even a novice politician knows an investigation doesn't have to turn up anything to ruin someone's career, reputation, and life. Usually it's sufficient just to call for an investigation and then sit back and watch as the press flies fast and loose with every unsubstantiated rumor that is fed to them.

It is not a particularly pretty game when politicians and press come together but it is not an uncommon one either.[55]

As it turned out, Don Fraser wasn't the only congressional gambler in town. He was preceded by another "public servant" turned high-roller. The town, of course, was Washington, D.C., where all human life revolves around an intricately linked set of floating political crapgames.

The object for the politically ambitious—and all are in Washington, D.C.—is to move up the power ladder with or without the use of loaded dice. The power itself need not be real, since the perception of power and influence is good enough for most.

At the end of 1975, no one was playing the game better than Senator Robert Dole, Republican from Kansas. He had already gone far, and he still had far to go. Along the way Bob Dole, like Don Fraser, would take a crack at Moon. Indeed, Don Fraser had actually been something of a student of Dole's, employing the same tactics and invoking the authority of Congress and several federal agencies to create the illusion of crime where none actually existed—a tactic the Kansan would find so successful in his quest to put Moon away.

Senator Dole—he has always preferred to be called Bob—had been moving up fast. From farm state congressman to senator in a few short years, Bob Dole was assiduously careful in protecting his home base. Unlike many who came to Washington, D.C., Dole's Potomac fever had not clouded his judgment about what came first. And what came first were Kansans and Kansas, especially in an election year.

He was lucky, too—or maybe his timing was nothing less than exquisite. By 1975, Watergate—President Nixon had resigned in disgrace little more than a year before—had ruined a generation of Washington Republicans, from senior figures like John Mitchell, the former attorney general, to junior-fry campaign officials like Jeb Stuart Macgruder.

But not Bob Dole.

Not that the Kansan Republican couldn't have been ground up by the scandal. Being innocent, much less good, had little to do with damaged or ruined reputations. A mere mention in the *Post* in a Watergate-associated story could be enough. And the senator from Kansas sat then on a very high and exposed perch. Not only was he a Republican senator, he was also chairman of the Republican National Committee.

But as chairman he was doubly fortunate. First, Dole was not a Nixon intimate. Second, the RNC, like its Democratic counterpart, has little to do when its party occupies the White House. And during Dole's tenure, Nixon-Ford-Rockefeller still held onto 1600 Pennsylvania Avenue.

And, of course, one other thing. Dole quite rightly helped himself through the muck of Watergate by shrewdly and carefully distancing himself—and the committee—from the scandal and Nixon. When the fever peaked during the House's consideration of the articles of impeachment, Dole was nowhere to be found among the president's shield bearers, much less spear carriers. And the man from Russell, Kansas, was spared the agony of voting on the articles in the Senate, thanks to Nixon's resignation on August 9, 1974.

Having survived, Dole would then flourish. In mid-1976, he was chosen by President Gerald Ford as his running mate on the Republican ticket that would, despite Watergate and a consequent thirty-point deficit in the polls, nearly do a Truman-Dewey against the Georgia preacher-politician, James Earl Carter.

The liberal elite didn't like Dole and he didn't like them. That became abundantly clear during the 1976 race. He was too strident and showed too hard an edge for that effete mob. And he was partisan too, favoring one-liners that made Republican county chairmen cheer and would-be Democratic intellectuals sneer, or cringe.

They were, for one, outraged by his refusal to call the Democratic party, the *Democratic party*. For Bob Dole, it was the *Democrat party*, the way Republican stalwarts had called it for years. Democrats liked even less his debate tactics with rival Walter Mondale when he accused the Democrats of being the war party. "Democrats always get us into wars," Dole charged, "including Vietnam." For liberal Democrats still feeling righteous about their opposition to that war, it was the ultimate calumny.

But Dole was better than that. He was funny. Witty, really. He could, in a line or two, deflate some awfully big political balloons in Washington, D.C., or, when he wanted to, cut with his verbal stiletto the very sacred cows grazing complacently in the liberal pasture. After all, you can denounce liberals, but you can't laugh at them and their whimsical pretensions at being *hommes serieux*.

But Bob Dole did just that, to their rage and fury. Surprisingly, some in the liberal media liked him. After all, a good quote can make a story, and a good sound bite saves everyone at Action News a lot of hard work.

Besides, who had ever heard of a funny Republican? It seemed so, well, oxymoronic, like Young Republicans, the ultimate contradiction in terms. At least, that's true if you're a with-it, New School journalist who has been freed of the duties that bound the older school: duties like reporting mere facts accurately and without noticeable bias, particularly political bias.

So Bob Dole was good copy and he would prosper. After his failed bid for the vice-presidency, the senator would become one of the leading lights in the struggle against the Carter-Torrijos Panama Canal treaties. His floor speeches pointing to General Torrijos' connection with drugs—a theme that would be resurrected by the Democrats a decade later for another presidential campaign—put the Carter administration in a state of near panic, if not shock.

And after that, Dole would emerge an even larger power in the Senate. After Howard Baker retired from that chamber, he would become the party leader in that body, first as its majority leader, then as its minority leader after the disastrous 1986 elections.

True, his bid for the presidency against Vice-President George Bush in 1987–88 did not fare very well—Dole like many of his congressional colleagues was a poor executive, that is, a bad manager of campaign staff—but inside the Beltway, Dole had risen to become a supremely powerful politician.

All that and more was in the future. But his restless ambition was very evident even in 1975.

As a left-for-dead veteran of World War II, with wounds that left him a shattered right arm, a passion for the handicapped, and a bitterness even friends did not bother to deny, Dole was a man on a mission.

The drive to get ahead, to win, also explains his ability to get on the Senate's power committees. In this case, it was the Senate Finance Committee, and, less important, Foreign Relations. And he did so in near-record time, carving out an important niche for himself. In a few years he was poised to become the ranking minority member and shadow chairman of Finance, the Senate's counterpart to the House's all powerful Ways and Means Committee. After the 1980 election and the Reagan landslide he became chairman.

Success in politics—electoral politics, at least—requires a keen sense of what the public wants or, better, fears or, better yet, loathes. By a process that no one, including Bob Dole's closest advisors of the time, can fully explain today, the Kansas senator had decided sometime in 1975 that America was menaced by religious cults, specifically the Unification Church.

Moon and his followers had first caught Dole's eye when the church sponsored a series of pro-Nixon rallies in late 1973 and early 1974. One of them took place smack dab on the U.S. Capitol steps. That was November 1973. For three days several hundred church members fasted and prayed for the embattled Richard Nixon, urging forgiveness and reconciliation from the Congress and the American people. Full-page ads in nearly every major daily newspaper across the country, paid for by the church, urged the same thing.

The rally attracted a lot of attention, but not much support. For someone from Russell, Kansas, the church must have seemed a little strange, not the least for coming to the rescue of a politically mortally wounded politician.

And they didn't go away. In May 1975, the church continued to be in the news. NBC, for one, had prepared a devastatingly critical documentary of Moon and his movement, complete with a sinister, vaguely oriental voiceover reading juicy, out-of-context portions of Moon's sermons and speeches.

American xenophobic fear of the Yellow Peril was alive and well in Burbank.

And it worked. The church-bashing documentary was a ratings bonanza for the otherwise weak network documentary shop. And the print media were not asleep either. Newspapers and magazines featured a plethora of stories about brainwashed and love-bombed "children" being "rescued" by their parents through the work of "professional" deprogrammers like Ted Patrick of San Diego, California. Never mind that Patrick like many of his cohorts had a long criminal rap sheet—everything from armed robbery to drug dealing and kidnapping—and the so-called "children" were all over the age of twenty, many with college degrees.

Yet even given all that, precisely why Bob Dole targeted the church is still not at all clear. Officially he would claim that constituent mail had alerted him to the problem. Perhaps, but in the mid-1970s the church had little presence in his state. Instead, Moon's missionaries were concentrating on the two coasts, more than a thousand miles in either direction from Kansas.

In fact, the only constituent of Dole's that ever talked to him about the church, as far as the record shows, is a Jean Tuttle from Manhattan, Kansas. Tuttle had a daughter, Sue, in the Unification Church. The daughter, according to her affidavit, was forcibly deprogrammed by her mother after the mother had hired Ted Patrick. The younger Tuttle resisted, eventually escaped, and remained bitterly estranged from her mother.[56]

But Jean Tuttle's one-woman war against the church hardly explains the letter Dole wrote the Internal Revenue Service on January 9, 1976—least of all why the letter was addressed to the IRS's commissioner, Donald Alexander. For all practical purposes, this one letter from Senator Bob Dole set into motion all subsequent events which, five years later, would result in the conviction and imprisonment of Moon.

Now it is not unusual for members of Congress to write officials in the executive branch. The amount of such mail, in fact, is substantial.

Still, this letter was unusual; extraordinary, actually. And as it was from a ranking member of the Senate Finance Committee, the congressional panel which directly controls the IRS's budget, it was one that Alexander could ill afford to ignore.

Only months before then-President Richard Nixon had run into a media buzzsaw over his attempted use of the IRS to shake up some of his political enemies. But that fiasco, and the lessons it should have taught, apparently escaped Dole.

He wasted no time beating around the bush. The eight-paragraph letter began:

A large number of my constituents have contacted me about the Unification Church headed by Mr. Sun Myung Moon. Their questions and statements raise doubt in my mind about the tax-exempt status of that organization.[57]

In the letter, no other religious tax abuser was mentioned. The finger of suspicion was pointed only at the Korean-based church.

But Bob Dole was doing more than raising suspicions. In fact, the letter read more like a memorandum for prosecution, a field commander's marching orders, than an inquiry from an elected representative concerned about his constituents. After telling Alexander that many of his constituents had offspring in the Unification Church, the Kansan made his case:

> As I understand, the first test for a tax exemption on religious grounds is that the group must be organized and operated exclusively for religious purposes. The information provided suggests the Unification Church may not meet this test in three ways.[58]

The information enclosed for Alexander included no learned legal briefs on the First Amendment and what churches can and cannot do as tax exempt bodies, but instead consisted of clippings of newspaper stories by "investigative reporters"—hardly experts on the Constitution, or on complicated tax questions for that matter.

Nevertheless, Dole then outlined his or, more correctly, Alexander's case against the "Moonies."

> Most of those contacting me question whether the organization is based on a bona fide religion or on mind control techniques. Parents of members and former members state that while initial entry into the group is clearly voluntary, the subsequent actions of members suggest the loss of any ability to make any reasoned or unguided choice about continued participation in the group.[59]

Having raised the spectre of brainwashing, Dole then proceeded to make it flesh and blood:

> This may indicate that the organization is maintained not by religious motivation, but by the calculated eradication or erosion of each member's ability to make an alternate choice. The well-documented process of training and initiation activities appears to

substantiate that the organization is based more on mind control and indoctrination than on religious faith.[60]

From that charge, Dole proceeded to another. The religion was no religion at all, but a money making enterprise, pure and simple. "Members," he assured Alexander, ". . . are subjected to great pressure to obtain funds. . . ."[61]

But Moon was not just making money, according to the Kansas solon, he was engaged in political activities, another taboo for a religious body, according to Dole's lights. Besides Moon's political statements, Dole charged that:

[T]he contacts of many followers with members of Congress suggest that the organization is being operated not exclusively for religious purposes but at least to some extent for political purposes.[62]

The second bone Dole had to pick was Moon's alleged pocketing of church funds for personal benefit. That, "as I understand," Dole said rather coyly, was not properly done by a tax-exempt organization and showed why Moon had a lifestyle above that which "could be reasonably expected for any clergyman."[63]

Which brings us to Bob Dole's principal conclusion:

Based on the facts reported by my constituents and by articles in the public media, it appears that the tax exempt status of the Unification Church is questionable. It is my feeling, on this basis, that an audit of the organization may be warranted.[64]

And for good measure, the Kansan added: "Your response would be greatly appreciated."[65]

Unfortunately, the public record does not contain Alexander's reply, but it can be safely bet that one was prepared. With great care. As a ranking member of the Senate Finance Committee— the oversight committee for the IRS—Dole had to be taken seriously and handled with kid gloves.

Alexander—or at least his legal counsel—knew perfectly well that Dole had made utter hash of the Constitution, the tax laws and the IRS regulations in his demand for an audit of the Unification Church.

It was clear that Bob Dole and his staff had done little to acquaint themselves with the rudiments of the First Amendment. Religious organizations had for nearly the lifetime of the republic been allowed to engage in businesses other than the immediate saving of souls. But the senator from Kansas did not seem to know that or, if he did, he didn't think such constitutional courtesies should be extended to the Unification Church.

As for religious organizations' not being allowed to engage in political activity, Dole was turning the First Amendment inside out twice over. America's religious sects and their leaders are permitted free speech under the Bill of Rights, like all other Americans.

Moreover, the non-establishment clause could in no way be taken as a prohibition of political activity on the part of the churches. In fact, the opposite was true. Congress (or any other branch of government) could make no laws limiting their right to do so, and American constitutional law took a dim view of Big Government getting itself into that business.

All in all, for a conservative Republican, Bob Dole seemed strangely indifferent to that deeply rooted conservative prejudice and principle.

And as a practical matter of fact, the nation's religious bodies have been political animals since Plymouth Rock. From Cotton Mather to Martin Luther King and now the Reverends Jesse Jackson and Jerry Falwell, America's divines have been playing hardball politics, often with far greater funding and far more sophistication—not to mention results—than the Reverend Sun Myung Moon could or would ever have. Few, certainly not Senator Robert Dole of Kansas, have ever questioned the tax-exempt status, for example, of the Roman Catholic Church because of its staunch opposition to abortion.

But even more disturbing in Dole's brief submitted to IRS Commissioner Alexander is the senator's reasoning. On what basis did Bob Dole draw the conclusion that the "Moonies" were a threat, turning America's children into brainwashed zombies?[66]

The evidence he cites to support his "suggestion" for a tax audit is laughable. It consists of organized, pressure group generated mail—certainly a politician and particularly a congressman should know how that's done—and newspaper clippings. Little old ladies in tennis shoes wave those around as proof of their favorite conspiracies.

But trendy news stories hardly constitute irrefutable proof of anything. "Facts," Dole called them. But who decided the allegations presented were facts? And how was it done? And these, of course, beg the basic problem of all human knowledge, which every epistemologist since Aristotle has known: that is, facts can explain nothing and have no meaning in and of themselves.

Any first year law student basing his brief on such "evidence" would flunk Rules of Evidence 101. Yet the ranking member of a powerful Senate committee was asking to be taken seriously by the chief of an equally powerful agency of the executive branch on the basis of such stuff.

And that brings us to the most disturbing aspect of the Dole letter. It's one thing for a citizen, and even a senator, to write to the IRS to complain about this or that. That's everyone's right. But it's a whole different matter when a powerful senator fires off a missive not only demanding what amounts to an IRS criminal investigation but going so far as to tell the top man at the IRS how to go about it.

Even Richard Nixon didn't go that far in his attempts to cause a few of his liberal opponents some financial discomfort at the hands of the IRS. Nixon, of course, had no direct control over the IRS's budget—that most sacred of all sacred bureaucratic cows—and even if he had threatened the IRS, there would have been no way to force the issue. It should also be pointed out that the Nixon plans to use the IRS were just that—plans which never materialized.

Dole's letter, on the other hand, had an immediate impact. Within days the IRS began what eventually became the most intensive and expensive criminal tax investigation of any religious figure in U.S. history.

But it gets better.

Senator Dole, of course, had no intention of keeping his letter to Alexander secret. Understanding at least the second law of political power, namely, power is publicity (the first being power is money), Dole and his staff issued a press release three days after the date of the Dole-Alexander letter (that is, about the time the IRS commissioner actually received it) disclosing the highlights of the note.[67]

Bob Dole's letter and press release calling for an investigation of the Unification Church was not meant as a one- or two-shot

affair—something to appease a few outraged hick constituents—
with no follow-up.

Dole wasn't just going through the motions, this time. He really
meant to bash the Unification Church. And bash them he did. The
letter to Alexander and the accompanying press release were only
the opening barrage of a carefully orchestrated attack.

Now, a general entering battle needs more than artillery. He
needs troops. Foot soldiers. And these Dole had. There may have
been a question as to who was commanding whom in this fight, as
we shall soon see, but at least the order of battle was pretty clear.

Unfortunately, Dole's allies were not exactly the stouthearted,
middle-American, plain-farm-folk Kansas constituents that the
senator had portrayed in his letter to the IRS. Instead, they were a
well-knit group of so-called "anti-cultists"—educated, affluent,
upper-middle-class, largely suburban Northeastern liberals—who
had formed an organization called Citizens Engaged in Reuniting
Families, or CERF, for short.

Most, but not all, of CERF's members were parents of adult
"children" belonging to so-called cults. Others were ex-members,
"professional" deprogrammers, and people who liked belonging to
a cause—especially if it attracted a lot of favorable publicity.

CERF's leaders were a Baptist minister, George Swope, and a
rabbi, Maurice Davis. Neither was from Kansas; both hailed from
New York's Westchester County. Swope and Davis, in fact, engi-
neered the 14,000 signature petition.[68]

They claimed the signers were all Kansans. Dole himself made
no such claim. In any case, the petition would lay the basis for Bob
Dole's expressed concern about the cult menace.[69]

A little more than a month after Dole zipped off his letter to the
IRS, both the senator and the CERFies had prepared a follow-up
attack on the Unification Church. It was nothing less than brilliant.

The CERF organization would call it "A Day of Affirmation and
Protest," one of those richly self-righteous self-accolades the "activists" so often wielded with deadly effect during the Vietnam War.

What it really amounted to was a bitch session on Capitol Hill. A
high-profile, orchestrated, well-publicized, one-sided bitch session. Speakers, all from a safely anti-cult point of view, tore into the
new religions—the Unification Church mostly—while their sup-

porters packed the room and cheered them on, and a handful of church members and their parents sat in stunned silence in the back.

It made for good theater—which was precisely the intent. Still, it was definitely not the routine, run-of-the-mill, three-ring political circus one usually associates with an election year. The tents were up on Capitol Hill all right, and lest we forget, 1976 was a very big election year, but the Day of A and P was more than that.

And it involved quite a bit of Chinese opera as well. The maestro-in-charge was, of course, Bob Dole, which is why it could be held in a hearing room in the stately Dirksen Senate Office Building, located only several stone throws from the U.S. Capitol itself.

The spacious wood-paneled chamber with its charming art deco brass fixtures looked damned impressive, as did its high-curved bench from which senators and staff looked down on witnesses and audience alike.

The room could seat four hundred people, not counting the media and their bulky equipment, and looked even bigger on television. As it did on that crisp, early February afternoon in 1976 when Bob Dole brought the event to order.

I say "event" because its chairman had a hard time explaining just exactly what he had brought to order. It was not a Senate hearing, Dole explained. Nothing official. To do that would have required some legislative pretext and the cooperation of his committee chairman. And there wasn't any on either count, despite Dole's best efforts.

The senator made that clear enough in his opening statement, which he read to the gathered multitude:

> I want to emphasize that this is not a congressional hearing. It is not any kind of investigation. It is not a public speechmaking forum. And above all it is not a debate between opposing points of view.[70]

He then added:

> I would remind everyone one more time that we are not taking any testimony and no one is under oath. Moreover, nothing that is said or done is to be interpreted as a prejudgment or stamp of approval by the legislative branch on anything.[71]

Well, that was true, technically at least. Mostly anyhow. It was not a formal hearing or anything equally official like an investigation. A congressional investigation, for one thing, would require the presence of those being investigated. And they would have their lawyers, and the right to reply, but neither Bob Dole nor the Ad Hoc Committee wanted anything like that. That would make it more like a debate with equal representation or a democracy with two opposing sides, and the Kansas senator wanted no part of that.

Still, not calling it a public speech forum seemed to be stretching it a bit, as only a politician can. Speeches were made. Lots of them. Vitriolic attacks and one-sided ones at that. And very public ones, too, thanks to the four television network crews and a dozen or more other TV camera crews who were present.

But let Bob Dole himself define what he had brought forth:

It is, very simply, an informal question and answer session involving two predesignated panels of participants whom I have brought together to discuss subjects of possible mutual concern.[72]

So, why, you might ask, in a Senate hearing room instead of, say, the senator's private office? Bob Dole, of course, had an answer for that one:

While it could very appropriately have taken place in my own private office, the widespread interest among both the general public and the press led me to select a larger and more open facility.[73]

And besides, the CERFies would have hardly settled for a Senate private office for something as officious as a Day of Affirmation and Protest. Affirming and protesting are not consonant with squeezing oneself into a small room while wedged tightly up against the water cooler. Particularly when there's no room for the cameras and reporters.

So it was to take place in a hearing room.

And the session would involve more than Senator Dole and a horde of unhappy anti-cultists. To listen to their complaints, the senator also "invited" a group of government officials. And where did they come from? The IRS, of course, but also from the Departments of Justice, Labor, and Health, Education and Welfare, not to mention the U.S. Postal Service, the Federal Trade Commission, and the National Institute of Mental Health.

True, those who came—there's no complete list of those investigative agencies Senator Dole invited/ordered to appear at the non-investigative non-hearing—were not bureaucratic heavyweights. They were mostly upper-level bureaucrats: an assistant secretary, a deputy commissioner, a special assistant, the directors of faintly obscure offices of the larger departments and agencies.

For example, it was not the chairman of the Federal Trade Commission who showed up for Bob Dole's "Moonie roast." It was the FTC's assistant director for evaluation, Bureau of Consumer Protection.

Nor was it the U.S. Postal Service's postmaster general who put in an appearance, but his assistant chief inspector of the Office of Criminal Investigations who made it to the hearing room that afternoon in February.

Of course, the question is: What were they doing there in the first place? The more cynical might observe that they were there because their superiors told them to appear.

Even a GS-12 can figure out that an invitation from a U.S. senator who happens to be a senior member of a powerful committee cannot be taken lightly. The same cynics might also add that their presence would help lend the appearance of an investigation without ever calling it that. That's called deniability which, of course, Bob Dole instantly invoked:

> I should stress . . . the members of the Executive Branch also have come here [sic] at my request are really themselves the audience. Their answers can, understandably, be phrased only in the most general of terms—but certainly, any disappointing limitations on the substance of the replies should be more than offset by the satisfaction of knowing those giving them care enough to listen.[74]

In case anyone missed the point, those who wanted a hanging that day were once more reminded by the Kansas senator:

> Many of the questions you may desire answers to have only come to the attention of these Federal officials within the last couple of hours, so we should all be understanding of the need for thorough processing and the inability to be candid in those instances.[75]

Dole's careful coaching of the anti-Unification Church audience of course gave away the game. Those federal officials had really no idea why they were there, except they had been told by their cowed superiors, quite probably that morning, to show up with bells on. In short, they were to serve as props for the show that Dole and the Ad Hoc Committee were determined to put on.

But they were not the only props. Bob Dole had not forgotten his fellow congressmen either. In a "Dear Colleague" letter dated a week before the event, Bob Dole invited them en masse to "a discussion-type forum" on the cult menace. Concerned parents from around the country would also be invited. So would executive branch bureaucrats.

There was no mention of refreshments.

Since congressmen are more sensitive to First Amendment questions than civil servants, Dole hastened to explain (as he hadn't with IRS Commissioner Alexander) that no one's religious freedom would be put at risk. And his colleagues who cared to drop in would have nothing asked of them. That did little to allay the fears of most congressmen, who previously had made it clear to Dole and his staff that they felt he was walking on thin constitutional ice with this inquiry, investigation, hearing or whatever the hell it was.[76]

In the end, only two colleagues appeared. Perhaps it was the lack of refreshments. Or perhaps it was too early in the afternoon: 1:30 P.M. left little time for lunch. Or perhaps it was just the press of business.[77]

They didn't miss much.

No sooner had Dole finished his statement, than he turned the meeting over to George Swope, who acted as the festivities' "moderator." Swope made it clear from the outset that he considered the proceedings his group's "day in court"—the beginning of what he hoped would be a thorough government investigation into Moon and the Unification Church, as well as other cults who were a "cancer in our national body."[78]

Forum? A polite exchange of views? Hell no, Swope wanted vengeance. Better yet, a public hanging:

We are citizens, concerned citizens, with deep, controlled anger resulting from psychological havoc in our homes, and a deep fear about the future of this nation we love. This deep anger and this deep fear will carry us united for months and years.[79]

Having gotten that off his chest George Swope then introduced the panelists, including amateur West Coast deprogrammer Daphne Greene; James Sheeran, the ex-FBI Special Agent whom we have already met; and a clutch of ex-church members like Greene's son Ford and Cynthia Slaughter. Mrs. Greene was no better nor worse than any of the rest. In her presentation, Greene offered a series of unsupported and often unconnected allegations based on her "research" which led her to ask finally: "Can a political ideology or a political philosophy get a tax-exempt status in this country?"[80]

Nobody bothered to answer that one.

Her son proved equally loquacious. He rattled on so long, in fact, that Dole had to cut him off, since the Greene family hour had already burned up too much of the forum's scheduled 120 minutes.[81]

Just how silly it got can be gathered by the insufferable Ford Greene's peroration which followed his lengthy description of his Life Among the Moonies (which lasted all of several weeks)— mostly spent in Boonville, California, a church retreat for wayward and mostly white and spoiled middle-class youth.

I quote:

> Will the Unification Church come up front and state its business? If Rev. Moon and the Unification Church can aid any flaw of ours, let them come forth freely under scrutiny so that we can be convinced that they truly have something to offer, are not trying to exploit the vulnerability of the United States of America, and make it clear that they do not intend—with no regard for America's people—to infiltrate a weakening society and overthrow the government.[82]

Actually, it got loonier. The idea had been to relate church horror stories to what its organizers hoped would be a slack-jawed panel of government officials. Unfortunately, it didn't quite work out that way.

Thus, we have ex-debutante Cynthia Slaughter from Grand Prairie, Texas, musing aloud:

> Are the mass marriages that were performed by Mr. Moon in Korea, are those valid according to American standards? Mr. Moon is not

an ordained minister. Can anyone answer that, or could we just put it up for further research?[83]

Unfortunately, since no one from the Bureau of Matrimonial Standards was present in Room 1202 that day, the question went unanswered.

Nevertheless, the matter of questionable marriages sparked another, yet weirder, line of thought. "Moonies," Ms. Slaughter volunteered, had to be prepared to marry communists.

What page of the *Divine Principle*, the main theological work of the Unification Church, is that on?

Breathlessly, they listened to the tale of yet another ex-church member, a David Geisler, who recounted a lecture he had heard in Columbus, Ohio. According to the church lecturer, Geisler recalled, it might be necessary to marry a communist "who might be high in the Communist party in order to convert her."

And that revelation prompted the young Geisler to disclose the church's larger plan, which made marrying communists seem like small potatoes in comparison. That was, of course, the church's secret march on Moscow. That is, Moscow, USSR, not Moscow, Idaho:

> . . . the big thing was the march on Moscow. It was a big slogan. They told us that the day may come when we would have to control these countries. They said it would take up to seven generations to bring the world under total subjugation. They said, for the time being, it might be necessary to control these countries forcibly, militarily, much the way they are being controlled now. In other words, we would be taking over the role of their Communist masters now. I think that the very close [*sic*] to what they are trying to do themselves.[84]

"If they are in cahoots with the communists," Geisler added in one of the afternoon's more notable non sequiturs, "I don't know. In my opinion, they are."[85]

And now that the cat was out of the bag on the "Moonie Mein Kampf" blueprint for world conquest—with or without the help of the Kremlin—the irrepressible Cynthia Slaughter offered this insight into contemporary political thought: "They live communistically. They promote socialism, which is closely related to communism."[86]

What did Senator Dole make of these extravagant adolescent fancies? We don't really know. The laconic Kansan said little after the opening, in part because he made it out of the room on several occasions to go and vote.

On occasion, the horror story gone wacky would turn into something even more sublimely silly.

Consider this one. An ex-member, Peter Tipograph by name, is telling his listeners about how "Moonies" are told to write "deceitful letters" to their loved ones to assure them that everything is all right.

This spurred Cynthia Slaughter to introduce a variation on the Tipograph letter theme by means of a young woman, for some unknown reason named only Marina, who told her tale from the Dark Side. Marina was from Peru and because she spoke Spanish was "instructed" to open other people's mail and read it to the church leaders.

It happened in Tarrytown, and one letter (it may indeed have been only one letter) appeared to be especially memorable for the haunted Marina.

> [I]t was . . . a love letter from one of the members. Actually it was from a husband to his wife. And when I say to them, "This is a love letter," I couldn't translate at all because I was very nervous.[87]

Suddenly, Cynthia Slaughter interrupted the proceedings. "Now that is tampering with personal mail, isn't it?" she asked the U.S. Postal Service representative, a Mr. Paul Coe.

The answer was no. The U.S. Postal Service's responsibilities end when the mail is delivered to the address of the individual.

That small setback, however, did not stop Miss Slaughter. She proceeded to bounce something else off the IRS representative:

> [A]re organizations that are against brainwashing but don't have anything per se to do with deprogramming—is this apt to jeopardize our tax-exempt status?[88]

And if you liked that one, how about the follow-up?

> If not, then why do we apply this in the opposite direction? Is it legal for an organization to be tax-exempt when it uses mind control and brain-washing techniques in holding its members? Is that a general question?[89]

At any rate, the IRS's Mr. Charles Rumph could not immediately recall any Postal Service regulation concerning non-profit
brainwashing.

Besides, he waffled, there are too many ramifications to the
question to answer it just like that.

O.K. But Rabbi Davis was not quite finished with mail tampering, so the U.S. Postal Service was not yet off the hook. CERF's
outgoing president observed: "You answered the question concerning ordinary mail. What is your answer, sir, if the mail is
registered mail?"

Nothing apparently stops the mail from being delivered, and
certainly nothing stops a civil servant from reciting standard operating procedure. So, according to Coe:

> Well, certified and registered mail are individual. A registered or
> certified article, of course, requires a signature on delivery. The
> article is delivered to the addressee or to his or her agent. Now, there
> is a provision for restricted delivery when the proper fee is paid. In
> that event, we would deliver the letter only to the addressee upon
> proof of identity.[90]

Still, the exact classification of the Peruvian love letter—whether
ordinary, registered, or certified—was never established in the
course of A & P Day.

From the merely adolescent, we now proceed to the utterly
childish—whether or not church members make it a practice of
letting the flag touch the ground at Boonville. Cynthia Slaughter
and Rabbi Davis had a field day with that one. But, there was more.
On occasion, the merely absurd turned into the nasty.

Just as he did during his bungled raid on the church training
center in Tarrytown, Jim Sheeran bulldozed his questions through
to the federal bureaucrats. The first was to the Labor Department
representative, a sweet-tempered man named Ronald James.

It took awhile, but finally Sheeran got to the point, which was:
Were the church leaders violating the federal labor laws by using
volunteers in profit-making businesses?

Well, it depends, James said. If the volunteers are not classified
as employees, then they are not covered by the Fair Labor Standards Act. And as far as the church was concerned, that was a
matter that could not be discussed:

I cannot give you a specific answer, just general guidelines. And I can indicate that there are some investigations underway, but I am not privileged to discuss those in any detail. In particular, I cannot discuss the matters which may come up for investigation by the Department of Labor.[91]

Not surprisingly, there was a good deal of this back and forth. The IRS was quizzed as to whether foreigners with permanent resident status were allowed to make money, tax-free—never mind the fact that the church members, rather than taking money from the U.S., had this peculiar habit of pumping millions from Korea and Japan into America.

To that one, the IRS's Rumph said simply that no comment could be made to a general inquiry. Furthermore, he said, the IRS was prohibited from talking about any specific organization when it came to taxes.

But Sheeran persisted. Shouldn't Moon be liable for taxes even if he is a religious leader? The IRS's Rumph demurred.

Well, what about a tax-exempt organization's investing money in legitimate businesses through its individual members?

With some exasperation, the man from IRS said: "I can't possibly answer that." And he didn't.[92]

But then why not ask the senator from Kansas? Sheeran was being no more presumptuous than Bob Dole when he wrote Donald Alexander a month earlier.

In any case, on and on and on it went. The Federal Trade Commission representative was pressed for answers on church consumer fraud. The FTC officer, like the other civil servants, politely begged off.

But then came Scharff. And there was nothing quite like Dr. Thomas Scharff, professor of pharmacology at the University of Kentucky and a loyal member of CERF. Like many members of CERF, Scharff had a son who was a member of the Unification Church.

Later he would be deprogrammed and become a zealous anti-church critic.

Dr. Scharff had a real bone to pick with the church. For starters, he presented irrefutable proof that Moon's minions had broken the law right there in Louisville. In exquisite detail Scharff laid out

the church crime: they had not obtained a solicitor's permit despite suspicion that they had raised as much as $30,000 selling
flowers the previous year.

> I might like to add two other instances here. Personal friends of
> mine, one at his home and one at a shopping center, were accosted by
> these cultists recently and in direct violation of the ordinance. And
> the one excuse for collecting money through selling whatever it is
> they were selling, was that they wanted to help families for delin-
> quent children. We have with us today. . . .[93]

Dr. Scharff was interrupted by Dr. Swope, who, sensing that eyes
were beginning to glaze over at this recitation of mayhem in
Louisville, wished to get on with it, and said so. Even Senator Dole
was moved to mention that the federal officials huddled in Room
1202 had no jurisdiction over violation of local ordinances.
Still, Dr. Scharff had the last word on that one:

> No, but the point, Senator, that I am trying to bring out here is the
> violation and the removal of these people from the normal ethical
> standards of the society.[94]

In other words, let's deport the suckers.
But the Kentucky pharmacology professor had another gripe
concerning Moon. It's best to let Dr. Scharff speak for himself:

> What can be done by the Federal Government to bring about an
> investigation of the Unification movement in the matter of aliena-
> tion of the Unification member from societal values through Unifi-
> cation indoctrination techniques? Is the Unification leadership
> inducing the members to practice deceit, to defy the law, to abrogate
> their important responsibilities to the Society?[95]

The U.S. Postal Service did not answer his questions, but someone tried.
Dr. Julius Segal from the Public Health Service attempted it. Yes,
he got a bit lost, but the sense of it was this: sure, the Congress and
the federal government were paying for research on the alienation
process. And they were getting some results. What results, precisely, were hard to tell. But, in Dr. Segal's words, there were
mitigating circumstances:

The problem, I am afraid, is that the issues are extraordinarily complex—much more complex than the interaction between the physical phenomena. And I believe it's safe to suggest that almost everyone who has experienced this phenomenon has their own individual hypothesis as to what is [*sic*] that triggers a change of attitude and values. And probably every such variable that the parents here might suggest is under scrutiny.[96]

Clearly, Dr. Segal was not serving up red meat to his audience, and one hot-eyed, anti-cult zealot was having none of it.

That was Mrs. Bruce Merritt, a psychiatric social worker from Boston, who had done her own research on scores of ex-members and found nothing complex about it at all. Or so she told the gathering:

Dr. Segal has said that there is an investigation going on. I would love to be able to speak with you afterwards to find out, because we have tried about ten million times, but have been unable to find out what's going on, because our findings are very much different from what you seem to be finding in your studies.[97]

And what about Mrs. Merritt's "findings"?

We definitely believe that brainwashing, mind control, persuasive coercion is occurring. We see very obvious common denominators where you can have five people from five different parts of this country coming out and saying the exact same thing, word for word. The technique is exactly the same, whether it be Reverend Moon's Unification movement, whether it be the Hare Krishna movement, whether it be anything else.[98]

Perhaps even the Baltimore Catechism, the Bible, or the Talmud. Who knows where this memorizing of religious passages will stop. No matter. Mrs. Merritt went on at some length in this vein and arranged for a follow-up meeting with Dr. Segal to compare notes.

Mercifully, history failed to record that exchange.

For the most part, "witnesses and panelists" made no effort at all to link their grievances against Moon to a federal question. Which explains the out-of-sync flavor of the whole wacko proceedings. But, on one occasion, the attempt was made, with odd results.

Dr. Frederick Bunt of New York's Case University, like most of
CERF's "experts," had a daughter in the Unification Church, but
his concern as an educator was that the church with one of its
educational fronts might attempt to obtain federal funding.

That is the federal question involved, although there was no
indication church members were even looking for a handout from
Washington, D.C. In fact, they weren't and apparently still aren't.

But Bunt's fear that this might be so proved a convenient hook
for unleashing his own diatribe against the Unification Church.
His real beef with the church was that it was indoctrinating rather
than educating the young. And that was, well, undemocratic.

The vile "Moonies laugh" at the notion of democracy, Bunt said.
They simply have no use for it:

> Lecture after lecture, there is no question permitted until it is over.
> Gross repetition with indoctrination as the sole purpose is exactly
> what education is for the Unification Church. Questions after the
> lectures are asked and answered in isolation, are perhaps vaguely
> answered or not answered at all, or treated as negative or evil feelings
> coming forth from the individual. Questioning the authority of the
> Church is the work of Satan, as the young people will attest.[99]

The good professor seems to have been encased in Saran wrap
for the last two decades. It is peculiar that he found the Unification
Church so uniquely in the business of indoctrination. American
academia has since Vietnam spawned thousands of would-be educators who have done little more than pass off their woolly headed,
left-wing politics as "learning" in the lecture hall.

And then one wonders why it isn't the business of a religion to
indoctrinate its followers into its beliefs. "Democracy" has precious
little to do with it, as anyone who grew up in the Catholic or
Lutheran educational system can well attest. Indeed, isn't the
essence of democracy and religious tolerance the freedom to
preach and proselytize without fear of government reprisals?

Such rather obvious anomalies, however, did not occur to Fred
Bunt—which led him to his crashing conclusion:

> Are we going to pursue the destruction of human and civil rights by
> the brainwashing and programming of your young people? No civil

liberty can be considered so important that it takes precedence over all other civil liberties, that is supersedes other civil liberties of greater or equal validity. Freedom of religion cannot be used to destroy life and liberty in our democratic type of education.[100]

Bunt's hyperbole, which bordered on hysteria, was more than matched by the wind-up furnished by the good Rabbi Davis.

The Unification Church affronted him in many ways. Church members were trying to convert Jews—at least in San Francisco and New York. That, in itself, was an unspeakable outrage. The Reverend Sun Myung Moon wasn't a Christian either, although he pretended to be one. Church members were selling flowers and candles and buying property in Tarrytown. A church kid would not visit his dying mother. An ex-member committed suicide. *Et cetera.*

Worse, Moon had political aspirations.

Part of them was Moon's plot to take over the Senate by assigning 300 pretty girls—three to a senator—to Capitol Hill, a variation on the previously discussed scheme to take over the Kremlin. Sometimes the point got a little lost in the bill of indictment. I quote:

> The 45 [Unification Church] organizations which go under different names, all of which belong to Moon, and all of which, incidentally, have been authenticated on television by a man in the back row—I saw it on television—these are the front organizations of Moon. I have prepared several kits filled with these materials, and you will be handed those kits to save time to peruse at your discretion.[101]

Davis went on, in much the same fashion and ended with a predictable, but still quite quotable peroration. It would also mercifully close the entire event:

> Senator Dole, ladies and gentlemen, the last time I ever witnessed a movement that had these qualifications: (1) a totally monolithic movement with a single point of view and a single authoritarian head; (2) replete with fanatical followers who are prepared and programmed to do anything their master says; (3) supplied by absolutely unlimited funds; (4) with a hatred of everyone on the outside; (5) with suspicion of parents, against their parents—

Senator Dole, the last movement that had these qualifications was
the Nazi youth movement, and I tell you, I'm scared.[102]

It was a conventional, even a trite analogy, but it didn't matter.
Davis received a standing ovation for delivering what must have
been the most outrageous overstatement in an afternoon full of
outrageous overstatements.

Sun Myung Moon, meet Adolph Hitler.

Needless to say, the rabbi's polemic never once touched on a
subject that remotely had anything to do with the business of the
federal government.

There was now nothing for Senator Dole to do except close the
meeting, since the federal officials, although invited, refused further comment.

Ironically, the most significant information to come from the
Dole non-hearing was not the testimony but rather what wasn't
said. And what wasn't said covers a myriad of myths about the
Unification Church which persist even today.

Not once, for example, did any ex-members or their parents
claim that they had been physically or sexually abused. No claims
of starvation, drugs, or sex. (Indeed, drugs, alcohol, and premari-
tal sex are forbidden by the church.) Likewise, no one even hinted
they were kidnapped or forced to stay in the church against their
will—unless you believe "love bombing" qualifies as a physical
restraint.

Remember, this was a convocation of the most vociferous and,
presumably, the most knowledgeable critics of Moon and his
church. Yet, for all the smoke, mirrors, klieg lights, and props, all
that really emerged from the hearing room that crisp, clear February day was hate. As they say in the newspaper business, there was
a lot of heat and no light.

Well, what to make of this?

No one could pretend—and Dole didn't even try—that this was
a serious examination of religious cults. All the presentations were
diatribes with no attempt to present evidence in a disciplined
manner. There were no real experts with serious qualifications,
although they would have been available if they had been asked.
But they weren't.

And from those who did show up to "testify?" What possible

information could have been gleaned by any responsible federal official?

It was simply assumed, for example, that the church members were an evil, brainwashing collection of religious fanatics which the First Amendment ought not to protect.

That made no difference, however, because the Dole circus had nothing to do with being serious about a problem—if, indeed, there were a problem at all.

But odd as the whole business was, it did serve two serious purposes for Bob Dole and his friends in the CERF and other like-minded organizations.

Beyond the preening and posturing of the participants, the Day of Affirmation and Protest was notable for getting the attention of the mass media. The three major networks were there as well as the infant Cable News Network. And they ate it up. So did the print journalists. The fact is, the media had been suffering from Watergate hangover since Nixon's resignation. That had been eighteen months before, and the "Moonie roast" served as a badly needed pick-me-up.

There had been little or nothing in 1975 that could even come close to Senator Sam Ervin's hearings or the House's impeachment proceedings. Indeed, until Watergate came along, a whole new generation of nouveau journalists had never been exposed to the joys of covering the natural and quite visual drama of congressional hearings.

The Army-McCarthy hearings were in the remote past. So was Senator Estes Kefauver's crime-busting extravaganza. Mere distant memories—if anyone remembered them at all. Watergate, however, was mainline news coverage. And if the reporter was lucky, a book might come out of it.

Also, gratification was instant. No long waits for investigations to be completed and trials to be held. The assumption was that the bastards were guilty as hell and it was a thrill a minute.

But, unfortunately, in February 1976 it was also over. The profession would not have the same pulse-quickening excitement until Ollie North gave us Iran-Contra.

Still, while Bob Dole's Kansas "Moonie roast" may have been an ersatz investigation, it was, nevertheless, the only picnic in town, and the media flocked to it and gobbled down everything in sight.

It made no difference that Bob Dole carefully caveated the event—you know, that part about it's not being a congressional investigation? He knew his print and electronic editors. No sound bites would carry that advisory.

Showing up with the camera crews, not the event itself, defines the importance of the event. That's elementary in the news business. It is the media version of the philosophic conundrum about a tree falling in the forest. If a hearing is held and no reporters are there to cover it, did it really happen?

The answer is no. So what the viewer would see is something that looked like a congressional hearing—it most certainly had all the trappings of one—and if all those very official people were present, something serious and important must be going on.

Ergo, the Reverend Sun Myung Moon and his Unification Church were a menace to America.

The second purpose the non-hearing served for Bob Dole was to put the federal government on notice that he was serious about what he had said in that letter to the IRS's Alexander. No matter how fuzzy-minded the CERFies had seemed that day, relevant agencies had better get cracking on doing something about the church or everyone from the IRS to the NIH would have to answer to the Man, a ranking member of the Senate Finance Committee.

That was never in doubt. Everyone got the message, and before the last of the CERFies had left town the bureaucrats were scurrying. Especially the IRS's Don Alexander.

How did the church members take all this? Not surprisingly, they weren't very happy and they let Bob Dole know it. They were completely unsuccessful in their attempts to cancel the forum, or even to change it. A specific request to have a chance to respond at the non-hearing was denied by Dole. The church members were to be tried before the TV cameras in absentia.

The Kansas senator, however, did agree to meet with Unification Church President Neil Salonen shortly after the Day of Affirmation and Protest. No cameras, no reporters, of course. Dole also took pains to write church officials his denial that the proceedings were official or that he was a supporter of Ted Patrick or any other deprogrammer.[103]

That, of course, was scant comfort to church officials.

Which is why, before the great day, Unification Church leaders had written every member of Congress in protest over what they called a trial-by-media event. They also arranged for an 800-parents-of-church-members telegram to be sent to Dole the day before the meeting, as well as a second telegram of protest signed the same day by 177 Protestant and Roman Catholic clergymen.

For their part, the clergymen expressed shock at what they called "a one-sided meeting" of one religious group's enemies.

"The closed format of the meeting," they said, "including your failure to provide any opportunity for the church to offer any defense of itself, is a threat to all religions."[104]

Needless to say, none of it did any good. Moreover, Bob Dole was not about to back off. A few months later, Dole wrote the Immigration and Naturalization Service about Moon and his planned departure from the United States.[105]

The federal bureaucracy had been put on notice in a variety of ways that it had better get cracking investigating the church or face the consequences from a powerful politician positioned to do each agency massive damage when it came budget-time.

Not surprisingly, the first to respond was the Internal Revenue Service. The IRS later explained to sympathetic journalists that its audit of Moon and the Unification Church came about through an accidental discovery by one of its agents who happened to be routinely pouring over Moon's 1974 tax returns in 1976 when he discovered certain anomalies. The fact that the auditor stumbled onto Moon's first U.S. tax return at precisely the same time Bob Dole's letter landed on the IRS commissioner's desk was, well, one of those funny Washington, D.C., coincidences.[106]

In any event, the IRS probe of Moon, his movement, and their tax-exempt status was officially announced in early June 1976 and had been leaked to the press a little more than three months after Bob Dole sponsored the Day of Affirmation and Protest on Capitol Hill.[107]

Indeed, IRS Commissioner Donald Alexander had hinted that such was the case in early February when he said that Bob Dole's letter would be "carefully examined and given consideration." That's as close to saying "yes" in bureaucratese as is possible in that difficult and often untranslatable tongue.

The Immigration and Naturalization Service also got the hint. By the summer of 1976, the INS was letting it be known that it was considering the deportation of hundreds of foreign church members for violating their visas. They were supposed to be "trainees," the service charged. Instead, they were peddling the usual line of church products. Fundraising, in short, was going on, not training.[108]

It was an old dispute between the church and the INS—and the church denied it all.

More important, the question had been quietly percolating in the U.S. courts for years—as is the case with most immigration questions—and, all things being equal, it would continue to do so for years. And years. Until 1979, when the U.S. Supreme Court in *Troyer vs. South Hampton* settled the matter by upholding the Unification Church members' claim that they were missionaries and, therefore, entitled to remain in the United States.

But other things were clearly not equal in 1976. By that summer, the Immigration and Naturalization Service began to act in untypically vigorous fashion. The foreign church members were going, and that was that. And so the press was informed.[109]

Why this unnatural haste? INS was in no mood to explain, but, like the IRS, spokesmen for the INS said the timing of their action and the letter from Dole requesting immediate deportation proceedings was purely coincidental.

Still, there would be a hiatus. Understandably, after the 1976 Republican convention in Kansas City, Bob Dole had things on his mind other than the church—even if its members were still tax-exempt and living and practicing their religion in America.

Dole, of course, and Gerald Ford were seeking the ultimate political prizes: the presidency and vice-presidency of the United States.

They would lose, as we all know, to a lay Baptist minister and nuclear engineer named Jimmy Carter and to Minnesota's own U.S. Senator Walter Mondale.

But not by much.

Despite the Watergate-imposed burdens, the Republicans nearly made it once again to the White House. For Bob Dole it was a moral victory. More important, it gave him priceless national exposure and national campaigning experience. And it didn't do his career in the U.S. Senate any harm either.

In short, after 1976 Bob Dole was bigger and more formidable than ever. And he hadn't forgotten the Unification Church either.

Panama and the canal treaties were one fish. The Unification Church was another. The canal debate took much of 1977 and the first half of 1978 for Senator Dole, a leader in the fight against the Carter-Torrijos treaties. But once that was over it was Moon's turn. And Bob Dole was looking for blood.

For church leaders and members alike, there was no respite. Following Senator Dole's non-investigative non-hearings, they were besieged by bags of hate mail, death threats, and a rash of uncomplimentary, if not outright slanderous, newspaper reports, magazine articles, TV series, and B-grade movies the likes of which hadn't been seen in this country since the Great Red Scare of the 1950s.

Within five months of the Dole non-hearings, a squad of IRS agents had taken up permanent offices in the Unification Church's downtown New York City headquarters while a team of field agents began round-the-clock surveillance of selected church members and their telephones. By the fall of 1976, the IRS had already expanded its so-called "routine audit" of Moon's 1974 tax returns to include all his and the church's financial activities.

About the same time that the IRS moved in with the church, the Immigration and Naturalization Service did something unprecedented. They set up a special New York office to do nothing but monitor the comings and goings of Unification Church members—preferably more goings than comings.

Remember, at any one time there were never more than 300 foreign church members in the United States, mostly Japanese, and all were here legally.

Now, consider this. During that same period there were an estimated three million illegal aliens, mostly Spanish-speaking, known to be residing on the East Coast, primarily in the New York City and Miami areas. And twice that number of illegals were believed to be living in the South, the Midwest and California. Yet nowhere else in the country had the INS decided to set up offices to deal specifically with a particular nationality, much less a religion.

Imagine the public outcry, the protests, and the lawsuits if the INS announced plans to set up a special office to monitor all

Catholic or Jewish immigrants—even illegal Catholic and Jewish aliens.

Incidentally, the INS was never able to put together a deportation case against any of the church members, but it wasn't for lack of trying or reluctance to spend millions of U.S. taxpayers' dollars for the effort.

When the INS couldn't find a legal way of barring Moon and his disciples from entering the United States, the agency turned its guns on their wives and children, but to no avail. The INS even went after a Korean children's choir, the Little Angels, which was sponsored by the church and performed recitals at the United Nations. That, too, failed, but the kids, aged four to twelve, learned a new American word: undesirables.

But the bad press, hate mail, and harassment by the IRS and the Immigration and Naturalization Service were only a small indication of what was in store for the church. By the end of 1976, local and state governments from Vermont to Oregon, from Georgia to California, had begun a systematic plan to rid their communities of any Unification Church members.

Local solicitation and licensing statutes were rewritten expressly to bar Unification Church members from doing business. When that failed, new ordinances were created to rezone or condemn the houses or apartments they lived in. Naturally, dozens of state attorneys general, always sensitive to the fears of registered voters, got into the act with their own investigations of the Unification Church peril.

None came up with anything, but no matter. Some church members were arrested and later released at the county line. Most, however, were merely run out of town. A few stood their ground, won lawsuits, and were promptly forgotten.

When the smoke cleared, no fewer than thirty-seven states, some with no church presence at all, had taken steps, in most cases flagrantly unconstitutional actions, to insure that Reverend Sun Myung Moon, his followers, and his religion didn't contaminate their communities.

While church members were busy putting out brush fires in America's grassroots and being held hostage by the IRS and Immigration and Naturalization Service, an even more ominous situation was developing in Washington, D.C.

Bob Dole may have been fighting a losing battle on the Panama Canal, but his kindred spirit in the House of Representatives, Donald Fraser, was planning to pick up the church investigation where the Kansas senator had left off several months earlier.

For the next two years, from 1976 to 1978, the Reverend Sun Myung Moon, and particularly his now more mature and wiser American followers, faced a multi-fronted battle with the full range of federal agencies, from the FBI to the SEC, INS, IRS, and FTC, as well as any number of congressional and state legislative committees.

Fraser, like Dole, helped the newspaper ink business flourish at the expense of the church, but the only scandal his eighteen-month Koreagate probe uncovered was the Congress's willingness to spend millions of dollars on an investigation which proved utterly meaningless.

But there was a silver lining for Fraser. His hearings, the myriad of ongoing federal investigations, and dozens of state and local anti-church actions were taking their toll on the new, barely formed church. And if Bob Dole or another prosecutor/politician wanted to step in, he'd find that the church had been softened up for the kill.

The legal and accounting fees alone were staggering. Millions were being spent yearly to defend the church before committees and courts while appeasing the seemingly insatiable bookkeeping needs of federal agencies. And, if that weren't bad enough, the battered image of the Unification Church following the Dole non-hearing had gotten even worse, if that were possible. Church members were now being beaten up on the streets.

By the end of 1978, many church members, particularly the Americans, felt like they had just done twelve rounds with Joe Louis with their hands and feet tied. To be sure, not one investigation had turned up anything even remotely illegal. And, yes, after two years of coming up empty-handed, IRS agents were pulling their hair out trying to find anything—a dime, a nickel, a penny misspent or unreported—but with no luck.

But more than a few American church members had had enough and were ready to throw in the towel. Some did and left the church reluctantly. Most stayed on, however, believing the worst was over.

Prophecy was obviously not one of their strong suits.

Fresh from his defeat on the Panama Canal, a now unencumbered Bob Dole would finish off Sun Myung Moon for good or, so he hoped.

Dole would use his accumulated power and prestige for a repeat of the 1976 mock hearings. What worked once should work again. Only this time Bob Dole was bigger and meaner than ever. A piece of cake, if you happened not to like Unification Church members. Of course it would all be high-minded. Good clean fun for the whole family.

Which brings us to this problem. As any good politician knows, an event, in order to be effective, cannot simply be staged. Certainly, the Royal Shakespeare Company is perfectly free to put on Hamlet at three in the morning, fifty miles north of Winnemucca, Nevada, in say, late December. But it's no one's fault if nobody shows up in a freezing Western desert to watch a seventeenth-century tragedy.

And Bob Dole understood the importance of proper timing and place.

Above all, timing.

That is why it was no accident that a repeat performance of the February 1976 Day of Affirmation and Protest was held in Washington, D.C., on Capitol Hill in early 1979.

February 5 to be exact. And Bob Dole was still very much the producer, director, and star.

But there was a problem. As the 1970s progressed, the fear of cults had begun to recede, if only gradually. Deprogramming was no longer in fashion. In fact, deprogrammers were themselves going to the slammer and citizens' groups, like the CERFies of the past, were starting to pop up and rail against the brainwashing and thug-like tactics of people like Ted Patrick—the same folks they had once employed.

Indeed, Moon did not seem quite as menacing as he once did. But the honeymoon didn't last long.

The Korean minister seemed harmless enough until the macabre spectacle of Jonestown, Guyana, jolted the nation's psyche in November 1978.

Again the panic button was hit as people followed the grisly story of the Reverend Jim Jones and the People's Temple.

Jonestown was the functional equivalent of declaring war, and the First Amendment was about to be carefully wrapped and put on a shelf for the duration of the hysteria.

The spectre of mass suicide—mass murder really—912 men, women, and children forced to choke down the cyanide-laced Kool-Aid at gunpoint—the last part somehow got missed in the informational stampede—revolted and just plain scared nearly everybody.

Religion and a fly coated, slow death in the steaming jungle were very powerful messages and the media transmitted them in Technicolor.

That a false prophet gone mad was the cause of this gruesome nightmare made it even more shocking and brought it a whole lot closer to home. And the Reverend Jim Jones, a Marxist, soon merged into another presence in the public mind.

Reverend Sun Myung Moon, meet Reverend Jim Jones.

Once more, familiar demons were on the loose, and cults were more than weird and crazy. They were demonic and deadly. And this was no Stephen King monster story either. It was real; every bloated body baking in the tropic sun was tangible. In the ensuing panic, distinctions, as usual, got lost. Wacko religions, all wacko religions, weren't just nutty, they were dangerous. And the anti-cult groups, which had fallen on hard times, made the most of it.

Naturally, their thoughts turned to their old friend, Bob Dole of Kansas. And the thoughts of Bob Dole of Kansas likely turned to politics—presidential politics, that is. It was not at all too early to think of the 1980 election. Jimmy Carter was in big trouble. Already fifty-five American hostages were being held in Teheran—kept there by another madman and religious fanatic, the Ayatollah Khomeini.

Construction workers in New York City were hanging out bed-sheet signs on skeleton skyscrapers saying, "Bomb Iran," and that meant big trouble for the little man from Plains, Georgia.

And the ex-governor of California was too old, too conservative, and too close to Hollywood to get the blue ribbon. As for George Bush—he was out of work.

Bob Dole was splendidly positioned, and, moreover, he could smell the trouble Carter was in better than most. It was time, in short, for the man from Russell, Kansas, to grab the spotlight.

Jonestown, Teheran, and Tarrytown, New York. It was a perfect fit, and Dole put it on.

Karl Marx once observed in an essay on Louis Napoleon, Emperor Bonaparte's slightly dizzy nephew, that if history repeated itself, it did so first as tragedy then as farce.[110]

That almost, but not quite, describes Bob Dole's attempt at holding a second "Moonie roast." Tragedy was not exactly what happened in 1976, but there was more than a touch of farce in A Day of Affirmation and Protest II.

To tell the truth, the U.S. senator from Kansas walked into a buzzsaw and never quite recovered from the experience—to the extent, at least, that he seemed subsequently to have given up the Great Anti-Cult Crusade.

How could it have gone so wrong the second time?

With Jonestown working in his favor, it didn't seem possible. But it was.

Let us talk about the things that Bob Dole did right. First, he prepared his ground carefully. Two weeks after the Jonestown disaster, Dole wrote a letter to Senator Russell Long, Louisiana's folksy chairman of the Senate Finance Committee. Dole, who expected and got the ranking minority spot on the committee in the coming 96th Congress, knew old Russell would listen.

What Dole wanted was for Finance to "review tax-exempt qualifications, procedures, and policing." And Dole wanted it "at the earliest possible date." In case Senator Long had not heard, there was a problem, and recent events in far-off Guyana gave Dole his peg:

> The proliferation of various cults under the protection of a tax-exempt organization is cause for concern. There is evidence that some organizations may be engaging in activities outside the protection of our tax laws. For example, I have been concerned about some of the activities of the Unification Church and other organizations under the leadership of Reverend Sun Myung Moon.[111]

What activities?

There have been allegations that certain tax-exempt organizations have engaged in systematic and planned violations of U.S. currency and foreign laws in connection with the movement of millions of dollars of cash into and out of the U.S. There may also be violations of tax laws through large cash transfers to individuals which were characterized as loans. Similarly, it has been reported that certain tax-exempt organizations such as the Unification Church have engaged in political, business, and other activities inconsistent with their tax-exempt businesses so as to render them ineligible for tax-exempt status.[112]

Bob Dole then threw his knock-out punch. He wrote:

The questions surrounding the Jonestown incident and the continuing activity of the Unification Church require action. The public needs protection from unscrupulous operations that flaunt the law for their own purposes. Tax-exempt status is a privilege, not a right.

In Dole's mind, Jonestown and Tarrytown were one, and by God, Senator Long and the Senate Finance Committee had damned well better do something about it.[113]

Meanwhile, the non-hearings would take place—not in the same old hearing room in the Dirksen Building—but across First Street in the older, even more elegant and, more important, larger Russell Senate Office Building Room 318, where the Ervin Watergate hearings had been held. It was the largest space available west of the city's RFK stadium.

That was all right. The press would like that. But, unfortunately for Bob Dole, it was also the location of the 1954 Army-McCarthy tournament, and that stirred reporters' memories—as they would remind their readers—of political witch hunts and congressional abuses of power, especially Republican abuses of power.

Still, Dole tried. He really did.

Once more the man from Kansas made clear to everyone that the meeting would be for the benefit of grief-stricken and outraged parents victimized by the cults. But that he, personally, was carrying no vendetta; merely obtaining information in an entirely unofficial manner. Again, this was no investigation. It was only supposed to look like one.

To be sure, the information was to be gathered from some awfully familiar sources: Daphne Greene of San Francisco for one; Ted Patrick of the Orange County jail for another; George Swope, of course; and Rabbi Maurice Davis, who was, like Swope, from Westchester County, New York.

In deference to Jonestown and to the congressman who inadvertently touched off the disaster, Leo Ryan of California, Ryan's chief aide, the lovely Jacqueline Speiers, would lead off the panel of witnesses.

Not just good television, but great television.

In fact, Jackie was picture-perfect as she testified before Dole and his colleagues. Dressed in a light spring suit, she carefully exposed her bandaged left arm—a small souvenir from Jonestown—for the benefit of the cameras. Besides expounding on her new-found fear of and expertise on cults, she was also running for her boss' old seat.

For Bob Dole things went wrong even before the great day in ways that the Kansas senator simply had not anticipated.

One reason: Round Two attracted unfavorable attention. And this time more than Unification Church members were unhappy about the set-up. The protests came not just from some hurriedly improvised and church-organized telegrams from people nobody in Washington had ever heard of before. Or cared about.

Now, we were talking political juice.

If the church members had been angry the first time, they were outraged now. And three years had toughened them up. Plenty.

Not only were they not willing to serve as doormats for Bob Dole's entry into presidential politics, they would be damned if they were going to be smeared with the Jonestown tarbrush as well.

They had been jerked around with the first Day of Affirmation and Protest; they had endured the Fraser subcommittee hearings; they were putting up with the IRS and the INS and all the other Washington, D.C., alphabet agencies. But by February 1979, they were mad, by God, and they weren't going to take it any more.

Not from Bob Dole. Not from anyone.

Firing off letters, telegrams, and phone calls, church officials made it clear they would not be fobbed off with a post-non-hearing chat in the senator's office. Not this time.

Neil Salonen, the church's normally soft-spoken American president, led the way. What diffidence he once had about addressing a United States senator had long since burned off in the heat of three years of non-stop combat. And the fact that, once again, no one in the Unification Church had been informed of the upcoming event, much less invited to testify, made him livid with anger.

Salonen wasted no time with pleasantries in his January 24 mortar lob. First, he bitterly complained that Dole had not informed him of his imminent lynching and that no effort had been made to hear his (Salonen's) view on the necktie party about to be held in his honor.

Furthermore, the list of Dole's attendees, he complained, "reads like a 'Who's Who' [sic] of anti-Unification Church persons, ranging in previously demonstrated bias from simple ignorance to convicted criminality."[114]

Warming to his work, Salonen dismissed the previous Day of Affirmation and Protest as a "forum for negative hearsay" and ended with a demand for an opportunity to have his turn at the microphone. The Unification Church, in short, was now impudently demanding equal time in place of the loaded, single-minded panelist approach Dole had used last time.

Surprisingly, Salonen's demand was listened to.

Sort of.

True, Dole at first decided that no church members would actually be allowed to say anything in Room 318 on that early February day, but others, sympathetic to the church position and critical of the anti-cultists, were invited.

What happened?

It certainly wasn't Unification Church pressure. They could still safely be ignored. Kansas was not under siege by strange oriental forces, after all. But something was going on.

For one thing, the intellectual climate had changed. Ideas do count, even in politics. And despite the Jonestown bombshell, 1979 was different from 1976. The anti-cultists were now on the defensive. Eminently respectable psychiatrists and psychologists were dumping cold water over the notion of brainwashing as a living, breathing, and believable phenomenon.

Mind control proponents were being ridiculed as either crackpots or highly unprofessional and/or opportunistic members of the mental health profession.

Theologians and constitutional lawyers were reminding America of its history of persecuting unpopular religions by first labeling them cults and then calling them un-American, with highly unfortunate results. In other words, they were talking about old-fashioned bigotry. And the media were beginning to tune in to the discussion.

And speaking of journalists, some of the brethren were noticing the awful methods—patently illegal methods—and pathetic results of the so-called deprogramming of innocent adults, who for the most part wanted only to practice their religious or political beliefs in peace.

In other words, it wasn't exactly a black-and-white issue any more. It was morning in America, and it came in shades of gray.

Also, in America, for every action there is inevitably a reaction, and despite the miasma of Jonestown, there was a strong reaction to the cult of anti-cultism—at least among the thinkers and doers.

And that Bob Dole had simply missed.

But he didn't miss the fact that representatives from the National Council of Churches were protesting—this time vociferously—his planned pseudo-investigation of the church.

The NCC did not accept the tried and untrue clichés Dole was still passing out about his little ole harmless town meeting. If the senator really was interested in obtaining information, the council asked, then why from only one source and a highly biased, thoroughly unprofessional, and discredited source at that?

Who knows? Bob Dole of Kansas might have been impressed by that argument. He was even more impressed by the fact that it was coming from the National Council of Churches.

Very establishment. Well connected. Respectable. More important, it meant lots and lots of voters. And Dole understood what lots and lots of voters meant.

And the council wasn't alone. The United Church of Christ, the United Methodists, the Baptists, the Presbyterians, the Church of the Brethren, the Lutherans, and the Unitarians also jointly signed a letter to Dole in protest. Others, like the Synagogue Council of America and Americans United for the Separation of Church and State, sent critical notes of their own.[115]

Suddenly, CERF and all those Kansas parents—all ten of them, no doubt—and a nauseatingly glib rabbi from Westchester, New York, did not seem like such a big deal.

Hell, maybe Davis and Swope and "Daffy" Greene were crackpots on an overextended ego trip after all.

In any case, two staff members from the National Council of Churches were asked to join the proceedings: Dean Kelley and James Hamilton, who directed the NCC's Washington, D.C., office. With the door cracked open a bit, others would squeeze through, too. Among those, Jeremiah Guttman, a constitutional lawyer from the American Civil Liberties Union, would speak. So would theologian Herbert Richardson of Toronto University.

There was one catch, however. Actually, two. First, the last-minute invitees were allowed only five minutes apiece. That did not go over as well with the First Amendment advocates as Dole no doubt had hoped. Maybe they wouldn't come.

And one of the prime movers for a balanced panel, Barry Lynn representing the Church of Christ, grumbled plenty: "Obviously that's not much time. We do believe that when something is funded by the taxpayers of America you owe a decent amount of time to opposing views."[116]

Lynn might complain, but he came, as did the other dissidents.

The second catch was that Dole was not about to give equality in numbers either. There were to be four dissenters, but more than a dozen to bash the cults, and they were to come first while the cameras were still rolling.

And that was not quite the end of it. Chairman Dole was even catching flak from his colleagues. This time they were not ignoring Brother Bob's invitation—they were showing up, and a number were lodging their own complaints about the handling of the panel. Two congressmen, a liberal Democrat and a moderate Republican, gave Bob Dole some congressional headaches all their own: Hamilton Fish, Jr., Republican, and Richard Ottinger, Democrat, to be precise.

Fish, in particular, could not be ignored. He was from a long line of distinguished Fishes. Ham, Jr.'s, father was once a powerful member of the House (one of the trio ridiculed by FDR in his scornful litany of Martin, Barton, and Fish). His grandfather had been a secretary of state.

Worse for Dole, Ham Fish had a daughter, Alexa, who was a contented member of the Unification Church and, unlike some of the parents pressing Dole, the New York congressman did not consider the church a threat to America. Besides, Fish wanted to hear the other side.

In fact, Fish had become so disagreeable on the subject of Dole's cult meeting that he and Ottinger forced the Kansan at the last moment to relent and allow Neil Salonen to make a statement.[117]

Even then, the wretched church members and their supporters were not pleased. The five-minute rule was still being protested. So was the imbalance on the panel. A ratio of thirteen to four or five did not sound right to them.

They were particularly sore about one of the proposed speakers: a woman who claimed inside knowledge that the church had a suicide ritual. (Like most religions, the Unification Church takes a dim view of suicide.) But Dole figured he had enough trouble on his hands and wisely decided to drop the would-be insider from the list of "witnesses."

All of this protesting left Dole and his staff a bit bewildered. What was the fuss? Nothing like this had happened last time. Now they had to defend themselves even from their own colleagues, the ultimate humiliation on Capitol Hill.

In a statement that Dole's office released shortly before the meeting, the scheduled forum was patiently and somewhat defensively explained: "It is very simply an information session for members of Congress and their staffs on the cult phenomenon in this country."[118]

Nothing else. Unfortunately, the familiar snake oil was not selling as well this time. In fact, it wasn't selling at all. Dole's colleagues knew damned well how the game was played: if it looks like a duck, walks like a duck, and quacks like a duck, it's not a simple "information session."

The statement was right, however, about one thing. Bob Dole had pitched this gathering for the benefit of his colleagues.

This time members of the federal government were not invited. They were already in Bob Dole's hip pocket, and most were still deeply immersed in the investigations of the Unification Church spawned earlier.

It was bitterly cold that morning as rush hour traffic crawled into the city. In the subfreezing weather, people were not in a good mood.

For those attempting to move up Constitution Avenue, it was a logjam. The farmers were in town, en masse, driving their tractors and combines toward Capitol Hill. Organized by a new radical movement in agriculture, the American Agricultural Movement, the farmers, too, were damned mad and wouldn't take it anymore. And they had turned the city's principal routes—the pride of architect Monsieur L'Enfant—into country roads.

The farmers had no interest in cults, just in crops and crop prices. The tractorcade of 30,000 farmers advanced slowly toward the Hill where the farmers would talk plenty to their congressmen about how they wanted the president and his secretary of agriculture, Bob Bergland, to implement in full the 1977 farm law.

But they were not alone that day. When the farmers got there, they found they had to share Jenkin's Hill with some 500 Unification Church members who were protesting Bob Dole's second attempt at "not" investigating America's religious cults.

For the examination of the cult phenomenon, participants and audience gathered in the Russell Senate Office Building on the third floor. That is, they did so after going through a gauntlet of armed Capitol Hill police and a metal detector thoughtfully placed next to the hearing room door.

Outside in the frigid air a Unification Church brass band played popular patriotic airs of the day, including the "Battle Hymn of the Republic" and "We Shall Overcome," while church demonstrators waved red, white, and blue banners proclaiming their displeasure with the proceedings inside. The signs were mostly about Bob Dole.

What the angry farmers and the equally angry church members thought about each other that morning is not recorded. But many farmers who entered the Russell Building to look for a farm-state senator or two paused to listen patiently to church sermons on the New Kingdom while church members passed out cookies. The two groups mingled on Capitol Hill in apparently patient good cheer: demonstrators, tractors, and brass band all making one joyful noise unto the Lord while Senator Robert Dole of Kansas served as the goofy locus point of it all.

One group wanted to be left alone; the other wanted a higher price for a bushel of wheat. Dole, they both thought, could help.

The church members, however, were not content to be kept outside in the cold. Several hundred of them crowded into the hearing room. But this time they dropped the dignified silence bit used in 1976 and reverted to a more traditional American mode of demonstrating that they had had it. The church members booed and hissed. Occasionally, they shouted "liar" at an anti-church spokesman. That shook up Bob Dole, as well as the eleven other members of Congress present.

But we are racing ahead of our story.

Also in attendance were more than a dozen camera crews who just happened to be in the neighborhood. Senator Dole had announced in his opening statement that the non-hearing "would not be a media event." Actually, in a way, he was right. The term "media event" hardly describes the five-ring circus and carnival midway proceedings that Bob Dole's pursuit of information turned out to be.[119]

The camera crews were more than matched by congressional staff aides from seventy congressional offices. After Jonestown, cults were hot.[120]

Henry Louis Mencken, the sage of nearby Baltimore, was right when he said that the United States of America was "the goddamnest best show on earth."

By the time everyone crowded in, it was strictly SRO—Standing Room Only—but this time the hot television lights were comforting to people who had just come in from the arctic air. Four hours later they would be sweating in their woolens.

Bob Dole gavelled the not-so-solemn assembly into something resembling a respectful silence and introduced the first witness. His self-named probe of the "The Cult Phenomenon in the United States" had begun.

Jackie Speier had survived Guyana. But only barely, according to her dramatic reconstruction. Her light, pale spring outfit made no sense considering the weather, but it looked terrific on television. Speier, after all, was a pro.

In a tribute to Jonestown, which had made this day's event possible, Leo Ryan's former aide was allowed all the time she wanted to expound her views on cults and their inherent dangers.

To the intense annoyance of the hard slogging anti-cultists, newcomer Speier also got most of the photos and hogged the news coverage. She dominated the *Washington Post* and *New York Times* stories, not to mention *Time* magazine's piece and the networks.

She and Jonestown were still news; "Moonie bashing" was not. And her long, curly, raven tresses and softly dramatic delivery didn't hurt either.

Speier first reminded the gathering that she was no expert on cults, but having said that she told Dole exactly what he wanted to hear. Based on her experience with exactly one group—an experience that consisted of talking to one hundred members of the People's Temple shortly before their deaths—Speier concluded that several of the women appeared to be programmed.

> These women [she said] showed little interest in career or college goals, expecting an early marriage within the cult to be their only option. It was a sad experience to see so many lost and misdirected people whose ability to seek individual goals had been destroyed.[121]

In other words, some female cult members didn't want to be doctors, lawyers, or members of Congress, the American yuppie dream. They just wanted to get married and have kids. Strange people.

Having secured that very slender database, Jackie Speier came to her significant conclusion that with ten million cult members loose in America, it meant: ". . . Jonestown—it can happen again."[122]

Except it didn't, and what if anything, the U.S. Congress could do about it even if it did happen, or what exactly constituted a cult in the first place were questions not addressed.

To do that, of course, would have required a serious effort on everyone's part. That effort, however, had nothing to do with the agenda of either Miss Speier or the anti-cultists from CERF, or Bob Dole, for that matter—who just a little bit later in the proceedings probably wondered why he wasn't outside in the fresh air in more familiar surroundings.

Speier came, was seen, got her press notices, and left. And it all went downhill from there. Way, way down. A string of anti-church speakers followed the original thirteen. And they stuck tightly to their scripts. No surprises.

Robert Boettcher, who was U.S. Congressman Donald Fraser's chief aide from the International Organizations Subcommittee, was fresh from his own investigation of the Unification Church threat to America. He predictably accused the Reverend Sun Myung Moon of perverting religion and being "a menace," to a chorus of jeers, of course, from church members in the audience who were by now feeling threatened themselves.

Harvard psychiatrist John Clark, a leading advocate of the theory that brainwashing and mind control were possible, launched into a new theme. Mass suicides were part and parcel of the cultist's mental make-up, along with other programmed responses. Cultists were zombies right out of a B-grade horror picture: "There are armies of willing, perfectly controlled soldiers," he told Senator Dole, and he warned that the U.S. government would have to act "before it is too late."[123]

Matching Clark in hyperbolic hysteria, shout for shout, was Richard Delgado, a law professor at the University of Washington, who, with Clark, was also very popular on The Great Cult-Bashing and Medicine Show circuit.

Delgado argued for federal legislation to require a "cooling off" period before a prospective member could join a cult. And why not also a spiritual "living will" to forestall future conversions? A third idea was to license cult recruiters—presumably by a government bureau. And finally, there should be—as a last resort—court-ordered psychiatric treatment for cult members.

A more massive government entanglement in religion could not possibly be imagined, although a state-required pause before religious conversion is amusing. Why not a blood and urine test too? With that in place, a lot of history could have been changed. Imagine St. Paul after his vision on the Damascus road being held by a Roman detachment while he thought it over. One question. How long should he have been held?

Still, as ludicrous as Delgado's understanding of contemporary American jurisprudence was, it was all taken as serious discussion by chairman Bob Dole, whose own feel for the Constitution was as sensitive as that of a milk maid wearing cement mittens.

However, Clark and Delgado were mild in comparison to deprogrammer Ted Patrick who came to the podium next.

Patrick by this time was in serious trouble with numerous law officials. He also had nothing new to say. Why should he? Despite his legal problems, the Chattanooga hustler had done pretty well for himself with the old formulas. Scare the white folks silly and mock their educated ignorance of the real world and the dark forces that inhabit it. For years it had worked like a charm—

"putting the Mo Jo on these kids" was the way he described his profession. And there was no point in changing his story in Washington, D.C.

So Patrick told Dole that a cult conspiracy was at work to turn America into a totalitarian country. In Patrick's comic-book fantasy, Moon and company were waging a war which was "one of the most dangerous . . . in the history of mankind."[124]

Talking about his work, Patrick described Unification Church members' minds as being "like containers, with the lids on tight; put them under the faucet and nothing can come in. What I've got to do is take the top off."[125]

Apparently the church members in the back row didn't agree. They yelled like hell at Patrick when he finished.

Other self-styled specialists in cult lore followed: Flo Conway, co-author of the anti-cult classic, *Snapping*, was one; dependable CERFie George Swope was another; but no one got the attention—not even Jackie Speier—or was able to work up the audience the way that the irrepressible Rabbi Maurice Davis succeeded in doing.

His appearance, as it turned out, was the rabbi's swan song in the national media limelight, and he made the most of it. Of course there was the inevitable comparison to Nazi youth, the disclosure of church death threats against his life, as well as his noble work in deprogramming fallen youth. But Jonestown helped juice up the by-now pretty stale Davis imagery.

One sample:

Every path leads somewhere. The path of segregation leads to lynching—every time. The path of antisemitism leads to Auschwitz—every time. The path of the cults leads to Jonestown— and we watch it at our peril.[126]

Jonestown was definitely the "boo" word that day, but the rabbi's peroration was even better:

I am here to protest against child molesters. For as surely as there are those who lure children with lollipops in order to rape their bodies, so too do these lure children with candy coated lies in order to rape their minds.[127]

All in all, it was a vintage performance, but Davis' absolute cause-and-effect rhetoric, of course, was inaccurate and inflammatory. As a contribution to the sum total of human knowledge it was less than zero. But it did prove how important Jonestown and the images it conjured had become in reviving the anti-cult mania. Manna from heaven, as it were.

On that day in February, Davis' rhetoric certainly inflamed the church members in Room 318. Rabbi Davis got their most heartfelt response. Cries of "garbage" and "liar"—this from a young black woman—rent the air, much to Chairman Dole's embarrassment as he vainly struggled to keep control by repeating assurances that he was not conducting an investigation. His colleagues from the House and Senate looked even more uncomfortable.[128]

Eventually, the dissenters had their chance, at the tail end of the hearing. Even Neil Salonen was given a few moments to read his statement. Naturally he was not happy with the testimony which preceded his. He also took a shot at Rabbi Davis, who had just finished giving his statement. Instead of making the Unification Church into a monster that it wasn't, "launching a reverse pogrom," he said, its critics "should be teaching their own faith."[129]

For Senator Dole, Salonen had this advice:

> [I]f we have done something wrong, then through the Justice Department or other executive agency, let us be charged, defend ourselves, and pay the consequences. To be held up to public ridicule with no chance to adequately defend ourselves is morally wrong.[130]

Salonen wasn't the only one worried about the inappropriateness of the forum or Congress' mucking about in religious affairs.

James Wood, director of the Baptist Joint Committee on Public Affairs, specifically warned against government meddling in matters protected by the First Amendment. "Government," he said,

> is not competent to judge which religious groups are good and which are bad any more than it can determine which religions are true and which are false.[131]

That sounded sensible, but unfortunately, if taken seriously, it would have put Bob Dole out of the cult-bashing business. Meanwhile, other critics of the anti-cult movement took their own shots—this time at the deprogrammers.

Herbert Richardson of Toronto University reminded Dole and everyone else that Ted Patrick was a convicted felon who had once slashed a young man with a straight-edged razor, a favorite weapon of street hoodlums, and, all things considered, was not the kind of person a parent should hire to abduct a son or daughter so Patrick could put the Mo Jo on them, whatever that was.

The ACLU's Jeremiah Guttman, looking prophet-like in a long, white beard, went for the jugular by accusing the deprogrammers of adopting Soviet-like practices themselves.[132]

Guttman then went after Professor Delgado's cult-curbing measures, calling them "constitutionally impossible." No government under the American system can monitor private conversation leading to a change in religious belief, he argued. As for "forced psychotherapy," it was, he said, "already against the law."

Guttman's civil libertarian position then touched off a debate between the members of Congress present as to whether they, the legislative branch, had any role when it came to matters of religion.

It was a good question. It should have been asked earlier—three years earlier so the grounds of inquiry could have been carefully understood and competently focused. Nothing like that ever happened, of course, and it was apparent that no one was interested in making it happen.

Religion is always a touchy subject, but Guttman at least admitted that Congress did have one legitimate area of investigation, and that concerned its legislative authority over tax-exempt institutions. What Congress could give, it could also take away. It could not, however, single out one particular religion for punishment, which, he opined, seemed to be exactly what was taking place here.[133]

Mercifully, it was nearly over. After four grueling hours of raucous debate, Bob Dole brought the session to an end. But as unpleasantly surprising as this second meeting was, the Kansan did not run up the white flag—not quite yet.

In fact, he promised more of the same.

As the number and prominence of so-called new religious groups rises, so does America's need to know and understand this development. There are questions that need answers. For instance, do these groups promote the spiritual liberation of true religion or the slavery of a psychological trap? In addition to what appears to be a very lucrative business, is deprogramming a synonym for kidnapping and a violation of an individual's First Amendment right to freedom of religion?[134]

Bob Dole seemed to have learned something from the two encounters, but not a whole lot. There was, of course, no self-evident need to know more about the new religions—at least by the U.S. Congress. As for the psycho-babble about programmed minds, what business was it of politicians to make distinctions between false and genuine religions?

The media were also more skeptical this time, even cynical about the whole business. *Time* magazine, for example, concluded:

[The anti-cultists] were unable to offer hard evidence of criminality, much less Jones-type mass murder. Nor did they define precisely what distinguishes a "cult" from an acceptable religion.[135]

Bob Dole's promise to do more proved hollow, however. After the February 1979 hearing, there was to be no more crusade against the cults, and against the Unification Church in particular. Memories of Jonestown would eventually fade, and other issues promised a bigger and safer return.

Whatever Bob Dole's second thoughts about thumping the tub and pointing with alarm at the nation's cults, a very big cat was out of the bag. Dole, whether he meant to or not, with his brace of ersatz investigations in 1976 and 1979, helped to legitimize legislative inquiries into new religions around the country.

Soon it became fashionable for state legislatures to do the same. Only in their case, the states were not nearly so delicate as Congress about the First Amendment.

In May of 1977, a little more than a year after the first Day of Affirmation and Protest, for example, no fewer than two state assemblies were busy at work doing something about the Unification Church menace.

In Texas, a resolution calling for the investigation of "so-called cults" was reported unanimously out of the Jurisprudence Committee of the state House of Representatives. The rationale for the resolution was supplied by anti-cultists like George Slaughter and

Gary Scharff, a former Unification Church member, whose father had made an appearance at the first Day of Affirmation and Protest.

The Texas resolution declared:

[W]hile some have claimed the so-called movements are religious in nature, others claim that they are subversive and insidious, and that cult members practice brainwashing and mind control, causing great fear among many, especially parents, that cults have mentally physically [sic] imprisoned many of our young people.[136]

Having stated the problem as they saw it, the state legislators called for its solution:

It's the duty of the state to protect the lives and well-being of its people. [A special interim committee shall] diligently inquire into every aspect of the cult movements in Texas to determine whether they are dangerous or harmless and report its findings to the 66th Legislature with recommendations for legislation to deal with the so-called cult movements.[137]

In Ohio, the Committee for Economic Affairs and Federal Relations of the state House of Representatives held similar hearings. Listening to deprogrammed church members and to parents of young adults still in the Unification Church, the committeemen heard the usual litany of warnings and pseudo-horror stories.

They were told the "Moonies" were a political arm of the South Korean government; that they solicited under false pretenses; and, of course, that they brainwashed their adherents into helpless, obedient zombiedom. One ex-member insisted that his old church was organizing "an elite para-military force, unquestionably loyal and devoid of individual identity."

Sobbed another, if the Ohio legislature didn't stop the "Moonie" tide with this SS force in embryo, in three years it would be too late. And Ohio would be among the first to go, since Columbus had a church center equalled in size only by that of New York City itself.[138]

And so it went.

Until the mid-1970s, official interest in the Unification Church tended to be passive and desultory.

The Unification Church was just one more, albeit rather unorthodox, religion doing a little missionary work in the United States. Nasty rumors circulating about them in Seoul's better bars were from low-grade sources whose stories rarely checked out—when anyone bothered to check them out.

That changed in 1976. The church had moved to America by then and Americans, after the battering of the 1960s, were definitely getting tired of the loud, the profane, and the weird. And they had never much liked foreigners, especially oriental foreigners.

As a consequence, new, exotic, and overseas religious cults proved easy to hate. Or to fear. Steven Spielberg's *Indiana Jones and the Temple of Doom* was still in the future, but it perfectly expressed what Americans already felt about any religion that wasn't at least vaguely Presbyterian in appearance. And sooner or later all grassroots phobias are detected by politicians; the "Moonies" proved to be no exception.

Besides, after Vietnam and Watergate the cults were something which could be loathed and despised by nearly everyone: black and white, men and women, young and old, straight and gay, liberal and conservative, Protestant, Catholic, Jew, and atheist.

We were coming together as a nation, ready to hang someone, anyone we all didn't like. And the Reverend Sun Myung Moon and his church were splendid targets. Hare Krishna, Divine Light Mission, and all the others were almost as eligible.

Congress got the message first. The American parliament is the most sensitive political instrument in the world. And members of Congress, when they get excited, are terribly good at telling other people what to do—usually people in the executive branch, who are not inclined to do anything out of the routine unless prodded.

And that is exactly what Senator Bob Dole and some of his colleagues did.

Actually, although the executive branch can be slow to move and stubborn in behavior, it is less a mule and more a cantankerous piece of machinery. It's hard to start and when it does it wheezes, pops, and backfires like Jack Benny's old Maxwell. But once kick-started, the damned thing is impossible to turn off. It just keeps clanking along, long after the prime mover himself has lost interest and moved on to other projects.

To be sure, even with Congress on their heels, the feds sometimes resisted. They had little interest in probing hard charges of church mind control and brainwashing—all staples of anti-cult propaganda which were soon amplified by the politicians.

Some agencies would resist. The Justice Department, for one, objected to probing into charges of brainwashing. Such investigations, Justice officials felt, would tread on very uncertain grounds, or at least on those protected by the First Amendment.[139]

Indeed, despite the political pressure, Justice dug in its heels on this one. And to his credit, then-Attorney General Benjamin Civiletti took the extraordinary step of holding a press conference to announce that previous Justice Department investigations into alleged church crimes, such as kidnapping and fraud, had turned up no evidence to support the charges.

About the same time in 1978, Justice's career lawyers got a break. It came in the form of a New York State Supreme Court decision overturning a grand jury decision in Queens which had indicted two Hare Krishna leaders for false imprisonment through the use of brainwashing techniques.

Judge John J. Leahy frontally attacked the basis of the grand jury's thinking with his blistering opinion.

> Religious proselytizing and the recruitment of a maintenance [sic] of a belief through a strict regimen, meditation, chanting, self-denial and the communication of other religious teachings cannot under our laws—as presently enacted—be construed as criminal in nature and serve as the basis for criminal indictment.[140]

Judge Leahy emphasized that the court's judgment was not meant for New York state alone. In fact, it was to be a "dire caveat to prosecutional agencies throughout the length and breadth of the land."[141]

But that legal victory was on a fairly narrow front. In other war zones it was still a pitched battle for survival.

Besides, as John Kennedy once said, there is always one dumb bastard that doesn't get the message. In the case of the Unification Church, there were plenty of dumb bastards who didn't. I speak of local officials—hundreds, maybe thousands of them—who went their own way with the First Amendment, Judge Leahy or no.

In the late 1970s, they worked very hard to run church members out of town.

Their favorite weapon? Withdrawing or denying solicitation permits. The reasoning was simple. If the church members couldn't engage in street sales of candles and flowers or if they couldn't solicit funds, they would go out of business or, better, just go home. In any case, the good burghers of Everytown, U.S.A. would sleep safely in their beds once more.

So, between 1977 and 1979, hundreds of communities in at least twenty-four states tried that approach. In Mobile, Alabama, the city council repeatedly denied a permit to the church for the purposes of solicitation.

In Arkansas, thirteen towns did the same thing, and in Illinois, city officials in Berwyn, Cicero, and Des Plaines, all suburbs of Chicago, refused to grant licenses because the Unification Church, in their view, was not a real religion.

In Lincoln, Nebraska, the state capital's mayor refused to issue permits, despite repeated requests. As a result, the church filed suit and a federal district judge issued an injunction ordering Lincoln not to enforce three sections of the city's solicitation ordinance.

In fact, the church took a page out of the book of the Jehovah's Witnesses—yesteryear's persecuted church—and sued any local official who attempted to stop them from working the streets. And in every suit they entered, the church won.

Meanwhile, back in Washington, D.C., the federal government swung into second gear (unless it's a war, the federal government never shifts into third). The Internal Revenue Service, the Immigration and Naturalization Service, the Securities and Exchange Commission, the Federal Trade Commission, and, naturally, the Federal Bureau of Investigation, continued with their investigations for presumed wrongdoing on the part of the Unification Church, if not of Moon himself.

Only Justice and the FBI showed some reluctance about pursuing the church. They had seen it all before. But now, by the late 1970s, there was a new director, William Webster, explaining to impatient members of Congress that the bureau did not lightly investigate religions if there were no suspicion of a federal crime.

Or as Clarence Kelley patiently explained to the Honorable Joseph D. Early in May 1977, the bureau:

> has received similar complaints from parents of other children who have joined the Unification Church organization. These matters have been discussed with the Criminal Division, United States Department of Justice, which has advised that such activity does not involve the violation of any Federal statutes. . . . In view of the above Department of Justice decision, the FBI cannot assist in checking on the physical wellbeing of individuals joining this organization.[142]

In other words, the FBI wasn't going to play nanny for America's parents who were wondering where their adult offspring were after 10 P.M. The boilerplate hadn't changed much, and the message was basically the same.

Meanwhile, the bureau patiently probed and poked around the edges of the Unification Church. Bits and pieces of information filtered into headquarters. Moon's bodyguards, for example, were reportedly proficient in judo and karate; they did not carry any firearms.[143]

In another report, the FBI checked out an allegation that the Unification Church director in Tennessee had threatened the life of President Carter. The charge proved to be false. The FBI's caution was exemplary and perhaps unique. The bureau had long been subject to politicalization—before, during, and after the J. Edgar Hoover era. With the pressure to become a political tool had come bitter experience. By the early 1970s the political pressure had nearly wrecked the FBI. It's not surprising, then, that Hoover's old agency should have become so advisedly cautious about pursuing dubious investigations.

Other departments that had not learned that political lesson were less cautious. In one case, the Immigration and Naturalization Service—taking its cue from Bob Dole and others on the Hill—was ready to move against the church. But INS was not just anxious to boot out a few questionable missionaries; it was after Moon and his closest associates as well.

And INS sought help from other government agencies. The CIA was one. The National Security Agency was another. In May 1978, INS Commissioner Leonel Castillo wrote the Director of the

Central Intelligence Agency, Stansfield Turner, a memorandum informing him that the service was looking for grounds to deport Sun Myung Moon, his wife, Hak Ja Moon, and his close associate, Bo Hi Pak.

What Castillo wanted specifically to know from Turner were the answers to three questions. Why was Moon arrested in North Korea in the period between 1945 and 1950? What could the CIA say about the Tong-Il Korean Cooking Institute? When had the diplomatic status of Bo Hi Pak been terminated?[144]

What answers, if any, the agency gave to the INS's queries is not public information.

The zeal of INS to pursue the church and its leader is amply documented. In fact, the Immigration and Naturalization Service yielded only to one other agency of government in its determination to hit the church hard.

I am speaking, of course, of the Internal Revenue Service. For years its agents poured over the Unification Church's books looking for evidence of tax evasion. They never found what they were looking for—that task would be left to an ambitious and frustrated federal lawyer. Ironically, by then the man who had originally supplied the impetus for "getting" Moon—the one individual who had put the whole rumbling, multi-billion-dollar machinery of the federal government in motion—had simply lost interest.

Bob Dole had other fish to fry.

CHAPTER IV

MISCARRIAGE AT JUSTICE

You're an attorney. It's your duty to lie, conceal and distort every-
thing, and slander everybody.

JEAN GIRAUDOUX

HE was short, round-faced, and plump. Physically, he was soft, but
anyone who thought that the rest of him was equally flabby would
very much regret it.

In a three-piece suit and wire-rimmed glasses, lips unparted in
a grimace, revealing that cobra smile of his, he looked like a lawyer.
And that was exactly what he was. Or had become. For no one,
although conceived in original sin, is born a lawyer.

Before the age of thirty, he had rocketed through the select
Bronx High School of Science as well as Columbia University
(where, as editor of the *Spectator*, he wrote fashionably anti-war
editorials), and then Harvard Law during the years on which *The
Paper Chase* is based.

No sweat. He was always at the top of his class. Maybe he wasn't
the most brilliant, certainly not the wisest. However, he out-
prepared everybody else. His professors loved that. The care with
which he paid attention to detail was worthy of a surgeon or an
architect. Or a chemist handling high explosives.

The diligence paid off at the prestigious Manhattan law firm

103

that took him aboard after he graduated *summa cum laude* from
Harvard. He out-libraried everyone at the law firm, too. He also
got results. Because of him, Paul, Weiss, Rifkind, Wharton and
Garrison settled more cases before going to trial than ever—to the
delight of their clients—and fattened the salaries of the partners
besides.

All that work might not lead anywhere. Years burrowed into the
books, on top of three years at Harvard, could well mean there
would be nothing at the end of the rainbow. An ambitious young
counselor needs an added edge, a few scalps hanging from his
belt.

So, he figured it out. It wasn't that hard. James Earl Carter
occupied the White House—it was the late 1970s—and the man
had a far better than even chance of staying put until January
1985. There wasn't a $1,000-grey-flannel-suit lawyer living in the
canyons of Manhattan who didn't think so.

So while others of his generation toiled on the briefs in the hope
that lightning would strike, the young lawyer executed an unorthodox maneuver.

He joined the Department of Justice. No, not the good, gray
building on Pennsylvania Avenue in Washington, D.C., filled to
overflowing with legions of aspiring young lawyers. Washington
was too far from New York, where the action was. He wasn't about to
become one of thousands of names in a government directory.
Instead he chose the office of the United States Attorney for the
Southern District of New York as an assistant U.S. attorney. Traditionally, this office was the most publicized regional arm of the U.S.
Justice Department, a place which had spawned more than its share
of crimebuster prima donnas and charlatans. It had also launched
the political careers of more than a few governors, congressmen,
and judges, to say nothing of rich and famous defense lawyers.

He had no patience with any starry-eyed notions about public
service. He knew that his public service requirements would last
two, better three, years—like the army in which he had no interest
at all—and that the purpose was to learn the prosecutorial ropes.
He knew how to prepare a case. He wasn't sure, however, if he
could do it before a grand jury. He damned well knew the competition at Paul, Weiss couldn't. He would learn the way he always had.

People would tut-tut about his arrogance. A touch too abrasive and all the rest. He had heard it all before. The point was the senior partners didn't care. What they cared about was winning. And money. In fact, mostly money. They damned well knew that arrogance usually helped. When money was involved they called it self-assurance instead. And they were right.

He had a tendency to show off with his new-found knowledge and his dog-eared legal Latin. That might get some judges irritated and confuse most jurors. A few years spent learning the ropes in the federal district attorney's office would refine his style as well as sharpen his skills. Prosecution, in fact, was a fine thing to do after all. Only moralistic fussbudgets saw anything wrong with being a prosecutor and using the position for self-advancement. Plenty of others had done so before him. Politically ambitious prosecutors are the stuff American legal and political history is made of.

For a young man in a hurry, however, the prosecution business had to be done just right. Right, in this case, meant jailing someone big. Big. Here, the soft idealism of the period conveniently served the young man's hard self-interest.

Otherwise, he might end up in the library forever. Not at Paul, Weiss either, but at increasingly lightweight firms, until he ended up in a Forty-Second Street walkup office. No thanks. With pressures like that, it was a relief when the perfect case came down the pike.

His name? Most likely you've never heard of him: Martin Flumenbaum.

His quarry? The Reverend Sun Myung Moon and his Unification Church. Though small in numbers in this country, church members attracted an enormous amount of attention, most of it unflattering, even in the early years.

By the mid-1970s Moon had become in the American public's mind—never too analytical at best—a kind of oriental Jack-the-Ripper, the personification to many anxious middle-class Americans of everything that had gone wrong since the sixties.

But was he a tax cheat too?

That's what the Internal Revenue Service wanted to know.

The Service, as it is known in government and legal circles, has always been a bit snoopy regarding previously unheard-of religious sects. It is almost axiomatic with the Service that, while

religion is protected by the First Amendment, the First Amendment was not intended to protect tax cheats who use religion,
especially patently false religion, as a tax shelter.

But it was difficult to tell if a religion was a cheat without getting
entangled in the religious question, something American courts
were loathe to do. The IRS has tried to define a church on several
occasions, never in brief form. A full discussion of the IRS standards can be found in the Appendix.

In any case, the Unification Church always has been and to this
day remains an IRS- and state-approved tax-exempt religious organization. In other words, a "church."

In 1979, a Memorandum of Law from the Justice Department,
the "church issue" memorandum, dealt with such organizations as
the Basic Bible Church of America, the Life Science Church, and
the Universal Life Church, Inc., which by all appearances were
formed for one purpose only. That was to make money for their
founders by selling information kits to customers showing them
how to use the religious clauses in the First Amendment to protect
their incomes from taxes.

Universal Life, for example, claims seven million ministers. It is
the oldest such tax dodge "church" in the country, having been
established in 1962 in its founder's garage. The UL has no creed
and believes in only what is right—whatever that is. Its chief
activity is to sell, for twenty dollars, an Honorary Doctor of Divinity to anyone, anywhere in the world. Needless to say, the doctorate
has no academic standing whatsoever.

UL will also, for a fee, grant church charters allowing its holders
certain tax benefits, in particular the legal right to "donate" half of
one's personal income to the church and take an automatic tax
deduction for the same amount. At the same time, the "church"
can provide housing, travel, and educational expenses without
having to count any of the funds expended as income. Plus possible relief from property and inheritance taxes.[1]

As one UL advertisement put it: "If the Government is going to
give a free ride to Billy Graham and the Pope, then why not let
everybody participate in these blessings."[2]

Indeed, why not? In *Universal Life Church, Inc. v. United States*,
the UL in 1974 received tax-exempt status from Internal Revenue
under Section 503(c), Title 26, United States Code.[3]

All this suggests that very grave problems arise when the question of a church and the power of the state to tax is raised—even in cases in which the "religion" under review by all common sense tests of religion is a fraud. The First Amendment and its case-law precedents erect substantial barriers against playing fast and loose with any religious body and its rights compared to established denominations.

Of course, religions are not automatically exempt from investigation by the Internal Revenue Service or other legal bodies.

In the case of the Unification Church, the IRS sent its greetings to Sun Myung Moon and his wife Hak Ja Han on October 12, 1976.

The Columbus Day note from the Service's New York district director said simply that the Moons' 1973 1040 tax return would be examined by IRS agent G. O'Donnell. It instructed the Moons to contact O'Donnell and arrange a date for a meeting. A reply, the letter said, within ten days would be appreciated.[4]

The letter from the IRS was hardly Moon's first brush with the American government. The Service, for one, had been working on the Unification Church for some time.

Six months earlier, in April, the IRS' Exempt Organizations Division had ordered a "temporary" freeze on all applications from Unification Church affiliates for non-profit status pending an investigation of the entire condition of the church's financial affairs. Four years later the freeze was still in force.

It is true that the mills of the gods grind slowly, but exceedingly fine. So, too, with the Internal Revenue Service. In the case of the Reverend Sun Myung Moon they ended up with nothing prosecutorial.

The American government is neither simple nor well coordinated. Merely satisfying the Service did not mean that everyone else in government was willing to allow Moon and his church to go about their business proselytizing like any other run-of-the-mill religion.

Under increasing political and public pressure the civil tax audit in 1976 suddenly became a criminal tax investigation in early 1978. By April 1980, the Justice Department had authorized a grand jury investigation to be carried out in New York's Southern District where the Moons had taken up residence.

Two months later the federal grand jury—the first of three—empowered to investigate Moon's tax returns from 1973 to 1976 was impaneled. The grand juries took their time, sixteen months in all, to hand down indictments against Moon and his colleague Takeru Kamiyama on conspiracy, tax evasion, and obstruction of justice charges—twelve counts in all.

A week later, October 22, 1981, the two defendants were summoned for their arraignment in New York City at the Foley Square federal complex, where they pleaded not guilty on all counts.

The process sounds simple and straightforward. Anyone who has passed Perry Mason 101 is familiar with the procedure: grand jury investigation, indictments, arraignment, the trial itself, the appeal process.

It is not quite that simple, however, especially on federal tax raps. Indeed, before any federal grand jury can hand down indictments, Justice Department regulations demand that all criminal tax prosecutions be approved by the assistant attorney general in charge of the Tax Division. That is in contrast to nearly all other criminal cases.

The stated reason for this procedure is that tax cases are usually far more complex than most federal crimes. For one thing, they involve the slippery question of intent, a central feature of the Moon-Kamiyama case. Another reason: Review by Washington helps ensure—it can hardly guarantee—a more uniform national prosecution policy on tax evasion.[5]

This last point leads to the unstated reason for departmental review. The fact that tax prosecution is liable to abuse is well known. Abuse by whom? Politically ambitious U.S. federal attorneys, for starters. They have a tendency to go after unpopular, but not necessarily criminal, figures who can only be tripped up on tax evasion charges. Add this to one other fact. Grand juries have long ceased being the first line of defense for Everyman; they have been turned into the pliant tools of prosecutors, especially bright, hard-charging, and glib prosecutors out to make a name for themselves.

Of course, that isn't in Perry Mason 101, but police reporters, even judges, are well aware of and disturbed by the trend.

The review process required by Justice in criminal tax cases is not a simple one. It takes time. The cases themselves are submitted either by the Internal Revenue Service or by any U.S. attorney's office from Guam to Maine. Unless the circumstances are highly unusual, the normal procedure is to submit them to the Justice Department's Tax Division after the investigation is completed.

Then begins a complicated seven-step procedure which is designed as much to protect the rights of the citizen as to crack down on tax cheats. Often, the procedure works well. Sometimes, it does not.

But we are anticipating events in the case of Moon and Kamiyama.

Step one involves the assignment of the tax case to a line attorney for review. The line attorney usually is a junior officer in the department.

When a conference is requested by defense counsel—invariably this is the case—the line attorney does a preliminary review of the case in order to prepare for the conference. This is step two.

Step three is the conference itself, in which the facts of the case are outlined in a memorandum.

After the conference, the line attorney reviews the case (step four)—this time in detail—including all issues raised at the conference, and then summarizes the evidence and makes a recommendation in the form of a prosecution memorandum: the key document in this long and involved process.

In step five, the "pros memo" is read and evaluated by a more senior departmental lawyer who adds his or her own conclusion to the document in the form of a supplemental memorandum.

The prosecution memo, along with the reviewer's comments, are in turn looked over by the assistant chief of the criminal section at Justice. If all three attorneys agree on the need for prosecution, the prosecution is authorized.

If there is no agreement among the three or if they agree not to prosecute—and this is the last stage—the pros memo is unloaded for a final decision onto the assistant attorney general in charge of the Tax Division.[6]

That's more or less what happened to Moon and Kamiyama, and yet there were irregularities that from the beginning muddied the federal case against the two men from the Orient.

There was, first of all, a basic conflict between the New York Southern District United States Attorney's office and the Justice Department. Conflict is not bad in and of itself. It is not even surprising. Tensions between Washington and the district offices are fairly frequent. A reversal of position and cover-up are, however, neither usual nor acceptable by any canon of justice.

And that is exactly what happened in the case of *United States v. Moon.*

In the beginning, the case went by the book. Moon's defense counsel requested a conference prior to the department's final decision on prosecution. At that meeting, held on June 22 and 23, 1981, the case was reviewed with Ralph Belter, the Justice lawyer who subsequently wrote the prosecution memorandum.

As is customary, Belter reviewed the case as he saw it, including the possible charges and the amount of money involved.

The principal item discussed was the $1.6 million of church funds deposited in Moon's name at the Park Avenue branch of Chase Manhattan Bank in the years 1973 through 1975. That money, Belter theorized, was taxable income belonging to Moon because he apparently had control over the funds for his personal, and not the church's, use.

As is the rule, defense counsel had a chance to rebut the charges. Moon's lawyers went over the tricky legal area of church monies and the role of clergy who act as trustees of funds. They also went over the facts of the case as they saw them. Those facts included a reconstruction of the sources of the $1.6 million Chase Manhattan Bank accounts—an exercise designed to demonstrate that the money had come from church members for the benefit of the church and not primarily for Moon. As a backup to the overall presentation, the defense lawyers provided copies of the "family fund ledger" and the "loan agreements."

These documents turned out to be crucial in more ways than one. Just what were they? The ledger is a simple chronological listing, originally written in Japanese and Korean, of the deposits to the Chase Manhattan accounts, along with a description of the individual church members or groups that provided the money. The so-called "loan agreements" were receipts showing funds obtained from various church groups, i.e., the New York, British, and West German branches of the Unification Church.

During the two-day conference, the defense lawyers never said the ledger or the agreements were records compiled at the time. Instead—and this is critical—they specifically told Justice officials that the documents were reconstructed from bits and pieces of information after the funds were deposited.[7]

Just why the documents were reconstructed is not very difficult to understand. In the early 1970s, the Unification Church in America was composed of Koreans and Japanese who were wholly unfamiliar with American accounting procedures. Those Americans who were in the church were often too young and inexperienced to be of any help. Indeed, most Americans of even advanced formal education know next to nothing about accounting unless they are accountants or in business for themselves.

Moreover, neither Moon nor any church members made any attempt to hide any of the financial transactions. They maintained their own internal records, albeit in Japanese and Korean, and they believed, as many Americans do, that a strict accounting of their deposits and withdrawals would be kept by the bank.

Concerning the latter, a senior vice-president of Chase Manhattan later testified that he had personally handled all the deposits and never perceived any attempt by Moon or his followers to cover up their finances. In fact, he said, nearly all of the deposits were in cash money which could easily have been kept in a safety deposit box, or in an offshore bank, or in a private safe, if the intention had been to cheat the federal government out of taxes.

At this point, the procedural tangle began. Justice's Tax Division review normally begins after the investigation is completed.

In the Moon-Kamiyama case, grand jury proceedings had not been completed even by the time of the June conference between Belter and defense counsel.

More than two weeks later, another grand jury again called Kamiyama and his assistant, Yukiko Matsumura, to testify. The pair told the jurors and the federal prosecutor as they had done previously that the loan agreement documents in question were in part reconstructed as long as three years after the funds had actually been deposited—in effect, a repetition of what defense counsel had told the Justice Department in June.[8]

The July grand jury proceedings provided the prosecution with testimony that the church financial documents were not contemporaneous, but reconstructed accounts based on incomplete records written in Korean and Japanese—documents that were not written with American accounting rules in mind. That brings us to the Justice Department's prosecution memorandum, the first of three "pros memos" by Justice.

The first prosecution memo was completed in the second week of August—two months after the conference and a month after the grand jury testimony of Kamiyama and Matsumura.

The memo's conclusions and recommendations were quite simple: the Justice Department found there was no reason to suspect that Moon or his followers had violated any tax laws. The evidence gathered, in the line lawyer's opinion, was simply insufficient to warrant indictment, prosecution, or trial.[9]

Normally, which is to say in 99 percent of the criminal tax cases referred to the Justice Department, that would have been the end of the matter, case closed. But that was hardly the situation involving Moon.

Curiously, two other prosecution memoranda were drafted a month later, in September, and approved by all the Justice Department's career criminal tax attorneys. They also recommended no prosecution. Why the need for an unprecedented three pros memos all saying essentially the same thing?

We'll deal with that question later, but it's only a small part of the puzzle. The second and third memoranda, also written by Ralph Belter, were completed during the first two weeks of September 1981. Yet on September 21, the Justice Department notified Moon's defense attorneys that prosecution had been approved.[10]

The notification was brief and austere. In a one-sentence memorandum addressed to Moon's lawyer, Bernard Bailor, John F. Murray, acting assistant attorney general of the Justice Department's Tax Division, stated:

> This is to advise you that the above captioned case has been transmitted to the United States Attorney for the Southern District of New York.[11]

In other words, Justice intended to hand over Moon and Kamiyama to the New York office for prosecution.

What had happened? To this day, the Justice Department has steadfastly refused to provide relevant documents, most especially the three prosecution memoranda, to any outside parties. Even the powerful U.S. Senate Judiciary Committee was denied access to the Moon records, forcing Senate investigators into the awkward, if not unprecedented, position of attempting to gather information from the Justice Department in a clandestine manner. In another era Justice's behavior would have been called stonewalling.

We, like the U.S. Senate, are left with a bit of legal construction to do ourselves.

Before attempting to unravel this mystery, let us look at one more puzzling, highly irregular procedure employed by the Justice Department in this case.

When Moon's counsel learned of the decision by Justice to prosecute their client despite the internal recommendations not to do so, they requested a second conference with Justice. That request was made on September 24. Nearly three weeks later, October 13 to be precise, Justice said no. A direct appeal to Attorney General William French Smith two days later was also turned down. The department rejected the request despite counsel's claim that the decision to prosecute was based on new evidence not available to the writer of the three prosecution memoranda and presumably not available to the three senior career criminal tax lawyers who had all previously agreed the government had no case against Moon.

The truth of Moon's lawyers' contention about new evidence is critical. If it is true, Justice regulations almost certainly require a second conference, because the conference is a procedure by which an individual is confronted with all the evidence that the government has assembled in regard to his alleged wrongdoing. His lawyers obviously have no chance to refute the new and additional evidence if they are not given a second chance.

Did Justice in fact have new and compelling evidence that would tip the scales? As it turned out, the answer was no. By violating their own regulations and denying a second conference, government prosecutors also negated the need to put their cards on the table and tip their hand.

Administration of justice should not be a poker game. The feds' attitude was similar to a famous scene in a W.C. Fields movie. A sucker comes up to the Great Man, who is playing cards, and asks him if this is a game of chance. Replies Fields: "Not the way I play it."

Justice seems to have played fast and loose with the rules. Still, what was the new evidence that it said supposedly undercut the three prosecution memos? In hindsight, we now know the prosecutors were concentrating on the reconstructed financial records, calling them back-dated and therefore false—leading to the obstruction of justice charges.

Yet, as we have seen, the reconstructed records were never presented as anything but that: honest attempts to piece together an accounting of the church funds eight years after they had been deposited and duly recorded by Chase Manhattan officials.

Moon and his lawyers certainly made no attempt to conceal anything, so what exactly was Justice hiding? Why, to this day, does the Justice Department acknowledge the existence of the prosecution memos but refuse to let anyone, including the U.S. Congress, see them?

To answer that question requires a clear appreciation of Justice's relationship with New York's Southern District attorneys, and one attorney in particular, Martin Flumenbaum.

Flumenbaum was young, ambitious, and in a hurry. He had for nearly his entire term been consumed with his one great case and one ambition: nailing Sun Myung Moon.

By late summer of 1981 he had spent more than two years investigating Moon and sixteen months trying, unsuccessfully, to persuade three grand juries to indict him. The Justice Department and the IRS had blown millions of dollars in taxpayers' money to underwrite thousands of hours of rifling private church records, tailing church members, wire-tapping church phones, and intimidating church leaders. Yet, for all those efforts, Assistant U.S. Attorney Martin Flumenbaum had failed to produce one shred of credible evidence which would warrant giving Moon a parking ticket, much less a jail term. And now here was a bunch of career Justice Department lawyers in Washington, obviously inferior to him intellectually, telling him that he had no case against the church.

By August 1981 it was clear to everyone, particularly the Justice Department's veteran criminal tax lawyers, that Flumenbaum had badly misjudged the case. What they didn't know was that he had one last desperate card to play.

Martin Flumenbaum was not about to take no for an answer. Even if the no came from Washington.

Like all great artists, Flumenbaum hated critics.

At age thirty-two, he was also not impressed with the solid graystone edifice that housed the Department of Justice. Buildings are only facades that men hide behind, and the men of Justice were jellyfish—and Flumenbaum would prove it.

He himself was a Carter administration appointee. To an ordinary man, that would suggest that he was in a poor position—a lame duck, as it were. Flumenbaum knew better. He, perhaps by instinct, knew that he was negotiating from strength, not the other way around.

It was simple. He knew the case, inside out. So did the professionals at Justice. He would not deal with them; instead he would deal with the political newcomers. Despite Reagan's margin of victory over Carter, Flumenbaum also knew that the Republican appointees would be cautious at first, afraid of the exaggerated attention paid by the media to the incoming crowd.

He also knew that Republicans, especially, are wary of the press, even terrified by the Fourth Estate. What could be scarier than the suggestion by some source that the Republicans were going easy on Moon—a man who had gotten his first political press notices defending an about-to-be-impeached Richard Nixon?

Moon meant Watergate, and a bright and shiny new administration was not about to have that dug up so soon. The Republicans had buried Carter, but they had not yet buried their own past.

It was a brilliant calculation by Flumenbaum. A bit ruthless perhaps, but what the hell, he certainly had the political and psychological nuances exactly right.

Flumenbaum was also working with another powerful ally: public opinion. In early 1981, the horror of mass suicide at Jonestown, Guyana, in 1979 was still very fresh in the minds of many Americans. The thought of making children strangle on poisoned Kool Aid did have a way of provoking visceral emotions about cults. Flumenbaum knew most people would reduce it all to a simple, but reverse, syllogism. People's Temple was a cult. The Temple was evil. All cults therefore were evil. Including the Unification Church and its un-American leader, the Reverend Sun Myung Moon.

Flumenbaum couldn't miss. He was about to squeeze off a skeet shot with a ten-gauge shotgun at a very fat, outsized clay pigeon. He was certainly not going to stand for anything as blindly provincial as a few Justice prosecution memoranda saying no. Flumenbaum therefore took the shuttle to Washington after the first August pros memo was released and argued vociferously against the recommendation. His trip was an unusual procedure, but the stakes were high—after all, a very important career was on the line, something that was not that difficult to understand in sultry Washington.

One trip to the nation's capital did not satisfy Flumenbaum. The career lawyers at Justice simply did not seem to understand the importance of the case. Cautious bureaucrats all, they infuriated the hard-charging Flumenbaum. So he went again. And again.

The process was frustrating. After returning from yet another of those seemingly endless encounters with the jello-like Justice Department, Flumenbaum turned down a ride from La Guardia Airport to the Manhattan prosecutor's office by telling his Southern District colleagues: "If they don't authorize prosecution, I'll take the subway back to Paul, Weiss."[12]

Just what was said or threatened at these meetings is still not known publicly. What is known is that by the third week in September the Justice Department, despite internal advice to the contrary, agreed to the prosecution.

The reversal seems to have been due to a combination of pressure from the New York office, led by its lead attack dog Martin Flumenbaum, plus a judicious amount of paper-shuffling from the civil servants. Shuffling takes place when no one around is senior enough and willing to make a decision. At the end of the Carter era and the beginning of the Reagan first term, plenty of senior Justice officials had already bailed out, making shuffling the favorite paper sport at Justice.

There is nothing sinister in that. Shuffling is perfectly normal during a transition when men and women exit government service. In Washington it is a fine art. Leaving too early strikes many as crass opportunism. You ain't paid your dues, buddy. But leaving too late may mean you haven't beaten the rush. Result? Not getting the job you wanted. Leaving really too late can make matters much worse—especially when your commander-in-chief has not been re-elected. That means unemployment, as many foolish Carterites found out.

Prudently, those at Justice who were about to join the private sector did not want to leave a poison cloud behind. None of the outgoing officials wished to appear soft on tax evaders—the public hates tax cheats; so does the press—especially when the alleged deadbeats happen to be the leaders of one of America's most controversial new religions.

Also, let's be practical about this. A green light for the prosecution did not mean that Moon would be railroaded into jail. The chances were in the real world that the Korean and his entourage would flee the country. Anyone in his right mind would do just that, knowing full well that the United States does not normally go through the difficult legal and diplomatic tangle of extraditing someone, anyone, on mere tax evasion charges.

In short, Moon could skip and that would be that. No harm done. So why stir up a lot of dust when more important matters were under consideration?

The trouble was the damned thing wouldn't go away. Largely because Sun Myung Moon wouldn't go away. His departure would have let everyone off the hook. Not to mention relieving the embarrassment the Department of Justice had suffered so far in this case.

Instead, Moon stayed. So did Kamiyama. Together, they stood their ground and went to trial.

Amidst the general consternation, only one man in government was entirely pleased with every development in the case. That was Martin Flumenbaum, anxious as ever for his first scalp.

But Moon and Kamiyama did more than not run away. What they did do proved terribly embarrassing for Justice and for both the Carter and Reagan administrations. It cost young Martin a few anxious moments as well.

The Justice Department has never revealed just why its leadership reversed course and decided to prosecute Moon and Kamiyama. Its flimsy cover story—as we shall soon see—does not hold water. Because the department has never authorized the release of any internal documents of the case, what I do know is a reconstruction at best.

Moon's lawyers, for example, believe that the man who made the actual decision was Deputy Assistant Attorney General Gilbert E. Andrews. Andrews was inexperienced in criminal tax procedures and took the unprecedented step of vetoing the recommendations of his entire criminal section after he met with New York Southern District U.S. attorneys, including Martin Flumenbaum.

To say the least, this was an unusual way of doing business.

But the indictment, trial, conviction, and a failed appeal did not end the defense effort to obtain information. The defense continued even after Moon and Kamiyama had finished their sentences.

Moon's lawyers' determination was nothing if not dogged, and a little scary to those who had participated in what had been little more than a legal lynching.

In fact, three years after Sun Myung Moon was notified that the government was prepared to prosecute, the stubborn Korean still would not let go. Having failed to obtain pertinent Justice Department documents, including the key prosecution memoranda, under the Freedom of Information Act, Moon's lawyers tried another tactic.

This time they enlisted Senator Orrin Hatch in the effort. Hatch, a conservative Republican from Utah, was a member of the Senate Judiciary Committee and also chairman of its Subcommittee on Constitutional Rights.

Hatch had already become interested in the Moon affair. As a Mormon, he was well acquainted with how unpopular religions can be treated in America, and not from simple abuse by a mob either. There was also the small matter of legal persecution.

Had the Reverend Sun Myung Moon been railroaded by an ostensibly legal process? Senator Hatch had his suspicions. In the summer of 1984, in his capacity as subcommittee chairman, Hatch requested and was granted a meeting with Justice officials in which he requested pertinent information about the decision to prosecute Moon. Specifically, he wanted to see the prosecution memoranda that had all originally recommended against taking Moon to the cleaners.

Now, when a powerful Senate committee chairman from your party (and its conservative wing to boot) speaks, you'd better listen. Justice did—up to a point.

Two weeks after Hatch's July 26 meeting with department officials, Justice's Robert McConnell signed a four-page letter attempting to explain what happened in the Moon case. McConnell was assistant attorney general for "Legislative and Intergovernmental Affairs (LIA)."

McConnell did not have line command of a substantive branch of the Justice Department, but he had attended the Hatch meeting, along with Roger Olsen, then deputy assistant attorney general, Tax Division.

McConnell's office, similar to those in all departments of government, was set up to handle the Congress. To massage it. To keep the guys who keep the money rolling in happy. And occasionally, to lobby it.

In other words, Justice's LIA was a first line of defense for the bureaucrats and the political appointees who did not want their names in the paper.

The Moon case, according to McConnell, was received by the Tax Division on June 8, 1981, from the U.S. Attorney's office in New York, which requested a review. That request, McConnell stated, was made only after "an exhaustive and detailed investigation conducted by career prosecutors and investigators" working in the Southern District.[13]

Then, according to McConnell, a staff attorney from Justice began to review the case. Two weeks after receiving the initial request from the U.S. attorney in New York, the conference was held between Justice attorneys and Moon's defense counsel.

So far we are on familiar ground. What happened next is also familiar.

McConnell continued:

Before and during that lengthy conference, a number of affidavits and various records were submitted to the Tax Division for consideration. Interestingly enough, many of these required translation. Since several matters were raised during the conference that had not previously been submitted for the Tax Division's consideration, these materials were forwarded by the Tax Division to the United States Attorney for the Southern District of New York. The Tax Division requested that the materials be translated and that the grand jury conduct additional inquiry into the areas raised by the defense attorneys.[14]

Next, the grand jury looked at those allegedly new materials. By early August, their work had largely been done. Justice's Tax Division attorney, as we have seen, wrote a prosecution memo recommending that the case be dropped. A senior reviewer in the

Criminal Section concurred. On August 21, according to the Mc-
Connell letter, the chief of the Criminal Section also turned
thumbs down on the prosecution route.

That made it three Justice officials who had said no according to
Justice's head of congressional liaison.[15]

Now comes the truly fascinating part. Having admitted that
senior Justice officials had found the grand jury evidence and the
efforts of the Southern District's U.S. Attorney's office somewhat
wanting, the prosecution unearthed a convenient "break" in the
case.

Something of a miracle, actually.

While the Moon matter was resting uncomfortably with Gilbert
Andrews, the grand jury, according to McConnell, established that
some of the testimony given by Kamiyama to the grand jury was
tainted with perjury.

In a crucial passage of his letter, McConnell then told Senator
Hatch:

> More importantly, the grand jury was able to determine that a
> number of documents submitted to the Tax Division during its
> June conference with Reverend Moon's attorneys had been pre-
> pared, not contemporaneously with the events in question as the
> Tax Division had been led to believe, but rather were prepared
> solely for the purpose of misleading the investigation. This devel-
> opment was first reported to the Tax Division in a memorandum
> from the United States Attorney for the Southern District of New
> York dated August 21, 1981, and received by the Tax Division on
> September 3, 1981.[16]

Because of this shocking "new" development, McConnell explains, a new conference between the prosecuting teams in Washington and New York was held. This time, the reluctant federal tax
attorneys agreed to prosecute, and Andrews then agreed to go
ahead, formally signing off on the prosecution on September 10.

The rest of McConnell's letter to Hatch was strictly for the
record. There was no question, he said, that the Moon-Kamiyama
documents were false. (An assertion.) The government lawyers
involved were motivated by the highest of professional standards.
(Another assertion.) Politics had nothing, absolutely nothing, to
do with it. *Et cetera*, etc., etc. . . .

And, oh, by the way, since you asked, Senator, the documents you requested will not be made available.

Why?

> [I]t seems to us most important that the Department adhere to its strongly held policy view that prosecution memoranda should not be released outside the Department. In this case, we deal with even more than our significant concern to safeguard our internal deliberative documents. Here, we discuss internal deliberative documents which reflect preliminary recommendations which were based upon materials which have been found by courts of law to have been false and which had been submitted to the Tax Division for the very purpose of influencing improperly this Department's deliberative process.[17]

In short, Senator Hatch, request denied.

Justice's letter did not satisfy Senator Hatch. It most certainly did not satisfy the defense counsel who were provided—as the Justice Department well knew—with a copy of the McConnell letter.

It didn't take long for Moon's attorneys to reply. Three weeks later, they had a full-blown response.

The first hole in the wall was Justice's odd review procedure. The first conference between Justice and the lawyers for the defense was supposed to have reviewed *all* the potentially criminal evidence.

The evidence that was found so scanty that even Justice officials thought it insufficient.

But when new evidence was allegedly developed—evidence that McConnell's own letter cited as crucial to the prosecution—no second conference was held between potential prosecution and defense. Not only was the conference not held, the request by the defense for a conference was denied.

Meanwhile, an inexperienced deputy assistant attorney general, Gilbert Andrews, was exposed to a lengthy and one-sided presentation from the Southern District U.S. Attorney's office. Defense counsel had no opportunity at all to reply to the new evidence— again evidence that the McConnell letter said was crucial to the case.

Not that Moon's lawyers didn't try. They made two requests for a second conference, and were turned down twice—the second refusal from Attorney General William French Smith in a one-paragraph brush-off that was no more than a typical staff-drafted answer: precise, bland, and beside the point.[18]

How come?

Justice merely replied that second conferences were unusual. It did not explain why, in the face of allegedly new evidence, another joint review was not necessary. Moreover, and much worse, the so-called new evidence led to a wholly different set of charges: perjury, conspiracy, obstruction of justice—charges on which Moon and Kamiyama were later convicted.

Even though the first conference covered only potential charges which were not used by the prosecution and even though a whole new set of charges was lodged against Moon, the government argued in retrospect that a second conference was still unnecessary. It is an utterly unfathomable assertion that rests on no known legal principle whatsoever. Why? Because if changing the whole nature of the case is not grounds for another prosecution-defense conference, what in the world is?

When in doubt, obscure the issue and plead standard operating procedure even when, manifestly, the matter at hand is not in the least bit standard. That's exactly what Justice did in the McConnell letter and the earlier brush-off letters from Attorney General Smith and Gilbert Andrews.

So, what about the new evidence that everyone at Justice and in the Southern District was supposed to have found so persuasive?

That evidence consisted of the so-called false documents provided by Moon and Kamiyama. Two types of documents were considered to be relevant by the government.

The first were handwritten journals that recorded the receipt of money from the Japanese Unification Church members, which money was subsequently deposited in the Chase Manhattan Bank accounts. The second were so-called "promissory" notes that reflected funds from other, non-Japanese Unification Church members and groups that were also put in the Park Avenue bank.

The government contended that these documents were false, not because they were inaccurate (which in some respects they were), but because they were not "contemporaneous," that is, they were put together after the events, in short, backdated.

The defense contended, however, that no one in the Unification Church ever said they were anything but reconstructed documents. Defense counsel made that clear during the first and only conference with Justice officials. Two weeks after that late June conference, Kamiyama under oath at the grand jury proceedings had said specifically that the "promissory" notes were prepared sometime in 1975, two years after the bank deposits were made.

The defense made two other points. First, the above facts were known to the government no later than several weeks before the first prosecution memo was written. Second, the reconstructed records had been put together long before any government investigation began. Since such was the case, how could the documents have been "prepared solely for the purpose of misleading the investigation," as the McConnell letter contended?[19]

But if the circumstances under which the documents were prepared were never falsely portrayed by Moon or Kamiyama or their lawyers, what about the mistakes contained in the reconstructed documents themselves?

No one denies that the documents were riddled with errors. After-the-fact attempts to figure out what, when, and who (in three languages involving money in several different currencies) is admittedly a confusing process. Were those errors significant? Were they done intentionally to mislead and hinder in any way a tax investigation?

This was apparently not the case.

Consider the errors themselves. One, for example, credited a California Unification Church with a contribution when, in fact, the contribution came from an individual member from California.[20]

Other things were wrong in the McConnell letter to Hatch, things that Moon's lawyers found disturbing. One was the assertion that Justice's Tax Division got the case in June 1981. But according to Moon's lawyers:

In fact, the case was first considered by the Tax Division at least a year earlier. At that time the Tax Division was requested to authorize a grand jury investigation of Rev. Moon. There is reason to believe that, even at that time, there was considerable doubt about the merits of the case but the investigation was nevertheless allowed to proceed. An objective accurate response to the Chairman's [Orrin Hatch's] inquiry must also cover this phase of the Tax Division's participation in this case.[21]

The defense lawyers also threw cold water on the notion advanced in the McConnell letter that the investigation of Moon was done by a thorough and highly professional group of career prosecutors.

That, as we have seen, is pure eyewash. The Southern District's leading investigator on the Moon-Kamiyama case was Martin Flumenbaum, barely past thirty years of age, and lacking a single day's experience in a courtroom. He was certainly no career professional.

To make matters worse, others on the prosecution team had also returned to the private sector—all of which was known to the Justice Department when the McConnell letter was prepared for Senator Hatch.

Another problem. While we know there is ample documentation in Justice's vaults about the recommendations against prosecution, there is no known paper trail within Justice that supports the reverse decision to prosecute. This, in and of itself, is highly unusual in this very unusual case. The earlier prosecution memoranda are known to exist, but what about the pros memo laying out the case for prosecution?

If such a memo does exist no one has ever even referred to it.

All we know is that the September meeting between Southern District and Justice's Tax Division lawyers took place, and that Gilbert Andrews shortly afterwards decided to prosecute.

So what really happened at that meeting? The argument that new evidence was presented as we have seen is tendentious—at best.

Far more likely, the Southern District crowd, led by Martin Flumenbaum, knew that this was going to be the last meeting. Flumenbaum's outburst mentioned in the *American Lawyer* article is proof of that.

If Justice would not budge even when confronted by legal arguments against phony "new evidence," then there was always the political squeeze. The Southern District mob was dominated by Carter-appointed Democrats and Justice by incoming Republicans.

Which returns us to this. What was in the prosecution memoranda that recommended against prosecution?

The first memo was written in early August; the second and third a month later. The latter two were likely attached to the first as a "supplemental"—thus bolstering Justice's contention that there had been only one review carried out by Justice.

But what did the memoranda say? We know that all three vetoed the idea of prosecuting Moon. Justice already admits that. The actual contents, however, have to be reconstructed from the odd bits and pieces supplied by Justice itself, primarily in its letter to Senator Hatch.

The McConnell letter listed three reasons advanced in the first pros memo. The first was Moon's apparent "insulation" from his financial affairs. The letter said:

> [T]here was evidence that interest income had been omitted from the returns, but it was difficult to tie Reverend Moon to the alleged falsities.[22]

The memo writer also had problems with a very large anomaly. If the Reverend Sun Myung Moon were a tax cheat who did not report personal income, then why did he not make a claim to a large charitable contribution to which he was entitled—according to Justice's own expert tax lawyer?

Quite obviously that fact alone not only radically undercuts the notion that Moon was a deadbeat, it just about confirms defense's contention that Moon's books were prepared by individuals unfamiliar and incompetent in dealing with American tax law and accounting procedures. Incidentally, the unclaimed but wholly legitimate charitable contribution, according to Justice, would have substantially reduced Moon's tax liability for the years under review, namely 1973 through 1975.

Finally, the senior reviewer at Justice could not make the connection between unreported income and Moon's personal involvement in the matter.

In McConnell's own words to Senator Hatch:

> The Chief of the Criminal Section concluded that the Government had a less-than-reasonable probability of conviction.[23]

So where are we? We have a divided Justice Department whose senior officers changed their minds about a prosecution that career lawyers said was a no-go. We also have political appointees in the U.S. Attorney's office in New York stridently begging to differ—one threatening to quit, or worse, if he did not get his way.

There was a sudden change of heart, but no documents are known to exist to explain the reasons why. The reasons offered to the defense team, which never had a chance to discuss the new evidence, appear for the most part flimsy.

And now, a decade after the decision to prosecute, we are still left in the dark. From stonewalling to limited hangout the irony is that a Republican administration ended up doing its best to advance the private fortunes of Democrat-appointed prosecutors.

Washington no doubt has stranger ironies, but it would be difficult to find them.

CHAPTER V

THE CASE OF THE MISSING TRANSLATOR

Finally, I accuse the first Court Martial of having violated the law in convicting a defendant on the basis of a document kept secret, and I accuse the second Court Martial of having covered up that illegality on command by committing in turn the judicial crime of knowingly acquitting a guilty man.

EMILE ZOLA

GETTING the Reverend Sun Myung Moon was not proving to be an easy task for Martin Flumenbaum, Esq. Despite the overwhelmingly negative public feelings about the Korean and his Unification Church, it was and still is hard in this country to prosecute simply because a man is unpopular.

How desperate the situation truly was for Flumenbaum is indicated by a brace of Justice lawyers who really thought there were no grounds for prosecution. Period. Ralph Belter, the department's Tax Division review attorney, the most unbiased and expert lawyer the government had on the case, concluded on August 4, 1981, that the Reverend Moon was not liable for any taxes in fiscal year 1973 even if all monies in his various accounts personally belonged to the Korean. As for the two following years, Belter reported that at best Moon might owe a grand total of $7,300 in taxes, but even that was not certain. Since tax liabilities of such dimensions were considered minor and disposed of ordinarily by paying a fine, Justice's top tax lawyer recommended no indictment. To do otherwise would have been absurd legal overkill in his view.

Belter's boss, Edward Vellines, assistant chief of the Tax Division, agreed. And his boss, Stanley Crisa, chief of the entire Tax Division, also signed off on the no-indictment recommendation, not once, but three times. By August 20 that triple negative recommendation had sailed up to Gilbert Andrews, acting deputy assistant attorney general for the Tax Division, a quickness in paper passing that approaches the bureaucratic speed of light.

This was getting serious. Martin Flumenbaum's whole case was at stake, two years of effort going down the drain because a coterie of fish-eyed, greenshade government lawyers thought his arguments for prosecution were for the birds.

Consequently, Flumenbaum wrote Andrews one day after Andrews got his memo from Crisa and company. Flumenbaum probably knew it would do no good to rehash the case as it had been presented, however. Wasting the taxpayers' money on a criminal tax trial involving less than $10,000 in liability just would not, no matter how much one flapped one's arms, excite the department's legal-eagles.[1]

And Mrs. Flumenbaum had not raised a stupid child. Anticipating trouble, he had prepared another approach.

But this time it would not be a frontal assault on Moon. Instead, Flumenbaum had been busy probing for weaknesses all along Moon's defense line. Now faced with ignominy and defeat, he launched an unexpected attack on the flank.

Flumenbaum selected as his target an associate of Sun Myung Moon, Takeru Kamiyama, a Japanese and a long-time member of the Unification Church. Kamiyama, who came to the United States in 1972, served as financial adviser to Moon.

The U.S. attorneys knew about Kamiyama's financial role, of course, and that is why Flumenbaum hauled Kamiyama before two grand juries in July 1981 to grill him on the finances of Moon and his church. After three full and exhausting days of questions and answers, Flumenbaum reviewed the testimony and found what he was looking for. Since Justice would not go for a simple tax evasion case, maybe they would buy perjury and conspiracy, six additional counts in all, obtained from yet another grand jury especially convoked for the occasion. Or so it was hoped. But more on that later.

The U.S. attorney wasted no time. It took not only a letter, but a personal, follow-up visit to Washington by Flumenbaum before Justice was willing to change its mind and buy his goods. But buy them it did: lock, stock, and barrel.

On September 10, 1981, Gilbert Andrews authorized the indictment. Flumenbaum had won another round, which proves, if nothing else, that persistence and no great reverence for authority do pay after all.

The charges of perjury against Kamiyama served as the bridge leading to trial and conviction of both Kamiyama and Moon on perjury and tax evasion indictments.

But how sturdy was that bridge? Was it a solid structure that could support the full weight of a federal prosecution?

A closer look at the proceedings suggests it was not and provokes questions about the entire judicial process.

In fact, it raises the direct question: Was perjury committed at all or only the appearance of perjury? Didn't the prosecution virtually guarantee the appearance of perjury before it actually happened by creating a perjury trap, a device not wholly unknown in American jurisprudence?

Furthermore, did the government have evidence that there had been a serious miscarriage of justice in the grand jury proceedings even before the indictments against Kamiyama were sought? And did the prosecution withhold that evidence from a grand jury, the court, and the counsel for the defense?

These questions and others revolve around the quality of the interpretation provided for Takeru Kamiyama (who spoke only limited English) and eventually led to two U.S. Senate committee hearings. Unlike many of their type, these hearings produced new legislation and federal laws designed to correct some of the grievous errors knowingly and unknowingly committed in the Kamiyama case.

For those who crafted the legislation—both Republicans and Democrats—the issues at stake posed serious dangers to individual rights under the Fifth, Sixth, and Fourteenth Amendments.

As Senator Paul Simon, a liberal Democrat from Illinois and one of the bill's co-sponsors, would put it:

> One of the most important improvements made in this section is the extension of the Court Interpreters Act to Grand Jury proceedings. Accurate interpretation is particularly significant at the Grand Jury level. An error in the interpretation of the testimony of an accused, or that of a witness, could result in wasted court time and money. More important, an interpretation error could result in the incarceration of innocent individuals.
>
> The Committee of the Judiciary heard extensive testimony in the 99th Congress about the dangers of this very problem. An attorney testified before the committee and read the statement of Takeru Kamiyama, a client who was sent to jail and convicted of perjury. His conviction was triggered by what amounted to an incorrect interpretation of his testimony before a Grand Jury.[2]

Very impressive. But the heart of the matter is summed up in two simple words: *due process.* That, as we shall see, was in short supply.

Before getting into the truly bizarre business of the inept interpreter and the missing translator, let us first refresh our memories about perjury. Once more the real world of perjury—lying under oath—is a bit different from what we see on old "Perry Mason" reruns. Although it has proven recently popular with prosecutors attempting to nail political appointees of the Reagan era, perjury is a rap not easy to sustain. That is so because the federal rules are stringent about it. Making a case on perjury is not ordinarily a matter of catching someone in a slip of the tongue or a mistaken response to a deliberately vague question. Moreover, in cases where witnesses have (at times) convenient lapses of memory, that in itself does not constitute perjury. The prosecution must prove that the "I don't remember" is false and any subsequent statement is also knowingly false.[3]

And as such U.S. courts have long recognized the potential for abuse by prosecutors when it came to perjury. "Perjury traps," in short, are nothing new.

No wonder then that the courts have established exacting standards of falsity and relevance which have to be satisfied if a perjury charge is to be sustained. As the Third Circuit Federal Court said in *U.S. v. Tonelli*, persons accused of lying under oath cannot be simply "assumed into the penitentiary."[4]

Perjury based on testimony in a language other than English is especially complex, as the *Kamiyama* case proved. Human languages are tricky. They are not one bit the tidy things we think they are as we work in our everyday world.

But for English-speaking Americans who rarely wander out of their monolingual culture, what happened to Kamiyama is difficult to understand and doesn't elicit much sympathy, if any. But it should.

Literate Americans who have read Franz Kafka's *The Trial* might remember (with a shudder) his story of an average man, Joseph K., who is caught up in a complicated and mystifying legal process where he can get no answers about what he is supposed to have done and what he is supposed to do. To him it is all murmurs and whispers. Baffling ambiguity.

Although Kafka himself lived in a bilingual world (Czech and German), the point of K.'s tribulations was not linguistic and cultural, but spiritual and philosophical. The fear and confusion of finding oneself in a new and vaguely threatening environment is nonetheless clearly sketched. Even to an American.

But imagine a different scenario. You are in a distant country where a language is spoken of which you have little knowledge. The culture is far different from your own as well. There is little that is familiar. You cannot even read the street signs. Suddenly you find yourself in trouble with the authorities. You are not sure exactly why because no one can explain it to you. When it comes to some sort of legal proceeding, you are still on your own. Everything said by the officials among themselves is, of course, completely incomprehensible to you. When they ask you questions, a stranger talks to you in broken English, apparently repeating what the others have said. Much of what the translator says is gobbledygook. It seems to be English, but many terms are unfamiliar, and the phrases put together don't make much sense. There don't seem to be any nouns or antecedents. The verbs are odd, stilted choices. It is all so vague, but then you don't have time to think about that because they are throwing a lot of questions at you at a very rapid rate. You wonder if your helper can keep up with all this. More than that you just wish he could talk to you in plain American so you could know what the hell it is all about. But he doesn't. Even when he makes some sort of sense, you are not sure how it relates to what was said before. Of course, you have no idea how your uncertain and somewhat confused replies are coming out the other end in the other language. All you know is that all of this seems important, and your fate depends on what is said. And still you are not sure what, after all, is happening. Nobody ever treated you like this in Sheboygan, but this is not Sheboygan.

Does that sound Kafkaesque?

It is. And it isn't some literary nightmare either. It happens. Sometimes in the courts of the United States. Some improvements have been made in recent years, but no one aware of the problem believes that we are anywhere close to a solution.

In contrast to what a majority of Americans think, we are far from being a single-language nation. Because of the increasing number of non-English-speaking aliens in the United States, both legal and illegal, the question of language and language competence in dozens of other languages from Polish to Pashto is growing, not receding, in importance.

At no time does it become more important than when the non-English-speaking person is enmeshed in the American legal system.

What happened to Takeru Kamiyama is a good example.

Takeru Kamiyama in his capacity as Moon's financial adviser was, naturally, a prime candidate to be a grand jury witness. The fact that Kamiyama spoke limited English even though he had been in the United States for eight years didn't hurt either—at least from the prosecution's point of view.

Speaking little English after so many years in residence may surprise some people, especially those who know only one language themselves, but it is very common. Particularly when two languages—in this case Japanese and English—are so very much unlike each other.

In Kamiyama's case something else militated against him. Unlike the fabled poor immigrant fresh off the boat, Kamiyama was not forced to learn English in order to survive. As an educated man in a structured environment, he could depend on others—in this case American and bilingual Japanese aides—to handle pesky problems with the language.

It was this linguistic cocoon that spelled so much trouble for Kamiyama and ultimately his superior, the Reverend Sun Myung Moon.

The nature of all grand jury proceedings also complicated the problem. The grand jury is an unusual institution in the world's legal systems. The Japanese don't have it, for instance. Because it is not a trial, certain procedures that are followed in bench and jury trials do not apply.

The grand jury's basic function in the American legal system is to determine if there is sufficient evidence to indicate that a crime has been committed. It does not decide on guilt or innocence, but whether or not there is enough proof for an indictment.

As such, grand jury proceedings are supposed to protect the individual and give him a chance to tell his side of the story without the elaborate and cumbersome procedures of an adversarial process in which prosecution and counsel for the defense can bang away at each other and the witnesses.

Because the atmosphere is supposed to be less hostile and more heuristic—or helping to discover the truth—witnesses face the jurymen and the prosecutor alone, that is, without benefit of counsel in the room. A witness or a prospective defendant can step outside and confer with his lawyer, but the witness for all practical purposes is on his own.

During the proceedings, any grand juryman can ask questions. Prosecutors can too, of course, but the assumption in a grand jury proceeding is that witnesses are not on trial. In many cases, it is the grand jury members who do most of the work, not the government attorney. Above all, the grand jury is not supposed to be the creature of the government, but an independent body. Increasingly, sad to say, that is not the case. With Kamiyama it wasn't that way at all.

Some things, however, haven't changed in a grand jury room. When a witness testifies, he swears the same oath to tell the truth as he would in a regular trial. And the penalties for perjury are the same.

That's one end of the stick. The other is the fact that the witness is still protected by the Fifth Amendment. He does not have to answer any question that might appear (not just would) to incriminate him. Protection from self-incrimination is still one of the few bedrock and basic rights of any individual in any and all American legal proceedings.

That's not just legalistic parsnips. Without the Fifth Amendment it would be a jungle out there. As a reporter who has covered more than a hundred trials and grand jury proceedings during two decades of investigative reporting, what I saw was and is not the Hollywood brand of courtroom justice we've come to know so well. Because the real legal world is coarse and brutal, only certain procedural rights contained in the Fifth Amendment can keep an innocent man's head above water, especially when the prosecution, for whatever reason, is after a conviction at all costs.

The grand jury serves as a central process in the American system of justice. It tends to keep the government honest and it protects the manifestly innocent from arbitrary prosecution. It also qualifies the guilty for later trial by handing up indictments.

Unfortunately, that old Roman caveat, *ceritus paribus* (other things being equal), did not apply in the Kamiyama case. For two reasons.

One, the prosecutor: Martin Flumenbaum acted more like an officer for conviction than as an officer of the court in the grand jury proceedings. He dominated them by asking all of the questions in a rapid-fire, prosecutorial manner. This was no search for the truth; this was pure adversarial behavior. And there was no defense counsel to object. Such behavior violated, from the beginning, the spirit of the grand jury proceeding and placed the witness, later the defendant, in an awkward if not totally compromising position.

Awkward is bad if you are an observer. Untenable is impossible if you are on the firing line, and that's where Kamiyama actually found himself. Why was he there? That's my second point. Kamiyama spoke little English. But in a grand jury proceeding in 1981, a witness had no right to his own interpreter. The foreigner took the interpreter he was given, leaving him with the loaded legal dice that the prosecution was playing with. Someone Kamiyama didn't know would do his talking for him at the grand jury proceedings.

To make matters worse, there were no checks in place in 1981 on the prosecutor's choice of a grand jury interpreter. He literally could have picked anyone off the street. The person he appointed as an interpreter needed no certification of competence. No test of any kind was necessary. Self-declaration was enough.

It was a perfect recipe for disaster. At least in terms of very basic notions of justice.

For starters, all interpreters are not equal. Nor are qualified ones to be found in great numbers—in any language. Quite aside from the question of basic competence in normal usage of a particular language, there are highly specialized forms of interpretation as well.

The kind most often seen by the layman are those involved in international conferences and forums like the United Nations or the Organization of American States.

There, interpreters provide simultaneous translation of speeches and comments. The vocabulary is highly specialized. Even the best of them find the job a strain, one that can only be done for a short period of time particularly when there is no prepared text from which to operate and the speaker is talking rapidly. That is why international organizations like the OAS assign three translators to each language. The interpreters take turns, only working for ten to twenty minutes at a time. Moreover, as any interpreter knows, translation is easier when one is already familiar with the speaker's style of speech. Interpreting for perfect strangers is more than a challenge; sometimes it is impossible.

A friend of mine who used to work at the White House recalls a time when our president made a phone call to another chief of state. The call was an attempt to defuse a potentially tense international confrontation. Because the other leader spoke no English, a highly trained State Department interpreter was chosen to handle the language chores.

Unfortunately, the interpreter had never before dealt with the foreign president. When the man got on the phone and extended greetings to our president, the interpreter's face went white.

"I can't understand him," he whispered frantically to a White House aide. He couldn't because he was entirely unfamiliar with the man's speech patterns and his accent. And, of course, there was also the small matter of the foreign president's being intoxicated at the time.

Once this fact was explained to the State Department expert, he settled down, relaxed, and came up with at least a competent performance. But it wasn't easy.

Interpretation is difficult even under the best of circumstances.

Intoxication hardly exhausts the potential problems. A few more are worth listing. The hardest form of translation is simultaneous interpretation; that is, the interpreter gives a running account of what the speaker is saying. Simultaneous translation is what you hear at the United Nations when, for example, the ambassador from Romania is blasting his colleague from Hungary.

The second most difficult interpreting chore is consecutive translation: a speaker finishes his statement and the interpreter then follows with his account. This is nearly as difficult as simultaneous translation and requires accurate and rapid note-taking, as well as a good memory.

Consecutive translation becomes even more difficult when the interpreter is responsible for translating for more than one person. If he must, in addition, translate in both directions for two or more people, the effort becomes Herculean. Even a well-trained interpreter's work decreases in quality if he labors for more than a half hour without a break.

Translation problems are even greater when the languages involved are very different. It is one thing to move from English to French or Spanish with their similar grammatical forms and high number of cognates—that is, words that look and sound the same in meaning—but it is quite another when the languages are polar opposites, such as English and Japanese. In Japanese verbs come at the end of a sentence and subjects often are omitted altogether, while past and present tenses are frequently confused.

On top of that, the cultural differences between Japanese and Americans are so vast that even when a word can be found to convey the meaning in one of these languages, it is often only an approximation. There is also all the cultural baggage that goes with any language which can add meanings that don't exist in another one.

Besides, some things can't be said at all in another language. Or if there is a word-for-word translation, the result can end up meaning nothing at all.

These are all difficulties that confront any interpreter, assuming that he is competent, well trained, and willing. Some aren't. UN translators, for example, who are considered the elite of the profession, wouldn't touch trial work with a cattle prod.

Why? Because, aside from the question of poor pay, language interpretation in a legal setting requires a specialized vocabulary that demands a detailed knowledge of the American legal system, as well as the legal system of at least the country of the people who need the services of the interpreter. And, moreover, often certain concepts of American jurisprudence have no equivalents in the other languages, a fact which compounds the problem.

So what happens if the interpreter isn't competent? Takeru Kamiyama's interpreter's performance became a classic in legal annals. But judge for yourself. For openers, look at the very start of the process and see how the court-appointed interpreter, John Mochizuki, handled even the most fundamental translation chores.

In a grand jury or a trial procedure, a witness is first sworn in. Then he's read his rights. Ordinarily this is a simple procedure.

But not so with Kamiyama. During the first session of the first day of the proceedings, July 9, 1981, Mochizuki's translation began to go wrong. And I am now quoting from the transcript as corrected from the original.

FORELADY: Do you solemnly swear that the testimony you are about to give to this Grand Jury in the matter now pending before it, shall be the truth, the whole truth, and nothing but the truth, so help you God?

INTERPRETER [in Japanese]: Regarding this present case, we would like here, to have you convey to us all of the truth er . . . only the truth.

WITNESS [in Japanese and English]: Yes.

PROSECUTOR: And in connection with your appearance before this Grand Jury you are entitled to certain rights. Let us explain to you what these rights are. First you may refuse to answer any question, if a truthful answer to that question would tend to incriminate you personally, in any way, shape or form. Do you understand this?

INTERPRETER [in Japanese]: And, er . . . in connection with your appearance in court today in accordance with a summons, there are several rights that are granted you. I will explain them to you. The first of these is, you can refuse . . . answers to questions such as would cause you to fall into sin. Were you able to comprehend this?

WITNESS [in English]: Yes.

PROSECUTOR: Second, anything you do say here today could be used against you, not only by this Grand Jury but in the court of law. Do you understand that?

INTERPRETER [in Japanese]: The statements you make today, at this Grand Jury, well . . . there may be occasions when they will be used to your disadvantage, and in addition . . . er . . . even in legal— subsequent ones, that is—proceedings, even in those that will continue hereafter . . . there is the possibility that they may be used to your disadvantage.[5]

Quite a verbal bog, wouldn't you say? And that was just the opening minutes of three grueling days of testimony. Start with the oath. It is familiar to Americans, but not to the Japanese. Japan is a nonlitigious society. As a result, the Japanese are truly fortunate to have few attorneys, little more than 14,000 nationwide. In America, lawyers crawl over the landscape like army ants in certain South American countries, seeking anything they can devour.

The Japanese therefore have difficulties with certain words like *oath*, which term the interpreter never explained. Instead, he simply suggested in a polite fashion that Kamiyama tell the truth. The translator did not add the phrase "so help me God" because the exact translation means nothing in Japanese. Because his Japanese was less than flawless he also did not use the legal Japanese equivalent, which is to swear by one's conscience. In Japanese courts, when a witness promises to tell the truth, a solemn little ceremony is performed during which he signs a document and affixes his seal. Thus in no way was the gravity of the grand jury proceedings conveyed to Kamiyama.

Nor were the witness's rights under the Fifth Amendment ever properly explained. Court-appointed interpreter Mochizuki made a hash—simply and totally—of the prosecutor's warning that anything said could be used for later prosecution. His testimony might only be used to his "disadvantage," whatever that meant.

It got worse. When the question of punishment for perjury arose—Kamiyama was eventually charged with six counts of perjury—the back-and-forth became another farrago of linguistic absurdity.

Again, I quote the corrected testimony:

PROSECUTOR: Finally, Mr. Kamiyama, if you should give a false answer or fail to testify completely and truthfully in response to the question that I ask you, you could be charged with a separate criminal violation for perjury or obstruction of justice. Do you understand that?

INTERPRETER [in Japanese]: And now, in today's questions and answers, er . . . if there are instances of false answers or failure to testify, there is the possibility that you may be charged . . . separately, that is . . . under criminal law.

WITNESS [in Japanese]: Does that mean, not the tax laws, but . . .?

INTERPRETER [in English]: Does that mean that on top of, or apart from the tax laws?

PROSECUTOR: That's correct. If you should testify falsely . . .

INTERPRETER [in Japanese]: Er, er . . .

WITNESS [in Japanese]: That means . . . ?

INTERPRETER [in Japanese]: Testimony . . . if . . . distorted the testimony . . .

WITNESS [in Japanese]: That means . . . that means I'll be charged with perjury, doesn't it?

INTERPRETER [in English]: Does that mean, once again, that I shall be charged for . . . er . . . I'm trying to find the right word . . .

PROSECUTOR [whispering]: Perjury . . .

INTERPRETER [continuing in English]: Ah . . . all right, fraudulent answers, or fraudulent . . . well, negligence of . . . er . . . testimony or . . .

PROSECUTOR: If you should knowingly and willfully give a false answer to the Grand Jury, that is a separate crime.

INTERPRETER [in Japanese]: Er . . . While knowing it, that is . . . er . . . matters that amount to crimes. That is the meaning.[6]

In short, quite aside from all the stammering, the interpreter did not even know the correct word for perjury in Japanese nor did he convey to Kamiyama the seriousness of the crime under American law. As for the warning concerning possible obstruction of justice charges, well, that simply fell through the linguistic cracks.

In fact, no matter how basic the legal vocabulary, Kamiyama's interpreter was ignorant of it all, right to the end. In the final afternoon session, for example, Mochizuki styles the grand jury "foreperson" as "the leader of this Grand Jury." But that's better than an earlier occasion when the interpreter said in Japanese to the bewildered Kamiyama that "four persons in the Grand Jury have decided on the next date" of his appearance instead of "foreperson."[7]

Just think of yourself in a Tokyo court dealing with this kind of gobbledygook.

And no one, least of all the U.S. attorney, seems to have given a damn.

On basic points, Mochizuki proved to be no more capable on later occasions. In the session on July 9, he called the oath a "declaration."[8]

As the grand jury proceeded, it also became evident that the interpreter made no attempt to improve his knowledge of either legal English or Japanese. For example, during the fourth session of the final July 21 proceedings, the prosecutor once more explained to the witness his "5th Amendment rights":

If you want to refuse to answer them, you can refuse to answer questions, but you have to answer whatever question I ask you. If you want to refuse to answer them, exercise your 5th Amendment rights, you can.[9]

That, however, is not how the translation came out. The interpreter rendered the statement thus:

I am now directing a question to you, but if you insist on rejecting it, er . . . the amendment of the fifth article . . . er . . . well . . . according to the . . . amended law, is it? . . . you have the right to reject. However, er . . . I would like to have you respond to what I have asked as far as possible.[10]

One more thing. As any beginning student of Japanese knows, a handy word one learns from the start is *hai*. Kamiyama frequently used it during the grand jury proceedings. It can mean "yes" and it was translated as such. *Hai* was the word Kamiyama used in response to the mistranslated oath. The problem is that *hai* means a lot of other things to Japanese as well. As Kinko S. Sato, a Japanese attorney who filed an *amicus curiae* brief for *United States v. Sun Myung Moon and Takeru Kamiyama*, wrote:

It is important to note here that in the context of spoken Japanese dialogue, the meaning of "Hai" is so vague, multifarious, and unspecific, and often does not mean what is meant by English "Yes."[11]

It can even mean the opposite, if the speaker is unsure of himself, and in the presence of authority which must be accorded an honorific reply.

Was Kamiyama's perjury conviction simply all the interpreter's fault for not making everything much clearer? It would be easy to say yes, but the interpreter in question had his side of the story, too. John Mochizuki, the unfortunate interpreter in question, later testified before the Senate Judiciary Committee's Subcommittee on the Constitution on Kamiyama's grand jury appearance. His testimony was not so much a defense of his work before the New York Southern District's grand jury as an explanation of why it went so wrong.

Although Mochizuki was indeed a professional interpreter of Japanese and English—he was Japanese-born, but moved to the United States at the age of twenty-six—he was only a part-time interpreter and had no technical training in legal work, although he had translated occasionally at trials (on four occasions) and had appeared before a grand jury three times.

By State Department standards, Mochizuki was competent only for casual escort service—hardly a pressure-filled job and one that requires language skills ranked well below what is needed for conference and trial interpreting. In fact, an interpreter with Mochizuki's experience and level of competence is no more prepared for service in the legal area than playing sandlot football on a few occasions makes one eligible for the NFL.

But Mochizuki related that his limited experience in handling trial situations was not his only problem. In his verbal statement to the subcommittee chaired by Senator Orrin Hatch, the interpreter recalled one disadvantage that he worked under:

> In this particular grand jury proceeding, the prosecutor asked questions in rapid succession which left me no opportunity to take sufficient notes. I had no opportunity to reflect before translating the questions and answers and to determine whether any corrections or clarifications were necessary.[12]

Note taking, of course, is the basic tool of a competent translator. Because Mochizuki took few notes, it was inevitable that he made mistakes and added things the prosecutor and witness never said, or left out words and phrases, even whole sentences, that they had said.

And finally, the interpreter was so cowed by the prosecutor that he never once asked the prosecutor simply to slow down—a routine request made by experienced interpreters.

In his written testimony, Mochizuki recalled something else. The weather was hot and muggy in New York in July that year. According to the interpreter, he and the witness Kamiyama "were kept waiting long hours in a room without air conditioning." It's not surprising that both Kamiyama and Mochizuki were a bit wilted when they finally arrived at the jury room only to face hours of grueling questioning. Even a competent interpreter, moreover, would have demanded relief after an hour. No such luck. Both were set up. To top it all, Kamiyama had a cold.[13]

So what do we have so far? First, the interpreter was neither technically proficient in either language nor professionally trained for the exacting job of trial work. Second, the interpreter was subjected to zero working conditions—the sessions were too long, he was forced to do two-way consecutive translations, and he had no familiarity with Kamiyama or Flumenbaum and therefore was incapable of dealing with the peculiar nuances of each man's speech.

But that is merely the beginning.

More revealing is how Mochizuki got the Kamiyama job in the first place. In his written responses to questions posed by Senator Hatch, Mochizuki said that he was not certified under the Court Interpreter's Act of 1978; that no one had ever asked if he were certified prior to his trial and grand jury work. When he asked the U.S. Attorney's office about how to become certified, no one had an answer.

Did the prosecutor, before any of Mochizuki's trial and grand jury experiences, bother to spend some time familiarizing the interpreter with even basic criminal law concepts and terminology?

Answer: No.

How did he get the job for the Kamiyama grand jury in the first place?

Simple:

[S]omeone at the U.S. Attorney's office once asked whether I had ever previously interpreted at a trial. I answered affirmatively. That is how I was placed on the U.S. Attorney's office list.[14]

If the interpreter was not up to par, how did the witness feel about the language barrier during the proceedings? Kamiyama stated, in an affidavit made in August 1985 from his Danbury prison cell that the whole grand jury process had left him:

emotionally unable to deal with the pressure of continuous questioning particularly when I experienced difficulty in understanding the ambiguous, confusing and sometimes incoherent and inaccurate interpretations of the prosecutor's questions. As a result, I was, at times, confused and my responses were not entirely clear.[15]

Of course, a man who has already been convicted for perjury and who has served four months in jail might well say something like that. But the circumstances described and Kamiyama's feelings are not the only evidence that something went haywire in that grand jury room in 1981.

Numerous students of Japanese and English have said that something was wrong. Among them seventy-nine members of the

Japanese parliament and nearly two hundred academics, lawyers, and other professionals. Even journalists.

In their view, expressed in a letter to Senator Hatch, "the law thus requires exacting proof of falsity and guilty knowledge, among other elements, as a prerequisite to a perjury conviction."[16]

The Japanese pointed out that because two languages had been in use during the legal proceedings and many errors had been made in translation, these errors "were viewed as intentional falsehoods."[17]

They added:

[This] represents the first such conviction based upon foreign language testimony in the recorded annals of American criminal law.[18]

It would haunt lawmakers from both American political parties for years to come. We had, to use an Asian expression, lost face.

The Japanese parliamentarians and professors were hardly alone in their view that a fundamental and literally unprecedented miscarriage of justice had taken place in an American grand jury room.

Several highly qualified translators, Japanese and American, have reviewed the tapes (not just the official transcript) of Kamiyama's grand jury testimony and found them wanting. Very wanting.

John Hinds, an associate professor at Pennsylvania State University, is fairly typical. Hinds speaks fluent Japanese and is a specialist in Japanese linguistics.

After comparing the tapes with the written English translations prepared for the indictment, Hinds rendered the following verdict:

I have determined that the translations contained in the indictment are highly inaccurate and do not approach the standard of care that should be expected even of a reasonably competent interpreter, much less that which would be expected of a competent translator.[19]

A bit pompous to be sure, but as damaging as that first cannonade was, Professor Hinds was only warming up with a little target practice. The linguist from Penn State also found:

Of a total of 39 question and answer pairs that I have examined, it is clear to me that in 16 instances the answer Mr. Kamiyama gives is simply not a response to the question posed by Mr. Flumenbaum. In 16 additional instances, there is considerable doubt about whether the answer Mr. Kamiyama gives, when correctly translated, is responsive or ambiguous. Thus, in no fewer that 32 of 39 question and answer pairs, the version of the conversation contained in the indictment deviates substantially from what a correct translation would have shown.[20]

In short, when Martin Flumenbaum was talking chalk, Takeru Kamiyama thought the prosecutor was talking cheese.

But does it make any difference? Did the egregious errors of translation lead directly to the perjury counts?

The experts think so.

The formula isn't simple, but any good lawyer can whip up a phony perjury charge. Watch carefully.

First, add one ruthless, ambitious, or desperate prosecutor. Next, mix in a grand jury proceedings in which two languages are involved and the intended target speaks only one. Next, stir in an interpreter who is qualified to translate little more than a luncheon menu. Then add one unprepared witness and pepper him with lots of questions. The questions should be about arcane subjects like tax law—American tax law, of course—and include complicated accounting procedures as well—again American. These topics, of course, should be totally unfamiliar to the witness and his interpreter. Finally, add a *soupçon* of legalistic procedure. In this case, keep the witness away from his lawyer.

Translation foul ups, in fact, were featured in all six of the perjury counts lodged against Kamiyama. These gross errors, however, did not deter Flumenbaum. The problem in the grand jury room was that the prosecutor asked one question, but the witness heard another and responded (accurately) to what he thought he had been asked.

That applied to questions that went beyond taking the oath and reading the witness's rights. It went to the core of the later indictments: lying to a grand jury.

Some examples:

First, Flumenbaum asked Kamiyama whether the Reverend Sun Myung Moon knew that Moon was a stockholder in Tong-Il—a

Korean industrial firm that made, for the most part, machine tools. The interpreter, however, changed the meaning and asked Kamiyama in Japanese if he knew whether Moon knew that stocks in his name were at Tong-Il? No mention was made of ownership in the Japanese translation.

The question of course is different, and the interpreter's version is an innocuous one. Based on the Japanese translation, Kamiyama replied: "I don't think he knows. Because I decided things and I did [them]."[21]

The prosecutor apparently came to believe that Kamiyama was lying to protect his boss on a question of stock ownership.

On a related question about Tong-Il, the prosecutor asked if Kamiyama had told Moon about his issuance of $50,000 worth of stock in the reverend's name. But the interpreter instead (again in garbled fashion) asked if Kamiyama had ever talked to anyone about stocks worth $50,000 in Moon's name.[22]

Again, Kamiyama's answer was no. But the question he answered was fundamentally different from the one actually asked.

Sometimes in the *Kamiyama* case the translation errors that led to perjury charges revolved around something incredibly basic, like the interpreter's inability to conjugate a verb properly.

For example, the prosecution asked if Moon carried a checkbook with him. The interpreter put the verb in the present tense ("is he carrying") and Kamiyama, answering the Japanese version, said "no."[23]

One final example of bad translation that led to the charges of perjury is an exchange on the so-called "family fund." The prosecutor was looking for evidence of misuse of church funds for personal use. The issue was a major item in the government's tax case against Moon, and it was crucial that the theme be introduced during the Kamiyama grand jury. Otherwise Kamiyama would not be a useful bridge for the prosecution of Moon.

Flumenbaum thus asked whether any money from the fund was ever used for the expenses of Japanese church members who had come to the United States.

It is a fairly simple question, but the interpreter got it fundamentally wrong, and then compounded his mistake. He asked:

> From the family fund did [someone] ever use the money to pay for
> the expenses incurred by the Japanese brethren coming . . . for the
> purpose of coming to the U.S.?[24]

First, the interpreter missed the pertinent point: Were the funds
used to support the Japanese church members while they were in
America? That was only the beginning. Kamiyama, confused at
this point, asked for a clarification; that is, did the prosecutor want
to know if the money was used to bring the church members from
Japan to the United States?

The interpreter, without asking for clarification from the prosecutor, answered Kamiyama's question as to what he thought
Flumenbaum meant. Result? Another comedy of errors and completely unprofessional conduct on the part of the interpreter:

> Yes, for the coming to this side, expenses like airplane fare, lay over
> expenses, for these purposes have the money from this family fund
> ever been expended.[25]

Trained interpreters don't do that, of course. But Mochizuki
was not trained for the job. In a sense, it is as useless to blame him
as to blame a child of four for not being able to drive a truck. The
problem is that he should never have been put behind the wheel in
the first place.

And that raises another even more fundamental question. Did
Flumenbaum know any better? And if he did, what did he know
and when did he know it? As an officer of the court he must have
known those interchanges between Kamiyama and the interpreter
were wholly against the rules. He should have stopped the proceedings right there. But he did not.

As a consequence, Kamiyama was left replying truthfully to this
totally erroneous extrapolation of the interpreter. Kamiyama said,
"There weren't such cases."[26]

Neither the grand jury nor the prosecutor could know, at least at
first, that Kamiyama had answered the wrong question. In so
doing Kamiyama once more would apparently commit perjury.

Was the prosecutor, Martin Flumenbaum, blissfully ignorant of
what was going on? There is evidence that he was not.

Here is what happened.

It did not take an especially astute observer to figure out that something had gone wrong during these grand jury proceedings. Very soon after the initial indictment against Kamiyama was returned, Flumenbaum sought out a small translation service, the Nihon Services Corporation located in Manhattan. He hired Eisuke Sasagawa to review the grand jury tapes and transcript for errors and omissions in the translation. At first, Sasagawa limited his work to those portions of the transcript that were immediately relevant to the perjury charges.

And now for another strange twist. Two weeks later, Kamiyama's counsel, Andrew Lawler, knowing nothing of Flumenbaum's arrangement with Sasagawa, also went to Nihon and hired another translator, Yuko Kashiwagi, who prepared a quick-and-dirty summary of Mochizuki's mistakes. On the basis of this rather thin presentation, defense counsel filed a motion to dismiss the indictment, unaware that a much more complete review was available, paid for by the U.S., and literally in the same building.[27]

Needless to say, Nihon's taking on two clients on opposite sides in the same case involved an ethical conflict of interest of which the firm quite naturally never bothered to inform anyone. But its commercial venality and legal neutrality had a decidedly one-sided edge. Flumenbaum received a detailed report. Lawler got a single page.

But let us return to the saga of Eisuke Sasagawa. In an interview three years after doing business with Flumenbaum, Sasagawa recalled in public for the first time his work for that U.S. attorney. In oral briefings, a written report, and then later a written analysis that ran for more than 400 pages, the translator said he had detailed for Flumenbaum the mistakes made in the grand jury room.

Sasagawa, among other things, informed Flumenbaum that the oath had not been properly translated and that the warnings on perjury and obstruction of justice had been hopelessly garbled. Furthermore, he advised Flumenbaum that the constitutionally critical Fifth Amendment rights had never been explained to the witness.

Sasagawa also pointed out that the grand jury interpreter had left out questions and added mistaken material, as in the case of the family fund question. Sasagawa also told him that the line of questioning regarding the checkbook had been botched.

In short, Sasagawa informed Flumenbaum that his entire case against Kamiyama, and by extension, Moon, had been built on an egregiously faulty translation and wholly false, oftentimes fabricated interpretations of testimony. What's more, the failure of the court to provide a competent translator also cost Kamiyama the most basic rights guaranteed under the U.S. Constitution.

So how did Flumenbaum react to all of this news? Sasagawa wasn't sure. When asked in an interview about Flumenbaum's reaction to the oral report on the failings of the grand jury, he said:

> He didn't say anything. He probably studied them carefully later, but he wore a "poker face" and showed no reaction. But when I gave comments on the translation he would often say, "That's good, that's good."[28]

Did Flumenbaum actually read and understand the import of Sasagawa's oral and written reports? Common sense indicates that he must have had grave doubts about the adequacy of the translation given in the grand jury room even while he pressed the Justice Department for indictments based on the same suspect grand jury testimony. After all, Flumenbaum asked for Sasagawa's independent review of the tapes on his own, and for a more detailed analysis of the grand jury translator's errors.

That review contained many of the same criticisms that other professional students of Japanese were to make.

But there was more, much more. In fact, Sasagawa's second lengthier report, delivered months before the trial actually began, was absolutely devastating. The whole flimsy facade that Flumenbaum had been carefully erecting for the perjury charges against Kamiyama—which you recall were the basis of the Justice Department's reluctant agreement to prosecute Kamiyama and Moon—had been dynamited by the Nihon translator.

Sasagawa found over 600 translation errors, more than 75 of which materially affected the perjury charges brought by Martin Flumenbaum. Put bluntly, Flumenbaum had no case according to Sasagawa. And his choice of Mochizuki as interpreter was ludicrous.

The Sasagawa report was radioactive. For Flumenbaum it couldn't have come at a worse time. The Justice Department had spent more than two years, three grand juries, and millions in taxpayers' dollars to get Moon and Kamiyama, and now, on the eve of what was to be *the* trial, a trial which would launch his legal career, up pops material evidence, solicited and paid for by Flumenbaum himself, which strongly indicates his case is nothing but smoke, and thin smoke at that.

So what's a young prosecutor to do? Well, the right thing to do is to turn over the material to the court and the defense and let justice take its course.

And what did Martin Flumenbaum do? He kept it to himself. Everyone remained in the dark: the grand jury, the defense counsel, the trial judge.

And later, years after the trial, appeals, and imprisonment of Moon and Kamiyama, when word of the Sasagawa report leaked out, the Justice Department too went into a stonewall mode. In August 1984, it refused to release the report under the Freedom of Information Act, a request made by the defense. The refusal, in itself, is an incredible development. Ordinarily, FOIA's are denied only if the national security is compromised or someone's life is at stake. Information manifestly cannot be denied because it could prove embarrassing to a government official. That's the law. The rules on this are very strict as any FOIA officer can tell you. Moreover, a refusal to release a relevant trial document is almost unheard of in my experience.

In any case, the District of Columbia's Federal District Court thought so too, and more than two years after Justice first refused to release the Sasagawa review, December 1986, to be exact, the court ordered it open and Justice reluctantly complied.

By the time Sasagawa's report became public, of course, both Kamiyama and Moon had already served their time in Danbury prison. When justice moves at all, it moves slowly. But there is no reason that it can't grind exceedingly fine.

And that is what I propose to do right now. By taking a closer look at the Sasagawa report. Because I have a copy. Looking it over, it is no wonder our Department of Justice did not want it made public.

It makes for unsettling reading. In fact, it is almost unbelievable. For more than 450 pages it rolls on, page after page of mind-numbing, eye-glazing detail. Mistakes, foul ups, and absurdities splatter nearly every page. Even a quick glance would convince anyone that the whole grand jury process was a travesty of justice.

It was Franz Kafka married to Lewis Carroll with Groucho Marx officiating and Chico and Harpo providing the music. But surreal as it was, it was no joke to Takeru Kamiyama and Sun Myung Moon, the only men to pay the consequences for this legal disaster.

Sasagawa, of course, was only doing his job. And he did it well. As a meticulous craftsman, the Japanese translator went over every bit of testimony, comparing what he heard in the taped testimony with what he read in the official transcript. He was appalled. And sometime in the spring of 1982, before the Moon-Kamiyama trial had begun, Sasagawa submitted the final version of his analysis, a three-inch-thick document, almost double the size of the District of Columbia telephone book.

Sasagawa, in fact, confirmed all the earlier mistakes made by Mochizuki that we have discussed: the horrible mangling of Kamiyama's Fifth Amendment rights, for example. He also devastated the government's case for perjury. But there was more, much more than that.

But before addressing the monster mistakes, let's take a look at some other problems that the reviewers missed.

Once again, Mochizuki was not a tested trial interpreter. And that meant more than being technically incompetent. He would interject his own opinions on matters that had nothing to do with what was said by either Flumenbaum or Kamiyama. And sometimes, his attention wandered. Towards the close of the third day, Kamiyama's answer to a question was omitted because Mochizuki was talking to the stenotypist.[29]

Mochizuki also had a habit of turning clear answers into vague, almost unintelligible responses. On a question about why Moon was asked to buy stock in the Tong-Il company, what Kamiyama actually said, according to Sasagawa, was clear enough:

> I said, "Reverend, I want you to give some money." Because it would be better for the company to have some of the luck the Reverend had. I remember having said, "Why don't you give about $1,000?"

But Kamiyama's interpreter rendered it:

> I recall I asked the Reverend to give us the money in order that the newly born company take a good faith and good omen from thereon.[30]

No mention at all of the $1,000. And while Mochizuki's version of the answer sounds goofy Oriental, it isn't what Kamiyama said at all.

Sometimes the interpreter's vagueness gave the impression that Kamiyama was deliberately evading questions when, in fact, he did answer. One question dealt with Kamiyama's asking the Reverend Sun Myung Moon to be chairman of the board of Tong-Il.

Here's Mochizuki's version:

I am not sure whether Reverend Moon gave it a very serious thought, but *I gather the impression* that his reaction was why not.

Kamiyama's answer was far more precise:

I'm not sure whether he gave a serious thought to that *but I remember now that I received his nonchalant reply, "That's OK."*[31]

Sometimes it was Mochizuki's poor English that got in the way. Kamiyama's interpreter not only had a weak grasp of Japanese, his English was also woefully bad, especially in the stress of the grand jury proceeding.

Here are two examples:

Well, in answer to your why question, I am facing my recollection back to '73. My work, day-to-day basis, was full of a variety and involved for me to try to recollect something from '73 is beyond.

And this:

As my movements and running around here and there, they got lost.[32]

Kamiyama of course said nothing as fractured as that, but how would the grand jurors know?

Although this was not an exam in English, the interpreter's tortured prose often did roll up black marks for Kamiyama. For example, when Kamiyama was clear, Mochizuki made him sound purposely evasive, a devastating impression to make, because grand jurors rule from impressions as much as hard evidence in deciding whether or not to indict.

When Flumenbaum asked Kamiyama if he made a loan agreement with Moon every time money was deposited into his account, the interpreter dutifully translated the parts about Kamiyama's agreements with the European and Japanese branches of the Unification Church, but left out Kamiyama's explanation of the loan arrangements with Moon.

That made Kamiyama look evasive (when he wasn't) and prompted Flumenbaum to repeat the question impatiently. That sort of thing happened all the time, which only served further to confuse and exasperate Kamiyama.[33]

Then there were times when all of the interpreter's flaws would get rolled into one huge and ever deepening morass of confusion, none of which added to Kamiyama's credibility. The following is as good a sample of verbal quicksand as can be found in this whole sorry and slightly dizzy affair.

It occurred near the end of the final afternoon session. Perhaps Mochizuki was punch-drunk by then, but in any case, the avalanche of errors went on for pages, burying any possible coherence.

It concerned stock in Tong-Il owned by Mrs. Moon. What Flumenbaum wanted to know was, Did she still have any shares in the company?

Mochizuki said that without her knowledge, Kamiyama put $14,500 worth of stock in her name, but did not tell her about it. That was accurate enough, but the interpreter omitted Kamiyama's additional statement that "I [still] keep the stock [ownership] for her."[34]

That little mistake soon got parlayed into another. Flumenbaum then asked why didn't Kamiyama transfer Mrs. Moon's stock from one holding company to another. The interpreter, however, asked the opposite: Why did you transfer? . . .

That, of course, completely confused Kamiyama who had done no such thing. So instead he attempted to explain there had been no transfer (which Flumenbaum already knew) and that the breakdown of the numbers came to $13,500 from the family fund and $1,000 from Sun Myung Moon.

Although Flumenbaum had not asked for such a breakdown, Mochizuki got that answer all balled up as well by omitting the source of the funds, thus making Kamiyama's answer both irrelevant and vague.[35]

And it gets worse.

Flumenbaum, despite the non-answer to his first question, wanted to know more about the source of the money for the stock. Did Mrs. Moon get a gift from the family fund, meaning, was the money from the fund considered a gift or a loan or what? The interpreter, however, misunderstood the question and asked Kamiyama if she "ever receive a gift from the family fund," thus obscuring the point of the question.

Kamiyama, by this time unsure of what was going on, went back to his original answer: $13,500 came from the family fund; another $1,000 from Moon. The stock was in Mrs. Moon's name and Kamiyama still held it. The interpreter, however, made another mistake. Instead of simply translating Kamiyama's barebones recital of the stock transaction, he began the answer to Flumenbaum's previous question—did she get a gift, which he had mistranslated—with a gratuitous remark, "I didn't see it that way," which, of course, Kamiyama had never uttered.[36]

By now neither Flumenbaum nor Kamiyama was even close to being on the same wavelength. One could argue, they were even in separate dimensions, lost somewhere in time and space. As for the grand jurors, one can only imagine what planet they thought they were on.

This time Flumenbaum can't be blamed for getting a little impatient. What he wanted to know was, Who owned the stock now? But Mochizuki couldn't even get that right. Instead, he asked, "whose name is that stock now?" confusing the ownership issue even further.[37]

Kamiyama replied simply that it was Mrs. Moon's stock. But when asked by Flumenbaum if it was her personal stock, the interpreter again extrapolated Kamiyama's answer by adding "I made it available in her name."

That sounded, once again, evasive to Flumenbaum, and no doubt by this time to the grand jury as well, so once again he asked if the stock were owned by Mrs. Moon. Unfortunately, that direct question was obscured yet one more time by Mochizuki who asked Kamiyama, was the stock "in her name?"[38]

Kamiyama, more confused than ever, asked, "since she doesn't know, what would that mean?" But the interpreter turned the confused question into a declarative, namely, she doesn't know about the stock. As Mochizuki had now left out the query altogether, it appeared that Kamiyama was stonewalling. And that misimpression was compounded by the next exchange.

Here, Flumenbaum still wanted to know if the family fund money was a gift or not. Kamiyama replied that from the family fund point of view it could be seen that way, but he could not be certain since Mrs. Moon was unaware that she had received the stock. Unfortunately, that relatively simple answer got twisted around by Mochizuki when he rendered it, "she still doesn't recognize it." Not recognizing stock is very vague in English and could be interpreted in several ways. Kamiyama's real answer was crystal clear and a repeat of what he had said before which had never been properly translated.[39]

The layers and layers of confusion of course did serve a purpose. They turned an innocent transaction into something darkly suspicious simply because Flumenbaum could not get clear answers to his clear questions. But the obscure questions and answers were provided by the interpreter, not the witness.

But these are only preliminaries. Now let us look at more serious mistakes uncovered by Sasagawa.

Example one: Flumenbaum asked Kamiyama if he had prepared all the checks for Moon. The interpreter botched this seemingly simple question by asking: "You mean that all the rest of the check[s] was previously written up so all he had to do was to sign [so he could sign] when you asked him to sign?"

Kamiyama nodded yes to the interpreter's question, and the prosecution would later argue Kamiyama had lied because the Reverend Sun Myung Moon's financial advisor did not, in fact, prepare all the checks for his boss.

The thrust of Mochizuki's question was not, Did Kamiyama prepare all the checks?—a fairly simple question—but whether he filled out all parts of a check in preparation for Moon's signature.

It gets worse. Kamiyama's answer to the next question made clear that when he arrived in the United States he let others prepare the checks because of his poor command of English. That should have negated even the uncorrected version of the previous question and answer. But it did not.

Why? Because Flumenbaum had the second answer expurgated on the grounds of its being a poor translation, even though it was not.[40]

Example two: the prosecution asked Kamiyama why Moon's name was used for the family fund. This time the interpreter got the question right, but the answer all wrong. Mochizuki speaking for Kamiyama said:

> As the money comes from overseas, and part of that money may become necessary as expenses to take care of the brethren, we put it in Rev. Moon's name, who legitimately represents International Unification.

What Kamiyama actually said, according to Sasagawa, was this:

> Well, it is because it is the money that came from Jap—, Jap—, uh— overseas and, furthermore, Rev. Moon represents the IUC, he represents it and the reason we put the money into that account in his name was, first of all, it came from overseas and, when the brethren came from overseas, *part of it* was put there.

> Part of it [I thought] could be used as expenses should there be a necessary an emergent problem. It could be taken from there. With this idea, I made them [pay as contributions].[41]

What Kamiyama made clear was that only a portion of the family fund money went into Moon's account, not all of it as Flumenbaum's handpicked interpreter had said. That small error would lead to yet another count of perjury hung on Kamiyama.

Yet Sasagawa was only warming up. Here is example three. But first a little background. Flumenbaum is quizzing Kamiyama on his participation in a business deal involving the purchase of an iron ore mine. What comes next is classic interpreter confusion which never did get sorted out:

> Q: You also gave $200,000, didn't you?

> A: That's right.

> Q: And you were supposed to lend more money than $200,000, were you not?[42]

That's what Flumenbaum said, but that is not what Kamiyama heard through his interpreter, who asked instead, was Moon's financial advisor "not supposed to *receive* more than $200,000?" That, of course, was the complete opposite of what was really asked.

Needless to say, Kamiyama was confused by the mistranslated question, and asked for a repeat. Flumenbaum asked it again, and once more the interpreter blew it. This time, however, Mochizuki simply went vague, avoiding the verb "to lend" entirely. As a consequence, Mochizuki rendered it as: "Was the deal supposed to be more than $200,000?" Now, thoroughly lost, Kamiyama gave a vague "don't know" answer—the kind that makes grand juries suspect you are up to no good—when in fact the witness had become totally baffled by one version in English and two different translations in Japanese.

And one more thing: the second translation error left the first uncorrected.[43]

This particular exchange also demonstrates another burden Kamiyama labored under. And that is, while Kamiyama did not speak fluent English, Kamiyama was no fool. He did understand some. In his workaday world it would have been impossible not to pick up bits and pieces of spoken English. But that did not help Kamiyama in front of the grand jury at all. In fact, it had the opposite effect.

Here's what happened. Kamiyama heard both the English and Japanese. In the case of the English he at least got the drift of what was being said. For short and simple questions, Kamiyama probably understood most of it. But he could never be sure. The interpreter's Japanese, however, was often wrong or vague or just off target. Kamiyama became at times uncomfortably aware of that and was then faced with a dilemma. Which version of the question should he answer? The one he thought he heard in English, and was not entirely sure he understood, or the one posed by the interpreter? That is and was a heavy burden to place on a witness, one quite unique, as we shall see. But the main point remains in place: Kamiyama's partial knowledge of English only added to the confusion and uncertainty he felt; a condition that Martin Flumenbaum in no way relieved, but rather made worse.

So what did Flumenbaum do about it? Nothing. Or rather, worse than nothing.

You will recall that Flumenbaum (who apparently had his own doubts about the quality of the interpretation) hired the services of Eisuke Sasagawa, who prepared his first report. That first report covered the areas of supposed perjured testimony, and in so doing blew away much, if not all, of the government's case.

At the same time, Kamiyama's lawyer, Andrew Lawler, with a wholly inadequate review of the testimony, filed a motion to dismiss the indictment. The evidence Flumenbaum had in his hand was not only relevant, but vital to that motion. But Flumenbaum said nothing at all about Sasagawa.

But that was only step one in this miscarriage of justice spun out over the next four years.

Still, it was not all smooth sailing for Mr. Flumenbaum. Lawler's motion, even though it was based on a less than thorough review, posed an awkward problem for the prosecutor, at least at first. In response, and with breathtaking daring, the U.S. attorney deleted several indictment specifications in the perjury counts. But please note the subtlety of the maneuver. He did so where the translation errors were, in fact, relatively minor, and kept those which were horribly and highly prejudicial to Kamiyama.

It was a stroke of sheer genius. By so doing, Flumenbaum seemed to establish his fairmindedness and generosity—even a small error results in a dropped specification—while, in fact, conceding nothing. It was a prosecutorial version of the pea-under-the-shell game. And there was yet another trick up the prosecutor's sleeve that we will get to presently.

But the problem was not quite solved. Lawler's motion forced Flumenbaum to recall the grand jury to consider the problem of interpretation. The most relevant piece of evidence, of course, was the first Sasagawa report. But Flumenbaum said not word one to the grand jurors about that report.

Even more breathtaking was Flumenbaum's placing Sasagawa on the witness stand in front of the grand jury. But the translator was not allowed to say anything about the errors he had found. Nor was Sasagawa allowed to prepare for his testimony with the details of his translation.

Instead, Flumenbaum used him to go over selected and very safe portions of the testimony, all of which gave the impression to the grand jurors that what errors had been committed were of a trivial nature.

As Sasagawa would recall in testimony before a Senate subcommittee:

> I made no preparations for the testimony, and I just answered either, "Yes" or "No." If I did say more, it was just a word or two, or a sentence or two. I didn't say much.[44]

Flumenbaum was almost home free, but not quite. At least one grand juror, warier than the others, expressed his concern that Mochizuki did not appear up to the job.

"Can you prove this interpreter is more qualified or more knowledgeable than the other one?" asked the grand juror. That dangerous question set off the following:

> MR. FLUMENBAUM: I think there is going to be a problem on the interpretation, no matter what it is. What you have to find, there is probable cause that the perjury was committed. I think based on Mr. Sasagawa's testimony, that the interpreter that was before the Grand Jury, apparently did a very credible job in terms of simultaneous translation.
>
> A VOICE: To me he [Mr. Sasagawa] seems more credible than the other one.
>
> MR. FLUMENBAUM: You also have to realize the other interpreter was doing it simultaneously and didn't have the luxury of making a tape and backtracking—
>
> A VOICE: A woman usually was here to interpret but wasn't. We had another man here.
>
> MR. FLUMENBAUM: We had Mr. Mochizuki at that time who is qualified, you know, interpreter. He wouldn't be before you if he weren't. As I said, I think the changes that have been brought to you indicate that Mr. Mochizuki did a credible job in terms of interpreting the transcript.[45]

Earlier, of course, Flumenbaum had also reassured them of his qualifications: "the interpreter that was before the Grand Jury, apparently did a very credible job .... We had Mr. Mochizuki ...

who is [a] qualified . . . interpreter. He wouldn't be before you if he weren't."[46]

With that misleading reassurance and without any mention of the Sasagawa report, the grand jury simply did as the prosecutor wanted it to do, namely, leave the misinterpreted parts of the indictment intact.

And now for the master magician's greatest trick, the one up the sleeve mentioned earlier. While the prosecutor convinced the grand jurors to keep the bad stuff, he did have excised from the record material with minor mistakes. That, as already said, gave Flumenbaum a patina of fairness. But it did something else that was far more important. By cutting out this material it very conveniently eliminated the context surrounding the supposedly perjured responses. Without it, the transcript with the translation errors really made Kamiyama look bad. With it, the issue becomes doubtful even with the bad translation.[47]

Once safely past the grand jury, Flumenbaum ordered a complete review of the transcript by Sasagawa, something the industrious Japanese completed before the trial began. Flumenbaum told neither the court nor defense counsel of either report. And, to make matters worse, he continued to insist in court that the interpreter was qualified. This occurred repeatedly during pretrial motions when defense counsel Andrew Lawler reiterated his arguments that the interpreter was grossly incompetent. Although he, too, had to know by this time that Lawler was correct, Flumenbaum argued passionately that the mistakes were only minor in nature.

And now a small setback for the U.S. attorney. The court had become convinced that the defense might have a point and therefore appointed during the pretrial proceedings a university student, Michiko Kosaka, as another translator. Miss Kosaka was no trained linguist, and she did not have much time, but her quick-and-dirty analysis resulted in Judge Goettel's dismissing certain specifications under one of the perjury counts, count twelve.[48]

But Flumenbaum didn't stop there.

Throughout the entire trial, and throughout the appeal procedure that went to the Second Circuit Court of Appeals and finally the U.S. Supreme Court, neither the courts nor the lawyers were ever aware that the basis for the perjury counts and the prosecution itself according to the Department of Justice rested on a foundation of wet sand. In fact, both Moon and Kamiyama went to jail before anyone other than government prosecutors learned of the Sasagawa translation.

And then only by accident.

According to a memorandum prepared by the Japan-based Association for Advancement of Human Rights:

> In August 1984, after Mr. Sasagawa was located in Tokyo, Ms. Kinko Sato, Esq., at the request of the Association for Advancement of Human Rights, interviewed Mr. Sasagawa. For the first time, Mr. Sasagawa revealed the existence of the complete re-translation of Mr. Kamiyama's testimony. He stated that his report pointed out inaccuracies in Mr. Mochizuki's interpretation and that he had delivered his report to the prosecutor before and during the trial. He also stated that errors were called to the prosecutor's attention whenever possible while he was working with the taped record of the proceedings.[49]

Armed with this knowledge, the defense attorneys would put into motion requests for the report, a process which would take two more years because of Justice Department stonewalling. And Justice did so despite the fact that Senator Orrin Hatch, chairman of the Senate Judiciary Committee's Subcommittee on the Constitution, wrote no fewer than three letters to Justice (December 1984, March and August 1985) asking for his copy of the Sasagawa report. Stretching executive privilege to the breaking point, the government's lawyers said no.[50]

As we have said, the *Kamiyama* case is unique because it is the first example of a conviction on perjury based on faulty translations carried out in a grand jury proceeding. The *Kamiyama* case is also unique in that it spurred an amendment to the Court Interpreters Act of 1978.

The amendment was introduced in the U.S. Senate in November 1985, and boasted bipartisan sponsorship, ranging from Republican Orrin Hatch of Utah to Democrat John Kerry of Massachusetts. The legislation was drafted after extensive hearings conducted by Senator Hatch's subcommittee in which the *Kamiyama* case was exhaustively discussed.

The bill that resulted from the Senate inquiry, S.1853, sought to remedy the worst excesses of the *Kamiyama* grand jury proceedings.

Throughout fifteen pages of turgid legal prose, the fingerprints of the *United States v. Sun Myung Moon and Takeru Kamiyama* were evident. The amendment was formally titled: the "Court Interpreters Improvement Act of 1985."

The amendment extended the constitutional rights of non-English-speaking persons to have access to proper interpretation at federal trials, to include all "judicial proceedings instituted by the United States." That important provision was quite specially meant to include federal grand jury sessions.

To make that expressed wish a practical reality, the legislation ordered the Director of the Administrative Office of the U.S. Courts to establish "a program to facilitate the use of certified and otherwise qualified interpreters in judicial proceedings instituted by the United States."[51]

To do so standards had to be established to certify interpreters, and their work had to be monitored. Initially, nine languages had priority in the certification process: Spanish, Italian, Chinese, Japanese, French (including Haitian Creole), Korean, Portuguese, Arabic, and American Sign Language.[52]

Besides putting some rigor into the selection process of federal interpreters, the legislation also directed that this previously slave-wage profession be improved by raising fees to the level paid by the State Department for conference-level interpreters. In the past, as might be guessed, skilled interpreters had often scorned court work because of the low pay.[53]

Finally, a defendant or witness in any federal judicial proceeding retained the right to waive his right to a court-appointed interpreter for one of his own choosing as long as that interpreter met the criteria established by the Director of the Administrative Office.[54]

In fact, the first awareness of the problem came to a court's attention in 1925 in *Terry v. State*, in this case, Alabama. But the landmark case that eventually triggered the Court Interpreters Act was *United States ex rel Negron v. New York*. The year: 1970.

Negron had been convicted in a state court for second-degree murder. His sentence was twenty years to life. Negron appealed to the U.S. Court of Appeals on the ground that he spoke no English and his court-appointed attorney spoke no Spanish.

But that was just the beginning. Fourteen witnesses had appeared at Negron's trial. Two spoke Spanish. A court-appointed interpreter translated the testimony of the English-speaking witnesses and Negron's testimony to the court. That was it. Everything else was left for Negron to figure out for himself, except on two occasions when the interpreter, on her own, explained to the defendant what she had happened to hear.[55]

In the eyes of the Court of Appeals, the fact that Negron was left to struggle for himself on his own to understand his own trial violated the basic notion of due process. The court reasoned:

> As a matter of simple humaneness, Negron deserved more than to sit in total incomprehension as the trial proceeded. Particularly inappropriate in this nation where many languages are spoken is a callousness to the crippling language handicap of a newcomer to its shores, whose life and freedom, the state by its criminal processes chose to put in jeopardy.[56]

The *Negron* case set off a wave of concern that eventually resulted in the 1978 legislation. *Kamiyama,* in turn, sparked the crucial amendment which extended the Court Interpreters Act to all judicial proceedings, including the all-important grand jury.

Negron got redress through the Court of Appeals and became a free man. Kamiyama was sentenced and served his time in jail.

As for Martin Flumenbaum, common sense itself raises serious questions about his conduct.

To be sure, Flumenbaum was young, ambitious, hungry, and even desperate for a big score. He probably still is. That is not a crime. If it were, most of America would be behind bars. But what U.S. attorney Flumenbaum did in pursuit of justice raises a number of disturbing questions.

Look at the record.

The grand jury was misled concerning the competence of Kamiyama's translator.

The U.S. attorney's duty in this matter was clear and simple. As the only officer of the court directly involved in the grand jury proceedings, it was up to the prosecutor to secure a properly qualified translator for any witness whose command of English was poor or partial. By the government's own translator's admission that was not done.

Yet on December 15, 1981, Martin Flumenbaum repeatedly assured the grand jury, and in answer to specific questions reassured the twenty-four grand jurors, that Kamiyama's interpreter was indeed competent, and any errors made were of minor significance. The truth is, the translation of the prosecutor's questions into Japanese and translation of Kamiyama's answers into English were often seriously in error and formed the basis of the perjury counts against the defendant.

Flumenbaum's doubts about his personally selected grand jury interpreter were proven by his hiring of Eisuke Sasagawa to review the transcript and tapes of Kamiyama's testimony. Sasagawa orally warned Flumenbaum of numerous and material translation errors. In addition, Sasagawa made two reports, the first before the revised indictment was handed down, in which the supposedly perjured parts of the testimony were reviewed and found grossly defective. The second retranslation which covered all of the Kamiyama testimony was completed months before the Moon and Kamiyama trial began. The grand juries, the court, and the defendants were not informed of this critically important information.

Failing to do so in the case of the grand jury probably corrupted the indictment process itself. The Fifth Amendment, which provides that no person "shall be held to answer for a capital, or otherwise infamous crime, unless on a presentment or indictment of a Grand Jury," may thereby have been violated.

Again the U.S. courts are quite clear on this. The prosecution does not have to disclose all the evidence to the defense or the grand jury.

But the U.S. Supreme Court has also established that "... suppression by the prosecution of the evidence favorable to an accused ... violates due process where the evidence is material either to guilt or to punishment, irrespective of the good faith or bad faith of the prosecution."[57]

Furthermore, under the rules laid down by *United States v. Ciambrone*, a Second Circuit Court of Appeals decision rendered a decade ago, evidence which tends to clear the defendant must be disclosed to a grand jury under the following rules: when it is known to the prosecutor; when it is substantial in negating guilt; and when it is likely to result in the grand jury's refusing to indict. In more recent cases, that third criterion laid down by *Ciambrone* has been virtually tossed out as speculative. But the first two remain in place.

There is no question that exculpatory evidence existed. There is no question that the evidence was substantial. Sasagawa had found some 600 errors committed by the interpreter, and many, if not most, were neither minor nor immaterial. What the translator gave the U.S. attorney was no obscure bit of evidence, but a body of facts that severely damaged, if not destroyed, the government's case for perjury and conspiracy.

The suppression of relevant evidence, in effect, corrupted the grand jury, particularly in its role as an investigative body which was supposed to act independently of either prosecuting attorney or judge. Remember, the grand jury's independence from the government was well established in American jurisprudence in such cases as *United States v. Phillips Petroleum Co.*, where the court held that the grand jury must be "apprised of the essential information which will allow it to make an informed . . . judgment as to whether it is appropriate to return an indictment in a given case."[58]

And the courts have held that when the grand jury's investigative function is compromised by the prosecution, the courts are directed in their overall supervisory role to dismiss any resulting indictment.[59]

But the role of the courts aside, the first duty of any prosecutor is not seeking criminal indictments or convictions, but to see that "justice be done."[60]

Flumenbaum, after learning of the serious and multiple errors contained in the translation, apparently did nothing to remove them from the transcript. Rather he kept them in while cutting other portions of the transcript which contained minor errors or no errors at all. That eliminated the explanatory context which would have called into question the only apparently perjurious Kamiyama testimony. Having trimmed the transcript, Flumenbaum then presented it to yet another grand jury which had no other evidence or testimony presented to it. That maneuver succeeded in obtaining a fresh indictment against Kamiyama. Thus, the U.S. attorney sought perjury counts on faulty evidence laundered through another grand jury.

The U.S. Federal Code's definition of perjury contained in Section 1623 is quite specific. Four elements must be present to establish the crime. First, a valid oath must be administered. Second, a false declaration must be made by one under oath. Third, the declarant must believe the statement is untrue. Fourth, there must be a relationship between the false statement and fact material to the court proceedings. A grand jury must find probable cause for each element, not just one or two, for a true indictment of perjury to be made.

These are stringent tests and not to be lightly considered. But in the case of Kamiyama, almost the reverse occurred.

Kamiyama was not properly sworn in, thanks to the evidence that Sasagawa and other experts presented. In fact, Kamiyama's prosecutor-appointed interpreter made a complete hash of the oath. He was entirely ignorant of the basic word *perjury*, and never properly warned the witness about the sanctions against lying under oath through six separate sessions. Mochizuki, for example, told Kamiyama he would be "criticized" rather than prosecuted for not telling the truth.[61]

Moreover, the perjured parts of Kamiyama's testimony have been shown to be the work of an unqualified interpreter's errors rather than any knowingly false declarations made by the witness as required in Section 1623. Thus, elements two and three were also missing for a true count of perjury to have been established.

Lacking these basic elements for perjury did not deter the prosecutor. Flumenbaum pruned and shaped the error-ridden transcript and presented it to a third grand jury in an effort to obtain the indictment.

In *United States v. Tonelli*, the court held that a count of perjury "may not be sustained by the device of lifting a statement of the accused out of its immediate context and thus giving it a meaning wholly different from that context."

The rationale for that ruling was supplied by a later case, *Van Liew v. United States*. In *Van Liew*, the court argued:

It is vital, of course, that the stream of justice not be contaminated by untruth . . . but the seriousness of the crime of perjury and the fact that it turns finally on the subjective knowledge and purpose of the swearer require that the government not be allowed to predicate its case upon the answer to a single question which in and of itself may be false, but which is not shown to be false when read in conjunction with testimony immediately preceding and following the alleged perjured statement.[62]

And there is something else. The government's casual use of multiple grand juries is—on its face—way out of line. Calling a second grand jury in a case is rare and done only in limited circumstances, none of which applies here. Assembling a third is, in my experience, unheard of.[63]

U.S. prosecutors also withheld exculpatory evidence from the defense, leaving them in the dark about material evidence that could have formed the basis of Kamiyama's defense for pretrial, trial, and post-trial motions and appeals.

The defendants were vaguely aware that another translator had reviewed the tapes as early as December 17, 1981, but they did not know the identity of Sasagawa until a year later. And it was another two years before they learned of the extent and nature of the translation. None of these discoveries was instigated by anything done by the U.S. attorneys.

Federal prosecutors are obligated to reveal exculpatory evidence to all criminal defendants as well as to the grand jury. Doing so falls within the rubric of the due process clause of the Fifth Amendment which guarantees a fair trial. Various court cases—most prominently the already cited *Brady v. Maryland* and *United States v. Agura*—also make clear the duty of a prosecutor in disclosing that evidence, even in cases where it is not requested by the lawyers for the defense.

The courts' teaching is very clear about when suppression is not permitted. The rules on suppression are again threefold. First, the evidence hidden by the prosecutor must be favorable to the accused. Second, that evidence must be material to the charges. Third, there must be proof that the government has suppressed the exculpatory evidence.

Again it seems evident that these criteria are clearly met in the *Kamiyama* case. But a word of explanation on materiality. Under one federal court ruling it was established "only if there is a reasonable probability that, had the evidence been disclosed to the defense, the result of the proceedings would have been different."[64]

Since Kamiyama's attorney managed to scrub one count of perjury from the indictment based on a wholly inadequate one-page review of the translation, the materiality of the Sasagawa complete review seems obvious.

It should also be noted that when Kamiyama's attorney requested "copies of any analyses or reports made by Mr. Sasagawa" on January 10, 1982, the prosecution denied that request more than a year later (March 2, 1983) without disclosing or denying such evidence existed.[65]

All in all, it was quite a performance.

I, for one, have never seen anything quite like it, and I have seen prosecutors work at all levels of government.

From the evidence, including evidence once hidden from the court and public, there's little doubt that some questionably legal acts took place in connection with the trial of Sun Myung Moon and Takeru Kamiyama. But that same evidence raises serious doubts as to whether the right men were accused of conspiring to lie, cheat, and defraud.

As for myself, I believe Emile Zola was right. The wrong man went to jail.

CHAPTER VI

THE TRIAL BEGINS

In times when the government imprisons any unjustly, the true place
for a just man is also in prison.

HENRY DAVID THOREAU

THE trial of Sun Myung Moon and his financial advisor Takeru
Kamiyama began with a bang and ended in a whisper.

The two were found guilty of all counts lodged against them by
the U.S. Attorney's office for the Southern District of New York.
The pair had faced thirteen charges, including conspiracy, perjury, tax evasion, and obstruction of justice.

The business took six weeks and nearly 7,000 pages of trial
transcript to get the job done, and when it was over much of the
media had long since moved on to other things. In fact, the media
had cleared out of the fifth-floor courtroom at Foley Square after
the first few days of the proceedings.

United States v. Sun Myung Moon and Takeru Kamiyama was—in
the words of one of the few veteran trial reporters who bothered to
cover the whole trial—"just another dull tax trial based to a great
extent on the submission of dull, dull documents and charts."[1]

Thousands of them. The government, in fact, submitted so
many pieces of paper that all parties to the trial—the defendants'

169

counsel, the judge, even the prosecutors themselves—were left confused by the paper blizzard. And what about the jury?

Before we turn to the evidence, however, we must meet the players.

THE PLAYERS

The man who stage-directed the whole effort—the man who, like the defendants, was also on the spot—was Judge Gerard L. Goettel. He was a slight man, fifty-four years old, both gray and balding. His features were no more impressive than his stature.

Judge Goettel was known as a decent, gentle man, but was not widely regarded as a legal scholar or as a particularly courageous member of the judiciary. He did not bang the gavel or exert the kind of tyrannical authority that only federal judges in a lifetime appointment can and do frequently display.

Goettel, something of a plodder, had labored for years in the federal system, fashioning for himself an uncontroversial career. He had begun as an assistant U.S. attorney, later becoming a magistrate. As a graduate of Fordham University Law School, Goettel had found no fast track to the top, or even the middle of the ladder.

As a magistrate, he handled the dullest of legal chores. Magistrates, in fact, act as little more than part-time law clerks for the federal judges in a serf-to-lord-of-the-manor relationship. But unlike the young clerks, the magistrates seldom rise or have hopes of rising to better things. Thus for years Judge Goettel had labored in obscurity, handling technical and civil disputes through consultation and mounds of paperwork. As a magistrate, he also advised his federal superiors on injunctions and other nontrial issues.

What magistrates don't handle are trials, with all their attendant pressures and difficulties. No wonder then that two years after the trial of the Reverend Sun Myung Moon, the *American Lawyer 1984 Guide* to federal judges criticized Judge Goettel for having trouble controlling his courtroom.

The criticism is not surprising since the chief virtue of a magistrate is to get the details straight, not to handle troublesome human beings. It's no job either for a jurist of large thoughts on legal philosophy. It also makes a man cautious.

At age fifty-four, with six years on the bench, Goettel was at the height of his career. He had sat through a score of tax trials over the years and was thus familiar with the intricacies of business law—a great help in the *Moon* trial. But his earlier cases had never been surrounded by such media attention, and Judge Goettel's inexperience with the press brought with it serious consequences.

He had not volunteered for the *Moon* assignment, but once picked by lot to preside he had not shirked it either. Still, as the trial proceeded, Judge Goettel showed his own uncertainty over where it was going. In this case, gentleness did not mask strength, but only weakness. At every point he resisted making hard decisions, even when he seemed convinced of the need to make them according to the law and fair trial procedure. For example, his early decision to deny a defense request for a bench trial (which would have rested the full weight of the case on his shoulders) and instead ordered a jury trial most clearly marked Goettel as a man not eager for responsibility.

Moreover, Judge Goettel's whole legal experience had been on the government's side of affairs. This judge had no difficulty understanding the prosecutor's position, even when he didn't agree with it. But the defendants' stand often baffled him. In virtually every case, his instincts lay with the government and, when in doubt—which this man often was—he followed his own prejudices. That came as no comfort to the defense.

Judge Goettel's lack of confidence in himself was in bold contrast to the prime defendant, the Reverend Sun Myung Moon. Moon played the part expected of a prophet and teacher. He was confident, stoic, good-humored. He spent a good deal of time comforting his entourage who, not surprisingly, looked on the trial as a humiliation and a disaster for the movement and its master.

Moon did not see it that way. Living in another world, with his own vision of human history, his attitude should hardly come as a surprise. But otherworldliness does not completely explain the Reverend Moon's good cheer, if not detachment. For one thing, Moon kept busy on all his religious and business projects throughout the trial. He got up early each morning and arrived at Foley Square hours before the trial began. He literally set up shop in a small room near the trial room. Koreans are an immensely practical people, making do with whatever is at hand, a common

circumstance in Korean culture. Sun Myung Moon was no different. But he had another advantage too: a psychological one. In
fact, the Korean cleric had been through all of this before and the
"before" had been worse.

Much worse.

As Moon pointed out to his younger followers, North Korean
trial procedures, not to mention their uninviting Communist slave
labor camps (all of which he had experienced thirty years before),
were infinitely worse. He had survived that. By vivid contrast, the
American experience was a piece of cake. The Reverend Moon let
it be known that conviction and prison would not faze him.

His close friend and advisor, the second defendant, Takeru
Kamiyama, was not so resigned and was much less cheerful. In
fact, he was morose, even depressed. He seemed to draw what
strength he had from Moon, who repeatedly encouraged his
friend to keep up a good front and reveal nothing to their prosecutors and persecutors.

Kamiyama showed every sign of battle fatigue. He nodded in
agreement when Moon spoke, but it was clear he was confused and
troubled. Kamiyama was Japanese and in his early forties, and as
such he kept to the old ways. Although he had been in the United
States for a decade, he had made little effort to adapt to the
strange American culture. His English was rudimentary; American folkways were utterly foreign to him.

The trial itself, as well as the grand jury proceedings before the
trial, were utter chaos to a man who knew little English and
nothing whatsoever of sophisticated legal procedures, much less
convoluted and highly technical U.S. tax codes. The result, as we
have seen, was that Kamiyama had several counts of perjury
slapped on him. The government accused him of lying to the
grand jury. In his own mind, Kamiyama had clearly lost face, and
in many ways he blamed himself, though wrongly, for the predica-
ment in which he and his spiritual father now found themselves. If
he had acted earlier to put church accounts into some kind of
order with professional guidance, would he and Moon now be
spending their days at Foley Square? The question haunted him
but, considering the government's determination to get Moon,
there was nothing Kamiyama could have done to have changed
things.

The government's aggressive attitude, however, gave little comfort to him. In the end, Takeru Kamiyama did not break, but the Japanese disciple was bent severely by the full weight of the federal government.

The strain that Kamiyama showed, and Moon did not, was not made any easier by the prosecution team. Three lawyers were assigned to the case by the federal attorney's office, but only two played major roles.

The first was Martin Flumenbaum, thirty-two, fairly fresh from law school, and new to the rough and tumble of criminal trial procedure. The Moon case was his: he had shepherded it from the beginning, constantly urging a reluctant Department of Justice to throw the book at Moon and his colleague. For Flumenbaum, it was a true case of good versus evil.

Still, Flumenbaum had nearly botched it. The grand jury proceedings themselves had been something of a shambles and the young attorney's ongoing argument with the Justice Department's tax division had become a legend in Washington, D.C., and New York City legal circles. So intent on nailing Moon was he that Flumenbaum had not mastered the intricacies of trial argument and evidence. And his inexperience showed.

It showed so badly, in fact, that the U.S. Attorney's office was not about to leave the case for the trial in the shaky hands of Martin Flumenbaum alone. He could still bungle it and thereby smash two years' delicate legal work into a thousand pieces. Not surprisingly, his superiors looked for help.

Enter Jo Ann Harris. Tall, thin, intense, middle-aged, and thoroughly professional. Although she had been called in to the trial at the last moment, at times she clearly displayed knowledge of the case superior to that of Flumenbaum, who had immersed himself in Unification Church minutia for years. Harris could sleepwalk through a trial and never miss a legal trick.

While her peers had dabbled a few years in prosecution and then moved on to lucrative law practices and partnerships, Harris had remained in government service. As a result, she was a finely tuned legal machine. She did not make mistakes; defense lawyers feared her.

Moon and Kamiyama's lawyers were not an odd couple at all. Both Charles Stillman and Andrew Lawler were pros, and they

wisely agreed to work together to present a joint defense of the two
men. Stillman was a New York lawyer; tall, thin, and graying.
Middle age had not wilted his humor or his courtliness—a trait not
that often found in hotshot criminal trial lawyers. He was also an
old friend and former colleague of Judge Goettel. Their relationship was clearly comfortable and relaxed. Perhaps too much of
both. In conducting the defense, Stillman counted on his relationship with Goettel and generally refrained from taking off the
gloves.

Younger than Stillman and even taller, Kamiyama's lawyer, Lawler, was built like a basketball player. Although Lawler was well
behaved like his counterpart Stillman, he was the more aggressive
and outspoken of the defense attorneys. At times, he would go
punch-for-punch with Flumenbaum and Harris, apparently not
giving much of a damn about his relationship with Judge Goettel.

Moon remained largely aloof to the planning of defense strategy. Often neither Stillman nor Lawler knew what their clients
expected. The diffident Kamiyama was no help at all, giving
Lawler special difficulties. Still, Lawler did his best.

These seven actors occupied center stage. The jurors and witnesses played their parts, of course, but the case against Moon and
Kamiyama prominently featured Goettel, Moon, Kamiyama, Flumenbaum, Harris, Stillman, and Lawler. These Magnificent Seven
were about to ride in one of the country's most complicated and
bizarre trials in this century. And the issue at hand was about more
than taxes. A lot more.

And then there was the jury. The Seven may have done nearly all
the talking, but in the end it was the silent twelve jurors in the box
(with their six alternates) who decided the fate of the defendants.
They were, thanks to the U.S. Constitution's Sixth Amendment,
meant to be the bulwark of a fair trial.

In English common law it is assumed that trial by one's peers is
inherently more just than trial by an appointee of the crown. But
like every good principle of government, the concept is one that
can be stretched beyond purpose and intent. Such was the case
with the Moon and Kamiyama jury.

To be sure, the jurymen were hardly less competent or more
prejudiced than many others in their situation. But in this case the
circumstances were far more complicated.

The defendants were not Americans, but orientals, poorly grounded in English, who ran one of the most publicized and least loved churches in the country. Not since Joseph Smith and later Brigham Young led their band of followers, the Mormons, into the vastness of the Great American Desert, had a religion been so roundly hated and suspected.

The jurors, who were finally selected from an extraordinarily large pool of candidates, denied having any real prejudice about the defendants—few confessed to such during the *voir dire* or jury selection process—but later evidence shows that many of the jurors did not like or trust either the "Moonies" or their leader, the Reverend Sun Myung Moon.

Which bring us to this point. The possibility of prejudiced jurors was only one part of the problem of selecting a dozen jurors to decide the fate of two individuals.

A second part of the problem was the question of the competence of the jurors to decide the facts of the case and render an unbiased and, even more difficult, an intelligent verdict. It was a sensitive issue, in part because it touched on class and ethnic considerations.

Selected for the jury were ten women and two men. Six were white, four were black, and two were Hispanics. Most were from the working class and lived in the city. Few were well educated and several had serious English language deficiencies. But as Judge Goettel advised the lawyers in the case, good Spanish and bad English could not disqualify a juror according to Southern District, New York, regulations.

In the Alice-in-Wonderland politics of New York City's ethnic politics, juror incompetence, in the language of the court, could not be held against anyone. That would constitute a form of discrimination.

Oddly, the lack of intelligence and sophistication on the part of the jurors did not especially alarm defense counsel. In fact, they reasoned—with considerable justification—that matters could have been worse. A more suburban, middle-class, college-educated crowd was likely to be more anti-church and considerably better able to obfuscate its biases—even to its own members.

After all, white, middle-class parents were the ones who feared Moon the most. It was Moon, they believed, who was snatching their kids and turning them into religious robots—slaves of a strange oriental sect.

With the simpler people sitting in the jury box—white, brown, and black—Stillman and Lawler hoped that they might have a chance at reducing the pool of prejudice to an acceptable level.

Still, they worried. The case was a complicated one that demanded not merely intelligence, but genuine analytical capabilities, to sift through the mountain of evidence offered up by both sides. Indeed, the issues involved had confused even the experts, who came up with differing versions of what had happened. Some of this was simply and, quite literally, due to the fact that the central facts of the case were unknowable, as we shall soon see.

In addition to the twin problems of jury bias and competence, the defense faced an equally difficult obstacle to obtaining a fair trial, one that they hadn't counted on and which proved far more unfortunate for their clients than either of the other two factors.

The problem was Judge Goettel himself, or, more specifically, the conscious or unconscious prejudice he displayed toward the Reverend Sun Myung Moon—his "state of mind," as the psychiatrists and legal scholars call it.

From the defense attorneys' standpoint, Judge Goettel's "state of mind" toward the case was anything but pure or impartial.

On the very first day of the trial Goettel sent shivers down Stillman's and Lawler's spines with an out-of-the-blue comparison of the Reverend Sun Myung Moon to Atlanta, Georgia, mass murderer Wayne Williams. Then, almost in the same breath, the good judge shifted into high gear comparing the Korean cleric with everyone's favorite villain, Adolph Hitler.

As bad as those remarks were, Goettel was only warming up. By trial's end, he had waxed analogous several more times, comparing Moon and his Unification Church operations to organized crime syndicates run by the likes of Al Capone, to the ultimate Dickensian crook, Fagin, who used little children to steal for him and, last, but hardly least, to Richard Milhous Nixon and his Watergate debacle.

Even from the very first moments of the trial, it was clear that the defense lawyers were fighting an uphill, losing battle with the court.

If the prosecuting team, on the other hand, had any worries, it certainly never betrayed any. Both Harris and Flumenbaum went out of their way to deny that the trial was particularly complicated—no more so than "dozens of white collar cases that juries in this courthouse hear year in and year out," as prosecutor Harris told Judge Goettel in the robing room halfway through the trial.[2]

It was a theme that the prosecutors had introduced early in the trial. In fact, Flumenbaum's opening statement to the jury established what the government expected of the jurors:

> This is not a complicated case. This is a simple case of tax fraud and obstruction of justice and perjury. Don't let your attention be diverted by nonissues and extraneous outside considerations.[3]

On the eve of the trial the defense lawyers were still not convinced that a jury trial was to be preferred to a bench trial by Judge Goettel. As a result, Stillman and Lawler once more moved for a bench trial. The judge denied the defense motion, but in so doing showed his inexperience with high profile trials and set off a media explosion.

In remarks that received wide publicity, Goettel mused upon the quality of the jury selected. "In attempting to get an unbiased jury," he said, "the leaning has been heavily towards people who don't read much, don't talk much, and don't know much because they are obviously the persons who start off with the least bias."[4]

That was, of course, clinically correct. But Judge Goettel was already in hot water and his inexperience led him to a worse conclusion. It became the newspaper lead across the country: "Conversely [the judge added] they might tend to be the less educated and less intelligent people."[5]

Goettel's remarks were featured on the *Today* show, and the *New York Daily News* ran the headline: "Moon Judge Hopes Jurors See the Light."

The jurors, who were enjoined repeatedly not to read or to listen to news about the trial, quickly got the court's word about them—and bitterly resented the judge's questioning of their intelligence. Mary Nimmo, the aggressive and talkative "forelady," was outraged.

She told her fellow jurors in the tiny, uncomfortable cubicle that served as their jury room at Foley Square that her daughter wanted to write Judge Goettel and tell him that momma was no "dummy."

All in all, it was an embarrassing beginning to the trial. It should also be noted that everyone in the case—judge, defense counsel, and the prosecution—promptly became exquisitely nice to twelve jurors and six alternates.

But the judge had done something else besides hurt the jury's feelings. He had—and by all indications unwittingly so—established a new standard the jury must meet. They must now prove their competence. And what better way to show they weren't "dummys" than to demonstrate they understood the prosecution's massively complicated case so well that they were willing to vote to convict?

Still, Judge Goettel had a problem on his hands. He knew that the defendants' lawyers had repeatedly requested a bench trial. Goettel himself had worried aloud that the appellate court might question his decision to impose a jury trial. But having denied the defendants' motion, he was stuck. Insulting a jury was only one more problem. Therefore a quick repair of damaged feelings had to be done to prevent the complete collapse of the trial edifice.

OPENING ARGUMENTS

Judge Goettel decided in his opening instructions to tell the jurors a little story. It was the oddest thing yet about this distinctly odd process.

In very, very simple words the court decided to talk about King Arthur and Camelot and bold knights and damsels in distress. And everyone was very happy except Arthur who couldn't find anyone who could locate the Holy Grail. So what's so special about a cup? The Grail, Goettel told the panel, if it could be found, would "cure the sick, feed the poor, it would do wonderful things for the realm."

The trouble was that no one around the Round Table could find it and they couldn't find it because none of the knights on search detail was sufficiently pure. That prompted a hard look for an innocent warrior who, in the end, turned out to be the son of

Lancelot, Sir Galahad. The young man had maintained his virtue despite dangers and temptations, and Arthur was certain he had found his knight.

Goettel then got to the point:

You are about to embark on a holy quest. You are searching for justice. During this quest you are going to be subject to temptation and dangers, just as Gallahad was. You were chosen for this mission not because you are the bravest and boldest, but because, in the opinion of the attorneys and myself, of the hundreds of people who are interviewed, you were the purest. You had the fewest preconceptions about the defendants, about the case, about the issues and we thought that you were the ones most capable of pursuin[g] this request.[6]

Whether Judge Goettel's well-intentioned story did any good is doubtful. But it was as close as His Honor could come to telling the jurors it didn't matter if they were dumb as long as they stayed away from people who sought to influence their judgment.

There of course could be no trial without the defendants' being accused of something. And that Martin Flumenbaum was eager to do.

The moment came on the morning of April 1. The trial was not held in Judge Goettel's usual venue; instead, it took place in the large ceremonial courtroom on the fifth floor. Full of brass and dark wood and Roman arches, the chamber breathed importance. There would also be plenty of room for the press and the curious. Two hundred people could be packed into the room, and the prosecutors promised to give everyone a good show.

After Judge Goettel finished, Flumenbaum got up from the leather-covered prosecutor's table and moved left a few paces to face the jury and offer the government's opening statement. An opening statement is an outline of the case the prosecution hopes to present to convince the jury that the defendants are guilty as charged by the grand jury. And in asserting Moon and Kamiyama's guilt, Flumenbaum wasted no time:

This case is about taxes and it is about fraud. It is about the obligation of every person who lives in this country to report all of his income to the government.[7]

An obligation which, Flumenbaum asserted, the Reverend Sun Myung Moon had over a period of three years repeatedly refused to meet. What the government proposed to do was prove that Moon had opened up three banking accounts in a midtown Manhattan bank, deposited an accumulation of $1.5 million in funds, and used them for whatever purpose he wanted.

The monies were not church funds at all, but Moon's personal property, Flumenbaum contended. In his words:

> [Moon] used them to pay personal expenses for his family, to make business investments in his name, to buy stock personally in his name, and even to personally guarantee loans to third parties, again in his name.[8]

Despite that and despite the fact that Moon had earned more than $100,000 in interest on the accounts, he had failed to pay the proper tax. Flumenbaum further contended that Moon, with the help of Takeru Kamiyama, had willfully filed false returns in a conspiracy to evade that tax.

Flumenbaum also charged that Sun Myung Moon had failed to report on his 1973 return that he earned $50,000 in income from stock which he had received from a Korean export-import firm of which he was the chairman of the board. The company? Tong-Il.

To cover their tracks further, Flumenbaum told the jury, the defendants had created other false documents to support their tax returns. They had lied to their accountants, they had lied to the Internal Revenue Service, the Department of Justice, and the grand jury investigating Moon's tax returns.

That, in very brief outline, is what Flumenbaum wanted to prove against Moon and Kamiyama beyond a reasonable doubt. But a simple and dry review of the charges was not entirely, as we shall see, what the young prosecutor had in mind. To nail Moon meant working on and, in fact, inflaming jury prejudice against him and his followers.

The *voir dire* had already shown that such bias existed, although Judge Goettel had already expressed the belief that such prejudice would fade in the bright sunlight of dull tax procedure. The Reverend Moon, very early in Flumenbaum's opening statement, was depicted as greedy and heartless, a businessman in clerical clothing.

> You will hear evidence about fund raising, and you will hear in early 1973 members of the church fund raised primarily by selling flowers. You will hear how Moon set quotas for the fund raisers, both American members of the church and members from Japan and Europe who were specifically brought over to help the fund raising effort.
>
> You will hear how in early '73 Moon set a quota of $80 per day, and how by the end of 1973 some of these fund raisers, these flower sellers, were netting $200 to $300 a day, all in cash.[9]

Cash. That four-letter word was used a lot in this trial. It was exploited to the hilt by the prosecution. Flumenbaum wanted to introduce the notion at the beginning of the trial. The fact that the Asian-dominated Unification Church usually did business in cash—with all of its illicit overtones in American society—would be introduced over and over again, albeit indirectly, by the prosecutors to the generally low-income jury.

Having jerked that chain, Flumenbaum went on to yank a few more—surefire efforts that were designed to elicit antipathy for the defendants above and quite beyond any crimes they were accused of committing.

One jibe was especially nasty. It involved Flumenbaum's accusing defendant Kamiyama of misrepresenting himself as majority stockholder of Tong-Il in order to extend his visa and his stay in the United States. The implication that an alien from the Orient was worming his way around the immigration law, the prosecutors obviously reckoned, would have a solid and negative impact on jurors who would have little love for "foreigners" cheating on their visas.[10]

Another chain-pull was equally nasty, but a bit more complex. It involved the alleged finagling in which Moon and his associates engaged in order to buy the Korean prophet a sumptuous home called East Garden: property to be held in his own name although church money had been used to purchase it. Even though $700,000 was involved in the buying of East Garden, Flumenbaum indicated all the fancy paperwork was designed for one purpose: to avoid any tax consequences for Moon.[11]

For jurors who themselves lived in modest bungalows and walk-ups, the thought of some foreigner living like a rajah at taxpayers' expense would prove, the government hoped, unbearable.

But the twelve-penny nail Flumenbaum saved to close Moon's coffin was the "charge" that Sun Myung Moon was nothing but a businessman using the church as a cover to avoid taxes so he could grow richer.

So, the young prosecutor told the jurors in his wind-up that Moon had been involved in numerous business deals. He had gone into mining and shipping of iron ore in Arizona. He had bought stock in a Washington, D.C., bank, hoping some day to take it over—a stock purchase he failed to tell his accountants about. He had tried to go into the paint business in England. And there were assorted publishing, seafood, and other real estate ventures.[12]

The oriental tycoon, the high-roller. Each thing Moon touched had a sinister, if not outright illegal, implication. Or so Flumenbaum told the green-as-grass jury.

All of this and more would be proved, Flumenbaum promised, with physical evidence—mountains of it—that eventually took the form of thousands of pages of documents; even the paper's water-marks would prove crucial to the case.

Martin Flumenbaum ended with a small flourish and a big bouquet to the jury. The case was not terribly complicated; the jurors could understand it after all. It was like a jigsaw puzzle. One piece may not make much sense, but all of them fitted together would give the jury the whole picture.

> [I]f you hold your judgment in suspension, if you review the documents with care and if, most importantly, you apply your common sense to evaluate the evidence, to judge the credibility of the witnesses, if you do all that, ladies and gentlemen, you will have no difficulty in finding both of these defendants guilty beyond a reasonable doubt of all the charges in the indictment.[13]

Charles Stillman and Andrew Lawler had a big problem and they knew it. Defending Sun Myung Moon wasn't going to be easy to begin with, but after Flumenbaum had finished an opening statement that made clear the government would not shy away from playing to jury prejudice, the two knew they were in deep trouble, before either had spoken a word.

Stillman went first.

Moon's lawyer was calm, careful, and courtly. He gave off no high-energy vibrations as Flumenbaum had.

Stillman began with an apology to the jurors. He knew that he needed to handle them with kid gloves. Their feelings had been hurt by Judge Goettel's early remarks; Goettel's children's bedtime story about King Arthur, he knew, had not helped much.

Stillman also knew that none of them was too happy about the grilling each had gotten during the *voir dire*. Much of the grilling had been done by Goettel, but Stillman and his partner had had a hand in it, too. The government's lawyers, Cheshire Cat-like, tended to disappear with only their grins remaining. They had fewer worries about facing a prejudiced jury. In fact, the more prejudiced the better.

And that bias was what Stillman had to remind the jury of—bruised feelings or no.

The *voir dire* had been conducted, he said:

... because you are being asked to judge another human being whose beliefs and religious practices are different from yours; another human being who has become a controversial figure in this country; who may not be liked by everyone but is a person just like you and me, who has an absolute and fundamental right to be judged fairly on the evidence in this case; who has the right to be judged without bias, the right to be judged without prejudice, who has the right to be judged on what he did or what he didn't do in this case and not for any other reason.[14]

And then the apology:

So we apologize for this intrusion into your privacy but I know you will understand why it was necessary. You have given us your word that you will be fair, that you will let nothing color your thinking except the evidence and the law as Judge Goettel will instruct you later in the case and we gratefully accept your word.[15]

But what was this business about? Why were Moon and Kamiyama in the docket? Stillman decided to approach the jury with homey analogies. The first one dealt with making pancakes.

The prosecution had presented its side, noted Stillman, but that wasn't the whole story. According to Stillman:

> You can take that pancake and you can pour the batter on the griddle and you can let that pancake sit on one side for as long as you want. But if you don't turn the pancake over and cook it on the other side, it is not a pancake.[16]

Stillman's side of the pancake was first to tell the jury that the Reverend Sun Myung Moon was above all a religious figure. His trips to America were part of his own vision about the future of the world, a vision which was primarily religious and political, not economic.

That vision, Stillman argued, attracted men and women, many, but not all, young—from Asia, Europe, and America—to spend full time supporting and evangelizing for their religion, "to help in accomplishing the goals that Reverend Moon viewed for his church."[17]

What about the money, the cash that figured so prominently in the prosecution's case? Stillman presented the defense's version of the matter:

> You will hear at that early meeting it was decided when a bank account would be opened for the receipt of some of their money coming to America, that the money should be deposited into an account in the name of the person who was the very personification, if you will, who was spiritual leader, who was in a very real sense the Unification Church International. Tha[t] is to say, the church in its international form as opposed to the American church, the Japanese church, the English church.[18]

That distinction later became a major issue in the trial as the jury attempted to follow a bewilderingly complex paper trail made even more confused by the various forms the Unification Church and its subsidiaries had taken during those years.

Regardless of the entity or entities involved, Stillman insisted, the jurors shouldn't get lost in the cash flow maze—cash that flowed in and out of numerous bank accounts. What was important to remember, he said, was that the money was used largely for church-related purposes.

So what about the big house called East Garden in Westchester County? Stillman answered:

> Yes,.it is a large house. Reverend Moon lives there. Mrs. Moon lives there. Their children live there. Other church members live there.
>
> Listen for the evidence of church business being conducted there. Listen for the evidence of church religious functions being held there. Ask yourselves whose house is this.[19]

Stillman then approached the delicate problem of Moon's tax returns. Moon's counsel painted a portrait of a preacher who had no intention of cheating anyone. This was no giant scam to make money for a man who only pretended to have a religion.

Instead, Moon and his followers simply assumed that the Reverend Sun Myung Moon and the church were nearly one and that its leader was a trustee of church funds. Much as Roman Catholic bishops act and have acted for centuries as "corporate sole" around the world, including the United States of America where their right to do so the law acknowledges.

Stillman then argued that, presented with this admittedly difficult task of separating church from personal monies, Moon's business assistant in the early years of the Unification Church's activities in the United States had figured the Moons' income based on personal expenditures and "added them together and reported them on Reverend Moon's tax return for his signature."[20]

Moon himself, Stillman added, was so uninvolved in the business that his personal assistant—by no means a professional accountant—was not able to get him to sign the return, which, of course, had to be sent back to the IRS. As a result, church members inadvertently allowed the U.S. government to add to its file on the Unification Church because an unsigned 1040 requires a separate form to be filled out acknowledging that the attached tax return was indeed Moon's own.

Unsigned returns are not usually part of elaborate and carefully crafted conspiracies to defraud the government.[21]

Why, if Moon were a mere cheat, Stillman asked the jury, would the church have hired the largest accounting firm in the world to prepare the religious leader's tax returns in the years after the 1973 fiasco?

Stillman asked the jury again and again to listen to the evidence in response to the government charge that Moon and his men had repeatedly lied to everyone. To be proved, the charge needed tangible evidence of deceit and mendacity—especially on the part of Moon, a man ever remote from mundane matters which did not in any way concern the church or his mission; a man who never once talked to the battery of lawyers and accountants hired to untangle his tangled financial affairs.[22]

Moon's apparent remoteness from his own finances was reinforced by a very elementary factor, Stillman argued. The Reverend Sun Myung Moon spoke practically no English; as a consequence, he allowed others who did to take care of his personal tax problems.

Here counselor Stillman was skating on thick ice. He knew perfectly well that the jurors, all English-speaking up to a point at least, had themselves over the years spent hours agonizing over 1040 forms and the accompanying incomprehensible instruction booklets.[23]

Having confronted one aspect of Moon's alien status, Stillman moved on to another, and that was the matter of cash. Cash was a major issue in this case and there was no point trying to duck it. Moon's lawyer did his best to make the issue a red herring:

> But ask yourselves, ladies and gentlemen, as you think about that, as you listen to the evidence, does that make it bad? You will hear . . . that in the Orient the use of cash is far more frequent, far more acceptable, indeed almost a daily part of life. Those folks over there haven't caught up with us. They don't have credit cards, they don't use checks the same way we do. Cash is used. That doesn't make it bad.[24]

Having tried to leap that hurdle, Stillman then gently jibed the government for its attempts to inflame the jury.

The money issue should not be allowed to sway opinion, he said.

> You cannot allow, and I say this most respectfully to you, you cannot allow some feeling that you might have that this is a lot of money for a house, you cannot allow those feelings to be in the way of your

judgment on the merits of this case. To do otherwise, ladies and gentlemen, would be an insult to your intelligence.[25]

As for the Unification Church's methods of fundraising, an issue introduced by Flumenbaum directly in his opening statement, Stillman replied that churches—all churches—need money. Regarding the Unification Church:

> [Their] church has raised money through the contributions from its members, through sales of items, through the opening and running of businesses. These may not be the methods that you use in your own church. You may not like them. But these church members have a right to go out and use their hard work to raise the money for their church's work.[26]

Inflammatory side issues were one problem, but the government's coming blizzard of evidence about Moon's financial affairs was another. Stillman knew perfectly well that the prosecution would introduce a mountain of paper. Unlike "Perry Mason," there are few dramatic surprises in any trial. Both sides have a right to know the nature and substance of each other's case. In most cases, the evidence to be presented is made available to the other side.

Stillman tried to prepare the jurors as best as he could for the upcoming avalanche. While they were being buried in paper, he pleaded, don't be impressed by the sheer weight of the thing.

It was to be a vain plea. But Stillman, undaunted, next introduced his most compelling theme in the entire Moon-Kamiyama defense.

He asked:

> [Why w]ould a person who had the cash money attributed to Reverend Moon, who wanted to cheat the government, who wanted to defraud the government, put it into a bank account at the Chase Manhattan Bank, and then, if you will, ladies and gentlemen, put right at the top of that account, and you will see it on the charts, Reverend Sun Myung Moon?[27]

Why indeed? It was a question that the prosecution never quite got a handle on. But Stillman knew a good issue when he saw one and decided to pour it on for the jury.

[W]ould a person setting out to cheat the United States of America
go about putting that bank account into his own name, not hiding
his name, say to the government "Here is the money" and say to the
government "Come get me?"28

It was Stillman's Parthian shot. Leaving the jurors a little puzzled, he hoped, Moon's counsel handed over the opening statement chores to his colleague Andrew Lawler. Lawler had a
narrower and in some ways more difficult assignment. He could do
nothing to undercut Moon, but Takeru Kamiyama was Lawler's
client and, as such, had a separate agenda.

Kamiyama, like Moon, faced tax fraud and conspiracy charges.
In addition, he also was confronted with counts of perjury allegedly committed before the grand jury session that had preceded the current trial at Foley Square.

People said that Lawler looked like Superman—at least the
1950s television version. He tended to tower over everyone, including his defendant, Takeru Kamiyama.

Lawler's strategy was to try to make the foreign seem familiar. It
would not be easy to remove the mystery surrounding Moon and
Kamiyama, but Lawler could not avoid trying if the two defendants were to have any chance of being found innocent.

After skimming over Kamiyama's biography, the defense counsel tried to overcome jury culture shock by explaining to the
America-centric jurors a few facts of modern life.

I would ask you to put aside certain views some of us may bring with
us, and that is the view of the United States as the source of all
money, as the source of all things for other people. That is, I think
certain of us are inclined to think that it is the United States that
sends missionaries abroad to other countries, it is the United States
that sends money to other countries.

The evidence you will hear is just the opposite: that is, missionaries
coming from abroad, from foreign countries, to the United States to
labor here, and money being brought in to the United States from
abroad to fund those church purposes.29

It was, of course, a novel, even startling notion that Lawler was
proposing to the unsophisticated jurors on the panel. But Lawler

knew that the defense had to confront from the start the jury's most basic prejudices if their clients were not to be eaten alive.

So why should a foreigner have the gall to come to the U.S. as a missionary? Who among us needs to be saved by them anyway? It was a question that Lawler couldn't avoid.

The reason for that . . . is that the spiritual leader of the Unification Church, the Reverend Moon, viewed the United States, the leader of the free world, as the most important country in the world, and thus the appropriate place to have the headquarters and to be the center of the international movement.[30]

It was important for Lawler to establish this reverse order of things. The jurors had to get used to Lawler's idea; the notion was critical to making credible the defense's contention that much of the money came not as the government attempted to imply with vague, suspicious origins but simply from devoted Japanese followers of Moon who entered the United States and placed funds in the care of their leader.

It was also an arrangement that the government stoutly denied as controversy gathered around what became known in the trial as the "family fund" issue.

But in making the strange familiar, Lawler was only getting started. He next drew a picture of Kamiyama himself. The man had come to the U.S. at Moon's request, but was ill-prepared to serve his leader as a financial advisor. He spoke no English, had no real knowledge of the United States and its diverse culture, much less its business practices and even less its tax laws.

Moreover, in those early years Kamiyama and his fellow Japanese were not thinking about pleasing the Internal Revenue Service, of which they had little or no comprehension, but about building a religious movement. Like all enthusiasts that flock to new religions, they felt that there was a world to save; don't mind the torpedos, full speed ahead. Now that may sound naive, but it's quite easy to underestimate the power of that kind of religious experience. And, of course, it's nearly incomprehensible to the secular-minded or the comfortably pious.

Saving the world takes money—lots of it. And Sun Myung Moon, to his followers, was nothing if not ambitious about saving the world. As a consequence, Kamiyama did in the United States what he had done with great success in Japan. He pushed street sales of flowers and candles—the original source of wealth for the Unification Church in Asia—and promoted other businesses he was familiar with, such as the importing and selling of ginseng tea and marble vases.

It was a typical Kamiyama effort. In fact, Kamiyama and his fellow Japanese did not have the faintest idea whether these products had any real place in the American market or if such a market could be created. Ginseng is, to say the least, an acquired taste, and marble vases for religious and decorative purposes are part of Korean and Japanese cultures, but hardly American.

They simply had no notion of cross-cultural marketing; they would have been bewildered if anyone had mentioned it. In the case of both ginseng and the vases, the demand for them in the United States was almost perfectly inelastic—in other words, they wouldn't be purchased by non-Asians in this country at any price.

Lawler didn't say all this—quite in that way at least—but it was something he strongly implied throughout his opening statement.

It would have been better if he had made the point explicitly, but to do so would have embarrassed Kamiyama and made him lose face with his colleagues—not to mention with Moon. The effect on Kamiyama would have been worse than being found guilty of the charges lodged against him. And Lawler knew it. Still, Lawler tried.

No, the American business ventures did not prosper, he told the jury, knowing, in fact, that they ranged from failure to fiasco to folly.

Skating lightly over that, Lawler then tried to explain the so-called "family fund." The fund's original impetus—money coming from the Japanese faithful—could be attributed, in fact, entirely to the miserable financial situation of the American Unification Church. The cash that the Japanese brought in—a few thousand dollars at a time—served two purposes.

In Lawler's words:

One, there was an awareness that the situation in the United States was not that great, and that is the church had not grown, that the funds were limited. The Japanese members as they came here did not want to be a burden on the church in this country if there was some emergency or some problem. So they brought money with them for that purpose.[31]

The second reason was that the money was needed for the evangelical effort. To the faithful that meant that the money was to be used for whatever reason the Reverend Sun Myung Moon had to advance the work of the church.

But the unusual aspect of the arrangement did not stop there. Lawler next had to tackle explaining another strange—to American ears—notion. That is, that the "Moonies" are a communal movement. People share from a common pot. In the case of the Japanese funds, the monies were simply pooled—no one kept separate accounts—and eventually those pooled monies were deposited in bank accounts in Moon's name instead of being hidden, figuratively, under mattresses.[32]

So how was all of this money flow kept track of? Badly. But let Lawler describe the chaos of those early years:

> Various members became bookkeepers, records were kept by the Japanese members, and in retrospect it is easy to see many of the members attempted to do too much, too soon, that they undertook tasks and responsibilities which by reason of their background and lack of understanding of our culture and business practices and the way things are done here, that they were really not qualified to do.[33]

Again that was euphemistic understatement and Lawler knew it. But dwelling on the business incompetence of the "Moonies" was a theme the defense counsel could only touch upon. Still, Lawler had to make the point. The financial records were a shambles; many were reconstructions made after the events. Mistakes had been made, and corrections inserted.

The government of course made the worst possible inferences from all of the financial confusion. Lawler pleaded with the jury to keep an open mind:

> The events took place as set forth in the document, but the documents were prepared later in certain instances, because the people with the responsibility to make the decisions did not fully understand the way things work in this country.

So, as opposed to the inference that the government would have you draw that certain of these things were done to fool the government in 1977 and 1978 when they began their investigation, I think you will conclude when you hear all of the evidence that by reason of lack of understanding, of mistake, confusion and of error, these events took place.[34]

The most important reconstructed financial document was the so-called "family ledger." The ledger was supposed to contain records of the transactions of the family fund; that is, the money brought into the United States by the Japanese faithful in the early and mid-1970s. The ledger—which the government put into evidence—was basically an edited account book that pieced together the who, what, and when of money brought into the United States on behalf of the church. It was at best an approximation, based on a mare's nest of papers written in Japanese by various amateur "Moonie" would-be accountants who were trying to keep track of hundreds of contributions.[35]

After arguing that the family ledger was never intended to be an accurate and contemporaneous financial record, Lawler came to his main point. If Kamiyama had little understanding of this country in the early years when his command of English was nonexistent, then it made little sense to think that Kamiyama could have engaged in a conspiracy to defraud the government, especially when he had little or no knowledge of American tax returns and other business documents to boot.[36]

With that point made, Lawler came to the end of the opening round.

It was going to be a long and confusing trial, he concluded. And it was going to be difficult for the jury to focus on the main issues. But would they please try? Once again, Kamiyama's counsel engaged in understatement.[37]

THE GOVERNMENT'S CASE

The jurors now were confronted with the real meat of the trial: the government's case against the defendants. Although the prosecution strategy appeared to be simple enough in outline, the government's presentation ground on for a full month. A battery of witnesses appeared, acting as vehicles to carry in the pile of evidence that Flumenbaum and Harris wanted to introduce in the courtroom—evidence that would dazzle the eyes and benumb the brains of a dozen jurors.

That process in itself took weeks. After the government witnesses had yielded their treasure-trove of documents, the prosecutors moved on to the church's witnesses. Of course the defendants themselves did not have to testify against their will—that is an individual right protected by the Fifth Amendment. The government, however, managed to procure the next best thing, or so its agents thought.

The prosecution subpoenaed top church officials—all Americans—and grilled them on the stand. Two final witnesses capped off the government's case. Both were former church members: one, Michael Warder, had held high positions in the American Unification Church and had once been in the confidence of Moon.

Warder, the government hoped, would supply the smoking gun, or at least seem to—enough to convince the jury of Moon and Kamiyama's wrongdoing. With that final flourish the government planned to rest its case, allow the defense to present its own, and then come back with a crushing closing statement.

On paper and in outline all of this seemed simple enough. The problem was that despite years of preparation, the government's case was confused, a mess—bewildering everyone involved, including Judge Goettel. Even the prosecutors seemed at times to be at a loss in keeping track of the charges, the witnesses, and the evidence. Above all, the evidence.

The confusion was there beginning the moment the government began presenting the evidence. In the eyes of the government, the case was anchored in the bank accounts of Sun Myung Moon, accounts established in early 1973. Broadly speaking, the government claimed that the funds in the accounts were not those of the Unification Church, but were intended for Moon's personal use. Calling it church money was merely a smokescreen to prevent a tax hit from the IRS.

The accounts were held, incidentally, at Chase Manhattan's Park Avenue branch. As a consequence, witnesses from the bank were

sworn in to authenticate a variety of bank documents and procedures. All of which was meant to prove what the defense had
long conceded: namely, that Sun Myung Moon had had three
accounts in his name at that bank.

There was, in fact, no mystery about Moon's having set up an
account at the Park Avenue branch of Chase Manhattan. Chase's
Park Avenue bank specializes in foreign clients, one reason why the
branch is located in midtown Manhattan, as opposed to Chase's
headquarters in the city's financial district, Wall Street.[38]

Testimony about the Chase Manhattan Bank accounts ran in
tedious detail for some thirty-five pages of trial transcript. None of
the testimony was particularly riveting, although it did boast a
couple of odd points. First, the prosecution focused on one particular cash transaction by Moon. Accompanying him to the bank
that day were several female church members. According to former Chase employee Charles Brinkerhoff, the original accounts
had been opened with checks. In a subsequent visit to the bank,
Moon made another deposit. To make the deposit, the church
members removed stacks of greenbacks from their pocketbooks.

The amount came to $100,000. All of it in small bills.[39] All that
cash. The jury had to think it suspicious.

That fact, to be sure, was highly gratifying to the prosecution.

There was another "oddity" about Moon's early bank transactions, however, that was not initially gratifying to the government.
Having carefully presented witness Brinkerhoff as a meticulous
banker with a steeltrap memory, the prosecution was chagrined
when his testimony turned troublesome. The Chase employee
recalled that Moon's first visit to the bank was in the company of an
American clergyman wearing a clerical collar.[40]

There was, indeed, an American that day with Moon, but he was
not a clergyman. The man accompanying Moon was Joe Tully of
the American Unification Church; but Tully wasn't wearing a
clerical collar, because he was—like all church members—a
layman.

A minor point but it would highlight the problem with the
Chase employee testimony. The prosecution witness could recite in
exquisite but pointless detail the nature of Moon's accounts, and
all the technical minutia associated with them, but the legal mean-

ing of it all eluded him. Through his testimony the government had introduced loads of evidence but it had not established any criminal intent or action.

Needless to say, that basic deficiency was not brought out by the prosecution, but by defense counsel on cross-examination.

Charles Stillman spoke for the defense:

> Q: You did not have a clue, did you, as to whether or not these were his funds or he was holding these funds for his religious organization; isn't that correct?
>
> A: Only knew that he wanted the account in his name. I did not know what the funds were.[41]

Already on the first day, the government had gotten itself tangled up in its own evidence. It was but a shadow of much more to come.

The initial problem with the prosecution's case involved counsel's inability to sort out the Chase Manhattan records and present them to the jury in some coherent form. The data turned into a miasma of every transaction connected to Moon's accounts. Checking, savings, and a number of time deposits were detailed: items related to the accounts filled ten fat exhibit books in all.

Not surprisingly, Judge Goettel (as well as defense counsel) was soon thoroughly lost in spite of Jo Ann Harris's attempts to navigate the rocky evidentiary waters with Chase employee Isabel Maddux. Here are Goettel, Harris, and Maddux—all familiar with financial matters—trying to make sense of records a much less expert jury was supposed to understand:[42]

> Q: And in the same book do you find Exhibits 110 through 117 which relate to a Chase Manhattan Bank time deposit No. 1856 in the name of Mr. Moon?
>
> A: Yes.
>
> THE COURT: Now you have got me confused. Are there separate books for 100 to 110 and 110 to 117?
>
> MS. HARRIS: Actually, your Honor, in some of those books there are more than one account and in some instances, unfortunately, the accounts span from one book to the next.

THE COURT: In any event, is 100 to 110 a separate book from 110 to 117?

MS. HARRIS: It is not.

THE COURT: That is all one book?

MS. HARRIS: That is all one book.

THE COURT: But there are two separate accounts in there, a savings and time deposit?

MS. HARRIS: That's correct.

THE WITNESS: There are two additional deposit accounts in the book.

MS. HARRIS: And the witness is correct. There is in addition to time deposit 1856, another time deposit in Mr. Moon's name of 1963.

Q: Is that correct?

A: That is correct.

Q: Does that take us through the book, Ms. Maddux?

A: No, there is a further time deposit, No. 2000.[43]

The trial was filled with moments like this. In fact, only two minutes after the above-noted exchange, the court, prosecution, and defense became entangled once again in an evidentiary question.

MR. LAWLER: Your Honor, I had 200 to 211D a minute ago.

THE COURT: 210D.

MS. HARRIS: Do you want me to back up?

THE COURT: Wait until they get through this. Then we will try and unscramble it.[44]

Later, in chambers, the normally mild-mannered Goettel exploded at a flustered Marty Flumenbaum:

What in God's name did you want to show the jury all of the papers that are pertinent to a letter of credit for? . . . One single document would cover that. . . . You are putting the jury to sleep by throwing all these scads of documents at them.[45]

It was a point that Goettel made again and again, sometimes within earshot of the jury. And the evidence never did get unscrambled in a way that a jury of limited capabilities could ever understand.

No wonder that even Judge Gerard Goettel, who would prove himself no friend of Moon's in the proceedings to come, at the end of the first day of the trial pronounced sentence on the government's presentation of its exhibits: "The handling of the evidence has just been a mess so far."[46]

The mess didn't get any better, but the trial moved on to other things. Having more or less established the basic facts of Moon's bank accounts, the prosecution introduced the second *bête noire* of the case: the infamous Tong-Il stock owned by Moon.

Tong-Il, it will be remembered, was a Unification Church company set up in part to import Korean ginseng tea and marble urns. The value of such merchandise in the United States had always been questionable. In a world of goods and services available to the consumer, neither was high on anyone's list in the United States, if indeed they appeared on anyone's list at all.

Still Sun Myung Moon's financial ties to the company were of keen interest to the bloodhound prosecutors.

The record showed that Moon had been chairman of the board of Tong-Il and that he had received $50,000 in stock, five hundred shares in all. His wife, Hak Ja Han, had received two hundred shares worth $20,000, and Moon's co-defendant, Takeru Kamiyama, was given one hundred shares valued at $10,000.[47]

For the prosecution that meant, of course, that Chairman Moon was nothing but a businessman after all. And that, as far as the government was concerned, was as good as being guilty.

The prosecutors also contended that the stock was a source of income for Moon that had not been reported to the IRS. It could not be, they said, merely church money kept in trust by the church's leader and founder. The government pointed out that Moon was also a salaried officer of the company and it insisted that payments of such nature, according to Judge Goettel's ruling, "can evidence ownership, control and dominion, which is the crucial issue in the case."[48]

Indeed, Moon did draw a salary from Tong-Il. It amounted to $20,000—a salary on which he duly paid income taxes. In any case, the defense argued, the stock—which earned him no income—was a gift or a loan. Which of the two it was, was uncertain, reflecting the vagueness with which the Asian-dominated church regarded such things (quite unlike the black-print, bottom-line mentality of the Americans, both in and out of the church). But whether gift or loan, in either case Moon would have no tax liability for the stock.

But the argument over Tong-Il was not the heart of the government's case. Nor was it Moon's three bank accounts at Chase Manhattan.

The government was counting on something else. The oldest story that divinity school professors tell their young charges is to make marginal notes when preparing a sermon. In addition they teach that when the hermeneutical point to be made is weak, the preacher can yell like hell. Chances are that the congregation will never notice the subterfuge.

The prosecutorial version of yelling like hell is to incite the jury against the defendant. Don't discuss the law or argue the evidence: just get a dozen men and women of the jury mad as hell at the defendant. In lawyerly language it's called engaging in "inflammatory and prejudicial" behavior.

Jo Ann Harris never studied theology, but she knew how to buffalo a jury. And under her instruction, so did her acolyte Martin Flumenbaum. Eventually.

And their conduct would raise the question of whether the real argument in the *Moon* trial centered on the big throbbing heart of dislike in America of strange foreigners who look like extras from an old Fu Manchu movie.

And whether the government of the United States would rely on crude bias—even racism—to convict a pair of orientals.

Let's consider how this was done.

It began on the first day of the trial when Flumenbaum attempted to enter into the record the weekly time and pay-sheets of the Tong-Il company. The purpose, the government lawyer said, was to compare Moon's salary with that of other employees. Flumenbaum knew of course that the latter made little or nothing in doing what they considered service to their church.

What Flumenbaum was doing was raising the spectre of young people working sweat shop hours for a Korean millionaire. While

Flumenbaum's assertion alone was grossly inflammatory, it also had nothing to do with the charges leveled against Moon, a fact which defense counsel Stillman pointed out to Judge Goettel.

At the time, however, Goettel's only problem with the myriad timesheets was a housekeeping one. The neat and tidy judge was appalled yet again by the government's attempts at "loading the record" unduly with "tons of documents." But not so appalled as to throw out any of the documents.[49]

Confronted on the larger issue of Flumenbaum's inflammatory and irrelevant assertions, the court was slow to grasp the point: "I see no problem with relevance and I see no problem with prejudice," Goettel ruled. Only later did it strike Goettel that the prosecution had been trying subtly to introduce the "slave labor" argument into the case.

To make Moon look like an oriental slave driver was only part of the prosecution's campaign to inflame the jury. Another aspect of the government's inflame-and-prejudge strategy was to highlight Moon's supposed total control over his followers. Although the effort to bring in brainwashing through the back door was of questionable relevance, church members who took the witness stand were nonetheless asked if they would do or say anything that their leader asked them to.

That's precisely what Jo Ann Harris asked one Korean advisor to Moon, Sang Ik Choi: "[Y]ou would come here and testify anything he wanted you to say, isn't that right?" Before the befuddled Choi could answer, the defense attorneys objected. Goettel, however, did not find the question particularly inflammatory—only that the grounds for making that assumption had not been laid.[50]

Occasionally, the government's tactic regarding brainwashing misfired. When another church witness was asked directly if she would lie for Moon, the woman, in effect, said no.

Takeko Hose had joined the Unification Church in 1964 in Japan, a true-believer if ever there was one. She had moved to the American mission field in the early years of the Moon campaign to save the United States; Hose was assigned to San Francisco.

Flumenbaum had little interest in Hose's activities within the early American Unification Church, but he did learn that the Reverend Sun Myung Moon had married the woman to an American Unification Church member. Next came the sucker question:

Q: And am I correct that when [Moon] asks you to do something you do it for him?

Over several objections from the defense, Hose was invited to
answer the question. Her answer was not what the prosecution
wanted to hear:

A: Depends on what he asks. Excuse me, it's too general to
answer.[51]

Still, Flumenbaum, the man who so artfully manipulated grand
jurys, their transcripts and witnesses persisted, effectively badgering the witness. For his trouble he earned a trip to the sidebar to
visit Goettel and two angry lawyers for the defense.

Flumenbaum wanted next to introduce statements from *Master
Speaks*, a compilation of Moon's sermons. Flumenbaum's plan provoked Stillman to argue that theological doctrines are not relevant
in a criminal trial. Goettel eventually got the point and ordered the
young prosecutor to move on to his next item.

Other arrows waited in the government's quiver. For example,
the prosecution repeatedly tried to get the allegedly lavish lifestyle
of Moon into the trial record, relevant or not.

Michael Trulson, a church member who worked at East Garden,
Moon's New York home, was quizzed over and over about details of
the buildings on the property, as well as Moon's cars and horses—
this although Trulson had no responsibility for either. Somewhat
surprisingly, this one incident did stir Goettel and the court found
the question irrelevant.[52]

Nonetheless, just about anything else was grist for the mill. The
prosecution team, for instance, brought a Washington, D.C., jeweler to the Foley Square courtroom.

Jeweler Alan Serman testified that Moon had purchased two
eighteen-karat Rolex watches in April 1973. The story of the gold
watches was, of course, what Harris and Flumenbaum wanted to
parade before the jury.

The government kept the question of the watches relevant by
eliciting from the jeweler information that Moon had paid for the
two items with a check from a checkbook that he had himself
carried.

As an aside, that apparently unusual fact got Moon's associate

Kamiyama into trouble, because the latter had earlier testified before a grand jury, claiming that he, Kamiyama, almost always carried the checkbook. As we have seen, Kamiyama's testimony about the checkbook was in response to a badly garbled question from an unqualified interpreter. No matter, in the end it got Kamiyama convicted on a perjury charge.[53]

But the effort to arouse smoldering resentments on the part of the jury was only one of several slightly disreputable tactics used by the government.

There were others, at least one of which operated on the assumption that the jury was not too bright. The prosecutors believed that if they employed repetition to drive home their points, the points would begin to stick like mud to the defendants.

One such mud-like *ad hominem* attack on Moon, as we have already seen, centered on his supposedly lavish lifestyle. At the very heart of that attack was the home at East Garden. The prosecution was especially fascinated by how Moon had acquired the estate and in whose name the property was held. While the details of deed transfers eventually glazed over the eyes of the jury, the physical size and monetary worth of the property—some $700,000—was pounded into the minds of the jury again and again and again.

For example, in her questioning of church member Bill Torrey, Jo Ann Harris dwelt on the East Garden acquisition:

> Q: When they told you that the property had been appraised at $700,000, you came up with $700,000 of loans from Mr. Moon to the church, correct?
>
> MR. LAWLER: Objection to the form of the question.
>
> THE COURT: I am not so much concerned with the form as I am with the fact that we have been over this three or four times.[54]

The prosecution was not stopped. After all, what was important to the government was the jury's getting into their heads the image of Reverend Moon living high on the American hog. Consequently, Harris took the point and then proceeded to repeat the question on financing. Defense counsel's objection was sustained, but the point was nonetheless driven home: Moon lived in a

$700,000 mansion and he was using church funds to support his elevated standard of living.

Bottom line conclusion: Moon and the Unification Church were phonies, cardboard covers for a money-making enterprise that spanned at least three continents.

Sometimes the repetition only added to the confusion— intentionally or not. It wasn't only the jury who got lost. At one point in the trial, prosecutor Flumenbaum quizzed the church's leader in West Germany about his knowledge of Michael Runyon, one of Moon's top aides in the American Unification Church.

When Paul Werner denied having any knowledge about Runyon, Flumenbaum tried again:

> Q: Isn't it a fact that you at Mr. Runyon's request met with attorneys for Reverend Moon in May of 1981.
>
> MR. STILLMAN: What does that establish?
>
> THE COURT: I don't know.
>
> MR. LAWLER: . . . It gives us something in common, your Honor.[55]

But Flumenbaum persisted until Goettel, thoroughly confused, invited the young prosecutor to the bench to offer an explanation. The explanation proved so tortured that the judge observed, out of the jury's hearing:

> Mr. Flumenbaum, unfortunately, has a curious way of approaching some of his questions which often gets him answers he doesn't want. If he asked the witness what the relationship between Runyon and Moon was to his knowledge, he might get a less restrictive answer.[56]

But Flumenbaum remained persistent, at least with other witnesses. One, Yukiko Matsumura-Fairbrother, another Japanese member, had helped to prepare the family ledger at the end of 1976 and the beginning of 1977. That fact, however, did not stop the prosecutor from asking questions about checks deposited in early 1975.

Lawler objected and the court, puzzled, asked Flumenbaum the purpose of it all.

MR. FLUMENBAUM: I want to show her the bank statement which reflects the $7,100 deposit.

THE COURT: I believe she already said she saw no bank statements.

MR. FLUMENBAUM: That is what she said, your Honor.

THE COURT: Yes. It won't change her answer to show them to her a second time.

MR. FLUMENBAUM: Maybe it will refresh her recollection.

COURT: I don't think so.

MR. FLUMENBAUM: I take it you don't want me to even try.

THE COURT: No.[57]

To go over and over again points already established in evidence, of course, was only one tactic to influence the jury. Evidence "clutter" was another.

Clutter is a legal tactic that the prosecution followed with a vengeance. The basic idea is simply to overwhelm the jury with "evidence"—both real and apparent. In tax cases, of course, it can be devastatingly effective. The suggestion is this: given all of this paper, the defendants must be guilty of something particularly to a jury whose mental capacities had already been publicly questioned by the presiding judge.

In the Moon trial, the prosecutors had to know very well that the jury would not and could not follow arguments about narrow and arcane tax matters. Knowing this, they proceeded to dump thousands of documents on the twelve men and women, most of whom were incapable of filling out a simple 1040 tax form. Quantity, not quality, of the paper introduced into evidence was what counted. For the jurors the sheer volume of documentary material suggested guilt.

When jurors are confused or bored, they naturally fall back on fixed views and familiar modes of thought; in other words, prejudices. And such biases were what the prosecution hoped would help to put Moon and Kamiyama away.

Not that the government was being particularly subtle about their "clutter" tactic. Judge Goettel would grow exasperated that first day of government exhibits and Chase Manhattan testimony though he would later seem to grow more patient with the prosecution. But defense counsel also caught on early and stayed exasperated.

One example of evidence "clutter" revealed itself in the prosecution's curiosity about another church purchase of property, the Belvedere estate once owned by Seagram distillery chairman Edgar Bronfman. The church had been late in its payments, and the whiskey king had made it clear in his correspondence with the church that he was considering foreclosure on the place—highly embarrassing to the self-sufficient Koreans. The church came up with the money in short order.

The whole episode was irrelevant to the charges laid against Moon and Kamiyama. When the prosecutors attempted to place the extensive Belvedere correspondence into evidence, defense objected.

Judge Goettel agreed to the cluttering charge. Or, he half agreed. Half of the Belvedere correspondence was declared inadmissable because of its cluttering effect, but the other half was not. The portion not permitted detailed how the arrearages on Belvedere were to be paid off.[58]

The document clutter also served to help nail down the prosecution's *sub rosa* contention that Moon was nothing more than a businessman in clerical clothing. The defense quickly caught on to this tactic.

For example, in what became known as the "668 series" of documents, the government submitted for the record dozens of checks issued by the Unification Church International involving transfers of funds among the church's various business enterprises. "All this 668 is doing," lawyer Stillman argued, "is loading this record with things that are just irrelevant."

Moon's counsel continued:

> The government seems to think that I am taking the position here that Reverend Moon was functioning as a monastic figure away from this. And I think that the examination, your Honor, of the other day

clearly indicates that that is not the position that we are taking in this lawsuit.[59]

Judge Goettel again sustained Stillman's "clutter" objection, but not without a stiff fight from the prosecutors.[60]

Midway through the trial the government's insinuations had apparently begun to penetrate not just the jury's subconscious but the judge's. *In camera*, Judge Goettel suggested that Moon was something worse than a businessman. In fact, the image of Charles Dickens' Fagin occurred to his Honor: "[Moon] has hundreds of people [read little children] collecting money and turning it over to him. . . ."[61]

It was a picture that Goettel never quite got out of his mind. The "Moonies" were all young waifs, Oliver Twists, learning to steal in the mean streets of Londontown.

Meanwhile, losing to Stillman's earlier "clutter" objection hardly discouraged the prosecution from evidentiary overkill. The government made a great fuss over having Pearl Tytell, a handwriting expert, verify the signature of Moon on a wad of checks issued by him in the 1970s on the Chase Manhattan accounts. The expert Tytell—those in the profession like to be called "questioned documents examiners"—gave her opinion that the signatures were genuine.

No one had disputed that the signatures were Moon's, but the government could not resist combining clutter with professional authority even if the point in question were, in fact, never in question, and had nothing to do with any count charged against Moon or his co-defendant.[62]

The government used the handwriting expert "tactic" over and over again, despite exasperated and usually ineffective objections by the defense.[63]

On at least one occasion the paper clutter was not even in English. One set of documents introduced into evidence dealt with Sun Myung Moon's background (birth and marriage certificates), along with similar information on his wife and children. Naturally, they were in Korean (or Japanese, it was never established which), and the prosecution did not have the slightest idea what they actually said.[64]

THE INVISIBLE TRIAL;
THE FORGOTTEN FIRST AMENDMENT

Beyond the "clutter" tactic, however—behind the paper confusion, the masses of irrelevant evidence, the repetition—was a larger purpose whose shrewdness became more evident as the trial wore on, the record became more confused, and the jury grew weary. For the prosecution, the real trial was not about specific criminal charges or evidence or exhibits. For the prosecution, there was a second, almost invisible trial, a *sub rosa* proceeding designed to play to jury prejudice by portraying Moon as a religous charlatan, living a lavish lifestyle while tyrannically exploiting followers blinded by their devotion.

Yet while the government tried to prove that Moon wasn't really a serious religious leader, it tried to do so quietly, through implication and through innuendo. Because to make Moon's religious vision the center of the trial would raise the very issue the prosecution most wanted the judge and jury to avoid: the fact that under First Amendment law religious leaders like Moon were permitted to act as "trustees" for co-mingled church and personal funds. That's right, in the U.S. it's absolutely legal for religious leaders to use church funds to pay, in effect, for their "parsonage"—the very thing the government held Moon had done and in so doing had somehow committed a crime.

But as hard as the government tried to prove that Moon was merely a businessman, the actual trial evidence showed something else. Not that it was particularly flattering to Moon. It did, however, suggest that he was a man seized with a religious vision who used business profits, if he could get any, to advance the cause. And, more embarrassing to church members, that his lack of business sense—at least in the Western world—had led the church into financial fiascos of the first magnitude.

Would a good businessman get himself into monumentally bad investments? The trial transcript offers two examples.

The first involved a straight-out-of-the-book confidence game in which the church got fleeced by an American con man named Frank Broes. No, Broes didn't sell them the Brooklyn Bridge or underwater real estate in Florida or a gold mine in California.

Instead, he sold them an iron mine in Arizona. High-grade ore, too.

Broes, perfectly aware that he was dealing with religious folk, appeared to be intensely pious to one of Moon's advisors, Sang Ik Choi. Although the prosecution tried to portray Choi as a shrewd man hiding behind the mask of a bumbler, in reality there was no mask, only bumble.

Choi tells the story:

> Then I come back and I called Reverend Moon, I found a very good Christian whose name is Mr. Broes. He's very faithful and also very good business which is iron ore. He like to help our group, are you interested.

> But then Reverend Moon told me, anyway he like to meet the people always. Okay, it is good people Christian. You can meet. Then I brought Frank Broes, Mr. Broes at that time, maybe a lawyer with him McCauley.[65]

Like taking candy from a baby. It gets worse. The church agreed to go into the iron ore and iron-making business. Broes' lawyer McCauley was to handle all of the legal paperwork. No one from the church except Choi, who used a dictionary for the hard words, bothered to examine the contract. After all, Broes was a Christian gentleman. On Choi's voucher of Broes' character, Moon signed the contract and the check.[66]

Broes, like any good con man, was talking big money. A cool $50 million was needed to get started. Of course, Moon and company only had to come up with $15 million to be partners in Stradco Iron (which, in turn, would produce a spinoff, the M&S Iron and Steel Company).

The iron ore magnate didn't get the $15 million. Even the church didn't hand out that kind of money as if it were pocket change to a favorite nephew. But Broes did get a check for $200,000. When church members had second thoughts about the iron ore business (having found upon closer examination that Stradco ore was low grade, even unmineable), they politely asked for their money back.[67]

Fat chance.

Broes kept the money, using it to buy an airport Ramada Inn in Jacksonville, Florida. Now, a motel doesn't look much like an iron mine, although Broes claimed, somewhat implausibly, that the motel also served as headquarters for the Stradco Iron Company. In any case, the return on investment in the motel was considerably and predictably more profitable than any iron mine. Meanwhile, the church, too embarrassed at having been suckered, took no legal action against Broes.[68]

But iron ore ventures were not the church's only entrepreneurial folly. It also poured money into a fly-by-night paint business in England.

"Microparticles" was the name of the paint company which signed an agreement with the Sun Myung Moon Foundation of Great Britain. Micro was owned by the Simmons family, Martin Allen, wife Daisey, and son Anthony.

But the Simmonses, in contrast to Frank Broes, were not out and out *artistes du flimflam*. Not at all. They fit more comfortably into the category of high, high-risk, venture capital. The Simmonses wanted to market a special paint that they had developed to stop rust corrosion. Well, why not? The church coughed up £50,000 British or $125,000 American to invest in the enterprise. In either language, it was a goodly sum.

It was a terrific idea on paper. There was just one problem. The paint didn't do what it was supposed to. In fact, instead of retarding rust, the stuff promoted it.[69]

Just how did the church get nicked this time? Yet another Korean advisor to Moon, David Kim, explained:

[I went to] factory myself and I was fascinated with the thing, the new invention by the scientist. Stainless steel powder which is not rusting. It was a very, very promising industry at that time.[70]

That was in 1973. Unfortunately, Microparticles had a problem. Kim explained:

Later, two or three years later when we have a wonderful market plan it turned out to be a failure. In other words, it turned out not to stick together. In other words, peel. More research was needed.[71]

It was all very embarrassing. So embarrassing, in fact, that defense counsel was not keen on dwelling on the subject. Nor was the prosecution keen on exploring church business misadventures. The government was anxious to paint Moon as a crafty profiteer; instead, the evidence painted a portrait of a rather unworldly figure who went along with the advice of old and trusted advisors who had even less business sense—at least as business is practiced in America.

What was the Reverend Sun Myung Moon? Businessman or prophet? Everything hung on the answer, or more precisely the jury's answer to that question.

In the prosecution's eyes, the answer was simple. Defense counsel naturally had a quite different view. Instead of dwelling on the embarrassing fact that the Korean and his associates did not understand the business cultures of America and Britain, Moon's attorneys attempted to win the jury by raising First Amendment questions.

The rights of the Reverend Sun Myung Moon and his church under the First Amendment run like a red cord throughout the whole story. If Moon was merely a man out for a buck, the First Amendment was not an issue. If he was more than that; if he really was a religious figure, then it applied. But where and how?

The First Amendment provides only a few signposts about what it covers. Needless to say, for example, in the amendment's clauses regarding religion, the Big Number One does not protect the chairman of the board of General Motors, even if he's a pious Presbyterian. The First Amendment does, however, give broad protections to churches and their leaders no matter how unpopular they become, provided that the institutions represent genuine expressions of religious belief, and are not simply crude tax dodges.

The question was discussed, but never resolved. The problem was that the government, court, and defense in the case had very different views on the man and on the First Amendment. Their splintered attitudes were, in part, a reflection of the inherent ambiguity of that great American constitutional question.

Nonetheless, for the government, a defense resting in part on

the First Amendment was a snare and a delusion; sound and fury
signifying nothing. The prosecution for the most part simply ignored the First Amendment question. Only at the very end of the
trial, in Jo Ann Harris's summation to the jury, did the government
even bother to address the matter directly.

Harris brusquely lectured the jury:

> There is nothing in this case that has anything to do with a tax
> exemption for churches. The First Amendment is an important
> constitutional part of our history and no one challenges that. This
> case is not about the exemption of churches. It is about personal
> income tax to an individual who happens to be related to a
> church.[72]

And that was that. No more was said by the government about
the tangled web of constitutional rights and protections afforded
America's religions, a web spun out in courts and legislatures over
the last two centuries. The government made its argument by
simple assertion and was confident that the jury would follow its
lead, rather than understand the complex tangle of law and precedent offered by the defense.

The defense, for its part, tried its best. All through the case
sensitive First Amendment questions surfaced—sensitive, at least,
from the defense's point of view. Often, in fact, the question of
constitutional rights was raised as a defensive tactic.

For example, during the testimony of church member Lewis
Burgess, the prosecution was eager to depict Moon not only as a
businessman, but as a viciously exploitative one. Burgess seemed
to provide the right opportunity to do so.

Burgess was an employee of Tong-Il—the ginseng tea and vase
importing company. Flumenbaum wanted to know what Burgess
did with his salary check. Flumenbaum of course already knew the
answer. Burgess, like other church employees, plowed his earnings
back into the firm, and thus, the cause.

Defense laywers objected vociferously to Flumenbaum's question on First Amendment grounds. In their view, the matter was
between Burgess and his church. It was not something to drag
before the jury in an attempt to inflame sentiment against Moon.
Defense noted:

Inquiring into that would be going into the reasons behind it and it
seems it would involve this witness' practice of his religion.[73]

Judge Goettel, however, was skeptical of the objection, so defense lawyers pressed the issue:

Some of the members did [contribute] and some didn't. It was up to
them. That should not be admissable against either defendant in
this case. It has nothing to do with their taxes. Everybody is entitled
to their money when they earn a salary and report it.[74]

Goettel did not see the defense's point at all. It simply went
beyond him. Kamiyama's lawyer, Andrew Lawler, sounded an
alarm which, in effect, described how the rest of the trial was
destined to go:

It seems to me that we are going step by step beyond that in terms
that are very prejudicial and that is by allowing the introduction of
the entire payroll here and an attempt to show that these people, all
of them church members, stockholders and employees are working
long hours and are underpaid and pouring their money back into
the church and it is going to tie in to the image they are attempting
to paint of the Reverend Moon which has nothing to do with this
specific tax case that is to be tried.[75]

In other words, Lawler argued, we are not dealing with a nebu-
lous point, but with a First Amendment right which protects religious practices as a religion's members see fit to exercise them. The
same amendment prevents those same faithful from being exposed in a prejudicial fashion to a jury which must determine the
outcome of a tax case involving a vastly unpopular defendant.

Lawler's argument made no difference. The court overruled the
defense's objection. It was as if the First Amendment simply didn't
exist. When the defense lawyers moved for a mistrial, arguing that
the government had gone into the area of questioning church
members "in pooling their resources for their mutual support,"
Goettel, as expected, denied the motion.[76]

That early exchange among the three—defense, prosecution,
and judge—was only a taste of what was to come.

Moon's lawyers tried again and again to tell the jury that the case was not a simple affair involving a couple of oriental businessmen trying to cheat Uncle Sam.

Stillman on one occasion during the cross-examination of Michael Warder, a former church official, attempted to elicit his recall of Moon's table talk about business and religion.

The government lawyers objected on the basis of hearsay and demanded a sidebar discussion with Judge Goettel and their counterparts acting for the defense.

Stillman defended his questioning of Warder by saying once again that he needed to spike the government notion that Moon was merely a businessman.

> And what I am suggesting to you is that there was in his mind . . . an effort to build a business and church together, this witness understood that to be so, he has so sworn to the grand jury. . . .[77]

For Judge Goettel that argument simply did not wash. To be fair to the court, the defense had not at that point presented a full-blown argument based on the Reverend Sun Myung Moon's unique status as leader of a fund-raising, worldwide religious movement. The government had no intention of dealing with the issue and had said so in no uncertain terms.[78]

The court itself was beginning to doubt that the prosecutor's principal contention was sufficient base for a legal case. Nor could the government simply evade the question of the Reverend Moon's roles as both a businessman and a church leader. After all, Goettel told Flumenbaum, "these people thought they were working for a higher cause. They thought they were advancing the Unification Church's movement internationally." Right or wrong, their belief, in Judge Goettel's view, could not be simply swept under the mat.[79]

Not surprisingly, Moon's lawyer agreed. In Stillman's view, if the "Moonies" were just businessmen, why had they devoted such efforts to creating a seminary or organizing religious conferences? He concluded:

> Your Honor we have a simple choice in this country. We can strip tax-exempt status from all churches, just do it. . . .
>
> But so long as we are going to recognize churches, then obviously we have to recognize this church as well.[80]

Judge Goettel's concern for the First Amendment question, however, had very clear limits. When the government went on a fishing expedition to discover how the Japanese Unification Church had created its assets and recruited members, the court quickly overruled the defense's First Amendment objections, not once but twice.[81]

Goettel, in fact, never viewed the proceedings as a tax case with significant First Amendment questions hanging over the whole. Not enough to make a difference, in any case. At the close of the trial Goettel made his view very apparent: "[M]y thought throughout this had been that even accepting the defendants' position [on the church's tax-exempt status] somebody avoided taxes on these funds."[82]

At least Goettel was candid, though belatedly so. But his candor did not alter this remarkable confession of judicial prejudice. And there wasn't a damned thing the defense could do about it.

If Moon and Kamiyama's lawyers could not convince the court that the First Amendment loomed large in this case, then they could hardly convince a jury of men and women not tuned into finely wrought debates on the rights afforded religion in the United States.

Moon's attorneys, in short, didn't get anywhere with their First Amendment defense of their clients.

So, the prosecution was breathing hard down the necks of the defendants with its success in scoring prejudicial points with the jury. The "clutter" tactic, the heap of evidence introduced by the government lawyers—most of it voluntarily surrendered by Moon and Kamiyama (a fact never mentioned in the course of the proceedings by anyone)—had its desired effect on the jury.

But it also became clear that the defendants contributed to their own problems. At the time, Moon was cheerful and spent much time encouraging his worried followers—including the morose Kamiyama. But some of the trouble the Korean and the Japanese found themselves in was of their own making.

This wasn't particularly surprising.

Although Sun Myung Moon may have been successful in Korea, and Takeru Kamiyama may have unlocked the riches of Japan for the struggling Unification Church, together they knew little about

American business practices and tax laws and its Rube Goldberg maze of procedures that even skilled accountants could get lost in. Nor did Moon's other trusted assistant, Dr. Bo Hi Pak.

This was especially true in the early years of the church in America. Financial records had been poorly kept, if kept at all, and they had been put together, not by professional accountants but by eager church members, most of whom were not American and spoke only limited English. Even the American members of the church who helped with the records knew next to nothing about basic accounting procedures, much less U.S. tax law.

As a result, the sloppy bookkeeping got Moon and his movement in lots of boiling-oil trouble.

But the trouble went deeper and hotter than mere bookkeeping problems. Even when competent accounting help was hired, communication between the bookkeepers and Moon himself was less than perfect. One problem was a compound of cultural and linguistic differences. Another was differing priorities. Moon had a religious vision, while the accountants and lawyers wanted to focus on the bottom line. The resulting clash of style and substance prevented the Unification Church's affairs from being as orderly as apple pie.

In truth, Moon was the founder and head of a religion, a church, and he cared little about earthly goods. Money, houses, cars, to his mind were and are to be used for the expression of true love and were also tools, if you will, to be used in spreading his religious beliefs. Moreover, church members and even Moon himself, I believe, held to the notion it was sacrilege to spend any more time than was absolutely necessary on such nonspiritual things as counting money or bookkeeping. Those church tenets became painfully apparent as the trial progressed.

Communicating with Moon on business affairs was often difficult, if not impossible. One example: a Chase Manhattan loan officer, Eugene Galbraith, recounted on the witness stand his problem in dealing with Moon on a business matter.

The church had arranged for a loan from the Bank of America to one of the church's subsidiaries, the Korean Cultural and Freedom Foundation. To obtain the loan, Moon and his associates had to pledge as collateral a sum of $250,000 in Moon's Chase Manhattan time deposit. If the KCFF for some reason could not repay, the quarter million dollars would be forfeited.

The terms of the loan made Galbraith nervous because he had not received either permission from Moon directly or any signed authority designating the ubiquitous Colonel Pak, Moon's representative on the project, to be the actual agent for the deal.

When Galbraith asked to speak to Moon, Pak demurred, explaining that the Reverend "was almost a holy figure," and therefore was not to be disturbed, particularly over such unholy matters as money.

Bankers don't care about things like that, and Galbraith did not plan to leave his backside uncovered. So, he insisted on speaking to the Reverend. Period. No talk, no collateral.

Reluctantly, Pak agreed and arranged for his boss to speak with Galbraith by phone. Galbraith explained to the court what happened next:

> I then explained to Reverend Moon that in signing this paper he was effectively saying if the Korean Cultural and Freedom Foundation at any time failed to perform on their loan contract and the Bank of America furnished us with a statement to this effect, we would forthwith charge $250,000 to his account, or time deposit, and pay it over to the Bank of America.[83]

Moon's response to Galbraith? "I have complete confidence in Colonel Pak." End of discussion. It was Galbraith's only communication with his customer. And that conversation was sufficient to pledge a quarter million bucks.[84]

Consider the case of Joe Tully, a church member who prepared Moon's first tax returns for the IRS. Tully knew next to nothing about 1040 forms, but at least he could read English. Tully testified during cross-examination from defense lawyer Stillman that the Korean did not want Tully to do anything less than a thorough job on the returns. That directive wasn't much help: Tully failed to have Moon sign his first tax return. Whether this was through sheer ignorance or inability to get access to Moon, Tully's failure was formidable proof of the church's disastrously poor business procedures.

Moon did little in the way of issuing tax and business instructions: not to the Peat, Marwick, Mitchell and Company accountants who were eventually hired by the church, but who never laid eyes on him; not even to his loyal subordinates, including Tully.[85]

As a result, the details of the church's financial matters were often left vague. When the accountants wanted to know Moon's connection with the church importing company (urns and ginseng tea), they had to get their answers through Michael Runyon, yet another young American member of the church who was unfamiliar with the exact structure of various businesses.

Certified public accountant Douglas Green explained to the court:

> Mr. Runyon was unable to ascertain an answer different than the representations that he had given us initially which is that it was his understanding that it was either a contribution or a loan but that he could not make a determination beyond that. That he found nothing that said it was anything either [sic] than that.[86]

Whether a loan or a gift, it was still not taxable, but such answers must have baffled Peat, Marwick. Communicating with Moon's top financial advisor, Takeru Kamiyama, was no easier. Possibly it was worse. Unlike Moon, Kamiyama was no unapproachable holy figure, but his command of English was, if possible, even feebler than his leader's.

Lewis Burgess, an American Unification Church member and an officer in Tong-Il, described for the court his reporting procedures to Kamiyama, an exercise conducted in pigeon English. Did it work? Burgess explained:

> I was never sure whether he understood what I was saying. Sometimes he misunderstood but he would nod his head like that, so I never talked about anything important with him directly because I didn't think he was really understanding what I was saying.[87]

When important matters were considered, translators were used, but the Japanese interpreters more than likely were totally unfamiliar with the language of American business.

It was all very odd. Even more odd was the government's notion that a religious movement in which communication between leaders and followers was either nonexistent or conducted in broken English was also capable of creating a monstrous conspiracy to defraud the U.S. government. The idea certainly tests the limits of human imagination.

But such was Jo Ann Harris and Martin Flumenbaum's story, and they stuck to it.

The confusion and sloppiness of the church's recordkeeping department did not get Moon off the hook. Nor was the issue merely one of bad form. The poor bookkeeping sent Moon and his colleague to the slammer. For the government, the issue was the weak point in the enemy lines, and there they focused their major effort.

Strangely enough, it was Judge Goettel, in a juryless courtroom, who summed up best the prosecution's case against Moon and Kamiyama:

> The government intends to prove that these documents [that composed the so-called family ledger] were fraudulently created. They intend to prove it in a variety of ways, some of which are less convincing than others, but certain of which will show that the documents were not created at the time they purport to be created.[88]

But this was a point much of which the defense readily conceded. The family ledger was a record of contributions to the church's work in America brought in largely by the Japanese faithful. According to the defense, these contributors typically brought with them several thousand dollars in cash in preparation for their stint of missionary work in the United States. All told, the contributions amounted to about $1.2 million spread over a period of four years.

No one ever argued at the trial that the family ledger was complete or accurate. Compiled from notes and other scraps of evidence, the ledger was a reconstruction done by various hands after the money had entered the United States and had been deposited into the Chase Manhattan Bank accounts. Takeru Kamiyama testified twice to the grand jury that the family ledger was prepared after the dates shown on the documents.

Finally, at no time was the family ledger put forward as a contemporaneous record. Nor was its creation ordered by the leadership of the church in order to cover the tracks of Moon's
supposedly real income, the defense argued.[89]

How sloppy was all of this *ad hoc* bookkeeping? Plenty, judging
from the testimony of Robert H. Elliott, Jr., a tax lawyer from the
firm of Caplin and Drysdale. His firm had been retained by Moon
to handle the civil audit of the Unification Church's finances.
According to Elliott, the family ledger was a mare's nest of almost
laughable, but not criminal, dimensions. In his first meeting with
Unification Church leaders, Elliott was told:

> Mr. Kamiyama kept notes of funds received and the people coming
> in, and that they had become confused or too voluminous and had
> been recopied into the books. They later corrected that to say that in
> fact they had been recopied twice. They had once been recopied on
> to a new list and about six months prior to that meeting, this list was
> prepared.[90]

On top of that, the recopied ledger based on Kamiyama's
confused and incomplete notes was prepared in Japanese in six
parallel columns, from left to right, the first containing the contributor's name. The next two columns listed dates, the first
signifying the day the member arrived in the U.S., the second
signifying the date of the member's contribution. The fourth
column noted the amount of money given by each Japanese
member. A fifth column recorded withdrawals, and a final one
gave a running balance to the ledger, a balance that was often in
error. It was purely a homemade job of cash accounting in which
even the simple acts of addition, and especially subtraction, were
often fouled up.[91]

No wonder. The ledger had been put together after four consecutive years of steady foreign contributions. The final compiler of
the family ledger, Yukiko Matsumura, another Japanese member,
had received few instructions about the task—none of them from
Moon or Kamiyama—plus a hodge-podge of odd-sized memoranda, written by various people, from which she was to reconstruct the cash flow. When she had finished the reconstruction,
Matsumura tossed out the original documents.

No one had told her to dispose of the documents; she had simply decided to be neat and tidy. Not surprisingly, Matsumura, six years after the event, had difficulty remembering any details of her ledger project.[92]

Needless to say, Yukiko Matsumura was not a professional accountant.

In any case, the family fund money detailed (more or less) in the family ledger was subsequently transferred to Moon's accounts at the Park Avenue branch of Chase Manhattan Bank.

But even these transfers to the bank were not efficient and businesslike. A lot of the cash was kept in an office in Tarrytown; specifically, in a small metal safe in Matsumura's tiny cubicle of a room that passed for an office. It wasn't petty cash, either, for which the would-be accountant was responsible. At one point, $150,000 was stuffed in the not-so-strongbox which Matsumura stowed in a small closet.[93]

The prosecution would have none of it. This casual approach to cash wasn't merely a peculiar oriental way of doing things, it was an outright lie. The family fund and the ledger—the prosecution's exhibit 863—were nothing less than a gigantic hoax.

Flumenbaum explained:

We don't believe the family fund. . . . What the family fund is [is] an attempt to try to tie up all the loose ends of moneys that flow to Moon. They account for both the household account and the personal account and all of that is strong evidence that all of [those] accounts are Moon's and Moon's money.[94]

That wasn't all there was to the prosecution's theory about the family fund. Because the fund was merely "a figment of somebody's imagination," in Flumenbaum's words, it followed that no Japanese church member ever carried more than pocket change in cash.[95]

Therefore, alleged the prosecution, the ledger had been created out of whole cloth only after the Internal Revenue Service had begun its investigation into Moon's finances. Instead of working from the mythical documents (so conveniently destroyed), the church's not-so-dumb creative accountants had worked backwards from entries in Moon's bank accounts in order to construct the fictional family ledger.[96]

There was just one problem, the government said. Church members had apparently made mistakes in working from the bank account records to create the ledger, which clearly explains why the family ledger had corrections patched over the original entries in order to keep the cover-up intact.[97]

That, at least, was the prosecution's contention. Convinced that the ledger was every inch a fake, Harris and Flumenbaum banged away mercilessly at exhibit 863, the evidentiary *pièce de résistance* of the government's case.

The allegations about the ledger's origin were all part of a magic lantern show on the part of the prosecution. The defense did its best to point that out to the jury. Stillman, for example, readily conceded the amateurish quality of the church's accounting procedures. He freely admitted its many mistakes and also the need to make corrections in such a way that they would never appear to be concealed. The family ledger was a reconstruction patchup job, and Stillman never pretended otherwise.[98]

But accounting mistakes, Stillman reminded the jury, do not disprove that the "monies were, in fact, being brought in by various Japanese members to be pooled for a common purpose."[99]

Stillman had a better argument and he saved it for last. It was an "Is this the way to pull off a tax fraud?" question posed to the jury.

> [G]iven all the time that they had to prepare it, when they realized that there were mistakes on it as they did, and there are crossouts and other numbers written in, but beyond that would you ever make a correction with a patch so that when it is submitted the government can do exactly what Mr. Flumenbaum did here, and that is he lifted up the patch and he saw what was underneath?[100]

Stillman's closing thought on this issue is worth considering:

> Is that the conduct of somebody who is attempting to fool the government? Or is that the conduct of somebody who submits a document ready to acknowledge that there are mistakes in that document and not seeking to hide those mistakes?[101]

There were other holes in the government's attack that the defense lawyers did not point out. The most important was the testimony of Yukiko Matsumura. In detail she recounted how the ledger had been created out of original memos. She flatly contradicted the government thesis that she had simply worked backwards from Moon's bank accounts—bank records, she declared under oath, that she had never seen. Moreover, Matsumura testified that she too had brought money from Japan, collected by her from friends and family.

The prosecution, both indirectly and directly, called Matsumura a liar. If the government's claim had been true, the number of possible perjury counts against her might have been staggering. But the government—in a non-action which suggests the level of confidence its lawyers had in their own thesis—never brought action against Matsumura's alleged lies on the witness stand. Nor did it bother to call to the witness chair any of the hundreds of Japanese mentioned in the ledger in order to grill them on their purportedly fake cash contributions to the church that were made upon entry into the United States.

The defense, it might be added, also did not call any of the Japanese faithful to the stand to rebut the prosecution's arguments about the ledger. The jury was left on its own to puzzle out which side was telling the truth.

But the allegedly false ledger was not the only prosecution attempt to find a smoking gun. Money was the root of the entire case against Moon, so the government sniffed in places other than the family ledger in search of hidden piles of cash that should have been declared as income.

Perhaps, Harris and Flumenbaum thought, undeclared cash was to be found in Moon's household accounts. It was worth a try. And try they did.

The so-called "household account" was set up to take care of the day-to-day expenses of running East Garden—the estate which was home for Moon, his family and staff, as well as headquarters of the Unification Church.

The government wanted to prove that the household account was funded by Moon's personal monies and should therefore be counted as part of the Reverend's income.

Moon's aide Joe Tully, however, testified to the contrary:

I didn't have any understanding that the account was in his name, and thus I had no reason to assume that they were his funds or incomes or anything of the sort.[102]

Despite Flumenbaum's badgering, Tully held his ground.

Sun Myung Moon and Joe Tully weren't the only ones to hold that viewpoint. Peat, Marwick, Mitchell and Company felt the same way.

For example, Peat, Marwick's CPA Douglas Green testified that meals for Moon's children were not taxable "because what was provided for the children was for the convenience of the church to have them there if Reverend Moon was going to stay for longer than a short duration."[103]

The government attempted to make several more assaults on the household account, but was unable to score any serious points beyond injecting several inflammatory suggestions that Moon lived quite well for a religious leader.[104]

The government's strategy to trip up Moon on the household account didn't work because under the First Amendment all clergy—Protestant, Catholic, Jewish—enjoy certain benefits related to their occupation as religious leaders. Those benefits are generally subsumed under the category of parsonage allowances. In the early years of the republic, American ministers and priests tended to be poor as church mice. In order to compensate for low salaries, the local parish or congregation provided housing and other household amenities to keep the parson and his family alive, if not well.

That tradition is kept alive in our tax laws, and Moon, like other clergy, took advantage of them.

The household accounts did not provide the *coup de grâce* so badly wanted by Flumenbaum and Harris. To find it, they had to look elsewhere.

And they did.

To put this case away, the prosecution needed more than piles of paper to impress the jury with "evidence" against the Reverend Moon and his financial advisor, Takeru Kamiyama. It needed more than questionable financial documents and allegedly jiggered household accounts.

In fact, if the government lawyers were not careful, the Korean fish might just slip away because despite a ton of evidence, despite an overtly friendly judge, despite the overwhelming community hostility against Moon and his movement, the legal defense was still credible. What the prosecution had established—putting

aside its innuendo and prejudice—was the confused state of Moon
and his church's finances in the late 70s and the government's own
confusion in trying to understand them. And that kind of confusion argued against the very charge the prosecution was trying to
make: a conscious, deliberate criminal conspiracy to defraud the
U.S. Government.

So the trial was slipping away. And that would be embarrassing,
not to mention damaging to promising careers.

The prosecution recognized that it faced a problem with its
barrage of paper evidence. Documents can impress a jury or put it
to sleep; the latter was something that the Harris-Flumenbaum
duo were not willing to take chances on. Harris' long trial experience told them that jurors tend to be persuaded by living human
beings, not dusty, dry, and dead documents. What would have
more impact than Moon's own associates on the witness stand,
spilling the innermost secrets of the church movement? Even better, they could quiz church dropouts who no longer had any desire
to protect their former Father.

And so they did. Understanding the rhythms of criminal trials,
the prosecution saved what they hoped would be best for last.

CHAPTER VII

THE TRIAL ENDS

This is a court of law, young man, not a court of justice.

OLIVER WENDELL HOLMES

THE church witnesses for the government testified in ascending order of importance to the prosecution's case: first, the current church insiders (all Americans), followed by former members, and finally the out-and-out apostate. It was a strategy that no prosecutor could resist.

It was a good strategy—at least on paper. But even the best laid prosecutorial plans can go awry. Some potential problems had already been anticipated by the government. For one thing, Harris and Flumenbaum knew perfectly well that the church members subpoenaed to testify were at best reluctant to appear at all. One reason: they had all been warned previously by prosecutors that they were on a long list of potential co-defendants and any misstep, just one wrong word under oath, could earn them an indictment and a long vacation in Danbury prison. Consequently they wouldn't be likely to chatter without reserve, and they would most certainly be hard to crack.

Loyalties run deep among members of the Unification Church. Even many former church members wish the movement well and hold no grudges. To its chagrin, the government soon discovered

225

that these well-wishers weren't apt to proffer evidence of criminal behavior on the part of the church. Why? Because the prosecution failed to appreciate one simple fact: persecution and hostility often only deepen bonds among members, or even former members, of a minority group under attack. The Mormons, Gypsies, Jews, and a hundred other ethnic, religious, or racial groups around the world can easily attest to the phenomenon. The prosecution's blind spot on the loyalty issue proved to be a costly mistake in the government's case against Moon and Kamiyama.

But before Unification Church members were dragged in to testify, the government needed to set the right atmosphere. Even before subpoenaing the reluctant church witnesses, the prosecution moved to brand them as unindicted co-conspirators. Sixteen church members were so labelled, representing a large pool of potential informers.

The government hoped that the unindicted co-conspirator designation would deal a devastating psychological blow to the religiously minded, middle-class Americans among the witnesses. To be accused of criminal behavior, or of even being associated with it, could open up many possible avenues of confession. The prosecution knew very well, too, that to the uninitiated, the system of criminal justice in this country is intimidating, even frightening. A witness, properly cowed with the threat of a perjury rap held over him, might be apt to say something he would otherwise keep to himself.

The conspiracy charge also served as a hint to the witnesses that cooperation with the government in the trial might just wipe away this unpleasant business forever.

It was of course a not-so-subtle form of legal blackmail.

This softening-up of the witnesses process wasn't exactly pretty, but the government was reasonably sure it would work. The prosecution was looking for a confession of personal knowledge of wrong-doing, or at least the appearance of it, by church insiders. Hearsay and rumor simply would not fly.

The strategy worked—up to a point. The prospective church member witnesses were, for the most part, distraught by the time the government was through prepping them to testify. Emotionally disturbed is a very soft way of putting it. Several of them never got over the experience.

The prosecution ultimately settled on calling only three current church members to the witness stand. If any of them cracked, then little else would be needed. If they didn't, it would be clear that additional church members would yield no better results. It would be best to move on to calling former members.

CHURCH MEMBERS

The trio of church members summoned by the prosecution to the witness stand included Joe Tully, Keith Cooperrider, and Michael Runyon. Two of the men were in their thirties; Runyon had just turned forty. All three were long-time members and held important positions in the American Unification Church. Most important, they had personally worked with Moon and Kamiyama.

Still, the government's strategy got off to a slow start: all three men had become ill before being called to testify.

Keith Cooperrider, for one, had pneumonia and was under a physician's care.[1]

A week later, Joe Tully's lawyer Michael Keegan reported that his client, too, was ill and violently so. No one was sure quite what Tully was suffering from, but Keegan gave the court a graphic description of Tully's problem:

He vomits, retches and develops diarrhea and is up the entire night. He is unable to function the following day until the late afternoon. He was under no condition to subject himself to the rigors of direct and cross examination.[2]

That wasn't the end of it. A week after Tully reported in sick, Michael Runyon did the same. Runyon had the flu and had to be put on antibiotics. The government's lawyers bitterly complained about the disruption to their carefully planned schedule, but doctors' reports kept them from pushing the absence-through-malingering thesis too hard.[3]

Judge Goettel was also annoyed at the delays. Like the prosecution, he suspected foot dragging by the witnesses—in a remarkably prejudicial comment, he called it "Moon fever." But it wasn't just Moon fever that kept Tully, Cooperrider, and Runyon from showing up as originally scheduled. It turned out they really were sick.

Winter had lingered late in 1982 in New York. Instead of welcoming spring in late March and early April, the city got socked with another winter blizzard. The storm came early in the trial and nearly forced its postponement while participants in the case struggled to reach Foley Square. The long winter had worn down everyone in Gotham, including a number of jurors in the case. Several in fact had to be dismissed and alternates placed on the front bench.[4] The doctors reports and the physical appearance of the witnesses would confirm their illnesses had been real.

Although still weak from their assorted illnesses, the three key church members eventually showed up in the courtroom; one, Michael Runyon, was threatened with federal marshals if he didn't show up. But the trio's ordeal had just begun. Before they got started in the witness stand, however, the witnesses were given one boon. All three, pleading their rights under the Fifth Amendment, were given immunity from any testimony they offered—perjury excepted, of course. Unlike many other legal procedural requests in the trial, the granting of immunity to the witnesses did not prove controversial. Judge Goettel was anxious to get on with the case and the prosecutors were anxious to get Moon. His followers weren't that important.

Bolstered by the court's pique over "Moon fever," the prosecution pushed for one more advantage before any of the church members climbed into the witness chair. The government's lawyers wanted all three men to be declared hostile witnesses.

The designation of the three as hostile to the prosecution had very practical consequences, of which the defense was painfully aware. The "hostile" label gave the government's lawyers a freer hand in grilling Tully, Cooperrider, and Runyon. Virtually no question, even those ordinarily considered leading or badgering, would be disallowed during direct examination.

More important, the prosecution could indulge in yet another privilege after defense's cross-examination of the witnesses. The government could raise entirely new subjects during redirect, introducing issues not included in the previous testimony. This was a privilege not ordinarily allowed the government.

The defense's objections to the automatic labelling of the church witnesses as hostile were brushed aside.[5]

Flumenbaum and Harris were to be allowed a free hand.

Were the church members really hostile? The trial transcript suggests not; in fact, at least two of the three men appear to have been the meekest of hostile witnesses. None of the three was actually overtly hostile, a fact that should come as no surprise.

Unification Church members, like many religious folk, are not red of tooth and claw. They actually tend to be quite respectful of authority, whether religious or civil. Docility, not hostility, is the typical attitude held by church members. This natural docility, combined with the aftereffects of illness and the intimidating atmosphere of a courtroom, hardly constitutes a recipe for producing hostile witnesses.

The "hostile" label given the three church witnesses ultimately proved to be an embarrassment to the prosecution—as well as a source of amusement to legal insiders. It also had the effect of tying the government's lawyers into knots. Even after his initial questioning of a sickly and pliant Tully, Flumenbaum persisted in characterizing the witness as hostile in Goettel's private chambers.

This time the normally get-along Goettel did not share the prosecutor's opinion. Gently dismissing Flumenbaum's characterization of Tully, Goettel suggested a different interpretation of the witness' effort to answer questions under oath:

> [Tully] is not demonstrating overt hostility. What he is demonstrating is a very cautious inability to remember. The answer is never yes or no. It is not, to the best of my recollection, or yes, it might have happened, that kind of stuff.[6]

Tully's caution on the stand was echoed by his fellow witnesses, Cooperrider and Runyon, which one fragment from Keith Cooperrider's testimony amply demonstrates:

> Q: Isn't it a fact that you were concerned about Reverend Moon's tax situation . . . prior to April 1st, 1974?
>
> A: I don't think I was involved in that concern.
>
> Q: You don't think you were involved at all?

A: I don't think so.

Q: Did you have any conversations with Mr. Salonen as to what constitutes a loan to Moon or a gift to Moon?

A: I don't recall such conversation.

Q: Did you have any conversations with William Torrey as to what constitute[s] a loan to Moon or a gift to Moon?

A: I don't recall such conversation.

Q: Did you have any conversations with Mr. Kamiyama about whether to call certain funds received by Moon gifts or loans?

A: I don't recall any such conversation.

Q: Did you have any such conversations with Mr. Matsuzuki?

A: I don't recall any such conversation.

Q: Did you have any such conversations with any attorneys for HSA [Holy Spirit Association]?

A: I don't recall such conversation.[7]

Cooperrider provided more than sixty "don't knows" and "don't recalls" to questions from the prosecution. Flumenbaum and Harris were naturally frustrated by Cooperrider's answers, but his responses were not entirely unexpected. Perhaps a more skilled questioner—it was Flumenbaum who tried to grill Cooperrider and his fellow church members—might have gotten more out of the witness. We'll never know.

Was it convenient amnesia, the programmed poor memory that skirts perjury without committing it and yet doesn't tell the prosecution anything useful?

But though "amnesia" is frequently the easy answer in cases both civil and criminal, with Cooperrider and the other church witnesses, the failure to recall events was not so easily attributable to a convenient lapse of memory.

Flumenbaum had clearly not prepared his line of questions carefully—a typical mistake by a novice prosecutor. Instead, he used a scattershot approach, hoping to hit a target, any target.

As a result, Flumenbaum was reduced to asking Cooperrider a series of questions about phone calls and conversations that occurred over the course of a decade. A back-of-the-envelope estimate suggests that Cooperrider's telephone conversations alone totalled more than 300,000, a fact that makes precise recall of individual calls understandably difficult.

Frustrated, Flumenbaum tried to zero in on finding a connection between Moon and an attempt in 1973 to convert his Chase Manhattan Bank accounts from taxable gifts to nontaxable loans.

Flumenbaum hoped to discover that Moon had given specific instructions regarding the attempt to convert the accounts, and he hoped that Cooperrider would provide the evidence. What Flumenbaum got instead was a hazy recollection about an incident in which the American Unification Church's President Neil Salonen instructed Cooperrider (Salonen's chief of staff at the time) to have a legal memorandum prepared detailing the tax consequences of loans versus gifts.

Although Cooperrider did not remember it, such a memo was indeed prepared and telefaxed to Salonen, who at the time was on a missionary swing through the U.S. with Moon. But Cooperrider could remember nothing about the memo and could not make any direct connection between it and Moon—or Kamiyama for that matter.[8]

With Joe Tully, Flumenbaum was not so gentle. From Tully, the man who had prepared Moon's 1973 tax return, the young prosecutor had expected much. When Tully did not deliver the keys to the kingdom, Flumenbaum tried another approach.

He accused Tully of backdating a document. The junior prosecutor's contention was that Tully and Kamiyama had concocted a scheme to cover up a Moon stock swindle involving the Tong-Il company. Flumenbaum's theory—like many others—was grabbed from the air. This time, he said, he would prove his point by comparing Tully's signature over a period of time to substantiate that Tully had indeed created a backdated document.

Because an individual's handwriting changes over time, the incriminating signature could easily have been placed at a time later than claimed. Or so a handwriting expert was prepared to testify.

Tully denied the charge, leaving Flumenbaum prepared to take him apart on the stand. Flumenbaum faced one major problem, however: neither the defense nor the court was willing to buy his backdating theory.

Moon's lawyers greeted the prosecutor's new theory with angry surprise; as far as they knew, Flumenbaum had dreamed it up on the spot, an evidentiary no-no. Under federal rules the introduction of evidence without letting the other side know beforehand is forbidden. Moreover, in this case expert testimony needed to be brought in—something Flumenbaum had not prepared.

Judge Goettel was also nonplussed by Flumenbaum's sudden introduction of the backdating theory. He was particularly skeptical of the idea of bringing in an expert to testify.

> I would be surprised [he said] that any expert could say that because a name is signed in this fashion it had to be at a different time when these were signed.[9]

Goettel might also have suspected that Flumenbaum's theory was a red herring, designed only to discredit a witness who refused to break under questioning by the prosecution. Goettel's suspicion was soon confirmed. Out of hearing of the jury, Flumenbaum promised, *in camera*, to provide expert testimony on the signatures when the trial resumed the following Monday; in fact, the prosecution discreetly dropped the subject the next week.

If Flumenbaum and Harris wanted something more from a church insider's perspective, they were left with the still bedridden Mike Runyon. With the threat of a visit from a federal marshal's posse hanging over his head, the forty-year-old Runyon finally made his appearance in the courtroom.

Runyon was groggy from his regimen of antibiotics when he took the stand. That was a good omen for the prosecution. Tired and sick as he was, Runyon might slip and let some kind of cat out of the bag and the government lawyer needed a few indiscreet kitties to show off to an increasingly restless jury. Just to be sure, Runyon was subjected to two days of questioning. But unlike the other church witnesses, Runyon wasn't so docile. When Flumenbaum shoved, Runyon shoved back a little harder.

Flumenbaum was anxious to get at Runyon, for good reason. In 1975 he had been the church's liaison with the Peat, Marwick accountants. Beginning in 1976, Runyon performed the same function with Moon's tax lawyers at Caplin and Drysdale. If anyone were the guardian of the family jewels, it was Runyon. The prosecution intended to make the most of him.

After a few feeble questions about the family fund and the by-now infamous ledger, Flumenbaum finally zeroed in on tax questions.

He went through the whole battery. What had Runyon told the accountants and the tax lawyers about Moon's stock in the Tong-Il company? Was it a gift or a loan or a payment?

Unlike earlier witnesses, Runyon did not struggle to remember. His answers tended to be far more precise than those of his peers. His patience under questioning, however, snapped when Flumenbaum asked him to explain why Peat, Marwick's accountants had posed certain questions about Moon's affairs:

> I don't know everything that goes on inside the heads of certified public accountants. I am not trained in that profession myself.[10]

Then Flumenbaum drilled again for new information on the family fund ledger, but came up with a dry hole. Runyon knew of the ledger, was curious about it because it was in Japanese—which he couldn't read—and half-remembered comparing the ledger's numbers with entries in Moon's Chase Manhattan accounts. But he couldn't be sure.

One item in the ledger especially fascinated the government lawyer: a record of twenty-eight Japanese bringing into the country exactly $2,500 each, a total of $70,000. Wasn't it rather odd that twenty-eight people would each be carrying the same sum of money? Flumenbaum, in fact, liked the question so much he asked it four times, and each time Runyon answered: "No, I wouldn't know."[11]

Flumenbaum also tried to establish a connection between Moon and Runyon via Kamiyama, and in doing so attempted to drive a wedge between Runyon's present testimony and his earlier testimony before the grand jury.

The strategy failed. Runyon merely got hotter under the collar, and the defense quickly raised an objection that the court sustained.[12]

Flumenbaum did not give up. He was determined to attack this witness in some fashion and thereby impeach Runyon's testimony. To do so, he moved to new ground. The ground he chose was the Diplomat National Bank, a federal bank located in the Washington, D.C., financial district.

Diplomat had gotten its start in the mid-1970s and was established to cater to the Asian community. The prosecution insin-
uated throughout the trial that Diplomat was somehow yet another
"Moonie" business. It was not. Despite its professed desire to help
out Asians in the Washington, D.C., area, the bank was, in fact,
largely a Korean creation, involving such prominent members of
that community as Jhoon Ree, the owner of a string of karate
clinics, and Tongsun Park, the Korean lobbyist at the center of the
Koreagate scandal of the mid-1970s.

Flumenbaum wanted to know what Runyon knew of Moon's
purchase of stock in the bank. Runyon claimed to know little of the
arrangement, but Flumenbaum persisted, repeating his questions
until they started earning objections from the defense lawyers. For
his trouble, Flumenbaum established no facts that were not already on the record.[13]

Flumenbaum was nonetheless determined to make one last attempt to get something out of Runyon. Anything. During redirect
he made another angle run at proving that Moon had exercised
direct involvement in his various business enterprises, a cor-
nerstone assumption of the prosecution's case.

To do so, Flumenbaum asked Runyon to look at cancelled
checks. Lots of them. The prosecutor wanted Runyon to identify
those that had been signed by Moon. One by one the checks were
offered to Runyon, who in turn verified each signature. Judge
Goettel, exasperated with the exercise and anxious to move on,
eventually snapped at Flumenbaum:

> Give him the whole batch of checks and look at all of them and tell
> us whether you can identify the handwriting other than the signa-
> tures on any of those checks.[14]

But that raised a problem. This "batch of checks" had all been
typewritten, Flumenbaum meekly observed to his Honor, except
for the signatures. "That ends that," Goettel said. "Did Mr. Kamiyama type, do you know?"[15]

Runyon didn't know, but remembered at least some of the
checks were typed in his office, but he could not recall which ones.
Nonetheless, Flumenbaum kept showing him checks and asking
the witness if they had been typed by him.

At that point, defense lawyer Andrew Lawler broke in: "Excuse me, have we switched topics now? Are we now on typewriters?"

Yup, sure are, Judge Goettel observed.

But Flumenbaum pressed ahead. If the check hadn't been prepared in Runyon's office, how about Kamiyama's? To which Runyon shot back: "Many times he [Kamiyama] didn't even have a desk."[16]

That did it. It had been a long week—it was now late on Friday afternoon and the courtroom exploded into giggles. Even Jo Ann Harris had had enough of her colleague's dithering. She put her face in her hands and slumped forward on the table, exasperated. Wisely, Flumenbaum closed the questioning and ended up with a zero for the day.

The dismal failure of the prosecution's strategy up to that point did not end the government's hope to get something out of the church members. The government still had two aces up its sleeve—or so thought Flumenbaum and Harris. What current church members wouldn't or couldn't say, former members would.

FORMER CHURCH MEMBERS

Michael Trulson was the first.

Trulson was then thirty-two, living in California, and out of work. He had left the church after being a member for seven years, but appeared to hold no grudges against Moon or the movement. That came as a disappointment to the prosecution, but Trulson was nonetheless a rare find. He had been an officer in numerous church enterprises, and best of all he once had been in charge of maintenance at Moon's East Garden estate. The latter position of course was of the keenest interest to the government.

The prosecution team did not take any chances this time. After Flumenbaum's inept performance with the earlier church witnesses, Jo Ann Harris took charge of questioning Trulson.

What was she after? Harris explained:

[Moon] was always concerned about how things are going to be financed and asserted control and considerable interest in money.

We also adduce from this witness how Reverend Moon conducted his business sessions with other members of the church and how he then operated all the various facets of the church, including business as well as the religious side of it.

We will get a picture of Reverend Moon as the man who was running the place and very much aware of all the financial situations.[17]

Harris' hidden agenda was to insert into the record a portrait of Moon's allegedly opulent life-style: details on the house, the cars, the horses, the tennis court, the size of the East Garden staff. The defense naturally objected when this kind of stuff was paraded before the jury, but Harris kept insisting that "in any tax case the Government is entitled to adduce life-style and other sorts of income."[18]

Judge Goettel did not buy the government's line. After some gentle badgering from the iron woman, however, the court backed down a bit to allow Trulson to relate his conversations with Moon about money—conversations usually conducted through a translator.

"Well, all right," said Goettel, "but just keep it down. Don't stir it around too much." The warning went unheeded. Harris was determined to show that in Trulson's talks with Moon the Korean had been in charge of everything, down to the last detail.

That was Harris' intention, but the plan didn't quite work out that way. Harris didn't have much more luck than Flumenbaum. For example, when Harris asked the ex-church member a series of questions about Moon's involvement on East Garden projects, the answers weren't quite those expected:

Q: Now, Mr. Trulson, did Mr. Moon sometimes initiate projects for the East Gardens property?

A: No.

Q: Let me show you something. Let me show you Government's Exhibit 875 marked for identification.

A: No, I don't recognize the document.

Q: All right. Would you read it to yourself and I will put the question to you again. All right. Did Mr. Moon sometimes initiate projects on his own with respect to the East Gardens property?

A: He never told me directly . . . I don't recall anywhere where he instructed me directly to initiate a project. It would be through someone else.[19]

Trulson's responses clearly didn't help the government's case. It was questionable that establishing the fact of Moon's control of East Garden improvement projects would prove very much anyway. In her questioning of Trulson, Harris certainly had not yet shown the relevance of the entire exercise.

Further questioning showed that Trulson had never had much direct contact with Moon—although it was clear that the latter's approval was necessary for all major projects. Undeterred by Trulson's less-than-satisfactory responses, Harris continued to chase her prey. Eventually, however, the normally unflappable iron lady was tripped up by her own attempts to snare the witness:

MS. HARRIS: Now, during your time in East Garden did you observe how Reverend Moon collected information and made decisions about those things that he had final decision-making authority about—that was a garbled statement. Do you want me to try that again?

MR. LAWLER: It will save an objection.[20]

Harris, rattled as she was, never managed to frame the question correctly. Instead, the gracious Judge Goettel did:

THE COURT: Are you asking him whether the process would be a question and answer kind of exchange, or a demand for written reports or something of that nature?

MS. HARRIS: Yes.[21]

But that approach didn't yield much either. Trulson's answer to Goettel's rephrased question:

I would very rarely give Reverend Moon a written report. He wouldn't keep it, I would give a very basic outline. As far as anybody else that I watched while at East Garden, all I remember is verbal. I never paid that much attention.[22]

This was not going as planned, so Harris tried a Flumenbaum trick: dazzle the jury with cash, forget the facts. The government knew that the witness had received a gift of a $100 bill from Moon. The government lawyers also knew that Moon had a habit of passing out C notes to other church members at East Garden. Where, they sniffed, did this money come from? It certainly didn't come from the Chase Manhattan accounts.

The court simply wasn't interested. "So what?" Judge Goettel observed. The prosecution dropped the issue.[23]

But it wasn't a complete shutout. Harris did manage to get Trulson to testify that Moon had displayed significant interest in the setting up of the first church-financed newspaper, *News World.* But it was a small victory for the prosecution. No one from the defense table had ever denied that the Korean took an enormous interest in larger church projects. It would have been strange if he hadn't.[24]

What that kind of interest proved in relation to the tax case, however, was another matter.

Although Trulson's performance on the witness stand had disappointed the government, it was not entirely a surprise. Trulson had left the Unification Church, but he had not shown any signs in the earlier grand jury testimony that he was overtly hostile to the church.

The next witness, another former church member, was a different story. Michael Young Warder had not only been a top official within the American Unification Church, his departure had not been a cordial parting of ways.

Warder was no groundskeeper. Prodded by his wife, who was heartily sick of her husband's working for and kowtowing to Asians, Warder took a walk, never looking back. His departure had badly shaken the church—the closely-knit American members in particular.

The prosecution had invested great hopes in Warder, and in his own way he did not disappoint. His testimony—indeed, Warder's motives—spelled trouble for both the government and the defense.

Since leaving the church in November 1979, Warder had had a tough time of it. Comparable employment outside the movement (among other things, Warder had been publisher of *News World* and president of the International Cultural Foundation, another key church organization) had proved very difficult to find. In fact, he had been without work for months after his exit from the church, and a nagging spouse was surely no help. Neither were three young children.

Warder drifted through a series of temporary positions with conservative think tanks, beginning with the Heritage Foundation in Washington, D.C. Typical of its genre, Heritage paid staff poorly and offered no security whatsoever. About all that could be said for Warder's jobs at Heritage, and later at the Ethics and Public Policy Center (also in Washington, D.C.), and finally at the Rockford Institute in Rockford, Illinois, was that none was church-connected.

All of this raised the ugly question of whether Warder had promised helpful testimony if the prosecution helped him to secure a job with the federal government, a job in which his former church affiliation might ordinarily create problems.

The makings of a deal between Warder and the prosecution were apparent even with only circumstantial evidence. For example, Warder turned over a dozen detailed diaries kept by him— ironically, at Moon's suggestion—between 1973 and 1979. The diaries were a treasure-trove of Unification Church information— just what the government had been seeking for years.

Equally tantalizing was Warder's grand jury testimony. In a grand jury proceedings, the prosecution's goal is to elicit enough evidence or the appearance of evidence to provide the basis for an indictment.

Warder had provided that with a vengeance.

Normally grand jury transcripts are sealed, but the record of one of several appearances that Warder had made for the prosecution became available.

At the grand jury, Warder seemed to be a dream witness for the prosecution. He virtually confirmed the worst suspicions that the government held about Moon and the Unification Church.

But did Warder tell the government what it wanted to hear? In many preliminary meetings with the prosecution was he carefully coached to give the government's spin on any and all of the anecdotes he related to both the grand and petty juries?

The reader must judge from the testimony. Here is a sample of Warder's wares.

Warder first told the grand jurors that at the time of the purchase of the East Garden estate, Moon told his followers that it had been done with "his money," undercutting the later defense claim that Moon was a trustee or a nominee of the church.[25]

Warder, however, was only warming up.

He also threw cold water on the family fund by suggesting that Kamiyama had concocted the story of Japanese members bringing in funds as a cover for his purchase of Tong-Il stock. Warder recounted Kamiyama's cynical observation that such a story would be difficult to check by American authorities. Possibly because Japanese all look alike. Exactly what was the actual source of the moneys for the family fund was not made clear by Warder; indeed, he was not asked that question by the prosecutor—a very curious loose thread.[26]

What the prosecutor really wanted was an explanation of why Kamiyama had needed to procure the Tong-Il stock. Reason? Kamiyama needed his visa renewed.

"In order to do that," Warder said, "he had to be a majority stockholder in a corporation. That was the tactic he wanted to use to ensure keeping a visa."[27]

Making Kamiyama look bad was only the beginning. The Kamiyama revelation was followed by Warder's vague allegation that church officials, including possibly Michael Runyon, had been busy backdating documents designed to create the illusion of a church pension fund, a useful device to avoid tax payments.[28]

But the accusations against Kamiyama and Runyon were small potatoes compared to taking on the Reverend Sun Myung Moon, the prosecution's next move.

Warder told of meetings attended by Runyon, Kamiyama, Tully, and Warder himself in which they agreed to have Moon "appear to be as removed as possible from the day-to-day workings of any of these activities." In other words, Warder and company had been involved in a cover-up; even the term "stone-walling"—made memorable by the Watergate scandal—had frequently been used, according to the former church official. Their meetings took on the added flavor of conspiracy when Warder noted that those involved "agreed" that all their conversations had never happened; they of course had never been recorded.[29]

Now Moon was directly involved. The problem of the church

money and to whom it belonged, according to Warder, involved a good deal of discussion:

> A: Well, one thing that was discussed had to do with Moon being in effect a trustee for the Church.
>
> Q: Or a nominee?
>
> A: Or a nominee or trustee, a representative of some sort, so he was holding money even though the bank account might be in his name on behalf of the Church.
>
> Q: When those discussions took place, were those discussions in the nature of planning what to do in the future, or of explaining transactions that already had taken place in the past?
>
> A: It was an attempt to explain things that had been done in the past.
>
> Q: Would it be fair to say that those discussions took place in the context of trying to develop an ex post facto explanation for what had occurred?
>
> A: Right.[30]

Warder threw a few other dirtballs at his former colleagues—several big ones—a rather remarkable achievement in testimony of less than twenty pages.

Warder's grand jury testimony was, of course, only the beginning. Warder had been questioned by a friendly prosecutor. Since no defense attorneys are present during grand jury proceedings, Warder was not subject to cross-examination.

But was there a deal between Warder and the government? Let's look at this more closely. In 1980 and 1981, Warder had ten meetings with Martin Flumenbaum, and during the first he was threatened with indictment. Until that first meeting, Warder had been very reticent in talking about his former church to anyone, least of all the feds. After that meeting, however, he had become very cooperative, turning over those fat and intimate diaries. Even something of a personal relationship developed between the former publisher and the prosecutor—Flumenbaum called him "Mike" several times during the Moon trial.

It was all very cozy, but was there more to it than mere coziness? The defense lawyers thought so, but couldn't prove it until a document fell into their hands very late in the trial. It was a letter signed by Michael Warder, attached to a resume which listed the Department of Justice as a job reference. Warder apparently had sent many of these notes around the sprawling federal bureaucracy in the hope of finding a good job. The matter was potentially explosive. The government team of Flumenbaum and Harris not surprisingly were outraged at the letter's introduction into evidence. Arguing on the basis of technicalities, they attempted to keep it out of the record, but they failed. Goettel allowed it to be placed into evidence anyway.[31]

Finding the letter came a little too late to make much of a difference. Warder had already testified by the time the letter was introduced into evidence. He had also been subjected to cross-examination, a process that tends to be a lot more impressive to a jury than an impeaching bit of evidence introduced at the tail end of a trial. Even in their summation to the jury, neither defense lawyer more than hinted at Warder's true motives for testifying. In the end, the Warder resume remained only a clue—a shred of evidence of a possible deal that Warder had made with the prosecutors. But the resume wasn't conclusive proof, and lawyers on both sides knew it.[32]

The question remains: did Warder stand and deliver during the trial itself? In the end that's all that counted. Everything else was only the overture.

And Warder had a lot to live up to. The media, which had long lost interest in a proceeding that had quickly become an exceedingly dry tax trial, pricked up their ears when they sniffed an "Ex-Church Member Discloses Sect's Top Secrets" sort of story. As we say in the newsroom, the story wrote itself.

On the stand, Michael Warder tried hard to live up to the advance billing. But a trial out in the open was different from a secret grand jury proceeding, so this time it wasn't so easy. He was nervous. Facing a room full of former friends, including his former leader, Warder was not in a comfortable situation. Warder's gaze never left Flumenbaum—in fact, he never once looked in Moon's direction. It was just Marty and "Mike."

Things went wrong for Warder from the start. What should have been a piece of cake nearly turned into a mistrial thanks to a near fatal legal *faux pas* on the part of Flumenbaum.

The young prosecutor began with routine questions about the witness' background, including Warder's first encounter with Moon. Before proceeding with that particular question, however, Flumenbaum paused and asked for a side bar; that is, a meeting of the court's officers out of earshot of the jury.

The following colloquy speaks for itself:

> MR. FLUMENBAUM: It might be out of an excess of caution I was going to ask him how he regarded Reverend Moon in '71, and I think he will say he regarded him as the Messiah.
>
> MR. STILLMAN: For God's sake.
>
> THE COURT: No. No. That won't go. It has nothing to do with this case.
>
> MR. STILLMAN: It will be like starting tomorrow morning. We'll pick a jury again.
>
> MR. FLUMENBAUM: I am glad I had a side bar.[33]

Having missed (barely) a nasty pitfall that might have caused a mistrial, Flumenbaum moved on to his main theme: namely, the current witness had enjoyed a special relationship with the Reverend Moon and thus was privy to the man's secrets—or at least to how Moon conducted his business. Unlike other witnesses, Warder was prepared to tell the prosecutor what he wanted to hear: that Moon took a deep interest in the details of running the movement including its businesses.

For example, regarding the church's religious training programs, Warder testified that Moon typically decided:

> [T]he length of lectures, what to do during non-lecture time; the number of days a person should hear lectures and the number of days that they should do fund raising; the number of days they should witness.[34]

The questions went on and on about who would fund-raise and for how long and how much—to the intense irritation of the defense, who charged that the questions were irrelevant, inflammatory, and trespassed on First Amendment ground.

Goettel did not agree.

Then Flumenbaum had Warder testify that, during his tenure

as president of the Tong-Il company, he had acted essentially as a figurehead, while Moon and his Asian associates conducted the real business of the firm. Whether any criminal activity had taken place, however, was hard to judge. The meetings involving Tong-Il were conducted—as was all church business—in a loose, informal, fluid manner and mostly in Korean, a language that Warder did not understand, except, apparently, the word for ginseng tea.[35]

After a short, sharp jab directed at Kamiyama's visa problem, Flumenbaum had his witness trot through a welter of documents detailing church operations in the business and cultural areas.

With the background established, Flumenbaum began playing hardball. First, he hit his favorite theme: the family fund and its ledger.

Dutifully, Warder repeated his grand jury testimony. In all of Warder's conversations with church leaders, especially with Takeru Kamiyama, had the subject of Japanese bringing in money ever come up? Warder asserted that his impression had been that the missionaries sent from Japan possessed little more than the blue suits on their backs upon arrival in this country.[36]

Except, perhaps, in one instance.

Warder proceeded to tell an odd little story that he apparently remembered only after appearing before the grand jury eighteen months earlier. Recalling a conversation that had taken place in late spring of 1974, Warder recounted being told by Kamiyama about the financing method for an upcoming science seminar in the U.S. The funding process was simple. Japanese attendees of the seminar were each to come with $5,000 in their pockets.

Kamiyama's explanation, Warder claimed, made him uneasy at the time. Although bringing such a sum of money into the U.S. was legal (in fact, more could have been brought in by declaring the amount on a customs form), Warder recommended a wire transfer of the money instead. Warder also told Kamiyama that to do otherwise would "cause problems" with the Immigration and Naturalization Service—problems left unspecified by Warder.

Kamiyama rejected Warder's advice. Why? Warder testified:

[H]e told me that the problem with that was that then there would be a trail of money which could be established at a later date, and that that would cause problems for the Japanese church relations with the Japanese government. That money, he told me, was money that was not shown on the Japanese church books, and because the income for the Japanese church was taxed by the Japanese government. So if it was brought in that way then there would be a trail and then possibly the Japanese government could go after the church for—to tax the money.[37]

Was what Warder was saying true? Who knows? Flumenbaum apparently couldn't have cared less because he didn't follow up on the response. Meanwhile, the testimony was a twofer. It helped to discredit the idea that there was a family fund in the first place, and it suggested not so subtly to the jury that if the "Moonies" were willing to break the law in one country, why not here as well?

But Moon was Flumenbaum's real target, not Kamiyama, and Moon he would have—with Mike Warder's help.

First, Flumenbaum tried a flank attack. No hearsay, Warder's testimony was to come only from his direct knowledge.

Here's what happened. According to Warder, in 1974 or 1975 the newspaper "publisher" needed more money to meet his church-approved budget commitment (presumably for *News World*). He had heard of the Chase Manhattan accounts and had asked Kamiyama's permission to tap that source.[38]

Nothing doing, Kamiyama supposedly replied, "that's Father's money, you can't—that is not accessible." This exchange allegedly took place several times. The implication is obvious. Warder's testimony about Kamiyama's comments directly undercut the defense's contention that Moon was a trustee of those accounts.[39]

But did it really? That question had to wait to be explored later during cross-examination. Meanwhile, it is worth remembering that several languages and cultures were involved in the exchanges detailed by Warder. It was only an assumption on Warder's part that, if he indeed said them, Kamiyama's words literally meant that Moon had possession of the accounts for private use. Just shorthand for indicating these accounts were managed differently.

Flumenbaum did not waste time exploring such possibilities. His tactics were classic. Hit and run. Suggest criminal intent where there was none and then move on. Flumenbaum continued to attack Moon, this time on the Diplomat National Bank stock issue.

In a long and contentious side bar, Flumenbaum told the court he wanted to go after the obstruction charge, using Warder as the chief witness. To do so, he needed to delve once more into the Diplomat Bank stock purchase by Moon and his associates. Flumenbaum made the request despite the government's previous promise not to do so; Judge Goettel had already decreed the topic to be irrelevant to the indictment, as well as quite probably inflammatory.

Flumenbaum then wanted to explore the Securities and Exchange Commission investigation of the church's bank stock purchase, somehow tying that investigation to the IRS tax probe that had begun at about the same time.

Flumenbaum's plans raised numerous objections from the defense. Even Judge Goettel had a difficult time following Flumenbaum's byzantine logic.

"How do you say the two merge?" he asked the prosecutor. "I don't understand that."

Flumenbaum tried to explain. With an air of rushed improvisation, he argued:

> Well, the question becomes, in Diplomat we have large amounts of stock being purchased, some of which comes out of Moon's bank account. How do you account for these stock purchases? How do you account for money—in addition to Moon, Moon gets stock, Kamiyama gets stock, somebody wants to know where is this money coming from? Are they acting in concert under Moon? What is the source of that money? Should we say it is church funds, should we say it's Moon's funds? What is the best explanation? And there are various conversations, and that impacts directly on the Chase account. Because that is the source of some of this money. And certainly the source of all the emphasis on Moon himself, and the bottom line is you have to protect Moon.[40]

It was a Niagara Falls-sized question with only a trickle of relevance to the case. Stillman and Lawler were quick to point that out. There was no secret about where the money had come from to buy the Diplomat Bank stock, Stillman argued. Flumenbaum knew as well as anyone that the money had come from the Chase Manhattan account. Nor was Stillman willing to let the government get away with making and then bending a promise. "[T]o now boot-

strap themselves into it I think flies in the face of the representa-
tions that they made to your Honor," he said.[41]

Like a dog with a rag, Flumenbaum wouldn't let go. He charged
that Warder and other top American church members had conspired to cook up a story for the SEC during that agency's investigation into the church. If there had been one cover-up, why not
another?

Flumenbaum faced one problem with that line of thinking.
Strictly speaking, the SEC inquiry wasn't relevant to any part of
the government indictment. Moreover, the Wall Street watchdog
had looked for—and failed to find—a church plot to take over the
Diplomat Bank by failing to file the requisite form to indicate a
change in ownership.

Faced with completely contradictory arguments from the prosecution and the defense, Judge Goettel typically waffled. Yes, some
of the issues were extraneous and possibly prejudicial. That was
not good. Indeed, that was bad. So, Goettel concluded:

> I want you to keep to a minimum the extent to which you have to
> touch on the substance of the Diplomat National Bank case which is
> a separate case and one which is not part of this indictment.[42]

Goettel's judgment on the Flumenbaum request was akin to
telling the fox he could enter the hen house, but only if he promised not to stay too long. The court's compromise, in fact, was a
cave-in to the prosecution, and the lawyers on both sides knew it.
Having broken one promise already, Flumenbaum happily agreed
to the new terms.

Why not? The "compromise" had cost the government nothing
and allowed Flumenbaum to do what he had intended to do with
Warder in the first place.

Skirmishes over, Flumenbaum was ready to launch the major
attack, the set piece maneuver of the whole trial.

First came a major assault on Kamiyama. Drawing on earlier testimony, the prosecutor asked Warder to recall a spring 1976 conversation that Warder had with Moon's financial advisor. Warder
recalled worrying about having to explain to curious government
investigators the source of the money used to buy Tong-Il stock.

No problem, Kamiyama had said to Warder. The money was to come from "a large number of Japanese individuals." It was the family fund story all over again, but this time on a larger scale.

But, Warder had asked of Kamiyama, What if even one of these Japanese money angels gets his story wrong? Kamiyama responded that there would be no slip-ups. Moreover, no government authority in Japan would report anything amiss to his counterpart in the U.S. because the two governments were not on such close terms.

The Kamiyama line, Warder claimed, was to be peddled to the SEC and the IRS, if necessary. As for Warder's own problem of explaining how he had gotten the money for his Tong-Il stock purchase, he was instructed to lie and say that it had come from friends and relatives.[43]

The second assault by Flumenbaum was directed at everyone else, including, of course, Moon. Flumenbaum invited Warder to recall a series of conversations, also allegedly held in 1976, that had featured Kamiyama, Tully, Runyon, and Warder—conversations about Moon's growing financial troubles with the American government.

The discussions revolved primarily around one question: To whom did the money really belong—Moon or the church? What were the tax consequences of both options? Underlying these conversations was the stated need to protect the founder of the movement: the Reverend Sun Myung Moon. Worries were expressed about the possibility that low-level clerks in the church could unwittingly get the church leaders into legal trouble. There was even some concern expressed about what a former member might say to the government!

Then, according to Warder, the group discussed the tactics to be followed if any of them were called to the witness stand. Should he plead the Fifth Amendment? Claim not to remember? Lie?

Warder then drove the nail into what Flumenbaum hoped was the church members' collective coffin:

> We discussed the possibility of somebody being a scapegoat, or fall guy in the proceeding where a person could simply say it was my fault, and that person would thereby protect Reverend Moon.[44]

Warder's comment qualified perhaps as a coffin nail, but certainly not as a stake driven through the heart of Moon's defense.

The admission fell short of Flumenbaum's goal. By Warder's own account, Moon had never been part of the series of cover-up conversations. The charges of conspiracy lodged against him remained unproven.

But Flumenbaum wasn't ready to give up. He had one more radioactive, he hoped, bit of dirt to drop on the church, courtesy of Warder. Flumenbaum wanted to know: Had the witness ever lied under oath for Moon? The record showed that he had, at least once before.

Warder said that, when he testified before the SEC, he chose not to remember or opted to change the emphasis of a particular conversation with another church member in his recollection for the record. In recalling one such discussion during his SEC testimony, he characterized the conversation as entirely theological in character, although banking was thoroughly discussed at the time.[45]

Why did Warder mischaracterize or "forget" the conversation? To help Moon, of course. Flumenbaum himself "forgot" to ask the next, obvious critical question: Was Warder prompted by anyone to do so?

In any case, Flumenbaum was soon off on another line of inquiry. Flumenbaum wanted to know more about Warder's confessed habit of signing false affidavits—as always, to help his leader. One of Warder's signed affidavits had asserted that *News World*'s board of directors was independent of Moon and the Unification Church. Warder's fib had nothing to do with any government investigation, but a good lie is always worth repeating.[46]

In spite of all the nasty stuff, the government hadn't yet nailed Moon. Flumenbaum still couldn't place the alleged culprit at the scene of any crime. To put it another way, Flumenbaum had landed some rabbit punches, but he hadn't severed anybody's jugular vein, least of all Moon's. Not willing to give up, Flumenbaum proceeded to elicit from his witness a recollection of a conversation with Moon in which the Korean allegedly ordered *News World* to publish articles that were critical of the Internal Revenue Service.[47]

That revelation brought the defense to its feet for yet another side bar with Judge Goettel.

Over the defense's protest, Flumenbaum pressed for permission to proceed with Warder's testimony about Moon's order to have negative newspaper articles about the IRS appear in the newspaper. The prosecutor also wanted Warder to talk about Moon's instructions to *News World* to file a request under the Freedom of Information Act to obtain all the "dirt" on him that the government had gathered.

Before the defense could voice any objection, the court stepped in to ask, quite rightly, that Flumenbaum show how the promised testimony was related to the indictment.

The obstruction of justice charge, Flumenbaum replied.

How so? Goettel asked.

Flumenbaum argued that Warder's testimony proved that Moon was aware of the investigations.

So what? responded the court. Marty Flumenbaum's rejoinder was a non sequitur: "[Moon] specifically directed [*sic*] smear campaign against Congressman [Donald] Fraser." That action, said Flumenbaum, showed that Moon was in control and was involved in actions designed to thwart the investigation.[48]

But the court didn't buy it. Goettel replied:

> It is one thing to oppose an investigation openly, it's another thing to obstruct justice by having people testify falsely. But I am not sure that the jury can necessarily discriminate between these two.[49]

But then Goettel became Goettel once again. Instead of throwing out the prosecution's whole line of questioning on the ground that it was not connected with any part of the indictment, Goettel once more compromised. Flumenbaum was allowed to ask questions about Moon's knowledge of the investigations and how he had acquired that information, but no details please.

Defense counsel Stillman protested. Flumenbaum was trying to pull off the same stunt that he had managed earlier with Warder's testimony regarding the Diplomat Bank, charged Stillman. The *News World* line of questioning had nothing whatsoever to do with the indictment at hand, not to mention the fact that the IRS had not been a serious concern of the church at the time of the alleged smear campaign.

Goettel shifted again.

It has got to be connected with the Internal Revenue in some fashion
or other. I realize that several of these things ran parallel to each
other for a while but it has to connect with the Internal Revenue.[50]

After stating (and restating) the guidelines of questioning for
Flumenbaum, and in the welter of exchanges, the court—
typically—forgot the main point. What did any of this have to do
with the charge of obstruction of justice that Flumenbaum had so
glibly thrown out only minutes before as his rationale for pursuing
the *News World* question?

After the side bar, Flumenbaum was allowed to ask two questions: Had Moon known that the IRS was investigating him? Did
News World file a FOIA (Freedom of Information Act) request?
The answers were, of course, yes. The second affirmative got a
caveat from the court that was addressed to the jury: FOIA requests were done all the time and they were perfectly proper.[51]

What the jurors made of the entire question-and-answer period
is a matter we won't go into here.

Such was the last shot (well, almost the last shot) from Flumenbaum and his star witness. It was now up to the defense lawyers to
launch their counterattack. For once, it was an aggressive assault,
featuring bitter exchanges between the two sides.

At one point Flumenbaum objected to a bit of testimony on the
basis of its being hearsay. Defense counsel Lawler was incredulous.
"They have spent most of their direct . . ." he charged before being
interrupted.

> MR. FLUMENBAUM: Mr. Lawler, if you want to have a speak-
> ing objection we can do it at the side bar. It is not appropriate in
> front of a jury and you know it.
>
> MR. LAWLER: Now you are making a speech and you tell me
> not to make one?[52]

Warder was not apt to be treated with kid gloves by the defense. His earlier testimony had already been peppered with
numerous objections from the defense, especially in the delicate
area of conversations with other church members. Where?
When? Who? Stillman and Lawler had kept asking Warder about
the alleged cover-up conversations. Warder could never recall in
precise detail.

Now cross-examination gave the defense a direct shot at Warder's testimony, and Stillman had the first go at the government
witness.

He took dead aim at Warder's truthfulness, a common tactic
among lawyers when a witness has admitted to lying under oath, as
Warder had confessed doing on several occasions. Early and often
the question came up, directly and indirectly, for the benefit of the
jury. The assumption that Warder could never be trusted ran
through the cross-examination.

Stillman then introduced another theme, this time focusing on
Warder's numerous meetings with the prosecution. He gently suggested that Warder's memory of events had vastly improved after
those encounters.

Stillman cited an instance before the grand jury in which Warder could not remember a specific conversation with Moon, only to
recall it later in his trial testimony. Why the sudden recall? Warder
mumbled something about documents refreshing his memory, but
wouldn't or couldn't say which ones.[53]

Stillman smelled blood. First, he read Warder's earlier testimony
to the grand jury about Moon's management ability:

> He didn't have a very good grasp [Warder said], it seemed to me,
> legal distinctions between corporations, at least he didn't act that
> way. He saw it all as one enterprise and under his direction.[54]

Only a moment before, Warder had told Stillman that Moon
"had a good grasp of the distinction between corporations."[55]

So, Stillman asked, which is the truth?

Warder was not stupid. He tried the long and complicated approach:

> Well, when we started the new corporations they were started for
> specific purposes. So I think that there was a grasp in the sense that
> these corporations were set up to accomplish certain things as dis-
> tinct entities. And it seemed to me at the time I was a church
> member, while I was a church member, that often times the distinc-
> tion was not significant in a functional sense.
>
> In other words, he would see all of these different distinct entities as
> under his control. So I think he did see them as separate entities, but
> he saw them all as under his control.

Now for me as a church member at that time given the responsibilities I had, it seemed to me at that time that there was no great
significance to those distinctions.[56]

Stillman wasn't satisfied. He still wanted an answer to his question. Warder had given two very different accounts of Moon's
management style. Was it Answer A or Answer B? Stillman never
got what he was looking for. All Warder did on restatement was
make more fudge.

Well, I think at times his grasp was quite good and at times his grasp
was poor. And I think he understood how he wanted to grasp at the
time he grasped.[57]

Right.
Stillman asked Warder if Moon had ever asked him to lie for the
cause—a question conveniently neglected by Flumenbaum. The
answer was flat out "no." Had he ever been coached by Moon to
give evasive responses to anyone in authority—a crucial point with
regard to the charges against Moon of conspiracy? The answer
was again "no." Would Warder have lied, if he had been asked?
"I think I probably would have," Warder confessed, falling into
Stillman's truthfulness trap.[58]
In other words, Warder had lied to the SEC, signed false af-
fadavits, and would lie if instructed to do so, all for no apparent
gain. The unstated question, and its answer, was obvious: What
would prevent Warder from lying once more for the prosecution if
it would keep him out of jail, land him a job, and make him a few
bucks?
In addition to tripping up Warder on the truthfulness question,
Stillman succeeded in driving a wedge between Warder's past and
present testimony on an important aspect of his former boss' role
in the church.
Moon's lawyer proceeded to stir up doubts about Warder's own
importance in the movement, which importance was a dead center
assumption in the government's case against Moon and Kamiyama. Although Warder didn't make it especially easy for Stillman, the defense attorney managed to get Warder to betray his
lack of knowledge about the inner financial workings of the

church. For example, Warder was forced to acknowledge that he knew almost nothing about Moon's tax returns in the years under question. Nor could he recall much of anything about the Chase Manhattan accounts and how they were set up. Nor had Moon ever discussed the accounts with him or how Warder should testify about them if asked to.[59]

With that, Stillman handed the baton to Lawler. Lawler, if anything, was even more scathing.

Andy Lawler, of course, was Kamiyama's lawyer. He naturally wanted to know more about the talk that Warder had with Kamiyama about the latter's visa problem. Lawler pushed hard, picking and probing till he found a weak spot in Warder's recollection. Like his partner for the defense, Lawler found contradictions between Warder's earlier grand jury testimony and his more recent memory. He asked Warder to explain an anomaly. If Kamiyama was so eager to be a majority shareholder of Tong-Il and thus get a trader's visa, and if Warder was part of the scheme, why was Warder's signature not on the stock certificate signing over the shares?

As president of Tong-Il, Warder's sign-off would have been normal procedure.

Warder could not explain: a strange thing since his memory of the matter had seemed so precise during direct examination.[60]

To close his cross-examination of the witness, Lawler wanted to go over Warder's testimony regarding Kamiyama and the family fund. Yes, Mike Warder had heard about the $50,000 brought in by the Japanese for the science seminar, but he had no personal knowledge about how it was actually done.

Lawler sprang his trap. "I understand that," he said, "but you have told us a lot about what other people told you." Indeed, Warder had not hesitated before to repeat what he'd heard from others; why the diffidence now? When what he merely heard would tend to reinforce the defense's contention that the family fund really did exist, a contention Warder had been perfectly willing to bring into question on the sole basis of what he had been "told." The fact is the most crucial testimony that had been offered by Warder (and encouraged by Flumenbaum) up to that point had, in fact, been merely hearsay.

Not surprisingly, Flumenbaum tried to cut off this line of inquiry. But the court allowed Lawler to repeat his question about the extent of Warder's knowledge of other money coming into the United States by way of Japan.

"I thought there was," Warder said, changing his story. A flurry of objections left the question vaguely answered, but not before Kamiyama's lawyer managed to take another crack at Mike Warder's earlier testimony.[61]

There was one other curiosity: the diaries that Warder had so carefully prepared and then turned over to the government. Before testifying, Warder apparently hadn't bothered to review them, with the exception of a couple of pages the government had specifically asked him to look at. During cross-examination it became clear that the entries he had reviewed did not deal with any of those damaging conversations he supposedly had with Kamiyama.[62]

Why hadn't Warder reviewed those passages in the diary that did deal with the conversations? Because there were few, if any. Warder knew it. So did the prosecution. As they say in South Philly where I went to school: "This dog don't bark."

That was it for Michael Young Warder.

Well, not quite.

Prosecutor Flumenbaum was less than ecstatic with his star witness' performance under cross-examination. The man had diminished in importance to the government's case. Key parts of his testimony had been impeached.

Warder's performance was not a strong one but Flumenbaum was determined to rescue what he could, getting in the last word on redirect. In what was an obviously rehearsed bit of business, the prosecutor asked Warder how he had changed since leaving the church.

Recognizing the softball, Warder belted it out of the park for the benefit of the jury:

At the time I was a member of the church I thought that the best good I could do would be to help Reverend Moon. And at the time I thought that by signing that document that we would help him. Since I have left the church I no longer consider that to be the standard of what's good, and I accept the authority of the Court and the government as an arbiter of right and wrong and other things, and the truth.[63]

The government wasn't quite ready to rest its case. Although its star witness had served as a kind of dissonant climax—like the last bar from a Charles Ives symphony—Mike Warder had not shone as brightly as the government's lawyers had hoped. The prosecution's contention that Warder was going to provide the *coup de grâce* to Moon and Kamiyama had gone a-glimmering.

It was worse than that. The burden of proof on the government was to prove beyond a reasonable doubt. Warder just hadn't come through. Yet the prosecutors were not without their reserves. To give their cause a dramatic finishing touch, the government saved for last a trio of "experts" to wrap up the case with bright ribbon and a pretty bow.

EXPERT WITNESSES

The first, Pearl Tytell, was a "questioned document examiner" or handwriting expert. Tytell had been in the business more than thirty years—a virtual fixture at Foley Square with some three hundred legal cases under her belt.

The prosecution had hired Tytell to review Unification Church records more than a year before the trial began. One of her specialities was and is the ability to date documents based on handwriting. Because a person's script changes over the course of time, Tytell tracks such changes to determine when a particular sample of handwriting was written. Although far from being an exact forensic science, the handwriting analysis procedure is one that's good enough to get people in or out of trouble.

Pearl Tytell was an expert. No one doubted her ability, including the lawyers at the defendants' table. Consider the authority with which she compared Sun Myung Moon's signature over the years:

> I call to your attention the difference in the style of the capital S of the first name, and you will note that the first four signatures in the group questioned have the print style S, whereas the last one above the legend, Exhibit 82, is the cursive style, or the regular S.

> It was noted among the documents examined—written by Mr. Moon—that around the very early years of 1974, and it is possible

there was a transitional period at the end of '73, when Mr. Moon first started to use the style of capital S that you see that used in Exhibit 82, that would be an identifying feature of when the signatures were written. It can clearly be used as a dating factor. . . .

The reason that I point out the difference of the capital S is because having taken the exemplars in 1981 the signatures that were written by Mr. Moon at that time of course used the capital S, the cursive style S, that he started to use around 1974. And that is why there was no signature written in 1981 that had the printed S. However, he still used the printed style S that you can see illustrated in the exemplars when writing his initials in order to identify each of the forms that he wrote.

And so that is where the printed style S's were taken and do compare as can be observed with the printed style S's in the signatures prior to the 1974 period.[64]

Tytell's recital was a show-stopper. The jurors' eyes did not glaze over; they followed her testimony with clear fascination. Here was a live human being who knew what she was talking about, sprinkling her testimony with enough jargon to impress without totally confusing them. Pearl Tytell, in short, was a pro.

Although the elaborate show-and-tell did not materially affect Moon, Tytell's testimony did have a profound impact on Kamiyama. The handwriting expert went through samples of the Japanese's handwriting and determined that his signature appeared on checks at various times, and that loan agreements bearing his name (and Joe Tully's) had been pre-dated. In other words, the documents had been executed after the date shown on the piece of paper.[65]

Tytell's testimony was elaborate and convincing. But was it relevant? The defense said no. In fact, Stillman and Lawler said so no fewer than four times. Stillman:

[W]ith respect to those items there has never been nor is there now nor will there ever be an issue with respect to those portions of the checks written by Sun Myung Moon.

What I am saying, your Honor, those portions he wrote we don't dispute it, we agreed to it a long time ago, we agree to it today.[66]

Protests of the defense duly registered and brushed aside, the government moved on to its second wrap-up "expert" witness, Herbert Rowe, an authority on the manufacture of paper. Indeed, the man had a Ph.D. in paper chemistry from the only school in the United States that grants such a degree, the Institute of Paper Chemistry of Lawrence University.

While Tytell was trial smart, Rowe was not. Rowe's inexperience, however, made no difference; the defense did not question the substance of his presentation.

Rowe had worked thirty-four years for Nekoosa Papers, Inc., and the man knew his paper. The government trotted him through his paces on the arcane topics of watermarks, bandmarks, and Dandy rolls. It's hard to imagine the jury sitting on the edge of its seats listening to this:

> A true watermark with a Dandy roll is made back when the paper is only 20 percent dry and it consists of roll that's called a Dandy roll. This is a large cylinder that has a shaft or journal through the center and supporting framework around which the circumference of which is covered with a wire screen, or wire cloth, and affixed to that wire cloth will be again designs, letters, numbers, pictures, whatever it may be that will be raised above the surface of the Dandy so that when it is run against the paper or around 20 percent dry the impression that's on the Dandy will be put into the paper by making the paper thinner at that particular point.[67]

Can the reader follow this? Did the jury? The prosecution and Dr. Rowe plowed on.

Nekoosa, for which the witness had worked since 1946, was the paper supplier for Xerox and its 1024 paper. In 1973, Xerox requested that Nekoosa change the paper mark used on the Xerox paper from a bandmark to a watermark. Dr. Rowe was in charge of the switch.[68]

The change resulted in a totally new watermarked paper that was available to Xerox beginning March 1974.

Having established timing of the Xerox paper watermark change, the prosecutor then asked the expert to look at various church documents related to the Chase accounts and Tong-Il. Flumenbaum asked Rowe to confirm that the documents had been written on Xerox paper that was available no earlier than the spring of 1974. Rowe readily complied.[69]

The paper expert's testimony raised an obvious point. The church documents in question were all supposedly written in 1973. Yet the paper they were written on wasn't available until March 1974. Once again the government had taken trouble to prove what the defense had already acknowledged repeatedly; namely, some church papers had been reconstructed or redone and backdated.

The prosecution next took a quantum leap. It argued that because the church documents in question had not been created in 1973, they could not have been created in 1973, 1974 or 1975 or 1976. Instead, the prosecution theorized, with no proof, all of the documents had been created in 1977 as part of an elaborate cover-up in order to protect Moon from the IRS investigation then under way. There was no evidence for the allegation; only wild accusation.

The defense naturally denied the prosecution's charge of criminal intent and argued once again that the documents had been redone in order to correct the incredibly sloppy or nonexistent recordkeeping that was typical of the early years of the Unification Church in America.

Dr. Rowe couldn't help defense counsel Stillman on that point. "Nice to see you, Doctor," Stillman told the government witness. "I have no questions, your Honor."[70]

Two expert witnesses down; one to go. But the defense was not so congenial to the prosecution's last "star" expert.

Surprise! That witness was none other than Flumenbaum himself. The young prosecutor had asked to take the stand—a somewhat unusual procedure to say the least—in order to tie up some loose threads.

The request was so unusual that Judge Goettel hesitated—Flumenbaum had difficulty getting his case precedents and exhibits straight, for one thing—but hearing no objection from defense counsel, the court gave its reluctant consent.[71]

The target of Flumenbaum-as-witness was Takeru Kamiyama. With something less than an airtight case established against Kamiyama, the prosecution had decided to change its strategy, and do the unusual. Flumenbaum in the witness box would give the jury one last impression: that Kamiyama was guilty of multiple counts of perjury. The perjury charge was, in fact, the strongest part of the government's entire case. If Kamiyama were convicted, there was a good chance that the jury would toss in his boss for good measure.

Flumenbaum began his witness stand grand finale with a hard-hitting jab at Kamiyama's grand jury appearances. A prime target was Kamiyama's testimony regarding his business visa: the prosecution contended that the visa had been obtained through a fraudulent purchase of Tong-Il stock—an accusation denied by Kamiyama under oath.[72]

Flumenbaum braced himself for what promised to be a tough cross-examination.

He was right. It got mean. And it got rough.

Lawler, Kamiyama's lawyer, began his attack by pointing out that Kamiyama had been dragged before, not one, but three grand juries in an obvious effort to wear him down. Wasn't it remarkable, suggested Lawler sarcastically, that it had taken three grand jury proceedings to find sufficient grounds to charge with perjury a man who had no lawyer present, who spoke no English, and who had no understanding of the American legal system?

The prosecutor in the dock appreciated Lawler's point, but he wasn't about to back off. Flumenbaum's response quickly escalated into the trial's sharpest exchange between opposing counsel.

Flumenbaum began by insisting that the foreman of the grand jury who conducted the July 16 session was at fault; the foreman had invited Kamiyama to appear knowing that he would appear before yet another grand jury, and knowing that . . .

Before Flumenbaum could finish his explanation, Andy Lawler objected on the basis of hearsay. The court agreed. But Flumenbaum would have none of it:

> MR. FLUMENBAUM: I was present, your Honor, so I don't believe it is hearsay.
>
> MR. LAWLER: Do you mean to tell us that the transcript reveals that the foreperson of the grand jury stated on the record that you are to return on the 16th before a different grand jury?
>
> A: I am sure Mr. Kamiyama wasn't told that, but—.

Q: Is there a transcript of that, Mr. Flumenbaum?

A: All proceedings before the grand jury are recorded, so there undoubtedly is a a transcript, that's my recollection.

Q: Are you telling us you have a transcript of that?

A: I am not saying one way or the other. I am just saying that he was directed to appear on July 16th by the foreperson of the grand jury, and my response to you was the foreperson of the grand jury at that time, and that grand jury knew that it would not be sitting and that Mr. Kamiyama's testimony would be taken by another grand jury on that day.

Q: I show you what is the last page of the transcript of July 9th [handing] and I ask you whether that refreshes your recollection that you were the one, Mr. Flumenbaum, who initially instructed the witness to return on the 16th.

A: No, that doesn't reflect that. It reflects that I requested—.[73]

Lawler, who towered over the diminutive Flumenbaum, was riled.

Q: I asked if it refreshes your recollection.

A: It requests—it states—

Q: Mr. Flumenbaum, you know the answer to that is yes or no. Does it refresh your recollection?

A: I can't answer that question the way you ask it.

MR. LAWLER: That's a fairly simple question, your Honor. It either refreshes his recollection or it doesn't.

MS. HARRIS: Objection.[74]

Jo Ann Harris knew that her colleague was going to get into trouble with his less than candid responses, but there wasn't much she could do. Judge Goettel was finally getting into the act.

THE COURT: Does it refresh your recollection?

MR. FLUMENBAUM: The—

THE COURT: Yes or no?

MR. FLUMENBAUM: Not to Mr. Lawler's question.[75]

Young Martin's snotty response did not amuse his Honor.

> THE COURT: My question is does it refresh your recollection
> as to the question he was asking you?

> MR. FLUMENBAUM: No, it does not as to the specific ques-
> tion that he was asking me.[76]

Flumenbaum's denial did not deter Lawler. He'd been waiting
for this moment: it was his turn to go for the throat.

> MR. LAWLER: Did you in fact on that date instruct the
> witness—did you in fact ask the foreman to instruct the
> witness—

> MR. FLUMENBAUM: That's an important distinction, Mr.
> Lawler.

> MR. LAWLER: Will you let me finish the question please, Mr.
> Flumenbaum? You are a witness now. Was it you who instructed
> the foreman to instruct the witness to be back here next Thurs-
> day, July 16th?

> MR. FLUMENBAUM: I did tell the foreman to instruct the
> witness as such.[77]

Lawler pushed hard on this point, with good reason. Technically, the prosecutor should not be telling the foreman and the
grand jury what to do. In the real world, this happens all the time;
Flumenbaum had manipulated not one, but three grand juries to
get the result he, not the jurors, wanted. And Lawler wanted that
on the record.

Lawler then accused the witness of entrapment. Flumenbaum
had asked Kamiyama about the Tong-Il stock and whether Moon
knew it was in his name or not. Kamiyama had denied it.

But Moon's signature was on the stock subscription. Kamiyama
had been caught in what the government contended was a lie. It
was Count Nine in the indictment.

Flumenbaum could have shown him the document first instead
of leading Kamiyama into potential perjury. But he didn't. That,
Lawler argued, should discredit Flumenbaum and his methods.

The prosecutor on the stand hotly denied everything. He was
saved by Judge Goettel, who ruled that Flumenbaum's procedure,
though perhaps questionable, was not legally improper.[78]

But Lawler persisted. The government, he charged, already had all the documents and facts about Tong-Il—thanks to the church which had surrendered everything that was requested. Asking an unprepared Kamiyama about something they already knew was not only setting him up, the questions were also immaterial to the grand jury proceedings—in other words, they were improper.

Lawler moved on to his next point:

> If in fact with respect to the Chase Manhattan Bank checks and with respect to that area and also with respect to the stock subscription agreement, if they had those materials in hand and that examination had already been done, then it was no longer material to the investigation to ask those questions. Unless they were testing Mr. Kamiyama's credibility, in which case, I would maintain, I am entitled to ask questions as to whether they had those documents available and whether a decision was made not to show them to Mr. Kamiyama.[79]

Judge Goettel by now had heard enough. "That doesn't strike me as the purpose of this hearing," he announced. That was that. Lawler had no further questions on cross-examination. The prosecution rested its case.[80]

Kamiyama now had problems. Moon's financial advisor, knowingly or unknowingly, had said things that were not true, aside from the translator errors that had been thrown into the perjury hopper by the government.

If Lawler could not explain to the jury the circumstances of Kamiyama's apparent untruths—the entrapment and the intimidating circumstances in which the questions were framed—then the facts, narrowly construed, would lead to a conviction on at least several counts of perjury. And if Kamiyama could be convicted, why not Sun Myung Moon, his friend and leader?

It had taken sixteen trial days and 3,300 pages of testimony to make the government's case, but on April 19, moments before Flumenbaum and Harris rested their case, they had at last made some kind of breakthrough on this point about Kamiyama's role.

Sun Myung Moon and Takeru Kamiyama were in deep trouble, and the defense knew it.

It was now the defense's turn. They had a lot of catching up to do. It was true that the prosecution team had had its share of disappointments. Many of their key witnesses, including Mike Warder, had failed to supply the smoking gun that would nail Moon. Yet little by little, by insinuation, assumption, and direct statement, by piling on a truckload of evidence—much of it marginally relevant—and by "expert" testimony, the government had at least put together a case. Add community prejudice and a jury that numbered no Nobel Prize winners amongst them, and the prosecution wasn't in too bad shape.

During the weekend after the government rested its case, the defense lawyers seemed uncertain as to how to proceed. How many and which witnesses should be called? As late as the final day of the government's case, the possibility was held out that the defense might not call anyone at all to the stand. Their strategy just wasn't clear.

One thing was clear, however: neither defendant was going to be put in the dock. It was the defense's right not to do so, of course, under the Fifth Amendment. But given Kamiyama's grand jury experiences, the remote chance that the two defendants would rise to their own defense disappeared entirely.

Indeed, a strong case could be made that eight years of continuous government harassment and the constant threat of criminal prosecution had effectively coerced the pair into waiving the most fundamental of all rights, the right publicly to defend oneself. After all, it was Moon's own public expression of outrage that had caused him to be forced to stand trial before a jury. And, it was the church's complete cooperation in handing over documents which had landed them in hot water.

In the end, the defense lawyers brought to the stand a string of witnesses, most of whom were members or who had worked for the Unification Church in some capacity. The general purpose of their appearance was to spike various parts of the government's case against Moon and Kamiyama. But unlike the government, the defense did not have a star witness and never pretended it had.

The first to appear was Bo Hi Pak's younger brother, No Hi Pak, a point of possible confusion that worried Judge Goettel, but not enough for him to clarify who was who for the jury.

No Hi Pak was the executive director of the Korean Cultural and Freedom Foundation in Seoul. It was the KCFF that borrowed the money from the Bank of America on the strength of Moon's collateral deposited in the Park Avenue branch of Chase Manhattan Bank.

The defense wanted to get on the record that the loan had helped build the Little Angels Art School, and that the school was a key part of the general education program of the Unification Church. In short, the defense wanted to show that Moon wasn't all business—something that the prosecution had steadily implied throughout the trial.[81]

As usual, the defense took only a few minutes to ask its questions, leaving the government the lion's share of the time. And Flumenbaum wasted no time in trashing the first witness for the defense. In a series of rapid-fire questions—which the interpreter had a difficult time keeping pace with—the prosecutor asserted that the KCFF was a political arm of the Unification Church—a theme that Congressman Donald Fraser had exploited in a Congressional investigation of the church. Moreover, Flumenbaum implied that the money passed to the foundation came directly from Moon, proving that within the "Moon Empire" funds were completely fungible. Separate legal entities were pure facade.

The assertion of course raised objections from the defense table and denials from the witness. But Flumenbaum ground away at his central points, effectively making speeches instead of asking questions—all for the weary jury's benefit.[82]

The court didn't seem to mind. Only once was an objection sustained, when Flumenbaum, having heard that Presidents Dwight Eisenhower and Harry Truman had once served as advisors to the U.S. KCFF's board, snapped: "And did anyone tell Eisenhower and Truman that Reverend Moon was involved in this?"[83]

Flumenbaum had gone well beyond the scope of the cross-examination and Goettel began a belated effort to rein him in. But not for long.

Flumenbaum now turned to Mrs. Moon. Did she, Flumenbaum asked Pak, receive a salary from the KCFF in 1972 and 1973? Pak wasn't sure. She had been with the Little Angels on a worldwide tour at the time in question, but he had no exact memory.

Flumenbaum pressed. Didn't she cook for the kids and act as a chaperone? What was her salary? Pak denied knowledge of any of it, but that did not stop Flumenbaum. He merely repeated the questions in slightly different forms, over rising objections from the defense—some of them sustained by the court. Sustained or not, it didn't make any difference, the prosecutor rode roughshod over the witness.

Then Flumenbaum came to the point. "Do you have any knowledge of an application made by Mrs. Moon for residence in the United States?"[84]

Pak did not know that answer either, but it made no difference. Flumenbaum asked the question again and again. For good measure he threw in a question about the Reverend Sun Myung Moon's visa application as well.

Having squeezed that grape dry, Flumenbaum ended his questioning of Pak, but not before suggesting to the jury that the loan to the Korean KCFF was nothing but an elaborate scam to provide employment for Mrs. Moon to help her get a permanent visa from the United States.

The scene was a textbook example of guilt by insinuation. In spite of ignoring the court's sustaining of defense objections, Flumenbaum got no reprimand.

Other defense witnesses had no easier time of it. Moon's lawyers would try to draw out something positive or at least mitigating, and Flumenbaum would slash away on a wholly unrelated subject.

Takeko Hose, a church member and a Japanese housewife married to an American, is a case in point.

Hose was an early church arrival to the United States and did her missionary work largely in the San Francisco area.

The defense wanted two things from Hose. First, what did the Reverend Sun Myung Moon think his mission was in the United States, and second, how did he, in fact, finance it?

Regarding the first point, Hose remembered a meeting held in March 1972 at which Moon had expressed his concern over the moral crisis of American youth—a subject not wholly implausible in the late 1960s and early 1970s when university presidencies went begging.

The defense's theme was not subtle. Moon was far more than a businessman. He was also on a mission. With a following in the U.S. that at the time numbered only in the hundreds, the question was, How was this mission going to be paid for?[85]

In reply, Hose recalled discussions among the American members that concluded that the Japanese Unification Church would provide the money which would be placed in an American bank account in Moon's name.[86]

Oddly enough, the subject of Moon and money did not interest Flumenbaum very much—at least with this particular witness. He had other things on his mind and wasted no time getting to them.

With not much delicacy, Flumenbaum delved into Hose's personal life. Who married you, Reverend Moon? Did Reverend Moon pick your husband?

The answer was yes to the first and no to the latter, and while Flumenbaum claimed he was only attempting to impeach the witness's testimony by showing bias, Stillman and Lawler were outraged. Defense counsel moved for a mistrial. The motion was denied, sparking another row at the sidebar.

Even the court was a bit disturbed at the prejudicial conduct of prosecutor Flumenbaum. In Goettel's words:

> I realize that this might have a slight amount of relevance to showing bias, but it seems to me that it has a potential prejudice far outweighing the reason for asking the question. Unless you know more about this than I do.[87]

Flumenbaum admitted he had no first-hand knowledge, only his "understanding" that the Reverend Sun Myung Moon chose all spouses within the church—an assertion that was not true, but was apparently based on his reading of newspaper accounts of church practices.

The court didn't buy it: "[T]he prejudicial impact exceeds the evidentiary value," his Honor said.[88]

But there was more to it than that, claimed the defense. Flumenbaum was trampling on theology and, by extension, the First Amendment.

"It seems to me," said Charlie Stillman, "they are trying to poison this record with this kind of stuff. It is improper and I just ask you to cut him off on this."[89]

Goettel did so. Sort of. "I want to keep out matters that go to theology and might prejudice the jury. To the extent that it's not essential you shouldn't do it," he admonished Flumenbaum. But once again the court handed the prosecution a straw, which promptly turned into a club.[90]

MR. FLUMENBAUM: Can I ask her if she refers to him as her true parents?

THE COURT: No. No. You can ask her whether or not she doesn't have great respect for him and great admiration and whether she doesn't like to serve his aims and things of that nature without getting into these theological—

MR. FLUMENBAUM: It is not theological. It goes directly to bias and directly to motive to lie.

THE COURT: No.[91]

Why take no for an answer when the next time you might get a yes? Both prosecutors had seen Gerard Goettel in action and they knew he could be worn down. But this time it wasn't so easy.

How about asking some questions about Reverend Moon as the Messiah? piped up Jo Ann Harris.

No, don't ask that, said his Honor one more time, breaking up the sidebar.[92]

Flumenbaum continued his pursuit of Hose, asking again the forbidden questions about arranged marriages. Hose, this time, answered the question. No, Moon had not picked her husband; she had.[93]

Barely deterred, Flumenbaum moved on to touchy questions about Moon's status as his flock's leader and master. Goettel allowed the questions. Flumenbaum asked if "members must be utterly obedient to him." That question, too, was permitted. Then he queried: "Have you heard him say that members cannot have a will other than his?"[94]

The question earned everyone another free trip to the sidebar. The defense once again was outraged. The government was not trying its case of tax fraud and perjury, insisted Stillman and Lawler. It was putting Moon and his followers' beliefs and practices on trial by putting them in the worst possible light.

Lawler reminded the court what the trial was supposed to be about:

[T]his is a criminal trial with witnesses testifying under oath. And the idea that in this religion or any religion where there may be doctrines of obedience which may relate to theological matters and abstract statements about the obligation of people who are participants to follow the guidance of the leaders with respect to these areas, those two things should not be confused and it should not be up to us to come back on redirect or recross—.[95]

Stillman added his two cents: "And it just seems to me absolutely outrageous that this is the way the government is going to try to prove that witnesses are supposedly lying."[96]

The court did not share the defense's outrage, but Goettel was a tad concerned. None of this would look good on appeal in front of an appellate court—a tribunal that tends to take things like the First Amendment quite seriously.

And so now did Judge Goettel, for the first time during this lengthy trial. Or, in his words:

> [T]he Pope is believed to be infallible in matters of Catholic faith but when he makes comments on the Polish situation or the Argentinean War and so on he is not speaking in the same context and consequently to try to couple his infallibility with his views on the Falkland Islands it seems to me a *non sequitur* and it may be well to do so here.[97]

Utterly impervious to all of the above, Flumenbaum proposed to question Hose about lying and cheating and Moon's condoning of the practice—in other words, the old "heavenly deception" smear that ardent antichurch groups had been pushing for years.

Goettel was cautious. Could Flumenbaum cite a Moon quotation on lying for the cause? Yes, sure, was the reply. No problem.

But there was a problem. Flumenbaum failed to produce. He did produce a Moon speech, however, dealing with the topic of disobeying parents and presidents.

But it says nothing about lying, said a puzzled and an unfathomably innocent Judge Goettel.

But Flumenbaum refused to quit the stage without getting something right:

> MR. FLUMENBAUM: That's one of the areas I want to get into. Here's the specific reference—.

THE COURT: We have already covered obedience. She said yes, she knew she was supposed to be obedient.

MR. FLUMENBAUM: This states disobeying laws.

THE COURT: This doesn't state disobeying laws. We have a president who wants to have more money spent on armaments, does that mean if I am opposed to that I am disobeying the laws?

MR. FLUMENBAUM: The context of that was the Immigration Laws and the difficulty they were having getting people into the country.

THE COURT: This doesn't concern lying at all. Tell me something else.[98]

Flumenbaum tried. He really did. Rummaging through his notes, the prosecutor did find the something else. How about showing that Moon approved of cheating? Would that do? The court was shown a sermon dating from 1973.

Goettel remained unimpressed and said so:

This particular quote here which concerns the Serpent and Esop [sic] and Jacob is almost a Biblical kind of lesson. And I don't think you can use this literally. I really doubt that most people listening to this would understand what it was all about.[99]

In other words, no, Mr. Flumenbaum could not pursue this line of questioning or, more precisely, interrogation.

Still, he would not give up, although this one sidebar alone had already consumed almost an hour:

MR. FLUMENBAUM: I can put on witness after witness on heavenly deception. We have avoided doing that and that goes specifically to fund raising. And if your Honor wishes we could do that. And it is based in part on speeches of Reverend Moon.[100]

The answer again was negative, but the unsinkable Martin Flumenbaum had one more request. Could he ask another question on the subject of obedience to Moon?

The defense chose to remain quiet while the prosecutor annoyed the court. The truth is Flumenbaum's desire to recite the whole "anti-Moonie" litany in court should have been grounds for mistrial.

Overall, Flumenbaum had not done well with this witness, although the defense made no large gains either. The prosecution fared better, however, with Isabel Maddux, the defense's next witness.

Maddux was not a church member, but an employee at Chase Manhattan Bank who had appeared on the first day of the trial as a government witness. This time she was asked by the defense to authenticate foreign exchange slips that indicated that money from Japan had indeed found its way into Moon's accounts during 1973. Maddux's testimony squared with what Hose had said earlier—all of which made the family fund not quite the family fraud that the government, based largely on hearsay from key witness Warder, had all along said that it was.

The prosecution did not contest Maddux's testimony about the documents, but Flumenbaum managed to obfuscate the issue with a variety of objections, at one point taking over the questioning of the witness through the *voir dire* privilege. His intent was to blunt the defense's point made to a jury that was already eyeing the clock.[101]

The trial was drawing to a close. The defense had one more witness, and like the prosecution it hoped that the best had been saved for last. That wish came true.

Margaret DeBoe was a staff accountant and a partner in the national accounting firm of Elmer Fox and Company. In early 1974 her company had been asked by church officials to take over the financial accounting for the Unification Church and its many subsidiaries.

In effect they were hired to develop the church's first real accounting system because, according to DeBoe:

> [T]heir books were quite elementary. They consisted basically of a cash receipts book and a cash disbursements book, and they wanted us to create for them ... a system of bookkeeping that would adequately document and gather their financial information.[102]

She added:

[A]t that point HSA had nothing but cash receipts and cash dis-
bursements journals, there were not collected in any one place information as to all the property that was owned, all of the furniture and
equipment, all the bank accounts, all the accounts payable, all of the
notes payable. The information just wasn't summarized in any one
place.[103]

It was strictly pop-and-mom store stuff, except that this particular shop was owned by Koreans who didn't have the remotest idea
of American accounting procedures or tax laws. Nor did they care
much.

Of course, those who had served as makeshift accountants knew
almost nothing about keeping books. That fact caused vast confusion when the professionals later tried to set things straight. The
amateur bookkeepers had been flying in a cloud bank with no
instruments. They had managed to make difficult the most elementary of accounting decisions. For example, it was nearly impossible to tell from the records whether money coming in was a
loan or contribution. If it was a loan, the money was a liability. If
such was the case, of course, it would make a difference in the
overall financial health of the church. But in many, many cases, the
record-keepers couldn't tell, and church officials couldn't remember. They simply didn't think in those terms.

Who knew? The scribbled bits of paper on which the incoming
money was recorded, when such bits existed at all, were often in
cryptic Korean or Japanese. Navy intelligence experts before
World War II had an easier job breaking Japan's Purple Code than
Fox and Company's army of accountants had in breaking the
church cypher. That's because there wasn't any. There was no key.
No pattern. Just chaos.

Fox ended up following the conservative accounting practice of
assuming, when in doubt, that everything is a loan. Others might
call this creative accounting. Under the circumstances there was
little else they could do.[104]

The whole business was a very messy one at best. A bit like
straightening up a ten-year-old boy's room after a few friends have
been over for the afternoon. "[W]e became aware of a lot of erroneous information and a lot of wrong accounts, a lot of omitted

items," said Margaret DeBoe in what might be considered the understatement of the trial.[105]

Actually, the church's record-keeping was even worse than an afternoon of children's games. Church money was difficult, if not impossible, to keep track of. In the early days of the church and its proliferating institutions, noted DeBoe, "moneys were transferred and they didn't really stop to consider whether it would be a loan that was to be paid back or if it was a contribution that was not to be paid back."[106]

As evidence of the church's financial ineptitude, not chicanery, mounted, Flumenbaum got restive. It wasn't long before he exploded in a series of objections. Goettel brushed them off. Perhaps the judge was impressed with a witness who not only knew what she was talking about, but whose testimony was relevant to the case at hand.

Stillman let DeBoe describe how Fox and Company proceeded to reorganize the Unification Church in America and its various entities. Not only had there been bookkeeping problems, but management difficulties as well. The management problems were quite basic, arising from an utter confusion over who was managing what, not to mention the even greater problem of distinguishing between religious and business activities.

Accountants and lawyers—not church officials—restructured the whole lot. For example, they created a new holding company, One-Up, which was "interjected" between the Unification Church International, which had itself been reorganized by Fox and Company as a nonprofit corporation, and the commercial businesses like News World, Tong-Il, and Oceanic Enterprises.[107]

Legally, the restructuring was a lot tidier than the oriental Rube Goldberg nonsystem that had been in place previously.

Stillman had another question for DeBoe. From her reading of the records, had large amounts of money come to the church from abroad and, if so, from where?[108]

Yes, there had been money from abroad; it had come primarily from Japan, replied the Fox accountant.

DeBoe's testimony had not been good for the prosecution's case, and Flumenbaum knew it. Which explains why the cross-examination of DeBoe took twice as long as the direct examination had, irritating Judge Goettel who, like the jury, was now looking at his watch.

"This is proceeding at a very slow pace, Mr. Flumenbaum," Goettel sighed at one point. "Is there any way we can expedite it?"[109]

There wasn't any way and for one good reason. Flumenbaum had to discredit DeBoe's testimony and he wasn't sure how to do it. His normal aggressiveness failed to cow the lady.

"Mr. Flumenbaum, I told you I don't remember," she snapped, when the prosecutor characteristically kept repeating a question that was not evoking the answer he wanted.[110]

Everyone was getting edgy by this time.

Flumenbaum persisted. Poking here. Prodding there. Looking for a soft spot somewhere. He picked out bits and pieces of the accountants' work and grilled her about minutia. He went over the East Garden loan again. Belvedere, too. But mostly he pushed one theme: How accurate could Fox's work be if it was based on information provided by church members? If members wished to lie and hide illegal transactions, he implied, the accountants would have no way of telling otherwise, would they?[111]

Technically, of course, the answer was no. The question was typical of Flumenbaum's approach to prosecuting. He didn't think it necessary actually to prove that church members had deceived their lawyers and accountants. He merely had to suggest that it was possible. Under that particular rubric of criminality, of course, we could all be guilty of something.

The government's junior prosecutor overreached himself at one point in the cross-examination of Margaret DeBoe.

The issue concerned a boat. What did she know about its purchase by the church in 1974? Before DeBoe could answer, an objection was raised and sustained. Flumenbaum asked for a sidebar.[112]

But before proceeding, class, let us refresh our memory of Basic Trial Procedure 101. In a cross-examination, the officer of the court does not raise matters that are beyond the scope of those raised during direct examination. Flumenbaum had turned the topic to boats. Boats? Who had said anything at any time earlier? No one, of course.

Gerard Goettel was incredulous. "After one month of trial suddenly we have a boat?"[113]

Yup, we sure do, your Honor. The boat was purchased by the

Holy Spirit Association, but used principally by Moon, Flumenbaum contended.

Goettel did not get the prosecutor's point:

> I am not at all clear as to why you are present[ing] this. I am not clear about a lot of things you are doing but I am particularly not clear about this. Explain it to me in a sensible fashion.[114]

Flumenbaum tried to explain but failed. Goettel listened once more and shook his head: "I still don't have the foggiest notion of what its got to do with this case, not even the slightest. I just don't understand it."[115]

At this point the proceedings took a distinctly humorous turn.

> MR. FLUMENBAUM: We think it is relevant to the question as to whose money it is in the Chase account.
>
> THE COURT: But the boat wasn't paid for out of the Chase account.
>
> MR. FLUMENBAUM: That is the point.
>
> THE COURT: Do you understand it?
>
> LAW CLERK: I'd like to hear it again.
>
> MR. STILLMAN: It seems to me, your Honor, if that is the clearest statement of relevance the objection ought to be sustained.
>
> THE COURT: I'm afraid I am going to have to because I still don't understand it.[116]

No, this portion of the trial was not written by Lewis Carroll or one of his lineal descendants, as some might suspect.

Although the boat issue was dropped, there was no mystery as to what Flumenbaum was about. Raising the topic had been grossly improper, but the prosecutor had never paid much attention to the niceties of trial procedure. Why should he now? Injecting the boat—one wonders why he did not call it a yacht—was simply another unsubtle neon sign flashed to the jury: Moon is a businessman who uses church money for his own private pleasure.

The court apparently had not yet fathomed the government's

strategy. It was a monument to Gerard Goettel's innocence. Such innocence, of course, is a virtue for some. But where a judge is concerned, it is disastrous for justice. The unvarnished truth was that Flumenbaum had no intention of being a good boy; if he played strictly by the rules, he would never win the case.

And Martin Flumenbaum wanted to win.

So did the defense. But unlike Flumenbaum, Stillman and Lawler stayed within the rules. One rule that Stillman invoked was the right to redirect. Meaning he could clean up some of the mess that Flumenbaum had left on the floor when questioning Margaret DeBoe.

And unlike Flumenbaum, Stillman got to the point. First, he established that DeBoe's work papers, which the government had tried to shred during cross-examination, in reality were painstakingly thorough and complete. Hardly the stuff of a cover-up. In fact, the papers filled a dozen large boxes.

Stillman, in short, was not about to have DeBoe's competence impugned:

> And you have done your best [Stillman continued] as you are here to try to identify bits and pieces that we have pulled out and thrown at you this last call it 24 hours; is that right, ma'am?[117]

Needless to say, the witness's answer was yes.
The final question from the defense:

> And did anybody at this point in time say to Colonel Pak, anybody say, by the way, for example, this earlier interest income somebody had better take care of it because some day the government might claim it is taxable income to somebody?[118]

Flumenbaum naturally objected. His objection was ignored, however. The court wanted an answer to the question. DeBoe's response? "Not as I can recall, no."[119]

The trial was effectively over. The defense had rested its case after less than three days of testimony, much of it taken up by prosecutorial cross-examination. The defense had produced only eight witnesses to the government's thirty-two.

What remained, after some *in camera* discussion of additional evidence, were summations by the prosecution and defense, followed by the court's reading of the instructions to the jury. In each case, the direct target was the dozen men and women who composed the jury. Until now, they had been silent and passive spectators positioned to one side of the proceedings.

Now, they were at the center.

SUMMATIONS

The prosecution had the first crack at the jury for the summation. The government lawyers were reasonably confident that they could get a guilty verdict returned on at least some of the charges.

But they were not about to take any chances. The summation was a thorough, businesslike presentation, lengthy on apparent facts and short on histrionics. It was also long, taking more than four hours to deliver. Jo Ann Harris ran the show—not the mercurial Martin Flumenbaum, whose tongue, on occasion, had run at flank speed.

Nothing about the prosecution's summation came as a surprise. The government had played hardball throughout the whole proceedings. It had also played fast and loose with the rules. And its lawyers had always expressed shock and indignation when they were caught at it. Let's review some of them briefly, since they would not be irrelevant to the final days of the trial.

Probably the prosecution's most egregious misuse of the system was the withholding of evidence from the defense. Under federal trial rules that's a big no-no. The government had practically made a habit of it in the course of the Moon-Kamiyama trial.

The prosecution's misuse of Federal Rule 16 had started early in the proceedings. Because the church was so quick to deliver documents—often keeping no copies for itself—the defense found itself in the position of not having papers belonging to its own clients.

The Tong-Il bank records were just one example. Over protests from the defense, Goettel merely shrugged and suggested that Stillman and Lawler could subpoena them.

And so they did. But the defense continued to insist that there was a larger issue at stake: the government should stick to the rules and not conceal evidence until its presentation in court.

The court was not swayed:

I say I don't have to order them because the rule says that they must produce under Rule 16 all documents that they intend to introduce in evidence on their direct case, and all of the documents which are necessary for the preparation of the defense. They know that already. I don't have to tell them that.[120]

Or so Goettel thought.

Two days later, the government had done it again, only with a slight variation. Instead of withholding evidence outright, the prosecutors simply kept it back until the last possible minute. They handed over the documents moments before the scheduled witness for the prosecution was to appear on the stand.

Protests from the defendants' lawyers earned them little sympathy from the bench.[121]

Bending, if not breaking, the rules was not the only unprofessional aspect of the government's conduct during the trial. In its eagerness to get Moon and Kamiyama, its lawyers sometimes came up with legal arguments that were contradictory in nature.

The government, in short, wanted it both ways. When it suited the government, it was Reverend Moon, the corrupt religious leader, and at other times during the trial, it was Mr. Moon, the unscrupulous business tycoon. Damned if you do, damned if you don't; either way church officials stayed in the cross hairs.

Such was the defense's contention, and the court was inclined to agree: "I get the strong impression it is a fishing expedition that will waste a lot of time," said Judge Goettel in reviewing and comparing the government's tangled lines of argument.[122]

Nevertheless, that was now history. The prosecution knew it no longer mattered what the defense lawyers thought or even what the court believed. Everything the government lawyers had done had one purpose in mind: will this argument or assertion move the jury one bit closer to a conviction or not?

If so, it didn't matter what the rules of procedure or even the law had to say about something. In the prosecution's summation, that became blindingly apparent.

Flumenbaum had carried most of the trial. After all, nailing Moon had been his all-consuming ambition for nearly three years. His fox terrier style of prosecution had served reasonably well in presenting the government's case, even though it ultimately got on the nerves of the court (not to mention the assorted gaffes and goofs that, at least in one instance, nearly ended the whole business in a mistrial).

Flumenbaum was still an eager amateur. A closing summation is not a job for such as these. Jo Ann Harris, on the other hand, was a professional. Seasoned and competent. She had faced scores of juries; Flumenbaum had not.

Harris' experience told in her every move. Her presentation to the jury would be long, longer than the film *Gone with the Wind*, longer even than Wagner's *Götterdämmerung*.

Harris' style was smooth and, in spite of the length of the presentation, nonverbose. Her words were simple—no fancy show-off legal terms that could alienate the jurors. Although she looked like a school marm, Harris did not intimidate the jury.

Harris was almost friendly as she walked the twelve men and women through the government's case. She took care to flatter them. Coming on like supersalesman Joe Isuzu, Harris opened with this hymn of praise to the jury:

> There really aren't quite the words to tell you how much all of this means to us just as human beings. More important, what you have done here by your service has made an important contribution to the administration of justice in this district. Jurors like you are the very key to the essential fairness of our criminal justice system. You are really what it's all about, and I want to thank you sincerely.[123]

Having begun on that melodic note, Harris quickly moved to the heart of the case. The defendants' guilt would be established, she explained, by documents and witnesses who were biased in favor of Moon and Kamiyama and hostile to the government.[124]

So, on to the basic character and motivations of the defendants. What were they? Greed, arrogance, and power, of course, but there was more. Harris offered a beautifully restrained leitmotif of xenophobia. Listen:

> They were [also] motivated by a contempt for our trust. They lie to their accountants. The evidence in this case has shown that. They lie to their lawyers. They move money and explanations for money around like they were playing monopoly.[125]

And after four more hours of this, Jo Ann Harris wound it all up without even a flashy peroration:

> In your deliberations what we ask of you is to be tough, be fair, use your common sense and render a just verdict. That verdict, we are confident, will be guilty on all counts.[126]

It was the defense's turn now. Charles Stillman spoke first for the Reverend Sun Myung Moon, followed by Andrew Lawler for Takeru Kamiyama. But as usual the defense was left in a hole before it even got started.

Jo Ann Harris had taken so long in her wind-up that Stillman was forced to spread his summation over two days. He began late in the afternoon of May 10, facing a jury tired and surfeited with argument and evidence. The jurors wanted to go home. Instead they got a ten-minute recess after which they had to listen to the lawyer for the defense.

Stillman knew the jury was tired, so he made it as easy on them as possible. Like Harris, he was a professional unwilling to put on a pyrotechnical display—a characteristic apparent throughout the long trial. But he had a client to defend, and he did so patiently and doggedly.

Stillman began with one example: the Korean Cultural and Freedom Foundation, hoping that tugging on that string might unravel the whole piece of cloth.

If the problem was merely a matter—and no one disputed it— of a $250,000 loan to build a school, why had the government felt the need to cart in hundreds of documents to prove the transaction? The question was more than rhetorical. Stillman offered the answer:

> I suggest to you, you can consider as you think about this evidence, that the purpose was to distract us, to take your eye off the key issues, as we think [they] are, and I hope to persuade you today and tomorrow, that they are.[127]

"There are more documents in this case than you shake a broom at," continued Stillman. "I would say a stick but it doesn't have the breadth of a broom," he added sarcastically.

Stillman, for the first time, was on a roll. He slammed his markers down hard on the table:

What was the purpose of Pearl Tytell telling us that Reverend Moon filled out the face, that is the entries on some of those checks?

What was the purpose of the paper test that we would have stipulated to?

What is the purpose of all the charts? I've asked them to take them down but who can ever forget the panorama of the charts?[128]

So if the real world was not on the government tri-color charts, what was the real world of the Reverend Sun Myung Moon? Stillman had a tough, uphill battle explaining it to twelve very plain men and women who had little or no knowledge of the world much beyond their own front stoops.

But Stillman tried, using common sense.

His thesis was that if the church were a criminal enterprise, complete with contempt for the Internal Revenue Service, the conspirators certainly had acted in a most peculiar way. Or as Stillman put it:

Now, I have been waiting and waiting and waiting for the Government's answer to the question, why would a rational human being, sitting with the cash they say he has, his own money, why would he take that money and walk to the Chase Manhattan Bank and say, "Chase Manhattan Bank, my name is Sun Myung Moon. I have this cash money. I want to put this cash money into your bank in an account in my name emblazoned on those bank charts."[129]

Why, asked Stillman, would Moon walk into a Park Avenue bank in broad daylight, open an account, lay down a paper trail a mile long, and then try and cheat Uncle Sam on one year's tax return? Stillman pressed hard:

Is that hiding something from somebody? Is this the way a person sitting with a cash hoard, conspiring from the moment he landed in America, according to the Government, is this the way a rational

human being would hide his money? I suggest to you ladies and
gentlemen, as we consider this evidence together, the overwhelming,
the ringing answer to that question is no.[130]

Rather, Stillman argued, the facts can be explained in a far more
rational and nonconspiratorial manner. Moon was simply doing
what he and his followers had always maintained he was doing:
namely, holding the money in trust for the movement. That had
always been the case, Stillman said, even before the formal organization of the Unification Church International.[131]

But it was the interest—some $100,000—that Stillman repeat-
edly went back to. He had to, because in his words, the fact that
Moon had not paid taxes on the sum was "the heart, the guts, the
innards of this case."[132]

And indeed it was.

The defense's assertion, of course, was simple. The money was
not Moon's in the sense of personal income, but was held by him
for the church's programs. And once more Stillman returned to
the unlikelihood of fraud carried out under such circumstances:

> Do you know what it means to defraud the United States? Three
> Assistant United States Attorneys, we had at least one Internal
> Revenue agent, paralegal, smart, intelligent, know those documents
> inside and out. You have got to be crazy to try to defraud those
> people when there is no need to.[133]

Stillman reviewed the documents with the jury from his
perspective—even the embarrassing episodes which featured
Moon and company being cheated out of $200,000 by Frank
Broes. Recalling the Broes scam, Stillman lost his cool for the first
time in the long trial. Raising his voice, he told the jurors:

> Where is the evidence, other than the evidence in this record that
> Frank Broes went to Mr. Choi and Mr. Choi who came here and
> swore and if you just want to disbelieve him because he is a Moonie I
> ought to sit down now. Forgive me, I didn't mean to raise my voice. I
> really should sit down now if that is so.[134]

That was Stillman's Parthian shot for the afternoon. But before
Judge Goettel gaveled the trial day to a conclusion, Moon's lawyer

confronted one other juror prejudice: if Moon was innocent, why was he being so thoroughly investigated?

The next morning, the defense went at it again. First, Stillman concluded. Then Lawler spent an hour doing what he could for Kamiyama.

Stillman was well aware of the many juror prejudices he had to address. He knew, for instance, that the jury was having trouble with the notion that the Reverend Sun Myung Moon had acted as a trustee for the church in handling the various bank accounts.

One particular problem the jury had was the admitted informality of it all, especially in the early years of the movement's existence in the U.S. But as Stillman explained, it wasn't necessary to have a twelve-page legal document to be a nominee of a trust:

> You don't need a single scrap of paper. That is to say, if you went to one of your loved ones and said, "Look, I want you to hold this for me, take care of it for me," that is a trust relationship recognized by the law.[135]

Technically, Stillman was right. Whether it made any impression on the jury was another matter.

But there wasn't time to worry about that. Stillman had another big prejudice to handle relating to the amounts of cash involved in this case. There was no point in being cute about it. Stillman had to face the problem directly. Characteristically, that's what he did.

> Now, an interesting thing happens in this Unification Church International and I think a rather dramatic thing. There was money coming from overseas, from Japan, in the early days. Money came in cash. In America, cash is not like it is in the Orient. Cash, we use cash in America, you are already suspect. What do you mean cash? Cash is bad. Cash is hiding.[136]

But it wasn't bad in the eyes of the church members, because they were Koreans and Japanese. As they became acculturated to the United States, they had started adopting American ways like using credit cards and check books.

By now, Stillman was working up a full head of steam, but as sometimes happens even with good lawyers, he made a mistake while continuing with the church and business theme.

Moon's lawyer argued correctly that other churches own businesses, citing the Mormons and the Catholics as examples. But Stillman's observations were a trial procedure error and Flumenbaum jumped all over it. Stillman, he charged, was commenting on something that had not been introduced into evidence. Contrary to popular belief and for those who are faithful watchers of "L.A. Law," an officer of the court cannot simply say anything he wants in summation.

Flumenbaum was right, and a valuable bit of evidence had to be omitted. Stillman had clearly blundered. The defense lawyers could easily have had expert testimony outlining the business practices of established religions. But they had not. And it badly hurt their case.

But Stillman recovered from his mistake and forged on.

He still had a mountain range of prejudices to scale. There was, for example, the small matter of the government's interjecting salary comparisons between Moon and church employees:

> The purpose of that, obviously, is to inflame you to say look, Moon is making all the money.

> Yes, Lewis [Burgess] drew a lesser salary. Yes, Lewis took his money with his church brothers and sisters. Yes, they contributed their money and they lived together for their common good, and there is nothing wrong with that.[137]

A related prejudice involved church fundraising practices. Stillman knew that middle-class Americans loathed them. Or were horrified. And there wasn't much he could do about it. Nonetheless, he did his best:

> Whatever we feel as human beings and we are entitled to feel this way and you are entitled to your feelings and we respect those feelings. I don't like fund raising this way, it is not right, you can do it differently. They have a right to do it. There is no charge here that fund raising is bad.

> But it has been injected into this case and I think that we should all face our own feelings. As I say, I respect them more than you could imagine. But it has nothing to do with this lawsuit.[138]

Stillman also had to deal with the church mansion, the $700,000 estate known as East Garden. Its existence couldn't be denied, so Stillman didn't try:

> The Government struggled mightily and finally I said all right, the house has a tennis court and remember the Judge pointed out it has a gazebo. It is a house in which this church leader lives, other members of his church live.
>
> It is a house in which, as we learned, church affairs are conducted. Religious affairs of the church, and yes, business affairs of the church are conducted there.[139]

Stillman left out the fact that East Garden had become worn around the edges. As one member familiar with the house pointed out: the linoleum on the kitchen had begun curling up around the edges as thousands tramped through it over the years. This was Moon's lavish lifestyle.

But Stillman could bash juror prejudices all day, and still have plenty of problems left over. And he knew it. One central issue that had been seriously dealt with during the main part of the trial was the conspiracy charge against Moon and Kamiyama.

Conspiracy, of course, was the foundation on which all the charges were built. It was key. It was crucial. Moon's lawyer took it on last. The evidence for the charge, he claimed, came from two sources.

The first was pure speculation. Moon and Kamiyama were close personally, therefore, "there must have been a conspiracy." But that was mere conjecture.[140]

Then there was the testimony of Michael Warder, the government's star witness. He had said under oath that he was prepared to lie for Moon—indeed, advance any conspiracy if he thought it would have helped the cause. The problem was, of course, as Warder himself had admitted under cross-examination, that no one had asked him to lie.

Stillman was running out of time. He had been talking to the jurors now for more than two and one-half hours, spread out over two days. But unlike Harris, he could not afford to talk and then simply stop.

He needed to build toward some kind of conclusion.

First, Moon's lawyer reminded the jury that the fact that the government was prosecuting his client did not mean that his client was guilty. If prosecution itself always meant guilt, Stillman argued, "we wouldn't need trials, we wouldn't need juries, we would simply lock up everyone whom the government wanted to lock up."[141]

Stillman then put his own spin on the concept of reasonable doubt. Beyond a reasonable doubt, of course, was the standard for finding a man guilty of a crime. But what exactly did that mean? Stillman used an analogy drawn from football:

> [I]f you looked upon it as reasonable doubt being a touchdown, one end of the field to the other, the government marches 99 yards, no touchdown. It takes 100 yards.[142]

Offering a useful illustration of reasonable doubt, Stillman reminded the jury of something he had said earlier:

> If you had the cash money, untraceable cash money and it was your money, why would you put it into a bank account in your own name?[143]

It was now Lawler's turn. He had an hour to sum up for his client. If anything, he had a tougher job than Stillman.

Like Stillman, he went for a weak point in the government's argument: that the case against Moon and Kamiyama was primarily a tax case. At the case's center were the Chase Manhattan Bank accounts. Lawler pointed out:

> And I say to you that if the government fails, if they fail to establish that fact, if they fail to establish beyond a reasonable doubt the identity of the funds in the Chase account, then the rest of the case fails too.[144]

Regarding Kamiyama's direct involvement in the alleged tax evasion, Lawler attempted to parry the government's sword play. Kamiyama, he pointed out, was a man who spoke no English and had little or no comprehension of tax laws—hardly someone who could be responsible for Moon's 1973 tax return.

The supposedly false information on the return was not a deliberate effort to deceive. It was only a badly bungled effort by Joe Tully, a man who was no accountant and whose only experience with tax returns was in helping friends in college with their 1040 forms. Indeed, considering the fact that Tully prepared Moon's return on the basis of a fiscal, not calendar, year and that he did not get Moon to sign it on the first go-around opens questions as to what happened to those fraternity pals at Stanford Joe Tully tried to help.

The bungled tax return constituted an odd sort of conspiracy, Lawler argued.[145]

I cannot imagine a better way of attracting attention, of making sure this return is noticed in the way it was done. And I submit to you that you can find that because of the way it was done, because of the mistakes that were made in the very filing, that there was no conspiracy underway then or ever.[146]

Lawler had spent nearly half of his allotted hour before approaching the perjury minefield. Understandably, he did so with caution, taking on the least explosive part of the government's charges first.

The first point concerned Kamiyama's testimony at the grand jury where he had stated that Moon had not signed any documents with respect to stock shares. As we know, Moon had, in fact, signed the Tong-Il certificates. But Lawler's point was there was no evidence that Kamiyama knew that Moon had signed. Rather than lying about it, he may have been just mistaken.

"[Y]ou will find not a bit of evidence that shows that Mr. Kamiyama was present when that document was signed or any evidence he ever specifically saw that particular document," Lawler told the jury.[147]

Kamiyama's attorney then attempted to sweep up another mine. This one concerned the government's query about a document that it failed to show Kamiyama, thus trapping him into making a false statement.

Lawler's comment drew a heated objection from Flumenbaum, forcing Lawler to rephrase his argument; rephrase, but not abandon.

In fact, he hit it harder than before:

> And I say to you that if the government is going to ask a jury to
> convict a man of a serious charge, if they are going to ask you to find
> beyond a reasonable doubt that he gave false testimony, then he was
> entitled to have that document shown to him, and in the absence of
> evidence that it was shown to him, in the absence of any evidence in
> this record anywhere that he had ever seen that document, then the
> [government has] utterly failed in its proof.[148]

Lawler plowed on. The question of Moon and the checkbook
was a tough one to defuse, and Lawler didn't quite handle it. But
then he had been left with little to say on the subject. Kamiyama
had flatly testified before the grand jury—or so it seemed, thanks
to the errors of Kamiyama's interpreter—that he kept the checkbook and that Moon had not signed any checks. But as the
government proved with hundreds of checks, Moon in fact did
sign them. Kamiyama's perjury could not be directly denied, only
finessed.

True, the prosecution, meaning Flumenbaum, had played it
cute before the grand jury by having on hand, but not showing,
checks with Moon's signature. But Lawler had a trick up his sleeve,
too. He reminded the jury that Kamiyama had in fact hedged his
grand jury answers by prefacing them with remarks like "As best I
recall," and "As I remember."[149]

Then Lawler made his main point:

> I say to you when you have a witness and you are questioning him not
> about what he did but about whether somebody else put handwrit-
> ing on a check and he is answering in terms of "As best I recall," and
> you are going back eight years, then before any jury should be asked
> to return a verdict of guilty, that person is entitled to have the check
> shown to him so he can say, "Yes, that is so, no, that is not."[150]

Lawler had done his best to make the government, not Kamiyama, the problem. The Japanese's attorney did not, however,
get the last word on the subject. Flumenbaum did, because under
trial procedures the government has the right to the final rebuttal.

Flumenbaum was not about to miss this opportunity. For an
hour and a half he hammered at the defendants with everything
he had. Now, as we know, rebuttals are supposed to be brief and to

the point, but the young Martin was no respecter of trial procedures.

Flumenbaum did not wait to get in front of the jury to open his attack; he began it in the robing room with Judge Goettel and the other trial attorneys.

The prosecutor had several bones to pick with Lawler's summation. First, Kamiyama's attorney had implied that a charge had been dropped against his client for lack of evidence. In fact, the charge had not been made because of the statute of limitations. Or so Flumenbaum claimed.

Second, Lawler, he claimed, had misrepresented the case in regard to the government's failure to present documents in question to Kamiyama, thus inducing his perjury.

Lawler *in camera* heatedly denied Flumenbaum's charges. Judge Goettel, typically, waffled and then once again postponed his decision.[151]

But that was only for openers—a small hint of the storm that was to come. Flumenbaum had gotten the signal to proceed. This trial was not going to go gently into the night. It ended instead with a bang, and not a whimper, and Flumenbaum made sure of the fireworks.

In a very real sense, this case was Flumenbaum's. He had nurtured it for years over the objections of his colleagues in the Justice Department. He could not and would not let go. With this last rebuttal opportunity, he would once more try the case—his way.

Ordinarily prosecutors, when they opt to do rebuttal, stick to the basic rule: make the rebuttal a rebuttal—a running commentary and refutation of issues and points raised in the defense's summation.

It is not an opportunity to say anything that comes to mind. It cannot be a chance simply to retry the whole case. Usually, with a certain amount of latitude given, that is what happens. It is, in the final analysis, a brief and concise reply for the benefit of the jury.

But those rules were not Flumenbaum's. He spoke for ninety minutes. He would have taken more, but the court virtually cut him off. This was no ordinary rebuttal in other ways, too. Ordinarily, summations and rebuttals are not peppered with objections from the other side. Jo Ann Harris got through four hours of summation without one from the defense.

Flumenbaum was different. He provoked a score of objections, some of which set off heated exchanges.

The bitter tone of the rebuttal was established early when Flumenbaum charged that the defense's case rested on a handful of witnesses "who would do anything, say anything, including falsifying documents, including lying under oath before a grand jury and, as I will talk to you later, before you right from that witness stand, to help Moon and Kamiyama."[152]

Flumenbaum didn't plan to yield a single inch. It wasn't long before the lawyers for the defense were weighing in with objections to Flumenbaum's rather interesting notions of what a rebuttal was all about.

At first Stillman and Lawler's objections were on the mild side. They soon learned that was a mistake. Even when the court sustained their objections, Flumenbaum had a habit of ignoring Judge Goettel and going on much as before. So they stepped down harder.

When Flumenbaum, for instance, raised the issue of David Kim's having received $75,000 in cash, Lawler strongly objected to it as improper rebuttal. Reason? The transaction had never been mentioned in anyone's summation. The court agreed.

But the young prosecutor did not, and so continued to harangue the jury on the point until he was brought up short by several more rounds of objections.[153]

No one could stop Flumenbaum now. He delved into anything he felt like. If Moon's household accounts annoyed him, he said so—three or four times—leaving the court to urge him to move on after the defense lawyers once more plied their objections.

Late in the day the clashes got so disorderly that Judge Goettel brought the lawyers to the sidebar. The huddle was called just after Flumenbaum finished castigating the defense once again for not bringing to the witness stand anyone with direct knowledge of the critical facts in the case, as he put it.

Lawler wasted no time, moving for a mistrial because, he charged, the government had violated the defendants' Fifth Amendment rights by questioning their unwillingness to take the stand in their defense.

The court denied the motion, but agreed that Flumenbaum had

gone too far: "The defendant himself can be considered a witness. You have to be careful about these comments."

Flumenbaum denied, somewhat unconvincingly, that his intention had been to suggest that the defendants were unforthcoming. In fact, he generously offered to make it better by telling the jury he was not referring to the defendants at all.

The suggestion horrified Goettel:

No please. You cannot do it now. The more you say the worse you make it. Just avoid any comments that have an ambiguous overtone.[154]

To be fair, Flumenbaum on occasion landed a good punch above the belt during the rebuttal. With the topic of witnesses still clearly on his mind, he pointedly asked, If the defense really believed in the family fund why didn't they call in at least one of those hundreds of Japanese who had ponied funds into the resource-starved American Unification Church?[155]

Why indeed? Considering the treatment accorded non-English-speaking Kamiyama at the hands of the prosecution, the answer is obvious.

Soon, however, he was back on the old track. He sneered at the defense's argument that if Moon were plotting tax evasion, he would not have been so obvious about it. "[I]t is an argument which is made in every single tax case," Flumenbaum told the jury.

"Objection, your Honor, I am not in every single tax case. I am just here," Stillman cried. That one stung. And it hurt. It was one thing to accuse his client of tax evasion, it was another to characterize his defense as a moth-eaten cliché, especially to the jury during rebuttal.[156]

The objection was sustained. The jury was instructed to ignore the government's remark.

Flumenbaum could not have cared less. He was reaching his crescendo, and he was going to beat this dangerous argument to death for the jury's edification.

Absolutely unfazed by the court's ruling, young Martin rolled on:

It is an argument that says if my client wanted to conspire to defraud the government why would he open an account in his name? Ladies and gentlemen, the sad truth is that once you are caught and once you are indicted it is very easy to say I couldn't have been that stupid. And if that argument were accepted there would never be any convictions in court cases.[157]

Lawler objected on the same grounds, and once more the court agreed. So what? was Flumenbaum's attitude. The objection rolled off.

Argued Flumenbaum:

There is always bank accounts involved. There is always a paper trail involved. The real answer to why you put the money in your name is simple, it's your money. You do with it as you please. It is a question of control, it is a question of power that you might believe that you are above the law.[158]

INSTRUCTIONS TO THE JURY

It was now Judge Gerard Goettel's turn to address the jury. Like all judges, he instructed the jurors in the law. They were to decide what the relevant facts of the case were and what the verdict based on those facts would be.

Goettel made no secret that this was a complicated case; it took over two hours for the court to read the charge. The case was also complex enough for Goettel to have copies of the charge prepared beforehand—a fairly unusual procedure—in order for each juror to follow along.

It was in keeping with Goettel's notion of being fair and impartial. To an extent and by his lights, he was. But Goettel's behavior through the whole trial had been odd and wobbly. Decisiveness was not and never had been his trademark. And his hesitation usually benefited the government.

His background showed.

For example, only moments after the defense rested its case, Jo Ann Harris raised an issue in Judge Goettel's robing room. The government wanted to introduce new evidence dealing with Mrs.

Moon's application for a permanent resident visa in the United States.

Before the defense could spring any objections, Harris explained why. It was the government's belief that the Reverend Moon's wife had lied about her status to obtain the visa. And her success in doing so had in turn led to Moon's ability to seek permanent residence in the U.S. as well which, in turn, gave him the opportunity to cheat on his taxes.

Or in Jo Ann Harris's words:

We think it demonstrates, again as a similar act, Mr. Moon's capability of forming the intent to file false documents with the United States, and we think it is very pertinent here for that reason.[159]

It was, at best, a rather irregular way of doing business. There is every sign that the decision to push the immigration issue was a last minute one, and not premeditated in nature. Apparently the prosecution had decided that after Mrs. DeBoe's testimony for the defense the government needed a new lift.

That it was a hasty decision by the government is evidenced by the fact that the documents submitted were sloppily put together.

And Judge Goettel was a bit put out. Neat and tidy these weren't, he complained; they even contained incorporation papers of the Holy Spirit Association. "I can't figure out what they are doing in the file since there is no indication they are resting on HSA for any purpose here."

"That's right," Harris sheepishly admitted.

"In the back," Goettel added, "there is a lot of papers I assume written in Korean or Japanese, I have no idea what they are. What are they?"

"Nor do I," admitted Harris.

"Do you really think you should be offering something when you don't know what it is?"[160]

The answer, of course, was obvious, but that hardly deterred the prosecution from pursuing its "similar acts" argument. That claimed Mrs. Moon had declared in her filing for permanent residency that she was a chaperone-cook-nutritionist advisor for the Little Angels choir; that she earned $7,000 for her work; and that as a permanently employed person in the United States she could support her husband until he found a job.

The defense lawyers protested this bit of legerdemain on the part of the government. "[T]here is nothing in this record to indicate that Reverend Moon was aware of anything that the government now says is false in his wife's application."[161]

But Goettel was not impressed. When Lawler broke in, the judge grew testy. "What are you doing back in here," he asked. "This isn't even being offered against your client."

When Stillman tried to explain that the two defense attorneys had an agreement to help each other, his Honor got nasty: "I do mind. You do yourself by yourself."[162]

From there it was a losing battle for both Stillman and Lawler. Stillman's argument that the case was a tax case, not an immigration matter, that there was no connection between the two, that the whole argument was convoluted, all fell on deaf ears. As did the fact that "similar acts" evidence had before only been allowed when prior criminal behavior had been established. Even Martin Flumenbaum had never argued that Mrs. Moon was a jailbird.

For the next half hour Stillman and Goettel contested the point while Harris and Flumenbaum remained silent. Why should they say anything? Suddenly, the court had become their chief advocate. Stillman cited case precedents. Goettel ignored them.

Getting nowhere, Stillman threw up his hands in exasperation: "But for the life of me, Judge Goettel, I don't see how some Immigration matter helps us advance this tax issue. That's my problem."

"Well," snapped his Honor, "it isn't your problem, it is my problem and since I see that it does—."[163]

Stillman's interruption did him no good. The court allowed the evidence in the record: the last piece that the jury received, thus guaranteeing its maximum influence on their thinking.

Gerard Goettel's bias for the prosecution in this last matter was extraordinary. It gave the jury a perfect bit of prejudicial evidence which Goettel nowhere officially recognized. To the twelve men and women of the jury, the immigration "special acts" evidence offered proof that the Reverend Sun Myung Moon and his wife had cheated to get into the country and once here were perfectly willing to cheat again—this time on their income taxes. To the man in the street it was devastating stuff.

The defense recognized it. So did the government. Only Judge Goettel did not. It only became blindingly apparent later when the Court of Appeals threw out the evidence and Goettel's rationale for its introduction. By that time, however, the damage was done.

No judge enters a case with an open mind. Like all other human beings, he begins with certain prejudices and predispositions and habits of thought that are the result of his whole life, on and off the bench. Gerard Goettel, of course, was no exception. What was the man's state of mind as he presided over a controversial case that he would just as soon have seen go to a colleague? The answer to that question will surely tell us something about how the case was conducted, including his instructions to the jury, who now faced him expectantly.

To be sure, Goettel was not in the habit of letting it all hang out as some of his black-robed brethren on the bench often did. Goettel, if nothing else, was careful in expressing opinions. Careful, but not abstemious.

Throughout the trial, Goettel had let his guard down on occasion, making a number of curious and negative references to the defendants by way of "innocent" analogy.

On the very first day of the trial as the lawyers discussed the problem of finding a panel of unprejudiced jurors for the defendants, Goettel had compared Moon's problem with that of Atlanta's accused mass murderer Wayne Williams. Indeed, in the comparison, Moon got the worst of it. To Goettel, Williams had jurors who only had to set aside their feelings related to the specific case. Moon, on the other hand, was unpopular for reasons that went far beyond what he was being tried for, namely, not paying taxes.[164]

But that had been merely a warm-up toss. One minute later, Goettel had offered an insight linking Sun Myung Moon to Adolph Hitler:

Think, if you will, of the following hypothetical. The Adolph Hitler is found alive and living in Hoboken, under an alias, of course. He has been living all these years on his ill-gotten gains spirited out of Nazi Germany. He is brought to trial for his tax offenses.

Having drawn this fascinating analogy, Goettel went on before the lawyers:

You poll the jury. You get the usual few percent who claim they have never heard of Adolph Hitler. You get a number of others who say that they have heard of him but they have no strong feelings about him. Then you get some others who say they have heard about him, they know his bad reputation, but they believe that they can put that behind them and nevertheless judge the case fairly.

And then came the snapper:

Do you think Adolph Hitler could get a fair jury trial on tax charges in this country today?[165]

From a killer of innocent children to the mass murderer of millions, Goettel's mind was clearly working in a way that did not favorably dispose him toward the defendants.

The Williams and Hitlerian analogies were mere preliminaries, tossed off before the trial had actually started. Goettel himself had only been warming up. Regarding Moon's guilt or innocence, for example, the judge at the sidebar had admonished the defense lawyers that their client wasn't off the hook simply because someone else had prepared his returns:

I would suggest to you that there is nothing in the law that says that the head of a large organization can avoid criminal responsibility by layering himself about three steps away from what is ultimately done and say that since I don't personally direct all these things you can never prove my personal knowledge of them and therefore I can't be criminally responsible.[166]

That observation might remind the listener of a criminal undertaking well known to viewers of, say, "The Untouchables." But Goettel hadn't been just hinting. He had said it directly in his next paragraph.

The organized criminal syndicates existed with great impunity in this country for long periods of time because of the difficulty in reaching the people on top, because of layers of persons below. It became impossible to prove that even the mob chief who never wanted somebody killed that the person who killed him, who never in his life had seen the mob chief was in fact doing it upon his directions. That is a problem of practical proof that the Government has to confront.[167]

When defense counsel somewhat timidly suggested that the court's knowledge of mob procedure was surely only by way of analogy, Judge Goettel had said, yes, of course, it was.

But he quickly had added that he had also used it because he had once written an article titled "Why the Crime Syndicates Can't Be Touched." Goettel had taken great pride in being part of an organized crime strike force, his greatest accomplishment. With Moon, it seems, he was reliving the whole adventure.[168]

Meanwhile, Goettel's earlier caveat was hardly convincing. Moreover, he just couldn't get the Mafia theme off his mind. Five minutes later the judge had gone back to the old stand. In this case, it was the "Moonies," all of them, who reminded him of the Mafia conspiring in the Adirondacks. Or in Goettel's words:

It always seems to me there was a fallacy in that reasoning in that when you get a lot of people who as their occupation in life is crime and who carry guns and have criminal records and happen to be in this remote section of New York at the same time, they weren't there to discuss the racing results.[169]

From Wayne Williams to Adolf Hitler and now Alphonse Capone it was an interesting trio of images. But Goettel had not finished quite yet. A few days later in the robing room, the judge had mused about the possibility that Moon's movement was a "Fagin-like operation" where hundreds of children were by theft and deception collecting money for their crime master. If that was the case, Goettel added, "[Moon] doesn't immunize himself against income by having the people who contribute say we are giving it to you for religious purposes."[170]

Comparing Moon to Charles Dickens' favorite villain was hardly a courtly boost to the defendants, and to the Reverend Sun Myung Moon in particular, but Judge Goettel still hadn't finished. Near the end of the trial, yet another analogy had struck the court as relevant. Why not Richard Nixon? If there were no actual existing records documenting a Moon conspiracy to defraud the government of a few thousand bucks, then perhaps it was because there were no Watergate-style tapes.

Judge Goettel said:

> [Reverend Moon] was not as foolish as the leader of another organization who made the mistake of keeping tape recordings of his meetings with people when there was something they didn't want known discussed. I grant you that is missing from here. We haven't got the Watergate tapes.[171]

One can almost hear the disappointment in Goettel's voice. The court had left out references to Attila the Hun and Jack the Ripper but not a kid murderer from Atlanta, Adolph Hitler, the *cosa nostra*, Fagin, and the disgraced Richard Nixon. It was an inkling to how Gerard Goettel saw this case.

And it wasn't good news for the defendants.

It was too late when Gerard Goettel finally read his statement to the jury. The charge was long, it was detailed, and for the most part it was even-handed.

The charge was divided into four parts. There were preliminary instructions; there were instructions on how the law applied to each count of the indictment; there were special instructions with respect to the evaluation of the evidence; and finally, there were some instructions as to how the jury should go about their deliberations.

The first part was mostly a plea for objectivity. "[Y]ou must not substitute or follow your own notion or opinion as to what the law is or ought to be."[172]

Fairness in this case was particularly necessary and Judge Goettel was not unaware of that fact:

> [T]he race, religion and ethnic origin of the defendants is of no consequence whatever. They are on trial in an American court before American jurors under the Constitution of the United States and considerations of race or religion must have no part in your deliberations. Indeed, you have taken a solemn oath to be fair and impartial to the defendants and the government alike.[173]

The court also reminded the jurors that they must not be swayed by the number of witnesses or which witnesses appeared for the defense and the prosecution. Nor should they be influenced by the rulings made by the judge—which was a good thing because while the prosecution rarely objected, the defense did, more than four hundred times—with the court ruling in the prosecution's favor by a three-to-one margin.[174]

Goettel then went through each count—all thirteen of them—line by line and cited the appropriate law and the standards of evidence that the jurors must consider.

But the key issue for Judge Goettel—the one the jury was to focus on—was whether or not the Chase Bank accounts and the Tong-Il stock belonged to the Reverend Mr. Moon for his personal use or for the church.

If the latter were the case, the jury had to understand the role of the trustee under the law, a role which Goettel spelled out with great detail and accuracy. "A trust is created when a person is given money or property to be held and used for the benefit of someone else," the court stated. He went on to remind the jurors that such an arrangement could be highly informal; it only required the consent of the parties involved.[175]

It is unnecessary for there to be a written agreement between Reverend Moon and the International Unification Church movement, providing he held the time deposits and Tong Il stock on behalf of the church . . . and you can find such an understanding on the basis of the party's conduct.[176]

Goettel also reminded the jurors that religious organizations have special rights under our system of government. Among other things:

[They] can invest and conduct businesses. While the income from such businesses is taxable, this fact does not make taxable the religion's income from other sources, including interest it earns on funds it has on deposit.[177]

They were special in other ways, too, the court pointed out:

A religious organization can properly pay the living expenses of its leaders or ministers in order to allow them to pursue its religious purposes and can make loans to its ministers or leaders on arm's length terms.[178]

Finally, Goettel gave some instructions as to how the jurors should deliberate. Each decision must be based on the evidence and the law. Opinions should not be changed—an honest conviction should not be surrendered "solely because of the opinions of your fellow jurors or merely for the purposes of returning a verdict."[179]

And if the jury got stuck, they could ask the court for help. If they needed evidence to be brought in, a written note would get them what they wanted.

The twelve were then sent to the jury room to deliberate. At last, it was their turn. It was May 12, six weeks after the trial had begun.

The moment that the defense lawyers had dreaded all along had arrived. This most complicated of cases was now in the hands of a jury. It was a situation that they had sought through pretrial motions to avoid. Judge Goettel had turned them down flat.

The quality of the jury had been a theme of the trial. The fear of prejudiced jurors had never gone away, even after the extensive pretrial *voir dire*.

Prejudice, however, was only one problem. Another was the capability of average men and women to follow the complex maneuvers they had been witnesses to. Or, for that matter, the some one-thousand exhibits presented in evidence, the lion's share of which had come from the government.

Occasionally, Moon's lawyer had gently reminded the court of just why the defense had asked for a bench trial. Judge Goettel, however, had brushed aside the concerns while the government lawyers sang the praises of the jurors. "This is a sophisticated jury who understands the evidence," Flumenbaum observed fatuously at mid-trial.[180]

But even Judge Goettel had not believed that one and had indicated so on a number of occasions. Often the jurors had been less than alert, judging from the several occasions when one or more were caught dozing.[181]

There had been simply no cure for that and, oddly enough, one makeshift juror remedy for wandering minds had not been encouraged: note-taking. Unlike the jurymen in *Alice in Wonderland*, Moon's jurors were discouraged from writing on their slates by

Judge Goettel after it was reported that at least one had been doing just that.

Under federal trial rules note-taking is not forbidden, but it is strongly advised against—which is what Judge Goettel did. There were two reasons for that, the court said:

> First, there is a worry that the juror taking the notes may miss the next testimony.

> The second problem is that we are concerned that the juror who takes the notes may become the unofficial recording secretary for the rest of the jury and that definitely is not allowed. No juror is allowed to show any notes to any other juror.[182]

The jurors, of course, weren't expected to remember all the testimony or even a part of it. They simply had to do their best and listen closely to the summations. If they needed a new look at the evidence or a portion of the transcript to review, it could be read to them. Otherwise, they were on their own.

The jury was locked up in a fourth-floor jury room—one that was deemed to be more comfortable than the one attached to the courtroom on the fifth floor. They were not sequestered. If the jurymen could not reach a quick verdict, they were to be allowed to go home each night.

That's exactly what happened.

At the beginning of their first full day of deliberations, the jury made several requests. The twelve wanted a blackboard and chalk which, after a search of Foley Square, were produced for them. Their other wants were not so easily satisfied. They asked for the text of Judge Goettel's charge and the transcript involving the testimony of four witnesses.

On this point, the jurors were under a misapprehension. The court could only read to them specific parts of the charge again— no copy would be allowed in the jury room—and relevant parts of the transcript, too, could only be read to them. Because their initial request amounted to two full trial days of evidence, Goettel suggested they refine the request.

By 5:30 P.M. the jury was deadlocked and elected to go home for the night.

The second full day of deliberation, Friday, May 14, saw more requests from the jury for documents. Unfortunately, the note was so badly written that Judge Goettel had to call them out of the jury room and ask for an explanation.

It was another tall order.

They wanted more information on Moon's interest-bearing accounts. They also wanted the family fund ledger in the English translation and in the original Japanese. There were also requests for the Tong-Il certificates and the charts covering the Chase Manhattan Bank accounts.[183]

At the end of Friday, there still was no verdict, and instead of laboring well into the night, the jury opted for taking the weekend off.

On Monday, May 17, the jury deliberated all day without making any requests. When the court had heard nothing from them by 5:30 P.M. they were brought in and sent home. The dismissal was the last one. The jury was close to a verdict.[184]

By two o'clock the following afternoon, the jury announced that it had reached its decision. Twenty minutes later, the foreman, Mary Nimmo, handed the verdict form to the clerk, who read it to the packed courtroom. The jury had found Sun Myung Moon guilty on Counts 1, 2, 3, and 4. Takeru Kamiyama was found guilty on Counts 1, 5, 6, 7, 8, 9, 10, 11, 12, and 13.[185]

It was a clean sweep. The only drama in the reading was the clerk's hesitation after the reading of Count 3.

Each juror was then polled to determine if what had been read was indeed his or her verdict. All replied in the affirmative although two of them seemed uncertain.

Judge Goettel thanked the jurors for their patience and hard work and promised to thank each individually later. He also praised the conduct of the lawyers on both sides and then promptly adjourned *United States of America versus Sun Myung Moon and Takeru Kamiyama.*

As reporters raced for their telephones—they still do that—a buoyant Reverend Sun Myung Moon thanked his lawyers and shook their hands. He then turned toward Martin Flumenbaum to shake his hand as well. But the prosecutor quickly gathered up his papers and left, studiously avoiding eye contact with the man he had just convicted.

It was a funny exit for a victor.

CHAPTER VIII

THE JURY

Jury: A group of twelve men who, having lied to the judge about their hearing, health and business engagements, have failed to fool him.

H.L. MENCKEN

So the trial was over. And no matter how much Moon's defense lawyers, or for that matter less partisan observers, argued that the trial had only established some financial mistakes of the sort no one involved in a criminal conspiracy would make, the fact remained Moon was headed for prison.

So why did the jury convict?

"I know every father thinks his daughter is pretty but mine really is," British journalist Douglas Hyde told an audience once to laughter. And, likewise, every defense lawyer with a well-known defendant who gets convicted claims pre-trial publicity is the real culprit.

So, did the second or invisible trial carried on by the Moon prosecution play to an already prejudiced jury? Was it with the assistance of a trial judge whose own bias was so deep and sweeping that he could not have done the defendants any more damage if he had tried? Did prejudice really have that much impact?

For an answer we must return to a time just prior to the trial.

The Reverend Sun Myung Moon's lawyers were worried men as the trial approached. With good reason. How was it possible for the

Korean and his Japanese disciple Takeru Kamiyama to get a fair trial on tax evasion and perjury charges? In New York City?

True, the trial would have little to do with the indictment. That was the trouble. Tax cases were something only an accountant could love. But Moon was different.

Moon's lawyers knew their client and his movement were among the most hated items in America. On anybody's list of unpopular men in America, Moon would have no trouble making it. Kamiyama, of course, didn't count.

For a dozen years or more the word "Moonies" had managed to find a prominent place in hundreds of ugly headlines, providing fodder, albeit largely unsubstantiated, for journalists. Unification Church members were easy targets and the country's libel laws seemed to have been suspended for the occasion. The church had made "brainwashing" a household word again. The thought of zombified Americans hadn't horrified the public so much since the Korean War, when the Chinese communists and Richard Condon gave us *The Manchurian Candidate*.

Now it was another band of orientals—but this time they were brainwashing our kids.

The trial was to be held in New York's Federal Southern District, which merely compounded the problem. It meant that the proceedings would take place in downtown Manhattan at Foley Square, New York, a place not unknown for ethnic resentment.

To add to the general bias, in the late winter of 1982 two more anti-"Moonie" books were published and a film, *Ticket to Heaven*, was enjoying a long run in Manhattan. *Ticket*, incidentally, was hailed by the *New York Daily News* "as an indictment of the Unification Church."[1]

These observations, of course, were all merely impressions. Strong ones, no doubt accurate ones. But Moon's principal trial lawyer Charles Stillman thought in early February that one thing was certain. Without hard proof, the court would not buy the argument of prejudice. Worse, the court would not accept the remedy either: a bench trial over one by jury.

It was a tricky question and Stillman knew it. Bench trials require the judge, instead of twelve jurors, to be—in legalese—the fact-finder. In plain English, the court decides on guilt or innocence as well as on sentencing, if there is a conviction. A bench trial is unusual, an exception to the Sixth Amendment privilege of trial by one's peers, but it is available. Under the right circumstances.

The problem was to make a convincing case to the court and to the prosecution. Bench trials were not (and are not) free for the asking—not under the Federal Rules of Criminal Procedure. Rule 23(a) had to be confronted, a rule that spelled out those circumstances in which a defendant could and could not waive his right to a jury trial.

For Stillman it was a nightmare judgment on which the whole case turned. Not just the trial itself, but the quite possible, and surely lengthy, appeal process that would follow.

That is why Stillman picked up the phone and called Stephen Roth. Roth was something of a legend. He was a pollster by profession, but his specialty wasn't product marketing or politics. Roth had founded a company called Litigation Services Group, a polling company that worked for, among others, lawyers and their clients. Stillman wanted Roth to do a telephone poll and find out how unpopular Moon was in the part of New York from which the panel of jurymen would be selected.

Roth, as usual, did his professional best. He surveyed a thousand people—an unusually high number—scattered over southern New York. His sample covered the whole demographic lot: rich, comfortable, and poor. Minorities, of course. With New York, naturally, it was vital that the net be cast wide lest some important group like left-handed Lithuanians be left out. So Roth tested the smart and the dumb; the suave and the ignorant. Everyone, in short, ended up in his polling universe.

Unlike many telephone polls, Roth's was not a quick-and-dirty effort. The procedure took several days, not overnight, which is how most are conducted. The unusually large sample and the length of the call—more than twenty minutes—gave the poll even greater credibility.

What Roth so painstakingly quantified came as no comfort to Moon's defense team. In fact, the results weren't as bad as they thought. They were worse. The Reverend Sun Myung Moon wasn't hated. He was reviled, loathed, and despised, thanks largely to nearly ten years of horribly negative publicity created by American politicians and served up by a gleeful press.

That bad? Consider. Exactly 76 percent of those polled reacted unfavorably to the name "the Reverend Moon" and a miniscule 3 percent favorably.

"Moonies," however, did better, sort of: 5 percent were favorable and 67 percent were unfavorable. To professional pollsters these were amazing "negatives."[2]

But that was only the beginning. A whopping 40 percent of the sample were ready to throw Moon in the slammer, never mind a hearing or a trial. The charges didn't matter either.[3]

Breaking down the overall sample into its components made for equally bad reading—if you were a lawyer for Sun Myung Moon. Those, for example, who would not jail Moon off the bat still had a 62.6 percent negative rating for "the Reverend Moon," 47.2 percent for "Sun Myung Moon," while "Moonies" got 51.4 percent. Moreover, among the more tolerant New Yorkers the positives were still a dismal 5.8 percent, 8.0 percent, and 9.1 percent.[4]

There was more bad news. The usual profile was not working. Among the more affluent and better-educated—"the Westchester resident," Roth called them—and therefore more tolerant, Moon's negatives were disastrously high. More predictably, the "don't knows" were very low. They were, it was clear, irretrievable.

What about the others? Minorities, working class, Catholic, the high school-educated? The negatives were high, but so were the "don't knows." This fact, Roth said, offered a small ray of hope. From among them "it is possible to obtain an objective jury— difficult but possible," he wrote Stillman on February 9.[5]

This was a slender thread indeed. In fact, Roth just about snapped it with this observation:

> Those that don't know Reverend Moon at present and are likely to listen impartially are most likely to have strong negative biases and therefore develop negative attitudes toward the case. This group includes the less educated and lower income.[6]

That's what Roth's data showed. Among Catholics, for example, nearly half would send Moon to a correctional center posthaste, while only 22.8 percent of Protestants were for instant jail. Jews only 11.5 percent. The figures for the lowbrows were even worse as Moon became better known.[7]

The bad news wasn't complete quite yet, however. Not only did

Moon have a comparatively—in fact extraordinarily—high-recognition, high-negatives problem, but opinions were strongly held. His lack of popularity wasn't broad and shallow; it was broad and deep. The man and his movement had hit a raw nerve and folks were just plain mad.

To test the intensity of public feeling, the respondents, at the end of the Roth questionaire, were given an open-ended question. How did they really feel about Moon and his church?

Typical responses included, "The man is a crook, he uses people for financial gain." So was "I think he's a big hoax, crook, just a racketeer." Can anyone doubt the gem-like flame of this response: "He brainwashes young kids . . . he's using it for his own personal benefit." Or "they exploit the young, receive too much tax free shelter. . . . [What] I dislike most about them is that he exploits the young and he hides behind his religion."[8]

Roth concluded that his vehemently negative results "are virtually unheard of in the modern-day United States" on any subject. "In light of this fact," he continued, "it must be anticipated that any representative jury panel will exhibit a strong negative bias and be predisposed against the Reverend Moon."[9]

Stillman wasn't surprised at the bad news, just possibly by the fact there was so much of it. Any lingering doubts that his clients could get a fair trial in New York of course were dispelled. There was no way in hell they could. That was that.

The problem was obvious. What wasn't so obvious was how to avoid this looming iceberg. The law, in fact, provided several remedies. All options were considered.

First, Moon's lawyers could have asked for a change in venue; that is, a different location for the trial. Because this was a federal case that could mean anywhere in the country. In ordinary criminal trials, local villains often have a better chance at finding an unbiased jury in another county, or even another state. Somewhere, anywhere, where the local and inflamed citizenry won't be.

In Moon's case, anything would have been better than New York City, but how much better? The church was almost universally despised, probably. One possibility, Utah, whose huge Mormon community possessed a strong memory of their own persecution, might have been better, but the actual site for the trial would be selected by the court. Defendants can't pick and choose where they will be tried.

Another way out of the dilemma was to request a continuance. The trial could be delayed by the court, *ad infinitum*. This procedure quite logically assumes that community passions eventually cool, leaving the defendant in a better position later rather than sooner.

Like change of venue, seeking a continuance didn't really cure the problem. Moon was not a mass murderer or a drug pusher. His alleged crime—tax evasion—had not aroused public hostility; his entire movement had. In addition, his unpopularity was not likely to lessen. In short, a continuance solved nothing either.

There was one last way out, and that was the course of action the defense team chose. They petitioned the court for a bench trial rather than a jury trial.

A bench trial meant throwing the case into the lap of the court for a decision on guilt or innocence. In fact, it was a desperate measure. Most lawyers would rather jump over the Great Wall of China than submit a client's fate to a judge—particularly a federal judge. Although almost unheard of, if requested, a bench trial is almost always granted.

But under federal trial procedure, the criteria for a bench trial request are found in Federal Rule 23(a). That rule sets out four criteria that must be met before a bench trial can be approved. First, the defendant has to put his request in writing. That sounds obvious, but the idea is sound enough: the accused must be fully aware of what he is doing before he waives his right to a jury trial—a basic right, squarely embedded in the Sixth Amendment.[10]

Second, the prosecution must agree to the waiver. Government approval is premised on the somewhat dubious (as we shall see) assumption that its attorney is acting in the public interest; i.e., saving the taxpayer unnecessary court costs (in this instance millions of dollars) while prosecuting a suspected criminal.

Third, the trial court must also give its consent. Fourth and finally, Rule 23(a) provides, somewhat redundantly, that the accused must "understand the significance of the waiver and that he exercises it voluntarily, knowingly, and intelligently.[11]

Strictly speaking, a bench trial is not a right of a defendant.

Whether he likes it or not, a trial by jury could be imposed on the accused although such instances are rare, extremely rare.

Case precedent lays out only two rules which prohibit a defendant from seeking a bench versus jury trial. The accused cannot waive his right simply to save time and expense. Most assuredly, he cannot seek a bench trial if he thinks the court will be more lenient or is already biased in his favor by either predisposition or fraud.[12]

The government and court must agree to a bench trial. Across the board, jurists and prosecuting attorneys much prefer a bench trial to submitting evidence to a jury, and why not? Juries are almost always composed of people who are somewhat unsophisticated and, to be blunt, don't know much about the finer points of jurisprudence. What's more, jurors tend to sympathize with the defendant, particularly in a tax prosecution where the universally despised Internal Revenue Service is usually involved in the case.

The requirement for government and court approval for a bench trial had never been an issue, not until Moon was indicted. It would later prove crucial in the trial.

As we have seen, with all the indicator lights of prejudice flashing red, Stillman and his legal team decided to waive a jury trial and ask for a bench trial.

However, something peculiar happened on the way to the court. The prosecutors said no. Under Rule 23(a) the government does not have to give a reason. In this case, federal prosecutors Jo Ann Harris and Martin Flumenbaum did. Their stated reason, however, was not the real one.

The government's lawyers could read poll results, too. It took no genius to figure out a conviction would be a lot simpler to obtain from a jury. Moon and Kamiyama were sitting ducks, and a hostile jury, fueled by the sort of emotion seen in Roth's poll, could do what a judge, even a judge friendly to the government, would have great difficulty doing.

Needless to say, that observation could not be offered as the reason for their refusal to approve the defendants' request for a waiver. Silence might look bad—if nothing else—on appeal. What could they say?

Nothing really, until Moon himself gave them what they were looking for. It was a matter of the duck paying for the hunting license.

On October 22, 1981, following his indictment, the Reverend Sun Myung Moon made a speech on the steps of the Foley Square courthouse in which he said that his legal difficulties were the result of racial and religious discrimination. Moon's statement was all the government prosecutors needed, a single straw that they could, and would, desperately grasp.

As every first-year schoolboy knows, speaking out publicly and protesting one's innocence—on the steps of a courthouse, no less— is perhaps the single most important fundamental right guaranteed by the U.S. Constitution.

It's no mere coincidence that the Founding Fathers placed free speech, along with its sister, freedom of religious expression, in the First Amendment to the Constitution. They knew how crucial both would be to the continued existence of a free, open, and just nation.

Now the U.S. government was about to use one of those sacred rights, free speech, as a hammer to deprive Moon of his other First Amendment guarantee, the right to practice his religion without government intrusion.

Having questioned "the integrity and motives of the prosecution," the government's lawyers argued, a jury trial was now necessary to repair the damage done to it by the defendant's criticism. This presumably would serve the public interest, which the government was duty bound to uphold.[13]

That was only the beginning.

Harris and Flumenbaum also argued that the judge, if a bench trial were ordered, would as the sole fact-finder in the case be subject to criticism no matter how he ruled. Thus, the jury should assume, and thus diffuse, the responsibility.[14]

An odd set of arguments; in fact, they were unprecedented. But the arguments were not laughed out of court. Instead, Judge Gerard Goettel considered them and waffled. He would not decide until the *voir dire*, the jury selection process, was completed. Then he would rule on whether the Reverend Moon would stand trial before a jury.

Did this make any sense? Moon's lawyers later, upon appeal, said no. In fact, they argued, everything was turned upside down.

The government had cross-wired the First and Sixth Amendments and gotten for itself a very peculiar end product. In effect, the prosecution argued that by the exercise of Moon's First Amendment rights, he had forfeited his chance for a fair trial.

Of course the government didn't put it that way. Lawyers rarely say what they mean. They use high-sounding legal language. The weaker the case, the more elegant the prose.

But let's take a closer look at the arguments advanced by Harris and Flumenbaum about why Moon should not be granted a bench trial.

The first thing that should be noted is that Moon's Foley Square statement—which was printed in a full-page advertisement in the *Times* two weeks later—was the sole reason under the rubric of Rule 23(a) offered by the government for its refusal to approve the waiver.[15]

The second observation is this: Judge Goettel didn't buy the government's argument, nor did he seem impressed with Harris and Flumenbaum's tender solicitations.

> Why are you allowing yourself to be led off by this red herring of prejudice resulting in this indictment? Almost every defendant who is of any public note who gets indicted says, "If I wasn't such and such, I wouldn't have been indicted." They say it continually.[16]

Judge Goettel was a lot of things, but one thing he wasn't was stupid. In fact, far better than the defense lawyers ever could, the court spotted the phoniness of the government's case for waiver denial. A red herring? It was a large smelly one that the prosecution team was dragging across Foley Square.

But it was more than a red herring. The government's argument, incredibly enough, ran against the spirit and letter of the Constitution and a string of Supreme Court cases a kilometer long. The right to criticize the government is one of the most basic rights any American has enjoyed since John Peter Zenger, the colonial journalist, took his whacks against a royal governor in the early eighteenth century. (He was tried for criminal libel and acquitted, a major victory for the cause of free press.)

As the high court put it a few years ago: "Criticism of the government is at the very center of the constitutionally protected area of free discussion."[17]

This was not about the proverbial yelling of "Fire!" in a crowded theater or the dubious rights of a child pornographer. This wasn't subversion; there was no "clear and present danger" alarm bell going off because of Moon and Kamiyama.

What this was about was political speech and the right to exercise it—in this case by a man who thought he had just been shafted by the Justice Department, with help from everyone's favorite bureau, the IRS. If free speech were rationed only to the contented, then the First Amendment would lose all meaning. The First was meant for people with grievances.

The point was made by the defense lawyers on appeal, although not much was made of it during the pretrial hearings.

There was another fallacy running through the government's interpretation of Rule 23(a). This was the assumption that by "protecting" the integrity of the jury system, the government was acting somehow in the public interest. The claim was not only maddeningly vague, it was also dead wrong. And full of mischievous consequences.

There was, in fact, no distinct public interest at play. Nor was such an interest recognized by the courts. It has always been presumed that a defendant's right to a fair trial (by whatever means) according to his lights is the overriding public interest. Otherwise, the Sixth Amendment becomes a dead letter, and not just for the individual involved.

As it turned out, the government did not even bother to assert that a jury trial would be the fairest procedure for Moon and Kamiyama. That small point was ignored entirely. Fairness, in short, had nothing to do with the government's objection at all. The prosecution simply used a spurious public interest to protect governmental institutions against the critical words of an indicted and justifiably outraged clergyman.[18]

As absurd as these arguments were, the prosecutors knew they wouldn't make any difference. Judge Goettel in the end refused a bench trial simply because the government had said no. Never mind the reasons. Goettel, of course, was simply reading Rule 23(a) as written and Goettel was strictly a black-print lawyer.

The trouble is that Rule 23(a) is not written in stone. It is not even the law as such or case precedent. Rule 23(a) is a federal regulation concocted by Justice Department lawyers. Moreover, the rule has been interpreted and reworked by the courts, and the courts' teaching on Rule 23(a) is very instructive.

The landmark case is *United States v. Singer*, heard by the U.S. Supreme Court in 1965.

Seven years before the court reviewed the case, Singer had been indicted and then convicted on thirty counts of mail fraud. His scam? He promised amateur songwriters he would market their tunes and make them rich beyond their wildest dreams . . . for a small fee, of course. It was, in the nature of these things, no big deal. Just your average penny-ante American flimflam. Often out of the small, mean, and sordid crimes great case law is made. This fact often comes as a shock to first-year law students, but it is true nonetheless. Our whole system of jurisprudence rests mostly on petty confidence men like Singer.

Needless to say, Singer just took the money from the suckers and ran—until he was arrested by a squad of postal inspectors.[19]

The *Singer* case became famous because he demanded a bench trial, rather than face a jury of his peers. His lawyer claimed his client had an absolute right to one, no questions asked. Singer's reason for wanting a bench trial, however, was not rooted in the fairness question. There was no community prejudice or hostility directed particularly at the con man. Singer had cheated people across the country, with the help of the U.S. Postal Service. It was a very ordinary swindle. No howling mob of his peers milled around outside the jail demanding his hanging forthwith.

Singer's request was based on mere convenience. He wanted to get the trial over with as quickly as possible—and save some money in the bargain.

But of course we are dealing with the American legal system. Exactly the opposite happened.

First, Singer's prosecuting attorney, without stating any reason, refused to approve the waiver. Singer appealed. Seven years later the case ended up in the U.S. Supreme Court. I suspect the Warren court took the appeal because it was the first time the high court had looked at the issue in some thirty-five years. As it turned out the 1965 decision leaned heavily on *Patton v. United States*.[20]

Patton had denied there was an absolute right of the defendant to choose his poison. The decision also upheld a general preference for trial by jury for criminal cases. Therefore "unreasonable or undue departures from that mode of [jury] trial" must be avoided.[21]

Even more specifically *Singer* upheld Rule 23(a):

> We find no constitutional impediment to conditioning a waiver of this right on the consent of the prosecuting attorney and the trial judge when, if either refuses to consent, the result is simply that the defendant is subject to an impartial jury—by the very thing that the Constitution guarantees him.[22]

The Supreme Court did not stop there. It also suggested—in contrast to *Patton*—that there might be circumstances in which the government's veto of the waiver could compromise a defendant's right to a fair trial.

"[P]assion, prejudice . . . [and] public feeling" would do that, the court argued in the *Singer* decision's fine print. But the observation was strictly an aside because the problem was not the issue to be adjudicated. Remember, the con man Singer was not worried about fairness, but only his personal convenience, along with his absolute right to choose between a bench and a jury trial.[23]

Although the *Singer* decision reinforced the notion that the government, under Rule 23(a), can exercise a waiver veto ostensibly to protect the jury system, federal courts since 1965 have also recognized the obvious fact that the prosecution is wearing two hats on this question. Worse, the hat it usually prefers to don is the one that makes conviction more likely.[24]

In fact there have been three instances in recent years in which federal judges overrode the government veto on the question of a bench trial.

The first instance happened three years after *Singer* and had a charming Alice-in-Wonderland complexity about it. In *United States v. Schipani*, as well as *Schipani v. United States*, the government originally agreed to a bench trial. Schipani was convicted for income tax evasion. Subsequently, however, the Supreme Court overturned the conviction for other reasons and ordered a new trial.

This time, the government attempted to rescind its original

waiver agreement. Schipani argued that the prosecution had no right to reverse itself. He still wanted a bench trial, despite the fact that the first judge had thrown the book at him.

Not surprisingly, the lower court had a difficult time figuring out the law in this unusual circumstance, but in the end the judge upheld the defendant's right to a bench trial, with or without the consent of the prosecution. The court did so primarily because the length of Schipani's rap sheet and his close ties to organized crime made a fair jury trial an unlikely outcome.

In the words of the trial court's opinion:

[N]o disinfecting admonition by the Court and no minor exclusion of evidence can prevent the jury from becoming aware of the stench [created by Schipani's Mafia ties].[25]

The next case, *United States v. Panteleakis*, opened even wider the breach in the government's absolute right to veto a defendant's waiver. Again the prosecution objected to a bench trial, and again a federal judge ruled otherwise. The reason once more was fairness and this time, please note, juror competence.

The case involved multiple defendants in a complicated Medicare fraud in which an understanding of byzantine accounting procedures would need to be mastered during a trial that was expected to last three to four months.

After reviewing the matter, the court found the government's objection to a bench trial "unreasonable and arbitrary." An ordinary jury just wasn't going to follow this at all, he reasoned. It would have difficulty even in keeping the defendants straight.[26]

The final case, *United States v. Braunstein*, was very similar to *Panteleakis* and came three years later in 1979. *Braunstein* too involved numerous defendants, as well as tax fraud, and, once again, medical public welfare payments. Once more the indicted asked for a bench trial, and the government said no. This time, however, the prosecutor offered no reason for doing so other than citing established policy. The lack of an explanation annoyed the court, which found the government's waving around of Federal 23(a) just a bit too arrogant. And, *Singer* or no *Singer*, the judge ruled that the fair trial requirement meant a bench trial for Braunstein and company.

The *Braunstein* decision went further than *Panteleakis.* The *Braunstein* judge decided that the apparently severe strictures of Rule 23(a) still fell under Federal Rule 2, a rule which dictates how the criminal procedure rules—including 23(a)—are to be construed.[27]

By citing Rule 2, the federal judge in the *Braunstein* case effectively injected the notion of equity into the rules game. That meant that if everyone followed the rules to the letter and yet justice was still denied, something was wrong with the rules. In such cases, fairness required an escape hatch. And the *Braunstein* decision restated an ancient principle of Anglo-Saxon jurisprudence: equity, or in other words, justice, applied in circumstances not covered by the law.[28]

None of the three cases overruled *Singer.* What they did do in the concrete circumstances faced by the judges in question were to supplement and to fill in the spaces left empty by the 1965 Supreme Court decision.

Now, none of the decisions negated Rule 23(a), much less threw out the concept of a jury trial. What they did was say that, in exceptional cases, the government does not have an absolute veto over how a defendant will be judged, whether by his peers or by the court. In other words, if Rule 23(a) remained rigid, justice could be denied.

Another point. The cases and the circumstances were roughly similar to Moon's. The trials had all been complex, multi-defendant affairs, in which the defendants had waived a jury trial, a waiver the government had elected to veto. The Reverend Moon didn't have just one reason to ask for a bench trial—he had several which federal courts had found acceptable in the recent past. (*Panteleakis, Braunstein* and *Schipani* were the case names.)

That's generally how a lawyer looking at the rules, laws, and precedents would have gone about discussing the issue.

Admittedly, to suggest that case precedents should have had a large say in Moon's proceedings seems a bit fussy and academic.

But did they? It is now time to part the curtain and look at how these things were really argued and decided *in camera.*

Did Moon's lawyers have any evidence that their client faced an almost certainly prejudiced jury? There was of course the Roth poll, but the results, it could be argued, did not prove the men and women on the Foley Square panel were prejudiced.

The poll aside, the likelihood of a fair jury seemed undermined by the results of the *voir dire* itself. For example, six of the twelve jurors knew that Moon wanted a bench trial—something gleaned obviously from the pretrial publicity. That known fact alone would hardly sit well with them. What's he trying to hide? was a natural reaction.

Moreover, that sentiment was most likely transmitted to the remaining half of the jury who were not aware of Moon's request. In the halls and at lunch, the jurors, we know, discussed the case and its details—even though they were instructed not to do so. It is likely that the bench trial request would have been disclosed, thus leaving the whole panel wondering about Moon's motives even before one shred of evidence had been presented.[29]

Of course, the news was far worse than that. Of the sixty-two men and women interviewed by the court during the *voir dire*, exactly one had heard anything positive about Moon—a statistic which tracked closely with the Roth poll. In this single case, "the positive" was absurdly trivial. The prospective juror had heard "a long time ago" that the "Moonies . . . were cleaning the street in Times Square."[30]

Only six of the sixty-two had never heard of the Reverend Sun Myung Moon or "Moonies" or the Unification Church—again, that ratio closely follows the Roth survey.[31]

What about the final twelve jurors, plus the six alternates, who served as the finders of fact in *Moon-Kamiyama*? Despite the extensive *voir dire* proceedings, the court did not find eighteen unprejudiced jurors at all. Exactly four of the group had not heard anything negative about Moon. Fourteen had.

Prejudice was only one-half of Moon's dilemma. The other was juror ignorance. Even Judge Goettel understood the problem. As he put it in a pretrial newspaper interview:

[I]n attempting to get an unbiased jury, the leaning has been heavily towards people who don't read much, don't talk much and don't know much because they are obviously the persons who start off with the least bias. Conversely, they would might [*sic*] tend to be less educated and less intelligent people.[32]

Goettel might have added, although he didn't, that those who might be least prejudiced initially were most likely to be highly negative about Moon once they had been exposed to him—or at least to the prosecution's version of Moon and his movement.

Goettel was aware of the competence problem. And he worried about it to the officers of the court:

They are probably quite capable of trying a simple criminal case. How good they are going to be in determining a tax case, if it gets more complicated and I don't know enough about the facts of this case to know whether it is going to be that complicated.[33]

Nor, as it turned out, was Goettel getting much help from the government on that score. Even well-disposed-toward-the-government Goettel was getting suspicious of prosecutors Harris and Flumenbaum. Was he being had? This was the judge's suspicion:

Every time I've tried to find out what is really involved there is an awful lot of well we don't want to be pinned down on this responses.[34]

Of course, the government lawyers knew that their case would be enormously complicated: that a thousand pieces of evidence, tens of thousands of pages, were going to be submitted—taxing anyone's intellectual resources.

Why weren't they more forthcoming? Goettel himself supplied the reason: ". . . if we get into complicated bookkeeping and accounting procedures and things of that nature, I am a bit concerned about them."[35]

That is exactly what the government had in mind. The prosecutors just didn't bother to tell the judge. The reasoning was sound enough, as Goettel himself made clear in the very next paragraph of the transcript.

I would have thought it fairer to have this case tried without a jury.[36]

Moments later, he added:

> But I do think I would feel better about the fairness from the position of the defendants had they been granted a non-jury trial.[37]

Why didn't he order one, although it was in his power to do so?

To answer that question we need to trace how Goettel got into this quandary, and how and why he never got out of it.

Judge Goettel characteristically had postponed the bench versus jury trial question until the last moment. He made no decision until the *voir dire* was complete and the eighteen jurors and alternates had been found.

Not surprisingly, once that unhappy process had been completed, the defense lawyers renewed their motion for a bench trial and asked that the court throw out the government's refusal to accept the waiver.

Defense lawyer Stillman argued first that the fact-finder, in this case the jury, was ill-suited to weigh this case. His reason was that many of the jurors carried a heavy load of prejudice, especially because a number of them had already discussed their preconceived notions among themselves—contrary to the court's order.

Moreover, Stillman continued, Judge Goettel had not given the defense enough peremptory challenges; that is, allowing them to toss out prospective jurors, no questions asked, no cause cited. The only thing the peremptories had accomplished, Stillman implied, was to weed out those potential jurors who were most blatantly anti-Moon.

The government meanwhile was enjoying a downhill run. The prosecutors didn't have to squander their peremptories on concerns about juror prejudice. Instead the government could use its uncontestable challenges to knock out "those people who seem knowledgeable, seem sophisticated and who gave what were the right answers for the exercise," in Stillman's words. What were those right answers? That they "could put out of their minds the bad things about which they heard and seemed to have the necessary sophistication to be able to do that."[38]

Objective jurors were the last thing Harris and Flumenbaum wanted. In one case, a prospective juror named Livingston, who had some legal training and who was probably the most intelligent-sounding of the sixty-two people questioned, was canned by a government peremptory.[39]

Stillman then retraced his arguments on prejudice based on the poll results. Earlier, when they had introduced the Roth poll, the defense ran into a court buzzsaw. Judge Goettel openly questioned the reliability of a telephone poll in which three of four people contacted invariably hung up before the poll was completed, a phenomenon well known to pollsters and taken careful note of. The judge's naive assumption was that only the people who really hated Moon waited patiently to vent their spleen, thus considerably distorting the results. Stillman hadn't been prepared for Goettel's objection at the time. But this was his last chance to plead for a bench trial, and he was now ready to respond.

The "disconnect" phenomenon, Stillman argued, was well understood by pollsters and not simply ignored, as the court apparently assumed. According to pollster Stephen Roth, the disconnects took place at a point in the phone call that indicated nothing in respect to attitudes and beliefs of the person at the other end of the phone line. It merely showed that of the 3,424 disconnects, 97 percent of them didn't want to be bothered with answering *any* questions.[40]

The court, however, was not much impressed either with the general community prejudice argument or the prejudice discovered during the *voir dire*. Or in Judge Goettel's words:

> I think most people have the good judgment to discount substantially [idle] chatter and hearsay and opinions which often are voiced with little or no basis.[41]

Only in cases of direct and bitter personal experience, the court argued, would prejudice have a fatal impact on juror objectivity.[42] Stillman wasn't buying that one.

> That might be true [he argued to Goettel] with respect to ordinary events in the lives of people. But I suggest to you . . . that that can't be true when the kind of thing that we are talking about is something that impacts the integrity of the family, something that impacts the relationship of a person to his or her children.[43]

And when it came to those things held most sacred by most people, especially lower-class Catholics—who represented a substantial portion of the minorities on this jury—Stillman argued that the jurors were not likely to set aside their prejudice at all. Period.

Of course Moon's problems did not end there, Stillman continued. Defense witnesses will be called. Many of them will be members of the Unification Church. With juror prejudice already in evidence, how objectively will the jury weigh their testimony? Or will they simply dismiss it as the words of brainwashed zombies? That, Stillman concluded, "deprives us of the opportunity to have a fair assessment of the evidence."[44]

Stillman concluded:

[I]t seems to me, your Honor, that there are so many threshholds that the potential jurors have to get by before they reach the merits, that it is just not fair to have to try a case in those circumstances, particularly where there is meaningful option to try this case in a fair and impartial way.[45]

Goettel listened but remained skeptical. After an hour of argument, Stillman was still going uphill. But now it was time for the government to restate its position on the jury waiver.

Harris did so by simply dismissing the problem of prejudice. In her view, the defense had not shown any substantial body of ill will against the defendants—only vague, general gossip, which was not the same thing: "not . . . in the real world and it certainly is not so in the law."[46]

Instead of prejudice against Moon and Kamiyama, Harris found mostly indifference on the part of the jurors: "these people . . . are totally indifferent to their client, their client's religion."[47]

No wonder that Jo Ann Harris could then observe, "I don't feel as if we have been in the same room for the last six or seven days, as we well have."[48]

Harris hadn't finished quite yet. She smoothly moved on to citing case precedents. The case most skillfully cited was the *Irwin* case, which had involved heavy and negative pretrial publicity directed at the defendant. A jury panel of 430 people had been summoned. But, according to the government lawyer, 90 percent of the potential jurors already had an opinion about Irwin's guilt and eight of the final twelve still expressed belief in his guilt before the trial began.

That, Harris argued, was manifestly not the case with Moon and Kamiyama. Indeed, no one on the jury had yet expressed the belief that either man was guilty. Message conveyed: be grateful it wasn't worse because it isn't so bad now.[49]

Judge Goettel, however, wasn't quite ready to buy Harris' happy talk.

> I'd be very concerned with [jury prejudice], for this reason. If there is a conviction here, the first point on appeal is going to be this jury versus nonjury question. An Appellate Court I do not think is going to be very happy with the government's position in demanding a jury trial, but I would believe that most appellate judges are not going to want to tackle this issue squarely. They will not like the fact that the rules seem to give an absolute discretion to the prosecutor and that except for a little bit of dicta in Singer, there is no authority for saying it can be overruled.[50]

Goettel was looking over his shoulder and he didn't like what he saw. The appellate judges were going to criticize him for ordering a jury trial.

> The trial judge should have been able to stop jurors talking in the halls [Goettel fretted]. He should have given directions that prevented that from happening. He should have taken additional steps.[51]

Sensing an opportunity, maybe their last, both defense lawyers, Stillman and Lawler, pressed the earlier points on jury prejudice, hitting the government hard for its low standard by which it found jurors to be free of prejudicial taint.

Judge Goettel wasn't ready to buy it. Indeed, he returned to one of his earlier themes. This case was not really different from others. Jury problems were always there; they would always be. If the court accepted the defense's standard for a fair jury "there will be no more jury convictions because I have been telling jurors until

I am blue in the face not to discuss the case ... and inevitably somebody always does. ..."[52]

Goettel's position was that there are always problems with juries. New jurors, he said, are strangers to each other. They have nothing in common except the case and that is what they will always end up discussing despite the court's admonition. Goettel added, that's only the beginning. They talk about it at home too:

> They may not have talked about the merits of the case, but they walked in the door and the very least they said is, "Hey, honey, you won't believe what case I am on," and then described it.[53]

Judge Goettel's defeatism, however, only riled the aggressive Andy Lawler. In an ordinary case, he retorted, such occurrences might not be so terribly harmful, but this was no ordinary case. And would the court stop acting as if it were?[54]

It was the last arrow from the defense's bow. Goettel stopped the arguments and announced that he would make his decision. Before making his announcement, however, the court went through a remarkably tortured summation of the case.

First, Gerard Goettel offered the thought that the *Moon* case offered conflicting principles. On the one hand, the defendants did have a right to a fair and yes, impartial, fact finder. On the other hand, there existed the public's right to participate in the case.

He conceded the first point was more important than the second. Goettel added:

> I believe that when a defendant in a criminal trial has reasonable cause for believing there is a substantial prejudice or bias against him personally and that when he wishes to waive a jury trial, that preference should not be overborne by the prosecutor's desire for a public trial by jury.[55]

That made it fifteen-love for the defense. Goettel's mental tennis match, however, had only started. In the very next moment, for example, Goettel changed his mind. Listen:

> But that is my personal view. It doesn't appear to be the law. The rule and the judicial interpretations of it seem to put no restrictions upon the prosecution being able to insist upon a jury.[56]

Score: fifteen-fifteen. Goettel's next move was to dismiss the defense's complaint that it had not been given enough peremptories. For the court, that problem was solved by doubling the number allowed Moon and Kamiyama's lawyers. Again, Goettel refused to acknowledge the extraordinary prejudice against the defendants. This was, once more, just another tax case.[57]

Thirty-fifteen. Prosecution in the lead.

It got worse. Goettel recritiqued the Roth poll:

I think it is fair to say that the general public image of the Unification Church and the Moonies has not been a positive one. So if a poll-taker wants to prod enough, I think he would come up with a 75 percent unfavorable group. But I think he does it by prodding persons who in some part are really not that interested and don't have that strong a feeling.[58]

So much for polling. To Judge Goettel, pollsters found what they wanted to find. The court's view was neither accurate, nor scientific, nor much beyond the man-in-the-street conventional wisdom on the subject. Like a politician who doesn't like a poll's results, Goettel was determined to dismiss the evidence out of hand. Period. And he did.[59]

That made it forty-fifteen.

Lastly, Goettel turned to the question of juror prejudice. On this he made his views quite clear:

You very rarely get a pristine jury. Jurors usually haven't heard of the defendant personally but they usually have strong feelings about the crime involved.[60]

The "so-who's-perfect?" argument gave him the opening that Judge Goettel wanted. Yes, of course, the jurors discussed the case in the lunch room. So what? All jurors do that. Furthermore, there was no evidence that such discussions had any effect upon the impaneled jurors. The court promised to give the jurors "a little sermon on the dangers of talking to people and maybe even threaten them again with contempt or sequestration"—a threat that in fact was not carried out, at least in regard to contempt and sequestration.[61]

To reinforce his conviction that juror prejudice was no problem, poll or no poll, Judge Goettel's happy thought was that this was really a tax trial, after all. It was a dull, boring affair the very dryness of which would allow "the more lurid aspects of de-programming and things of that nature" to fade away.[62]

Game, set, and match for the prosecution.

Having thus turned down the request for a bench trial, Goettel then unburdened himself. Law or no law, fairness or no fairness, this particular judge did not want to take this case all on himself.

[A]ttorneys try a better case to a jury. They put it in more dramati-cally and more understandably. When they have a Judge, they let the Judge do all the work and just throw in everything but the kitchen sink and let him determine what is and what is not important.[63]

Goettel's observation suddenly changes to petty complaint:

Of course, I have an awful lot of responsibilities and I have an awful lot of things to decide in every case and in every matter before me. I don't look to acquire more responsibilities than I have to. So having the jury make the determination of guilty or innocent is just fine by me.[64]

It was an extraordinary admission. Judge Goettel did not want this case. He was making no pretense that he did. Let this cup pass from me, and Lord, if you don't, at least give it to the jury, he was saying. Not very judicial. And even at that, the court would admit one final time that a nonjury trial would be fairer to the defen-dants.[65]

What could he do? Nothing, he thought.

Goettel was wrong. Rule 23(a) was not so inflexible. The courts, including the Supreme Court in the *Singer* case, had left him with a choice. He could have overridden the prosecution's veto. But he didn't.

Goettel was led by the nose by the prosecution on this question, and his subservience to the government attorneys wouldn't stop there. Moon and Kamiyama were stuck with a jury trial. Not just stuck, but inevitably sunk by it.

The *voir dire* was the process of selecting the panel of jurors who, at the end of a grueling seven-day process, were chosen to be the fact-finders in this case.

Although the concept which underlies the *voir dire* is simple enough, the actual procedure is not. *Voir dire* is an examination of potential jurors by the court, the prosecution, and the defense. All officers of the court have the right to question these potential jurors to determine not only their ability to render an impartial verdict, but their ability to understand the trial itself. In other words, are they smart enough to know what's going on? The problem is delicate, but it comes up more often than you might think. It haunted the trial of Sun Myung Moon.

In the *Moon* case—which was a complicated tax trial—the question of juror intelligence played an unusually large role in the *voir dire* process, although the issue of juror prejudice quickly overshadowed the consideration of juror competence.

A panel of 200 jurors was rounded up—an enormous number that could not be properly accommodated in the courtroom. The winnowing process—to the discomfiture of Judge Goettel—took seven days, an almost unheard of expenditure of time for a *voir dire* in a criminal tax trial.

Voir dire is not simply a matter of somebody asking a potential juror questions, even if there are 200 waiting to be grilled.

First, the court must swear in the panel. Then the judge must tell potential jurors something about the case. Then he gives instructions about the nature and obligations of jury service. In this case, that meant informing the panel that the trial would be a long one, along with the usual warning against reading or listening to anything about the case during and after jury selection.[66]

After these preliminaries, potential jurors (in this case all 200 of them) fill out a simple form that requests basic information: name, address, phone number, number of dependents, *et cetera.*

In the Moon case, one other question was asked: Would a lengthy trial be an intolerable burden on the juror? Not a few would say yes.

Judge Goettel seemed happy about being able to have a relatively tidy courtroom once again. Those jurors who raised an objection to long jury service were first questioned by the judge (with all lawyers present) in the robing room, out of earshot of the other jurors.

Most excuses were accepted after a few questions by the court, although several were persuaded to remain on the panel; reluctantly to be sure, but they stayed on for the duration of the *voir dire*.

Having purged the panel of the reluctant and unwilling, the next step was to probe the remaining potential jurors for bias or incompetence. The process is by no means a simple one, nor the results all that satisfactory.

With the real *voir dire,* just about everyone gets into the act. First, the court has its own set of questions—in this case, Judge Goettel had a couple dozen. These questions were meant to be merely preliminary in order to weed out those obviously tainted: Do you know personally the defendant? The prosecutors? The defense lawyers? That sort of inquiry.

The prosecution and defense had their own questions, too, which raised the total to eighty-five queries, not counting follow-up questions in case any juror's answer required clarification.

During the *voir dire* there is often much haggling among the officers of the court on the exact wording of questions or whether they are proper in the first place.

The *Moon-Kamiyama voir dire* was no exception. The court and the lawyers quarreled on every conceivable subject. They even argued about who, exactly, should be questioned for bias.

Judge Goettel wanted to save time by examining only those potential jurors who raised no objection to serving during a long trial. That sounded sensible—why prolong the proceedings unless absolutely necessary? Defense counsel, however, wanted to question even those who might ultimately be dismissed for hardship reasons. They argued that their purpose was to increase the size of the juror sample to show the extent and shape of the root difficulty posed in this court-ordered jury trial.

As defense lawyer Charles Stillman put it: "[The] overall problem of the bias, prejudice, hostility and the hatred in the community . . . ."[67]

Moon's lawyers had not given up on their quest for a bench trial. In case of the need for appeal, a large sample of jurors who had proven to be biased would dramatically reinforce the findings of the Roth poll. The lawyers said or, more accurately, shouted out loud and clear, that Moon had no chance of getting a fair jury trial, his basic right under the Sixth Amendment.

Judge Goettel was "sympathetic" to defense's argument for questioning the whole panel, but said no just the same. Again.

However, that was only the beginning. The defense, prosecution, and court clashed repeatedly over what were proper questions to ask of prospective jurors.

Based on the Roth poll, Moon's lawyers were certain that any panel, no matter how large, was poisoned by deep-seated prejudice against their client. Their other basic point, however, was that it would take a variety of questions to smoke out juror prejudice, a process that required approaching the issue from a variety of angles, some of them frankly devious.

The court repeatedly expressed confusion over the defense's problem. The prosecution was more than happy to agree with Judge Goettel.

As a result, question after question designed to tease out juror prejudice was ruled to be out of order. When in doubt, Goettel asked the prosecution to reinforce his own belief that juror prejudice was not an overridingly important issue.

Could a juror be asked if he were a member of a labor union? Moon's lawyer asked.

Why?

Because the Unification Church relied on unpaid, volunteer labor; it was likely that that fact could rub some people's nerves raw. In New York City, a militantly organized town where doing anything on a volunteer basis probably violated some union rule, the question was a natural to elicit prejudice.

Sorry, but the judge did not agree. In the words of His Honor: "I am not going to ask that."[68]

When the defense attempted to ask questions to elicit attitudes about religious leaders and their life styles, because Moon's East Garden mansion had already gotten plenty of negative press comment, Judge Goettel failed to see the point:

> You have to face the fact [Goettel told defense lawyers] that people's reactions to the way various religious leaders live depend upon their views as to that religion and whether they are members of it and what-have-you. . . . I just won't ask that question.[69]

Which, of course, was the point of asking the question in the first place. Judge Goettel believed that any potential juror who was forced to deal with that kind of inquiry was having his beliefs subjected to unwarranted intrusion. The juror's rights were thus being violated, and that was simply unacceptable.

It was an odd sort of symmetry. The juror, after all, was not on trial; Moon was. Whose rights in this case were more important? The court seemed to suggest that a potential juror's rights were at least as important as the defendant's even though Moon, not the juror, was the one in danger of prison.

Judge Goettel's curious doctrine of equal rights for jurors extended to other proposed questions. When defense requested the privilege of asking potential jurors, "In your opinion, is it right for religious groups like the Unification Church to use church funds for business ventures and investments?" Judge Goettel expressed bewilderment over the purpose of the question.

Defense lawyer Charles Stillman tried to explain:

> It is designed to provide some insight into the jurors' attitude. One of the problems we have here is that I think that most jurors speaking about so-called established religions would be perfectly prepared to say, "Yes, it is all right that the Catholic Church owns New York City, and it is all right that the Mormon Church owns Utah," but the people may have some different views, and we have seen that through our survey about the rights of the Unification Church, Reverend Moon's church, to own businesses, to own properties. It seems to us that we just had to start to dig into this question because there will be an abundance of testimony in the course of this trial with respect to the ownership of businesses, with respect to the ownership of property by the Unification Church. I think it really goes to the very essence of this lawsuit.[70]

Both court and prosecution stoutly resisted Stillman's argument. If questions about property had to be asked, each side was inclined to leave out any reference to the Unification Church or, worse, the "Moonies," to the intense objection of defense counsel. In the end, the general subject of church investments was allowed but the questions could not be phrased to refer directly to the Reverend Moon or his Unification Church.

The term "Moonies" was something the prosecution particularly wished to avoid, and once more Moon and Kamiyama's lawyers objected. The prosecution did not want to raise the spectre of prejudice. The defense most certainly did. Otherwise, Moon's lawyers argued, it would be difficult, if not impossible, to detect juror bias.

To put it in defense lawyer Andrew Lawler's words: "What the government is attempting to do is totally undercut the purpose of this *voir dire*."[71]

Both court and prosecution repeatedly did so with Judge Goettel ruling one question after another as inappropriate. Sometimes reasons were given; sometimes not.

Could defense ask potential jurors how they felt about people living together in communal fashion, something church members did, albeit with strictly gender-segregated sleeping arrangements?

No, defense lawyers could not.

How about asking, "Do you feel that the only true religions are the ones that have been around for centuries?"—a question lifted from the Roth poll. More than 32 percent strongly agreed with that proposition (in the poll's total sample). Judge Goettel didn't like the question, however.

He gave no reason, he just didn't like it. As for any questions regarding religion, the court delivered this blanket opinion:

> I consider it improper to ask a juror about religious preferences and political questions which are sacred matters under our Constitution, and nobody should be required to disclose these sort of matters.[72]

Besides, it wasn't nice. Still, Moon's lawyers pointed out, this was no time for false gentility. Prejudice isn't nice either, and it would materially damage the chance of a fair trial for their clients.

As lawyer Stillman put it:

> I think that a lot of the questions that we have to ask to test the bias and prejudice here are questions that we as Americans don't like to ask because they probe the very essence of a characteristic that we are taught not to like, but it seems to me the only way that we can ask a stranger about his or her feelings on the subject is to ask unnice questions.[73]

"Unnice" is putting it mildly, but accurately. Judge Goettel seemed obtuse to the argument.

The debate over what constituted proper questioning of potential jurors was only the beginning of the *voir dire* and the defendants' problems in getting a fair trial.

The second problem was Judge Goettel's decision not to sequester the jury. He made the decision knowing full well that the *Moon-Kamiyama* trial would generate a hurricane of publicity. In such cases, judges usually attempt to provide shelter for the jury so that it can deliberate on the evidence without outside interference.

Sequestering is nothing more than providing that shelter. Jurors are literally shut off from the world, housed in a hotel under conditions that, as Judge Goettel put it, "insulate them from exposure to extraneous publicity that might affect the fairness of the trial."[74]

That means no exposure to newspaper, magazine, radio, and television stories that deal with the case at hand.

Jurors, however, do not enter a monastery. They can remain in touch with family members, business associates, and their physicians, but communication is restricted to the essentials. For a lengthy trial—which Moon's was—sequestering imposes hardships, but again, as most judges know, justice is a balancing act. The rights of the defendants to a fair trial are weighed in balance with the inconveniences suffered by the jurors.

Judge Goettel decided that juror comfort was more important. Instead of sequestering them, the court issued only a warning "to absolutely avoid reading, hearing, overhearing, watching, seeing and talking about the case outside the courtroom."[75]

To make sure, the court added the following warning:

> You must avoid all contacts with representatives of the press, the lawyers, defendants, witnesses, and any spectators in the case, and I will issue orders designed to insulate you from contact with the press, the lawyers, the defendants and the spectators.[76]

Judge Goettel warned the potential jurors that if exposure to the press coverage of the trial became an issue, he just might be forced to sequester the jury.

How effective these warnings were, including his threat to sequester the jury if and when, will be seen later.[77]

How effective the *voir dire* process was in detecting bias and incompetence is our present subject. As will be seen, finding prejudice—especially juror prejudice—is not easy when the questioning has been sharply limited.

Most people are cagey about their biases. Few admit to having them. They prefer instead to waltz around their biases or directly deny that they have any.[78]

There are, of course, exceptions. In the Moon *voir dire*, several potential jurors volunteered their prejudices.

Susan Hill wrote on her jury card "because of religious beliefs and the reputation of the man I do not feel my feelings would be prejudicial." After she was questioned, it became clear that she meant that she would, as a Catholic, be prejudiced against the leader of the Unification Church.

Although Goettel expressed some skepticism that Hill's stated prejudice was her real reason for wanting to be excused, he excused her anyway, and then threw the defense attorneys a curve ball. He counted Miss Hill as a defense peremptory challenge based on bias.

Moon's lawyers, knowing full well that they had entered no challenge because Hill was a volunteer drop-out, and knowing that such challenges would be limited in number, were flabbergasted.

Charles Stillman asked, "I didn't know I had—there is no totting up on this one, is there, your Honor?"

The court had just that thing in mind. At some point, Goettel added cryptically, it "might become important."[79]

If the court treated prejudice gingerly even when it stood up and said boo, the prosecution was having its doubts too.

In the case of Susan Hill and one other potential juror, B.A. Zilkowski, who volunteered that her church (Methodist) and pastor were strongly anti-Moon and had convinced her of Moon's iniquity, prosecutor Jo Ann Harris said that the real reason for their wanting to be excused was their fear of being tied up in a lengthy trial.

"They have heard three months," said Harris. And that, in her opinion, was enough for them to cop a hardship plea.[80]

This preliminary screening of potential jurors was only the beginning. There were six more days of *voir dire* aimed at potential jurors who wished to serve or at least entered no objections to being part of a *Moon-Kamiyama* jury.

One question that the *voir dire* process poses is: How much prejudice is enough to disqualify a juror? That wasn't clear in *Moon-Kamiyama*; perhaps it never is. The examination of potential juror Wilfredo Llenza is a case in point.

Llenza, a man of obviously limited education, knew next to nothing about the Unification Church, but a number of his answers were nonetheless troubling to the defense.

Was it right for religious bodies like the Unification Church to use church funds for business ventures?

Answer? "No."

Is it appropriate for religious groups to ask for money at airports and on the streets?

"I am not for it," was Llenza's answer.[81]

Do religious cults exploit their followers and brainwash them into joining the church?

"Yes."[82]

True, he wasn't good about the actual identity of the cults who engaged in these practices or, in Mr. Llenza's words: "Different religions out on the street there, you know. I don't know the names."[83]

Do churches abuse their tax-exempt status?

"It's a hard question. Let me see. To a certain extent," said the potential juror.[84]

The defense particularly wanted to pursue the brainwashing angle, pointing out that it was vital to do follow-up questions in order to draw out jurors reluctant to discuss certain topics, much less their own most tightly held views.

The court agreed, albeit reluctantly.

The follow-up, however, was something less than satisfactory. Potential juror Llenza related a tangled (and probably garbled) tale based on what his brother told him about their former brother-in-law who had become a "Moslem" (highly unlikely). The man had been told that the world would soon end and to buy sacks of beans. Consequently, the brother-in-law lost an enormous amount of weight, got into trouble with the law, and then disappeared, never to surface again.[85]

A fascinating story, but no one bothered to explore Mr. Llenza's feelings about brainwashing. Instead, the topic shifted to religious people selling flowers—and Unification Church members do sell flowers. The court, however, did not get around to asking how Mr. Llenza felt about such practices.[86]

Although the *voir dire* established that at least one potential juror thought that religions abused their tax free status and that some engaged in brainwashing and involved themselves in business, these were not deemed adequate grounds for automatic dismissal.

How much bias is enough to disqualify a potential juror? Evidently it had to be a lot, a whole lot.

There were other difficulties as well. One was the problems encountered when dealing with the more intelligent juror. He (or she) is distinctly aware that his deepest feelings are being probed in the presence of a number of people. Uncomfortably so.

Not a pleasant experience for anyone. The smarter ones often resort to careful understatement, if not downright subterfuge, in their responses.

Potential juror Joanne Lenard was an outstanding example of this particular problem.

Had she heard anything critical about Moon or his church?

Well, "Yes."

Anything specific?

"Not really."

How about Moon's life style?

"I don't know whether it is rumor or fact, but I guess he doesn't live too humbly," Mrs. Lenard replied, with a true masterpiece of carefully nuanced ambiguity.

When asked if she had seen television shows on the church, her answer was yes. What was the impression given? "I am not too sympathetic," she said.

Why?

"I guess I feel there is a little bit of brainwashing going on."[87]

"Not too" and "a little bit" were beginning to establish a pattern of evasive understatement. What about using church money for business ventures?

No, it wasn't right. After all, it depended on where the benefits would go. "I mean if they reinvest and it goes back to the church, fine."[88]

The only thing Mrs. Lenard was absolutely clear about with no euphemisms employed was the question of solicitations. She didn't like them. Period. In her words, "I never approved of that." And "I don't like any door-to-door people."

Why? "Begging isn't nice. [S]o to speak."[89]

Well, O.K. To his credit Judge Goettel brought up the brainwashing question once more. Would the fact that the Unification Church has been accused of brainwashing, rightly or wrongly, affect Mrs. Lenard's impartiality?

"I am not sure."

"I guess that would be possible."

Unfortunately, "possible" is not good enough, as the court rather astutely pointed out.

"I would try."

Oddly enough that response was good enough for Judge Goettel. So what about the church's allegedly abusing its tax exempt status?

"As well as others, I guess," she said. Back to nuance.[90]

Now for the fundamental question. What was her gut feeling about the Reverend Sun Myung Moon and his followers?

"I guess I feel that the young people become mesmerized or something, and they feel he is a terrific leader and bigger and better things and he can accomplish them," was Mrs. Lenard's reply.

Are these beliefs misguided?

"I suppose to a certain extent."[91]

Could she put these feelings aside and judge Moon on a tax case impartially? Judge Goettel gently asked.

Having delivered this royal softball, the answer, of course, was yes. The rest was pro forma, even though Mrs. Lenard admitted at a later point that she was "old-fashioned" and that "Moonyism" was a "kind of a new-fangled thing."[92]

What about that? The question lay lingering in the robing room. After Mrs. Lenard left, the three sides had at it once more.

Defense lawyer Andrew Lawler—Kamiyama's attorney—pointed out the obvious. This potential juror was intelligent and was not about to be trapped in an overt bit of bias.

"I suspect," Lawler said dryly, "if we were sitting around a cocktail party and the same discussion was going on, we would get different answers."

"I think that is obvious," said the judge. "After a few drinks I become indiscreet also, but that is not the point."[93]

What Judge Goettel thought the point was exactly was never made clear.

The defense attorneys were clear about Mrs. Lenard. In Charles Stillman's words: "She is not a juror we should have, your Honor."

His Honor, however, did not see the matter in such stark terms.

"The issue is," he said, "whether she is so clearly biased as to be somebody who is susceptible of being challenged for cause, and that is a more difficult question."[94]

Later, Moon's lawyers challenged Mrs. Lenard for cause. The ever-cautious court, however, only reserved its decision.

And what about Rosa Grant?

She too had the usual juror reluctance to be frank—at least at first. On questions she had clear feelings about, however, she minced no words.

Church and business did not mix because "at church we have envelopes, and we put a donation for the whole year . . . whatever you can afford." If a church invests what's left over, forget it. That is wrong.

Ditto to churches sending their members out to solicit.[95]

As for cults' brainwashing children, the answer was "yes," without any caveats.[96]

What if the Reverend Sun Myung Moon opened a church next door? "Well, I wouldn't like it." Do some churches abuse their tax-exempt status? "Yes."

Are the "Moonies" a cult? "I don't think it's a real religion, really."[97]

The Moonies are only out for the money, and Moon ought to pay taxes like everybody else: "Even if you hit the lottery or the Zingo, you have to pay tax on that, so why shouldn't he pay taxes on what he has?"[98]

So much for carefully made arguments about the First Amendment.

Now, overall, Grant's testimony might strike a person as being that of a woman who has little use for the Reverend Moon, "Moonies," and religions who do not operate by her "put in the envelope on Sundays" rule.

The prosecution, however, would only admit to Rosa Grant's

being a "close case," while Judge Goettel assumed that she might be a bit off-base. The court also asserted as a general rule, "[S]o long as the juror believes that they can put aside these kinds of rumors, I don't think they are challengeable for cause. If they have been personally involved, that's something else again."[99]

Quite needless to say, the defense attorneys did not buy this minimalist approach when dealing with jury prejudice. As Andrew Lawler suggested, the *voir dire* was, at best, a hit-or-miss approach to detecting bias.

"If you don't hit that precise button," he said, "a person can walk out of here or perhaps not even realize that they have heard this until they get on the jury and it starts to come back to them."[100]

It was a thought that would torment the defense throughout the trial.

As a classic example of cagey evasion, juror Mary Nimmo surely won the prize. Although she was later reported to have offered unvarnished and derogatory opinions of Moon and the "Moonies" to other jurors before and during the trial, she was the soul of broadminded discretion during the *voir dire*.

Have you heard that the Reverend Moon owns businesses? Yes, but she couldn't recall any. How about soliciting funds? She didn't know, but it was O.K. when her church did. Do cults brainwash? Mrs. Nimmo had heard that, but didn't know it for a fact. Are the "Moonies" a real church or a cult?

"I don't know."[101]

Well, try.

"I really don't know," she said, "if it's a cult or a religion. It's supposed to be a religion, and I would like to think it's that until otherwise proven differently."[102]

So much for Judge Goettel's questions. But the defense attorneys were no more effective than his Honor in breaking through Mrs. Nimmo's screen of detached reasonableness.

What criticism have you heard lodged against Moon or the church?

"Well, he gets all these young people to work for them. They work for little or no money. It's become a big organization. He's become a very wealthy man."[103]

Anything else?

"Somebody has told me that one of his children was going to

Rockland Country Day School from Westchester. Now, I don't know if he was or not . . . that's the only thing I really know about him."[104]

Later, Mrs. Nimmo offered a different version of that observation to other jurors, but for the moment she was content with this bland observation.

And she was not challenged.

The clever and evasive juror was hardly the only problem. Nor was mere bias. There was, too, the question of sheer competence.

One potential juror, Eugene Scott, a retired gentleman, perhaps best exemplifies this problem. He had no prejudice against Moon, the "Moonies," or the Unification Church because he had never heard of them. He wasn't interested.

Scott believed that churches should not own businesses because his own church did not. Church members should not be out soliciting money because his church's members didn't do that either. No church should brainwash people for the same reason. Nor should its members live communally "because that's not religious."[105]

Although Mr. Scott had not heard of the Unification Church, he was sure it wasn't a real religion. Why?

"My belief is three different denominations—Protestant, Jewish and Catholic. That's what I go by. Any other ones come, he's just hooey, nothing to me," he said, explaining his simple creed.[106]

As for the question about whether it is all right for religious groups to support political candidates, Mr. Scott had difficulty understanding the question.

"Is it all right if the Pope tells people who to vote for?" asked Judge Goettel.

The answer:

What I said, I believe in three different denominations, see. So, therefore, the Pope have the regulations, the Jews have the regulations and the Protestant have the regulations. So I'm on the Protestant Council.[107]

While court and prosecution chewed over other questions that might be asked of Scott, the defense attorneys pointed out the painfully obvious: the man was not qualified to sit on a jury for a complicated criminal tax case. (He eventually was shown the door.)[108]

Mr. Scott's lack of qualifications was underlined when, after a second round of questions, the juror had difficulty in finding his way out of the room. Embarrassed, Stillman repeated the incompetence argument.

Judge Goettel, however, wasn't sure.

> I think we would all agree that he is not a highly educated person and that his intelligence level may be less than average. However, I have never heard that that is any grounds for excusing a juror.[109]

It was a rather extraordinary standard to apply, especially in a trial where some 1,000 separate exhibits were ultimately placed in the record, and where arcane rules of accounting complicated enough to bewilder a jury of certified public accountants were slowly unraveled. Merely excusing the intellectually incompetent wasn't the entire solution, however. One Hispanic juror not only did not know much, she had to struggle with the English language during her *voir dire*.

When the court asked her if she thought the "Moonies" were a cult, she replied yes. Pressed to define a cult, she answered: "I don't know, because, you know, I hear people say that."

When asked if she had been audited, the reply was: "What you mean audited?"[110]

Needless to say, defense attorneys expressed their concern about the woman's command of English, while Judge Goettel reminded them of the facts of life in New York's Southern District:

> I am not telling you that her English is perfect, but I am telling you that it is no worse than about ten percent of the jurors we get in this district, and we have been strictly admonished not to disqualify persons of Hispanic origin because their English isn't good.[111]

And that was that. The problem once again was that of perceived juror "rights." Why does a person who speaks English poorly have a right to be a juror when much of the testimony will be beyond his or her comprehension? The right certainly isn't a constitutionally based one, yet no one challenged that assumption at Moon's *voir dire*.

The question of jurors' intellectual competence was the smaller of the two problems. The bigger one was hidden—and not so hidden—juror bias, especially among the more intelligent potential jurors who bent over backwards to appear untainted by prejudice.[112]

The *voir dire* is an old-fashioned method rooted in the nineteenth, if not the eighteenth, century, a method which does not take into account human psychology as we now understand it.[113]

That the *voir dire* was outdated occurred to lawyer Stillman in the third day of the proceedings. After consulting with a psychologist he explained to the court that the technique was not working. And why should it?

During the *voir dire* the presiding judge first enjoins the whole panel to be fair and impartial. Having been told that, they are interviewed one by one about possible prejudices. Let Stillman explain:

> They sit beside you as the supreme authority figure here with the majesty of the Court and the robe, and in the presence of all of us professional looking people, and they are now being asked to say to you that they harbor biases. That they can't—they have to say to you they can't be fair.[114]

Judge Goettel, however, was skeptical. How do the defendant's lawyers know that?

Because the Roth poll showed that a large body of negative public opinion about Moon existed? How would it manifest itself in the court room? Stillman thought he knew:

> In this situation we are seeing people who are hinting at the very same—that the catchwords are the same and yet the folks are not able to honestly look you in the eye and say, "Yes, Judge, I have a bias."[115]

The court would have none of it. The poll, Judge Goettel suggested, was a near-hoax. Three-quarters of the people surveyed, he said, did not fully participate or respond. The ones who waded through all the questions were obviously people who had strong and negative views about the church, thus grossly distorting the results.

Anti-Moon bias, in short, was not rampant in New York, and most of the prospective jurors were being honest and forthcoming. The prosecution was only too happy to agree.[116]

Oddly, though, the defense lawyers did not defend the poll results very vigorously, until it was too late to make a difference. They didn't say, for example, that all telephone polls have a very high percentage of nonrespondents because it is easy to hang up, and that is why their results are given a higher margin of error than polls conducted on a face-to-face basis.[117]

Instead Stillman proceeded to make several challenges for cause based on answers given by potential jurors. Most were denied—usually with no explanation.

At times, it got exasperating. When Judge Goettel refused to accept a challenge for cause against one juror who expressed hostility to religious leaders other than his own, the court mused: "I understand it is the fact that we are dealing with religious leader . . . but I am wondering . . . whether one person's firmly held view is adequate grounds for excusing him."[118]

Sounding unlawyerlike, the exasperated Stillman shot back: "I hate to keep repeating it, but I must—a religious leader is on trial and this man says that that is hooey, I think that is not fair."[119]

It made no difference. Virtually every challenge for cause was disallowed.

Behind the scenes, the potential jurors—strictly against the orders of the court—babbled constantly about the case in the jury pool, the halls, cafeteria, and restrooms.

With gossip about Moon flowing freely, Judge Goettel knew, understood, and appreciated the fact that those few who might originally have been relatively free from prejudice would now be contaminated by those who were not.

Invariably, people trust those with whom they have immediate and personal contact, as opposed to strangers—even well-known strangers like Dan Rather or James Reston. That thesis, a bedrock hypothesis of most public opinion research, was first spelled out more than thirty years ago by Paul Lazarsfeld in his *Two Step Flow of Communication*.[120]

A review of the twelve men and women who were selected for Moon's jury reveals disturbing trends. Nearly all of them had heard, seen, or read media reports about Moon, and few—if any—of those reports were positive. Many were downright hostile.

Worse, half the actual jurors admitted or suggested that they were aware that Moon had requested a bench trial because, in effect, he did not trust them to render a fair verdict. It takes no Sigmund Freud to figure out that such knowledge hardly works in favor of the defendant.[121]

All of this, after all, should come as no surprise. A look at the whole *voir dire* sample—all sixty-two potential jurors interviewed—reveals that exactly one person reported hearing anything positive about Moon and his church.

Joining the single positive reaction were a half-dozen others that showed ignorance of the Reverend Sun Myung Moon, the Unification Church, the "Moonies," brainwashing, *et cetera*. That meant fifty-five—a staggering 89 percent—of those actually interviewed in the *voir dire* had picked up negative information about the defendant.[122]

Let's look at real people and not just statistics. In a review of the jury members (twelve sitting and six alternates) prepared by Moon's lawyers, the following turned up.

The jury foreman, Mary Nimmo, thought that the Unification Church was a cult "making money on young people" and she "wouldn't have wanted my children to have been a part of it."[123]

Juror Esperanza Torres knew about a case of deprogramming in which the parents "rescued" their daughter, and Torres concluded "that the parents were right." Moreover, she had seen the Reverend Sun Myung Moon on television once speaking through an interpreter. For Torres that wasn't right either.[124]

Another juror, Amerria Vasquez, had heard that Moon and his followers "indoctrinate the young people in the church" and "are taking over New York City." The menace of "Moonies" was alive and well in Ms. Vasquez's mind.[125]

These were jurors who actually served on the *Moon-Kamiyama* jury. They had survived the *voir dire*. They had survived all the challenges, peremptory and for cause. Clearly something had gone terribly wrong. There was worse to come.

The *voir dire* statements made by actual jurors tell us something else, too. They are not just your general run-of-the-mill opinions. The statements dealt with the fundamentals: home and family and protection of the young from foreign—in this case, sinister oriental—mind control, that is, brainwashing.

On top of that, the menace was a religion that no one understood and was entirely new to the American religious landscape. Finally, many of the actual jurors were women of Hispanic origin, the most socially and culturally and religiously conservative subgroup in the entire American population.

If there was a threat, these women would kill to protect the family and established religion. This was not and could not be to many jurors merely a trial about taxes.

The defense knew that. So did the prosecution. It is not clear what the court really thought about the case.

What does all this mean? Moon and Kamiyama were supposed to get a fair trial or, at least, some semblance of an impartial jury. Perhaps Judge Goettel meant to do the right thing. Well-intentioned, but hopelessly naive and weak (he never did stand up to the prosecuting team—especially Jo Ann Harris), Goettel put his trust in several elements that he thought would give the defendants the benefit of the doubt.

What were they? On the face of it, the statistics are impressive.

The court called a much larger than normal venire: a panel of 200 potential jurors. It was a huge crowd; so huge, in fact, it was nearly unprecedented. The bailiffs literally did not know where to put some of them during the lengthy *voir dire*.

Speaking of the *voir dire*, the near seven-day examination of potential jurors was both prolonged and detailed by conventional standards. The court meant it to be that way.

Judge Goettel also deliberately gave the defense more peremptory challenges than normal: twenty instead of ten—although as we have seen the number was ten fewer than defense counsel requested.

None of it worked, however.

Still, the numbers are impressive. Nearly seven days of *voir dire*. More than two thousand pages of transcript. Two hundred people impaneled with fifty-six excused for hardship reasons. Sixty-two more were interviewed out of which the eighteen were selected. Seventy-two remained in case they were called.

Underlying the numbers, however, was a great deal of *sturm und drang* of which we have already seen a little bit. Defense counsel, in selecting out the most obviously biased and incompetent, quickly used up their twenty peremptories. A desperate quest for five more at the end of the *voir dire* was turned down.

Moon's lawyers managed to persuade the court, without issuing a formal challenge, that six other candidates were not fit jurors, but just barely. Eleven more challenges for cause were denied by Judge Goettel.

Of those eleven, ten served as regular jurors and one became an alternate.

In the end, Moon's jury was loaded, indeed stacked, with men and women the defense attorneys had challenged for cause: an extraordinarily high number.

It was a clear warning of things to come. And an indication of the sort of problems that would surface in the secret tape recordings made by John Curry of juror Virginia Steward.

CHAPTER IX

THE TAINTING OF
A JURY

*A courtroom is a place where Jesus Christ and Judas Iscariot would
be equals, with the betting odds in favor of Judas.*

H.L. MENCKEN

So now we come to the secret tapes. And secret they were.

The truth is that on the central question of jury tainting, the
proceedings were held *in camera*, in secret, with witnesses, prosecutors, defense counsel, and judge sworn to secrecy.

The record of these discussions was supposed to remain under
wraps, sealed presumably forever, a luxury not even extended to
the nation's most sensitive intelligence.

With secrecy, of course, it is always a question of *cui bono* and in
the *Moon-Kamiyama* case, the sealed court records show beyond a
doubt who benefited from the secrecy, and it was not the defendants. Nor for that matter the American system of justice.

But the court did. And the government. And the jurors. The
foreman in particular. Still, their conduct would have remained
under cover. Forever. Except for one thing.

I obtained those sealed transcripts.

The following account of the court's attempt to determine whether the Reverend Sun Myung Moon's jury was biased and compromised is based strictly on the official and secret written record. Nothing is inferred except when I plainly say so.

While it is true that there is little in life that speaks for itself, this case is one of the exceptions.

There were two tapes. They record the post-trial phone conversations of one Moon juror in which that jurywoman made some remarkable disclosures.

It is the second tape that contains all that was necessary for defense counsel to move for an inquiry relating to jury conduct. Predictably the government objected.

The request for a hearing was granted and it was held—or sort of—by Judge Goettel.

The result, as we saw in the opening chapter of this book, was serious questions about a prejudiced jury foreman, Mary Nimmo, another juror who felt she and her family had been threatened by the defendant, two other jurors who complained of pressure in the jury room, newspapers available to the jury, and finally, the jury's defensive decision to delay the announcement of their verdict for the sake only of the appearance of impartiality.

The Steward-Curry tapes thus provided the ammunition for the defense's argument that the jury had been tainted and its deliberations hopelessly compromised.

The real fireworks, however, hadn't even started yet.

But first there was a side issue. The issue in question was money. As we have seen, those who made the tapes possible, Messrs. Curry and Romanoff, did not enjoy the highest of reputations—especially Bruce Romanoff. The prosecution dwelt on the unsavory characters of the two men at great length as we shall shortly see.

That the pair were in it for money—to be obtained from the Unification Church—seems, under the circumstances, quite obvious and inevitable.

Before exploring the money angle, however, it should be made clear that neither Romanoff nor Curry had done anything illegal. Taping telephone conversations without permission is not against the law in New York, as it is in other more civilized places like Baltimore, Maryland. Perhaps taping without permission is not nice—Mrs. Steward later became angry when she found out—but it is not illegal.

The prosecutors knew perfectly well that such was the case. And that is why in their cross-examination of John Curry about his taping of Mrs. Steward, the question of whether or not Curry had asked permission to tape never arose. How Curry got the tapes was immaterial. Although the government labored hard later on the "corrupted circumstances" argument, it never once specifically raised the matter of how the tapes were made.

The government also knew that taping and wiretapping to collect evidence is often done by police agencies, federal and local, without formal permission or court order. The information gathered on the tapes may not be introduced in court, to be sure, but surreptitiously gathered evidence can be used for other purposes—as leads, for example, to other evidence obtained legally.

Negotiating over payment for the tapes isn't illegal either. Defense counsel and friends of the defendants have every right to develop evidence that supports their case as long as they remain within the law, and buying evidence isn't against the law.

But what about the money? That, too, is a confused tale, but considering the nature of the gentlemen, that should not be too surprising.

The clearest evidence on this point comes from Romanoff's sealed September 30, 1982, testimony. As usual, the ever cagey ex-P.I. waltzed around the question. No, he did not ask for payment at first contact with David Hager.[1]

In fact Romanoff attempted, in baldly self-serving fashion, to look good on this point. He never asked for money either from the start or even after he turned over the first tape, he said. Monetary abstinence, albeit temporary, was made by Romanoff to look like a virtue.

Indeed, the idea of money seems, according to Romanoff, to have been John Curry's all along and the sum mentioned was $5,000 for himself and Virginia Steward. As for Romanoff, he did not discuss his cut with Curry—according to Romanoff.[2]

In fact, according to him, he was not expecting any money whatsoever. Really? Upon direct questioning from prosecutor Jo

Ann Harris, Romanoff, Brooklyn's answer to San Francisco's Sam Spade, replied coyly:

> Well, if they [Moon's attorneys] were kind enough to be authorized to pay it I would be happy to accept it, yes.[3]

Exactly when did the question of money arise with David Hager or the defense attorneys? Romanoff was a bit vague on this, but the chronology went something like this. After the two tapes had been played to both Hager and the attorneys, Charles Stillman and Andrew Lawler, the subject of money came up.

First, the attorneys rejected out of hand Curry's idea of payment to Mrs. Steward. But what about Curry and Romanoff? The ex-detective told the court:

> Oh, Mr. Hager did say that he thought I would be entitled to a fee for all this trouble, and I responded to him that I had not been looking for a fee, but if he thought a fee should be paid I would be happy to accept it.[4]

Virtue preserved. Sort of.

As for an amount, Romanoff testified, nothing specific was discussed by David Hager or Bruce Romanoff, but Romanoff in a subsequent conversation with Curry suggested that the fee would not be anything like $5,000, but $200 instead—an amount mentioned by Hager—even though in testimony a few minutes earlier Romanoff had denied any specific sum had ever been mentioned.[5]

Can anyone sort out this confusion? No. John Curry's testimony was cut off by Judge Goettel before such questions as fee requests were discussed. Moreover, despite the presence of Stillman and Lawler, the court showed no interest in asking either of them whether the question of money arose and how it was handled. As for the original contact man, David Hager, he was never summoned *in camera*.

In the end, Romanoff and Curry got nothing for their efforts. No money of any kind was given to them. We have only Romanoff's word that Hager mentioned the sum of $200. Even that fee, by Romanoff's own testimony, went unmentioned by Moon's defense lawyers.

Money, in short, played no part in obtaining the Steward tapes except, perhaps, in the greedy imaginations of Curry and, quite probably, Romanoff.

Meanwhile, the Steward-Curry tapes were as welcome to the court and prosecution as a stinkbomb at a high school prom and both judge and prosecutors seemed to be holding their noses for the next six weeks as the court, in September and October 1982, reluctantly examined the evidence of jury tainting. Like some of the jurors at the *Moon* trial, Judge Goettel gave every indication of wanting to go home, justice aside.

The secret sealed transcripts and memoranda of law tell their own story about Goettel's hearing.

For openers we have the government's September Memorandum of Law submitted to the court *in camera*. This thirty-four page confidential document outlines the government's case against holding a post-trial inquiry into the jury tainting question.

If nothing else, the memorandum leaves no doubt about the prosecution's position. Despite the Steward-Curry tapes, the government saw no reason for any inquiry. Period.

Its arguments are a mish-mash of impugned but unproven motives of defense counsel (among others); relevant but inaccurate observations on the substance of the tapes; and accurate but irrelevant characterizations of the parties (Romanoff in particular) involved in making and delivering the tapes to defense counsel.

There is also the expected farrago of case precedents that suggest that defense counsel had not met the minimum standards for a jury inquiry. So many precedents are thrown out, it is clear that their sheer number were meant to overwhelm. Relevance, however, is another question as we shall shortly see.

As for the government's style in presenting its case in the memorandum—here is a sample:

> The motion [by defense counsel] relies, in total, on two tape recordings of conversations with Juror No. 3 [that is, Mrs. Steward] surreptitiously merchandised to the Unification Church by a convicted felon, with connections to organized crime, whose record is strewn with instances of obstruction, abuse, and misuse of the justice system. The two tapes, in spite of the best (or worst) efforts of the felon and his cohort to lead this juror down the garden path, do not contain statements which, even if true, would provide a basis for

setting aside the verdict. Indeed, putting aside defendants' tortured theories, they do not contain statements admissible under Fed. R. Evid. 606(b) as a basis for any further inquiry of this or any other juror.[6]

Polemics and hyperbole—hardly dispassionate legal analyses. But then the prosecution in the *Moon* case had always relied on emotion and prejudice—never directly, of course—in an indirect fashion. So it was with its Memorandum of Law. Why change now?

In the government's attempt to discredit the defense's claims, it also pursued several lines of simultaneous attack.

In good tactical fashion, the government first pushed against the weakest point in the opposition's defense: the "corrupt circumstances" argument. Not only did the government claim that circumstances surrounding the acquisition of the tapes somehow tainted what was said; but the government offered a vision of the hell that comes about by merely examining the evidence. It became known as the "cottage industry" argument.

> [To accept the evidence] is to invite every unscrupulous and greedy opportunist in the City with a tape recorder to prey upon jurors in direct contravention of sound public policy.[7]

In pursuing the corrupt circumstances argument, the government not only cited known facts (such as Romanoff's background), but it also simply and casually assumed the evidence of wrongdoing, or the appearance of it, whenever it could. For example, the government's memorandum suggested that it didn't know whether or not Bruce Romanoff had contacted David Hager even before the tapes were recorded, suggesting, therefore, that Hager and the Unification Church might have ordered the taping in the first place. Later evidence shows that no such order was given, but that did not prevent the government, without a shred of evidence, from assuming the worst about the actions of the defendants and their supporters.[8]

Bruce Romanoff, as we have already seen, was subjected to heavy verbal artillery fire from the government. Three pages are devoted to his character in its Memorandum of Law. The character description, however, is entirely irrelevant, as any first-year law student knows. If evidence were automatically tainted because of its source, every police department in America would go out of business. So would every district attorney's office, to say nothing of federal prosecutors themselves.

Law enforcement officials depend upon paid informants, many of whom are far less savory than Bruce Romanoff. They also frequently rely on hardened criminals to appear and testify in court as government witnesses, usually in exchange for immunity from prosecution or in a plea bargaining deal designed to reduce their own sentence.

Those legal precedents went unmentioned, of course, by the government in its Memorandum of Law.

Having attacked the messenger, what about the message—the tapes themselves?

In predictable fashion, the prosecution sought to destroy their credibility too, by presenting the tapes as a manipulated affair by Romanoff and Curry in which the juror, Virginia Steward, was snookered into saying things she didn't mean.

But let the prosecution speak for itself:

> The facts, to the extent we know them, lead inevitably to the conclusion that there were a number of unrecorded (and perhaps recorded and not disclosed) contacts between John "LNU" [that is, John Curry] and the juror prior to and in between the making of these telephone tapes. We have, at this time, no idea of the conditioning or pressure that may have occurred which led this juror to contradict directly the content and tone of the statements she made to the *Prospect Press* immediately after the verdict, when the deliberations were still fresh in her mind.[9]

The government failed to produce a shred of evidence to support these allegations in its memorandum. Later, as we shall see, despite efforts to support the charges of conditioning and pressure, the government failed again to produce the evidence to support its assertions.

Never lingering on any particular unproved point, the prosecution then produced another argument to discredit the Steward-Curry tapes. This one was a first cousin of the manipulated statement theme, in which John "LNU," a.k.a. Curry, is supposed to have coached the unwitting Virginia Steward into saying things that contradicted her earlier interview in the *Prospect Press.*

The government cited various "leading questions" put to Steward by Curry as evidence of the latter's coaching. Admittedly, John Curry's remarks are pretty crude.

The following are cited as examples by the government of manipulation of Steward by John Curry:

> He [Moon] might be a prophet, who knows—you know if Jesus Christ came today, they'd probably get him for tax evasion?

> What was their opinion of him before the trial started, though? That he was, uh . . . he's a charlatan.

> Yeah, well I wouldn't want to be on it, I, I keep picturing Jesus Christ on the stand, you know, think of it?

> That's what Pontius Pilate said, he's gonna wash the blood off his hands, you know?[10]

At first glance, the government appears to have a good case with the coaching argument. Running through that argument is the lawyer-like assumption that Curry was out of order for asking "leading" questions.

But this was a phone conversation, not an interrogation in a court of law. And more important, a close look at the Steward-Curry tapes shows that the government once again played around with the facts in its memorandum, letting the reader, in this case the court, make assumptions that are not warranted.

The argument was all sleight of hand. Curry's statements are more gratuitous than leading or manipulative. None of them forces comment from Steward. Her damaging comments in regard to the trial came unprompted. If Curry had been brighter, he would have said nothing at all except an occasional sympathetic "uh-huh"—the standard technique of a skilled interviewer when the interviewee is on a roll.

In fact the celebrated Pontius Pilate comment cited by the prosecution had just the opposite effect from what the government attorneys claimed, and resulted in nearly turning off Steward from any further substantive comment.[11]

The government's point was merely suggestive rather than analytical. But not willing to rest on its laurels, the prosecution tried another wholly nonlegal approach before getting to the substance of the defense motion.

This time it used a bit of amateur psychology. Thus while disarmingly observing that "[W]e are not licensed to practice anything but law," psychology is precisely what the government's lawyers practiced on pages 14 through 16 of its Memorandum of Law to the court.

The prosecution portrayed Mrs. Steward's taped comments as nothing more than the product of an unbalanced mind, one wanting "to step away from responsibility," the result of mere "manifestations of post-verdict introspection."[12]

Aside from its pop psychological woolgathering, the government produced no evidence to support this analysis of Steward's state of mind. It patronizingly refused to examine the substance of her remarks, although it was willing enough to commend her judgments offered to the Brooklyn newspaper.

So having attacked the charges of jury tainting on several peripheral fronts, the prosecution in its memorandum then launched its main assault: the legal one involving whether law and precedent allowed for the kind of evidence that the defense wished to submit on behalf of its motion for a post-trial inquiry.

The legal arguments presented by the government are a classic example of "lawyering" a brief to death. Although short on analysis, the brief is long on case precedents cited: no fewer than twenty in a space of fifteen short, double-spaced pages. They come exploding out like popcorn from a pressure cooker: *United States v. McKinney, United States ex rel Owen v. McMann, Bulger v. McClay, Remmer v. United States, Smith v. Phillips* and *King v. United States*, to name only a few.

Even for trained lawyers, this kind of brief causes the eyes to glaze over.

The prosecution's real argument stripped of the precedent panache—some of it questionable—asserted that the defendants had not provided sufficient evidence of jury tainting to justify an official inquiry.

Mrs. Steward's comments about bias, especially bias expressed

by Mary Nimmo, are reduced *ex cathedra* into "harmless gener-
alized community knowledge and common gossip."[13]

Having diminished the problem to common gossip, the government brings in the stern standard contained in *United States ex rel
Moore v. Fay:*

> [N]ot every violation by a juror of the Court's instructions with
> respect to third party communications, nor every irregularity in a
> juror's conduct, automatically compels . . . vacatur of a judgment of
> conviction. The dereliction must be said to deprive the parties of the
> continued objective and disinterested judgment of the juror, thereby
> foreclosing a fundamentally fair trial.[14]

As was usual with the government's memorandum, the document cited an abstract and unquestionably reasonable principle in
case law, and automatically assumed it was relevant in *United States
v. Moon, et al.*

The memorandum does the same thing with questions involving
prejudiced jurors' misrepresenting their true views before a trial
begins under *voir dire*, where *United States v. Mulligan* is cited to the
effect that "[e]very incorrect answer given on *voir dire* [does not
call] inexorably for a new trial. . . ."[15]

Finally, the prosecution shifted to one other standard found in
King v. United States in which predictably the court refused the
defendant's motion for further inquiry into the possibility of jury
tainting.[16]

In summary then, the government attempted to reduce the jury
tainting question to one of small talk by one disgruntled juror,
recorded under dubious circumstances, which if allowed would
further corrode the jury system. In so doing, the prosecution
surrounded the kernel of its argument with a hard shell of precedents.

The memorandum, in short, looked formidable despite the
noted reservations.

But was it?

Defense counsel did not think so, evidenced by its reply to the
government's memorandum. The defendants' reply, also placed
under seal, made a number of critical points against the prosecution's arguments.

The first was that the prosecution sought to narrow the scope of the problem and thus leave out the embarrassing questions— embarrassing, of course, to the government's case.

In so doing, the defense argued, the prosecution had set up a straw man by pretending that the defendants were arguing for a new trial basing their arguments solely on the contents of the Steward-Curry tapes.

According to the defense counsels' reply:

> At this stage, defendants are seeking only an inquiry to determine whether the extra-record, prejudicial matters referred to on the tapes did in fact penetrate the jury room and, if they did, whether such contamination was the result of improper outside contact with the jury, and/or misleading answers on voir dire, and/or juror concealment of bias.[17]

The Steward-Curry tapes, in brief, defense argued, were not meant to be any sort of final proof of jury tainting, only sufficiently worrisome to launch a further inquiry into the possibility of such.

That inquiry, the reply argued, would involve further questioning of Mary Nimmo's conduct. It would explore Mrs. Steward's assertion that newspapers had been available in the jury room—a question that the government's memorandum ignored entirely. It would also examine juror Esperanza Torres' fears of harassment— another subject left untouched by the prosecution.[18]

Having expanded the confined space which the government lawyers wished to preserve in their argument, defense counsel moved next to the question of the authority of case precedent upon which the defense based its motion for an inquiry.

The defense's reply argued that the government had fundamentally misused the authorities it cited. The cases were either inapplicable, it said, or in fact supported the defendants' request. *King*, for example, was irrelevant because (a) the affidavit had been submitted four years after the trial and because (b) *King*'s lawyer tried to contact the jurors in order to give them a multiple-choice form in an attempt to determine the extent of their contamination by the media.[19]

Defense argued that the government's attempt to equate *Moon* with the *King* case, where the resemblances were few and the differences basic, was bizarre in and of itself.

In short, *King* was irrelevant.

Other cases cited by the government, like *Smith v. Phillips* and *Remmer v. United States*, dealt with tangential questions, the defense contended. They, in fact, called for a "full hearing" to examine "the entire picture" when the question of juror bias was raised (*Remmer*) or when the very issue at stake was the mental attitudes of the jury when it came to determining juror bias (*Smith*).[20]

Finally, it might be asked how serious was the government in its efforts to discredit the Steward-Curry tapes? In the course of its memorandum, the government's lawyers slyly suggested that they reserved doubts about the tapes' authenticity, but failed to follow up on that question.[21]

The prosecution could have subjected the tapes to voice analysis—a not very difficult or expensive test—but did not do so. Meanwhile, in its treatment of case law, there was a show of legal analysis but little substance with regard to the central questions at issue.

Still that did not matter much. The government's case against conducting an inquiry beyond the defense counsels' formal written argument was not tested either by the court or, for that matter, the defense during the *in camera* proceedings that began on September 3 and stretched spasmodically until mid-October 1982.

Judge Goettel, for example, admitted reading only the *Moten* case and not the score of other cases that both prosecution and defense had cited in their briefs. So much for the legal house of cards constructed on both sides, the prosecution in particular.[22]

In the first skirmish, the tone was set for the rest of the post-trial inquiry. In an informal setting which was designated as nonconfrontational, the prosecution pressed its basic case, namely, that the evidence presented by the defense had not crossed the threshhold of jury manipulation. The defense countered that it had, but Moon's lawyers did not pursue these arguments very vigorously.[23]

The other prosecution strategy was to delay the process as long as possible in the hope that the jurors would get wind of the proceedings and then prepare their own carefully recollected version of the events surrounding their deliberations.

And in that the government succeeded. But it did not succeed in quashing an inquiry altogether. Indeed, the government's lawyers, Jo Ann Harris in particular, did not fight very hard to prevent one from taking place once it became clear that Judge Goettel was willing to go ahead with one.

But the prosecution did convince Judge Goettel that the circumstances surrounding the acquisition of the Steward-Curry tapes were questionable, and the court held open the question of the government's implication that the recordings may have been done through collusion among Virginia Steward, Bruce Romanoff, and John Curry.[24]

Judge Goettel also signalled his belief in the "so what" school of thought. What if the jury was not completely free of prejudice? What difference does that really make?

> Well, I know your [defense's] approach is going to be that in every jury deliberation there are a lot of matters considered by a jury that should not be considered by a jury and a lot of things said that should not be said and that per se is not enough to open up the jury's verdict.[25]

This preliminary thrashing-out of the issues on September 3 clearly established the pattern of the post-trial inquiry. The prosecution found the whole process unnecessary; Judge Goettel was openly skeptical about the business.

On this last point, Judge Goettel also made clear that he had more important things to do than lead an inquiry into jury conduct in the *Moon* case:

> I am going to be in Hershey, Pennsylvania, next week. I should tell you I have a large class action on trial and it probably will be on trial for many more weeks. It involves a great number of attorneys and what-have-you, that definitely limits the amount of time that I have available for some time to come.[26]

One other characteristic of this peculiar inquiry also was revealed in this first head-to-head encounter of September 3, and that is the curious passivity of defense counsel. Only once was there a flash of protest. It came after Judge Goettel's recital of his busy schedule and his intention to wind things up "probably without further oral hearing."

In response to that, attorney Charles Stillman reminded the court:

> We started this case with our deep concern about a jury trial. Then we went through a process of trying to find a jury, because the Government wouldn't go along with us on going to trial without a jury. . . . [W]e lived with the nightmare from of our point of view with the jury feeling that Sun Myung Moon is a brainwasher who takes advantage of children.[27]

Stillman's protest went nowhere—in fact, it quickly degenerated into an exchange with Judge Goettel on why the defense did not challenge Mary Nimmo and thus prevent her from becoming juror and foreman.[28]

When Stillman was able to steer the conversation back to the topic at hand ("the bottom line is, we didn't get a fair trial"), Judge Goettel continued to ignore that sensitive subject by observing:

> But the way you are going to raise this and the reason you are pressing this now is that you want to make sure you have a complete record on this when you go on appeal, because this adds a lot to your appellate points.[29]

Clearly, in Judge Goettel's mind the inquiry could never lead to a new trial, and since the whole business was meant for the record that would be taken to the Appeals Court, there was no hurry or even need to examine the witnesses in any case.[30]

Incredibly enough, defense counsel meekly accepted Goettel's version of what these proceedings were really all about.

There was one last question about the September 3 proceeding, one that haunted the whole inquiry: namely, How would the court summon the witnesses? Defense counsel was eager to issue invitations to them in the least threatening or intimidating manner. Defense protested, for example, the idea of serving the witnesses with a subpoena by a U.S. marshal.[31]

The fear? That under any kind of threat, witnesses would retreat into a defensive clamshell in hope of avoiding further trouble. As it turned out, the issue of intimidating witnesses played the decisive role in the next round of hearings.

So, finally, more than four months after the conviction of Sun Myung Moon and Takeru Kamiyama, Judge Gerard Goettel initiated a half-hearted attempt to determine jury conduct.

Only five witnesses were called and only three jurors: Virginia Steward, Mary Nimmo, and John McGrath testified. No other jurors were asked to appear, despite a clear suspicion of perjury by at least one of them. Then too there were numerous other instances in which jurors in the record were cited by name for possible improper conduct.

As Judge Goettel predicted, there was no retrial and whatever appellate points could be gleaned out of the inquiry would have to be enough for the defense. The question of justice and the adequacy of the jury system in this case was shunted aside.

The examination of the sealed records shows the inquiry began with the September 30 examination of Bruce Romanoff. Romanoff was followed the next day (October 1) by the grilling of John Curry, the man who had started it all by taping two telephone conversations with his friend and Moon juror, Virginia Steward.

Romanoff had been summoned to testify by subpoena, including a subpoena *duces tecum*, a term which meant that the unlicensed investigator had to bring in all documents (including tapes) relevant to the inquiry.

After Romanoff was read his rights and warned of criminal penalties for perjury, the government prosecutor, Jo Ann Harris, grilled him about the tapes.

Romanoff answered that he had indeed brought the two Steward-Curry tapes, and that they were the originals. No copies had been made by him.

As for Curry, Romanoff was not sure if his partner had made any duplicates.[32]

In discussing Romanoff's first contact with John Curry, the ex-P.I. said that Curry had called him after the *Moon* jury's verdict. Curry told him that a close friend who had served on the *Moon* jury was

> sorry that she voted for the defendants to be guilty when in her heart and head, I recall that, she felt that there was insufficient proof of his guilt.[33]

There were other jurors who felt the same way, Curry reported, and the "forelady" had been "quite strong in convincing the jurors to vote guilty.[34]

What did Romanoff do then? The high-minded, civic thing of course, as Romanoff cagily pictured his motives. According to him, he told Curry to urge Steward to report her concerns to the court. Since John Curry was too timid, Romanoff volunteered to contact the defense lawyers. Nothing else was suggested. Nothing about tapes, and certainly nothing about a bounty for bringing them in. Perish the thought.[35]

On further questioning, however, Romanoff admitted to telling Curry to tape any further conversations with Steward, and to try and get "as strong and good a conversation on that so I [Romanoff] could take it the defendant's attorney. . . .[36]

A few days later, according to Romanoff, Curry brought in the first tape and Romanoff contacted David Hager. Clearly Hager was not impressed with the quality or substance of that first tape, and Romanoff, realizing that little would be gained with this first recording, told Curry to get a "second tape with greater detail as to what occurred in the jury room."[37]

Did Romanoff coach Curry on what to say to his friend Virginia Steward?

No. Well, not exactly. Romanoff did instruct Curry to ask Steward about identifying those jurors who felt as she had about the verdict.[38]

A few weeks later, Curry turned up with the second tape. Romanoff swore that in the interim he had no further contact with his part-time operative on this matter.[39]

Nevertheless the government lawyers kept after Romanoff to go further and then further into the chronology, prompting Judge Goettel to complain about the time—it was then 7:00 P.M. That was followed by an open accusation from defense attorney Lawler that the government was stalling.[40]

There was, of course, more to it than nitpicking, delaying tactics. The prosecution was also trying, through its extensive questioning of Romanoff on the fee issue, to lay the basis for a "cottage industry" argument.[41]

That is, the government wanted to shift the focus of the inquiry from jury conduct to an examination of the motives (read, greed) of Romanoff and Curry.

The prosecution was only partially successful. Yet, all in all, it had been a good day for the government on this first hearing. Romanoff came off as a slick, self-serving operator whose grasp of chronological details was faulty and at times contradictory.

Defense counsel at least got the tapes on record and pressed to get the first juror, Virginia Steward, to appear as a witness during the *in camera* proceedings.

But before that, John Curry was asked a few questions. But even before Curry was summoned on the second day of the proceedings, the prosecution once again attempted to attack the integrity of the tapes as if that were the chief issue, an argument that drove defense counsel Charles Stillman to exclaim at one point: "I think you are making a mountain out of a molehill. . . ."[42]

Still it was Andrew Lawler, Kamiyama's lawyer, who brought the argumentative Jo Ann Harris to earth:

> It seems to me that we are placing the emphasis on this tape. The tape is really just a foundation to attempt to convince the Court that we have to speak to the juror. Since everyone is in agreement that we have to speak to the juror, to continue to speculate or spend a lot of time over the circumstances under which a tape was made doesn't seem productive for our motion, which is really permission to examine jurors for purposes of seeking a new trial.[43]

In the end, Judge Goettel reluctantly agreed, despite further niggling from the government lawyers.

Things were not looking up for the defense at all. For example, instead of a nonthreatening invitation by phone to testify, Curry was brought in via subpoena. Although first assured that he was being called as a witness, the court read him his rights and warned that criminal charges would be filed against him later . . . if. Curry was also advised that he had the right of counsel, which the Brooklyn handyman refused—initially.[44]

He was a lamb on the block as the prosecution wielded the axe. After setting it up with questions on Curry's background and his relationship with Romanoff, the government aimed its blows on the tapes.

According to Curry, he recorded the tapes, then gave them to Bruce Romanoff who, in turn, returned them to Curry. Curry then claimed he had lost the tapes:

I can't find them. I lost a camera, several other items, in a bag in my car.[45]

Curry's statement contradicted Romanoff's recollection of keeping the originals and playing them for David Hager. Whether Curry was talking about losing copies or simply forgetting that they had not been returned to him or that something else happened was never cleared up in the inquiry. The point became important because it caused Judge Goettel to stop the questioning and reflect on Curry's lack of counsel.[46]

Although Judge Goettel made clear he did not believe that Curry was intentionally lying—there was no benefit if he were—the warning was significant for the court's later course of action.

Meanwhile the prosecution, not defense counsel, took the lead in directly examining John Curry. Once more a chronology was laid down regarding phone conversations and face-to-face meetings with Virginia Steward as well as with Bruce Romanoff.

It should be remembered that the hapless Curry had no knowledge of the court's examination of Romanoff or that the court possessed the actual tapes and transcripts of his phone conversations with Steward.[47]

In recounting for the court that tangled maze of conversations with various people, John Curry made statements that Judge Goettel found internally contradictory and in contradiction with Romanoff's statements—which they were, in part. Picking up from an earlier theme, Judge Goettel told both prosecution and defense counsel (Curry being absent) that he would warn the witness about the consequences of perjury and the need for counsel.

That was agreeable to defense counsel, but once again Andrew Lawler reminded the court that the questioning of Curry had gotten off the track. The proceedings to date had featured the government doing the direct examination, which was an attempt to impeach the accuracy of John Curry's recollection of events that had occurred more than two months in the past.

Lawler argued that all of this was beside the point. The point was to get the most accurate background so that the inquiry would get on with it and talk to Virginia Steward. Curry's credibility, in terms of the defense's motion, was irrelevant. Consequently, John Curry should no longer be left in the dark about what the government, defense counsel, and the court already knew, with the tape transcripts in front of them.[48]

This sensible procedure was objected to by the government and once more Judge Goettel agreed with the prosecution. The court also then raised Jo Ann Harris' favorite spectre: the possibility of collusion between Curry and Steward to make a for-sale tape.[49]

No wonder. The issue of collusion was brought up repeatedly by the prosecution. But first, John Curry had to be finished off.

That was done with near surgical precision by the court, not the prosecution; but not before attorney Stillman attempted to inject a note of sanity into the proceedings.

He pleaded with the court: "Ask the direct question: Didn't you [Curry] tell Virginia Steward that you were going to pass this information on to somebody?"[50]

The answer to this question might have laid the factual basis for the collusion charge or a count of perjury against John Curry. But that was not to be. Instead, Judge Goettel postponed that direct and simple approach and opted for an indirect one.

Sensing that the defense had completely lost control of an inquiry that they themselves had requested, attorney Lawler protested, "somehow it has become the Government's proceeding here." Instead of a probe for jury misconduct, he argued, the whole business had become an effort to discredit Curry and Romanoff, and possibly Steward; if not the Moon jury.[51]

Lawler of course was right, but his statements put Judge Goettel in a huff. Brushing aside defense counsels' arguments, the court announced archly:

> There is just one little problem. This proceeding isn't your proceeding and it isn't her [Harris'] proceeding. It is my proceeding. I intend to get everything out in the proper fashion at the appropriate time.[52]

Having regained control, the court then decided to do things its own peculiar way. First, Virginia Steward was summoned to court by a U.S. marshal who served her a subpoena, rather than by a nonthreatening phone call. Next, John Curry was marched back into the courtroom and reminded of the horrible consequences of committing perjury.[53]

Faced with that, and a reminder that counsel was available to the witness-turned-possible-criminal, John Curry meekly took Judge Goettel's advice, explaining:

> As far as dates are concerned and conversations are concerned, it's, to me, the least of my worries. I lost my wife thirteen months ago. I got four children home. I've got four grandchildren home. I have a lot of pressures on me.[54]

Three days later, on October 4, the thoroughly intimidated John Curry returned to court accompanied by counsel, the court-appointed James Cohen.

The government prosecutor, Jo Ann Harris, proceeded to ask Curry a series of questions—eleven in all—including ones answered earlier by the witness. This time, however, to each question, John Curry pleaded the Fifth Amendment.[55]

What had begun as a supposedly nonadversarial proceeding, Judge Goettel had—by his usual loose hand—turned into a shambles. Curry refused to answer anything put to him including a question on collusion and all other matters pertaining to the recording of the crucial second tape.

Thus the earlier interruption of Curry's October 1 testimony had been exquisitely timed for the prosecution and was thoroughly bad news for the defense.

Having eliminated Curry before he could testify on the major questions dealing with the background of the Steward-Curry tapes, the government went for the kill.

Without Curry's uncoerced testimony, the prosecutors were now free to impugn the recorded conversations. They began by asking the court to issue a trial subpoena ordering Virginia Steward to bring in her long-distance telephone records.[56]

The subpoena would serve two purposes. It would, along with the accompanying U.S. marshal, further intimidate Steward, and it could lay the basis for suggesting collusion on the part of Curry and Steward.

Defense counsel protested, of course. The inquiry was not a trial, and Steward's toll records could be obtained from the telephone company. And after lengthy argument on this seemingly technical point, the defense attorneys' objection was sustained by the court.[57]

It was small change in the face of the defense's other defeats. They resumed two days after John Curry's disastrous second appearance, when the lady who started it all, Virginia Steward, took the stand.

The testimony of Mrs. Steward was critical to the defense's motion. At the least, she had to corroborate what was on the tape, and at best furnish more details about what had happened during the *Moon* jury's term of service.

To do that the witness needed to be in a frame of mind that would facilitate, not retard, cooperation. We have already seen, however, that the court had decided on the intimidating approach: a U.S. marshal with subpoena in hand.

Actually, it turned out to be worse than the defense had ever imagined.

When the marshals attempted to serve the subpoena at Mrs. Steward's country trailer on October 4, she was not home. Family members did not know when she left or when she would return.

Odd, thought the officers. But it wasn't. Virginia Steward had had another argument with her husband, and was thinking of leaving. Permanently.

The U.S. marshals next sought out Steward at her job, but found she had been fired on June 8. On the night of October 5, the marshals waited for her return home. When she did that evening, they tailed her and served her the subpoena plus a restraining order that forbade her to speak to anyone—John Curry by name—about the *Moon* trial.

The already harassed woman asked what this was all about— her family had only told her that "the cops" were looking for her— but the officers would tell her nothing.[58]

Sensing that the woman had been through enough already, the defense again pleaded for a nonadversarial proceeding.

According to attorney Stillman:

It is our deep concern that somehow this proceeding will drive Mrs. Steward to the protection of the Fifth Amendment, in which event we will never, at least through her lips, find out what happened. . . . I have this terrible concern that somehow the process could intimidate her into not simply coming forward and telling us what if anything happened in connection with the matters raised by our motion.[59]

As a practical course of action, Stillman then suggested that Mrs. Steward be told (unlike John Curry) of the tape recordings, and then reassured that she has "zero to be afraid of . . . here." Telling her this would also lessen the pressure on Steward to clam up for fear of getting her old friend John Curry into trouble.[60]

Stillman's second idea was to lessen the threatening circumstances by not reading her rights, but simply asking her what happened in the jury room.[61]

It was a sensible procedure. If one's purpose was to get to the truth. Judge Goettel said no. With a wave of the hand and an airy remark about Earl Warren's turning over in his grave at such a notion, the court rejected all defense proposals and brought in Virginia Steward.[62]

The intimidation machinery went immediately into motion. Steward's rights were read; she was repeatedly asked if she wanted an attorney. A stunned Steward took the stand assuring the court, "I didn't do nothing wrong. . . ."[63]

Then the prosecution opened up on the woman as if she were a member of the Charles Manson family. What followed were questions about contact with other jurors; records she had kept about the trial; and, of course, the number and nature of her contacts with John Curry. Bruce Romanoff. David Hager. And then there was the matter of a payment of a fee.[64]

Except for Curry, Steward knew nothing about nothing. Nor did she know about the tapes of her telephone conversations with Curry. Steward, in fact, was indignant. She angrily accused Curry of invading her privacy and denied he had ever told her he was taping the conversations.

Now that Steward's righteous anger had been thoroughly

aroused, Judge Goettel decided to play the tapes in court. The effect on the juror was devastating. She went silent—as defense counsel had feared—refusing to add anything to what had already been said on the tape.

The only conversations that she had had with Curry on the trial had been recorded on the tapes. No more took place, she said, clamming up entirely.

Under more questioning, Virginia Steward continued her retreat. She felt betrayed by Curry ("to think that someone I have known after so many years") and was in no mood to go into the whole business:

> I said I don't want to get into it, I don't want to be bothered with it, I'm glad it's done and over with.[65]

Virginia Steward was speaking in the past tense, but even an amateur psychologist could see that the "defense shields" had gone up. Questioning her was useless. Still defense counsel tried fighting an uphill battle all the excruciating and tortuous way.

What about Mary Nimmo's talking about brainwashing, as Virginia Steward had recounted to Curry in the second tape? No, she couldn't recall saying that. As for brainwashing children, that had been said before the trial began, and the details were now cloudy.[66]

The questioning of Steward was going so badly that Judge Goettel became embarrassed. Goettel, however, thought that the problem was the quality of the questions rather than the procedure he, himself, had ordered—against the advice of defense counsel.

It was too late. Neither Stillman nor Lawler could elicit any more from Steward on any of the points brought up in the two tape recordings. She adamantly refused to add anything new, and on occasion her memory of her past statements totally failed.[67]

For example, after she acknowledged that Mary Nimmo made a remark about Moon's son being a troublemaker, Steward said she "just dropped it." As for newspapers, yes, they were in the jury room, but Steward could not any longer remember if they had been read by the jurors. At another point, Steward corrected her earlier statement about Mary Nimmo's having said that Moon should be deported. Upon reflection during the October 6 hearing, Steward decided that the comment had been made by someone else—a person she could no longer recall.

In the case of Esperanza Torres, the frightened juror had become an "excitable . . . Spanish girl." Was her experience with the BB gun and the automobile accident the result of "Moonie" intimidation?

Answer: "[I]t could have been. She didn't know." And at another point, the alleged threat was only from "a somebody" not further identified.[68]

Defense counsel, having exhausted their attempts to draw out more from Mrs. Steward, handed over the questioning to the prosecution.

That is when Jo Ann Harris went in for the kill. Sensing Steward's anger with Curry, the government lawyer asked sweetly: "[D]o you feel that he was twisting your words, putting things out of context, is that what you mean?"

Answer: yes.

Defense counsel objected. And was overruled.

Harris then asked the juror if, after the jury was impaneled, "Did in fact as far as you know everyone follow the Judge's orders?"

Answer: yes.

Another objection and a move to strike the answer. But too late, the court overruled.

Harris, however, was not finished quite yet. Just one more question. It regarded Virginia Steward's interview by the *Prospect Press*. Was the article accurate in all respects?

Defense again objected, but Steward's answer was allowed to stand. Yes, her views had been correctly reported and by implication they reflected what she believed then and now.

Prosecution had thus quite neatly come full circle, with Mrs. Steward leaving defense counsel sprawled in the dust.[69]

As for Virginia Steward, she needed no warning from the court: "I'm not going to talk to nobody. No way. Not now. I'm sorry if I caused any problems to either one. I'm sorry."[70]

Although Steward never took the Fifth Amendment, it did not really matter that she had not. A more intimidated witness can scarcely be imagined, as her final comments on the stand indicate.

Still, despite the Virginia Steward fiasco, the defense lawyers attempted to rescue something. At a minimum, they wanted the Moon jury foreman, Mary Nimmo, to answer the questions raised, albeit reluctantly, by her co-jurywoman.

Not surprisingly, Judge Goettel didn't quite see the point. Maybe Mrs. Nimmo had deep-seated feelings about the Reverend Sun Myung Moon, and maybe she didn't. Nevertheless, his Honor would only "with an abundance of caution [be] prepared to call her and allow questioning of her on the point."[71]

Now the court's mind shields went up. Judge Goettel signalled the defense that he had no intention of calling the rest of the jurors, no matter what Mary Nimmo had said. Moreover, when Charles Stillman wanted to bring in at least Esperanza Torres, Goettel promptly mind-read her outbursts as "absolutely irrational thoughts and she had enough sense to realize they were irrational."[72]

It was an astonishing analysis of the record, but it went unchallenged, leaving Judge Goettel with the final word: "You have a long way to go before you convince me that she [Torres] should be brought in on that."[73]

Still, if nothing else, that statement did show how Gerard Goettel thought about the inquiry. It was necessary, he thought, in *pro forma* fashion to be conducted for the record, so to speak, but it would never change his mind.

That left the defense lawyers with Mary Nimmo as their last card. Nimmo, however, proved to be a most formidable witness, as we soon shall see from the sealed transcript of the October 7 proceedings.

Before Nimmo was asked a single question, the rules that had applied to the three previous witnesses were suddenly changed. For instance, Judge Goettel explained to Nimmo that allegations had been made against her as a juror and foreman, but that she was not a defendant. While Nimmo was reminded of her right to counsel, no perjury warning was issued.

Moreover she was allowed to violate the secret, closed-door proceedings by bringing along moral support in the form of her husband, a New York City policeman. It is doubtful that she needed her husband though. Before defense counsel had a chance to ask a single question, Nimmo angrily demanded to know which juror had ratted on the "fore-lady."[74]

The court declined to name Virginia Steward, but it made no difference. Mary Kathleen Nimmo was now in charge.

That was evident from defense attorney Stillman's rattled first question, which was half-formed and then withdrawn. It would go downhill from there for the Reverend Sun Myung Moon's lawyers.[75]

Mary Nimmo was neither awed nor cowed by the court and the legal apparatus around her. Unlike Steward or Curry or even Romanoff, she had her story and she stuck to it. Needless to say, she had done nothing wrong.

Under direct questioning from defense attorneys she denied no fewer than twenty-eight times or professed not to remember saying or doing anything that was prejudicial to Sun Myung Moon and his associate Takeru Kamiyama.[76]

It was a breathtaking performance.

Did she say Moon brainwashed children?

No, she had not.

Did she say that Moon kept children from their families?

No.

What about Moon's child being a school troublemaker?

Mary Nimmo couldn't recall.

Could she remember anything about Moon and the Unification Church?

Her answer was a classic in studied vagueness:

I had remembered something about when he had a thing at Yankee Stadium, he had a big fund-raising or whatever at Yankee Stadium. That was one of the things I had remembered about him.[77]

Perhaps there was one other tiny thing she remembered: "[P]eople sold flowers for him."[78]

But it was all so unclear as to what she knew before the trial and later. One thing was certain though. According to Mary Nimmo, before the trial "I didn't know too much about Reverend Moon. . . ."[79]

No matter how the defense went at her, she was not to be shaken in her account of saying and doing nothing prejudicial to the defendants.

Asked again about the subject of "Moonie" brainwashing, Mary Nimmo suddenly began to sound like a lawyer herself:

> I can't remember if I had heard it, but even if I had, I would have—I wouldn't have paid much attention to it, because I have no proof. It was all hearsay. You can't believe everything you hear. People have different views on different things.[80]

Nor could she remember much about newspapers being in the jury room, although she was jury foreman. Of course, Mary Nimmo had not read them—she was too busy perusing the novel *Airport*. Had anybody else read papers or discussed articles about the case?[81]

She didn't know. It was a complete blank to her.

What about Esperanza Torres?

Nimmo could recall very little. Torres came back from the courtroom once, she recalled, very excited. But the rest was a blur. Yes, Mary Nimmo remembered hearing second hand, something about a BB gun, but that was it. She did not believe it was connected to the case, and she knew nothing about Esperanza's car being rear ended.[82]

As for juror John McGrath who chided Nimmo on being prejudiced, according to Virginia Steward, she did not remember much about him or the remark either. What she did recall, however, had a totally different ring to it:

> I might have said something that I was waiting for the defense, I got to hear their side of the story, you know, I can't wait for that because there's got to be two sides to it, because right now we are being shown one side and it can make you—it can sway you. And maybe that's what, something I said. But I did say that was the biggest part, I wanted to hear the other side, the defense side.[83]

Well, then, what about Virginia Steward? A comment to her about brainwashing?

She couldn't recall. All she could remember was that Steward got irritated at her once, but Mary Nimmo could not say what it was about.[84]

And so it went. Mary Nimmo did not say anything wrong or couldn't remember if she had. She was the perfect juror and held no biases against the defendant. Indeed at one point she declared:

I came there—all the testimony I ever heard there I said to myself I don't have to worry about what he [Moon] did, who he did [sic]. All I am here for is to judge on tax evasion. And I couldn't have cared less, frankly.[85]

According to Mary Nimmo the trial foreman kept a totally open mind on the subject of the defendants and their alleged wrongdoings, as she had been charged to do.

It was a superb performance, and the defense counsel did not lay a glove on her. Nor did the court interrupt and furrow its brow over possible perjury.

Not once was Mrs. Nimmo reminded that she might be the target of possible criminal charges nor was it suggested to her that she should seek counsel. And with that, she left the stand never to return.

At that point, counsel for the defendants threw their last bolt.

[G]iven the direct conflict between the two jurors [Andrew Lawler argued], we would request that your Honor issue a call or subpoena for the other jurors who have been identified as having been present at some or all of these conversations.[86]

Especially, Esperanza Torres.

No. Flatly denied, Judge Goettel ruled. Moreover, he said, the case for jury misconduct was actually weaker than before the inquiry had started. Mary Nimmo's testimony had apparently struck no sparks of doubt. All Judge Goettel would acknowledge was that the recollections of Virginia Steward and Mary Nimmo were not in agreement, but "[w]hether that difference *has any materiality* vis-a-vis the defendant's motion is something I am not prepared to decide at this time."[87]

All that Judge Goettel was willing to contemplate was to summon John McGrath, the other juror who had allegedly heard Mary Nimmo's prejudicial remarks.[88]

Despite protestations from new defense lawyer Laurence Tribe about Mary Nimmo's testimony having been in direct contradiction to Virginia Steward's testimony and her taped remarks, the court remained firm.

If from this trio [Romanoff, Curry, and Steward] good cause exists for voir dire'ing [Goettel explained] every member of a jury, we are going to have an awful lot of these proceedings in the future.[89]

And that was that.

John McGrath's testimony was strictly anticlimactic. Nothing was developed from his abbreviated testimony, which took place a week after Mary Nimmo took the witness chair.

With McGrath, it even began wrong for the defendants. Before he took the oath, the juror explained that because of his job he hadn't slept in at least thirty-six hours.

John McGrath's big problem was he could not remember much about the trial proceedings of just a few months before. Indeed, when it came to remembering anything concerning one of the more important events of his entire life, McGrath seemed to suffer near total amnesia. Mary Nimmo was a blur. He had no recollection about her criticism of the Reverend Mr. Moon's son. He remembered nothing about Esperanza Torres' complaint about a BB gun or an automobile accident. He recalled nothing about his supposed remark to Mary Nimmo about not being prejudiced. And nothing about anyone saying anything about brainwashing or deportation or, well, anything at all.[90]

In fact, John McGrath could not "recall anybody saying anything negative" before, during, or after the trial; this, of course, despite the fact the jury convicted Moon of some very "negative" things.[91]

The only point he could remember was the newspaper article that had suggested that the jury members were "dummies," but McGrath did not take it very seriously, although Mary Nimmo seemed a bit upset. But he insisted it was not important, and the moment passed.

His non-remembrance of things past on these questions might surprise some, but it was John McGrath himself who provided a clue as to his lack of memory.

When asked if he had been friendly with any particular jurors, such as Virginia Steward, McGrath said no. He explained:

Well, to tell you the truth, I think I was mostly friendly with everybody. That's kind of my personality. I get along well with people and

I don't think there was anybody there could say I actually favored anybody, you know. I just get along with a lot of people.[92]

A man like McGrath who gets along with everyone is not about to answer hard questions about other people's words or actions that would get them—or himself—in trouble.

For all practical purposes, the inquiry was now over. Despite a last-second plea by Professor Tribe that more jurors be quizzed, Torres in particular, Judge Goettel turned thumbs down.

The court was tired of the proceedings. Romanoff and Curry were sleazy. Probing jury conduct is a bad business in any case. The Steward-Curry telephone logs suggested collusion which, to be sure, could not be proved. Mrs. Steward, Judge Goettel said, was not credible, but Mary Nimmo was—"for a variety of reasons"—left, however, unexplained.[93]

Still, it was an amazing list of material facts upon which the defense counsel hoped to build their case. Without question, a juror had expressed grave reservations, albeit privately, about the jury's decision to convict the Reverend Sun Myung Moon. In telephone conversations and under oath this same juror had confirmed that the jury foreman had made prejudicial statements to other jurors about Moon, his family, his religious beliefs, and his honesty.

Another juror, McGrath, hadn't denied that those conversations had taken place, only that he couldn't recall them exactly. All three jurors questioned, Steward, Nimmo, and McGrath, had acknowledged hearing or knowing of another juror's hysterical claims during the trial that she was being followed by "Moonies" and even threatened with physical assault.

And, again, all three jurors who had been called to testify had admitted that the jury as a whole had violated the fundamental rules of the court by reading and watching news reports and openly discussing rumors and hearsay while the trial was taking place.

Despite the judge's and the prosecution's efforts to intimidate witnesses, the defense had shown beyond a reasonable doubt that the jury which had decided Moon's guilt or innocence had been tainted from the start, poisoned from within and predisposed to a guilty verdict. At the very least, even a skeptical court would have wanted to hear the testimony of one or more jurors.

Not so Judge Goettel.

He not only refused to hear any further testimony but also threatened the defense lawyers with criminal prosecution if they ever made contact with any of the jurors again no matter what the circumstances or what the jurors had to say.

On top of that strange, if not unconstitutional, directive Judge Goettel slapped a permanent gag order on the defense lawyers, who were forbidden, under pain of criminal penalties, from discussing the post-trial hearings.

Needless to say, Judge Goettel was hardly sympathetic to any further defense motions. To Professor Tribe's appeal to vacate the judgment of conviction and order a new trial for Moon and Kamiyama, the court had only two words:

Motion denied.[94]

CHAPTER X

AMICI, APPEALS, AND PRISON

The income tax has made more liars out of the American people than golf. Even when you make a tax form out on the level, you don't know when it's through if you are a crook or a martyr.

WILL ROGERS

A STRANGER group of bedfellows would be hard to imagine: the Reverend Jerry Falwell, former Senator Eugene McCarthy, the late Clare Booth Luce, Harvard law professor Laurence Tribe, and Senator Orrin Hatch. What could all these people with such disparate philosophies possibly have in common?

Politically and personally very little, perhaps nothing at all, with one notable exception. That single thread also ties together the liberal American Civil Liberties Union and the Southern Christian Leadership Conference with the conservative Freemen Institute. The same thread connects Baptists and Presbyterians, the Roman Catholic Church and the National Council of Churches, not to mention the avowedly Marxist Spartacist League as well as the states of Hawaii, Oregon, and Rhode Island.

Between 1982 and 1984 all the above and more than thirty other individuals and organizations entered *amicus curiae* (friends of the court) briefs to the United States Supreme Court in what to the untrained eye was a minor tax case involving an unpopular religious figure whose Asian origins and unusual theological notions had earned him in this country a small following and little sympathy from established religions. Moreover, the issue had already been settled by the lower courts. Or had it been, really? The petitioners emphatically didn't think so.

Amicus briefs, incidentally, are a familiar part of Anglo-Saxon jurisprudence. They are the legal version of political lobbying. Yet such briefs cannot simply be direct and naked statements of political interest on behalf of the petitioners. They must be framed in legal form and substance, outlining before the Supreme Court a substantial federal question in which basic constitutional principles are at stake. They should be dispassionate, learned, and heavily laced with case precedent. And, despite the reputation of much legal opinion in this country, the briefs should be short, clear, and to the point.

Indeed, even a casual reading of the briefs, from religious and secular groups, from Protestant, Catholic, and Jewish organizations, from religious conservatives and fundamentalists as well as liberals, suggests strongly that the officers of the court for the prosecution committed gross breaches of American constitutional law and procedure. Moreover, these same officers either deliberately or through ignorance casually demolished a plethora of principles involving American religious protection rights that go back before the nation's founding to the roots of Western civilization itself. Or to be more precise, if one *amicus* can be believed, to the fourth-century Edict of Constantine which, in effect, lifted the Christian church from its status as a much maligned and persecuted cult to an established religion.

It should be added in regard to the *Moon* case that, although the defense had friends of the court, the *amici* were not necessarily friendly to the defendant. Legal counsel for the mainline religious bodies went out of their way to disassociate themselves from the theology of the Reverend Sun Myung Moon's Unification Church. So did the Marxists and representatives from three black minority groups.

The fastidious and thoroughly establishment National Council of Churches of Christ, representing thirty-two American Protestant and Eastern Orthodox bodies, made brutally clear that their filing did not represent any agreement with Moon's faith, or sympathy with him.

More than forty *amici curiae* briefs were filed in the *Moon* appeal case alone. Some came from flyspeck groups, but combined, the briefs represented the voices of some 160 million Americans. If these organizations spoke only for 160 Americans, however, the constitutional questions regarding individual rights would remain on the table. In theory, at least, there would be even more at stake since the rights of a minority were being abused.

One issue the *amici* involved themselves in was a defendant's right to a fair trial, the very heart of the Sixth Amendment. In the 1965 *Singer* case, as you may recall, a defendant was denied a request for a bench trial, but as the *amicus* brief filed by the American Civil Liberties Union in the *Moon* case pointed out, *Singer* had only established the right of denial if a bench trial merely served the personal convenience of the defendant. In the *Singer* case the defendant had only wanted to save time. His request for a bench trial had nothing to do with seeking protection from a prejudiced jury.

The ACLU, incidentally, was not impressed with the government's fretting over the integrity of the jury system either. As its brief acidly observed: "[T]he government's objection appears to confuse means and ends. A jury is not an end in itself, but the means by which a fair and impartial factual determination may be reached."[1]

But if the American Civil Liberties Union was not impressed with the government on this point, another civil rights *amicus* brief, this one submitted by the National Emergency Civil Liberties Committee, a collection of 1950s radicals, thought even less of Judge Goettel's ruling on bench-versus-jury trial.

The committee's brief, drafted by the late Leonard Boudin, father of 1960s self-styled revolutionary Kathy Boudin, took a dim view of Judge Goettel's reasoning. According to the judge, the jury would be "if not totally free from bias, by and large capable of putting aside the bias."

Wrong.

At least that is how the Civil Liberties Committee saw it. Being "by and large" free of prejudice is not good enough, it argued, and jurors who do not read, talk, or know much are "hardly the jury of one's peers in a complicated tax case."[2]

An *amicus* brief submitted by the Institute for the Study of American Religion called the refusal to grant Moon a bench trial only "the most recent manifestation of a tragic history of unfair and unconstitutional efforts in America directed against new and unpopular religions currently called cults."[3]

As a result of its research, the institute concluded that the court had horribly underestimated the effect of prejudice on religions struggling to become established. In contrast to Judge Goettel, who found the Unification Church question *sui generis*, the institute's brief charged the matter was nothing of the kind.

The institute's brief pointed out that at one time or another Baptists, Unitarians, Catholics, Jews, Mormons, Adventists, Amish, and Jehovah's Witnesses had been the object of hate and suspicion as well as legal discrimination. For example, the now commonly accepted name for the Society of Friends, "Quakers," was originally a term of derision, intended to wound the sect's members. Three centuries later it was the turn of the "Moonies."

Another issue. The Reverend Sun Myung Moon's troubles did not end with a biased jury deciding on his tax returns. The U.S. government also moved to restrict his freedom of speech before, during, and after the trial and the appeal procedure.

The American Civil Liberties Union, for example, flatly contended that the government's opposition to a bench trial because Moon thought his indictment had been politically motivated had been "irrational" and a clear violation of the First Amendment.[4]

But Moon faced another, even bigger problem; an issue that many *amici* contended was almost totally ignored by the court.

As the Catholic laymen's *amicus* brief pointed out, religious tolerance was a slow and evolving concept that long preceded the founding of the American republic. In fact, the concept's genesis sprang from the ancient Christian church fathers who attempted to fashion ecclesiastical freedom after the fall of the Roman Empire. Nor was the work finished when the First Amendment was ratified in 1791. The meaning of the amendment and its Religious Clauses have changed over time.

In the words of the Catholic Laymen:

By trial and error a compromise and equilibrium has been attained in the United States between the freedom to worship and the power of the state. Certain relationships are the concern of both the religious and secular orders, although for different purposes. But control over the religious order, through an unwarranted extension of power granted by the people to the secular order, would be a constitutional disaster.[5]

Not only was the Reverend Sun Myung Moon's religion relevant to the trial, even more vital was his position as leader of his church. To the Catholic laymen, the lack of specific attention to this matter in the judge's instructions to the jury was especially troublesome. In their *amicus* brief, they concluded:

If permitted to stand, the principle ... could readily be applied against those who hold office in the Roman Catholic Church, as well as against leaders of other hierarchical religions. The weapons fashioned by the government in this case—hauling a religious leader into court in part *because* of his ecclesiastic office, and then denying the significance of that office when it sheds critical, exonerating light on actions taken by the religious leader and his followers, is a weapon that this Court, faithful to the precepts on the Religious Clauses, must not permit civil authorities to wield.[6]

The government's determinedly secular approach to the *Moon* case had also trampled on another aspect of the First Amendment's religious clauses. It did so, according to the *amici*, by refusing to recognize or accept the religious nature of the Unification Church and the Reverend Sun Myung Moon's role as its leader. The government had accomplished this by insisting (with the court in agreement) that the Unification Church did not really exist because it had no formal corporate status.

The clearest expression of this refusal to acknowledge this issue was Judge Goettel's instructions to the jurors, which had omitted mentioning that the group had to accept the church's definition of itself as a religious body unless previously proved otherwise in court—something which, in fact, had not been done or even attempted.

Because the church had no legal existence, the government could then argue that the business ventures it had engaged in by use of the money from the two Chase Manhattan Bank accounts became proof that no religious trust existed. The prosecution, in short, had considered Moon, for purposes of trial, to be just another high-ranking businessman.

In so doing, both judge and jury had failed to understand the unique position of the Reverend Sun Myung Moon in his church. The Reverend Moon was more than a trustee of the church's money; he was the very embodiment of the movement, the defense had contended. The concept, too, was understood by the leaders of more conventional church bodies. The Catholic Laymen brief, for one, accepted the Reverend Sun Myung Moon's position as one analogous to that of the Pope.[7]

Moreover, the *amici* also recognized that religious leaders, particularly those who found new religions, exercise great personal control over their movements "lest the movement be subverted or destroyed."[8]

Joseph Smith, Brigham Young, and Mary Baker Eddy come to mind. So do John Calvin and Martin Luther, not to mention St. Paul, and yes, Jesus of Nazareth. The Moon-as-just-another-businessman argument also disturbed the religious *amici* in another and very basic way that touched their own interests as well.

As the National Council of Churches pointed out: "[C]hurches routinely and necessarily invest their funds in 'business ventures' as part of the effort to sustain and spread their spiritual mission."[9]

As a further consequence of the judge's instructions, the jury was left to its own devices to reach conclusions on complicated state-church questions without any guidelines from the court on a subject matter thick with law and precedent.

That mistake, the Catholic laymen and others argued, had opened up a Pandora's box of problems:

> [The court] allowed the jury to impose its own lay standards as to whether the funds in question were properly treated as the Church's or as the personal property of Reverend Moon. The ultimate result of this intrusion is an overturn of church-state equilibrium by administrative fiat and an excessive government entanglement with religion in violation of the First Amendment.[10]

That intrusion had the effect of casually giving a secular jury the power to judge religious doctrine and practice. Such involvement has been viewed by the Supreme Court since 1944 (in *United*

States v. Ballard) as improper and excessive entanglement in religion.

As another friend of the court, the Catholic League for Religious and Civil Rights, put it:

> [T]he largely unlimited jury inquiry into religious purposes licensed by the decision below gives no assurance that courts would treat a Catholic bishop in such a deferential manner.[11]

That, of course, is an understatement. American Catholics, who have often been at the wrong end of community prejudice in our history, understand that a breach of that size in the wall separating church and state might be the undoing of far more than one Asian religious leader.

In conclusion, the Catholic laymen drew the larger lesson:

> The resulting precedent [established in *United States v. Moon*] is bound to be far-reaching and deleterious to churches everywhere in the United States. This is a clear violation of the anti-establishment tenets of the Constitution.[12]

The National Council of Churches agreed, stating that Moon's First Amendment rights had been egregiously violated by the trial court when it allowed "the government to use Reverend Moon's religion *against* him, while forbidding Reverend Moon at critical junctures to use his religion in his defense." It was the best of both worlds for the prosecution; hell on earth for the defense. Or so the friends of the court contended.[13]

Perhaps the chop logic of the American courts was finally best exposed by the Mormon *amicus* brief:

> [T]here is a crime if there is no religious purpose, the jury says there is no religious purpose, therefore there is a crime. The syllogism should have been: There is a crime if there is no genuinely held religious purpose: the jury says the religion's stated purpose is (or is not) genuinely held, there is (or is not) a crime.[14]

Logic, however, was never the guiding star in the *Moon-Kamiyama* case. As Sun Myung Moon and Takeru Kamiyama were about to find out—again.

Once the Foley Square jury had delivered the verdict in May, counsel for the defense pored over the trial transcript in June and then presented a handful of post-trial motions to the trial judge, Gerard L. Goettel. Goettel considered the motions two months after the conviction.

Post-trial motions are part minuet, part Chinese opera. They are carefully choreographed and the results are almost always known in advance. There is little room for surprise or improvisation. But, like Peking opera, there can be noisy distraction while the real plot is unfolding.

Defendants rarely have their motions granted—whether the request is for a new trial or an outright acquittal—unless dramatic new evidence comes to light, a development that happens in the movies more often than in real life.

Post-trial motions are also a dress rehearsal for the appeals court, the next major link in the long legal chain of redress that convicted defendants often pursue, something that both the prosecution and defense are intimately aware of while the post-trial motions are being argued and considered.

In the matter of *United States of America v. Sun Myung Moon and Takeru Kamiyama*, the defense motions sought to overturn the trial verdict in two ways: acquittal under one set of motions; a new trial under the other.

The motions also asked for an investigation to determine whether or not the government had "selectively" prosecuted Moon and Kamiyama.

Professor Laurence H. Tribe of Harvard University, the new man brought in by the defense for the post-trial process, led the way.

Although a brilliant constitutional lawyer, Tribe was no ancient doyen of the law. At age twenty-six he had begun to teach at Harvard Law School. Tribe had barely turned forty when he accepted the post-trial assignment from Unification Church members anxious for some fresh blood in the defense's line-up. They wanted a legal heavyweight in this last round in the Foley Square arena.

At first glance, Tribe was a distinctly odd choice. He was well known for his liberal beliefs, something that was in contrast to the conservative, anticommunist views of the Reverend Sun Myung Moon and his followers. But Tribe had been born in Shanghai, China, the son of immigrant Polish Jews who had suffered at the hands of both Hitler's Nazis and Stalin's Communists.

In his legal career he had, unlike many liberals, defended the weak and genuinely unpopular, including several marginal religious groups.

The last point in Tribe's favor was that he was a winner. Accustomed to arguing before appellate courts and even the U.S. Supreme Court, the man from Harvard Law School had already won a key victory for the church's tax appeal case in New York State courts—a decision that had provided recognition of the Unification Church as a legitimate religion.

Tribe had his work cut out for him. This was Moon and Kamiyama's last stand—at least with Judge Goettel. Tribe asserted in the course of oral argument that the court could and should act as "the thirteenth juror," ready to undo the mischief created by the first dozen.

Under Tribe's supervision 400 pages of legal argument were prepared raising some thirty issues. Expecting a routine defense effort, and thus caught by surprise, the government lawyers turned nasty.

But one thing Harvard academics can do is dish it out as well. Professor Tribe told Judge Goettel:

> When I came into this case, I knew it was a large case and the constitutional issues distressed me. I didn't anticipate I would have to or be able to produce 600 pages of papers. Contrary to the government's snide suggestion that we are more interested in the weight and bolt than in the substance but the reason is that this trial was so rife with constitutional error, error that is not too late for your Honor to correct.[15]

In the post-trial procedure Tribe, as counsel for the defense, made his presentation to the court before the government.

For the most part, Tribe's brief was simply a distilled version of what the defense had argued during the long pre-trial and trial phases. In contrast to Charles Stillman, however, the professor from Harvard sprinkled his argument with learned references to other cases like *United States v. Kuch, Mullaney v. Wilbur* and *Jones v. Wolf*, often without further explanation as to what they actually contained.

Tribe's style seemed to annoy Goettel who, after all, had not gone to an Ivy League law school but had attended the more plebeian (and Catholic) Fordham. Taking a more academic approach than Stillman, Professor Tribe stuck with the defense's principal trial argument, an argument anchored firmly in the First Amendment.

Specifically, Tribe restated Moon's defense by asking what limits the U.S. Constitution and the First Amendment place on the government's ability to prosecute tax fraud cases against religious leaders who hold property in their names, but do so for the benefit of the religion?[16]

Moon's counsel argued that there were indeed limits on the government, but conversely, that did not mean that there was a total exemption from prosecution. Religion, in short, did not enjoy a completely free ride, thanks to the First Amendment. Tribe brought up the issue because the government in its post-trial submissions to the court had said that the "free ride" was, indeed, the defense's claim. But the prosecution's version of the defense argument was a straw man. "[T]hat ... is utterly remote from the motion that we make in this court. . . ." Tribe told Judge Goettel.[17]

Goettel was not convinced. In fact, he became the prosecution's echo on this major point:

> You are virtually suggesting to me that I must accept the church's view of the Reverend Moon and, having done that, I must not question anything he does.[18]

Tribe denied the assertion again. "[R]eligion is not an absolute shield," he countered. Nowhere in the defense's position was there a claim of absolute immunity from prosecution on the basis of the First Amendment. In fact the government, Tribe argued, could have established tax fraud by legitimately stripping away First Amendment protections of the Unification Church and its leader if—and this was the Big If—the prosecution had attempted to show that the religion was a sham or if it had "clear and objective evidence" that Moon had been given assets specifically for his personal use.

Or, finally, if the government had shown that in the course of diverting funds for personal use from the Chase Manhattan Bank accounts, Moon had under-reported the money for tax evasion purposes.

The prosecution, however, had not done any of these things. Instead, the government had ignored the possibility of diversion and focused on the interest generated by the Chase savings account. As a result, the government lawyers had virtually ignored the First Amendment question, and had treated Moon like any other business tax cheat. Or so Tribe argued. For all practical purposes, the First Amendment had disappeared, during the course of the trial, into thin air.[19]

Tribe's words rang a bell with Goettel. The judge, who had shown so far only a limited and restricted interest in the First Amendment, found to his amazement that major religious leaders who would not be caught dead with the Reverend Sun Myung Moon were agitated enough about the trial to write him. Personally. Goettel acknowledged:

I have received fifty, perhaps one hundred, letters from prominent church leaders, Protestant and Catholic church leaders, decrying the fact that a religious leader could be prosecuted for merely holding church funds in his own name.[20]

The outcry had obviously come as a shock to Goettel, but the letter campaign was not enough to move him much. The ever-helpful government lawyers managed to minimize the importance of the letters. Jo Ann Harris, for one, labelled them "one dimensional," showing a "misinformed or misguided view of this case."

Tribe, however, had dug up the first real doubt the court had entertained about the case since jury selection. Tribe now pressed as hard as he could. Moon's lawyers weren't the only ones who were worried about the cavalier treatment the First Amendment had been given during the course of this trial.

What had happened to one Korean minister on the fringes of Christianity could happen to the staid, respectable, mainstream and orthodox clergy. Tribe explained what these religious leaders were worried about:

> [I]t exposes every religious group to the danger of a civil jury verdict or a criminal jury verdict which disregards the intent of the donors and treats the ultimate use by the recipient, by the person holding the funneled funds, as dispositive. It seems to me very clearly established in the law . . . that the mere fact that the trustee may use some of the money for his own purposes, though it may bear on a charge of diversion and a claim that the taxes should be made on the money so diverted, does not in any way negate the controlling intent of the donors and the existence of a religiously imposed charitable trust.[21]

Tribe then hit another point, and it came very close to home with Goettel. The professor from Harvard had to tell the judge to his face that his instructions to the jury had been faulty, even fatally flawed:

> [I]n carrying out the instructions that were given to the jury, even if we were to assume that the jury is composed of very well educated, brilliant individuals, any reasonable jury would have supposed that the mere fact that they in their own common experience would regard some of the expenditures that Reverend Moon was required to make as nonreligious, not by the church's own definition by that their secular definition, would destroy the existence of a fiduciary relationship. Not only is that not the law in New York but I am convinced that the Second Circuit would not say that is the law under the First Amendment.[22]

As Laurence Tribe knew, the jury had not been composed of brilliant people at all. None had college degrees and most had shown a remarkable ignorance of anything outside their immediate, small, and personal world—a problem that Judge Goettel had worried about out loud at the start of the trial. When the bench's instructions left out a relatively complex explanation of what a trust relationship was—how could this jury be expected to make well-informed judgments?

The question is not entirely rhetorical. In fact, the issue was the core of the defense's post-trial motions.

Goettel would have none of it. Calling the defense's position "schizophrenic," the judge rejoined that Moon could not have it both ways. The Korean could not be the personification of his church and thus do anything he wanted with the money, and at the same time have a trust relationship with his followers. "He can't be a trustee for himself," said Judge Goettel.[23]

Tribe again tried to reacquaint the court with the First Amendment, the meaning of which Judge Goettel did not seem to fathom. The First, Tribe argued, does not force any legitimate religion to choose between the two possibilities outlined by the court. Other religions did not. The Unification Church should be no exception—unless the government had proved that the Reverend Sun Myung Moon's religion was a fraud—which it hadn't.[24]

Tribe also argued that the prosecution carried out an invisible trial relying on the defendant's unpopularity to sway the largely uneducated jurors into a conviction. Moreover, the question of religious prejudice, Tribe stated, made it impossible for the defense to describe the Unification Church's theology, which would have explained Moon's unique position in the movement.

Put another way, tails the government wins, and heads the defense loses. It was a perfect legal Catch-22, and the only hope that defense counsel had was to argue before the bench that this particular post-trial motion for acquittal be granted.[25]

The court was very uncomfortable with defense's line of argument. Judge Goettel did not like having the selective prosecution argument sprung on him after the trial. He replied (correctly) that the usual procedure was to argue that issue before a trial begins.

The Moon trial, however, had been an unusual case—to say the least—and the argument about selective prosecution rested on the vindictive way the government had demanded a jury trial.

Goettel would not budge. He had not wanted a jury trial either, but had felt handcuffed by the Sixth Amendment and legal precedent. He felt that the *voir dire* process had proved satisfactory. It was time to move on, and so he concluded:

[T]here is nothing more you can say in that regard that is going to change my view on it. If there is going to be new law, it will come from an appellate tribunal.[26]

Nor would Goettel accept Laurence Tribe's thesis that a trial judge can and should act as the "thirteenth juror" to correct miscarriages of justice brought about by both juries and prosecution:

I don't think the Supreme Court . . . would necessarily endorse the thirteenth jury [sic] approach, and particularly in this circuit which has always taken the view that district judges can and often do make errors, that jurors never make errors, that they would endorse the thirteenth juror approach.[27]

With that turn-down, Laurence Tribe had pretty well shot his bolt. It was now the turn of Kamiyama's lawyer. Andrew Lawler's focus was on the government charges of conspiracy. That is, that Moon and Kamiyama had engaged in acts of concealment to further advance their conspiracy to avoid the payment of taxes on the ownership of stock in the Tong-Il company.

If no concealment had taken place, then the whole conspiracy thesis began to fall apart. Lawler duly argued:

[T]here was no effort to conceal the fact that stock was in the name of Reverend Moon. Stock was placed in his name, documents were drawn up by attorneys that placed the stock in his name, he signed a stock subscription of agreement, indeed when the accountants were first retained, Peat Marwick, they were informed that there was stock in the Reverend Moon's name in Tong Il even though that stock was placed in his name in 1973, not a year about which they were going to review the tax returns.[28]

Without evidence of concealment, Lawler argued, the government's only other option to prove conspiracy was to introduce direct evidence of such a conspiracy—something the prosecution had failed to do.[29]

Judge Goettel was sympathetic to the argument, but the issue of concealment was still on his mind. "Moonies" just had to be sneaky. What about that story of Japanese members bringing money into the United States? Goettel mused:

Well, that seemed to me [Goettel argued] to be a very, very difficult argument to accept because, if hundreds of Japanese would decide to come to the United States and make small donations, a few hundred dollars each, they would be bringing yen, they wouldn't be bringing small American bills and the stuff wouldn't all come in a little brown paper bags at once. They would bring their yen in, they would convert it to a single traveler's check and turn the money over in that fashion.[30]

The court's one description of low international finance was quite extraordinary, as defense counsel pointed out. Lower income Japanese brought money into the United States in exactly such a fashion. Unlike Americans they were used to cash—not Karl Malden traveler's checks. And selling yen first and buying dollars in Japan at a familiar Japanese bank—where the price is better—made perfectly good sense.[31]

The family fund, in short, was not evidence of concealment, it was merely evidence that other cultures sometimes do things differently from Americans. That rather obvious fact of life, however, seemed totally to escape the court.

Lawler then attacked the perjury counts against his client. With time short, Kamiyama's lawyer could not go over all of them, but he focused on count nine which charged that Kamiyama had falsely told the grand jury that he never talked to Moon about the Tong-Il stock transfer.

Lawler's position was simple. The government had produced no direct or circumstantial evidence that Kamiyama had lied to the grand jury, even though, in Judge Goettel's words, "It sort of boggles the imagination to believe that the two of them never discussed it."[32]

That was, of course, pure speculation based on common sense on the part of Goettel. As a result, Andy Lawler had to restate the basic laws of evidence:

The issue was whether Mr. Kamiyama knew that and as to that particular question, again, the government failed to introduce any evidence. They failed to prove the circumstances under which it was signed. They failed to prove that Mr. Kamiyama was present at the time it was signed. They failed to prove that he had ever seen the documents prior to the time that they introduced it here in court and indeed this is not a situation where you might reasonably infer that someone in Mr. Kamiyama's position must have seen this and understood it, again, because the record is clear that in 1973 [when the stock was transferred], Mr. Kamiyama could not read English.[33]

Lawler's argument made no impact on the court. Judge Goettel merely handed the baton to the government, Jo Ann Harris, to be exact.

The prosecution was in the cat-bird seat. They had a conviction and a friendly judge who was not about to make waves by calling for a new trial, much less acquit the defendants. Not surprisingly, the government's strategy was simply to stand and hold. New arguments posed by the defense were simply ignored, especially those that were unanswerable, as was the case with the conceal-ment cum conspiracy charge.

The prosecution could also afford to be sarcastic, an attitude displayed by Harris throughout the post-trial motion hearing. The defense's work was "second guessing" and "wishful thinking about what might have been."[34]

The government lawyers never frontally took on the principal defense arguments, most prominently, the role of the First Amend-ment and the question of selective prosecution.

But then why bother? They knew that the case would go to the appeals court anyway. There was not the slightest chance that Judge Goettel would do anything radical.

And they were right. Laurence Tribe's closing arguments, even if correct, made no difference to the outcome of the post-trial session. There was an invisible trial going on—a concept first outlined by Tribe in discussions with Moon and Stillman a month before their July date in court. It was a trial which prevented Stillman and Lawler from making a full-blown defense based on the church's theology. Nor would it do much good to argue that Moon's religion and his position in the church needed to be dealt with in front of this particular court, as Judge Goettel's rulings proved:

> With respect to the motion for judgment of acquittal and the motion for a new trial and also the motion for an evidentiary hearing on selective prosecution, it is the view of this court that all of these motions must be denied and I do deny the motions.[35]

Having denied all motions, there was nothing left for Judge Goettel to do but pass sentence on the defendants. He did so two days later.

The sentencing procedure is normally simple. Before passing sentence, both counsel for the defense and the government prosecutors can make arguments about the severity of the penalty to be exacted—nothing more. The defendants have an unlimited right to speak on their own behalf—something that both Moon and Kamiyama refused to do. Under general procedure, defense counsel speaks first, while often the government does not speak at all, leaving sentencing in the hands of the court. The Moon case was to be different, as we shall see.

Tribe, Stillman, and Lawler spoke in order to mitigate their clients' sentences. The Harvard professor went first. Not surprisingly, he argued that an appropriate sentence would not include imprisonment. Why? Because a man who was fully aware of widespread hostility against him and his message had nevertheless returned voluntarily from Korea to the United States in order to undergo the trial. He deserved consideration for his cooperation.[36]

Secondly, a jail term, in Tribe's words, "would send a chill through the religious community." He added:

> Rightly or wrongly, to them it would say, there but for the grace of the Internal Revenue Service and the United States Attorney's office go we. If our religious believers and practices should fall into disfavor, perhaps we, too, will find that what we all believe is true of our assets when we entrust them to our leaders will be second guessed by Internal Revenue officials or by a jury.[37]

As for the government's anticipated contention that a jail term would deter other tax cheats, Professor Tribe called the idea "inherently incredible." He explained:

> Rightly or wrongly, they would view his imprisonment, if they thought about it at all, as the price he paid for running a church whose members he marries by the thousands in Madison Square Garden as part of the faith they find bizarre, not as proof that tax crime does not pay.[38]

Moon's first lawyer, Charles Stillman, spoke next, and offered an appeal that was more personal than legal or logical.

There was first the question of willfulness. If Moon were a

common tax cheat why did he go to the bank and open the account himself? Why lay down a paper trail that probably goes from here to the moon and back? Why sign all those easily produced documents? In Stillman's words, "that direct, powerful piece of willfulness testimony was never supplied."[39]

Stillman then made the character argument. From personal knowledge, he knew the Korean to be sincere in his beliefs and devoted to his cause and to his family. Besides that, Moon was a first offender. A prison sentence, he warned, would only "satisfy a public blood lust for Sun Myung Moon." And letting him off with a suspended sentence would take, Stillman admitted, an act of courage on the part of the court.[40]

Not a pretty thought, that last one, but accurate enough.

With that Moon's lawyers left it in the hands of Judge Goettel. But not before the government had one more crack. Jo Ann Harris noted once again that the government had treated the defendants like any "corporate executives" who have committed tax fraud. Prosecutor Harris therefore urged a "straightforward approach" and a sentence that would treat them "like any other businessmen caught and convicted with these kinds of serious crime."[41]

Harris was too delicate to call directly for a jail sentence for both defendants, but she left no doubt what "Maximum Jo Ann" wanted.

Delicacy was not Martin Flumenbaum's leading characteristic either. Typically, he weighed in with a tire iron.

> I agree with Mr. Stillman and Mr. Tribe that this is a complex person who stands before you at sentence, but I also agree that he has violated the law on numerous occasions. He has shown a disregard for law and he should be sentenced accordingly.[42]

Finally, it was Judge Gerard Goettel's turn. His remarks are worth considering at length. Unlike the TV version of justice, sentencing by the court is often not just a simple reading of the defendant's fate.

It is also the court's last statement on how the trial judge has conducted the case. It is important because district federal judges know that others above them are watching. They most certainly want to make the best case they can in this final appearance, no matter how weary and how sick they are of the whole business.

In *U.S. v. Moon and Kamiyama*, Judge Goettel wanted to do his best. And, in fact, the sentencing ritual perfectly showcased the court's strengths and weaknesses.

Above all, Goettel apparently favored neat balances, after which he would make pseudo-Solomon-like decisions. Often, however, the rulings were more on the order of Messrs. Laurel and Hardy.

The record will have to prove my point. A word of warning. Judge Goettel really loved carefully calibrated judgments that served merely to rationalize what he had already decided. For the record, of course. In short, the good man had his thumb on the scales of justice all along.

An example.

The court at the beginning of its sentencing statement contrasted the letters it had received from the non-Unification Church religious leaders and Unification Church members with the "goodly number of unsolicited letters" from parents of church members who wanted the good Reverend strung up on the nearest sour apple tree.

Having struck that exquisitely perfect balance, Judge Goettel offered his judgment on the matter: "I do not believe it is proper for this Court to consider the religious overtones of the letters written pro and con."[43]

Thus Judge Goettel ended as he had started. Religious controversy on both sides was thus in perfect equilibrium. One side cancelled out the other. Therefore, ignore the question entirely. It was as neat and elegant as a mathematical formula. Result: the First Amendment and its relevance to the case had been once again avoided in a mock show of judiciousness and decorum. The First Amendment had become moot because of the judge's own version of a popularity poll.

Having disposed of the First Amendment question, Goettel then gave his final judgment on the jury.

It is my sincere belief that the jury treated the case [without prejudice]. They deliberated for the better part of five days. I think they took the issues as presented to them and that they were not influenced by any extraneous considerations of the defendant's religious mission.[44]

With the jury problem out of the way, Goettel then reinforced his original belief that the First Amendment played little or no part in the trial. Having disposed of that small but troublesome matter, Goettel was able to state his basic philosophy about sentencing: "I have attempted to treat him [Moon] as I would anyone else who was charged with tax evasion and conspiracy."[45]

Beneath this ultra-thin veneer of liberality was nothing less than the government's whole case. Reverend Sun Myung Moon was nothing more than a tax cheat, and should be judged accordingly.

Leaving one judicial balancing act, Judge Goettel moved on to another one. This time, Goettel counterpoised the fact that Moon had no criminal record in America—a major consideration in suspending sentence, as in the case of Lt. Colonel Oliver North— with, ahem, the good Reverend Moon's legal difficulties involving the authorities of North Korea.

Of course, the legal system then prevailing in the People's Republic, Pyongyang division, left something to be desired— something even Goettel admitted. But the court's mere mention of Moon's experience in a North Korean concentration camp threw the whole question of prior arrest record under a cloud. Goettel's final judgment that he would treat the defendant, Moon, as a man with no previous criminal record somehow itself became an act of judicial equity if not charity.[46]

Except, of course, it wasn't.

But now the time had come to sentence the prime defendant. The crucial matters for the court, in its judgment, were two. First, Goettel said, Moon had involved others in the tax cheating, and by doing so had caused the court to endorse entirely the government's case on conspiracy.

Second, Goettel added, there was the small matter of deterrence. If Moon were to be let off lightly, white collar criminals in every nook and cranny of the land would be immeasurably heartened. Let the court explain itself on this one:

If the Reverend Moon gets a suspended sentence, there are going to be millions and millions of people in the general public who will say very skeptically that when the poor get caught even for minor amounts, even for welfare cheating, they go to jail, but when the rich and powerful get caught and can hire the outstanding kind of lawyers that have represented the defendants in this case, persons who can speak as eloquently on their behalf as Mr. Stillman and Professor Tribe just did, that the rich and the powerful go free.[47]

The assertion proved wrong on several counts. First, it was wrong factually. Second, public reaction should have no effect on sentencing, something Judge Goettel himself had earlier made clear. Third, it was another example of misplaced analogy on the part of the court.

Regarding the first error, it is not true that poor criminals are treated worse than their white collar colleagues. Virtually every law enforcement officer knows men (the majority black) who have committed violent crimes in this country and have not been put away.

Second, who cares what the public thinks or may think? The central object of justice—especially when administered by a federal judge—is to be totally impartial, unswayed by mob opinion. Of course, that is an ideal, and a genuine one. That is why federal judges are given lifetime jobs with, among other things, salaries that, according to the U.S. Constitution, may not be reduced. No other federal official in either the legislative or executive branch is provided such protection. Or anywhere else for that matter. On this planet, it is an American exclusive.

Third, the equating of the Reverend Sun Myung Moon with the rich and powerful proves only that Judge Goettel, after six months' experience with the case, still had not grasped the central issue and continued to harbor the same biases that he had from Day One. Moon's chief characteristic as a defendant was not that he was rich and powerful—at least these were not the salient questions—but that he was a foreigner who happened to head one of the most misunderstood and feared religions in America.

All of that, however, totally escaped the court, even at the end of the trial. Judge Goettel then proceeded to the sentencing itself. He handed down no light sentence. After all, he was not facing some killer, rapist, or drug dealer. This man had been convicted of evading several thousand dollars in income taxes. About $7,400—

the big huge sum of seventy-four hundred dollars!—was owed to the IRS. And for that Moon got eighteen months in jail and was fined $25,000, plus, naturally, the costs of prosecution.[48]

What followed in the sentencing ceremony was all anticlimactic. Defendant Takeru Kamiyama had yet to be disposed of.

His lawyer, Andrew Lawler, gamely pleaded for clemency as well. He made, of course, the character arguments. How Kamiyama had sold his blood to earn money for the Unification Church in Japan. His endless hours of work for the cause—without apparent remuneration. In his plea, Lawler also reminded the court that Kamiyama was a family man and a man of no prior record.

The government had the last word. As usual, Harris deferred the heavy stuff to Flumenbaum who wielded his tire iron once again.

Kamiyama, Flumenbaum told the court, because of his religiosity, had committed serious crimes for the sake of his religion. Or to quote him:

> [T]he recurrent theme that comes through Mr. Kamiyama's actions is to do whatever is necessary or whatever Mr. Kamiyama wants to be done and that is glorify the aims of Mr. Moon.[49]

He was waving the red rag of religious prejudice, knowing full well that the issue no longer mattered. So did Lawler, who didn't bother responding.

No wonder. Goettel agreed once again with the government's position. Indeed, the positions of the court and government were almost indistinguishable. Said Goettel:

> Regardless of the benign motives of the defendant, he committed some serious crimes and I consequently feel that some sentence is necessary.[50]

But because Kamiyama was, after all, a relatively minor figure who had been roped into trouble, the court decided to throw Kamiyama in the slammer for only six months coupled with a fine of "only" $5,000.[51]

Oh yes, there was one small matter that boomeranged on Goettel. It was very embarrassing. Because the court had sentenced

Moon to more than a year in jail, the leader of the Unification Church was eligible for deportation. Judge Goettel had not realized that expulsion was a possibility, and so three weeks later, the whole cast was once more in his courtroom.

The government's lawyers were naturally eager to rid the country of Moon. Therefore they argued that Judge Goettel did not have to issue an opinion on the matter, leaving the Immigration and Naturalization Service a free hand to carry out its will after Moon had finished his sentence.

The prosecution had guessed that Gerard Goettel would once more cave into his desire to get out of this legal briar patch.

But for once they guessed incorrectly. Goettel was annoyed that the government was going to the well one more time. He did not like the brief prepared by the government attorney. He was bothered by the evasive answers he got from the government's lawyers during oral argument on the issue.

Yet, Goettel was not sure. Let us follow him through his quandary:

> The whole thing revolves on the sentence. I indicated on sentencing that it was a difficult sentence. The parameters ran anywhere from a suspended sentence to few years in jail. It was an unusual case with unusual considerations. I came out with an eighteen-month sentence. I haven't heard from anybody who approved of the sentence yet. I heard from a lot who felt it was too much and a lot who felt it was too little, and maybe both were right.[52]

Wonderful. In the end, Goettel was convinced that deportation on top of jail time was too much. "Excessive" was his word, and he recommended no such action.

That did it. Moon would not be forced to leave the United States. Two days later he got his green card back.

Nine months later, the defendants took their case before the Second Circuit Court of Appeals. But before oral argument was presented to the three-judge panel, there were several legal hurdles to overcome.

First, the defense, Laurence Tribe taking the lead, had to sharpen the arguments in the form of a new legal brief. Just before Thanksgiving of 1982, Moon's lawyers pulled together a new seventy-five-page argument.

The appeal brief dealt heavily with constitutional and procedural questions—not surprising because Professor Tribe was its chief author.

The defense's brief completed, it was the government's turn to respond. It did so two months later. The prosecution was not about to break new ground. Its lawyers kept in a hull-down position, largely ignoring the constitutional questions and concentrating instead on their facts of the case: bank accounts, backdating, perjury.

The government's presentation was not elegant, but the appeals court had to pay attention. So did the defense, which was allowed to file a second brief in response to the government's.

The preliminary skirmishing over, the whole crew gathered once more at Foley Square to listen to oral argument before Judges James Oakes (the senior magistrate in the Second Circuit), Richard Cardamone, and Ralph Winter.

There had been a few substitutions since the last great game. Charles Stillman was on the sidelines. Laurence Tribe now quarterbacked the defense team.

And unlike some fading stars of the NFL, Stillman had taken his replacement very well, thanks in part to a bit of deft diplomacy on the part of the Reverend Sun Myung Moon.

On the opposite side of the field, all was good cheer. Jo Ann Harris had gotten a promotion; so had Martin Flumenbaum—thanks largely to their nailing of Moon. Harris was now executive assistant to U.S. Attorney John Martin; Flumenbaum had been made a special assistant U.S. attorney.

Harris and Flumenbaum were awfully confident that they could make the conviction stick. For one thing, the pair knew that the three appeals judges could not totally immerse themselves in the case. Their workload was already heavy, and besides, *U.S. v. Moon and Kamiyama* had already generated 12,000 eye-glazing pages of transcript—six novels the size of *War and Peace*—most of it incredibly boring and often difficult to follow, even for an experienced jurist.

Needless to say, the three appeals judges had no time to read the transcript. Nor did their clerks. They relied on the appeal briefs with their attached documents. But what they really depended upon was the distillation of the original oral arguments.

Such is life in the busy world of the federal courts of appeal.

The oral argument phase was actually fascinating (as it often is)—at least to nonlawyers. Each judge had prepared himself for the case—sort of—but there was plenty of room for very basic, naive, even fatuous questions on the part of the appeals court.

Much of the argument was merely a repetition of the familiar. Certainly the battle lines were well drawn. The defense, now led by Tribe, stressed the constitutional issues of the case. That was the Harvard professor's strength. Besides, appeals judges like to think of themselves as second string Supreme Court justices, mulling over weighty federal issues and not just pothering about exactly who killed Joe Schmoe.

The government stuck to the "proven facts in the case," an approach that had worked to its advantage so far.

The central battle that was waged during oral argument ended up being fought on Tribe's chosen terrain. The fight boiled down to the nature of trusts, and their relation to the First Amendment. The government contended the notion had been cooked up by a desperate defense at the last moment. Tribe denied that accusation and said that the issue had been central to the defense's case all along, beginning with the pretrial motions.

The appeals judges proved to be as confused about this issue as Judge Goettel had been. Judge Winter, for example, asked whether Moon's buying a watch was not an outright personal use of the Chase account funds. In response, Tribe told the bench that such a purchase would be relevant if the case revolved around the issue of diversion of funds. Tribe pointed out that instead "the issue in this case was whether the corpus of the trust belonged to him or belonged to those who gave it to him within the religion."[53]

Winter was still not satisfied. Wasn't what Moon and Moon alone wanted to have done with the money decisive?

Tribe said no: "There is no evidence that his judgment was conclusive. He was surrounded by a circle of elders who in concert made decisions."[54]

The man from Harvard then quickly slapped down another contention of the government, that if the Reverend Sun Myung Moon invested in secular business, like iron ore mining, then he was nothing more than a businessman in religious clothing. Tribe refuted the government's argument:

The implication the government makes is that when money is invested in an iron works, let's say, you have got to be an iron worshiper for that to be a religious investment. There is no such principle in our law. The Catholic Church and every other church can invest in conventional businesses, and unless it is shown by evidence, which simply wasn't present here, that he was free to do whatever he wanted, we would submit that it is a very fundamental defense.[55]

At that point a sympathetic Judge Oakes managed to clarify Tribe's rather labored argument. Oakes said:

The defense is a defense to the charge that the assets in the Chase account were the Reverend Moon's for his personal use. The charge was not made that he failed to pay tax on income that he did use from that account . . . for his personal purposes.[56]

Grateful for the help, the professor from Harvard promptly agreed:

That is exactly correct. And one could always prosecute tax fraud by a religious leader by proving that he did not pay income tax on money he made personal use of . . . which obviously couldn't be proved here, or by proving that the intent of the donors was not to advance the religious faith.[57]

Again, Tribe drove home his central point. If there had been a diversion of money, the government had not proven it. It had not even tried. Even if Moon had pocketed church money for personal purposes, that did not negate the notion that Moon was a trustee for the bulk of the funds. A trustee, that is, and not the personal owner of the money. That, Tribe argued, was the law. But it was not what the trial judge, Gerard Goettel, had told the jury. The instructions to the jury had been wrong on this fundamental point, and that constituted reversible error.[58]

After Tribe came Lawler. The dogged lawyer for Takeru Kamiyama went after one major issue, the so-called "prior act" evidence.

Lawler reminded the court "that there is no more sensitive issue than the introduction of prior act evidence, particularly under circumstances where there are multiple defendants."

That was a masterly sample of legal understatement.

What was going on here? Prior act evidence is exactly what it sounds like. It is evidence of acts done or not done by the defendant before the alleged criminal activity has taken place. When it is introduced legitimately, prior acts evidence can add context to the case of either the government or the defendant. It can, for example, explain motive.

But used wrongly, such evidence serves only to inflame the prejudices of the jury. Which, Kamiyama's lawyer argued, was exactly the intention of the prosecution when it submitted proof, for example, that Kamiyama had not filed a 1973 and 1974 income tax return.

Kamiyama in fact had not filed, but then he was not charged with that offense in the bill of indictment. The introduction of that evidence therefore was prejudicial to Lawler's client. As Andy Lawler put it:

Having planted this evidence in the record, having the jury read to them the fact that Mr. Kamiyama had failed to file returns for 1973 and 1974, the government never utilized it again, the jury was never informed by them the purpose for which it was supposedly introduced which only went to a collateral issue. It sat there and it severely prejudiced him.[59]

Nor was that the only dirty trick the government played in its prosecution of Moon's financial advisor, said Lawler. Kamiyama's lawyer accused the prosecution of virtually manufacturing the counts of perjury against him.

But let Andrew Lawler explain it:

[I]t is clear that the government, although they had Mr. Kamiyama before the grand jury and were questioning him about events which had taken place long ago, made no attempt to refresh his recollection even under circumstances as set forth in the count when he was saying, "As best I recall," or "as best I remember"; that the way they handled the entire issue of translation under circumstances where we have a perjury prosecution for foreign language testimony that was given and the teaching of *United States v. Bronston* as to the necessity of precision in any perjury prosecution. . . .[60]

But the government's flim-flam hadn't ended there. Lawler was just warming up:

> [T]he way they handled his testimony before the grand jury, in that [the prosecution] froze in effect his testimony before an accommodation or substituting grand jury, and then read it to the investigating grand jury at a later date, and then in attempting to sustain those perjury counts, maintained that all along this accommodation grand jury had been acting in an ancillary capacity to the investigating grand jury, even though that particular element was not charged in the indictment nor was it proven at trial.[61]

Playing games with interpreters and manipulating multiple grand juries was explosive stuff, but Lawler had run out of time. After a few perfunctory questions from the bench, the appeals court turned the floor over to Jo Ann Harris to begin her solo final pitch for the government.

There was nothing new in her presentation, but occasionally the court asked embarrassing questions. Judge Cardamone, for example, asked—when Harris claimed Moon had been hiding his assets from the IRS—how the Korean could hope to conceal his accounts at a Chase Manhattan Bank?

Lacking a good answer, Harris bobbed and weaved. Like the skillful legal boxer that she was, the prosecutor simply pointed out that other tax cheats had left paper trails before.

As for the fairness of the jury trial, Harris once more defended the procedure and the unexceptionalness of the defendant. Not once did she mention his unpopularity, choosing instead the term "high visibility," which of course is a euphemism if ever there was one.[62]

On the central question of the First Amendment and its relationship to trust law, Harris would not budge an inch. When Judge Oakes asked her about the practice of other religions in this regard, Harris casually brushed him off:

> I don't know that how other churches operate is particularly pertinent here. . . . [T]he real point here is that the government proved that the moneys were not the church's; or, put the other, which was really what our burden was, the government proved beyond any reasonable doubt that those moneys were Moon's personal funds.[63]

As is usual in appeals court proceedings, the defense had the last word. Tribe would save his most explosive rhetoric for the finale.

All through the trial, Tribe charged, the government had used "[i]nnuendo and smear ... to make it look like there was no religion here." That action alone, Tribe argued, constituted grounds for reversal.[64]

In summary, Tribe made a final pitch for his defendant:

> In this case it seems to me plain that there was the wrong tribunal, wrongly charged, on insufficient evidence; that the evidence was further poisoned by highly prejudicial and inadmissible similar acts evidence.[65]

Any federal circuit court of appeals carries a heavy load. So it is not surprising that it was six months later that the Second Circuit came to its decision, rendered in September 1983.

Moon and Kamiyama lost again, but this time it was a split decision. The senior justice, Judge Oakes, agreed with the defense's major contentions.

Oakes concurred with Tribe that Judge Goettel's instructions to the jury on who "owned" the funds in the Chase account were faulty. He rejected the government's contention that the defense had raised the trust issue at the last moment:

> The defense position was clear and consistent throughout the proceedings. That position on the trust was all important because the question of beneficial ownership was "central to the determination of guilt or innocence."[66]

As a result, Judge Oakes found both the trial court and the government's case insufficient to prove guilt on either Moon or Kamiyama's part.

Unfortunately for the defendants, his colleagues did not agree. Judge Cardamone wrote the majority opinion, and it was a brief one. Essentially, and unsurprisingly, the decision upheld (for the most part) the government's thesis of guilt and commended Judge Goettel for conducting a fair trial under extraordinarily difficult circumstances. Cardamone affirmed the conviction of the defendants on all counts, except one lodged against Kamiyama. That was count number seven which the majority felt had been entirely conjured up by the prosecution and was not worthy of consideration.

Laurence Tribe had one more card to play before appealing to the U.S. Supreme Court. Encouraged by Judge Oakes' dissent, the defense filed a request for a so-called *en banc* review two weeks after the appeals court decision. *En banc* simply means that the entire Second Circuit would consider the case. Such reviews are rarely granted; this one wasn't either. Consequently, the defendants and their counsel announced in November 1983 that they would go to the U.S. Supreme Court.

Such appeals come in the form of the petition for *certiorari*. They are neither easy to obtain nor simple to file. In the case of Moon and Kamiyama, extra time had to be requested from Justice Thurgood Marshall—who oversaw Second Circuit cases—to finish the new brief.

When it was completed in late January 1984, the new brief, as is customary, had first to be sent to the U.S. Solicitor General for his opinion before being sent on to the Supreme Court. In turn the Solicitor General had to file within a month his opinion on whether he thought the court should take up the question.

Although the Solicitor General is a member of the executive branch, the history of that office shows that he may not always agree with U.S. district attorneys or their supervisors in the Department of Justice.

The office, in fact, over the years has come closer to being the judicial rather than the executive branch, so much so that the Solicitor General has often been called the "tenth justice."

For reasons that have never been made clear, the Solicitor General had difficulty in writing his opinion on the *Moon* case— problems that required asking and getting two additional delays of thirty days each.

As an experienced constitutional lawyer, Professor Tribe knew that his arguments had to be succinct and involve substantial federal questions if the busy high court were ever to review the case.

Consequently, Tribe boiled down his previously lengthy briefs and focused on three issues. First, Tribe wrote, because the trial court had accepted the government's demand for a jury trial, the judiciary abdicated its duty to assure a fair trial. Second, allowing jurors to substitute their uninformed opinion on the constitutionally sensitive question of church property violated the religion clause of the First Amendment. Third, a criminal conviction based on a highly questionable theory of federal tax liability violated due process.

Despite hopes that the Solicitor General would at least agree that the issues raised were important, this was not the case. In early April the government's thirty-one-page response was entirely negative. Not only did it recommend that the Supreme Court deny review, it rather patronizingly told other religions that the Reverend Sun Myung Moon's conviction did not threaten them in the least.

The opinion knocked the wind out the defense. Tribe and the others knew perfectly well that the Solicitor General's advisory is accepted by the Supreme Court 70 percent of the time. The odds for reversal, in short, were now very long.

It wasn't over, however, until the Supreme Court made up its own mind, and here is where the situation becomes both complicated and opaque. Indeed, the court's decision-making process remains nearly invisible to outsiders, including prosecutors and defendants.

Yet, some of it can be pieced together.

First things first. Defense counsel had, after the issuance of the government's opinion, the right to respond—briefly. All the issues had to be boiled down to ten pages, which Tribe did, using all of the allotted time—six days—to do it. The new brief arrived at the Supreme Court, literally, with only minutes to spare.

Moon's appeal was handled like all the others that came to the court. Each justice received copies of the petition and a summary. In addition, they were orally briefed by their clerks on its contents.

Then the case was reviewed in a weekly "*cert*" conference where the justices alone were present. In these all-day sessions, up to a hundred *certiorari* petitions are reviewed to determine whether or not oral argument will be heard. In most cases, agreement to do so requires either a majority or unanimity of the court. In a few rare cases, four justices can insist on a full review and get it.

If this sounds like the nine justices have a lot on their minds, that is exactly right. Add the fact that a number of them are men long beyond their prime suggests another sort of rough justice.

How does the system work at all? The answer is simple and in four words: the clerks do it.

In an ordinary bureaucracy, that would not matter much. Surely it is no secret that political appointees new to government and their jobs rely on career civil servants for information, for background, for an institutional memory.

In the case of the judiciary and the Supreme Court in particular, clerks have no institutional memory. The court's law clerks are very bright, but also very fresh out of law school. Worse, they serve for only a year.

Yet their influence is great. They summarize *cert* petitions; they even recommend to the justices whether they should be considered or not.

According to one close student of the high court:

> Clerks play an indispensable role in the justices' deciding what to decide. . . . [Justices] voted overwhelmingly along the lines recommended by their law clerks. . . . Clerks would look very powerful indeed if they were not transient in the court.[67]

The problem is that such an arrangement is inevitable simply because of the burden on the court. In a litigious society such as ours the use of clerks is necessary, unless the size of the court were to be changed—which it can be only by congressional statute. Or if younger justices were appointed to the court, and the infirm, if not senile, ones somehow gracefully but firmly retired. Not likely. The last president to walk into that buzzsaw was Franklin Roosevelt in 1937, and he was accused of "packing the court." None of his successors has ever forgotten that one.

There is one more thing to say about clerks: they are extraordinarily intelligent, at least based on law school grades, but they are also very young, and they often lack the experience to make seasoned legal judgments. Like everybody else, they have too much work to do to reflect properly on what they are doing, even if they have the maturity to do so.

So what happened to the petition?

It was denied, of course. But unlike the other critical turning points in this case, the denial had the air of lifeless anticlimax. No packed courtrooms. No robed judges. No lawyers playing point and counterpoint.

Only a piece of paper, the so-called "*cert* denied" roster, posted at the castle door. It appeared on Monday, May 14, 1984, two years after Sun Myung Moon and his lawyers first assembled in the Foley Square courthouse. As is customary, no explanation was given. There was and is no way of knowing how much interest the court took in the case or how controversial it had been. The appeal might have been a dead letter from the beginning. Then again, maybe it wasn't. Who knows? Certainly the government's final brief did not help. But in the end, trying to figure out what really happened is all guess work.

Laurence Tribe tried to get hold of internal Justice Department memoranda that he rightly suspected had recommended against prosecution, but he was unsuccessful. With the possibility of new evidence denied him, he was out of options.

And that was that. The legal process had come to an abrupt end, and the Reverend Sun Myung Moon had run out of cards to play.

Still, it was not over.

For one thing the once hostile media took a second look—albeit not in the news pages but rather by the editorial writers and the columnists.

The liberal *Los Angeles Times* shortly before the Supreme Court decision thought that the trial and conviction of Moon and Kamiyama were a miscarriage of justice. In the words of the *Times*:

> The Supreme Court should reverse Moon's conviction and reaffirm the principle that the First Amendment makes no distinction between popular and unpopular religions or orthodox and unorthodox faiths.[68]

Columnists, both liberal and conservative, struck similar themes. Leftwing Catholic writer Colman McCarthy admitted to a moment of elation when Moon had been convicted two years earlier, but now (that is, February 1984) he was having second thoughts.

McCarthy, a columnist for the *Washington Post*, had for years defended the down-and-out and the picked-on minorities. Now he was worried that he had somehow missed one. Certainly, other religions' support for the Reverend Moon's rights were decisive in McCarthy's change of heart:

> The national concern generated by the case isn't wasted. Moon's unpopularity is unimportant. Even then, the personal attacks against him are similar in meanness and bias to those vented historically against Jewish, Christian and Moslem leaders when they were newcomers bringing a minority religion into the community.[69]

Two months later, McCarthy's fellow columnist at the *Post*, Bill Raspberry, made a similar sort of argument. Moon clearly was unpopular and the jury trial seemed unfair, reported the veteran black columnist. Raspberry too was impressed with the groups that were coming out in support of the Korean:

> Why are these people, whose judicial concerns tend toward the legal rights of poor blacks, moved to support a controversial Korean nearly all of whose American followers are white?[70]

Raspberry of course was stating the issue in baldly racial terms—something customary in these sorts of discussions—but the fact that the Southern Christian Leadership Conference and the National Black Catholic Clergy Caucus were supporting Moon's plea for a Supreme Court review was enough for Raspberry:

> I still don't know whether the Rev. Moon was guilty of converting the church's assets to his private use and failing to pay the appropriate personal income taxes. The government claims it has solid evidence of a massive effort on Moon's part to deceive the Internal Revenue Service. Maybe it does. Still, the amicus briefs made a compelling case that the Supreme Court should at least take a hard look to satisfy itself that the controversial minister did in fact get a fair trial.[71]

But if Raspberry was not sure about Moon's guilt or innocence, conservative columnist James J. Kilpatrick voiced no doubts:

> Viewed simply as a matter of criminal law, the record does not establish Moon's guilt. Viewed as a matter of constitutional law, the record raises most serious issues under the First Amendment.[72]

And the Sixth as well. For Kilpatrick, the government's refusal to waive a jury trial was "almost unheard of" and an act of "pure vindictiveness."

The columnist's conclusion:

> Moon was denied a fair trial. It is not necessary to like this Korean guru to say, as I must, that he got a bum rap. It is small wonder that other churches are alarmed.[73]

All true, but a little too late in the game. The First Amendment worries had all been there from the start. But it took others—in this case within the religious and civil liberties communities—to remind some of the media, at least, that a war was going on, and supporters of the First Amendment were losing it.

Despite the Supreme Court's denial of the *cert* petition, the now desperate defense tried a few more slightly unorthodox maneuvers.

They were inspired by justifiable fears on the part of church leaders that Sun Myung Moon in jail would not be secure. He had had innumerable death threats in his life; and even in a less dangerous lock-up like Danbury, he would be pretty much on his own if anyone wanted to stick a knife in his back.

It would be easier there than say a high security place like Atlanta, where in-danger guests of the federal government can be placed in minimum-access, highly secure, would-be fortresses.

The fear of assassination more than anything else impelled this last effort to avoid incarceration. But what could be done?

Rejected by everyone out of hand was an appeal for a new trial. No new evidence had been discovered, thanks to Justice's stone-walling of the release of internal memos. Such an appeal would go nowhere. So that was out.

That left the defense with a strategy to reduce the sentence; a plea, in fact, for community service instead of time in jail. The hook was that the only man who could grant such a boon was Gerard Goettel.

That's right. Gentle Gerard himself.

Well, even the staunchest supporters of Laurence Tribe among the church leaders believed that the professor was not of much use any more. The man from Cambridge, Massachusetts, was absolutely anathema to the trial judge. As far as Goettel was concerned

the boy hotshot from Harvard had announced to the world he was
seeking a new trial because the original trial judge—Goettel—was
an utter incompetent. Simply put, Goettel could not stand to be in
the same room with Tribe. It was Harvard v. Fordham, and in this
football game Fordham was going to win.

No wonder then that there was a decision to hire new counsel
one more time to make the final approach to Judge Goettel. The
freshman lawyer, Michael McAllister, did his best.

But he was holding a pair of deuces and he knew it. Moreover,
his plea to Judge Goettel for an extension so he could study the
case went over like a cement cake at a kids' birthday party.

Goettel, annoyed and tired of the whole nightmare case,
snapped: "[Moon] has had a two-year delay already because of
appeals. Now he's acting like the little boy who killed his parents
and then asked for sympathy because he was an orphan."[74]

Well, not quite, but Goettel's impatience, if not his usual mal-
aprop analogy, was understandable. Remarkably enough, though,
he granted the extension. A month later, July 18 to be exact,
Moon's new lawyer, McAllister was ready to make the plea for an
alternative to jail. But Goettel had already made up his mind.

Stripped of legal niceties, Goettel's opinion was just this: forget
it. Your man is going to the slammer. It would be the rough sort of
justice that Judge Goettel said it would be.

Two days later the Reverend Sun Myung Moon, along with
Takeru Kamiyama, walked into Danbury federal prison in Danbury, Connecticut.

In the end, the Reverend Moon served thirteen months there—
getting five months off for good behavior. His companion Kamiyama served four months with two taken off for the same
reason.

Outwardly, Danbury appeared to be a soft prison. No bars on
the cells, no walls, no barbed wire. It was set on a hill with a nice
view of a river valley. The amenities included a gymnasium, a
swimming pool, a weight-lifting room, and yes, ping-pong and a
pool table.

Moon loved pool and quickly established a reputation for being
the best snooker artiste in prison.

It was no Hungnam, North Korea, but jail it still was. The life
was regimented, shut off from the outside. Moon's job was in the

cafeteria, setting the tables at mealtimes and washing the dining room floor. He never complained and on several occasions quietly did the work of other inmates who were too ill or depressed to leave their beds.

Prisoners were frequently subjected to strip searches and no one talked back to the guards. No sex.

There were several other rules. Moon could not conduct business, that is, the making of money—a tough rule for all the white-collar criminals at Danbury—and he could not proselytize. The North Koreans also had that last regulation.

Moon didn't break the rules. But there was more than one way to preach the Word. St. Paul in jail had managed to get his message across by saying nothing about his beliefs, but living them by example. Practicing what you preach can be the most powerful way of all to send a message.

Many in the Danbury population could not deal with the disgrace and shame of incarceration. Some of them could not bear it at all, and broke. Attempted suicides, withdrawal, whatever, were fairly common in the minimum security federal pens like Danbury and Allenwood. Those who broke down rarely recovered.

If the Reverend Sun Myung Moon felt any of that kind of desperation, he did not show it. He was outwardly cheerful and friendly with everyone. He talked to them as best he could in his broken English. With church visitors, he conducted the affairs of the church. There was no let-up on that.

By all accounts Moon's fellow prisoners liked him—and they were a tough audience to please. Even this collection of middle-class men gone wrong could be tough and derisive. Moon's financial advisor and bunkmate was immediately nicknamed "Half-Moon." No one got to know Takeru Kamiyama: he left after four months.

In an extraordinary turn of events, prisoners wrote letters about Moon. No more prepared to like him than anyone else, those who wrote expressed a very high regard for his courage and compassion.

The strangest of these epistles, I suppose, was addressed to *Hustler* magazine by a Danbury convict and a fan of publisher Larry Flynt.

Hustler, which is notorious for its bad taste in both pictorials and

text, had portrayed Moon in an imaginative and unflattering account of life in Danbury. The article apparently got the goat of
inmate Justin Ignizio, who wrote:

> I work side by side with the "Rev" in the kitchen and have seen him
> do all that has been asked of him, smiling and without complaint, (I
> wish I could say the same of all the other inmates here) including
> washing toilets and mopping floors. He never puts on any airs and is
> just one of the guys. I have my visits on the same days as the
> Reverend and see him to be a devoted husband and a loved and
> loving father. Maybe this country wouldn't be in the sad shape it is in
> if we had more men like Reverend Moon around.[75]

Moon was held in equally high regard by other prisoners who
were more than willing to give press interviews on the subject.
One, Bill Sheppard, told a magazine reporter:

> I saw how he [Reverend Moon] treated people. He was tremendously
> respectful to everyone and their opinion . . . and he was respected by
> everybody, no question about that. He gained respect and people's
> image of him and the general atmosphere of the prison began to
> change. I was fortunate enough over the period of time he spent in
> prison to get close enough to him to know that he's not an act. He is
> who he is.[76]

What did Moon think of all this? No one really knows. He kept
his thoughts to himself. One thing is certain, he never complained.
He certainly was smart enough never to give any pleasure to his
many enemies by showing that he thought Danbury was some
form of disgrace or even burden. For him it was not even a trial and
tribulation sent from God.

He actually left some with the impression he rather enjoyed it. In
any case, one prisoner related the following story. "Gee, Reverend,"
he recalled to a magazine reporter, "what do you think of America
now?"

The reply: "Is still better than communism. . . . This is not a
jail."

"What do you mean this isn't a jail?" the inmate asked. "What
is it?"

"I have been in Korean prison," said Moon, who was incarcerated by the communists between 1948 and 1950. "That is prison. This is country club."[77]

The Reverend Moon may have actually thought that, but his followers wanted desperately for him to be out of Danbury. They needed a full-time leader. Even with all the church business that could be done at Danbury, it wasn't enough.

As usual, the efforts to obtain a parole for Moon were both comic and another sad judgment on the American legal system. The truth is that despite Moon's exemplary record in prison—and no one disputed that—his gross public unpopularity made prison and parole officials nervous.

When bureaucrats get nervous, they resemble frightened rabbits in the road frozen by oncoming headlights. They stand absolutely still, paralyzed by fear. To be more precise, the bureaucratic bunnies pass the decision on to somebody else, if they can.

In Moon's case, they froze. Moon's first parole hearing took place in October 1984. The session was delayed because the government had not yet figured out what the Korean's exact tax liability actually was.

That's right. In this whole Kafkaesque process with its 12,000 pages of transcript and 1,000 pieces of evidence assembled over the course of two years by a regiment of government lawyers, and literally millions upon millions of dollars in taxpayers' monies spent to investigate Sun Myung Moon over some seven years, nobody, *nobody* had figured out exactly what the man had supposedly failed to pay Uncle Sam.

Indeed, in all those mountains of pages of trial transcript, nobody had ever asked. Neither the IRS nor the Justice Department knew for sure. In fact, it took the green shade boys another two months of frantic pencil chewing to come up with an answer and even then they weren't exactly sure. Of course, by that time Moon had already served one-third of his sentence.

But the comedy was only beginning. Because Moon still refused to admit guilt, the board of examiners that interviewed him at Danbury was left with something of a dilemma. How could it recommend a parole when an innocent man claimed he was innocent?

The entire situation was, well, embarrassing. The recommendation sent by the board to the regional parole commissioner in Philadelphia was not at all welcome. In fact, the whole Moon matter was such a hot potato that the potato got passed to the Southeast parole commissioner in Atlanta from whence it was lobbed to Washington, D.C., to three national parole commissioners.

Because the three could not agree, the recommendation was forwarded to the ultimate arbiter, the U.S. Parole Commissioner himself, Benjamin Baer.

Baer refused to rule, sensing that no consensus existed in the ranks below him. As a result he faxed the potato, by pre-set arrangement, to the Southwest regional parole commissioner in Dallas.

And he said no.

The entire parole request had taken seven months, ending in April 1985 when the Danbury show was almost over anyway. Because of good behavior, Moon was released early, provided that the rest of his term be spent at a half-way house in Brooklyn. Forty-six days later, on August 20, 1985, the Reverend Sun Myung Moon became a free man.

There's one more important footnote to this rather sad page in American jurisprudence. Moon and Kamiyama stood trial, were convicted, sentenced, and then jailed on a voluntary basis. That's right.

As foreign nationals, neither the Reverend Sun Myung Moon nor his disciple had to submit to any of the rough justice handed out by the American courts. Tax evasion is considered by most civilized countries to be a "political crime" and, therefore, not subject to extradition or prosecution in another country. On top of that, neither man had any travel restrictions placed on him by the courts or federal government.

Moon and Kamiyama could have simply boarded a plane and left the U.S. at any time, up to and including the day they both surrendered themselves to the guards at Danbury prison. No questions asked. Indeed, there were officials at the Justice Department who fervently hoped and expected Moon would do just that: leave the country. And, of course, he did. Many times before, during, and after the trial the Reverend Sun Myung Moon flew to

Korea and Japan. But he always returned to New York, much to the surprise and dismay of his persecutors.

Which leaves us with an uncomfortable question: if the guilty man flees—and we have always assumed running away was proof of guilt—what then of the man who remains of his own free will and pleads his innocence, who endures the "fair" trial and judicial "due process" you've now witnessed, able to leave at any time but never does, and who voluntarily stays and serves the felony prison sentence awarded him?

Is that man guilty?

It's a question worth pondering.

CHAPTER XI

THE DEPROGRAMMING CULT

All looks yellow to a jaundiced eye.

ALEXANDER POPE

IT was not the best of times. It may have been the worst of times. It sure wasn't Morning in America.

The sixties wasn't even a traditional decade. It extended for ten years all right. The beginning, however, was in 1965: the year of Watts and Da Nang. The ending was in 1975 when Gerald Ford drew the poison of Watergate by pardoning Richard Nixon—an act that cost him the presidency and gave us Jimmy Carter.

There was more to it than that. The known, safe, and predictable world of a comfortable American middle class had quite suddenly dissolved into seeming chaos—thanks to television. It just didn't seem fair. It sure as hell was not reassuring.

The problem wasn't just the "underprivileged" who were bent on violence. There was, too, the nation's future elite on prestigious university campuses. They were a minority, but they got a huge amount of attention. So did their faculty advisors who railed against an "Amerika" grown old, corrupt, and, naturally, imperialistic, hence Vietnam.

419

A good many more of that generation took it a little easier. Politics of the street took second place to casual sex in the dorm. Recreational drug use was popular, with few at that time inveighing against mind-altering substances—still fewer politicians of liberal persuasion. That was another time.

All, of course, were against The War. Some were righteously indignant about it. What you didn't know could be learned at campus teach-ins, one of the more curious intellectual rituals of the time.

Things weren't so bad in America, but much of the nation's elite pretended that they were. A familiar litany of complaints about racism, sexism, and, yes, imperialism were thrown about. Pollution, too. America's economy was poisoning the planet.

The time was not an easy one for the American family—at least the white, middle- and upper-middle-class American family. "Ozzie and Harriet" and "Leave It To Beaver" were over and something else was taking their place. Just what, these Americans didn't know. Charlie Manson and his "family" gave them a glimpse of hell after the Tate-Bianca murders in 1969: killings of such brutality that even hardened police officers had retched at the sight.

If *Helter Skelter* wasn't enough, what dark things were going on in all those other communes to which young and radical Americans flocked by the late 1960s in search of an alternative lifestyle?

Their parents didn't know. Their parents were scared.

The fright took different turns. Smart politicians like Richard Nixon figured out that a lot of Americans over thirty were getting tired of the noise. Nixon called them the Silent Majority: a shrewd assessment that said most Americans did not share the values of their garrulous intelligentsia and its acolytes in the media. They weren't guilty, but they were getting angry.

They were a small majority in 1968, and a thunderous one by 1972: the doubts of the late sixties had turned into a roaring protest vote by the early seventies.

Middle-class America was quite definitely fed up. Radical politics were out. Radical lifestyles were out, too. Soon, radical religions were questioned.

At the end of that turbulent ten years, attention was paid to different phenomena. Their apologists referred to them as the "new" or "alternative" religions. Their detractors called them "cults" and branded them dangerous.

Then all hell broke loose. Younger clergy pushed for new things: Political and social engagement. Causes. Folk masses. Forget the organ and Bach. Bring in the guitars and John Lennon. Middle-class America yawned and dropped out, and sought after more conservative churches, even fundamentalist ones.

Others went elsewhere, but not in great numbers. In the thousands, not the millions, as their enemies implied. These drop-outs were mostly young, almost always white and middle-class—usually upper-middle class.

Instead of becoming hippies, however, and adopting a hedonistic lifestyle, they were attracted to religions with an odd mix of theologies that preached and practiced an austere way of life. Drawn from various parts of the globe, the new sects often originated in the Far East. The oriental angle was one of the causes of anxiety. The mysterious East was just too much for insular, provincial Americans and Canadians—Hare Krishna and the Divine Light Mission, both from India, the Unification Church from Korea. Yet these small sects created a furor far exceeding their numbers. The threat spawned a cottage industry in the United States and Canada. The captains of the new industry sought to convince us that the cults were dangerous, that the industry's methods for fighting them were legitimate and, what is more, the only way.

A lot of people who laughed at the notion of a communist bloodbath in Southeast Asia agreed that cults were a menace. NBC in 1975 put together a documentary on the new religions which helped scare the hell out of America.

Indeed, virtually the whole Anglo-Saxon world, including Australia and Great Britain, was washed with the new hysteria.

Why?

Well, after the long period of social and political turbulence, many of the new religions were easy to dislike. Noisy kids in silly orange robes chanting God-knows-what were, at the least, annoying. Proselytizing peddlers in the nation's airports were hardly more popular. Mere annoyance turned to fear, if not panic, in 1979. The event that sparked the fear happened not in safe and sunny America, but in a remote jungle in the Essequibo, a part of

South America claimed by Venezuela and owned (sort of) by Guyana, a bankrupt socialist country on the edge of nowhere.

The heart of that darkness was Jonestown. The colony was the brainchild of a white, former fundamentalist Church of Christ minister, Jim Jones, who had taken his mostly black flock from the safety of San Francisco to Guyana in a fit of paranoid persecution.

Jones and his People's Temple of course made headlines after their grisly mass suicide (although many of the "suicides" were forced by the reverend's armed guards). Jones' final act of insanity was set off by an investigating congressman anxious to know what his former constituents were up to in the Essequibo.

His curiosity did him no good either. Congressman Leo Ryan was murdered at the Jonestown airstrip by the Temple guards. Ryan himself was soon forgotten by America, but the poisoned Kool-Aid was not. Nor was the death agony of the People's Temple members: men, women, and children.

Cults were no longer zany-silly, they were crazy-dangerous.

For every perceived problem in America there is very soon a perceived solution. In other words, somebody is going to make a buck from somebody else's worry or misfortune.

Is that a tad cynical?

Let me introduce Ted Patrick. He was a professional "deprogrammer," a profession he invented himself in the early 1970s. He is now a convicted felon, sentenced to do time in a California jail for kidnapping and false imprisonment.

A self-described high-school dropout whose father ran numbers in Chattanooga, Tennessee, Patrick would, for a time, convert the fear of strange new religions into a flourishing and profitable business. He convinced parents that their adult children who belonged to these new faiths had become mindless robots—zombies, to use Patrick's favorite description—that he alone could save.

To some, he was a hero in a war against a hideous threat to our young and the American family. To others he was a con-man—a good-times-loving hustler who cashed in on America's latest scare by victimizing parents and children alike while casually disregarding basic constitutional rights contained in the First Amendment.

Let Our Children Go!, published in 1976, is Patrick's own book— his beliefs cum biography. The work is also a handbook on how to "deprogram" someone out of his or her cherished beliefs—not, as we shall see, always religious ones.

According to Patrick, he just fell into the business.

It was the summer of 1971. Patrick was living in San Diego with his family. He had moved there some years back from his boyhood home in Chattanooga.

Tennessee was not at the time a land of opportunity for blacks. Patrick was a ghetto kid with little formal education but an accumulation of street smarts. He had tried a series of jobs but had no career.

At various times, he had been a shortorder cook, a chauffeur, a barber. Also an undertaker's assistant, a masseur, a floor sweeper. Once, he had opened up a night club—the Cadillac Club in Chattanooga—and then another. The latter failed, though Patrick is unclear as to the reasons, citing only "political enemies."[1]

California proved to be easier pickings. He became a political organizer in San Diego—an early version of the "community activists" that began to flourish in the turbulent sixties. Not surprisingly, Patrick got his first big break in 1965.

In the aftermath of the Watts riots in south Los Angeles, Patrick attracted attention by keeping Logan Heights, the black section of San Diego, cool and quiet. His success eventually earned him a brief stint as "special representative for community relations"—a gift from Governor Ronald Reagan.

The job had one of those euphemistic titles that implied, but did not actually say, what Patrick was supposed to do, namely, keep things from reaching a flashpoint, especially in summer. In the late sixties, the community relations business was definitely a growth industry. Money was being pumped into community relations by willing local, state, and federal governments, and most taxpayers weren't objecting.

Ted Patrick and the other Ted Patricks prospered—for a while. One lesson learned by Patrick was that scaring the white middle-class silly can be profitable. Not a bad achievement for a tenth-grade dropout from Chattanooga.

As Patrick himself put it in his book:

In the past few years I have spoken on college campuses all over the country from Boston to California, and I can't let help [sic] thinking at times, when I'm addressing a history class, or a sociology class, or participating in a seminar with PhD's, [*sic*] that for a black from Chattanooga, *a tenth grade dropout,* whose parents and relatives and friends once despaired of my ever being able to utter an intelligible sentence [Patrick had a congenital speech defect], everything considered I haven't done too badly with my life. I don't feel that I owe anyone an apology.[2]

But time was clearly running out for the community relations business by 1971. If we are to believe Patrick, his new career in fighting cults began about that time quite casually, actually by accident on the Fourth of July.

According to Patrick, he was getting ready for his annual Independence Day bash at a Mission Beach hotel. His son Michael, then fourteen, had come back late from a fireworks display.

When he finally returned, the boy looked funny, and Patrick knew something was wrong.

The first thought that passed through my mind was, "He's been smoking grass!" He looked vacant, somehow—glazed, drifting.[3]

Marijuana or alcohol wasn't the mind-altering force with which young Michael had a close encounter. The glassy-eyed stare came in the wake of a brush with a wandering band of believers called the Children of God. Each time Michael and his cousin wanted to leave this creepy bunch of guitar players, according to Patrick, "they grabbed [them] by the arms, made [them] look into their eyes."[4]

As "the man" from community relations, and action-oriented anyway, Patrick began checking around, he says, after that episode.

What he found out, he didn't like. The so-called Children of God were snapping up a lot of San Diegan youngsters—twenty-six by Patrick's account—and nobody was doing anything about it.

So Patrick did his own hands-on investigating of the California cult by pretending to join the COG. As a black forty-one-year-old, his recruiters might have been suspicious, but they weren't. With their dilated pupils and "empty, staring" eyes perhaps they didn't notice that Patrick wasn't young, white, and rich—the supposed quarry of the Children of God.[5]

In any case, Patrick and the other recruits soon found themselves on a bus heading for a COG country camp.

He didn't like the camp. The kids acted funny, including the new recruits. "Instantaneous hypnotism," Patrick thought, drawing on his vast knowledge of human psychology. He began to get suspicious:

> During the forty-five minute ride, we sang songs and read the Bible and talked about our private lives with our so-called counselors who were very interested to know how much money we had in the bank.[6]

Thus Patrick concluded:

> [W]hatever the Children of God's real business was, it had nothing to do with religion and a hell of a lot to do with turning a rapid buck.[7]

A business with which he, Ted Patrick, was all too familiar. Patrick soon discovered another trait of the COG cult. They were turning the kids against their parents.

> "Your parents are the enemy!" the Elder shouted [recalls Patrick]. "You have to surrender your whole life to God, you have to give him everything, one hundred percent. . . . And that means giving up your parents too. 'He that loveth his father, mother, sister, and brother more than Me is not worthy of Me.' That's what the Bible says. . . . If you believe it, then you believe you gotta hate your father and your mother because they're evil, because they're of Satan, because they *are* Satan."[8]

For Patrick, a black son of the South with its own tradition of hell-raising preachers, "this was pretty feeble stuff," but we are told, "not many of the middle-class white kids in the room had any experience at all with real evangelical preaching, and they gobbled it up. . . ."[9]

Then there was the pressure. Doubters and skeptics were hammered at by COGies until their defenses were broken down and they became one of the group.

Patrick recalls:

I was never left alone, not for a minute, not even to go to the toilet. After I signed the application—admitting to possession of a car, some stereo equipment, and several musical instruments—I went back to the living room and sat down on the floor again to listen to another lecture and to hear more tapes. . . . I was getting tired and very thirsty. But when I would mention to one of the leaders assigned to me that I would like a glass of water, he would reply, "You're hearing the living word of God. Isn't that more important than a glass of water?"[10]

Apparently not.

The ordeal continued. Not for Patrick so much. He was tough. But what about the kids? Patrick had his doubts:

[They] looked soft and pampered and vulnerable. I tried to imagine what kind of hell they were going through, what kind of pressures motivated by the desire to eat, drink, and sleep might be at work forcing them to sign anything, to agree to anything. I recalled tales of brainwashing sessions reported by American prisoners of war coming home from Korea and resolved that when I got out of there I would look up some of the literature on the subject of mind control and brainwashing, because what I was witnessing sounded pretty much like what I'd read about in the papers in the fifties.[11]

Thus Patrick introduces his other grand theme: cults engage in mind control—brainwashing, if you prefer.

Deprive a person of sleep and feed him little—oatmeal and stew were the sole items on the menu at Camp COG, we are told—and pretty soon the victim is over the edge. Not insane, exactly, but programmed. The talk, of course, is endless.

You don't hear individual words anymore [Patrick recalls], just a stream of babbling and shrieking. I guess that's when the programming starts becoming effective—when the conscious mind stops functioning out of weariness and all that propaganda begins to seep into your unconscious.[12]

For Patrick, it was enough. He had seen the doorway of hell, and he intended to get out while the getting was good.

Not surprisingly, Patrick conned his way out of the camp—rather easily, I might add—in order to tell his story to the world.

But the world wasn't interested in Ted Patrick's discovery. At least not at first.

Patrick's first move, characteristically, was to organize a group: something he was good at. The organization consisted of parents with children in the Children of God. Patrick's outfit was called, almost naturally, Free the Children of God, Free COG, for short. The organization was not enough.

What Patrick wanted was official action—the moral equivalent of sending in the Marines. He wasn't getting any.

I tried to impress on the authorities the dangers of the setup at Santee [the COG camp]. But no one was interested. Free COG wrote letters to congressmen, senators, the Justice Department, even the President, and received form letters in reply. We got a lot of helpful publicity, but no one would take official action.[13]

Trivial issues, like freedom of religion and the First Amendment, prevented these spineless bureaucrats from becoming involved. They just couldn't see what the real issue was. And for Patrick the issue was simply this:

Psychological kidnapping was the issue—brainwashing was the issue, white slavery, prostitution, fraud, false advertising, alienation of affection.[14]

Because no one in officialdom seemed to care, Patrick decided to go ahead and take action himself. He informed the Free COG members at a meeting in August 1971:

[We had to] bodily abduct the children from the communes and colonies they were living in. I did not feel that I would be disregarding the free choice of those young people who had become members of the cults. Once they had been programmed, like the kids I watched at Santee, there was no longer any question of their exercising anything that could reasonably be called free will. They stayed with the cults because they had been programmed to stay, brainwashed into believing that it was Satan who was tempting them to go.[15]

What the Free COG parents thought about that fateful meeting in San Diego is not recorded. But it is clear that from the beginning these parents and others like them would play a very important role in Patrick's deprogramming mission.

From his legal research, Patrick tells us, parents would not be prosecuted for kidnapping their own children, even if they were no longer minors. Or so he hoped.

Ted Patrick, entrepreneur, had worked out his own rules for "deprogramming"—something that was entirely of his own invention. In a way, the techniques, and especially their sale, were quite brilliant and served him well in his own self-declared war on the cults.

Here were the beginning rules:

> The first rule was always to have at least one of the parents present when we went to snatch somebody. The parents would have to make the first physical contact; then, no matter who assisted them afterwards, it would be the parents who were responsible.[16]

Because a parent, *ipso facto*, could not commit a crime against his own child, neither could by extension Santa's helpers. In other words, Patrick could not be deemed an accessory to kidnaping.

That was important because California's legal code imposes equal penalties on both the directly guilty and accessories to major crimes.

Of course, after the snatch, the real fun would begin.

For Patrick, the chance to test his theories came within a few days of the Free COG meeting.

A frantic parent had lost a daughter to the Children of God. The girl had dropped out of the University of Southern California and was being held captive in a COG community, based in Phoenix, Arizona.

For a first time, the snatch was understandably crude. The girl was grabbed in the middle of a Children of God meeting by an accompanying USC classmate, and then stuffed into a car. Patrick was safely in the chase car.

Apparently Tommy Trojan made something of a hash of it. In any case, a long three minutes went by before Patrick and company were wending their way to San Diego—a mere 350 crow-flown miles—over some excruciatingly hot desert in August.

Nevertheless, this was the first deprogramming grab in U.S. history.[17]

Once in San Diego the group checked into a motel, in case the cops were on the trail. At the motel, a room on the fourth floor was selected by Patrick: too high for the girl to try to jump and escape. Patrick relieved the girl of her Bible—after all the book, in his words, had become "a device for self-hypnosis" for the COGie— although others might call it a familiar object of comfort and reassurance in a terrifying situation.[18]

According to Patrick, the "child"—her age is never given— called her captors Satan and quoted programmed Bible passages at them. Patrick, in turn, read them back to her, placing the Scripture into the proper context. Or so he says.

The routine became a familiar one as the years and deprogrammings went by for Patrick. He was self-taught in the Bible, and as in many other branches of human knowledge, Patrick needed no instruction from anyone.

What followed was a genteel debate as to whether God was a God of wrath or love. Patrick, he says, softened her up by pointing out that He was the latter and that her parents were the instruments of His love.

After a good deal more of this, Patrick reports that she gradually began to listen, slowly recovering her faculties. Her recovery, he said was "exciting to watch."[19]

It was also pretty easy.

> After two days of talking, with three of us taking turns, she suddenly gave in. She snapped, just as if someone had turned on a light inside her. The change in her appearance, her expression, her eyes—it was startling. I was amazed. It was like seeing someone return from the grave. It was the most beautiful thing I'd ever seen.[20]

Praise God.

There is more good news from "Reverend Ted." It took three people, according to Patrick, working *ad seriatum* to break her, but she'd been "deprogrammed."

Patrick said it was "the first time I'd ever used the word."[21]

The process took two days—a fairly short period compared to what became the deprogramming standard of four days. This deprogramming was far from the last. The daring strike at the COG commune got Patrick almost instant notoriety, earning him the sobriquet "Black Lightning."

He wore the name proudly.

As time passed, deprogramming techniques and strategies became more and more complicated—and a lot rougher. Consider Patrick's own account of the deprogramming of Wes Lockwood.

Lockwood had been a student at Yale when he became interested in the New Testament Missionary Fellowship, a tiny sect led by an obscure fundamentalist evangelist, Hannah Lowe.

Wes Lockwood's father Joseph came to Patrick in January 1973 seeking help. Wes, we are told, had been trapped far more subtly than any Children of God victim.

Consequently, the snatch was more difficult.

The young Lockwood was grabbed off a New Haven street and shoved into a car by his father with the help of the senior Lockwood's brother-in-law. But the lad resisted, and Patrick had to come to the rescue:

> Wes had taken up a position facing the car, with his hands on the roof and his legs spread-eagled. There was no way to get him inside while he was braced like that. I had to make a quick decision. I reached down between Wes's legs, grabbed him by the crotch and squeezed—hard. He let out a howl, and doubled up grabbing for his groin with both hands. Then I hit, shoving him headfirst into the back seat of the car and piling in on top of him.[22]

From Connecticut they drove to Pennsylvania, Lockwood resisting all the way. Hours later, the Lockwoods and Patrick were in a small western Pennsylvania town where another father whose son had been deprogrammed by Patrick provided the safe house for the deprogramming.

Young Wes, according to Patrick, fought to escape and failed. When he was locked in a room, Patrick tried "to reason" with him. Lockwood would not listen. He sang, spoke in tongues, danced around. Patrick kept at it, with hours and hours and hours of "talking."

For Patrick talking wasn't much fun. Wes Lockwood never told his side of the story, but according to the First Deprogrammer:

I'm a man of action. I don't like sitting in an airless room day after day talking. I'd rather be out in the open, on the move. But I had to admit that Wes was so strong he was stimulating. I love a good fight and he was putting up a beauty.[23]

Wes Lockwood resisted, at one point, according to Patrick, getting into a knock-down wrestling match with his father. Patrick had to separate them, and suddenly the fun and games were over. Patrick commanded after throwing the young man on the bed:

Now you sit there, sit your ass down, and if you so much as move a muscle again I'm going to knock the shit out of you. You understand?[24]

Patrick assures his readers that he usually did not use such language—heaven forbid. Others, however, have a somewhat different story. But we'll save that for later.

Having gotten young Lockwood's attention, Patrick tells us he began what, by now, was his usual deprogramming procedure.

I was able to begin talking to him, analyzing his beliefs, showing him the contradictions he was hanging on to, pointing out step by step what had happened to him and forcing him to think about who Hannah Lowe really was and what she really represented. I knew once he began to listen to me that it was only a matter of time before he broke. I don't think his beliefs were all that structured or complicated, otherwise he wouldn't have had to throw up that smokescreen of frenzy and craziness and physical energy. . . . Anyway, around midnight he snapped.[25]

Snapping simply meant that the young man broke down, cried and embraced his father. Then he phoned his mother.

Young Lockwood next volunteered that his friend Dan Voll, who also belonged to the New Testament Missionary Fellowship, should be hustled out of the organization.

Dan Voll was another story. He didn't break. But let Ted Patrick tell his version of events.

The snatch was set for Harlem in January 1973. It was to be

carried out by Patrick and the young man's parents. Unfortunately, the deprogrammer's program did not work out according to schedule. Nearly everything went wrong.

> [Dan Voll] was kicking and screaming and a crowd was beginning to gather. I pounced on top of him and got my arms locked around his shoulders. Mr. Voll got his legs and we tried to lift him. But we kept slipping, and then some guy was climbing all over my back yelling, "Let that boy go, let him go, damn it!" I gave him a hell of a kick in the shin, heard him shriek, and let him fall away off me.[26]

It got worse. The driver, the abductee's mother, panicked, forgot about her job at the wheel and attempted to explain to the gathering crowd what was happening.

Eventually the Voll family and Patrick got away from their audience—a block away, where they were arrested by an assembly of New York City's finest.

Six months later, Patrick was in court on unlawful restraint and assault charges. It was his first such appearance; it would not be his last. Nor would his defense strategy change much. The Voll trial pretty well established the pattern of putting the cult and its beliefs on trial rather than the act of abduction and, in other cases, false imprisonment.

In the summer of 1973, the New York jury bought the defense's argument and found Patrick not guilty.

So the deprogramming continued with a vengeance. Hare Krishnas; followers of Brother Julius; Love, Israel; the Alamo Foundation; and the Divine Light Mission, to name only a few. Some of them were real enough religions, though exotic. Others plain wacky. But dangerous?

Patrick reserved special attention for members of the Unification Church, the "Moonies," a religion which he describes in his book as a compound of "Manichaeism [sic], Nazi-style anti-Semitism, Calvinism, and the most discredited aspects of pre-Reformation Roman Catholicism, including the selling of indulgences and a doctrine of 'indemnification' for the sins of one's ancestors."[27]

Snatching Unification Church members after a while almost became a pastime with Patrick. He seems to recount those adventures with special relish. Ex-church members also became useful in pro-Patrick testimonials. One, Winnie Swope, was a college student who had become a member of the movement.

By the time Patrick got to Swope, his techniques had been considerably refined.

For one thing, Patrick was no longer present at the abduction, if he could help it. Once the snatch was completed, however, Patrick entered the room and started to talk. And talk. And talk. He claims to have popped her out of her religious trance in twenty-four hours.

Rehabilitation, a return to normalcy, was supposed to keep the freshly deprogrammed "child" from getting any ideas of going back to the cult. Patrick had a pseudo-technical term for this phenomenon.

He called it "floating," and naturally he had a remedy. In the case of Kathy Crampton, a member of a Seattle-based new religion called Love, Israel:

> She would drift in and out mentally; you can see this happening with kids: the old vacant look will return, they get restless, they begin to express doubts. It's important for whomever is with them— preferably their parents—to recognize these symptoms and make a vigorous effort to bring them back to reality. Occupy their minds. Talk to them. Get them involved in some physical activity. *And keep an eye on them to make sure they don't suddenly bolt.*[28]

Patrick also had picked up an entourage. Middle-class parents, anxious about their straying lambs, proved to be less-than-perfect accomplices in such small matters as kidnapping, assault, and false imprisonment.

At first, the extra help was on a pick-up basis. In Detroit, for example, in the summer of 1973 Patrick offered $50 to recruit "four black thugs" in a "dingy bar"—his words—to help grab a girl off the streets at seven in the morning.

In one truly bizarre incident, Patrick was asked to deprogram no fewer than four members of one family, the Goskis: two brothers, a sister and the sister's husband—followers of Brother Julius, a former engineer from Brooklyn who thinks, quite naturally, that he is Jesus.

Abducting four people at one time presented problems. Patrick recruited a man named Goose to help. Goose appeared in many of Patrick's subsequent kidnappings. There is no better description of this gentleman than the one provided by Patrick:

> Goose is big, about six-foot-five, and strong as iron. He wears his hair long, with a sweat-band around it. His arms are tattooed, and when he goes out on a mission he wears heavy boots, a leather vest, and black leather gloves like a strangler. I think all that is part of *psyching himself up*. At heart he's really a gentle man, but when he gets riled, he has been known to become aggressive.[29]

Unfortunately, when thugs and sadists in leather outfits are hired to provide "security" for an illegal act, things are liable to go wrong.

During the snatch of one of the Goski family, things went very wrong indeed. Conveniently, Patrick was not there.

The simple snatch turned into a brawl. Patrick's goons were attacked by other cult members. The encounter wasn't just a matter of fists and feet this time; Mace was used, liberally sprayed on all those who objected to Ronnie Goski's kidnapping. The heavy muscle tactics did not succeed.

This description of Patrick's method of operation comes exclusively from Patrick himself. Others who experienced a Patrick deprogramming had somewhat harsher judgments to make, and as time went on and the snatchings piled up, the snatchees began to fight back.

I have over thirty affidavits from individuals who were subjected to forceful deprogramming. Most of the affidavits were recorded in the middle and late 1970s and the early 1980s, at the height of America's hysteria over cults.

Sherrill Anne Westerlage is a fairly typical example. A member of the Unification Church, she was abducted in September 1975 and subjected to a week of Patrick's deprogramming technique.

The deprogramming didn't work. Seventy-five days went by before Westerlage made her escape and returned to her church.

Westerlage was twenty-five at the time of her deprogramming. Unlike others, she was not grabbed off some city street. Instead, she was lured from New York to her parents' home in Dallas under the impression that her father was dying from a brain tumor—a favorite deprogrammer trick.

What happened next is from Westerlage's own sworn affidavit:

> Ted Patrick, his bodyguard, "Goose," and Cynthia Slaughter, helper of Ted Patrick in his deprogramming, came to my parents' home in Dallas on the 23rd of September. [For a week] I was absolutely forced to endure his verbal abuse, obscenities and spiritual harassment for stretches of 12 hours at a time. Ted Patrick determined when I slept, ate, took a shower [or] listened to him. He was in absolute control of our house, completely manipulating my parents. All of the windows in the house were nailed shut, the locks on the outside doors had been changed and the door knobs removed. The telephone was guarded at all times. All of the neighbors had been warned to notify the police, that if I should by some chance escape I should be returned immediately. . . .[30]

Patrick, Westerlage recalls, slept in her bedroom while she was ordered to sleep in another room with her mother and the inimitable Goose who, according to Westerlage,

> was 26 years old at that time and is really a "tough" guy with his mod clothes, straw hat, long shoulder-length hair and ever-present cigarette, hanging out of his mouth. He never wore a shirt, shoes or socks and always walked around in a very leering way.[31]

Apparently Goose and Westerlage never hit it off.

> Every morning when I was woken up, he was standing 5 feet away in the door-way watching me, with his usual attire. He always guarded me if I was in the bathroom. . . . Goose occasionally called me under his breath a "cold bitch" etc. and even remarked that if I were not a girl he would knock my head off, as he was so disgusted with me.[32]

For a week, Westerlage was subjected from 9 A.M. to 2 P.M. to the attentions of Cynthia Slaughter or Goose. After that, Patrick took over with sessions lasting until four o'clock in the morning.

These encounters hardly consisted of the quiet talk that Patrick depicts in his book. According to Westerlage, they were more like brutal interrogations.

He accused me for hours of being a whore, a prostitute, selling myself to the devil, worshipping a Satanist snake, being no good, rotten, a God-damned bitch. . . . He didn't call me this just one time, but repeatedly, over and over and over, for hours, screaming, yelling, and shouting it to me. And during these outbursts, he would forcibly rock my chair back and forth and take my hand or stroke my arm.[33]

Patrick also made it a practice to ridicule his victims' beliefs. In the case of Westerlage, he ripped up, page by page, Unification Church literature. A favorite technique was to remove photographs of the Reverend Sun Myung Moon from Patrick's briefcase and decorate them with mustaches, beards, and so on. The Korean divine was also accused of the usual run of sins; he became an oriental cross between Adolph Hitler and, naturally, Charles Manson.

The week of deprogramming in Dallas was followed by two weeks of rehabilitation, the object of which was that Westerlage sign an affidavit that the Unification Church had "psychologically kidnapped" her. During the next forty-seven days Westerlage was kept under strict supervision; she was never left alone or allowed to make a telephone call in private.[34]

Sue Tuttle, another Unification Church member, was picked up by her mother in Pittsburgh, for breakfast, she thought. Two of Patrick's assistants went along, however, and she was taken instead to a remote, rural Pennsylvania motel whose owner had entertained Patrick's deprogrammings before.

Tuttle was accused by Patrick of being a prostitute of Moon's and a whole lot worse. In addition, local school superintendents were brought in to watch, and an NBC camera crew was allowed to film part of the proceedings for what would become its 1975 anticult documentary—a favorite of Patrick's, who showed the program incessantly in later deprogrammings.[35]

In the course of this exercise, another facet of deprogramming emerged: the final rupture of family ties.

According to Tuttle:

Since I am a so-called zombie, how are my mother and I supposed to communicate? Nothing that I could say could be relevant. He [Patrick] effectively destroyed our relationship. He played on her emotions with so much fear and turmoil and mistrust and formed a wall between us which will stand for many years.[36]

This is the saddest and most persistent theme that runs through the literature of those who were not successfully bludgeoned into giving up their beliefs.

The cottage industry that Patrick began was hardly confined to his efforts. A perceived need had been created. A market that needed suppliers.

America soon got them.

They came from every walk of life, these new deprogramming "professionals." For some, deprogramming soon became a fulltime occupation or sometimes, more accurately, a blood sport. It was profitable, too. Parents paid as much as $25,000 in fees and expenses for their services.

Still others deprogrammed part-time. No special qualifications were required, of course. Needless to say, there was no licensing procedure as the deprogrammers worked in one of those gray areas of the law: a gray area in this case that cried out for clarification.

The "sons" of Patrick were hardly ever leading citizens. Usually they had no qualifications whatsoever for counseling. The rough stuff, however, often came naturally to them. Galen Kelly was a licensed private eye. Joe Alexander, Sr., was a used car salesman. Some were former cult members and others were parents of children who belonged to the new religions. Others simply liked to hurt people—especially if their subjects were defenseless and the law couldn't or wouldn't interfere.

Not surprisingly, the Patrick imitators were often more callous and brutal than their godfather. That fact clearly comes out in the affidavits and testimony of those snatched by the likes of Galen Kelly and Joe Alexander, Sr., who worked with his son, Joe, Jr.

Laura Jean Wilson, a member of the Unification Church, was snatched by her parents and the Alexanders in Delaware and taken to a Ramada Inn outside of Philadelphia. Although Wilson was twenty-four years old, her appeals to the police and hotel manager got her nowhere. She was, of course, not allowed to see an attorney—a standard practice of all deprogrammers, including Patrick.

All the usual procedures were followed: the locked rooms, the nailed windows. In this case, however, the Alexanders played rough in their subduing of the unwilling Wilson. She was hand-cuffed, and forty-one days later she still had scars on her body as a result of the Alexanders' notion of deprogramming.

As for her actual treatment, Wilson's testimony is illuminating:

> For hours they talked to me, and I had to listen. They played cassette tapes of former members' opinions and non-members' theories about the church. I had to read several papers written by "ex-cult" members and negative newspaper and magazine articles. They played a tape of a friend of mine being deprogrammed.[37]

In all, five people hammered at her for three days, although they were careful to hide their real techniques from the parents of Wilson.

> They would keep talking and pressing material on me until I agreed with their viewpoint. When my parents were in the room, the talk was light and about general topics, even some joking. But when my parents left the room, the talking and the pressure would start up again.[38]

Evidently satisfied with their deprogramming, the Alexanders took Wilson to a "rehabilitation center" where she was also closely watched. Her parents left Wilson at the center and returned to their home in Pittsburgh.

There wasn't much in the way of recreation at the center (a favorite technique of Patrick); instead, the experience consisted mostly of more pressure. In their casual comments, the new team of deprogrammers—a younger and clearly less experienced bunch—tended to be more indiscreet.

Wilson recalls one encounter:

> They often spoke about my church and other religious groups in very scornful terms, ridiculing the church leader and joking about the church traditions. Joe, Tim, and Gifford Cappellini, their attor-ney, spoke about their kidnapping experiences with pride. The night they returned from trying unsuccessfully to kidnap Kate

Kennedy in Chicago, they told many such stories, and I heard Gifford exclaim several times, "I love chasing Moonies!"[39]

Just one more thing. Before Wilson could leave, there were a few papers she had to sign. One of them, a so-called Living Will, would have given the deprogrammers the right to "physically remove" her if she rejoined the church. She was also to sign a statement saying that because she may have been a victim of brainwashing, the deprogrammers had temporary guardianship over her for two more months. Of course, there was the usual codicil saying Wilson had not been coerced into signing any of the above.

Wilson refused. She managed to talk her way out of it by promising to live with her parents and attend Pittsburgh University. At her earliest opportunity, however, she went back to the Unification Church in New York. The Alexanders did not bother her again.[40]

As the years went by the used car salesman and his son seem to have developed something of a roadshow. In August 1983, they turned up in, of all places, Auckland, New Zealand, where the Alexanders oversaw the deprogramming of yet another Unification Church member, Maree Patricia Ryan. The encounter would consist of all the tried and true techniques of harassment and ridicule. The senior Alexander was very much in charge.

Joe, Jr., however, got in his licks as well. According to the terrified Ryan:

He said such things to me as "Bitch!", "Smart-arsed bitch!", "You're just acting like a jerk!", "Little Miss Arrogant!"[41]

The harassment went on for ten days, with the promise of a lot more. In New Zealand, however, the police apparently did not approve of false imprisonment, especially when carried out by foreigners. When the cops showed up the Alexanders' show was already over, and Ryan promptly submitted an affidavit and filed it with her solicitors. Meanwhile, the American deprogrammers scooted out of Auckland before being charged with violating Section 209 of New Zealand's Crimes Act of 1961.[42]

Galen Kelly often proved inept and brutal in his methods. In one snatch in New York, the private detective did not even bother to bring along a relative of the victim.

According to the sworn testimony of Krzysztof Hempowicz:

> Eventually . . . I was completely pulled onto the floor of the van and the door was closed. When the van started to move one [of] the men was holding my arm, and Galen Kelly was sitting on my chest with his hand over my mouth to prevent me from shouting out for assistance. At one stage Galen Kelly had his hand clamped so tightly over my mouth I feared I might be suffocated. One of my arms was twisted in such a way that it caused me considerable pain.[43]

Hempowicz was to be spared the Kelly deprogramming technique. Only minutes into the snatch, the police stopped the van and ordered Hempowicz's release.[44]

How many were involved in deprogramming at the height of the anti-cult hysteria? No one really knows, but if the casual and part-timers are included the number may have been as high as three hundred although probably fifty to sixty constituted the truly hardcore.[45]

They had their counterparts in Canada and England as well. In Canada, Professor Paul MacPherson held people in his home in Guelph, Ontario, until American deprogrammers arrived to whisk their subjects off to the United States, thus avoiding the Royal Canadian Mounted Police who tended to take a dim view of deprogramming.

Lawyers, of course, played their part in keeping their deprogrammer clients on the streets or out of court, protected from subjects who fought back with civil law suits.

Even more important than legal counsel was the respectability that deprogrammers acquired from supportive professionals in the field of psychiatry and clinical psychology.

Deprogramming was made possible by the psychological gloss the technicians, who themselves had no formal training, received from academic psychology.

The key work in their arsenal was a seminal book on brainwashing written by Yale psychiatrist Robert Jay Lifton in 1961. Titled *Thought Reform and the Psychology of Totalism: A Study of "Brainwash-*

ing" in China, the Lifton study provided the basic rationale for deprogrammers.

Quite simply, Patrick and company were fighting an evil they thought had been imported from Red China by the new religions. Lifton gave them more than a red herring. In his famous Chapter 22, Lifton breaks down the thought control process into eight categories: milieu control, mystical manipulation, the demand of purity, the cult of confession, the sacred science, loading the language, doctrine over person and the dispensing of existence.[46]

Lifton's categories were intended to describe a political movement's method of imposing its political ideology on a mass population. The deprogrammers simply borrowed the categories and applied them to the new religions—and they did so with little or no systematic and first-hand research into the movements. Indeed, the only record of any deprogrammer who acquired first-hand knowledge of any cult related to Patrick's celebrated two-day stint in a Children of God camp in 1971.[47]

Lifton helped the anti-cult movement in ways other than his Chapter 22, which had been written a decade before deprogramming got its start in San Diego. Well after the anti-cult hysteria was under way, Lifton wrote an article titled "Cult Process, Religious Totalism, and Civil Liberties" which this time stated explicitly that political thought control could apply equally well to religions. In so doing he denounced "destructive cults" and their manipulation of a "totalistic" environment.[48]

Lifton, although personally supportive, was by no means an activist in the movement. Others in the profession were. Two come to mind.

First, John G. Clark, a professor of psychiatry at Harvard University. Clark, unlike Lifton, worked closely with the deprogramming movement in its war on the cults. From his research on fifty cult members over a period of four years, the Harvard psychiatrist argued that, while brainwashing within religious cults is a real phenomenon, the mental illness it induces may not be made apparent by ordinary psychiatric methods. In other words, an apparently normal person is not normal—he is merely hiding his illness—if he belongs to a cult.[49]

Clark played a vital role in a new strategy desperately needed by the deprogramming movement in the middle 1970s. Forced abductions even with the presence of parents were rapidly becoming legally dangerous.

A legal breakthrough came with the aftermath of Patrick's attempted deprogramming of a Hare Krishna adherent, a twenty year old named Edward Shapiro. Despite Patrick's best efforts, he failed, and Shapiro, the son of a physician, returned to his religion.

Lee Coleman, a psychiatrist and a student of medical involvement in the deprogramming movement, describes what happened next:

> At this point Ed's father asked a nearby psychiatrist for help. Dr. John G. Clark, *despite never having examined Ed,* told a local court that he was "incompetent as a result of mind control." Based on such opinions, Ed was unable to gain access to money he was to inherit; it was turned over to his parents. Later, Ed was even forced to enter a mental hospital, in order, as Dr. Clark later explained, "to have determined whether Edward Shapiro has been subjected to coercive persuasion or mind control, and the extent, if any, to which such mind control prevents or precludes diagnosis of mental illness." To see, in other words, why he looked so normal.[50]

The young man was sent to a psychiatric hospital where he was diagnosed by Clark as a paranoid schizophrenic.

But Clark's snap diagnosis was overruled by a board of psychiatrists at the hospital who found after two weeks of tests that Shapiro was neither sick nor incompetent nor under mind control.[51]

Despite that setback, Clark would persist.[52] According to Biermans:

> In a number of similar instances, he gave sworn testimony that members of the Unification Church were subject to "mind control" simply by virtue of the fact of their membership in the Church.[53]

In one legal case, a civil suit against the Unification Church, Clark testified that the young woman who remained a church member did so because she was in a trance-like state. He did that despite the fact that he had never met, much less tested her.[54]

That kind of testimony also got Clark into trouble in later years. Clark, however, was not alone among mental professionals in advancing the agenda of the deprogramming movement.

Even more active than Clark was (and is) Dr. Margaret Singer, a psychologist who also shared the belief that cults were psychologically dangerous to their members, and that, indeed, all members by virtue of their membership demonstrate behavior bordering on the psychotic.

Like Clark—and even more so—Singer propounded her "clinical research," frequently appearing in various court procedures involving cult members, their parents, and the deprogrammers.

Singer specialized in testifying at hearings involving conservatorships, in which parents of adult children sought to regain a role as guardians because of the alleged mental incompetence of their offspring. This technique flourished among deprogrammers after the rougher methods advocated by Patrick began to go awry and deprogrammers like Patrick and Kelly found themselves in jail.

In San Francisco in late 1976, for example, Singer testified in support of parents of five Unification Church members who wished to place their children under their parental care.

Her expert testimony, according to Lee Coleman, was based on a single test administered by Singer on the five somewhat unwilling subjects.

> She had previously given each of the five the Draw-A-Person test and testified that in her opinion, the drawings reminded her of those produced by the Korean War prisoners-of-war she had studied in the early 1950s. The drawings showed, she claimed, that each of the five was the victim of brainwashing. Dr. Singer could think of no other reason that their drawings were so primitive, looking like a small child's stick figure.[55]

Her recommendation? That the San Francisco Five be sent to the Tucson Center for rehabilitation.[56]

Singer's testimony in a later 1986 San Francisco case, *Molko and Leal v. Holy Spirit Association*, earned her the most notoriety. David Molko and Tracy Leal were ex-Unification Church members who, after deprogramming, filed a suit against the church for brainwashing, false imprisonment, deception, and emotional distress.

In support of their claim, Margaret Singer (and psychiatrist Samuel Benson) in their *amicus* brief said that Molko and Leal's decision to join the church was the result of "coercive persuasion" or "systematic manipulation of social and psychological influences." That, they argued, had made the pair incapable of rational choice. Once they were in the movement involuntarily, they suffered the damage done to them as claimed.

Singer and Benson once again put forward the all-purpose formula based on earlier research with no specific examination of the facts in the particular case. Neither had examined either Molko or Leal before, during, or immediately after their involvement in the Unification Church.[57]

For the most part the ever-cautious professional psychological and psychiatric associations stood aside and for a while sheepishly ignored the whole controversy.

While the cult experts helped, they could not alone create a culture of fear surrounding "the cults" that the deprogrammers thrived on for over a decade. That required the media—print and electronic—plus a good dose of the popular literature that soon got attached to the cult phenomenon.

The media got to the story, especially irresistible after Jonestown. Even before Jonestown the 1975 NBC "documentary" portrayed the new religions in the most sinister light possible. A CBS *60 Minutes* interview with Ted Patrick gave the deprogrammer the strictly kid glove/star treatment rarely accorded anyone on what is supposed to be investigative journalism's prize show.

Even movies about the cult menace, like *Crazy for God* and *Ticket to Heaven* (which mainly focused on the Unification Church, or thinly disguised imitations), were cranked out with a single message: the cults were dangerous because they dragged off America's young to a fate worse than death, a zombie-like existence in the service of a horrible oriental menace.

Newspapers of course reveled in their discovery. Moon alone seemed good enough to fill a newspaper morgue with stories. The headlines said it all: "Bizarre Plot to Rule the World," trumpeted the *San Francisco Examiner.* "Parents Fight Brainwashing by Bizarre Sect," informed the London *Telegraph.* And why not? "I Was a Robot for Sun Myung Moon," read the title of one article in demure *Glamour* magazine. The ordinarily staid *New York Times Magazine* cover story (May 1976) keyed on "the anguished parents who have lost their children to . . . this devil who enslaves young Americans by means of brainwashing and mind control."[58]

With copy like that, Ted Patrick and his movement needed no press agent. The media generated their own hysteria.

Pop literature helped, too. Sometimes such writings took some odd but effective forms. For example, under the imprimatur of Boys Town and the Boys Town Center, an attractive twenty-page pamphlet, *Cults and Kids*, was written in the early 1980s by the center's science writer Robert Dellinger.

The essay was a non-stop endorsement of the brainwashing cult menace thesis. All the usual authorities were cited; most prominently, Margaret Singer.

As for deprogramming, a San Francisco deprogrammer, Neil Maxwell, a pharmacist with fifty deprogrammings under his belt, was cited as an authority. He would gush:

> I think it's a fantastic process. It's very similar to surgery to correct a condition that can't be corrected in any other way. It's not a harsh confrontation process but rather a kindly exchange of information.[59]

Worried parents then are advised in the pamphlet to seek help with such organizations as the Citizens Freedom Foundation and the American Family Foundation, another anti-cult organization headquartered in Lexington, Massachusetts, which, in addition to everything else, issues a newsletter targeted to college students.[60]

Then, of course, there was a rash of anti-cult books, some of them, like Lifton's, aspiring to scientific validity. The best-known probably—and a virtual bible of the anti-cult movement—is Flo Conway and Jim Siegelman's *Snapping*. Its subtitle, *America's Epidemic of Sudden Personality Change*, is a paranoid's delight. Released at the absolute height of the hysteria, 1979, *Snapping* confirmed the worst fears of anyone remotely concerned about America's new religions.

Conway and Siegelman's thesis is simple. Mind altering techniques—chanting, touching, physical duress, fatigue—change the quality of information that enters the brain. The result? "Information disease." The only way a human being can be cured of this new malady is, of course, by deprogramming.[61]

The pop literature on the cult menace and the deprogramming cure is studded with accounts from former members. No doubt the best example of the genre is Christopher Edwards' *Crazy for God*, a 1979 account of his seven months in the Unification Church.[62]

Evidently this overwrought, adolescent, and somewhat suspect account of life as a Unification Church member has become something of an embarrassment to the anti-cult movement. It is rarely, if ever, mentioned in the literature despite the book's glowing dust cover send-offs by Rabbi Maurice Davis and Dr. John Clark. Edwards was deprogrammed in early 1976 by Ted Patrick, and his story sounds like the extended apology for himself that is common among cult apostates. He was not responsible for anything he did simply because he innocently joined the movement where without his knowledge, he was programmed.

Edwards' story is very melodramatic and unconvincing. In fact, the tale sounds exactly as if his experiences were drawn from a deprogrammer's manual, with added bells and whistles for dramatic effect.

Lured to the Unification Church camp near Berkeley, California, for a weekend, young Edwards, then a recent graduate of Yale with money from his prosperous parents and nothing to do but cultivate a vague adolescent search for the meaning of life, slowly finds himself trapped in a cult. Through endless lectures, silly games, love bombing from other members, and lack of sleep and little food, he soon becomes a semi-zombie, complete with glassy stare.

Eyes are big with Edwards, as witness his prose:

> I glanced into the mirror as I brushed my teeth. Back and forth, up and down. . . . Suddenly, my hand froze. Foamy Crest toothpaste dribbled down my chin as I stared into the glass. I hardly recognized myself! My face was red and perfectly smooth. My eyes were wide as a child's, as round as oranges. My eyelids, which normally partially hooded my eyes, were now glued to the skin above them. The change frightened and fascinated me. *I had the same glassy stare as all the others!* I was one of them, then, wasn't I? I must be deeply spiritual after all, just like they'd said. Maybe that's why my eyes look so strange. But *why* glassy?[63]

Unable and unwilling to escape, he finds salvation only because his parents have him abducted and deprogrammed. But not until we get a rich and fruity display of melodramatics.

In one scene, he assures that for the first time in seven months (!) he was assailed by thoughts of fleshly lust in the form of one Jennifer, a round-faced, smiley church member who mildly, very mildly reciprocates.

In high Victorian fashion, the mere idea drives him—well—hysterical:

I held my hands to my ears as words streamed through my mind: God is evil and evil is good. God is Satan is God is Satan. I am God. I am Satan. Help, help, God. Spirit world, rescue me, Jesus Christ, rescue me if you exist. I am love, I am love. I am hate, I am hate, I hate, I hate, I hate, I hate. God is love, God is love, God, God is.[64]

And more:

I collapsed on the floor, rolling around on the carpet, tucking my knees into my chest. I sucked my thumb, curled up in a corner, stared at the smiling picture of Reverend Moon in the center of the room. I faded into unconsciousness, chanting, "God is love, God is love, God is love."[65]

Complete with a lady-like swoon, this is the most contrived mad scene since Ophelia did her thing in *Hamlet*, Act IV, scene 1, right before that last dip in the pool.[66]

Ophelia, poor soul, did not have the services of a skilled professional deprogrammer.

Edwards, however, is careful not to cross the libel line. Real people in the Unification Church are given slightly altered names. Sun Myung Moon, of course, was impossible. But Mose Durst, then-president of the American branch of the Unification Church, becomes "Dr. Dust." Moon's right-hand man Colonel Bo Hi Pak is transformed into "Colonel Peck.

Atrocity tales by former members of any faith, it should be added, are common throughout history. For one thing, they are a comfort to the teller of the tale because all human beings have a habit of reconstructing their past to adjust to present circumstances.

In the end, *Crazy for God* was really no worse than all the other overwritten, menace-of-the-cult treatises that entertained and frightened the public for the better part of a decade. Besides making their authors richer, they also accomplished one other objective, albeit inadvertently: they helped set off a backlash.

It couldn't last, of course. Even good things don't, and increasingly a lot of Americans decided that deprogramming wasn't such a good thing.

So what did in the movement? Deflated the hysteria? Got some of our finest deprogrammers thrown in the jug?

Well, Americans always move on to fresh challenges and new worries, but the exaggerations of the anti-cult cult surely helped.

By the early 1980s it became apparent, Conway and Siegelman to the contrary, that millions of young Americans hadn't suddenly disappeared into the twilight zone of zombiedom. A robot army of white, upper-middle-class dropout Yuppies were not about to seize control of the capital under the command of Generalissimo Moon.

In fact, the deprogramming movement and their psychiatric auxiliary corps had yet to produce one certifiable zombie for us lay yokels to marvel upon and wonder at.

Was America being treated to yet another *Wizard of Oz* routine? In spite of all the Great Oz-like warnings from the anti-cult movement not to regard the little man behind the green curtain, folks were beginning to get suspicious. Perhaps the Great and Terrible Oz was only a lot of smoke and a good sound system after all. People gradually began to figure things out. They no longer accepted on faith the nightmare Wonderland of the deprogrammers. They began to accept plain, humdrum reality.

A little academic research helped, too. Robbins and Anthony, for example, discovered that many people left the Unification Church and other new religions easily and voluntarily. Very few people who attended seminars offered by the new religions ever actually joined them.[67]

As for those Unification Church members who remained in the movement, a 1979 study of seventy-four practicing members, by Professor Thomas McGowan, concluded: "There is no evidence of so-called 'brainwashing' in either the written replies or the oral interviews." He added that most who were interviewed appeared to be relatively independent young adults who had already given up their parental religion before joining the Unification Church.[68]

In fact, virtually the only evidence of discontent with the new religions and accusations of brainwashing came from one source: those who were forcibly deprogrammed. For reasons already cited, that evidence for most analysts is *a priori* tainted.

The attack on the deprogrammers' most sacred assumptions did not stop there.

Such stand-by civil liberties organizations as the American Civil Liberties Union entered the fight pretty early against the deprogrammers. For the ACLU, the matter was simple. Adults were being deprived of basic rights at the whim of parents and guardians, with the help of hired hands.[69]

Organized religion in the form of the National Council of Churches also weighed in and so did groups like Americans United for the Separation of Church and State. For them, the small sects were being persecuted for their odd religious beliefs rather than any identifiable crime.[70]

Even the sleepy mental health profession began to wake up and take a look at what some of its members had wrought.

The first to be shot down over the blue skies of Massachusetts was John G. Clark. His conduct during the Shapiro case at last got the attention of the Massachusetts Board of Registration and Discipline in Medicine, the state's medical licensing board. The board did not move at all until some Scientologists brought the Shapiro matter to its attention.

Thus cornered, how did the board respond? I quote from their findings:

> There is no recognized diagnostic category of mental illness of thought reform and mind control. . . . Moreover the basis on which this diagnosis was made seems inadequate, as mere membership in a religious organization can never, standing alone, be sufficient basis for a diagnosis of mental illness. . . . There seems no factual basis either for the conclusion that Mr. Shapiro was mentally ill, or that he was a danger to himself. Again, this invites the concern that the judgments were entirely based on the subject's religion.[71]

No disciplinary action was taken against Clark.

Margaret Singer too was attacked by her colleagues. Louis H. Gann of Stanford University and its Hoover Institution concluded this about Singer's research:

> Her work, unfortunately, suffers from a variety of disabilities. These include a lack of historical perspective; an inadequate knowledge of comparative theology necessary for a researcher concerned with the subject of religion; an apparent failure to grasp the varieties of religious motivation; a seeming unwillingness to consider adherence to orthodox—or even bizarre—religions as a legitimate form of behavior guaranteed under the Constitution; and a remarkable propensity for drawing sweeping conclusions from inadequate evidence.[72]

But it was Singer's *amicus* brief in *Molko and Leal* that got her into trouble with the American Psychological Association and its Board of Social and Ethical Responsibility for Psychology. In a memorandum, the board lashed out at Singer, her Task Force on Deceptive and Indirect Methods of Persuasion and Control, and its report on cults.

The memorandum concluded.

> [The Board] is unable to accept the report of the Task Force. In general, the report lacks the scientific rigor and evenhanded critical approach necessary for APA imprimatur. The report was carefully reviewed by two external experts and two members of the Board. They independently agreed on the significant deficiencies in the report. The Board cautions the Task Force members against using their past appointment to imply [the Board] or APA support or approval of the positions advocated in the report. [The Board] requests that Task Force members not distribute or publicize the report without indicating that the report was unacceptable to the Board.[73]

In other words, Singer's task force on deception was engaging in deception itself. The shot across the bow from the APA, although late in coming, was devastating to Singer and her colleagues on the witch-hunting task force. The end was in sight already when the court in *Molko and Leal* accepted an *amicus* brief submitted by a score or more of scholars. They found:

Specifically, the conclusions Drs. Singer and Benson assert cannot be said to be scientific in any meaningful sense, and the methodologies generating these conclusions depart so far from methods generally accepted in the relevant professional communities that they are incapable of producing reliable or valid results. Stripped of the legitimating lustre of a scientific pedigree, plaintiff's purported scientific claim of coercive persuasion is little more than a negative value judgment rendered by laypersons about the religious beliefs and practices of the Unification Church.[74]

Stripping away the authority of psychology and psychiatry badly hurt the anti-cult movement, but the obvious excesses of the deprogrammers themselves also made a large contribution.

Patrick, for one, didn't know where to stop. In Salt Lake City he admitted deprogramming four Mormons. And why not? To the First Deprogrammer, Mormons were only "mindless robots" and the Mormon Church "is the biggest cult in the nation."[75]

Why stop with Latter-Day Saints? Patrick and his colleagues, in the twilight of forced deprogramming, snatched a Roman Catholic, an Old Catholic, and charismatic Episcopalians.[76]

Patrick's troubles really began when he kidnapped two sisters in Denver in 1978 at the request of their Greek Orthodox parents. Their crime? They had chosen to live away from home and no longer participate in the life of their church. But they had joined no other religion.[77]

The Denver job got Patrick oceans of bad publicity.[78]

Other cases got him into even hotter water. In June of 1980, Black Lightning snatched a thirty-five-year-old woman and held her for thirty-one days. Susan Wirth, who has a Ph.D. in Spanish literature, was handcuffed to a bed for two weeks and denied food, water, and sleep. Her problem? Wirth's mother did not approve of her radical political beliefs and paid Patrick $27,000 to make her "normal."

The Wirth snatching quite logically led to his next crime, the abduction of Stephanie Reithmiller in Ohio in 1981. Reason? Her parents objected to their adult daughter's living with another woman in an alleged lesbian relationship.

If that leaves the reader with the suspicion that Patrick was losing his marbles, remember that two years earlier Patrick had abducted and deprogrammed Janet Schumacher of Salem, Oregon, because her mother objected to her fiance. He was supposedly exercising "mind control" over Janet.[79]

The Patrick-style deprogramming, after a total of 1,600 snatches by 1982, was rapidly self-destructing. The only purpose to his activities apparently was the love of the chase, the brutality of lording it over hapless, white, mostly female victims with the shield of parental consent. And, of course, the sweet smell of money.

Then too there was the growing suspicion that the parents of these deprogrammed adult children were not entirely volunteers in these escapades. Evidence began to surface that deprogrammers were directly attempting to create demand for their own services. Attorney Jeremiah Guttman of the American Civil Liberties Union in 1977 learned of deprogrammers who obtained a list of Hare Krishna devotees' parents and gained admittance to them by pretending to have a message from their offspring. Only then did the "salesmen" attempt to sell the deprogramming service with a $1,500 down payment.[80]

The effect of all of these machinations no doubt gave many pause for thought.

Patrick was first convicted in May 1975 in Orange County, California, for kidnapping and unlawful imprisonment. That got him two months in jail. A year earlier, he had been convicted in Denver for false imprisonment. He was sentenced for twelve months, released after two weeks, and then jailed later for violating probation. In 1980 he was convicted in San Diego for the usual crimes and sentenced to a year in jail. In 1985, California Superior Court Judge Norbert Ehrenfreund imposed a three-year jail term on Patrick. In October 1981, he was indicted in Ohio for the abduction, assault, and sexual battery committed against Stephanie Reithmiller. In October 1987, Delaware police issued a warrant for his arrest on another kidnapping charge.[81]

As if that were not enough, Patrick was in trouble in other ways as well. In a 1979 *Playboy* interview, Black Lightning claimed he had $60 million in lawsuits pending and had already spent $200,000 in legal fees.[82]

Chalk up some of that to street hustler braggadocio, but his civil suit troubles were real enough, and the costs incurred may help explain his frantic search for subjects, no matter what their background.

As for Galen Kelly, he was convicted in March 1979 for assault in connection with an abduction. Nine months later the detective lost his pistol license after carrying an unregistered weapon in a struggle involving yet another false imprisonment. Kelly's idea of abduction? Pistol-whipping a bystander who tried to rescue the "subject."[83]

Joseph Alexander, Sr., was indicted in California in March 1981, for two counts of conspiracy, one count of kidnapping, and one count of false imprisonment. His son, Joe, Jr., was indicted three months later in Denver on a charge of kidnapping, and later convicted.[84]

These are only the highlights. Moreover, since deprogrammers started at such a low level with Patrick and the Alexanders, it is not any surprise that during the boom years of deprogramming, truly genuine scum were attracted to this pseudo-profession.

Robert Brandyberry is only one example. Brandyberry has been repeatedly accused of sexually abusing his "subjects" and even his fellow deprogrammers—to such an extent that former deprogrammer Gary L. Scharff made that accusation in writing to author John Biermans. In early 1988, Brandyberry was indicted in Denver on kidnapping and false imprisonment charges. Convictions against other deprogrammers picked up. Suddenly, America's heroes in the Great Zombie Wars of the 1970s weren't looking so good.

The rap sheet on Patrick and his fellow deprogrammers is only the surface of the real story. The real story is what happened to the law in the course of the deprogrammers' legal saga.

As usual, Ted Patrick was the man in the middle. The first fact to understand is that Patrick did little or nothing different from the first snatching to the last. What changed were the perceptions by judge, jury, and prosecutor of what Black Lightning was up to.

Patrick, from the start of his legal troubles, used a "necessity" defense. It would soon be used by other deprogrammers in copycat fashion. Rooted in common law, justification by necessity merely meant that Patrick and the parents were kidnapping in order to prevent a greater harm from happening to the child.

Thus a forced removal was, in effect, a rescue operation for the person—whether he or she wanted it or not.[85]

At first, the necessity defense worked. In New York in 1973 Patrick used that defense and was found not guilty for the abduction of Daniel Voll.[86]

In that trial, Judge Bruce Wright, incidentally, allowed the defense broad latitude in investigating the sect under question— namely, the New Testament Missionary Fellowship—and he further permitted the jury to become involved in value judgments about the sect itself.

But, according to legal scholar John LeMoult: "No evidence was offered to show that this group was engaged in anything unlawful or even mildly improper."[87]

Patrick scored again with this defense, this time in Seattle, Washington, where a federal district judge dismissed kidnapping charges filed by Kathy Crampton citing "necessity" and a lack of criminal intent on Patrick's part.[88]

The string ran out with the Crampton case, however. In Denver, in the Greek Orthodox case, Patrick was convicted of false imprisonment. The real blow came in the Colorado Appeals Court, which rejected Patrick's necessity defense. In its view:

> First, for the choice of evils defense to be available there must be an imminent public or private injury about to occur which requires emergency action.[89]

The court also argued that Patrick and his brethren would have had to prove that a particular religion was doing real injury and do so *in camera,* that is, without the jury present. No longer could deprogrammers "try and convict" a religious sect's beliefs in an effort to sway the jurors. That was found to be a violation of any religion's First Amendment rights.[90]

People v. Patrick blew a gaping hole in Patrick's defense. When judges and juries focused on the law rather than sentiment, the flimsy necessity defense collapsed like a pasteboard skyscraper.

How really flimsy the necessity defense was all along becomes even more obvious when the federal kidnapping statute itself is considered.

The statute applies to:

[w]hoever unlawfully seizes, confines, inveigles, decoys, kidnaps, abducts, or carries away and holds for ransom or reward or otherwise any person, except in the case of a minor by the parent thereof when: (1) the person is willfully transported in interstate or foreign commerce.[91]

And where was the Federal Bureau of Investigation in all this? Until the late 1970s, there was only one federal prosecution of a deprogrammer under the federal kidnapping statute. And this particular case is a very sorry example of selective enforcement, a selectivity not guided by the law, but by other and immaterial considerations.[92] But despite the federal government's reluctance to be involved, the classic defense of the deprogrammer was pretty much in ruins by the late 1970s.

Other legal battles, however, lay ahead.

There was much more to the process than the arrest, conviction, and jailing of a few deprogramming vigilantes when it came to the law. In fact, the war had only begun, and is still being waged on a wide range of fronts—who, for example, gets control of junior's legacy?

Still, by the early 1980s, things had progressed a long way from a time when local cops had not only looked the other way as the deprogrammers plied their trade, but had actually assisted in the abductions. (In one case in Minnesota from 1976, Nancy Lofgen, a member of a fundamentalist sect, was thrown into a car by county sheriff's deputies who wore no uniforms or badges.[93])

To paraphrase Bob Dylan, you don't need a weatherman to figure out a that hurricane is coming. So those who remained in the business of breaking the faith of sect members decided to use other and safer tactics.

Some advocates of the practice began denying that they had ever believed in forcible deprogramming. Instead, they were simply recommending the use of entirely legal means such as discussion with new-religion believers. This method became known in the trade as "soft" deprogramming.

One of the new methods called for parents of adult children to file for a writ of habeas corpus before a judge. The parents under this maneuver had to prove that their offspring were being "wrongfully denied liberty."

The problem with this approach was that, even if successful, it did not restrain the object of the writ from returning to his religion whenever he wanted. There were other problems, too.

Helander v. Salonen, a 1975 case before the District of Columbia Superior Court, was a parental attempt to seek a writ of habeas corpus in order to extract a daughter from the Unification Church. The plaintiff's contention was that the daughter remained within the church because of psychological pressures. The court, however, found no evidence of mind control and dismissed the suit.[94]

For these reasons, obtaining such a writ soon went out of fashion. A more successful legal approach that was combined with so-called soft deprogramming was to obtain a conservatorship on the part of the parents on behalf of their (usually) adult children.

It was also fairly easy to obtain one, thanks to the probate conservatorship law. According to Coleman:

> State law permitted such conservatorship not only if the person was of "advanced age, illness, injury, mental weakness, intemperance, addiction to drugs or to other disability," but also if the person was "likely to be deceived or imposed upon by artful and designing persons." With a law as vague as this and a cooperative psychiatrist, parents could almost count on a favorable verdict.[95]

The law later was amended to eliminate the artful and designing clause, but parents and their support groups made the most of it while it lasted. In the San Francisco Bay Area in the last half of 1976, for example, judges granted two dozen conservatorships of Unification Church members.[96]

In Arizona, conservatorships proved nearly as popular—stimulated by Joe Alexander, Sr.'s, Freedom of Thought Center where the average cost of deprogramming was $9,700.[97]

Although the guardian and conservatorship laws, then and now, were designed to provide protection for the elderly and mentally incompetent and their property, the deprogrammers used them to restrict a person's religious beliefs.

Soon standardized forms for conservatorship were provided to parents by the deprogrammers and their supporters. According to Siegel:

These standardized forms contain allegations that the church to which the proposed ward belongs has used "coercive methods" to effect the conversion, including "sleep and food deprivation, enforced isolation and prohibition from communication with friends and family and other psychological manipulations."[98]

The advantage of these fill-in-the-forms, besides convenience, was that the custodee need not know anything about them, and thus had no opportunity to defend his or her own sanity. The other advantage was that the process could give the parents or guardians thirty days of conservatorship—no questions asked—giving the deprogrammers plenty of time to do their work.

Once the court order had been obtained, usually by a team of two lawyers and a psychologist, the subject could be seized by the police and then handed over to the deprogrammers. The "Legal Deprogramming Kits," as they were called, were truly a gift from the gods.[99]

For a while the ploy worked. Deprogrammers were delighted. Subjects and fees were once more rolling in—with no risk at all. Best of all, it was legal.

Unfortunately, the good times didn't last. Something called *Katz v. Superior Court* got in the way.

The case had a very routine beginning. Again, San Francisco; 1977. Parents filed for conservatorship of their adult children— five of them in one fell swoop. For Alexander the nice part about the arrangement was that doing them in multiples saved on paperwork, while increasing the number of clients.

San Francisco Superior Court Judge Lee Vavuris was cooperative, too. He handed the kids over to the parents without any question. This time the wards—all members of the Unification Church and all over twenty-one years of age—proved mentally competent enough to fight back and took their complaint to the California Court of Appeals.

The Appeals Court took a different view of the proceedings. The court judged that the parents had not proved their case. The conservatees in question were neither insane, nor incompetent, nor unable to manage their property. And these were the only grounds recognized for a conservatorship to be granted.

Furthermore the legal process could not specifically be used to

deprive these adult children of their religious freedom or—worse
news for the Alexanders—be a means by which they could be
involuntarily deprogrammed. To grant conservatorship in this
case was, in the court's opinion, little more than a license to kidnap
"for the purpose of thought control."

The Court of Appeals added:

> We conclude that in the absence of such actions as render the adult
> believer himself gravely disabled as defined in the law of this state,
> the processes of this state cannot be used to deprive the believer of
> his freedom of action and to subject him to involuntary treat-
> ment.[100]

Katz was a terrible setback for West Coast deprogrammers. *Katz*
did something else, too. It revealed, for the first time, the mindset
that had taken hold of many local and state officials in the first
years of deprogramming. Perhaps inadvertently, Judge Vavuris
expressed it perfectly in his opinion on the original question of
conservatorships. He said:

> [W]e're talking about the very essence of life here, mother, father,
> and children. There's nothing closer in our civilization. The family
> unit is a micro-civilization. That's what it is. . . . One of the reasons
> that I made the Decision, I could see the love here of a parent for his
> child, and I don't even have to go beyond that. Even, our laws of this
> State, the Probate laws have all been set up—the laws of succession,
> children succeed to the estate of their parents if the parents die
> intestate. So the law looks at that binding thing between a parent
> and a child. It is never-ending. No matter how old we are, it's there.
> And that was one of the things that influenced this Court.[101]

Very moving, but Judge Vavuris was speaking as a cracker barrel
philosopher, and not as an officer of the court. The judge's opinion
nowhere contained any findings of fact that disclosed the grounds
for, much less justified, the action taken.

As an editorial in the *New York University Law Review* commenting on the *Katz* case stated:

> It is certain . . . that the court was wrong when it myopically claimed
> there was no need to "go beyond" the love of a parent for his child,

because in so stating, it ignored the central First Amendment questions presented by the case. The court thus allowed its visceral response to numb its institutional responsibility, which demands a greater attention to and analysis of free exercise issues whenever that constitutional clause is implicated.[102]

Nevertheless, Judge Vavuris put in bold relief the hidden prejudice of many court and police officials. For them, the deprogramming and conservatorship questions were simply defenses of the family against an evil and unscrupulous force—namely, the new religions.

Hidden prejudice is difficult to combat. Vavuris, by bringing it into the open, tore away the legalisms behind which the anti-cult forces had hidden so successfully for so long. Once the prejudice was revealed, the case was open to reversal, which is precisely what happened in *Katz v. Superior Court.*

The news was not all bad for deprogrammers, however, in other parts of the country—especially the Midwest where conservatorships have enjoyed a longer and more profitable run.

In the late summer of 1977, a Wisconsin judge found a thirty-two-year-old woman mentally incompetent because she belonged to a fundamentalist sect called the Disciples of the Lord Jesus Christ. The court gave the parents temporary guardianship over her and her children.

According to Boothby, the story has more than the usual number of grim overtones:

> According to testimony at the hearing [Darlene Sense] was incompetent as a result of her membership in the Disciples. . . . Mrs. Sense was never notified of the hearing. The judge also agreed to seal the court records to keep the plan secret, thus foiling any rescue attempt. In addition, Mrs. Sense of course was denied the right to obtain her own counsel or to secure witnesses on her own behalf. The transcript from the secret hearing held on April 11, 1978, further indicates, unbelievably, the discussion between the judge and the lawyer seeking Darlene's conservatorship concerning the logistics of Darlene's abduction.[103]

Even more unbelievable, when Sense finally obtained her release with the help of another judge and filed suit against her captors and the accomplice judge, the U.S. District Court for Wisconsin's Eastern District ruled, in May 1980, that the judge was not liable due to judicial immunity. The rest, however, settled out of court, paying Sense $25,000.[104]

Still, the handwriting was on the wall for that particular deprogrammer tactic.

And yet another tactic backfired.

We return to a matter already mentioned, *Molko and Leal v. The Holy Spirit Association*. Deprogrammers in this case had persuaded two ex-Unification Church members to file a civil suit against their church in the hope of legally establishing the concept of brainwashing: the fundamental notion that supposedly legitimized the deprogrammers' dubious enterprise.

It was a disastrous failure. Both the original court and the Appeals Court threw out the case in no uncertain terms. The Court of Appeals derided the "expert opinions" on brainwashing, calling them little more than "veiled value judgments concerning the outlook of the Unification Church."[105]

The court also castigated the experts, Singer and Benson, for entirely ignoring the question of religious teaching and the spiritual nature of its hold on the faithful—as is the case with any religion.

For the court to do so, in the judges' opinion, would cross the fine line that separates church and state. And that the Court of Appeals would not accept. In its words:

> If liability could be imposed in such circumstances, any disaffected adherent could bring suit alleging that he had been "brainwashed" by the religious organization, and courts would have become entangled in determining which former adherents acted out of true faith and which were subject to "mind control."[106]

In this, the California Court of Appeals was returning to a solid body of constitutional precedent found in opinions that the U.S. Supreme Court had been arguing since *Reynolds v. United States* in 1878, but which until now had been studiously ignored by lower courts in the deprogramming cases. That is, the lower courts often ignored grave First Amendment and Fourteenth Amendment questions.[107]

Molko and Leal was a legal rifle shot aimed right at the heart of the deprogramming business on the grounds already established by the Appeals Court.

The California court had just one more thing to say. It dismissed entirely the plaintiffs' claim that they had been deceived. Nor, it said, were they forcibly kept in the church. "To the contrary," the court argued, "plaintiffs were at all times free to maintain contact with non-members as they did." And the judges added: "the techniques used to recruit and indoctrinate plaintiffs . . . are not materially different from those employed by other organizations."[108]

But the courts were not quite ready to junk their arguments completely.

The most significant reversal for the Unification Church came from the California Supreme Court in October 1988 when it overturned some of the important findings in *Molko* that had been handed down by the San Francisco Superior Court and the California Court of Appeals. The 6–1 majority in the State Supreme Court found, for example, that the church could be sued for fraud and brainwashing because the First Amendment, while protecting religious belief, did not necessarily protect some forms of religious conduct, including fraudulent conversion.

In the words of Justice Stanley Mosk:

> The challenge here is not to the church's teaching or to the validity of a religious conversion. The challenge is to the church's practice of misrepresenting or concealing its identity in order to bring unsuspecting outsiders into its highly structured environment. The practice is not itself belief, it is conduct subject to regulation for the protection of society.[109]

In effect, Mosk was resurrecting the brainwashing controversy, even though the idea had been steadily discredited over the last decade. Thus, although acknowledging that the concept was controversial, the majority opinion still treated such experts as Margaret Singer as authorities who provided "a scientific basis" for the phenomenon.

With that mindset, it is no surprise that Mosk concluded:

> While some individuals who experience coercive persuasion emerge unscathed, many others develop serious and sometimes irreversible

physical and psychiatric disorders, up to and including schizo-phrenia, self-mutilation and suicide.[110]

That, of course, once more opened the barn door. If brainwashing were real, then the state had a substantial interest "in protecting individuals and families from the substantial threat to public safety, peace and order posed by the fraudulent induction of unconsenting individuals into an atmosphere of coercive persuasion."[111]

The California Supreme Court in this case did so by reversing the two lower courts and holding the church liable for fraud, infliction of emotional distress, and restitution.[112]

The Unification Church and its supporters in the mainline churches could take some comfort in the court's simultaneous dismissal of deprogrammer Neil Maxwell's suit against the church. They could also find solace in that Leal's charge of false imprisonment was also thrown out.[113]

All the old smears were still alive and well, however. Despite the warning from the lone dissenter, Judge Carl W. Anderson, that brainwashing and heavenly deception "fail to constitute those gravest abuses" and that the California State Supreme Court by believing otherwise was entering "a theological thicket," the matter now could only be settled by the U.S. Supreme Court.[114]

The Unification Church, in short, had not yet overcome the legal difficulties spawned by the deprogramming cult. It was not yet to be "just another church."

CHAPTER XII

THE REVEREND SUN
MYUNG MOON

Men make history and not the other way around. In periods where there is no leadership, society stands still. Progress occurs when courageous, skillful leaders seize the opportunity to change things for the better.

HARRY S TRUMAN

LIKE most founders of the world's religions, the Reverend Sun Myung Moon came from the humblest of circumstances. His rise to wealth, influence, and, of course, notoriety is remarkable even when compared to that of other world prophets.

Sun Myung Moon was born in 1920 in an obscure part of what was then the Imperial Japanese Empire: Korea or *Chosen*, as the Japanese insisted on calling their colony. The name was an adaptation of the old Chinese name for Korea, *Choson*: Land of the Morning Calm.

To be precise, the Moon family for generations had farmed near the coastal village of Jung-ju located near the Yellow Sea in what is now North Korea. Jung-ju lies approximately fifty miles from the Yalu River and the Chinese border near the fortieth parallel.

A less promising place for a prophet and world religion to begin

463

could hardly be imagined. Korea was starkly impoverished. Worse yet, since 1910 the country had been occupied by the Japanese who viewed it as their back door to that great prize, Manchuria.

By the 1930s, *Chosen* was more than conquered territory. Korean culture, including the language, was to be eliminated entirely, and Koreans were to become permanent second-class Japanese. But that was all in the future when the Moons of Jung-ju had their fifth child, a boy, Sun Myung. Eventually there were three more children; the size of the family was typical for Korean farmers.

The land near the Yellow Sea where the Moons tilled the soil was relatively fertile. It was also well watered by large rivers which tumbled down from the jagged, snow-capped mountains, cutting southwest from the central Hamgyong range, the spine of the northern part of the Korean peninsula.

Life was hard and living conditions primitive. The large family lived in a compound featuring a thatched roof house surrounded by a low mud wall. There was no electricity and no running water. Diets were simple: fish, rice, and fermented cabbage, the fiery *kimchi*. Winters were harsh—far more difficult than ones in southern New England, which shares the same latitude as the northwest portion of Korea where the young Moon endured his childhood. Luxuries were nonexistent.

Poverty, however, was hardly the only early and formative influence on Moon's life. Far more important than mere grinding poverty was the peculiar nature of Korean history and Korea's acceptance of Christianity.

Indeed, these two factors have done the most to shape the man and his movement. They also help to explain the unusual nature of the Unification Church's history in Korea and, later in the United States.

To Americans, the history of the Korean people is one of small triumphs. Although a highly homogeneous people, the country has been divided since the end of World War II. That division has made the Korean peninsula one of the world's flashpoints, as dangerous as the Middle East.

The Communist north's dictatorship is controlled by the world's most durable tyrant, the half-mad Kim Il-Sung, who intends to bequeath power to his equally deranged son, Kim Jong Il. The Democratic People's Republic is almost a purely totalitarian monolith. No dissent of any kind is tolerated in this highly militarized state which has less than half the population of the south, but larger and better-equipped armed forces.

In the south, the Republic of Korea is emerging as a genuinely democratic government after more than thirty years of authoritarian rule, often by military strongmen who nonetheless took turns in power and had their rule ratified by some form of election.

Again, in contrast to the north, South Korea has been rapidly building (over the last two decades) one of the world's most vibrant economies. Growth rates of 15 percent per year are not unheard of for this country which is nearly the same size and shape as the state of Indiana. Its greatest resource: forty million hardworking people.

North Korea, with its creakingly old-fashioned, iron-like Stalinist command economy, has fallen far behind its southern brother. Like Cuba, North Korea constitutes one of the genuine embarrassments of what's left of the socialist camp. Worse, North Korean diplomats have used their diplomatic pouch privileges to smuggle and sell illegal drugs for hard currency in a desperate effort to fill in the huge gaps in North Korea's international trade account.

More than forty years of bitter division between north and south hardly begin to tell the sad story of Korean history. Of far greater importance is the Korean War, launched by the north in June 1950. A wholly unprovoked attack, North Korean aggression at first nearly overwhelmed the lightly armed fledgling South Korean republic. Only the hasty entrance of American ground forces, and more important, American air and naval units, prevented complete defeat.

South Korean and poorly trained American forces took a battering in their southern Pusan redoubt. They would have remained pinned down there forever except for a daring landing, further north at Inchon, which General Douglas MacArthur hoped would split the North Korean forces in half.

MacArthur was right. The aggressors were hurled north of their original start line on the thirty-eighth parallel. Within a few months, South Korean, American, and a smattering of other United Nations' contingents were racing even further north. By November, some units had reached the Yalu River dividing Korea from the newly founded People's Republic of China.

The sense of victory, however, was short-lived. The thin winter line along the frozen Yalu was smashed by a million-man "volunteer" Chinese communist army which succeeded in driving the U.N. and ROK forces back down the peninsula. In a desperate series of counter-attacks the allies managed two months later in January 1951 to establish a line of defense: a line that slashed across the peninsula some fifty miles below the south's capital, Seoul.

The commander of the U.S. Eighth Army, General Matthew Ridgway, was not content to sit on the southern end of the Korean peninsula without another fight. He pulled together a dazed and defeated armed force and turned it once more into a fighting machine.

In two months Ridgway's forces had recaptured Seoul and the overextended Chinese were in full retreat. Three weeks later, U.N. forces had pushed the communists north of the thirty-eighth parallel. There would be more fighting, and one more large-scale Chinese offensive, but by the summer of 1951 the war of movement was over.

The war itself was not. Despite peace talks which began in July 1951, the fighting and dying went on for another two years until an armistice was signed on July 27, 1953. No peace treaty was signed; technically both sides are still at war, a fact that North Korea fully understands, as evidenced by a long series of provocative actions which continues today.

Still, it is the cost in human life that is at the center of our story. For the Korean people the price was appalling. The physical destruction alone had wiped out the little progress that had been gained by Japanese forced-draft development in the thirty-five years of their rule.

The capital, Seoul, had been shattered in the conflict, changing hands no fewer than five times—block-to-block and house-to-house fighting each time had left it a charred and smoking ruin.

The damage was little compared to the loss of human life. Americans remember that the Korean "police action" cost fifty thousand American lives—approximately the same as the Vietnam conflict. By the 1970s, the Korean War had so receded from the American memory that *M*A*S*H*, an unrealistic "antiwar" film comedy (and later an equally successful television series), could become a box office success.

Even the heartless barons of Hollywood might flinch a bit if they ever bothered to learn that the war inflicted 3.8 million casualties—two million of them civilians—mostly women and children, in a population of scarcely more than thirty million people. And that does not count the suffering of tens of millions more— two million of them North Koreans fleeing the terror of war and the Kim Il-Sung murder machine.

That bitter war was not the only tragedy suffered by the Korean people. Japan's forty-year rule, interrupted only by defeat in the Pacific, was hardly more pleasant. In fact, it was harshly dictatorial. The Japanese considered the Korean people to be slaves and their economy a merely convenient supplement to that of the home islands. After defeating the Russians in the 1904 war, Japan was free to establish a one-sided protectorate over the Korean peninsula in 1905. Five years later, it annexed Korea outright after failing to stamp out Korean resistance with half-measures. The Japanese then turned Korea into a full-blown colonial police state. They showed the Koreans no mercy whatsoever.

As only one example of Japan's tyranny, the rice grown on the peninsula was forcibly taken and the subject population was fed with the inferior and highly unpopular barley and millet imported from Manchuria.

The economic development which took place in the form of railroads, port facilities, and mines was done to benefit the imperial Japanese economy. Period. As for the Koreans themselves, the Japanese could not have cared less.

At only one point did the Japanese overlords ever loosen their hold a bit. After World War I, Japan's governor-general made some conciliatory gestures because of the worldwide popularity of Wilsonian principles of self-determination.

That liberal mood would not last long, however. By 1931, in reaction to Korean restlessness, the Japanese army put its iron boot down. No dissent of any kind was tolerated. The Korean language was targeted for extinction. It was against the law for the language to be written in any form. Koreans were ordered to register with Japanese names. Worship at Japanese Shinto shrines became obligatory even though there was no history of Shintoism in Korea. It was as if an invading army had ordered Americans to become Hindus and speak Hungarian.

Because Koreans were kept close to starvation—a hungry people have no time to think of revolution, only of feeding themselves and their young and helpless—more than a million were forced to go to Manchuria to work in Japanese-run mines and mills. A million more were sent to Japan to be factory workers. Working conditions were horrible. The worst part of it was that these Korean workers were little more than slaves with families torn apart.

Thousands were exported to the Pacific where, in combat conditions, they were forced to build military facilities for the Japanese army and navy. Tens of thousands of defenseless Koreans died, caught innocently in the crossfire. The Japanese only recently have offered an apology and some compensation. Full "compensation" is impossible. The real cost, even to the buoyant Japanese economy, would simply be too high.

But the Japanese and two wars were not the only scourges suffered by the Korean people. Their whole history is a bloody tale of one foreign invasion after another. There were, of course, brilliant periods of independence and high civilization such as the Silla Kingdom of the eighth and ninth centuries and the apex of the Yi dynasty during the fifteenth and sixteenth centuries.

Far more common, however, were internal division and its inevitable consequence, foreign conquest. Korea has, with one notable exception, suffered nothing but evil from outsiders. The country endured 148 invasions between the beginning of the Koryo dynasty in 918 A.D. and the Japanese annexation in 1910. Invaders have included Chinese (of various dynasties), the Mongols in the thirteenth century, and the Japanese in the sixteenth century. They all fought to possess the strategically placed peninsula. Only the Chinese at various times left the Koreans with anything of value, Confucian thought in particular.

As a natural response to these repeated man-made disasters, the Koreans attempted to insulate themselves from the outside world. From the early seventeenth century until the late nineteenth century, Korea became the Hermit Kingdom, where foreign travel was forbidden—it was against the law to build oceangoing vessels—and no foreigners were allowed into Korea. The penalty, incidentally, was death.

Predictably, Korea's insularity produced a stagnation that made

Japan's early twentieth-century conquest a relatively easy affair. Korea became a backward and impoverished backwater which fell far behind its Asian neighbors, let alone the newly powerful nations of the West.

Despite their bitter experience with foreigners and their own penchant for going it alone, the Koreans proved to be a remarkably resilient people. They had to be. The alternative was cultural and even physical extinction.

The only grand exception to the bitter rule was the United States. To the surprise of Koreans, north and south, President Harry Truman ordered U.S. forces to stem the communist tide. Without American intervention, Pyongyang under Soviet and Chinese tutelage would have been the master of the peninsula—a dagger directed at Japan. The Americans, unlike all other visitors to Korea, demanded nothing in return for their efforts. Indeed, with large aid programs, the United States effectively rebuilt shattered South Korea. To this day, the U.S. remains the country's leading trade partner, absorbing—as a growing number of American politicians have pointed out—a large trade imbalance.

The seemingly inexplicable American generosity—wholly unique in Korea's entire several thousand-year history—made a profound impression on an entire generation of Koreans. Only lately have some of the new generation of Koreans, who missed the war and its bitter aftermath, had the luxury of questioning the American alliance.

But American influence is of relatively recent origin. The U.S. first appeared in the south after the defeat of Japan. The Soviets occupied the north as a result of their declaration of war on the Japanese empire six days before that country's surrender. The dividing line, the indefensible thirty-eighth parallel, was agreed upon at Yalta and reaffirmed at the post-Roosevelt Potsdam Conference of the wartime allies.

Under that agreement, for five years all of Korea was supposed to be under the joint trusteeship of the United States, Great Britain, the Republic of China, and the Soviet Union. Elections were supposed to be organized for the entire peninsula, but Moscow refused to play the democratic game in Korea just as it had in Eastern Europe. Elections in the south were held anyway in July

1948, and after the government of President Syngman Rhee took office the following month, American military forces began to withdraw from the peninsula.

In turn, the Soviets established a typical "people's republic" and placed their agent Kim Il-Sung on the throne. But Moscow's forces did not withdraw. Instead, the Soviets directed a crash program to construct a formidable Korean war machine.

Still, what the United States did in 1945 was not the first time America had influenced Korea. Sixty years earlier, American missionaries arrived for the first time on the peninsula. What they did set in motion the second major influence that shaped Sun Myung Moon and, indeed, much of contemporary Korean culture.

As I indicated earlier, the Moons were humble farmers who accepted Christianity in 1930. The impact that had on the lives of two adults and eight children can scarcely be imagined.

The effect of the coming of Christianity for the Moons and the other farmers and fishermen of the small villages which hugged the Yellow Sea can hardly be exaggerated. On top of that the Moons had become Presbyterians. The Presbyterian church encouraged literacy so each could read the Bible for himself—and herself. And they read and reread the canon, interpreting the ancient texts and fitting them to their own limited experience of time and place.

Sun Myung Moon himself was ten before he attended his first Presbyterian service. He soon began reading the Bible to himself and learned to recite Christian creeds and prayers, from the Lord's Prayer to the Nicene Creed.

Of those early years, Moon told some of his American followers in 1965:

> I had a very strong desire to live a life of higher dimension. When I was 12 years old, I started praying for extraordinary things. I asked for wisdom greater than Solomon's, for faith greater than Apostle Paul's, and for love greater than the love of Jesus.

Four years later on a cold Easter Sunday morning, April 17, 1936, the young Moon was praying on a mountainside near his home when, according to Moon, the spirit of Jesus Christ appeared to him and spoke at length about the state of Christianity and the world.

The visionary Jesus told the Korean lad to continue his mission on earth so that mankind would, finally after two thousand years, receive God's full message to the world.

Moon refused. In fact, he refused twice. Finally, he relented. Years later he would tell his followers that he had done so for two reasons. First, if he did not take on the job, the Lord might not find anyone else. Second, Moon knew that if he began the messianic mission on his own, he would have the option of giving up at some point in the future. If he made the promise to another, in this case Jesus, then he would be bound to see it through to the end.[1]

Like St. Paul after the vision on the road to Damascus, Sun Myung Moon spent the next few years in study, prayer, and fasting. And like Paul and other saints such as St. Anthony, Moon sought solitude, where he struggled with the great cosmic forces of evil.

Combining ancient Christian heritage with Buddhist self-abnegation, Moon adopted early a life of physical discipline of an utterly rigid self-denial. It was fortunate that he did. Without that training, it's unlikely he would have survived the trials ahead.

Moon, however, was no hermit. He continued in the world, gaining a formal education, first at an old-fashioned Korean school which taught Confucian virtues and classical Chinese learning and later at a technical junior high school where he first studied electrical engineering. He followed a pattern typical of restless and ambitious farmboys around the world.

Having exhausted all possibilities of further formal learning in impoverished and backward Korea, Sun Myung Moon then went to the metropolitan Tokyo.

It was 1939, and although Japan's prestigious public universities were forbidden to the inferior Koreans, the Koreans were allowed to attend private schools. And that is what Moon did. He entered Waseda University—supposedly one of the best—and continued his education in electrical engineering.

The young Korean was nineteen and already physically tough. He needed to be. A Korean student in a hostile and militaristic Japan bent on further conquest—the brutal bombing of Shanghai had occurred two years before—Moon should have treaded softly while carrying no stick at all.

While he pursued his studies, Moon had to support himself through physical labor. His family was too poor to pay for his education. He labored at a coal works—at that time coal was Japan's chief source of energy. The coal came from the captured mines of Korea's north and Manchuria (now styled *Manchuko*).

In his spare time, Moon kept up his religious studies. A fellow Korean student recalls that Moon read, marked, and inwardly digested the Bible in three languages: Korean, English, and Japanese.

Sun Myung Moon, however, was not simply an overly bookish boy from the Korean provinces. He also became a political activist leader—a quite dangerous thing to be in pre-war Japan. Along with other Korean students, Moon demonstrated for Korea's freedom from Japanese control. The results were more than predictable.

For his troubles, he was picked up by the security police several times, interrogated, and brutally tortured.

When he refused to divulge the names of his fellow "conspirators," the security police relented and he was let go.

For Moon, the youthful rebellion against his Japanese masters was not purely political in intent. Instead, as he would later recall, it was an act that was as religious as it was political.

Theology and politics became inextricably intertwined in Moon's mind—a source of much confusion to friends and critics of the Unification Church alike. But always, Moon insisted, his political views were driven by a deeper religious belief.

His late 1930s university-based protest—indeed, his entire life in Japan—seemed to him to be comparable to Moses' time in Pharaonic Egypt: a sojourn in a hostile land where he would be tested in order to learn God's will and how best to serve and save his people.

But before that he would have to spend nearly the entire war in Japan. And Tokyo was increasingly dangerous. By 1944 air raids carried out by giant four-engine American B-29s—the Superfortresses—rained death on Japanese cities.

Moon survived, however, and by early 1945 he was once more in Korea, which was, not surprisingly, a backwater of the war. For all the hardships of the Koreans, the war itself was a relatively remote affair for the people of the peninsula.

Sun Myung Moon was nearly twenty-five when he returned to

his homeland. The Japanese were still in charge, wielding their whips over the despised Koreans. Job prospects, especially in the professions, were virtually nil for any returning Korean student.

Young Moon showed no real interest in becoming an electrical engineer—at least full time. His mind was on God, and Unification historians agree that by the time of his return from "Egypt," Moon was eager to begin his mission.

Instead of returning home or even to Pyongyang, Moon settled in Seoul, then and now the peninsula's largest city. His idea was to find existing Christian groups and try to convince them of his special mission: the one commissioned by Jesus on the mountaintop a decade earlier in 1936.

Moon found no immediate takers despite the fact that religious enthusiasm was again at a peak in Korea. He finally found his first spiritual home in Seoul three months after Korea's liberation from Japan—that is, in mid-November 1945.

Moon targeted a church run by one Elder Kim, a mainline Protestant who ran a seminary and ministered to a large congregation in the South Korean capital.

Sun Myung Moon might have remained in that church, but Kim would not accept Moon's claim to be on a special mission as Korea's prophet. Kim's rejection of Moon was soon followed by that of other church leaders in Seoul. All that Moon was capable of doing, it seemed, was to attract individual parishioners from other congregations; he never won over organized churches as a whole.

The cold reception in Seoul did inspire a change in his plans. According to Moon in later years, he was told by God in a vision to return to the north. That was in June 1946, several months after meeting Elder Kim.

By this time, Korea had been divided de facto into two spheres of influence: Russian and American. And they were growing further apart by the day. Moscow, for example, had already rejected the U.N. resolution calling for Korea-wide general elections, and it had prevented the U.N. Commission on Korea from crossing the thirty-eighth parallel.

In the meantime, by early 1946 the Soviets had set up a Provisional People's Committee for North Korea stacked with Russian-trained Korean communists who had spent the war in the Soviet

Union. Backing this Soviet-imposed committee was a Russian-trained, twenty-thousand-man North Korean police force. By August, it had become the Korean People's Army.

The young Kim Il-Sung would make the arrangement official by naming himself premier two years later.

Despite the growing communist cloud, the north's provisional capital was alive with Christian fervor, far greater than that in Seoul. New churches were multiplying in the north and communist persecution of Christians (as well as all other religions) at first only increased their zeal. In mid-1946 a revival—perhaps Korea's most fervent—broke out in Pyongyang. Church bells called the faithful daily to 5:00 A.M. prayer services. Because tens of thousands showed up at these affairs, the small buildings that passed for churches could not hold them and soon the Pyongyang revival became an outdoor spectacular.

The communists, needless to say, were alarmed by this outpouring of religious enthusiasm. To their credit as Machiavellians, they understood that religious belief could not be destroyed in one fell swoop. Instead, Kim Il-Sung moved slowly to close the churches. He also knew that since the end of the war no fewer than 170 new sects had emerged in his country. The sects were often a colorful combination of orthodox Christianity and native beliefs, producing a bewildering variety of doctrines, creeds, and practices.

Fortunately for the communists, the older, established Christian denominations did not get along with the newcomers. And among the latter there was often a rivalry which came close to open warfare. Koreans like to win, and the timid concepts of Confucianism and traditional Buddhism held no great attraction for them. Christianity, with its more aggressive, pugnacious ethic, better fitted the Korean temperament.

The rivalry also suited Kim Il-Sung's needs quite handily.

Sun Myung Moon eventually became one of many targets in Kim's scheme to wipe out the Christian movement in the north—once and for all.

In Pyongyang, Moon added to the general religious uproar by preaching in the city's squares. Some local Christians considered him dangerous and more than welcomed the police who forced him to move on. Still, he persisted. Although after two years Moon had won only a handful of followers, he had at least become well known in the communist capital.

Moon got his first break in Pyongyang when he linked himself to a charismatic leader who happened to be a woman. This Korean woman evangelist, Ho Bin Hur, had attracted a relatively large following. According to Unification Church accounts, she and her followers prepared special clothes for the coming Second Advent of the Lord. They made three suits and three robes for each year of Jesus' life. At each stage, the group was guided by revelations received by its prophetess leader.

At one point, she received a revelation that Jesus had not had enough food to eat when he was alive, so they began preparing huge meals for him.

Her most distinctive belief? Christ would be born again in Korea from a mother's womb. Thus, her sect's name: *Bok Joong Gyo*, or Inside-Belly Church.

Her success was so great that her flock was able to purchase one of the few decent homes in Pyongyang to serve as a sanctuary. As one of the city's stranger religious groups, *Bok Joong Gyo* was a prime target for police repression. On August 11, 1947, the preacher, her husband, and the twenty-seven-year-old Sun Myung Moon were rounded up by the government police. They were accused of deceiving people and enriching themselves at the expense of their followers—a not-unfamiliar charge.

In North Korea the consequences were severe. While in jail, Moon, believing his arrest was a sign from God, passed a message to the woman urging her to understand his mission and work for him rather than the other way around. That message written on a chopstick wrapper was thrown away by the lady preacher and soon found its way to prison officials.

The chopstick message earned Moon a rigorous interrogation from the police and then torture.

The episode was reminiscent of his experience at the hands of Japanese police during his college days. Indeed, the North Koreans used methods of torture learned during forty years of domination by the Japanese.

But this time, for Moon, the torture was much more brutal. He was hung up from the ceiling with his hands tied behind his back.

Beaten until he was unconscious, he was cut loose to drop to the cement floor, doused with water until he came to, only to be strung up and beaten again.

This procedure was repeated until he couldn't be revived.

At the end of October, after more than six weeks in jail, the would-be prophet was thrown out the back door of the police station, half dead from internal bleeding, into a snowdrift.

Luckily some of his few followers found him and nursed Moon back to health with herbal medicines.

At first, he vomited blood every day. His condition was so grave at one point that his followers began preparing for his funeral.

Even for the physically durable Moon, recovery was not easy—it took three months.

Moon, inspired by the persecution, once more returned to the squares of Pyongyang and once again began to preach. This time he began to attract followers. Unfortunately, the converts came from existing churches. This, of course, annoyed the local clergy just as it had done in Seoul. They, in turn, wrote letters to the communist authorities, who arrested him one more time.

But this time it was no ordinary detention. Moon was put on trial the following April. It became, in fact, something of a show trial, one which piqued the interest of North Korean communist officials from surrounding provinces. It was meant to be a textbook example of how Christianity should be suppressed in a model communist state.

The trial lasted one day in a not-quite-completed courtroom. The room was jammed with Christians, communists, and Moon's few followers. The prisoner, head shaved and hands manacled, was charged with "advocating chaos in society." After some perfunctory questioning of Moon by the prosecution, the complaints from other Christians were read and the verdict was pronounced.

Moon received a five-year sentence to be served at the Tong Nee Special Labor Concentration Camp in the port town of Hungnam, some one hundred miles northeast of the capital.

Tong Nee was not a pleasant place. In fact, it was a slave labor camp whose fifteen hundred prisoners loaded sacks of nitrogen fertilizer on railroad cars bound for the Soviet Union. North Korea's exports from Hungnam were partial payment for the Russian arms that Kim Il-Sung was desperate to obtain.

The factory complex had been built by the Japanese before the war, and at that time it had been the largest plant of its kind in Asia. It was meant to revive Korean agriculture for the benefit, naturally, of the foodstuff-hungry home islands.

The Hungnam complex had been manned by a Korean labor force who had little to say about its running. Nothing had changed when the Korean communists assumed command.

The regimen was brutal.

First, the hardened fertilizer had to be blasted loose by primitive hand tools. Then the inmates, Moon among them, filled eighty-pound rice straw sacks with the chemicals. The ten-man work groups had a quota of 1,200 to 1,500 bags per day. For those teams which did not meet the goal, their already skimpy food ration of boiled millet, sea weed soup, or polished rice was withheld.

Prisoners' families were allowed to bring in supplementary food packages, and Sun Myung Moon's mother would make the journey bringing rice powder, wheat, and barley. These visits to Tong Nee, in fact, were the last occasions on which Moon saw his mother. In the chaos of the war which soon followed, the whole family—Moon excepted—disappeared in the night and fog.

In the meantime, prisoner Moon had to learn to survive. Inmates were expected to live only six months. Many did not survive that long.

Short on food and rest, and overworked besides, prisoners also faced the special discipline of Tong Nee. Prisoners, for example, were required to write letters of self-criticism every month to the camp commandant. Sun Myung Moon, prisoner 586, refused.

Otherwise, he kept quiet. Preaching in camp of course was forbidden. Instead, he kept his discipline of prayer and performed a variety of good deeds for other prisoners, including sharing his already pathetically inadequate food ration.

Much later he would tell his followers about those years:

I never prayed from weakness: I never complained: I was never angry at my situation: I never even asked His help, but was always busy comforting Him and telling Him not to worry about me.[2]

To outsiders, such a statement might seem presumptuous. After all, an ego big enough to presume to comfort God Almighty is an ego strong enough to overcome anything, including a stint in a North Korean concentration camp.

Students of the concentration camp experience know that the survivors are very special human beings. They must have the self-discipline to act and to function without resignation, self-pity, or useless anger.

Sun Myung Moon was obviously one of those individuals. In the first few months of imprisonment he gave away half of his meager ration. His generosity proved to be an effective survival tactic. Simply, Moon learned to live on next to nothing and when he resumed eating his full allowance, it seemed like enough.

Life at Tong Nee was never easy. Moon contracted malaria in the camp and suffered horribly from chemical burns caused by the nitrogen fertilizer.

It was not "safety first" at Tong Nee.

But it did not last forever either. Moon, in fact, never finished his sentence. After he had spent nearly three years at the death camp, the North Koreans decided to make some changes. In the spring of 1950, Kim Il-Sung was preparing for war with the south. Even Tong Nee was not exempt from the effort. Camp officials began to separate the prisoners into categories. The young and fit were to be drafted into the growing North Korean army. Political prisoners with long sentences were useless and promptly executed. Others were shipped out to Chinese-held Manchuria.

A few months after this process began, the North Koreans attacked the south, en masse, crossing the thirty-eighth parallel and throwing the Republic's lightly armed troops back to a small enclave around the southern port town of Pusan.

Life at Tong Nee, however, did not seriously change until August 1950, when American B-29 bombers, left over from the Tokyo run, raided Hungnam. Their target? The Tong Nee factory complex.

The U.S. Air Force did a thorough job. Three hours of bombing demolished Tong Nee. While workers and officials had bomb shelters, the prisoners were left out in the rain of 250-pound bombs. Many died. Those remaining had their new assignments expedited. No wonder.

The following account of Moon's release was given by Won Pil

Kim on October 14, 1978, exactly twenty-eight years after Moon was released from Tong Nee:

> The frontlines of the war were changing in favor of the U.N. forces. They landed in Hungnam even before they reached Pyongyang. The communist jailkeepers were desperate and began executing the prisoners. . . . They called out the prisoners by number and gave them the order to bring with them three days' food rations and shovels. They deceived the prisoners into believing that they were being transferred to another prison, but in actuality they were being taken to a nearby mountain where they would dig their own graves before being mowed down by gunfire.
> However, before they got to all the prisoners in the cell, the U.N. forces, which had already landed at Hungnam, started marching to the city. The communists could not cope with the crisis, and leaving the prisoners behind, ran for their lives. . . . It was October 14, 1950.

Moon left Hungnam for Pyongyang, one hundred miles away. He was fortunate again despite the difficulty of the trek.

As he reached the outskirts of the capital, so did the U.N. forces driving in from the south. Kim's Russian-trained and equipped army had simply collapsed in the aftermath of the Inchon landings. The aggressors, in short, had taken a terrible beating.

Now a free man, Moon searched for what remained of his followers in the rubble of war. Despite his single-mindedness, he could find only a few of the faithful from the old days. One of them, Jung Hua Pak, had shared the hard life of Tong Nee with him. The rest—and there were not many—were straining to survive.

The respite from communism in Pyongyang was a brief one; three months later the Chinese volunteers who had crossed the Yalu in November once more took the northern capital.

Moon, still in search of disciples, waited until the last moment to evacuate in early December. He left with only two followers—Pak and Won Pil Kim—all that remained from his Pyongyang and Tong Nee days.

To be a refugee is never an easy experience—especially when one is putting distance between oneself and the communists. This particular exodus, however, was worse than usual. It was already well into the harsh Korean winter: howling north winds frequently accompanied temperatures of ten and twenty degrees below zero.

The primitive roads and mountain passes were not only clogged with ice and snow, but jammed with soldiers, their equipment, and millions of terrified men, women, and children desperate to escape the Chinese and what remained of Kim Il-Sung's rabble army.

Making matters even worse for Moon, Pak's leg had been broken in Pyongyang by a mob who found out that he had once been a North Korean army officer.

Besides the clothes on their backs, the three possessed a couple of rucksacks and a bicycle. It was a most unlikely escape. Nevertheless, they did escape.

Won Pil Kim recalled:

> At that time, it was common for many to leave their wives and children behind because of the inclement weather, for they thought they would return home in a matter of a few days.

Those few days have since stretched into thirty-nine years.

At first, Pak rode on the bike while Moon and Kim pushed. When that proved too painful, Pak was hoisted on Moon's back where he clung for the remainder of the tortuous journey. Despite the terrible conditions, no food, and sub-zero weather, Moon forced-marched eighteen miles a day with Pak on his back until the trio arrived at the port city of Haeju on Korea's west coast, seventy miles due south of Pyongyang—only days ahead of the Chinese.

Kim recalled:

> We had to cross over part of the sea to get to an island about two and a half miles from the shore. We had to wait until the tide was out in order to cross. We had just walked almost 25 miles the night before and didn't arrive at the shore until one or two o'clock in the morning.
>
> Now I had to carry the bike on my backpack, while Father Moon carried Mr. Pak, who was about his own weight and size, on his back. It was pitch dark, of course. A tiny oil lamp was burning on the island, and that was the only thing we could really see. At least it was a reliable guidepost.
>
> The sea was still deep in many places at low tide, and we had no way of knowing where it was shallow and safe for us to walk. It was very perilous, to say the least. If we stayed in one spot a few seconds too

long, our feet could sink too deep for us to pull them out and go on. . . .

We finally made it to the island. . . .

They had hoped to catch a boat and escape in relative safety and comfort across the Yellow Sea. These frail fishing craft were already loaded with desperate refugees, and the three men with their Japanese-built two-wheeler turned southeast, crossing the frozen Imjin River near the thirty-eighth parallel.

We pushed forward, walking over the ice. Many airplanes were zooming low over our heads; we heard the strafing from the air and machine guns were returning the fire from the ground.
We realized that perhaps the Chinese communists were already close by. Across the river, the U.N. soldiers were putting up barricades to defend the last battle line.

They arrived in Seoul, ironically, on Christmas Eve nearly three weeks after fleeing Pyongyang.

Wartime Seoul proved to be no haven. The three of them, with their prisoner haircuts, were frequently stopped by suspicious South Korean police and were forced to recite their unlikely tale. Because none of them qualified for the volunteer army, they eventually got refugee cards—the first official papers any of them had possessed since entering Tong Nee.

Less than a week after their status had been determined, however, the evacuation of Seoul was announced. Once more Moon and his tiny flock headed south, first along the eastern range of the Sobaek mountains, then through the centuries-old Moongyeong Gate, and finally to the ancient capital of the Silla dynasty, Kyongju.

In Kyongju, the exhausted Pak, claiming that his leg was better, asked to stay in the old capital, at least for a while. Moon and Kim, however, walked another twenty miles south to Ulsan, where they caught a cargo train and held onto its sides for the thirty-five remaining miles to Pusan and safety.

For Moon, the odyssey from Hungnam to Pusan was five hundred miles long; it had taken four and a half months.

By that time U.N. troops were counter-attacking further north, relieving Pusan from any immediate worries over liberation by the

Chinese. That, too, was another miracle, and Moon was grateful to the U.N. forces, especially the American Eighth Army which, along with the ROK troops, bore the brunt of the fighting.

Sun Myung Moon had proved at least one thing by the end of January 1951. He was a survivor, a brilliant survivor who showed an amazing ability to save himself, as well as others, under the most extremely adverse conditions imaginable. Beyond his extraordinary determination, however, he had little to show for his missionary efforts. Although he had suffered the disappointments of St. Paul, it must be said that, for all the risks run and the pain suffered, Moon had gathered but one follower by the time he arrived in Pusan: Won Pil Kim.

Pusan was a mess. The port city had become home for thousands of refugees uprooted in a war which would not end for another two years. There were formal refugee camps, of course, but many lived with friends and relatives in crowded wood and tin shacks. The especially bitter winter of 1950-51 added to the misery. Only Pusan's port helped keep the city alive.

Sun Myung Moon was one of the lucky ones. Although malnourished, bearded, and grimy, his once white clothes almost black from grease and dirt, he was recognized by a fellow student from Japan: Duk Moon Aum, who was now an architect and generously offered his classmate shelter.

Moon accepted, and went back to his life of hard labor, working in the busiest place in town: the docks. In his spare time, he rested and prayed and gave free haircuts to the bedraggled refugees.

Still, Moon went days at a time without food. To make some extra money he and his disciple, Won Pil Kim, began to paint souvenir pictures of American soldiers. They worked from photographs, using oil paints applied to a stiff card. It brought in a trickle of money, barely enough for survival.

Won Pil Kim recalled the time:

I had a job painting the barracks of a U.S. Army post. As a joke, I did a portrait of someone there. Father took one look at it and encouraged me to do more. I did this work in spare moments after my day's work at the U.S. Army post. When I came home after 5 o'clock with new orders, I would start painting right away and continue until midnight or one o'clock in the morning. But before I got home, Father had already bought the necessary supplies, and he made the frames as well. He watched over my shoulder until I finished. When I went to bed, he stayed up to frame the portraits and he would have them all ready for me by the next morning.

Soon the painting venture became a regular assembly line. Won Pil Kim would paint only the heads and Moon would do the uniforms and background and framing.

By July Moon had also built, with his own hands, a primitive hut on a hillside near Pusan. The hut was hardly more than a lean-to made of earth, rock, tin, wood, and cardboard from U.S. Army ration boxes. The floor was sand and covered with typically Korean straw mats. It served as church and home.

Twenty-four years later Moon recalled that first church:

The original home was much smaller . . . there was no room to lie down, except diagonally. The surroundings were not so holy. . . . We built a ditch to lead the water out of the house. This was the first Unification Church under the sun. Can you imagine who would ever visit us?

With his humble church intact, the thirty-year-old Moon began to dream of things to come:

I went to the mountain to pray many hours. I would look at the ships in the harbor, and think of how I would reach the other ends of the world. . . .

The Moon hovel soon had its first visitor, a woman who was also a minister. She had heard of the odd religious couple living on the hillside and hoped to convert them. Instead, she was converted herself.

By this time, Moon had also begun transcribing his revelations, which were laboriously taken down by pencil in two worn note-books. Often he woke Won Pil Kim in the middle of the night so that he could read back what Moon had dictated earlier.

These jottings became part of the Unification Church's central source of doctrine, the *Divine Principle*. Pusan, however, was hardly a stunning mission success, at least on a visible level. In nearly a year, Moon had only attracted two other followers, the female preacher and Hyo Won Eu, a cripple who nevertheless became Moon's first lecturer, an eloquent orator who usually spoke from a stretcher.

As a consequence, Moon moved once more to the north. His first stop was Taegu, some sixty miles northwest of Pusan, and there he experienced some success. Initially.

His preaching began to attract converts. Moon was now a polished public speaker with a powerful message. He was lean, strongly built from years of hard labor, and still young. Being a true survivor, he also had a forceful and confident personality.

Taegu's women flocked to hear the preacher from Pusan. All in all, it was Sun Myung Moon's first missionary success. Except for one thing. The husbands of Taegu were outraged. Added to the chorus of male complaints were the usual noises of disapproval coming from the established churches.

Late in 1953 Moon headed again for Seoul, and six months later he had attracted enough followers to found officially his movement. On May 1, 1954, the movement was called the Holy Spirit Association for the Unification of World Christianity. The name was a mouthful, but it accurately summed up Sun Myung Moon's message. In abbreviated form the organization became known as the Unification Church: *Tongil Kyohe* in Korean.

The Reverend Sun Myung Moon and his flock soon found their first permanent headquarters: an old Shinto shrine which they renovated. To overcome the church's total obscurity, Moon circulated a typed two-page proclamation in "Korean English." It was sent to Western embassies and military installations.

That message proclaimed to "Dear Persons, Christians and Other Religionists, Truth Researchers":

> Our association is ready to speak the following subjects any time at your request to any-body who is especially interested in truth, "Where human-kind is Destined to go", unknown fact in the Bible, and new interpretation of the Bible, etc. . . .[3]

Having whetted the appetites of the readers, the new church promised more:

> Once you hear by accident even one of the subject any time you will be inspired soon, and you will find yourself in Holy Spirit. We are

spreading new truth to every person in the world by ordinance of the Lord, Father of human-kind. . . . DO NOT miss the chance to hear while you stay in Korea. New ideal world is approaching day by day awaiting the "Latter Day," of the earth-final judgement.[4]

Despite this earnest and first appeal to the West, there is no record of any foreign resident in Seoul taking interest in the new church.

Still, Seoul was not without possibilities. Moon's flock was growing and he had a base of operations. But the old troubles from Taegu soon made their appearance.

Women loved most to hear the new prophet announce the Lord's new dispensation. Why not? He was attractive, sincere, and charismatic. What's more, he exuded confidence, and those who listened were struck by this man who appeared to know what he was talking about. Because it was difficult to stop the Reverend Sun Myung Moon from preaching, services often went past midnight and curfew hour.

The men and women, therefore, had to spend the night in the old Shinto temple, now decked out in red paint.

Husbands and fathers were in a dither and Moon would have to watch his step.

That was only the beginning of his problems in Seoul. Soon there was more trouble; this time with a twist. In late 1954 the president of Ehwa University, a Methodist women's college, decided to launch her own investigation of the new Unification Church. She had heard that students from Ehwa and Seoul University were hanging about the old Shinto shrine, turned Christian-sect headquarters, and that bothered her.

So Ehwa's president sent several female faculty members to the little former shrine on Pak Hak Dong Street for a first-hand report. The uproar at Ehwa went into hyper-drive when the investigators and three other faculty members joined the Reverend Sun Myung Moon's church instead. They took with them a hundred students. Faced with expulsion from school, only fourteen remained with Moon. But the professors stuck it out and two of them, Young Oon Kim, who had headed the religion department, and Won Pak Choi, a professor of English, became major figures in the church and among its first missionaries to the United States.

The Ehwa episode took its toll on Moon and his followers. Once again, he had made powerful enemies, including Ehwa's vice president, a woman whose husband happened to be Speaker of the National Assembly, Korea's unicameral legislature, and a regime intimate.

The doughty vice president organized the students' parents into an angry association which promptly filed a formal complaint with the government. They charged that the Reverend Sun Myung Moon was leading a dangerous sex cult—"a church of fornication"—a provocative title that soon found its way into Seoul's newspapers.

That one charge, proven later to be false but which would be recycled in America twenty years later, soon made Sun Myung Moon and his tiny Unification Church famous in Korea. It was not the kind of publicity he was seeking. Many members, especially the younger ones, left under pressure from parents and neighbors. In the tightly knit Korean society, the effect was devastating.

In 1955, within a space of six months, Moon and his remaining band were forced to relocate no fewer than three times. They finally ended up in southern Seoul in a Japanese-style house. Their long Sunday services soon attracted attention. On one occasion a mob lobbed rocks at the house, breaking all the windows and knocking in part of the roof.

The pattern of persecution of Moon and his followers was now well set, and only the hardiest of the faithful remained to enjoy their hard-won notoriety.

Sun Myung Moon's troubles did not end with angry parents and irate neighbors. In July 1955, some of Seoul's "finest" picked up the preacher on a Monday morning and subjected him to an all-night grilling.

Moon was placed under arrest and four other followers were picked up for good measure. Later they were transferred to the high-security Sudaemun prison where they were placed in separate cells. While they were in jail, the church struggled on, with little money and no charismatic leader. It all but shut down.

The Reverend Sun Myung Moon, fortunately, was no longer in North Korea. His compatriots were soon released, though Moon himself spent three months in jail before going to trial. Needless to say, the Moon case was the talk of Seoul in 1955. The Ehwa parents presented their charges of sexual misconduct and the government added a count of draft evasion. Despite Moon's innocence, few would have predicted an acquittal.

Nevertheless, he was found not guilty on all charges and in October of that year he was set free by a reluctant Korean court. It was the last time that the leader of the Unification Church would run afoul of the law in Korea, north or south.

The cost of his notoriety was high. Almost ten years later, church membership was a relatively modest 32,491 attending some 891 churches.[5]

What did the struggling little Korean church look like in the 1950s after its time of troubles? A word snapshot of the movement was provided by a visiting American missionary who had been stationed in Australia. The Reverend Joseph McCabe arrived in Seoul in June 1956 and was warmly welcomed by Moon and his crippled aide Eu, who had stuck with the leader since the old Pusan days.

McCabe noted that among Moon's followers were two college professors, two physicians, an ex-labor minister, and a Korean air force colonel.

The Unification theology, McCabe tactfully noted, was not quite Pentecostal, "yet the Spirit of the Lord [is] manifest among them, as some have visions, others have tongues and interpretations, while a spirit of prophecy is exercised by others in private. . . ."

McCabe wondered at the power of Moon's preaching and prayer and the resultant "fervor and sincerity" of the worshippers.

As for the physical environment, the American observed:

The meeting place is an old hall in an out of the way spot. . . . I reckon the Seoul hall is the most inaccessible I have been in. There are no seats as in other churches: everyone sits on the floor. Half an hour before the service is due to begin we have a time of singing, and the place is packed. . . . It is a hive of spiritual activity.[6]

McCabe also observed the emphasis on teaching, lecturer Eu carrying the main burden by talking from five to six hours a day from the *Divine Principle*. Church doctrine could be covered in two days and examinations were administered frequently. Classes ranged from as few as five or six to as many as thirty or forty.

In 1956, McCabe estimated that the Unification Church totalled no more than 1,200. Sunday services attendance in Seoul
ranged between 300 and 400.[7]

The Unification Church grew slowly throughout the 1950s in
Korea, but at the end of the decade its doctrine and practices were
well set. The *Divine Principle* had already been translated into
English. That 1959 edition is still the official version used by the
American church.

Some of the church's best-known practices were also part of the
ritual. The seven-day fast to be observed in the first three years of
church membership had now become a fixed tradition. Arranged
marriages took place in 1960—including the Reverend Sun
Myung Moon's marriage to Hak Ja Han—and the extended evangelical campaigns in search of converts began in 1957—soon to be
dubbed "pioneering" in America.[8]

Sun Myung Moon's prophetic role in the movement had also by
now been well established. After an intense reading of the Bible
following his conversation with the spirit of Jesus, Moon thought
he had worked out the "unsolved mysteries" of the Old and New
Testaments—as many before him had claimed following the Protestant Reformation.[9]

Moon proclaimed that these new ideas were checked with ultimate authority: Jesus and God the Father. In a test of his faith, it is
said, Moon's views were rejected twice, and it was on the third time
that God confirmed his view of Biblical truth.

God was not the only entity featured in these celestial revelations. The Reverend Sun Myung Moon also asserts that he had
conversations with holy men from both the Old and New Testament in order to clarify the most obscure portions of scripture.[10]

These are not small claims. What precisely constitutes the core
of Unification theology? What is the message that the Reverend
Sun Myung Moon wished to transmit throughout the world?

From a layman's point of view it is, in fact, a complex compound
of traditional Christianity, some familiar heresies, and wholly new
material. Little wonder that traditional Christians in Korea and
elsewhere sometimes find themselves uncomfortable in the presence of Sun Myung Moon's theology.

The theology is, first of all, Bible oriented.

As in traditional Christian belief, God created man in his own image. But the first Adam fell into sin. Unification theology holds that he did not do so as traditionalists argue—rebelling against God by eating forbidden fruit. Instead, he (and Eve) did so by engaging in forbidden love, in other words, sexual intercourse at an immature age. According to Moon, their sin was not pride or rebellion, but was explicitly sexual in nature.[11]

God's plan for the redemption of mankind involved the second Adam: Jesus Christ. In that, Unification theology tracks with orthodox Christianity. However, Moon's theology states that Jesus did not complete his mission. By dying on the cross and being resurrected, the core event for conventional Christians, Jesus only gave man spiritual salvation. Mankind was not yet restored to God's original ideal and every human being on earth remained condemned to suffer.

In short, mankind needed a Third Adam to restore mankind to God's own image. The Third Adam, of course, is the Reverend Sun Myung Moon. That astonishing claim raises an interesting question about who is superior to whom in the greater scheme of things. For example, if Jesus did not succeed in the second half of the mission, and Moon has, who is the greater?

Church doctrine indicates that Moon is. A proposition which, needless to say, scandalizes orthodox Christians.

Still, Unificationists claim to be Christian in much the same way that early Christians, particularly those who followed Peter instead of Paul, claimed to be Jews.

The affinity of Unification theology with both Judaism and Christianity is natural because it teaches that God works primarily through Judeo-Christian history in His attempt to save mankind.

The church is close to Judaism in the sense that its view of the messiah is non-trinitarian. It is Christian in that it recognizes the messiahship of Jesus of Nazareth.

Unlike many Christian churches, however, the Unification Church is eclectic. It teaches that there is truth in each of the world's major religions and that God works through those religions.

Church doctrine is a body of thought worked out by Moon over time and with much struggle.

By the late 1950s, it was time for the Korean prophet to move on to other worlds.

With a settled doctrine and a stabilized base in Korea the restless leader began having the same thoughts he had once had on that Pusan hillside looking at the harbor and the world's shipping below.

The time had come, Moon thought, to spread the message beyond the homeland. According to Moon's sense of dispensational geography and salvation history—*heilsgeschicte* to the Germans—God had decreed that Japan and the United States were to work with the "Adam nation," Korea.

These three countries, in unison, would help reconcile humanity with God, and thus heal the rift that had begun in the Garden of Eden six thousand years ago.

The first target: Japan. Only one missionary, a former Christian minister, Sang Ik Choi, was sent there by the church in 1958. Altogether it was an unlikely enterprise. Almost everything about the effort smacked of failure. For example, although the Japanese had lost the war, they still viewed Koreans with utter disdain. Moreover, Moon's notoriety had long since spread to the nearby home islands, and a Unification missionary was not likely to receive a warm welcome.

In fact, Choi was soon jailed for six months because of his overly zealous proselytizing. Japan, in its Grand Tradition, had always treated Christians and near-Christians with the greatest possible caution—that is, when it didn't just execute them. Korean Christianity, however, came in for a good deal worse than the Japanese equivalent of a cold shoulder.

Once Choi got started, however, he could not be stopped. He made inroads into the Japanese Christian community, and even more important, he gained converts among Japanese Buddhists. A former Buddhist leader, for example, became the Japanese Unification Church's first president. In a few years, members in the Japanese church surpassed in numbers their Korean brothers. The Japanese experience taught the Koreans an important skill: how to make money to sustain the church.

It is not terribly surprising that the Japanese would know how to make money. The skill, however, made the difference between modest success and failure for Sun Myung Moon.

Despite strenuous efforts for nearly a decade, the Reverend Sun Myung Moon and his Korean flock were always close to the poverty line. Very little separated Moon in Seoul in 1961 from his 1951 tin-and-cardboard hovel in Pusan.

Moon's church was not much different from other impoverished Korean religious groups of the time. Members had little because the republic itself was desperately poor. Churches with foreign sponsors could eke out a living of sorts. Those without, like the Unification Church, either perished or went into business.

The businesses, at first, were simple ones. Production and sale of ginseng tea—a Korean obsession—marble vases, and simple machine parts. Later, members went into titanium refining.

Because members worked long hours and profits were reinvested and spread around to the various companies, most of these companies were barely kept afloat in the early difficult years when church members knew a lot about the *Divine Principle* and precious little about business.

Real success came only when these products were marketed abroad to the United States and most especially Japan. The basic entity for marketing was Tong-Il Enterprises: the most famous of the Unification businesses.

It was not, however, an immediate success for Tong-Il. Low profits, heavy government red tape, and poor management added up to an uninspiring bottom line.

The Japanese, in fact, taught Sun Myung Moon how to make money—intelligently. Japanese church members started with nothing more than their hands and their heads. No secrets, no gimmicks. They began doing the simplest of things: collecting scrap paper and metal to pay their living expenses while they went about doing their mission in life, witnessing. Scavenging, furthermore, was easy and they could set their own hours rather than punch a Japanese time clock. Later, they learned that selling flowers was even more profitable. It was as flexible as collecting scrap, but it made more money. Highly congested cities filled with people who delighted in a bit of beauty to take home to inadequate housing were a ready-made market for the simplest of God's creations: flowers.

After the flower trade, other businesses were developed. In Japan these enterprises generated millions, and within a few short years, billions, of dollars in revenue.

America, the archangel nation, however, was proving something less than angelic in the early 1960s. After six years of missionary work in San Francisco, for example, precious few Americans showed any interest in the church. East met West and the latter just shrugged.

Not until the late 1960s, when Sang Ik Choi, fresh from his success in Japan, came to California, were any substantial numbers of followers recruited. Even then, his first converts were primarily Asians, not Anglo-Americans. The missionaries persisted, however, and by the early 1970s, the Reverend Sun Myung Moon was ready to take his message personally to America.

The road from Jung-ju had been a long, long one, the suffering and reversals many. Moon had known hard labor, grinding poverty, and physical pain, much pain. He had lost his entire family in a war that had wrecked his nation. He had been persecuted by the police of three countries. He had been thrown into jails and concentration camps where there was little or no chance of survival. Tortured and beaten with rods of iron, he had preached and no one had listened. He had clashed with established churches and been vilified by the very Christians he hoped to convert. He had been pilloried and falsely accused by the press. He had been hounded and threatened by angry parents. He had suffered stoning and assassination attempts at the hands of his countrymen. He had lived through slavery under two of the most brutal regimes of this century and had gone on to complete an epic five-hundred-mile exodus through some of the harshest terrain and deadliest conditions on this planet.

Somehow, the Reverend Sun Myung Moon managed to survive all these adversities.

Now, all he had to do was survive America.

CHAPTER XIII

THE PRESS

News is the first rough draft of history.

BEN BRADLEE

History is bunk!

HENRY FORD

THAT the Reverend Sun Myung Moon has not enjoyed a good press in this country is a gross understatement. His media coverage hasn't been merely bad; it has been devastatingly awful.

Faced with such sustained blasting, Iran-Contra's Ronald Reagan would have been impeached and Watergate's Richard Nixon shot. At least one public relations firm, when hired a few years ago to improve Moon's image, had immediate second thoughts and dropped the account. Why? Because the gents at Burson Marsteller became worried about their image if they should take on the Korean religious leader. That is absolutely nothing unusual for the star-crossed Unification Church and its leader, the Reverend Sun Myung Moon.

The negative image of the Unification Church and Moon has endured, is carved in granite, and is unlikely to change. For most journalists—print or electronic—that is not only a given, it is also meet, right, and salutory that it should be so.

To the scribbling set, Moon, the "Moonies," the Unification

Church and anyone associated with them are all suspects in, if not guilty of, dark and dirty deeds, and beneath contempt. Beyond redemption. Actually, in reviewing the American press' coverage of the church story over the last score of years, my conclusion is that Nazis would have gotten more sympathetic treatment.

Hyperbole at the least?

As Richard Nixon was fond of saying, let's look at the record. After more than twenty years as an investigative reporter, I think I can recognize when a guy is getting a fair shake by the media. I also know lazy journalism and pack reporting when I see it. And I can spot "research" based solely on the newspaper's (or magazine's) clip file. What has been forgotten by many in the media is the old *Chicago News Service*'s dictum: "If your mother tells you she loves you, check it out."

There is also a powerful instinct among reporters to run with the herd. Journalists, like cattle on the range, tend to follow leaders wherever they go, and don't bother to ask questions. That is why the national media—the news magazines, the *New York Times*, and the *Washington Post* in particular—are so powerful.

Little old ladies in Des Moines may not read the *Post* or the *Times*, but the *Register*'s editors do, and they take their cues accordingly. Sometimes it isn't even that indirect. Stories supplied by both major papers' news services are frequently reprinted in the provincial journals.

That circular flow of information often squeezes out aspects of a story that remain unexplored. Little things like the First Amendment.

To digress for a moment.

There is a tradition cherished by this country's free press that holds that the media do not serve the Powers That Be. More than that, there is the belief that not only does the press not pander to the authorities, it takes them on, front and center.

The crusading journalist has long been a part of the national mythology. Like most myths, there is a core of truth there that should not be dismissed lightly.

Solid reporting and letting the chips fall where they may, no matter how unhappy the high and mighty, is the stuff of investigative journalism.

James Gordon Bennett (a Scotsman by birth) of the *New York*

Herald, who was the very prototype of a tough American newsman, said it best: "A newspaper's job is to comfort the afflicted and to afflict the comfortable."

The trouble is that while we often pay lip service to Bennett's credo, we equally often fail to do the job. Good journalism sometimes means going out on a very long limb. It certainly doesn't mean reporting what is fashionable.

During the 1970s, in the throes of Watergate and the frenzy of the press that ensued, the doctrine that the media's role had to be and always was an adversarial one became fashionable. As it turned out, the only adversary was the American government, preferably run by Republicans. Only the U.S. government could stonewall, prevaricate, dissimulate, and lie. The presumption was, it was guilty as charged.

Well, there is a certain amount of truth in that. But it is not revealed truth. And it is awfully simple-minded. And so very selective when it comes to many in contemporary American journalism. But to be selectively adversarial is to serve someone else's agenda. If the American press wants to be taken seriously and, more important, to remain independent of faction and partisanship, then it had better re-examine some of the comfortable assumptions it has entertained for the last couple of decades.

What has this got to do with the Reverend Sun Myung Moon? Consider his story.

Even though much of the press coverage of the Unification Church took place during Watergate and the years just following, the whole situation got turned inside out and backwards. The government was given the benefit of the doubt when some agency launched an investigation—even when it wasn't really the government talking, but mysterious and unnamed "official sources" speaking from behind a cloak of absolute anonymity.

At other times, the government was urged to take on the Unification Church with greater zeal than it had shown. This note was trumpeted from both the news and editorial pages, not to mention the electronic media.

How come the sudden change in the rules?

Fairness and accuracy most certainly were, and are, not the norm in the media treatment of the Reverend Sun Myung Moon and his movement.

The story about the story is not a simple one. In fact, the American press treatment of Moon falls into three periods. The first—which stretches roughly between 1970 and 1973—is the "Look What Crawled from under the Rock" period.

The second is labelled "The Moonie Menace," in which the spectre of an alien nation was raised by our national media, which should have known better but reported otherwise.

Finally, there is stage three which can be summed up as "The Empire Strikes Back."

But before exploring these themes, a question, one I don't quite have the answer to: Why should a small-membership movement (30,000 adherents in America is the biggest number ever claimed) receive so much attention? And the church got attention! From the press, the government, the public. Such odd-duck religious organizations as the Christadelphians and the Theosophists have more members. No, size is not the answer.

Quaintness in their theology? But most religions, including Christianity, have some pretty far-out notions that contradict everyday common sense. Otherwise they would not be revealed religion. Virgin Birth? A Three-in-One God? These concepts may not seem strange to us, but only because we are used to them.

Did God talk to the Reverend Sun Myung Moon? The Almighty has talked to a lot of individuals over the years—and some of them were a little peculiar. From St. Paul to Joan of Arc to Joseph Smith. Did He and his angels really communicate with all, some, or none? Reports of such occurrences are not unprecedented.

How about the church business empire? The Unification Church by even the most liberal accounts took in each year far less than, say, the electronic religious empires of Jim Bakker, Jimmy Swaggart, and, of course, Billy Graham. That doesn't even take into account the mainline denominations who have grown financially fat with bulging stock and bond portfolios.

In fact, it's safe to say that a single Roman Catholic religious order, not the Catholic Church entirely, but a simple religious community like the Franciscans, the Trinitarians, or even the Sisters of Charity or the Little Sisters of the Poor, is far more financially well-heeled than the Unification Church in America could ever hope to be.

Of course there were the allegations of brainwashing and mind control of America's young—much of it pure bunk. But bunk that was never carefully dissected by the press. Why?

When a good portion of American youth in the 1960s was tripping on God-knows-what to God-knows-where, the media treated it as a good story, not a national menace. After all, some of the boys (and girls) in the newsroom were themselves doing a little flying without a license.

But when a small portion of the druggie set got off the chemicals with the help of Puritan lifestyle religious movements like the Unification Church, all hell broke loose. Why?

The story.

Phase I: Look What Crawled from Under the Rock.

Press coverage began slowly in the first years of the Unification Church's mission in America. Although the movement's first adherents kept themselves busy proselytizing—in the early 1960s, especially in the San Francisco Bay area—they drew little attention.

This was not surprising. All sorts of strange things were going on in the Golden Gate City, thanks to the good climate and tolerantly cheerful ambience of California. Who would be apt to notice an obscure Korean-based religion?

Indeed, little really happened until the Reverend Sun Myung Moon himself arrived in America from Korea in 1971 in order to jump-start his American movement. After a dozen years in the United States the church had few members, numbering in the low thousands.

One way to gain followers, of course, was ginning up publicity, a strategy that the church began to follow, starting with a seven-city speaking tour for Moon in early 1972. The tour drew some press, but not much. The *Washington Post*, for example, did an interview with the Reverend Moon for its religion page which sketched out the background of the church and Moon's beliefs, described by the paper as "post-Christian."[1]

The *Post* piece was small potatoes. About the only real publicity the movement received was related to a bus breakdown in Maryland that left church members scrambling to find the funds to repair the vehicle.[2]

Meanwhile, the local papers that were covering the national tour stopovers kept the stories low-keyed. Puff pieces really, based on interviews with church members and short descriptions of the movement's leader and his beliefs.[3]

The bad stuff (press-wise) really started at the beginning of another national tour of twenty-one cities with a brief *New York Times* piece focused on the movement's penchant for mass marriages—in fact, only one example was cited—and the then-recent purchase of two estates, one in Tarrytown, New York, and the other in nearby Irvington.[4]

The *Times* article was only the opening volley compared to a double-barrelled blast of publicity provided by the nation's two biggest news magazines, *Time* and *Newsweek.*

Although the stories were somewhat overshadowed by the Yom Kippur War which had started shortly before the press run, Moon was now national news. The two stories led a healthy and long shelf life in newspaper clip files around the country.[5]

Of the two, the piece in *Time* was the fairer. It also had all the familiar elements of a thousand other stories about Moon. His followers were "well-scrubbed" and "neatly barbered"—this was not a compliment, by the way. Being unkempt and unwashed was still considered fashionable in the 1970s.

Moon's so-called business empire was catalogued, and it was suggested somehow that religion and business (at the time reported to be a paltry $15 million worth) did not mix.

Then there was Moon's odd speaking style. Observed *Time*:

> On stage, Moon sells his ideas like a tub-thumping evangelist slapping his fist into his hand to make a point, belting out his words in enthusiastic Korean which an aide quickly translates.[6]

Moon's lifestyle, felt to be luxurious, was contrasted with the austere life of his followers who devotedly "rise at dawn" to sell flowers, candles, and peanuts on the mean streets of America's cities.

Newsweek was less kind; indeed, openly hostile. The leitmotif was sarcasm and ridicule. As a from-under-the-rock creature, Moon got it with both barrels.

Sample:

Would you believe:
—that the fall of man occurred when Eve was literally seduced by
Satan behind Adam's back?
—that Jesus' mission as "the second Adam" failed because he was
killed before he could find a perfect mate?
—that when the Messiah appears on earth as "the third Adam" he
will restore the Garden of Eden by marrying a perfect mate?
—that the Messiah will be born in the "new Israel"—Korea—by
1980?
—that only the righteous parents who form faithful marriages will
be welcomed into the coming Kingdom of God the Father.[7]

The sneering *Newsweek* editors who put that piece together
revealed more about themselves than they did about the Unification Church.

For example, the Unification Church myth about the Garden of
Eden is no crazier than the orthodox Christian belief that the Fall
recorded in Genesis was precipitated by eating a piece of fruit
from a forbidden tree.

As for Jesus' failure, that particular belief was also held by many
in the gnostic movement which challenged Christian orthodoxy in
the old Roman empire—a rivalry that lasted for centuries.

In short, *Newsweek's* ridicule could also have applied to most
other religious beliefs. But Moon's movement was small and weak.

Aside from the sarcasm, there were the other themes. Luxury
living, of course, and the mass weddings. Also, the church members
were no longer merely well scrubbed, but paramilitary in nature as
well. What passed for paramilitary was a checking of "pocketbooks
and packages" at the door of a Carnegie Hall meeting.

Contemptuous quotes from old Korean rivals are cited and
treated as gospel. Moon's anticommunism was depicted as a mere
ploy to gain official South Korean government support.[8]

The *Time* and *Newsweek* pieces—the first real attention paid by
the national media to the Unification Church—soon found their
way into the clip files of the nation's newspapers from Tampa to
Takoma. Such is the power of these mighty organs of some fact
and lots of opinion.[9]

It was not long before such "Moon-mocking" stories became standard fare for the rest of the press pack. One favorite device was to attend a Moon meeting or a banquet and whack away in the ultra-hip new gonzo journalism style. The chief requirement in this particular approach to news is the liberal use of adjectives and the present tense. Add lots of spleen and venom and no research.

Tom Basham's piece that appeared in the October-November 1973 issue of *Performance* is typical of this school of journalism. He describes a typical "Moonie."

> The look on this guy's face is unearthly. He is about 22 years old, wears neat, wire-rimmed glasses, and a conservative brown suit, has close-cut blonde hair and resembles the earnest chemistry majors who assisted Fred McMurray in "Son of Flubber."[10]

The paragraph is a classic. It conveys no real information at all. It leaves only the impression of a writer who is showing off. Even the stereotype is not original. Of course, a reference to a movie or a television show must be included. Literary allusions are out. *Son of Flubber* is going to be recognized by his public.

Having started a portrait of a church nerd, why let so much fun go?

Thus, the second paragraph:

> He is a disciple of the Rev. Sun Myung Moon, intercepting would-be gate crashers at the banquet kicking off the Reverend's Washington lectures. He is standing outside the Continental ball room of the Sheraton-Hilton with this benevolent, spaced out expression on his all-American face.[11]

The all-American face crack is no compliment either. But he has not finished with his victim quite yet.

> Is this guy on something? That humanoid smile, those glazed eyes, that kind but firm hand on your elbow as he parks you just outside the entrance doors and tells you radiating peace, love and salvation—to wait here.[12]

The aren't-I-clever? reporting approach to church members was just beginning to become popular as was the fixed description of members as Zombies.

The followers were only part of the story as Basham demonstrated in his piece. The real target was the Korean at the podium. Here's how Basham saw him:

[Moon's] subject is God's hope for Man and his approach is complementarity [*sic*]. God the object, man the subject: God the alpha, man the omega. Most religions place God too high. Man and God must be brought closer together, like father and son. Life is a circle. He sounds like daffy duck.[13]

Now for the zinger conclusion:

"God exists for you," the translator renders. "He is you . . . and you is He."[14]

The journalist's message is clear and simple: foreigners are funny, at least those with anticommunist credentials. They talk funny. Like a "Loony Tunes" character. And, of course, they can't conjugate a simple English verb.

How terribly droll. How terribly bigoted. But typical of the first wave of reporting on Sun Myung Moon. A mere warm-up compared to the second round.

Phase II: The "Moonie Menace."

Suddenly the foreigners weren't so funny anymore. Daffy Duck was out. Frankenstein was very definitely in. Reports, largely from America's heartland, began to portray something more ominous than a road company of the *Mikado*.

The "Moonie Menace" stories largely coincided with the rise of the so-called deprogramming movement in which self-styled professionals promised to "rescue" adult "children" from the country's new religions—cults, if you prefer—usually at very stiff fees that worried parents gladly forked over.

The Unification Church with its foreign origins became the favorite whipping boy of deprogrammers like Ted Patrick. He believed in hard deprogramming in which his "clients" were forcibly abducted and held against their will until they broke.

Some did. Others refused. Still others escaped or lied to Patrick and then returned to their religion. At first deprogrammers like

Patrick and the stories that church apostates told were treated with great respect by the media.

The *Omaha World-Herald* (in a 1973 front page story) was pretty typical. The story told the tale of Kim Craig, a religious drifter, who was enticed into the Unification Church by a girl who lured him with smiles and religious fervor.[15]

According to Craig, the Unification Church was "an army of brainwashed zombies . . . children who would do or die for their leader."

Craig charged that members were subjected to "daily indoctrination" and kept busy—day and night, up to eighteen hours per—selling peanuts, candles, and flowers. Reading was confined to Moon's *Divine Principle*, and days of fasting were enforced.

According to Craig the regimen had a sinister purpose: "They weaken your health by fasting, break your will and reduce you to nothing."[16]

Or how about the sympathetic account of a "deprogramming" performed by Ted Patrick on a former University of Texas co-ed as portrayed in the *San Antonio Light*?

Patrick, along with a San Antonio minister and the woman's parents, spent three days hammering at her. In the language of the article, "only the Moonies indoctrinate." Patrick and company were merely calmly, but forcefully, chipping away at her defenses.

The woman's story of having been kidnapped by Patrick and her parents was merely "a tale." The woman, according to the reporter, "is having to cope with two personalities, two beliefs, two realities."[17]

It simply did not occur to the reporter that the woman had a perfect right to her beliefs. Nothing was said of Patrick's fee or of his background, a rather sordid past which included several felony arrests and imprisonment.

Some of these questions began to be raised in later days, but almost never without prompting from nonjournalists who began to see the deprogramming movement as a far greater threat to human liberty than any cult, including the Unification Church.

The press themes were repeated endlessly—all from interviews with former church members, many of whom had been forcibly "deprogrammed." The formula, in fact, hardly ever changed.

Still, the Unification Church would have probably remained a minor menace had it not been for Watergate. The Reverend Sun Myung Moon's decision, late in the scandal's history, to rally around the American presidency and ask the nation to forgive, love, and unite around all involved in the crisis—Richard Nixon most of all—provided just the right exotic fuel to send Moon and his movement into outer space.

Needless to say, by the time of the church's Washington-based Watergate rallies and vigils, held in December 1973 and January 1974, Richard Nixon had long been a villain to most of the nation's press. To newsmen he was already guilty of all sorts of high crimes and misdemeanors; clobbering George McGovern in November 1972 probably being the most serious. Indeed, the antipathy for Nixon by many journalists was hardly news at all.

No wonder then that Moon's theme that "in a war of hatred, there are no winners" got thoroughly lost. To the press, the Korean Reverend was giving aid and comfort to the enemy. The American media, by and large, were in no mood to forgive. They wanted to hate and defeat their enemy, Richard Nixon.

Dan Rather probably summed up the press attitude best at a now-famous Houston news conference in which he asked Nixon if he were a crook. That heavily loaded question—which Nixon fell for—was not viewed as out of line and off the wall by a huge majority of the American version of the Fourth Estate. Most were sorry that they hadn't the chance to do the same.

The combination of Moon and Nixon was just too good to resist. It was an intoxicating brew to pep up a story that was beginning to show its age after eighteen months. Ultimately, the mixture was nearly lethal to the church.

The first casualty was the Reverend Moon's rationale for the Unification Church's involvement in the crisis. His words, supposedly aimed at bringing Americans together and saving what was left of the American presidency, got lost fast.

Moon's Oval Office meeting with the embattled chief executive on February 1, and Nixon's walk-through of a rally of church members reinforced the media's conviction that the Unification Church was the last redoubt of fading popular support for King Richard.[18]

No wonder that by mid-February Moon was no longer on the religion page. Instead, he was featured on the front of the *Washing-*

ton Post as a Nixon-backer in a story that jumped to nearly a full page inside. Eighty-five paragraphs.

The story was a classic *Post* attack piece. Old enemies from South Korea were dredged up, supplying damaging, but unverified, accusations against Moon. Not to mention the use of guilt by association—a technique the *Post* had deplored when that tactic was employed by the late Senator Joseph McCarthy of Wisconsin.

For the *Post*, supporting Nixon was bad (and odd) enough. But this major-league exposure of the Reverend Sun Myung Moon and his movement by the newspaper had other themes to knead as well.

In part, it reworked the *Time-Newsweek* stories but added dollops of allegations about illicit sexual rites during the church's early history, with the *Post* limply concluding that "[T]he record is not clear." And then there was lots more about the financial secrecy of the church industrial empire. And of course there were the usual suspicions raised about the movement's anticommunism and its ties with the authoritarian South Korean government.[19]

One wonders if the *Post*'s reporters would have been equally disturbed if there had been church ties to communist North Korea.

Sources? For such a long piece loaded with such high explosive allegations, the documentation proved remarkably scanty. Exactly seven sources were cited, five identified by name, four of whom were from the Unification Church or were church-related, including the then-president of the American branch, Neil Salonen, and Moon's principal advisor and translator, Colonel Bo Hi Pak.

The rest of the sources were either old enemies from Korea, like Kim Kwan Suk, then General Secretary of the Korean National Council of Churches, or unnamed Korean emigrés living in the United States. Also included was an anodyne comment from a nameless State Department "spokesman."[20]

Even for the *Post*, this was a bit on the thin side. But the prestige (and literary license) gained from the *Post*'s Watergate reporting, and the ethics of the new journalism, kept the church story from being scrutinized and questioned.

The *Washington Post* piece was only one of the opening salvos in the battle against Moon and his followers. Naturally, a blockbuster story from the newspaper that was bringing the nation fresh and daily revelations on the inner workings of the Nixon administration was not about to be ignored especially one involving a key presidential ally. Soon other newspapers reprinted the story, including the *Des Moines Tribune*, the *Charleston Sunday Gazette-Mail* (West Virginia), and the *Hartford Times* (Connecticut), all of which subscribed to the *Post*'s national news service.[21]

Lesson learned: friends of Richard Nixon can expect no quarter and no mercy.

Having established that negative matrix, the local papers wove in some of their own themes. Of course, by now the "Moonies as Zombies" leitmotif expanded upon by the deprogrammer set had been swallowed by credulous small-town reporters.[22]

Another theme also emerged in stories about Moon: Christian clergy denouncing the Unification Church as heretical. In Missoula, Montana, the local ministerial association released a pamphlet attacking Moon's beliefs and the regimentation of his followers. In Salt Lake City, members of a local church handed out anti-Moon tracts at the convention center where the Korean was scheduled to speak.[23]

Less than four months later, the fun was over. Richard Nixon resigned, banished to San Clemente, California. Suddenly the Moon-Nixon connection was old news, and the church was no longer a front-page item. But stories about the church appeared once in a while as the search for dirt continued.

Chief among the would-be investigators was the Republican Senator from Kansas, Robert Dole, who almost single-handedly whipped the media and the federal government into a feeding frenzy with the Unification Church and its leaders as the main course.

The press, both print and electronic media, were more than willing to oblige Dole, providing the senator with huge chunks of air time and print space. Thus, he had plenty of opportunity to bamboozle the public and press into believing the small Unification Church had somehow managed to replace drugs and rock-and-roll as the biggest threat to American youth.

This was pretty heady stuff, particularly for a politician looking to make a national name for himself in the post-Watergate era.

Enter Donald M. Fraser, an obscure congressman from Minne-

sota who nevertheless headed the International Organizations
Subcommittee of the House's International Relations Committee.
Fraser was then a liberal Democrat keen on gaining a seat in the
U.S. Senate. Bob Dole's successes and the *Post* story which alleged
the close ties of the South Korean government with the Unification
Church and its allied organizations provided the incentive to begin
the search.

The House investigators, however, did not make the mistake of
leaking their "findings" to the *Washington Post*. That no doubt
would have been too obvious. Instead they gave the story to the
New York Times, which in its good, gray way had shied away in the
past from sensational stories about the Reverend Moon and his
movement.

The piece, written by reporter Ann Crittenden, was another
blockbuster, ninety-three fat paragraphs running for more than a
full page. The headline said it all: "Moon's Sect Seeks to Build
Support in the U.S. for South Korean Regime."[24]

By then—it was May 1976—Nixon had been largely forgotten;
Watergate was alive only in the hearts of hardcore Nixon-haters.
Thanks to Koreagate, the church members were once more vul-
nerable. Not only were they Korean, but the clip files, especially the
Post story, had already made a link between the movement and the
South Korean government, a target that had become a favorite of
the liberal press after the fall of South Vietnam.

With neither Vietnam nor Nixon to kick around, Korea—that is,
South Korea—seemed only too natural and inviting a target. In
any case, the *New York Times*, having been left in the dust on
Watergate, was not going to resist a handout from a congressional
subcommittee.

Not coincidentally, the article appeared one month before Fraser
opened his hearings on the very same subject. The lead summarizes perfectly what the *Times* set out to prove:

> A number of individuals and organizations connected with the Rev.
> Sun Myung Moon, the wealthy industrialist and evangelist, have
> intimate ties with and have received assistance from the South Ko-
> rean Government and the Korean Central Intelligence Agency, ac-
> cording to former Korean and American officials and former
> members of the Moon organization.[25]

At least, in contrast to the *Post*, the *Times* had its sources up front. How good those sources proved to be will be taken up shortly. The *Times* story also had its share of caveats, something that earlier reporting by others had omitted.

In fact, the story's major cautionary is worth quoting:

> It is open to interpretation whether these activities are legal or illegal, and whether some of the Moon groups have violated statutes governing the activities of tax-exempt organizations or requiring registration as foreign agents. But enough evidence exists to raise questions in the minds of a number of government officials.[26]

The caveat ends in an editorial judgment. And as it turned out the judgment was shared by only a few, mostly in Congressman Fraser's office, and found to be wrong, but only after a long and expensive congressional investigation.

In outline, the story was really quite simple. The South Korean government, after the fall of Saigon, became fearful that its chief ally and nearly sole supporter, the United States, might desert the ROK as it had its Vietnamese allies. This drove Seoul to use all of its resources, including the Reverend Sun Myung Moon and his multiple organizations, to lobby the American government, both the executive and legislative branches.

Naturally, the logic of such an effort being undertaken by a threatened country which already had experienced a bloody invasion and war was ignored. Who cared what the South Koreans felt or feared? To the relentless Fraser and his allies in the press, it was a totally irrelevant question.

What mattered to them were the links between an obscure church and Seoul. Those ties, they believed, included funding, as well as use of the diplomatic pouch to bring in funds (possibly illicitly) and secure communication channels from the South Korean embassy in Washington, D.C. Just why the ties were needed was not explained in the article, but the close association between the Korean government and Moon was asserted.

There was also the small matter of the KCIA, which enjoyed the same press in the United States as the church. The church and the KCIA were supposed to be one, fused into one dark menace.

According to the *Times* account, Colonel Bo Hi Pak acted as a

INQUISITION

liaison between the KCIA and the American intelligence community (while serving in the South Korean embassy in Washington, D.C.). Church members in Korea, it further charged, were encouraged to cultivate relations with the KCIA.

Finally, Kim Jong-Pil, who founded the KCIA, had become the honorary chairman of the Korean Cultural and Freedom Foundation, one of the many Unification Church-connected organizations that roused the curiosity of the Fraser subcommittee and the *New York Times*.[27]

Kim Jong-Pil's roles in both organizations may not seem like a well-documented linkage, and it begs the question of criminal or even unethical behavior, but the connection seemed enough at the time for both the congressional and journalistic investigators to sound the tocsin. Apparently, the unspoken assumption of the media and the U.S. Congress was that working for or working with one's own government was *a priori* wrong, even evil, for anyone in any country—as long, of course, as it was aligned with the United States.

The *Times* story looked good. At least on the surface. Far more skillfully done than that of the attack dog of the Democratic party. And unlike the *Post* piece, the story seemed to be amply documented and more or less narrowly focused. But was it? A closer look raises some doubts.

First there was a great reliance on unnamed U.S. officials, current and past, chiefly from the Department of Justice, although a straggler from the U.S. Customs Service—equally anonymous—managed to wander in at an appropriate moment.

Of course, there was the usual dependence on Korean emigrés and defectors who were—like all deserters—making a profession of railing against the then-current government in Seoul—a regime they had learned to hate but were unwilling to confront on home ground. Several of the sources were former embassy officials in Washington who had for years peddled their wares to anyone willing to buy.

There were also drop-out church members eager to supply their own damaging testimony against Moon. Ex-member Ann Gordon, for example, who had been deprogrammed the year before the *Times* article appeared, described church-lobbying practices with the U.S. Congress:

We were told to be somewhat vague when dealing with the Capitol Hill contacts in order to protect our presence there, but we were trying to influence our contacts to support Moon and South Korea.[28]

Behind this screen of relatively anonymous but impressive sounding sources was exactly one source: the House Subcommittee on International Organization's chairman, Congressman Donald Fraser, and his closest staffers, top aide Robert Boettcher in particular. What Fraser & Company had gathered in a totally secure and controlled environment, they promptly handed over to the *Times*. And the *Times*' reporter and editors gobbled it all down without an apparent second thought, but with lots and lots of relish.

So much for adversarial journalism. "We are adversaries only when it suits us," seems to have been the operating philosophy of the *New York Times*. Meanwhile, basic fairness, even straightforward journalistic practice, got entirely lost in the rush to print.

In short, the preliminary and largely precooked Fraser findings were reproduced faithfully in the *New York Times* account, like some kind of journalistic photocopying.

Unfortunately for Congressman Fraser and the *Times*' credibility, once their sources were subjected to closer scrutiny, the tale of church and South Korean intrigue to influence the American political system began to fall apart.

Before proceeding further, one classic bit of newspaper "reporting" bears looking at. It is contained in the *Times* story's twentieth paragraph.

In that key and revealing paragraph, the *Times* quotes an unnamed Justice Department spokesman who said (actually the word was "insists") that the department had seen no evidence directly linking Moon and Colonel Pak with Seoul. At the same time, an equally anonymous former senior official government official told the *Times* reporter that he could recall an intelligence report dating from the early 1970s which placed Colonel Bo Hi Pak at a meeting with Korean President Park Chung Hee in which they discussed financing one of Pak's numerous projects.

The alleged Pak-Park meeting is a very slender thread on which to hang a heavy story, but that single, quite raw intelligence report seems to have formed the basis of the Fraser investigation as well as the accompanying *Times* account. Incidentally, the unnamed "former senior government official" showed up at other equally critical points in the story and appeared before the Fraser subcommittee in executive sessions.

What the *New York Times* did in its mammoth story on the church's political influence in the United States was essentially to justify the Fraser subcommittee's investigation. Indeed, the preliminary conclusions of Fraser & Company are the heart of the article.

Such justification in the press is not unknown. But in this case, it carries some pretty ugly overtones. For the showcase newspaper of the powerful American media to form a working alliance with a committee of the U.S. Congress, in pursuit of an unpopular religious leader in allegations that later proved to be exaggerated or dead wrong, was and is not a pretty sight. In fact, the activity is both ugly and dangerous to anyone who professes to have liberal concerns about the big guy versus the little guy.[29]

More scare stories followed, of course. Increasingly, the "Moonie Menace" story went along two tracks. The prestige media—the *New York Times* and the *Washington Post*, in particular—took the elevated approach. High politics. Grand questions of state. National security interests. Great principles. The propriety of a religious movement's serving the agenda of a foreign government . . .

To be sure, all of this noble high-mindedness also helped to carry out the political agenda of the very same stuffed-shirt establishment liberals. To a man and woman, they despised South Koreans for their obstinate, humorless anticommunism.

America's tabloids couldn't have cared less about South Koreans. But they liked the church story just as much as the higher-toned press; even more, and their treatment of the Unification Church story followed a distinctly lower track.

For example, the *New York Daily News*, in a piece that appeared in tandem with the *Times* article, followed a totally different line of attack. The springboard for the *Daily News* story, which appeared in mid-1976, was an actual event. Unlike the *Times'* approach, the angle was focused on the church's Yankee Stadium rally. Covering the rally was only a platform to support one more "Moonie Menace" story.

Forget foreign intrigue. This was a domestic plot. According to the *Daily News*, Moon in 1973 had announced his wish to organize a Christian political party in which the separation between church and state would be dissolved.

From that fantasy sprang the plot itself. But let the *Daily News* tell the story:

> Those fighting Moon say what frightens them most is Moon's ability to move followers around the country. He has the potential voting force to sway congressional and local elections, they say, if he gets hundreds of members registered in one spot. The critics note that Moon is aided by the recent Supreme Court decision supporting 30-day residency requirements for voting.[30]

The thought that several thousand members of the Unification Church would rattle around the country—along with their eighteen-hour-a-day peanut peddling schedules—and still find time to establish residency in order to re-register so they could then vote in close elections seems absurd. The idea that the outcome of those elections, dictated by a master electoral strategy plan to have Moon come to power or at least exert great influence on our defenseless republic, is, well, a tad farfetched.

Let's face it. The story about Moon's alleged desire to take over the United States was ludicrous from the outset, absurd, paranoid blather. It was the kind of crank nonsense—"my mother was captured by an alien spaceship, and the Air Force knows and doesn't care"—that reporters from the old school put in the circular file along with the latest two-headed dog story.

Yet the *Daily News* swallowed the story, hook, line, and sucker. Nor did the *Daily News* ever quite quit. After its Yankee Stadium stories, it followed up with other church horror stories, including a softball interview with leading Unification Church basher Rabbi Maurice Davis.

Sample quote from Davis, who was the sole source of the story: "Moon's goal is political power in America and the world. Just like Hitler, he spells it out but nobody pays any attention. I've asked the kids, 'How far would you go for Moon.' They say, 'I would have killed for him.' "[31]

High track or low track, the last word on this particular round of church-mauling by the American press was left to the big two news magazines: *Time* and *Newsweek*. The two magazines ran major stories on the Unification Church in the same week, dated June 14, 1976.

Only seldom do great minds think alike, but pack journalists always think alike. Reason? They talk to each other, read the same things, and largely share similar, privileged, upper-middle-class, liberal Democratic backgrounds. Consider the *Time* and *Newsweek* pieces written to update their earlier estimates of the threat posed by the church empire after the rally at Yankee Stadium, the pieces written by the Pete and Repete of weekly U.S. journalism.

The reader can guess which is which.

Pete opened with a little history: "In 1948, Moon was arrested in North Korea for what his followers say were his religious and anti-Communist activities; his opponents maintain he was jailed for practicing ritual sex."

So did Repete: "According to a former North Korean army officer who was in prison with him at the time, Moon received a seven-year sentence because he had contributed to 'social disorder.' He had been proclaiming the imminent coming of the second Messiah in Korea. . . . When the Chinese pushed the U.N. troops out of North Korea in 1950, Moon fled to the south and later started a church in Seoul. In those days, say early members of the sect, ritual sex characterized the Moon communes."

Pete on the Big Investigation: "Rep. Donald Fraser whose subcommittee on international organizations has been looking into the U.S. activities of the Korean CIA, says, 'We've got testimony that suggests that there may be an effort by the Unification Church to serve in part the interest of the KCIA.' "

Now Repete: "Since some government officials believe there are extremely close ties between the Moonies, the Korean CIA and the Park regime, such investigations plus Moon's often unsavory publicity may build up enough resistance in Congress to be reflected in votes against aid to South Korea."

Pete on the Threat: "Despite repeated denials that he is involved in politics, Moon held prayer vigils for Richard Nixon during his impeachment hearings and he maintains a 'ministry' on Capitol Hill made up primarily of attractive young female Moonies who regularly visit Congressional offices to 'talk to whoever will listen.' "

Repete: "To some spectators in New York City in the weeks leading up to his [Yankee Stadium] rally, his cadres of short-haired, fresh faced youths marching and singing together were a reminder of early Nazi days. So are the anti-Semitic doctrines expressed in Moon's religious writings though many of his followers are young Jews."

Pete on the church danger to the young: "The next phase involves what Moon critics claim is 'a systematic effort to brainwash' the recruits by physical isolation, exhausting activities and alternating rounds of positive and negative reinforcement."

Now Repete: "Once seduced into their weird new world, converts are surrounded always by warm, supportive Brothers and Sisters and are reassured by smiles, friendly pats and handholding called 'love bombing.'... Yet there is little evidence that the Moonies' efforts contribute to anything but Moon's coffers and the glassy-eyed behavior of the youngsters has so alarmed many parents that they have resorted to illegal kidnappings and 'deprogrammings' to retrieve their offspring."[32]

Time or *Newsweek?* It scarcely matters. Aside from small discrepancies about exactly when and where Moon engaged in sex orgies (were they held in Korea North or Korea South? 1948 or 1951?), the two articles were similar in style and messages. Both authors had looked at the same clip files; both had been spoon-fed by Don Fraser's subcommittee "findings"; both had the same midseventies liberal mindset about South Korea and about what was the main threat to freedom; and, finally, both were flat, dead wrong. Little has changed. Yet there is nothing magical about Tweedledumb and Tweedledumber news magazine journalism. Despite the likeness of the two stories there was no plagiarism in the case of *Time* and *Newsweek*.

The very similarity of the articles, however, isn't very reassuring.

But the Yankee Stadium story was only one small benchmark in the American Fourth Estate's war on the Reverend Sun Myung Moon and his band of followers.

In fact, the whole theme of "Moon-as-Menace" climaxed with the Fraser hearings, which finally got under way in the spring of

1978. Fraser & Company of course had already cultivated the major media—*Time, Newsweek,* the *New York Times,* and the *Washington Post*—by feeding them juicy morsels garnered from his closed door sessions with "friendly witnesses." The witnesses naturally agreed with Fraser's central thesis: that the Reverend Moon and his movement were arms of a foreign power, namely, South Korea. In Fraser's mind, South Korea, although once a wartime ally, was now a dictatorship and like South Vietnam deserved to be thrown to the wolves from the north.

So what if both communist states were far crueler tyrannies? Fashionable liberals in those days were decidedly anti-anticommunist. Indeed, they gloried in it. And Don Fraser, if nothing else, was a fashionable type of liberal.

But even liberals can get mean. For all their homilies on tolerance and individual rights and a devoted belief in their own nobility, they can play dirty too. And that is exactly what Fraser did at the beginning of a second round of leaks to the press just when public hearings on Moon were about to open.

Fraser was no fool about the media. He too understood the double-track strategy. Some forms of dirt are not usually printed by the highbrow press. As a consequence he took the low track for his opener and selected the *Chicago Tribune* to carry the garbage.

The old *Trib* by the mid-1970s was no longer the lusty "World's Greatest Newspaper" that it had once been under the irascible Colonel Robert Rutherford McCormick. McCormick had liked big stories, and smelly ones, too. But they also had to have strength and honesty. And truth. When McCormick went for a man, he did so front and center, not from behind.

But those days were long gone by 1978. The new editors had removed the U.S. flag from the *Trib* masthead. In earlier years the banner had decorated the front page, in case anyone, anywhere, would somehow forget, for one instant, that the old girl was an *American* newspaper.

More than a flag was now missing from the *Trib,* however. Also gone was the paper's brashness, its guts, and its unstudied humanity.

The *Tribune,* sadly, had become a pale copy of its East Coast "betters." The change meant, among other things, that sob sister reporting was now *de rigeur* at the *Chicago Tribune.* Every cliché of the new journalism was faithfully copied. Its editorials were even more limp-wristed than the *Washington Post's*.

Moreover, where once reporters on the old *Trib* would have looked twice at a story handed out by a government official— what's the mayor trying to hide now?—the new *Chicago Tribune* never thought to ask.

The headline on the Fraser-fed *Tribune* story pretty well conveys the flavor of the piece: "Moon Church Traced from Sex Cult." Thanks to raw U.S. government reports, the *Trib* reconstructed the early history of the Unification Church.

Hints of the sex scandal had already appeared in the news magazines, but they had been buried in the main story. Now "the sex cult" theme was the lead.

According to the *Tribune*:

> Diplomatic cables said that the church patriarch, the Rev. Sun Myung Moon, headed a Korean cult that "interprets the Bible in sexual terms." The KCIA decided to use Moon in a scheme that grew to include other Koreans bribing congressmen, the documents said.[33]

The raw cables, of course, were provided free of charge from the Fraser-run subcommittee. That was only the beginning.

The *Tribune* continued:

> A cable sent to Washington from the American Embassy in Seoul on August 26, 1966, describes an initiation ceremony for the church involving sexual relations. The cable said the church refers to such initiation as baptizing. The author of the cable quoted Thomas Chung, president of the Koreans' Student Association in Washington, as saying: "Colonel Pak was in trouble because he had attempted to initiate into his church [i.e., to have sexual relations with] the wife of a visiting ROK [Korean government] official [either the minister of national defense or the chief of staff]."[34]

Why student leader Chung qualified as a source on these matters is not made clear by the article.

But the *Trib* had not quite finished:

> That cable also quotes another intelligence source: He said that the church interprets the Bible in sexual terms and maintains that

religious experience is interrelated with sex MUN SON-Myong [sic], leader of the church, was once arrested because of the sexual practices of the organization.[35]

There it was. All the garbage Fraser and staff could find by picking through piles of raw intelligence reports that had accumulated over the years. These were reports that the intelligence agency had clearly labeled as unverified and probably unverifiable. As raw reports, intelligence experts know that they were hardly worth more than barroom gossip. That was in fact what they were.

Fraser and his staff knew as much. Journalists, unless they have been around intelligence reports for a very long time, usually do not. Fraser knew that a government document can take on credibility and authority merely because it is a government document.

Add the word *intelligence* and suddenly all the caveats in the world cannot alter the impression left. Which is, of course, "guilty as charged."

One does wonder why an "obscure cult with a shady past which included bizarre sexual rites" would be chosen by the KCIA as a principal in South Korean influence peddling in Washington. The *Tribune* never stopped to ask that particular question in its breathless haste "to break" the story. And Congressman Donald M. Fraser, Democrat of Minnesota, was certainly not likely to raise the subject with the *Tribune* either.

But for all his success with the media, Chairman Fraser was not about to neglect the home folks. After all, he was running for the U.S. Senate. Why should the *Post*, the *Times*, and the *Trib* get all the action?

Four months after the hearings, the congressman helped the hometown *Minneapolis Star* write a series of articles investigating the church.[36]

The content was for the most part anodyne. The *Star* reporter goes to a church camp and makes the usual complaints. Breakfast is spartan: "only" fruit and cereal or pancakes. Water or milk. The lectures are too long. And yes, not enough sleep, although the wake-up call is at 8:00 A.M. Nothing much sinister in that.

In one of the *Star* articles, the reporter quotes at length a scholar's sympathetic views on the church—views that include a knocking down of the sex cult stories that Congressman Fraser had so assiduously succeeded in spreading only months earlier.[37]

Still the stories were not a total loss to Fraser. The *Star's* article dealing with Moon's troubles with the U.S. government gave some comfort. Although the article reported that the Justice Department and other federal agencies had not found much to pin on the Reverend Sun Myung Moon, it did quote in a favorable light Congressman Fraser's allegations.

For example:

Fraser's subcommittee investigators have found that the Unification Church owns about $16 million worth of heavily mortgaged real estate in the United States and frequently transfers millions of dollars in and out of the country, [Michael] Hershman said.[38]

It continued:

The subcommittee has information indicating the church is a majority stockholder in Tong-Il Industrial Corp., a Korean firm selling weapons material to the South Korean government.[39]

Moon's refusal to appear before the Fraser subcommittee was depicted as a "he must be guilty" impression as well. Still, Fraser's attempted manipulation of the hometown press was not as successful as earlier ventures.

Perhaps the "Moonies-as-Menace" theme was wearing a little thin by the time the news reached Minneapolis. In any case, the *Star* was not alone in stifling a yawn. The national media were getting tired of it too.

But exhausting one vein of fool's gold did not mean that the folks in the Fourth Estate weren't looking for another. And they found it when Moon's tax troubles began to mount in the late 1970s.

Phase III: The Empire Strikes Back.

Of course, the menace stories never went completely away, but as the trendsetter, *Time* magazine, observed in April 1985, "[T]here seems to be much less hysteria about Moon now than there was in the late 1970s." *Time*'s role in hyping that hysteria went delicately unmentioned. Absolute amnesia set in about its earlier piece that had compared clean-cut church members to equally clean-cut Nazi youth.[40]

Time's jocularity at the expense of the church was not, however, the principal theme that our news establishment was pounding home in the early 1980s.

No doubt inspired by the Internal Revenue Service and the Justice Department's investigation of Moon's finances, the media began doing lengthy exposés of the church's business "empire." They also wrote about businessman Moon, who Midas-like (allegedly) accumulated treasure by exploiting his followers and using the clerical cover to divert attention away from his dazzling wealth.

Moon's lifestyle—the mansions, the limousines, the bodyguards—had long since become a staple of reporting, but the notion of a business empire coiling its tentacles worldwide, well, that was an octopus of entirely another color.

The classic in this genre—which was to be imitated by scores of others—was no doubt the *Wall Street Journal*'s exposé in February 1982. Although the *Journal* had paid little heed to church members during the previous decade, its 1982 piece made up for lost time.

The *Journal*'s angle was the trailblazing "rich as Croesus and twice as bad" leitmotif that ran through much of the reporting on the church in the early- and mid-1980s.

The article's thesis was stated clearly in the second paragraph:

> Though many churches run businesses, few have extended their temporal enterprises so far—or met with such stiff opposition—as the Holy Spirit Association for the Unification of World Christianity, better known as the Unification Church. The full extent of these church-linked holdings isn't known, but like the church, they appear to be spreading rapidly in many countries.[41]

What did this purported empire consist of? The *Journal* suggested a huge conglomerate involving communications, entertainment, food retailing, banking, and fishing. It was impressive.

But what did this transnational complex of enterprises really consist of ? The authors eventually got around to a description, but first the necessary background had to be included, in case any *Wall Street Journal* readers had forgotten about the Unification Church.

Thus, after going through the familiar litany of charges about brainwashing, ties to the South Korean government, and Moon's tax problems, the authors returned to the main theme: the church as business empire. The mainspring of this empire, the article said, was the $20 to $25 million that the church members earned from street sales of flowers and candy.

We are then to be introduced to an associated theme. The authors continued:

> Much of this income has been channeled into a variety of businesses around the world. The aim of the expansion, concludes Robert Boettcher, who was [Fraser's] subcommittee staff director of the congressional investigation, is to further Rev. Moon's ambitious dream of unifying business, politics, culture and religion into a global theocracy that he would control. "To succeed," Mr. Boettcher says, "he needs money."[42]

In other words, Moon, Inc., was not just another would-be General Motors out to make a buck wherever it could find it, but a global conspiracy to create a theocracy under the scepter of Father Moon.

Such fantasying is not reporting business news as we know it. But there was more, of course.

Much was made of the precise ownership of the businesses and their relationship to the Unification Church and the Reverend Sun Myung Moon. It was not clear in the *Journal* article why this was so important except that the businesses were "enriching [the church's] coffers."[43]

What is wrong with raising money is not explained either, but when one begins with a conspiratorial assumption, why spell out the problem? Just let the reader do the rest.

As for the multinational conglomerate, closer inspection of the church's businesses suggests something else.

The food retailing "empire" turned out to be seventeen convenience stores in the Seattle area. Go N Joy Food Corp. hasn't exactly challenged the Seven-Eleven or even Texas' beloved Maverick Markets, but the *Journal's* perception of this small store "empire" was spiked with fantasy.

Quoting an ex-church member who attended a leadership meeting in 1980, Moon allegedly disclosed plans to build a chain of no fewer than 5,000 convenience stores to gross $750 million a year.

Naturally, that was only the beginning. Let the *Journal* explain the rest:

> Mr. [Michael] Lisman quotes Mr. Moon as saying that these "store churches" would put church members in touch with five million people daily. "Then in America," he reportedly said, "we will have a friend everywhere. How quickly, how incredibly fast we could grow."[44]

The banking component of the empire turned out to be plans for church members to buy controlling shares of stock in a small Washington bank that catered to Asian Americans, the Diplomat National Bank with its sole branch on K Street.

Even the *Journal* authors admitted that the venture went haywire when the Securities and Exchange Commission filed a complaint saying that the purchase by church members violated an agreement that no single entity could own more than 5 percent of the bank's stock.

To be sure, there was then and is now an argument over whether the twenty-two church members constituted a single entity or not. The fact that the shares were sold and the church entry into small-time banking came a cropper is not debated. Nevertheless, the Diplomat Bank fiasco became a fixture for *Journal* and other media reporting on the church business empire.[45]

As for the entertainment empire, the evidence in question consisted of one church-financed movie, *Inchon*, which cost $42 million to produce and made no money whatsoever. The film, which the *Journal* reporters acknowledge was a commercial disaster, was somehow supposed to constitute proof of a hugely successful, multisegmented business empire.

The same is supposed to apply for the church "communications" conglomerate which consists of several small-circulation newspapers, including the *Washington Times* and its companion news magazine *Insight*, which for all their reporting excellence lose pots of money.

And so it goes for the church's fishing armadas—also money losers—and its newspaper ventures in Uruguay, a tiny South American nation sandwiched in between giant Argentina and colossal Brazil.[46]

The South Korean enterprises—which are among the only real profit makers in the "Moon empire"—are mentioned only in passing by the *Journal* reporters. Air rifles, stoneware vases, lathes, and paint chemicals after all are not terribly sexy.

In its totality, even when listed in a thirty-seven-paragraph exposé, the church empire isn't all that much of an empire, either standing alone or in comparison to real business conglomerates or the holdings and investments of other churches.

Other churches own or operate businesses and control huge sums of stock in Fortune 500 companies, but nowhere are the vast holdings of the mainline denominations, including the Roman Catholic church, ever cited in any of these pieces.

If they had been, the Unification Church business balloon thesis would suddenly have lost all of its moist, hot air.

To get a more realistic handle on just how exaggerated and distorted these tales of Moon's wealth are, one need only look at a couple of facts.

According to a government survey conducted in 1983, combined yearly contributions to all churches in America topped the $35 billion mark while total real estate holdings for all religious denominations approached $1 trillion, mostly in tax-exempt properties.

That same year, 1983, the relatively tiny Mormon church reported an annual income of nearly $2 billion against total assets of $9.8 billion.

Quite literally, God only knows how much all the other mainline churches received that year, because most never report their income or holdings to the public or, for that matter, their congregations. Even the few that do issue fuzzy financial reports which only outline, in the vaguest terms, the general health of their church.

As just about any big-city tax assessor will tell you, church-owned property usually accounts for the largest share of privately held, singly controlled real estate throughout the U.S.

As I said, ignoring other religions and their financial practices and performing hatchet jobs on the Unification Church was a formula so good it was worth repeating. Over and over in true clip-file, herd-journalism style. The trouble is, that wasn't good reporting. No real independent research was ever done. Wholesale and sweeping assertions were made without any proper documentation. Their mere repetition was authority enough. Apparently no research was thought necessary.

After all, they are only "Moonies," and as such hardly entitled to the respect and fairness accorded people of other faiths.

Newspapers had once swooned at the thought that a Korean evangelist was worth a total of—get this—$15 million. Yet TV evangelists even in the early 1970s were pulling in many times that per year in direct mail donations. Billy Graham, the Bakkers, Jimmy Swaggart, Oral Roberts, Rex Humbard—and a score of others—were awash in an ever rolling stream of God's greenbacks.

But until the Bakker scandal broke, along with stories of their displays of vulgar wealth, Moon was looked on by the media as a model of clerical extravagance. Yet no one, no reporter, no editor from any major newspaper or network (the *Charlotte Observer* excepted, hardly a media mogul) ever bothered to check the very stuff of modern American televised religion before delivering his (or her or their) grand *pronunciamientos* on the subject.

Thus, the truly sinister aspect of the church story is not the Reverend Sun Myung Moon or his following or their hopes and dreams. It is the national hysteria that was aroused and inflamed by the American media. Despite the media's pretensions of being adversarial and skeptical, they worked hand-in-glove with the powers that be.

Hunting the weak was no triumph for my profession. Nor was carrying out the not-so-hidden agenda of powerful congressional committees. But it is a useful reminder of how comfortable we have become, and how powerful we are. And how, on the trail of Sun Myung Moon, American journalism somehow lost its way.

It forgot that allying with the big shots and pillorying the unpopular is not necessarily what we are all about.

Nor is copycat, clip-file journalism.

But in the case of the Reverend Sun Myung Moon and his movement that is exactly what many of us did. And the practice still goes on.

CHAPTER XIV

KOREAGATE

*There are some politicians who, if their constituents were cannibals,
would promise them missionaries for dinner.*

H.L. MENCKEN

THE Reverend Sun Myung Moon's troubles with the United States
government did not begin or end with the executive and judicial
branches—impressive as these problems proved to be. Moon and
his Unification Church also ran into the buzzsaw of a full blown
congressional committee investigation that stretched over nearly
two years and cost the American taxpayer more than one million
dollars.

The Moon investigation did not rank with the Joe McCarthy or
the Estes Kefauver hearings of the 1950s or the Sam Ervin-
Howard Baker investigations that gave us Watergate twenty years
later. But in its own way, the Fraser probe of the Unification
Church, and of Moon in particular, does rank as a textbook example of congressional abuse of power.

In the end, the investigation yielded precious little—certainly
nothing in the way of new legislation, the supposed central objective of such hearings. It did, however, unintentionally create new
precedents in the tricky area of the Congress and the First Amendment. The hearings certainly brought no glory to the chairman of

the Subcommittee on International Organizations, Congressman Donald Fraser, nor did they further his political ambitions, the one clear and obvious purpose the hearings were intended to achieve. Fraser shortly lost his own House seat in a failed bid for the U.S. Senate.

The subcommittee's final report, issued on Halloween in 1978, was by all accounts a masterpiece of beautifully packaged assertion and innuendo. The report once again raised the spectre of a "Moonie Conspiracy," the more outlandish versions of which, suggested that world dominion was the goal of its leader, the Reverend Sun Myung Moon.

Fraser and Moon were an odd couple. On the right was the Reverend Sun Myung Moon, a Korean religious leader and prophet. His beliefs, a blend of Christianity and elements all his own, embraced not only a religion but a strident anti-communist political philosophy as well. They also had a large streak of historicism—the belief that history has some final purpose—that intrigued and often confused observers, including members of Congress. As a consequence of Moon's world vision theology, he saw communism at that time as the great enemy of God. Indeed, he unblushingly called the Soviet bloc not merely an evil empire, but the Antichrist itself. On top of that, according to Unification theology, in the great struggle with that adversary, America was to play a special role in the salvation of the world.

Meanwhile, on the left was Congressman Donald M. Fraser of Minnesota, a liberal Democrat who ran the Subcommittee on International Organizations according to his own agenda, whether its mother committee, the House International Relations (now the Foreign Affairs) Committee, liked it or not. Fraser was a new-generation liberal; that is to say, one who shared the attitudes and beliefs of the George McGovern wing of the Democratic party. Liberal in his support of spending at home, stingy on defense, and frankly isolationist in outlook, Fraser was also a severe critic of any use of American force and a determined enemy of noncommunist, but authoritarian, regimes abroad.

It is no wonder that these two men clashed. The real wonder is that the confrontation had not happened earlier. What Fraser wanted was an investigation that would prove, above all, that Moon and his church were agents of influence of the South Korean government, specifically the Korean Central Intelligence Agency, an organization that had achieved great notoriety by the middle 1970s. Fraser's accusation about the KCIA was central to all other issues for the subcommittee, and both sides took great pains either to prove or deny it.

The KCIA was hardly the only issue, however. No more so than was the fate of Corporal G. David Schein the single factor that sparked the celebrated Army-McCarthy hearings of the 1950s But it formed the leitmotif that seemed to run through all the alarms and excursions that mark every big-time congressional investigation.

Was the International Organizations Subcommittee's investigation of Korean-American relations nothing more than a fishing expedition? Many have concluded exactly that, but they would also add that few fish were ever actually landed—certainly not Moon or any of his principal followers.

The congressional investigation of the Reverend Sun Myung Moon is only one chapter in the bizarre history of the Korean's stay in America. Moon first arrived in 1971 and by 1978, despite (or perhaps because of) massive publicity, the number of the faithful by the church's count only amounted to 37,000 (by some hostile press accounts the figures were as low as 4,000 members).[1]

So, then, how can such a little church get into so much trouble so soon? With difficulty, but it can be done, and the Reverend Moon and his Unification movement succeeded in doing so, all in less than five years.

Moon's beginnings, as we have seen, are somewhat obscure given the fact that he appeared to have emerged from the ashes of prison camps in postwar Japan and communist North Korea. Officially, he established the church in Seoul, Korea, in 1954: the date of its origin became a vital issue in the subcommittee's investigation. Today it claims three million members in 123 countries, although the bulk of the followers are in Japan and Korea.[2]

Recruiting in America began in 1960 and was especially active on the West Coast. It was not until the ferment of the early 1970s, however, that this tiny neo-Christian movement began to get attention. With so many cults and sects flourishing in the lush subtropical California climate, it took time for the followers of the Unifica-tion Church, later to be derisively known as "Moonies," to be distinguished from the myriad of pop religions.

Even a Korean minister who claimed to have talked with Jesus was nothing truly out of the ordinary. But stories about forced recruitment and retention of followers through sophisticated brainwashing techniques most certainly did get Unification Church members a kind of attention they had not exactly bar-gained for.

In response to the Unification Church and other unpopular new religions, a whole new American industry grew up: de-programming. Followers of the Reverend Sun Myung Moon were deprogrammed by "professional" deprogrammers like Ted Patrick and Daphne Greene. Deprogrammers usually but not always acted at the request of worried parents, although the "children" were adults over age twenty-one. Moreover, deprogramming was often no more than a euphemism for kidnapping.

Occasionally deprogrammers made the society pages. In one case the publicity had curious repercussions.

In May 1978 a cocktail-party-cum-buffet was held in the swank Washington Sheraton-Carlton Hotel to honor Daphne Greene, a San Francisco housewife who had become a volunteer deprogram-mer after her two children joined the Unification Church.

Her hostess and ardent admirer was Sonny Adler, who with her husband Warren published the chic boutique Washington maga-zine *Dossier*. There was no mystery about the Adlers' fondness for Daphne, and it had nothing to do with their being in the same social set.

The Adlers too had "lost" a son, David, then twenty-six, who was "saved" for them by Mrs. Greene. "She brought my son back from the dead," Mrs. Adler repeated to her guests—an observation well within earshot of *Washington Post* reporter Joseph McLellan.

As for son David, he told the *Post*: "I was brainwashed to the point where I trusted those people completely, and they took advantage of me. They exploit your best motivations. The kids in there are the best kids in the world, but they're under mind con-trol."[3]

The quote of course rounded out a nice twelve-inch story on the "Moonies," and encapsulated perfectly liberal, upper-middle-class

America's mindset on the Unification Church. Vietnam, drugs, and Richard Nixon, held no greater terror for them than the evangelist from Seoul.

The piece was typical of the *Post*. In a few hundred words it carried a message and dropped a lot of Washington names besides, including that of then-FBI-director Judge William Webster who, in fact, had nothing at all to do with the story, much less the church.

Nonetheless, the *Post* piece did have two genuine bits of news in it. One was that one of the guests at the affair was Senator Robert Dole of Kansas. The other was that no fewer than four members of the Fraser subcommittee had joined the "Moonie" bashing party.

In addition to the brainwashing scare, by 1977 one more ingredient had been added to the stew, and that was Koreagate. Not only were prominent Koreans involved in this murky affair, so was the United States Congress.

In brief, the facts:

The Korean CIA in the mid-1970s decided that South Korea's future lay in keeping the U.S. Congress a firm ally of the Republic. The notion was not altogether farfetched. Although the United States had been a loyal ally of Korea since the 1950-1953 war, the American pull-out from its Vietnam commitment stirred some not-so-outlandish second thoughts in Seoul about Washington's reliability.

For Korean intelligence officers courting Congress that meant something direct and crude. To keep one's friends, give them gifts. In this case, the "gifts" took the form of plain white envelopes stuffed with $100 bills.

These Korean Express payments, as they became known, were delivered through a most curious mailman. He was a self-described Korean businessman and socializer who sought out Washington's powerful and invited them to his own posh Georgetown Club. This gracious host on lower Wisconsin Avenue was none other than Tongsun Park.

Park's friends? Invariably members of the United States Congress, House and Senate. They were, for the most part, not Republicans.

After Watergate and the perceived abuse of power by a Republican president, it was inevitable that the nation would be treated to

Watergate's mirror image involving congressmen and its perennial majority party, the Democrats.

The episode soon became known as Koreagate. The name was a not-too-imaginative retread of Watergate. It stuck, though few now can remember what the fuss was about. The deputy counsel for the Committee on Standards of Official Conduct of the House of Representatives in the committee's hearings conducted in October 1977 summed it up this way:

> The evidence shows that tremendous sums of money were provided to Korean agents, including, but not limited to, Tongsun Park. The evidence further implicates other high ranking officials. . . . You have direct testimony, some of it extremely vivid, of the formulation and effectuation of a sophisticated well-defined plan to exert influence on American officials.[4]

One member of the committee, Congressman Bruce Caputo, a young Republican from New York, put it even more bluntly:

> [T]hroughout that time all these people were reporting to Tongsun Park, who was talking to the KCIA chief in Washington and to the KCIA director in Seoul. Does that suggest to you a pattern of influence and positioning of agents here on Capitol Hill?[5]

Congressman Caputo summed up the whole damp and dirty cloud of Koreagate in those few words. Korea. Its intelligence arm. Agents on Capitol Hill. Influence. Easy money. An assumption of wrong-doing.

Koreagate was almost like its damp and dirty predecessor, Watergate, and just as inviting to a new breed of Washington journalists who had learned there is gold in toppling the high and mighty. But what was it really about?

A small lesson in Korean geopolitical history is required before we go further. The Republic of Korea lies on the southern half of the Korean peninsula. The peninsula is a small and narrow appendage of the Asian landmass. Roughly north of the thirty-eighth parallel, South Korea faces its totalitarian twin, the People's Democratic Republic of Korea, which for four decades has been under the unquestioned rule of Kim Il-Sung.

Kim launched the Korean War in June 1950 in the hope of

unifying the peninsula by rapid conquest of the south by force of arms. In the attempt, he had moral and material help from his giant communist neighbors, the People's Republic of China and the Soviet Union. Kim failed.

The conflict was a combination of blows to the head that South Koreans have never forgotten. Nor have they forgotten that the war technically has never ended. There is no peace treaty, only an uneasy armistice. Moreover North Korea, mainland China, and Russia have remained in place, geographically, and, so have their communist regimes. Things are changing now, but it was not apparent at all in Seoul in the mid-1970s.

South Koreans, who had fewer resources and a smaller army, saw themselves forever exposed to danger. Their only non-hostile near neighbor, Japan, to the east, was the peninsula's former colonial master. The Japanese during their occupation of Korea from 1905 to 1945 had been unimaginably brutal, intent on wiping out the Korean identity entirely.

For South Koreans, the single exception to this bleak rule of life was the United States of America. In the entire 2,000-year history of the Korean people, no foreigner had brought anything but trouble. In 1950, President Harry Truman ordered American troops to resist North Korean aggression. In the end, the decision would cost 50,000 American lives and produce an uneasy stand-off.

Truman's intervention was an act of God for South Korea. And Americans became for a while gods. They not only spent blood and treasure—their own—in the Republic's defense; they helped rebuild that war-torn country. By Korean standards, American assistance was a miracle, but it was absolutely necessary if South Korea were to survive as long as its hostile northern neighbor remained armed, alert, and unrepentant.

Key to the ROK's survival was the retention of American combat troops in South Korea. The Americans were not stationed in some safe rear area ready for evacuation in case the going got hot. Instead they were placed in the north of the country, athwart the main North Korean invasion route to Seoul, the capital.

If the Korean civil war were to resume, the Americans would be the tripwire guaranteeing a full United States response à la 1950. Or so the South Koreans hoped.

That hope, however, was shaken by America's slow and painful withdrawal from South Vietnam in the early 1970s. When Saigon fell to North Vietnamese tank regiments in April 1975, Korean qualms turned to panic. Would America forget its other Asian ally?

Seoul's fear was expressed quite succinctly by a former official of the Korean government to the House Official Conduct Committee in October 1977. He was General Hyung Wook Kim, a former director of the KCIA who fled South Korea in 1973 after a falling out with President Park Chung Hee.

But General Kim was still a patriot. He told the committee:

> Our purpose and our desire at that time was to have U.S. Congress not to reduce its military and other aid to Korea. Even until 1969 Korea could not manufacture even a single bullet. And I thought it was a good idea. I thought it was a very conducive idea that this Congressman from the United States and others would help Korea in furthering Korea's interest in terms of security. However, the direction took another course, since the revision of October revitalization of the Constitution. Otherwise, there is no support from the United States; no one in Korea would be able to sustain its power. And therefore, the effort of the Korean Government shifted away from our original desire, to maintaining U.S. support for the dictatorial policies that were carried out in Korea.[6]

General Kim had his own obvious reasons for dividing his government's concern about America into two parts, but his final comment is relevant:

> While I was in the office I had offered my help in terms of rice concession only once. That is all I want to say about that.[7]

And that is exactly all General Kim did, or rather did not do. No matter. The members of the committee had no interest in rice concessions or why South Korean officials were so nervous.

To James H. Quillen, a Tennessee Republican, it was all so incomprehensible:

> I can't imagine [he told General Kim] a stable government like South Korea embarking on such a program to a country that has

supported always and still supports the government of South Korea against the government of North Korea. To me, the semblance of offering favoritism, offering money, offering other gratuities, to me just stinks to high heaven.[8]

Empathy has always been in short supply in isolationist Washington, but the congressman's indignation rings somewhat hollow. After all, the subject of money and the Members is not exactly a question of water and oil. The two do mix, in fact, rather well, like water and whiskey. It was, however, a delicate time. Congressmen were investigating their own, en masse, as they do now, and public handwringing was the order of the day as long as it did not tear down the temple.

The point Congressman Quillen missed, of course, was the heart of Koreagate: rice. In this case, the short-grain, glutinous variety which can be found only in one place in the United States: California.

Rice, even to the uneducated, is associated with Asia. That is what they eat. Rice is the staple of the Orient. It is not merely the bread of Asia. It is the meat and potatoes as well. South Korea's population in the 1970s (thirty-eight million people) was packed into a country the approximate size of South Carolina.

Despite growing prosperity, by the late 1970s South Korea could not feed its rapidly expanding population. With all their other security worries to deal with, South Korean officials began to panic. Without an adequate supply of food, even the toughest of regimes fail.

As early as 1967 South Korea needed to buy annually 200,000 metric tons of rice. Despite great efforts, demand had outgrown supply. It was, as they say, a lot of rice. The rice had to be glutinous, or sticky rice, because that is the kind that Japanese and Koreans eat. Long, loose-grain rice to a Korean is not food.

South Korea selected Tongsun Park as the middleman. And like Iran-Contra, two entirely different problems got intermingled to the detriment of the people who started the whole business.

The 1967 rice sale was made through an established import-export firm from Philadelphia. Woodward and Dickerson of Philadelphia, Pennsylvania, had been impeccable since its founding in 1873.[9]

The deal was straightforward. California pearl rice obtained from the Rice Growers Association of California (whose lawyer was the former mayor of San Francisco, Joseph Alioto) was sold to South Korea.

The problem began after the sale was made. As the middleman on the deal, Park had made millions. But on orders from the KCIA he began to distribute at least some of the profits quite lavishly beginning sometime in 1973. The money all went in one direction, toward Capitol Hill. Over a period of seven years, the cash amounted to $9 million. And the merchant of rice was not bashful about his conquests when reporting to his case officers in Seoul.[10]

Occasionally the gift-giving became too obvious and Park would get into trouble as a result. The wives of two members of Congress, Mrs. Kiki de la Garza of Texas and Mrs. John T. Myers of Indiana, would tell identical stories to the House ethics committee.

Formally titled the Official Conduct Committee, that body heard from the women that each, during a trip to South Korea in August, had been offered an envelope of cash for her husband's campaign expenses. Both strong-minded women instinctively refused the money. Their husbands also agreed that accepting the cash was a bad idea, and the money was returned.[11]

While Park was busy making American friends, he was not always appreciated by his fellow Koreans. Consider the testimony of Keun Pal Lee, who served as a political third secretary in the Korean Embassy in Washington.

In Mr. Lee's words:

[Park] was considered an arrogant and cocky young fellow, overstepping Ambassador Dong Jo Kim's territory as chief of mission here in the United States.[12]

No wonder. Park had a way of sweeping out of his limousine in front of the Korean Embassy on Sheridan Circle and stepping up unannounced to the second-floor KCIA station chief's office. The habit annoyed other diplomats, including Korea's ambassador to the United States.

All very interesting, but what did Park and rice and the KCIA and the American Congress in its pursuit of truth, justice, and plain white envelopes have to do with the Reverend Sun Myung Moon?

Not terribly much, but the record of the Official Conduct Committee of the House of Representatives does bear scrutiny on this point.

In the three days of exhaustive hearings and months of investigations of the Korean government, its intelligence agency, and the legislative branch of the United States of America exactly two references were made to Moon or the Unification Church or any of its members.

The first appeared in the testimony of the same Mr. Lee. The committee was told that the former Korean cultural and informational attache had offered committee members a copy of a letter from President Park Chung Hee addressed to 60,000 "prominent Americans" (obviously a close-kept secret) praising the work of the Korean Cultural and Freedom Foundation (KCFF). The KCFF, which would feature later in the Fraser committee investigation, was a part of the so-called "Moon Empire."[13]

In contrast to the allegation in Mr. Lee's testimony, the letter, written in October 1970, is a vague one. It praises the work not of the KCFF directly, but one of its offshoots, Radio Free Asia (RFA). The praise is for broadcasting to Vietnam a program on American prisoners of war. That program, President Park wrote, would "give some comfort and assurance to suffering families in the U.S. that they are not alone in their fight for the return of their loved ones."[14]

Clearly Park's letter was meant to remind Americans of what a valuable ally South Korea was to the United States. It had little or nothing to do with promoting the Unification Church, the KCFF, or even RFA. (In any case, Congressman Caputo was wrong when he suggested that the letter was soliciting contributions to the unmentioned KCFF.)[15]

Koreagate's second tie to the Unification Church was revealed in the testimony of a former Korean Embassy employee in Washington. Under questioning from Congressman Caputo, Keun Pal Lee recalled a Lieutenant Colonel Han (he could not remember his full name) who served as assistant attache during Lee's tenure.

What was Colonel Han's role in Koreagate? Well, really he had none. According to testimony, Han simply resigned his position at the embassy and began working for Sun Myung Moon in New York City.

Han's other connection to Moon? Keun Pal Lee supplied the answer:

[W]hen I was the chief of the consular section he used to bring in the passports for both Mr. and Mrs. Sun Myung Moon whenever he made trip to the United States for the purpose of securing visas for them. So, I understood at the time that had some sort of relationship with Moon's church even then.[16]

That was that. It was all the information on Moon's connection with Koreagate as far as the committee could discover.

So far this was not political nitroglycerin. At least not yet. Other elements were needed. One must have an unpopular religious movement from the Far East. Add its exotic leader. Mix in a scandal involving the man's government, including the regime's intelligence arm, and *voila*—we have quite suddenly a very explosive mixture.

Or so the chairman of the House Subcommittee on International Organizations, Donald M. Fraser, thought. The subcommittee was one of nine organized under the House of Representatives' then Committee on International Relations.

As a subcommittee chairman, Fraser, like many of his colleagues, ran his fiefdom pretty much as he liked. In the 1970s and 1980s, the petty nobility of the House and Senate were after all no longer under control of the leadership, much less the full committee chairmen.

They chose the subjects they wished to investigate, hired whatever staff they pleased, and wrote the reports they wanted. The subcommittee chairmen were subject only to the criticism of the minority party. In the case of the House of Representatives, the minority was a near permanent (that is, an impotent) one. In nearly sixty years, two generations, the Republican party had enjoyed a majority in the House for only two years.

Fraser's subcommittee hardly confined itself to the rather dry subject of international organizations like the United Nations and the Organization of American States.

Fraser, in fact, made his subcommittee the liberal House organ for human rights. In the late 1970s human rights was the fashionable liberal foreign policy cause, surpassing even arms control. Conservative critics, however, like former UN Ambassador Jeane J. Kirkpatrick, had long accused liberals like Fraser of being highly selective in their judgments on human rights abuses. These same critics also charged that, while great attention was and is paid by American liberals to violations committed by authoritarian governments that are friendly, or at least not hostile to the United States, liberals ignore totalitarian governments with anti-American sentiments.

A review of the Fraser subcommittee's work on human rights seems to bear conservative critics out. For example, in the five years after 1973 it spent 120 days investigating human rights in all the expected countries anathema to American liberals: Argentina, Chile, El Salvador, Guatemala, Haiti, Iran (under the Shah), Indonesia, Nicaragua (under Somoza), Paraguay, the Philippines (under Marcos), Rhodesia, and Thailand. And, of course, South Korea. Hardly a *bête noire* was overlooked (in those busy productive years) by Chairman Fraser who, in addition to everything else, after January 1977 was given the full support of the Carter White House.

During the same period, only two weeks in total were devoted to the likes of North Korea, as well as Cambodia, Cuba, the Soviet Union, and Vietnam. That is about a 10–1 ratio.[17]

By early 1977 it had occurred to Congressman Fraser that something more than human rights in Korea needed investigating. South Korea with its overly long-lived Park regime, its anti-communism, and its quaintly fierce attachment to the United States was an ongoing temptation to investigate.

Koreagate only added spice to the stew. Like a new television situation comedy series, however, it had to have a hook to freshen up an old formula. In the case of the Fraser subcommittee, the hook was supplied by the Reverend Sun Myung Moon and his Unification Church. While others would investigate Koreagate, the International Organizations Subcommittee would probe the Unification Church and its ties to the Korean government, and in particular Korea's own Central Intelligence Agency.

To do the investigating, Fraser needed money. He got it. The initial amount totalled $300,000. Later, he received another installment, this one amounting to well over $300,000. With the money, the subcommittee chairman hired staff: lawyers, analysts, and field investigators, for eighteen months.

Although the previous history of the Fraser subcommittee suggested the investigation would turn out to be unfair, one should not always be guided by prejudice. A better test regarding the question of bias would be the composition of the investigating team. Fraser did not disappoint.

Of the thirteen new staff positions created especially for the probe of Sun Myung Moon, exactly one was given to the minority, that is, to the Republicans.[18]

The slight did not go without notice or protest. The feisty ranking Republican on the subcommittee, Congressman Edward Derwinski of Illinois, sent a "Dear Clem" letter to Fraser's nominal superior, Congressman Clement J. Zablocki of Wisconsin, Chairman of the International Relations Committee.

Derwinski also protested the large amount of money the investigation was allocated.

> Members of the Committee should fully understand that, in allocating $365,500 for the Korean inquiry we are paying a high price in terms of "opportunity costs." The Committee, and the House as a whole, now has $365,500 less to spend on research and investigation into other problems in the international arena.[19]

The committee could look into the military balance of power in Central Europe, Derwinski fumed, or some other threat to American and Western security like the alleged inability of international nuclear agencies to detect diversions of nuclear bomb material.

Moreover, the Illinois congressman said, the expanded subcommittee staff would be dedicating thirteen man-years to the investigation, which was exactly three times the amount of research done by all the House subcommittees in the previous year, 1976. Where, Derwinski implied, is the sense of proportion in all of this?[20]

Not only was the probe costly in staff time and money, Derwinski contended, the Fraser probe would also be redundant, merely mimicking the work of the House ethics committee, the Department of Justice, and the Security and Exchange Commission.[21]

The hardheaded Derwinski wasn't quite through. Less than a

month later, the Illinois Republican made a statement to the House Administration Committee's Subcommittee on Accounts, which oversaw and gave approval to House committee and subcommittee budgets.

In that statement, Derwinski bluntly told his congressional colleagues:

> In pondering the wisdom of this inquiry, one must also evaluate its foreign policy implication. Why are we picking on South Korea over the other countries we have similar relations with? Is singling out one of our few solid Asian allies really called for, especially when it could provide a series of deeply destabilizing events affecting both the security of our remaining troops in South Korea and the stability of the Far East generally?[22]

Nor would Derwinski let the subject lie there. Charging that Fraser was driven by an "obsession," the Illinois congressman suggested to the Budget Subcommittee that a time limit be placed on the inquiry and no extra staff be hired.

If the subcommittee would not accept that suggestion, Derwinski pleaded that Republicans be allowed a modest one-third of the new staff.[23]

Derwinski's objections were brushed aside, as he knew they would be. The Budget Subcommittee like all the other committees and subcommittees of the House and Senate were dominated and controlled by Democrats. Even the modest request for one-third of the new staffers was shunted aside.

Fraser, on the other hand, got everything he wanted. In the Committee on International Relations' resolution adopted by the House on February 3, 1977, one day after its introduction, his subcommittee was given a green light to "conduct a full and complete investigation and study of" U.S.-Korean relations involving all "agencies, officials, employees, and agents of the Government of the Republic of Korea and of persons and organizations acting on behalf of, under the direction of, or in cooperation with, such agencies, officials, employees, or agents. . . ."[24] In short, the Fraser subcommittee received *carte blanche* to investigate anything remotely connected to South Korea.

But there was more in the resolution.

The Fraser subcommittee could also examine "all aspects" of U.S.-Korean relations that dealt with political, military, intelligence, economic, educational, and informational "relationships" between Washington and Seoul as well as the usual array of agents and organizations acting under orders or working with the same.

In case anything had been omitted from this extremely broad charter, the resolution added a final general provision permitting the subcommittee (and, of course, its chairman) to examine "such related matters as may be appropriate."[25]

In other words, stripped of the legal gobbledygook, the Fraser subcommittee could do as it damned well pleased on anything even remotely connected with South Korea, the 1977-78 political season's least favorite American ally since South Vietnam.

What investigating South Korea had to do with "international organizations," the supposedly real work of the Fraser subcommittee, was never explained. Neither was the fact that this investigation was not being carried out by the Subcommittee on Asian Affairs.

Even within the House there were rumblings of discontent, and they were not confined to the much exercised ranking minority member of the Subcommittee on International Organizations.

The chairman of the full committee was not quite sure the South Korea probe was necessary in the first place, and he was a lot less certain at the conclusion of the process.

Clem Zablocki was a tough, old-fashioned Catholic Polish-American from Milwaukee. He never did understand "the San Francisco Democrats"—to use Jeane Kirkpatrick's later lugubrious phrase—and he knew that Fraser was one of them. Zablocki's doubts about Fraser's "witch-hunt"—a term that fellow Pole Ed Derwinski had already affixed to the man from Minneapolis' idea of a full and fair investigation—were expressed, however, only after the final subcommittee report was issued.

Zablocki's opinion raised eyebrows on Capitol Hill. Ordinarily, a full committee chairman writes an introduction to the subcommittee's published account of its final report. In doing so, the chairman gives his imprimatur to the work of the subcommittee chairman who is from the same political party.

In the case of the Fraser report, Clem Zablocki had other

thoughts: in fact, Zablocki washed his hands of it, and, moreover, said so. In his words:

> The findings, conclusions, and recommendations in this report are those of a majority of the members of the Subcommittee on International Organizations and do not necessarily reflect the views of the membership of the full Committee on International Relations.[26]

That the majority of the subcommittee would sign the report was a foregone conclusion since the panel was stacked not only with Democrats, but Vietnam-War-style liberal Democrats at that. The chairman's disclaimer, however, was not at all a foregone conclusion, but it proved to be an embarrassing epilogue to an investigation that Congressman Derwinski had long warned his colleagues about.

But we are getting ahead of the story.

Before Zablocki's disavowal of the subcommittee's report, there was one more storm warning. Again it came from a Democrat, Georgia's John J. Flynt, chairman of the House ethics committee. In opening his own Korean hearings on October 19, almost nine months after the Fraser subcommittee began its work, Chairman Flynt quoted extensively from the opinions of the late Supreme Court Justice Robert H. Jackson.

It was not an idle or merely literary choice by Congressman Flynt. As he knew full well, Jackson had been an ardent believer in the First Amendment and the rights of genuinely unpopular minorities (who by definition have no fashionable defenders). Even more than Justice Hugo Black, who had a Ku Klux Klan membership to live down, Jackson had believed in a literal reading of the Constitution when it came to basic human rights for Americans and for anyone else who became enmeshed in the American machinery of justice.

After all, it had been Jackson in the dissenting opinion in *Korematsu v. the United States* (1944) who had defended a Japanese-American's right to sue the American government for forcibly relocating him and his family during wartime, a privilege not extended to Americans of German and Italian descent.

So Flynt quoted Jackson, and not Black, much less Douglas. His citations served as a warning to congressional witch-hunters. Four years before *Korematsu*, Jackson, who was then U.S. Attorney General, had said:

> [T]he most dangerous power of the prosecutor: that he will pick people that he thinks he should get, rather than pick cases that need to be prosecuted. With the law books filled with a great assortment of crimes, a prosecutor stands a fair chance of finding at least a technical violation of some act on the part of almost anyone.[27]

Jackson had continued:

> In such a case, it is not a question of discovering the commission of a crime and then looking for the man who committed it, it is a question of picking the man then searching the law books or putting investigators to work, to pin some offense on him.

> It is in this realm, in which the prosector picks some person whom he dislikes or desires to embarrass, or selects some group of unpopular persons and then looks for an offense, that the greatest danger of abuse of prosecuting power lies. It is here that law enforcement becomes personal, and the real crime becomes that of being unpopular with the predominant or governing group, being attached to the wrong political views, or being personally obnoxious to or in the way of the prosecutor himself.[28]

In an eerie foreshadowing of his *Korematsu* opinion, the future Justice Jackson had concluded with this observation:

> In times of fear or hysteria political, radical, religious groups, often from the best of motives, cry for the scalps of individuals or groups because they do not like their views.[29]

Jackson's words were a warning that Chairman Flynt would take seriously in his investigation of Koreagate. To see how seriously his colleague from Minnesota took them, read on.

Having collected his budget and staff, Fraser moved quickly to lay out what he had in mind.

On April 4, 1977, after two months of preliminary investigation, the subcommittee issued, under the full committee's name, its guidelines for the investigation.

There was not much in the way of intellectual coherence in the guidelines, but in the U.S. Congress such qualities in a one-party organization were seldom, if ever, required.

The ten-point list of charges was arranged in no discernible order; the list instead was a casual collection of accusations that indicted anything that appeared to be South Korean.

The thrust of what Fraser really had in mind came out loud and clear in the first point on the list. The subcommittee would investigate:

> Operational ties between the Korean Intelligence Agency and organizations headed by the Rev. Sun Myung Moon[.][30]

As for the other nine points, they were a hodge-podge of charges already proven, assertions that were never proven, and connections that were never established. All of this, of course, was suffused in a fog of innuendo that depended on prejudice for proof when it came to pinpointing actual wrongdoing.

Except for the first charge, the subcommittee's *magna carta* to itself consisted mostly of apples and oranges. There were the already well-known complaints about the South Korean government ("influence-buying by the Government of the Republic of Korea") and sinister suggestions about church leaders (they tried "to gain control of an American bank").[31]

Of course, the overall mandate was wider still. The subcommittee would also "examine allegations of improper or illegal activity in the conduct of relations between the United States and the Republic of Korea."[32]

Fraser claimed to have long been interested in these questions (since 1975) and he promised to conduct the investigation in order "to identify sources of discord, corruption and distortion of national interests with a view to having them corrected." In addition, and perhaps more modestly, the subcommittee promised to provide "some guidelines of the proper conduct of relations" between the U.S. and Korea.[33]

Modesty aside, for the up-front $700,000 in taxpayers' money, what did the subcommittee actually prove and what did it provide?

The answer to that question is the subject of the remainder of the chapter. Before we proceed, however, it's necessary to ask an even more basic question. And that is, what damned business was it of Congressman Fraser in the first place to launch this investigation?

In an era when the United States Congress seems to run everything except perhaps most of the nation's railroads, the question might seem odd. But it is not, and this is why.

Historically, the investigative power of the American Congress was based on a sensible requirement; namely, the need to know in order to pass good legislation. Congress of course still does this on occasion by making laws just the way that the textbooks in high school civics insist on describing the process.

But the investigatory power of the Congress has gone well beyond the original intent. The American Imperial Parliament can hold hearings to elicit information leading to legislation, of course. But it can also sniff out anything any part of the executive branch is up to. Actually, the Congress can do just about anything it wants. And that amounts to whatever any chairman thinks will benefit himself or his most important constituents—largely the same thing. In the case of the Fraser subcommittee, the staff that wrote its own investigative mandate did not bother to suggest that there was a legislative purpose for the eighteen-month mission on which it was about to embark.

The subcommittee's staff simply assumed that it had every right to poke and probe into anything that the subcommittee pleased—even if it had little or nothing whatever to do with international organizations.

And why not? Chairman Fraser was mounted on his favorite hobbyhorse; and so it was that he rode off into the sunset, his saddlebags stuffed with the taxpayers' hard-earned dollars. The unspeakable in pursuit of the unfindable.

Cynics of course contend that the United States Congress' present power to punish is unlimited. Iran-Contra is often cited as an example of this. They may, in fact, not be cynics but realists after all. But a hardy band of dissenters insist that the American Constitution, the Supreme Law of the Land, did create limits to government intrusion—even for the legislative branch.

Limitation of congressional power is an ancient and yet shocking notion and worth exploring before examining the particulars and details of Fraser versus Moon.

Consider this: the subcommittee's agenda, stripped of the high-minded and high-browed palaver about pursuing the national interest involving Korean-American relations, was based on a deep and abiding desire to fry Moon and his followers.

To do so, however, involved the subcommittee in delicate constitutional questions. We begin, for example, with the First Amendment.

The Founders of our nation correctly recognized the mischief legislatures could inflict upon the rights of individuals. They fashioned our fundamental laws in such a way as to ensure that individual rights were not trampled upon.

In Moon versus Fraser, First Amendment issues quickly emerged. The subcommittee insisted on probing the inner core of Moon and his Unification Church. And the core means precisely that. Fraser and his cohorts were intent on passing judgment through their "investigation" on the nature of church beliefs.

To say the least, Fraser & Company did not approve of these beliefs, but that the investigation grossly intruded into religious faith never bothered the investigators. So much for the First Amendment.

In one other general area the subcommittee showed an equal understanding regarding basic constitutional limitations to the power of the Congress. Chairman Fraser assumed that Moon and his followers were wrong to express political opinions. Mere expression, in fact, was quickly converted into a shadowy conspiracy in order to—what else?—rule the world. This comic book premise, which would have shamed the publishers of *Superman*, engaged grown men and women for a year and a half. Bravely, the members of the subcommittee, its chairman, and a full field army of investigators battled to prevent Moon's threat to human history and life on this planet as we know it.

Treading on sacred constitutional ground can make even a member of Congress wary—at least for a while. Chairman Fraser made the appropriate noises at the very beginning of the probe. During the pre-probe part of the process which began in mid-1976 Fraser said:

Many people have contacted my office regarding this hearing and seem to have the impression that the subcommittee is investigating the Unification Church, which Sun Myung Moon heads. Let me say at the outset that this is not the case. This hearing is not concerned with the religious philosophy or practices of the Unification Church. Those are protected by the First Amendment and those rights are inviolable.[34]

A man who could confuse theology with philosophy in one muddied and muddled sentence does not merit much trust from theologians, philosophers, or even the casual student of the U.S. Constitution.

But much worse followed.

Like any good game hunter, Fraser began slowly and carefully. In the tradition of all congressional investigations, the hunt did not start in the hearing room with witnesses, spectators, and reporters. The lights, cameras, and network exposure would come later. Or so it was hoped.

Demonstrating a noncombative spirit, Fraser met with Neil A. Salonen, president of the American branch of the Unification Church, a month before launching the probe. (Salonen was to be the investigation's first witness.) The meeting was a get-acquainted session and went very well, or so the hapless Salonen thought.

Salonen brought with him official church documents outlining the work of the Unification Church, the Freedom Leadership Foundation (FLF), and the International Cultural Foundation—all of which were founded by the Reverend Sun Myung Moon.

In some detail, the goals and purposes of each were outlined by Salonen, after which Fraser and staff asked questions. Salonen answered them. The atmosphere was deceptively mild and cordial.

After several hours of pleasant exchange, the private meeting broke up. Salonen and his fellow church members were convinced that they had explained their side completely and that Fraser and his staff had been satisfied on all counts.

Then the hammer dropped.

Three months later Salonen was invited back, this time to appear before a public hearing on the same day that three critics of the Unification Church just happened to be scheduled to speak.

Salonen refused; although pro and con witnesses can appear on the same day, the usual practice is to separate them. If that is not possible, an effort is normally made at least to balance the testimony from each side. Congressman Fraser made no such attempt.

When Salonen did appear later in executive—that is, secret—session of the subcommittee, his testimony was promptly leaked to the press by the chairman in violation of the subcommittee's own rules. The leak was only a sample of what was to come. It simply set the pattern for what became the norm of the Fraser subcommittee's behavior.[35]

As already pointed out, the late Justice Jackson's worry—that a prosecutor too often found a prospective "criminal" and then searched the lawbooks for a proper crime—seemed to fit perfectly the *modus operandi* of this subcommittee.

The perpetrators had, of course, already been found. They were Moon and his followers. The question then became: What was the nature of the crime these people had committed?

Fraser and his eager-beaver staff of young and ambitious lawyers and investigators readily found the answer to that all-important question.

Any good crime story needs a surrounding milieu, and the Fraser subcommittee supplied it. The milieu was colored with one overriding assumption, one master premise upon which everything else was to be based. That assumption, that premise, of course was never proved. It didn't have to be. The subcommittee started its investigation in the belief that the Unification Church members were up to no good simply because they were "Moonies." And thanks to years of bad publicity about "brain-washing" the young, the "Moonie Conspiracy" could safely be put into the "everybody knows that" category.

Justice Jackson knew of what he spoke.

A corollary assumption that the Fraser subcommittee cited over and over again was that the conspiracy was advanced by "the Moon Organization," a tightly interlocking array of foundations and institutions—front groups, really—acting on behalf of Moon and his overall ambition to run the world.[36]

Is this an exaggeration? I quote from the subcommittee's "Conclusions":

The U[nification] C[hurch] and numbers of other religious and secular organizations headed by Sun Myung Moon constitute essentially one international organization. This organization depends heavily upon the interchangeability of its components and upon its ability to move personnel and financial assets freely across international boundaries and between business and non-profit organizations.[37]

Of course, that was only the beginning. The Fraser report's conclusions also asserted:

The Moon Organization attempts to achieve goals outlined by Sun Myung Moon who has substantial control over the economic, political and spiritual activities undertaken by the organization in pursuit of these goals.[38]

The report continued:

Among the goals of the Moon Organization is the establishment of worldwide government in which the separation of church and state would be abolished and which would be governed by Moon and his followers.[39]

Having spelled out the goal of the "Moon Organization," the Fraser subcommittee laid bare the means by which Moon would effectively destroy the American Way of Life. Here's how the church would do it:

The Moon Organization has attempted, with varying degrees of success, to gain control over or establish business and other secular institutions in the United States and elsewhere, and has engaged in political activities in the United States. Some of these activities were undertaken to benefit the ROK Government or otherwise to influence U.S. foreign policy.[40]

The tie with the ROK of course was the heart of the Fraser probe. Without it, the chairman and his subcommittee were, among other things, in shallow constitutional water. Therefore, the Fraser report's conclusions hammered home the alleged link between Moon and Seoul:

While pursuing its own goals, the Moon Organization promoted the interests of the ROK Government, and at times did so in cooperation with or at the direction of ROK agencies and officials. The Moon

Organization maintained mutually beneficial ties with a number of Korean officials.[41]

At first reading, the charges are either hair-raising or utterly laughable. First how about the specifics? Let us hear more about the "Moonie" plot to rule the world. What about those institutions and businesses that are supposed to further this modest ambition of the Reverend Moon? Which ones are the Fraser report talking about?

What about the political influence of the Moon Organization? Where, when, and with whom? And please, let us have more on the church ties with the South Korean government and the KCIA.

Finally, there is the larger issue that newspapermen call the "so what?" question. So what? What does any of this prove? Are we being had by somebody else's hidden agenda, and if so what is it?

It is hard to believe that a religious organization that could claim no more than 37,000 followers in the United States at the time of the Fraser investigation was in a position to scrap the American Constitution, and in particular its First Amendment. But that is what the Fraser subcommittee would have had us believe, and more besides.

It emphasized also that Moon intended to be the leader.

To gatherings of his followers, Moon makes it clear that he would occupy the position of authority in the future world order which is his goal.[42]

Although the subcommittee's staff had no trained theologian, or even one on call, that did not stop it from making key judgments about the Reverend Sun Myung Moon's religion, judgments that should have been the result of a sophisticated theological analysis; in this specific case, the interpretation of one of Moon's beliefs.

As a whole, Moon's beliefs were never examined by Fraser. Instead, and in Joe McCarthy-like fashion, the International Organizations Subcommittee focused on a single belief of the church— and managed to get that wrong.

The report quoted the following remark made by Moon as proof that he intended to create his own theocracy, abolishing separation of church and state.

The time will come, without my seeking it, that my words will almost serve as law. If I ask a certain thing, it will be done.[43]

That statement was a reworking of a passage from the gospel of John 12:48, in which Jesus explained his mission to his disciples.[44]

Moon's followers insist that his message was no more political in nature than the Nazarene's. Both, they say, were talking about moral teaching, not secular legislation; both were saying that the teaching will or will not be accepted by those who choose to listen—in other words people have free choice.

As such, this kind of pronouncement is hardly different from the view expressed by every prophet, true or false, that has ever wandered through human history. Nevertheless, the religious naifs on the Fraser subcommittee interpreted a moral observation intended to comfort a few modest followers into a *Mein Kampf*-style proclamation.

But one can't hope to rule this world without an apparatus of some sort. In Moon's case, Fraser & Company spun out a web of businesses and foundations that all formed a huge international empire. Spider-like, Moon's enterprises secretly crept out, unnoticed, seeking whom they might devour.

The subcommittee was disturbed by the fact that the Unification Church and its members owned a variety of enterprises in the first place, even though for centuries churches worldwide have owned businesses that have had little or nothing to do with matters of the spirit.

With that presupposition carefully planted, the Fraser report went on to pillory particular church enterprises. (They were apparently only interested in some of Moon's organizations.) One prize example of this was Tong-Il Industries. The reason for interest in Tong-Il is simple. Based in South Korea, the firm is a defense contractor. The owners of Tong-Il, or at least the major stockholders, are members of the Unification Church. By Korean law, this enterprise and thousands of other companies are required to contribute to South Korea's defense if the government finds it necessary. As the country has been under the communist gun for nearly forty years, that South Korean government requirement is not altogether mystifying.

The opportunity to brush the Reverend Sun Myung Moon, a

man of religion, with the tar of the name *arms merchant*, was simply too good for the subcommittee to resist. So it didn't.

Fraser and his investigators dropped what they thought was the big one on Tong-Il, accusing the firm of manufacturing, or wanting to manufacture, the local version of the M-16 rifle.

The Tong-Il smear is a near-perfect example of living and breathing liberal McCarthyism. Relying on prejudice and callow assumptions, the smear simply glided over inconvenient facts and assumed that the case was proven.

Fraser's subcommittee apparently had yet to hear of the classical Christian doctrine of the "just war." During most of Christendom's history, it has not been considered shameful for anyone, including a religious man, to contribute to his country's defense.

And no one on the subcommittee contended that any South Korean government had been revanchist, bent on attacking the North.

The subcommittee also seemed unaware that mainline churches in the United States, including the Methodists, the Presbyterians, the Baptists, and the Disciples of Christ, have long held stock in defense industries. These churches have not necessarily linked their portfolios to any just-war doctrine. "Morality is fine," the late Kaiser Wilhelm II is once supposed to have observed, "but so are dividends." I suspect a lot of Presbyterians think so too.

As for Tong-Il, the company produces in the main low-technology machine tools including lathes, milling machines, and boilers. Also needles. General Dynamics it is not. Instead, Tong-Il also makes machine parts that others turn into military goods. It denies making the M-16 rifle or ever having wanted to. The Fraser report did not bother to furnish proof on the M-16 question nor did it establish the immorality of manufacturing such a weapon other than to assert a glib and conventional 1960s-style pacifism.[45]

Then there was Il Hwa. The subcommittee thought a great deal about Il Hwa because the Korean pharmaceutical company, owned by a long-time Unification Church member, was indicted for non-payment of taxes in Korea. The Fraser report also happily announced, citing a Korean newspaper account, that Il Hwa had transferred some $6.2 million to the Unification Church without making any tax payment.

The story is not pretty, but what the Fraser report left out was also interesting. Although the report was issued at the end of October 1978, it failed to mention that Il Hwa's owner had been cleared of the charges in a Korean court in May, five months before the subcommittee released its findings.[46]

News travels slowly from the Far East, I suppose, but not that slowly. That wasn't the worst of it. The subcommittee fumbled it once more on the Il Hwa case. In their eagerness to get the church on anything, the boys on the Hill blew a big hole in their main contention.

A major premise of the larger argument was that Moon's organization and the Korean government were in cahoots. Yet when that same government indicts a company, Il Hwa, owned by a church member, it is offered as proof of Church illegality.

So which is it? Were the church members and the Korean government bad guys in bed together involved in some kind of planetary conspiracy or were church members in Korea, like all Korean citizens, being monitored closely by a virtuous Korean government?

But Korean-owned businesses in Korea were not the only problem, as Fraser and friends saw it. There was also the affair of a Washington, D.C., bank, the Diplomat National Bank. Put together in 1977, the Diplomat was supposed to be the country's first Asian bank.

The Fraser subcommittee found the bank interesting for two reasons. First, Tongsun Park owned shares in the bank, as did members of the Unification Church. The Fraser report also accused the church of attempting to gain control of a majority share of the stock, which, if true, isn't illegal. Nevertheless, the attempt to control Diplomat Bank stock was supposedly done in a sneaky, sly fashion. At the same time, Fraser hoped to establish a link between the bank, the Unification Church, and the Korean government by way of Washington's favorite rice merchant.

The subcommittee could not do that for a simple reason: there wasn't any link. It should have been obvious, even to a congressional investigator, that if Unification Church members, including Moon, wanted to conceal their purchases of bank stock, they wouldn't have purchased shares in their own names.[47]

It was never very clear why Congressman Fraser thought that the Unification Church and its interest in the Diplomat National

Bank constituted something sinister. Only the cloud of innuendo surrounding the Reverend Sun Myung Moon and his church can explain how that suspicion could ever have been taken seriously.

Church businesses were only part of the apparat, of course. There were the various church-sponsored foundations, even a little kid's choir, that aroused the suspicion of the intrepid congressional gumshoes.

Two of the foundations figured most prominently in the Fraser probe: the Freedom Leadership Foundation and the Korean Cultural and Freedom Foundation.

The sin of the FLF, according to the Fraser subcommittee, was its involvement in American politics. At a time when the Nicaraguan Sandinistas (whose party hymn still identifies the United States as the enemy of mankind) employed (and until recently continued to employ) U.S. public relations firms to curry favor on Capitol Hill, this may sound rather quaint.

But the Fraser report identifies the FLF as "the political arm" of the Unification Church—an accusation that FLF spokesmen vigorously denied in the Fraser hearings—denials that were simply ignored.

What made the FLF "political" and therefore unacceptable to the McGovernite liberals on the subcommittee? Simple. The FLF's principal purpose was to prepare and distribute anticommunist literature. Doing so is protected by the First Amendment, but the subcommittee chose to ignore that point and made their charges all the same.

Unfortunately for Fraser, the Internal Revenue Service didn't agree with the implications of the report. And the IRS still doesn't. The IRS listed the FLF as a tax-exempt educational organization, a status which was not changed despite an IRS investigation, the results of which were known to the Fraser staffers before the report was written. Instead, the subcommittee relied on the unsubstantiated testimony of two professional ex-church members who had never worked at the foundation in question.[48]

Who is to be believed? The Fraser subcommittee's work has already been examined and found wanting in a number of areas. As for the IRS, it is known for its thoroughness in finding ways to extract income from individuals and organizations.

The Korean Cultural and Freedom Foundation, the KCFF, also

drew its fair share of flak from Fraser & Company. This time, the issue wasn't what the foundation did, but who ran it. KCFF's president, Bo Hi Pak, was known to be the closest associate of Sun Myung Moon. Pak, someone with a high profile, was an easy target. Or so the subcommittee thought.

Oddly enough, the Fraser subcommittee wasn't interested in the Moon-Pak relationship. Perhaps they thought exploring it further was merely beating an already dead horse. Instead, it was another dying nag the members wanted to flog. Pak, the subcommittee said repeatedly, was an agent of the Korean CIA, and the KCFF was nothing more than a front for Korean intelligence.

When that rather nasty accusation did not fly, the subcommittee tried a new approach. Using the testimony of yet another disgruntled ex-church member, Pak and the KCFF were accused of trying to "influence" wealthy Americans and raise money for Moon's empire through the back door.

Here is where the kids' choir comes in. The KCFF was and is the sponsor of the Little Angels Korean choir and dance troupe. The children have performed for years around the world. The troupe's first patron was President Dwight Eisenhower. The children are welcomed as ambassadors of good will for Korea in the tradition of the Vienna Boys Choir. Church spokesmen deny that any effort has been made to exploit the kids for the church's purposes.

The denial did not stop the Fraser report from stating:

> Little Angels concerts often provide the occasion for Moon and his top followers to mingle with politicians and endorsements were used in Moon Organization literature to enhance Moon's image and have pictures taken.[49]

The subcommittee, however, never produced the pictures or literature or any other tangible evidence that the "Moonies" had ever done that. This, of course, begs the question: So what if they had?[50]

The Fraser subcommittee, having saved America from the menace of oriental child dancers, naturally had to detail other examples of church attempts to influence politics.

Again the presumption that political activity by church members is wrong in and of itself is a powerful leitmotif in the subcommittee's report. But is the indignation a case of naivete or merely dissembling? It's hard to believe that these dedicated public servants could conclude what they did and still pretend that they operate in the center of the American political system.

American religious denominations have fought inside the political system tooth and nail for what they believe since the nation's founding. Churchmen weighed in for and against slavery before the Civil War. In our time, the hottest social issues, including school prayer and right-to-life, have been led and financed by America's manifold religious groups.

For the liberals on the Fraser subcommittee, the year of our Lord 1978 was not too long after America's left-wing clergymen waged war against this country's involvement in Vietnam.

Apparently any involvement in politics by the Reverend Sun Myung Moon was different for the Fraser subcommittee. His influence in politics was bad and that simply was a given. The subcommittee ignored the fact that such examples of influence were found to be ludicrously few.

Three examples will suffice.

First, there is little doubt that the first time many Americans ever heard of Moon was in the final days of the anguished Nixon presidency. Watergate brought this unusual Korean out into the open in support of a beleaguered chief executive.

Yet church members, with reason, deny that their efforts during the Watergate crisis were directly political or even indirectly partisan in defense of one Richard Nixon. Moon's campaign, labelled the National Prayer and Fast Committee, or NPFC, came about as the result of one of Moon's numerous revelations.

The basis for this particular campaign was religious, not political. Forgiveness (not necessarily of Nixon alone), Love, and Unity were the themes.

In the Reverend Sun Myung Moon's one meeting with Nixon, the conversation began with a prayer. It is the sort of thing preachers do. They also preach. Which is what Moon proceeded to do to Nixon, who is himself a sort-of Quaker.

Moon exhorted Nixon to tell the truth (really!) and requested the president's support for a movement of prayer and fasting. Moon also warned against the communist enemy.[51]

This is not exactly the stuff of Washington novels, but it is the stuff that actually gets said in the Oval Office—even, or perhaps especially, in moments of national crisis.

The tale becomes even sillier. The next target of the Fraser probe into church political influence peddling was the NPFC's three-day prayer and fast session on Capitol Hill. Admittedly prayer on the Hill is a long-established ritual characterized by a lot of moist, hot air. So why not include the Almighty in congressional doings? Such occurrences are taken with a grain of salt anyway.

Moreover, the contention by the Fraserites that the NPFC's session was a pro-Nixon demonstration is belied by the speeches and the literature handed out at the vigils. Nothing was said in support of the president to the detriment of his congressional Democratic (and by this time even Republican) critics. Instead, the soothing syrup of mutual forgiveness and national unity was administered.[52]

The event was not, in short, political hardball.

The final example offered by the Fraser team was church participation in election campaigns. That is, members of the Unification Church actually helped in congressional campaigns. Again, one gets the feeling that the subcommittee members and staff were being totally disingenuous. Religious groups involving themselves in electoral politics? From what distant planet had Fraser and his staff so lately come?

Let us look at the specifics.

The Fraserites hinted of a dark Moon Organization conspiracy to bore within Congress by supporting and getting elected legislators sympathetic to the Cause. Only three instances, however, were cited: two involving House and Senate races, plus one involving a seat in the strategically vital New York State assembly.

The Freedom Leadership Foundation, which the subcommittee identified as the church "political action arm," was fingered as the conduit for the church's campaign activities.

What precisely was the church's role in these three political races? The church members and groups did next to nothing. In the 1974 New York congressional race, three unpaid FLF volunteers took time off to work for Charles Stephens in his race against incumbent Richard Ottinger. They had done the same when Stephens ran for the New York State Assembly two years earlier. Finally, the Fraser subcommittee accused the New Hampshire

Unification Church of supporting a Republican candidate for the U.S. Senate. Again, several church members had simply worked part-time for the candidate as volunteers—handing out bumper stickers on weekends.[53]

And that was that. The Fraser machine had labored and labored and labored again, and this time, it had produced a bumper sticker.

In each case, the church-supported candidates also lost. Not only was their effort a drop in a very large bucket of campaign effort across the country, it was also on the lowest possible level.

So, why the worry? Besides the general anti-church bias, church member support of Stephens against Ottinger might have caused the subcommittee chairman's ire. Richard Ottinger was a liberal Democrat of exactly the same persuasion and generation as Donald Fraser. Two peas in a pod could not have been closer.

But all of the political wheeling and dealing, even in the subcommittee's eyes, was only a side show compared to the middle ring under the Big Top. The featured attraction of the Fraser circus was the church-KCIA connection. Or alleged connection, because as it turned out, the church-KCIA link wasn't much of an act either.

Fraser's pitch, like any good barker's, was shouted loud and clear about what the customers would see before the customers got inside the tent. In this case, Fraser told the press on March 15, 1978, that the Unification Church was founded by the KCIA's director Kim Jong-pil in 1961. Not too surprisingly, Fraser got his headlines in the *New York Times*, the *Washington Post*, and most newspapers in Japan.

As proof, Fraser released intelligence documents purporting to prove the illegitimate birth of the Unification Church. Although Fraser and his McGovernite allies were no friends of the CIA, what the agency said this time was taken as pure gold.

The intelligence is suspect and the documentation skimpy. There were, in fact, three reports about the Unification Church. One mentions the church by name, two others refer to the "Tong Il Church" which Fraser and I presume refers to Moon's church.

The first CIA report, dated February 26, 1963, says that the Unification Church was founded by an ex-KCIA chief, presumably Kim. But the document in question is a raw field report—they

come in by the thousands every day to the U.S. intelligence community. As such they are clearly labelled tentative and unrefined
because, among other things, they have yet to be substantiated by
proven sources.

The other two documents, dated December 18, 1964, and January 4, 1965, were also field reports and had no solid substantiation
either. In fact, they merely repeated the 1963 story about Kim and
the Unification Church and added no other details.[54]

Unfortunately for Fraser, and despite eighteen months of looking, the link between the church and the KCIA was never forged.
He came up with nothing more than the old field reports. He
couldn't find anything because there wasn't anything to be found,
something that was ruefully admitted on page 354 of his subcommittee report.[55] Moreover, the subcommittee couldn't prove that
the Unification Church members were also "agents of influence"
for the Korean government.[56]

Although the report contained more accusations of church-ROK
links, all of which proved insubstantial, one particular example
helps illustrate the Fraser mentality.

As part of the overall accusation that Bo Hi Pak was an agent of
the KCIA, a Korean defector in testimony to the subcommittee
said Pak had a secret and direct cable channel to the Blue House,
the Korean executive mansion. Fraser and his staff took up the
mantra also by hinting several times that Pak had such a link to the
Korean president. Pak denied it and challenged the subcommittee
to produce intercepts proving the tie. Intercepts, of course, could
have been produced. The U.S. National Security Agency is in
business to intercept communication links. But the subcommittee
couldn't produce any because the intercepts didn't exist.[57]

So what had all of Fraser's sound and fury produced? Not very
much, it seems. Certainly no evidence of wrongdoing. Laws had
not been broken. Although plenty of accusations had been made,
more often than not the accusations themselves violated the constitutional rights of the accused.

But worse, the very accusation that had sparked the hearings in
the first place was never proven. Indeed, buried in the Report was
an admission that the church was not a part of official U.S.-Korean
relations and had never been.

So what did the Fraser subcommittee recommend in the end?

More investigations of the Unification Church by the federal government. Investigation would come in the form of a coordinated effort by numerous agencies, including the Immigration and Naturalization Service, the Internal Revenue Service, the Securities and Exchange Commission, and the Federal Trade Commission.

The INS was to figure out a way to keep foreign Unification Church missionaries out of the United States. The IRS, despite its earlier best efforts, was to try again to nail the church on some tax charge.

The SEC and FTC, meanwhile, were supposed to reopen their investigation of the Diplomat National Bank. They did not do so.

Fraser also wanted the U.S. government to investigate supposed church violations of the Arms Control Act. And what about a "Unification Crusade Army" and "paramilitary discipline"? Those questions, too, were supposed to be investigated. Perhaps the FBI could get into the act.[58]

From a supposedly objective and dispassionate investigation of Korean-American relations, the subcommittee reduced the probe to screaming in the night over a fantasy church militia.

After the Fraser subcommittee had exposed such a dangerous menace, one would suppose that Moon's "empire" would strike back.

It did, sort of. At first church members rather naively believed that cooperation with a congressional investigation was the right thing to do. In fact, they made the subcommittee's investigations easy by giving them box-loads of documents. Only later, when they realized that the church was getting the axe, did they fight back. The members did so by appearing at hearings, usually without subpoena, in the hope that their side of the story would get reported. It didn't.

Leading the counterattack was the Unification Church's top representative in the U.S. and confidant of the Reverend Sun Myung Moon, Bo Hi Pak, who testified before the subcommittee on March 22, April 11, and again, on April 20.

Apparently realizing there wasn't much percentage in restraint or civility before the Inquisition-like panel, Pak threw caution to the wind and on his first day of testimony stunned the packed hearing room with an uncharacteristic verbal assault on the subcommittee, its actions and its motives.

In a prepared opening statement, Pak accused Fraser and his staff of violating the church's First Amendment rights and attempting to undermine South Korean-U.S. relations. He also hinted there was a strong odor of racism and bigotry surrounding the hearings. He put it this way:

> I am here today because I am a Korean disciple of Reverend Moon and a member of the Unification Church, and a dedicated anti-Communist. "Korean" is a dirty word these days and everything "Korean" is suspect. Also, to be a "Moonie" in this country is very unpopular and the cause for anti-Communism is practically dead now. Yet, I am all of those unpopular things. However, Mr. Chairman, I will not recant any of those qualifications. I am a proud Korean—a proud "Moonie"—and a dedicated anti-Communist and I intend to remain so the rest of my life.[59]

For the most part, Pak sidestepped or declined entirely to answer most of Fraser's inquiries, responding instead with criticisms of his own about both the questions and the subcommittee's sessions. Already confused by the aggressive and defiant witness, Fraser was completely flummoxed when, after testifying, Pak insisted on ending the session with a prayer.

Pak's second appearance before the subcommittee on April 11 didn't go much better, though Fraser and his staff seemed prepared and determined to head off another Pak fillibuster.

When Pak asked to read an opening statement, Fraser denied the request and began his inquiry. Pak refused to answer any questions until he had read his prepared remarks. After several exchanges, Fraser finally relented and said he would allow Pak five minutes for his comments. Pak refused and demanded "19 minutes and 45 seconds." The chairman threatened Pak with a contempt of Congress citation. Pak was insistent. Fraser gave him fifteen minutes. Pak accepted and, once more, tore into the subcommittee and Fraser personally, accusing him at one point of being "an instrument of the devil."[60]

And, again, Pak closed his testimony with an unsolicited reading of the Lord's Prayer.

Pak's third and final appearance before the subcommittee came on April 20. Once again Fraser attempted to bore in with questions, and once again Pak refused to cooperate until he had an opportunity to read from a prepared statement. Fraser relented, but this time Pak's remarks were directed specifically at the chairman himself, who, he intimated, was a communist sympathizer or worse.

Brandishing newspaper and magazine clips, Pak said there was sufficient evidence to suggest Fraser was little more than a communist stooge and the hearings were designed to destroy the alliance between South Korea and the United States. He high-lighted one article in which a former Polish intelligence officer, who defected to the U.S., claimed that Fraser was considered an agent of influence for the Soviet Union. Then Pak delivered his summation.

> Today in this Subcommittee hearing room we have raised portentous questions which demand answers. What if, as the evidence suggests, you, Mr. Chairman, are secretly working to undermine Korean-American relations? What if you are an ardent supporter of the Troskyite-Communist Party? What if you are the "agent of influence" for Moscow here on Capital Hill? If these things are true, then the government of the United States is itself in grave danger. America's very survival and the security of the free world are at stake.[61]

Pak again attempted to close his testimony with a prayer, but Fraser cut him off explaining he was late for a plane back to Minnesota where he was campaigning. But before Fraser could reach the door, Pak grabbed the microphone and insisted on a prayer for a safe journey on the chairman's trip to Minnesota. The room exploded in laughter but Pak prayed anyway.

When the leaks and charges continued to pour out of the subcommittee to friendly media, the Unification Church and Bo Hi Pak on June 22, 1978, filed a lawsuit for a damage award of $30 million against Fraser and two of his investigators.

The suit charged that the three had conspired to violate the constitutional rights of the Unification Church and Pak.[62]

Then the church quickly assembled a book refuting the Fraser subcommittee's report. It wasn't very slick, but *Our Response* made its points in 128 pages. All in all, the book was more carefully argued than anything the subcommittee had offered. But vindication it was not.

One other question hangs in the air. Were the church members themselves victims of a conspiracy?

Under American law, conspiracy is something one can be easily indicted for, but rarely convicted of. Nevertheless, Fraser's conduct and the conduct of his staff are most certainly worth looking at.

Abuse of power is easy, and the Fraser subcommittee seemed bent on proving how easy abuse was.

Some abuse is already apparent. But more examples are worth examining. One has already been mentioned in passing: the use—or rather misuse—of the media.

Fraser and the subcommittee loved publicity and they knew how to get it: by throwing the first punch and serving up red meat, to use a colorful mixed metaphor. I have already mentioned the opening round in which the Unification Church-KCIA connection was trumpeted to the press at the beginning of the hearings.

In the spirit of the lynch mob, the hanging always comes first, then the trial. In that spirit, Fraser and associates also promptly leaked testimony that was supposed to remain confidential. With Fraser, confidential testimony didn't stay that way long.

Members of the subcommittee and the staff knew that by selective leaking they could control the spin of the story and the direction the investigation was taking. Besides, the leakers knew that reporters would be eager to grab anything with a "secret" label on it. Write first, ask questions later, is the usual procedure in these cases.

In one case, the confidential testimony of church President Neil Salonen was given to the *New York Times*. The *Washington Star* also got material connected with that testimony. One staff member even talked to the U.S. Communist party's newspaper, the *Daily World*.

It wasn't just the church members who complained. So did a subcommittee member, Republican William F. Goodling. In April 19, 1978, Goodling said in a session of the hearings:

I am, needless to say, very upset that when we have executive sessions I either hear on television or read in the newspaper what took place. I hear from time to time that the Chairman approved. Well, in my estimation the Chairman has no legal right . . . to approve anything that anyone has done in Executive Session without the committee itself giving him that prerogative.[63]

In fact, Chairman Fraser had rather casually broken the rules of the U.S. Congress, specifically Rule 3.4(g) which prohibits such leaks. The chairman was following his own rule; namely, a chairman can do anything he wants or thinks he can get away with.[64]

But Fraser and his staff hardly stopped at breaking a House rule or two. Another interesting practice was the purchase of witness testimony.

Five of them were given $2,000 "consulting contracts" by Chairman Fraser. The "witnesses" were either ex-church members or left-wing critics of the South Korean government. One was a Korean defector. No one, naturally, was hired to "consult" on the other side of the question.

Fraser's reward of friendly sources for the kind of testimony he wanted to hear did not go over well with the minority. Congressman Derwinski, for one, warned that doing so had "all the appearance of a payoff to witnesses for their testimony," and that he was neither consulted on the matter as ranking minority member nor would he give, *ex post facto*, his approval.[65]

At times, the dirty tricks operation bordered on the ludicrous. Two examples will suffice.

In April 1978, Fraser subcommittee staff handed over to the *Chicago Tribune* supposedly official U.S. government reports tracing the origins of the Unification Church to "a small-time Korean sex cult."[66]

The second sample of Fraser foolery was supplied directly by two of his so-called investigators. In early February 1978, two staffers, Edwin H. Gragert and Martin Lewin, attempted to conduct a search of a Unification Church in Northwest Washington. They had no warrants and they had no real business there.

Like a scene from an Abbot and Costello movie, the pair lied about their identities (they claimed to be architects) while browbeating a receptionist into letting them have an unescorted look around. They did not get it.

None of this amateurish nonsense would have been remembered except that the church receptionist later saw the "architects" at the Fraser hearings. When a church official asked Lewin about the incident, he lied twice about it, only later admitting the truth.[67]

What the Fraser sleuths did was neither very nice nor very intelligent. It certainly was not conduct worthy of a congressional committee staff member. But such conduct was in its own dumb way a vivid example of the Fraser subcommittee's very essence: vindictiveness mixed with incompetence.

But what about their leader, Donald Fraser?

What was this Unification Church investigation all about? After all, it had dragged on for nearly two years and had cost more than $685,000.

The hidden agenda of the subcommittee was neither simple nor straightforward. To be sure South Korea was investigated and whenever possible portrayed in the worst possible light. The man from Minnesota could do no less. After all, he had done it before. With not a lick of concern about the implications for this country's basic security interests.

Hitting the church, however, was something different. The church, by 1978, was a convenient target of opportunity. The church was wildly unpopular, and throwing mud at it was easy. The mud might possibly even stick. If it didn't, who would care? Except the church members themselves, who didn't count anyway.

But why do that?

The answer involves far more than mere "Moonie bashing." Politicians don't do something for nothing. In Fraser's case, the chairman had grown tired of the House and wanted to move to the Senate. Was it a mere coincidence that the Unification Church investigation in 1977-78 coincided with the Minnesota Senate race also scheduled for 1978?

As they say in Duval County, Texas, "not hardly."

In fact, Fraser himself made no bones about exploiting the investigation for his political advantage. On campaign flyers, released prior to the party primary on September 12, Fraser bragged about his role in saving America from Moon:

> Don Fraser was the first to discover Korean CIA activity in this country aimed at manipulating U.S. policies. Don Fraser is also investigating links between the KCIA and Rev. Sun Myung Moon.[68]

It was an artful smear, of course, reporting that he was "investigating" not "proving" the tie, because by then Fraser knew he could not do it. But a smear is still a smear, and for a politician professing liberal values, it is something worse than that.

In the end, ironically, his efforts would do Don Fraser no good. Not only did he not get his prized seat in the U.S. Senate, Fraser did not even get his party's nomination. Perhaps, one day he will make a national comeback.

CHAPTER XV

A MATTER OF
SELECTIVE
PERSECUTION

*So long as society is founded on injustice, the function of the laws will
be to defend injustice. And the more unjust they are, the more
respectable they will seem.*

ANATOLE FRANCE

AMONG the more compelling arguments against the indictment
and imprisonment of the Reverend Sun Myung Moon is the one
summed up in two words: *selective prosecution.* In a strict legal
sense, *selective prosecution* means that the government goes after
one individual while ignoring others who have committed the
same crime.

That's bad enough, but in the case of the Reverend Sun Myung
Moon the very definition of selective prosecution took on an entirely new, more sinister meaning. Not only was he tried and
convicted for operating his church in much the same manner as
mainstream U.S. religions do, he was also persecuted by federal
officials who refused to investigate less-publicized religious scan-

dals involving blatant criminal misuse of tens of millions of dollars in charitable funds.

You may never have noticed or even heard of these scandals. But that comes as no surprise. They were all left under the rug by a timid legal system and a passive press.

The scandals involved more than $50 million in squandered religious donations, entailing hundreds of potentially criminal acts from tax evasion to fraud, conspiracy, obstruction of justice, and theft. Tens of thousands of church-going Americans, many old and poor, were bilked out of their meager incomes or persuaded to contribute unwittingly in efforts to cover up potentially embarrassing church financial scandals.

It's a sad fact of life but religion and scandal really do mix. Especially if it involves those two hardy perennials: money and sex.

A miscreant minister or a peccable priest are the stuff of which juicy stories are composed, ranging from hometown, backyard gossip to lavish musicals—witness the stunning success of a stage version of *Elmer Gantry*. *Gantry* is based on an almost forgotten 1925 Sinclair Lewis novel about a tent preacher with a wandering eye and a perpetually dry throat.

Elmer's recent popularity was considerably enhanced by the coincident revelations of wrongdoings committed by television evangelists, ranging from the merely incredible Jim and Tammy Faye Bakker to the sizzling antics of Jimmy Swaggart.

Not to mention Oral Roberts, who announced that God would kill him if the faithful did not cough up their widow's mites. Why? To pay off the huge debts incurred after Roberts' Oklahoma-based building frenzy went into hyperbolic overdrive.

He still owes a trunkful of money, but brother Oral is still with us.

So as the Holy-Roller-and-Holler-for-Jesus electronic tent and sawdust freak shows come tumbling down we should remember that religious scandals are nothing new in America or anywhere else. They no doubt go back at least to ancient Egypt where the priests of Amon amassed enormous wealth and political power on the strength of their claim that they held the secrets that could guarantee everlasting life. For a few coins.

In America we do things a little differently.

Established churches tend to go about their business without the

glare of publicity. The fringe groups—from the electronic fundamentalists with their perspiring preachers to the more sedate, but
vastly more mysterious, Unification Church—get and have gotten
the lion's share of the attention.

Presbyterians don't.

God knows, the low visibility of their scandals is not because they
or the Episcopalians or the Lutherans or the Catholics haven't ever
been naughty. They all have their hidden dirty linen; it's just that
we in this country arc squcamish about having it taken out of the
closet.

America is the only country in Christendom that has no strong
anti-clerical tradition. Just why that is so is a bit mysterious. Maybe
we are simply a whole lot more innocent than other peoples. But
we are also—thanks to the wisdom of the Founders—without an
established church. Religion in this country is pluralistic, diffuse,
scattered, and fragmented. In other words, it does not present a
single, fat target for the critics to bang away at.

Furthermore, many insist we're not even a Christian nation.
When Supreme Court Justice Sandra Day O'Connor (in a recent
private letter) suggested that we were, the resulting storm of publicity got her off that tack real fast.

We are also suspicious of Holy Joes, the name we Marines routinely used for chaplains. It is, however, a carefully circumscribed
suspicion.

Take Nathaniel Hawthorne, for example. A New Englander and
the descendant of the region's first settlers, the Puritans, Hawthorne's great commentary on his ancestors and their religion
(found in *The Scarlet Letter*) came a safe two centuries after their
heyday. And then, of course, his vehicle was fiction.

Hawthorne's novel nonetheless packs a wallop. The piety and
downright nastiness of the Puritans comes through in this tale of
adultery and persecution.

The novelist, however, saves his greatest scorn for the Reverend
Mr. Arthur Dimmesdale, the pale divine who stands in judgment
over Hester Prynne.

Dimmesdale is Hester's secret lover but refuses to take his medicine until the very end. Hawthorne makes it clear that Dimmesdale's sin wasn't bundling Hester, it was his cowardice in leaving
her holding the bag.

But, significantly, the novel's theme of clerical sin and hypocrisy was limited to exploring those vices within a society that had already vanished.[1]

Our reluctance to look at the business of religion and how it is conducted is still very much with us.

That's true for the media as well. In an age of investigative journalism, with its attitude that anything goes and nothing's sacred, those things that are supposed to be sacred still lead a remarkably charmed existence. At a time when every secret of the White House, the Congress, the CIA, the Pentagon, and even that bastion of hush-hush, the Supreme Court, has been ventilated, not so those of the established churches. They rarely if ever are the subject of sustained investigation.

Only small, new religions and cults get that treatment. Television programs which feature priests as characters remain properly worshipful in their attitudes toward the clergy. "Father Murphy" is no more and no less the compound of sentimental hokum that *Going My Way* dished out for us in 1943. Father O'Malley never retired; he just went in for a retread.

How far would Hollywood have gotten without Spencer Tracy, Pat O'Brien, Bing Crosby, and all those other friendly-tough, streetwise padres who were as clichéd as the bumbling vicars who appeared in all those English Ealing comedies?

Answer: not very far—at least with America's urban, working-class, Catholic movie-going audiences that were the heart of Hollywood's cash flow in the 1940s and 1950s. The O'Boyles, and their Italian and Polish and German counterparts, did not go to the opera on Friday night. They went to the Rialto. And they did not want anyone cracking wise about their church.

Nobody did. Nobody dared.

The hands-off attitude continues to this day, but does not change the fact that the American Roman Catholic church has had its share of serious scandals, most but not all of a financial nature.

From a poor, immigrant, outcast church of a few thousand souls at the turn of the eighteenth century—a church and its flock which inspired horror and persecution from the dominant Protestant majority—the Roman Catholic church grew to become by far the nation's largest denomination.

In numbers, wealth, and raw political power, there is no match for the American Catholic church anywhere within Christendom, a fact of life that the Vatican is fully aware of.

Rome worries about its North American flock, as well it might. When scandals have hit it, as they do now and then like meteors from the cosmos, you can bet they are not talked about in public. They don't even leave a streak in the night air, if it can be helped.

Let me give some examples from my own reporting.

How about Boys Town?

I thought that would wake you up. Not *the* Boys Town? Omaha, Nebraska? Father Flanagan? Spencer Tracy? Mickey Rooney? O.K., the Mick was a rotten kid in the movie but he got straightened out in the last reel. Didn't he? Say it ain't so, Joe.

Sorry, it's so.

Spencer Tracy received an Oscar in 1938 for his role in that picture. Hollywood got rich.

So did the real Boys Town. Its annual appeals—one of the very first direct-mail operations—netted millions, then hundreds of millions, of dollars as the years passed.

Boys Town's population, however, remained roughly the same—about one thousand kids in trouble—while Father Flanagan's heirs continued to rake in the big bucks. By the early 1970s, the town was pulling in $25 million a year, had no debts, and, oh yes, I nearly forgot, assets worth $250 million, a lot of it kept liquid. Only a fraction was spent on the boys, who still lived in spartan conditions worthy of any Catholic seminary, one of which I attended. Marine boot camp was better. More food.

Only when the tiny, weekly *Sun* newspapers of Omaha started poking around was a financial disclosure forced out of Boys Town's Monsignor Nicholas Wagner.

That black cat out of the bag, the cash horde began to be spent. The dormitories on Boys Town's 1,500 acres were fixed up, made liveable actually, more staff was hired, and two $70 million child welfare institutes went into construction. And the heart-rending appeals for money were toned down. A little.

While the Boys Town story did not reveal misspent funds, it certainly raised serious questions about charitable fund-raising schemes run amok. There were no priests, as far as I know, caught with sticky fingers, but to some the whole thing smacked of fraud; not criminal fraud necessarily, but civil fraud which, put simply, is an abuse of trust. The scandal lay in the fact that loyal Catholics were being asked to dig down deep every year for a cause that had gone from worthy to wealthy. Money that could have been spent on their own kids, many of whom were living less well than the Boys Town crowd. Nobody told those decent Catholics either. The money just came rolling in, leaving Boys Town's managers wondering what to do with the stuff. So they did nothing, until a couple of reporters got curious.

No reflection on the *Sun* newsmen, but this story never made it big. Despite the fame of Boys Town and a Pulitzer Prize to the *Sun* papers, editors around the country shied away from this story. Television reporters did not descend on Omaha en masse. It was a nonevent.

Boys Town is hardly the worst example of financial finagling to be found within the Roman Catholic Church in recent years. After all, a real financial scandal involves criminal fraud and deception and perhaps high living on the side—all at someone else's expense.

For this, turn to the Salvatorian Fathers, who filed for bankruptcy two years before Boys Town erupted, in November 1970 to be exact.

Filing for bankruptcy under Chapter XI of the federal bankruptcy laws was not as commonplace then as it is now. For a church order it was unprecedented.

The good fathers had raised millions of dollars selling unsecured bonds and life insurance policies to trusting (and mostly poor and elderly) Catholics. The money was squandered on high-risk investments managed by a crooked lawyer, with the result that some 2,400 cash-strapped creditors were left holding the bag. As a result, the faithful were granted an even more impoverished last few years of life.

The Boys Town fathers had too much money; the Salvatorians didn't have any. In fact, they were $8.6 million in debt—at the time, 1972, the biggest financial failure of any Catholic order in the country. The federal bankruptcy court in Milwaukee took six years to unravel the mess and in the end the good fathers were not held criminally liable. Go and sin no more, said the court, no penance required. Case closed. The Security and Exchange Commission, however, was not so charitable. It did launch its own investigation—after all, some $17 million just disappeared somewhere inside the Washington Beltway on dubious development projects—but that, too, came to nothing.

In the end, no Salvatorian got whacked by the SEC either. All were found to be innocent dupes or "wholly inexperienced in commercial affairs," in the words of the SEC report.

The shady lawyer in the case, Victor J. Orsinger, wasn't so lucky. At least he ended up in the slammer. His 3,200-acre, 37-room mansion-in-Virginia's-horse-country lifestyle suddenly, if temporarily, came to an end.

That didn't help the creditors much. Few of the mostly aged and poor Catholic faithful got their money back. Most just gave up and received nothing. Others died waiting.

Florence Bates of Duluth, Minnesota, had invested $1,300 and figured she was owed $451, but didn't ask for it. Bates was seventy-seven and did not want to die before her financial matters were settled.

Others were even more pathetic. Helen Geary of Washington, D.C., had worked for forty years in an Arrow shirt factory—her greatest pleasure was saying the rosary during lunchtime at the factory.

Later she invested her entire life savings in religious bonds, thinking that they would help people much like herself. Earlier and shortly before Geary was to retire, she had a nervous breakdown which disqualified her for a union pension. The earnings from the bonds, somehow, were to help make up for this catastrophe.

At the time of the order's financial failure, Geary was confined to a nursing home, after taking care of her sick brother for many years. Now ill herself and alone, with virtually no money other than a modest Social Security check, Helen Geary pleaded for her money. Actually, Geary herself didn't write the court. She couldn't. She had become too distraught and depressed to act. So a friend at the home carried on the correspondence.

The $8,000 that belonged to her would have kept Geary in some small comfort. Instead, she got less than $2,000. No horse country estate for her. And no Catholic charity stepped in to make up the difference.

Is that a scandal? The Salvatorians' professed innocence doesn't mean that a lot of people didn't get hurt. They did. Helen Geary was only one example.

But the Salvatorians were hardly alone in that regard.[2] Some were not so guileless.

There were, for example, the Pallotine Fathers of Baltimore, Maryland.

In the 1970s this small but extremely well-heeled missionary order ran a massive and sophisticated mail order appeal from a warehouse in Baltimore. The clerical letter campaign worked— just like Boys Town. This obscure order, with no visible accomplishment or cause, managed to haul in $15 million a year for the "poor and needy."

Less than 3 percent of the funds went to the missions.

According to the *Baltimore Sun*, in a series of stories which generated virtually no interest nationwide, the Pallotine money went to a variety of causes. One of them was former Governor Marvin Mandel, later to be convicted of graft. He received $54,000, a cash payment delivered to him in a briefcase by a priest messenger to help finance a messy divorce settlement.

Why was a Catholic order paying for a divorce with other people's money? Mandel wasn't even Catholic. He was, however, governor at the time, and the Pallotines wanted a little juice in Annapolis. They got it, but it didn't last long. Marvin Mandel eventually went to jail.

The bare bones of this tale don't even begin to describe adequately the sheer sleaze of the Pallotine operation. In 1974 the order had hit its stride. That year 1.6 million computerized letters, cards, and "sweepstakes" fliers were sent out to the Catholic masses. The mailings were so large that the Baltimore post office granted the Pallotines their own zip code.

The appeals were richly illustrated with pictures of starving, hollow-cheeked, pot-bellied youngsters staring at the reader.

"Help these children with your contribution," one appeal implored. "They are but a sample of thousands of children in the Pallotine Missions who are either starving, sick or naked. . . ."

Quite cynically, it added these breathtaking lies: "Our funds are sent directly to our missionaries in the field (no middlemen). We employ no professional fund raisers. We have no executives to pay. We prepare our own mailings."

The money rolled in. Usually in small amounts—one, five, and ten dollar cash donations from poor, decent Catholics who couldn't stand the thought of a hungry child.

These good people often sent in a letter, too, with their prayers—thinking some good father would read it. But the Pallotines couldn't have cared less. The trust shown in the letters makes truly pathetic reading.

One Vermont woman, aged 74, wished to send more than the $10 offered, but it wasn't possible. She had a heart ailment and lived in a $100-a-month unfurnished, unheated house in the country.

All the old lady wanted from the Pallotine fathers was for them to pray for her.

Her letter and thousands like it were promptly pitched in the wastebasket once the money was extracted from them. And although a Mass was promised for every contributor by the Pallotines, none was ever said. None means zero. That woman probably died in the dark and the cold without a prayer from the Pallotines.

The truly obscene aspect of the Pallotine operation is what they actually did with all that money.

In that bonanza year of 1974, the Pallotines of Baltimore managed to send a grand total of $260,000 to the order's missions (and the children); Marvin Mandel and company got the rest . . . over $14 million.

Most of the money was funneled secretly into wildly speculative land ventures and unsecured loans to Maryland "businessmen" who were linked to the Mandel administration through various state contract frauds.

The remaining bags of cash were used to invest in Florida real estate, orange groves, condos, and beachfront hotels, including one which, a *Sun* reporter discovered, served as a front for an old-fashioned house of sin, a brothel.

As former Vice President Spiro Agnew could tell you, Maryland is a state with a long and dishonorable record of thoroughly corrupt politics where a few in government and a few in the private sector work together and grow rich.

Even by Maryland standards, the Mandel administration managed to set some records. And the Pallotine Fathers—and not innocently this time either—were very much part of the scams.

Despite the public heat from the *Sun* articles, there wasn't any stampede by law enforcement officials to set things right. Indeed, the federal government, and this includes the U.S. Postal Service which knew for years that something wasn't exactly kosher with their largest Baltimore client, dithered for months while the money continued to roll in and the Pallotine priest executives quietly left town and moved their headquarters to New Jersey.

Since most of the funds raised came from out of state and the U.S. mail service was used to conduct the fraud, the responsibility for investigating and prosecuting the case fell squarely within the jurisdiction of the federal government. Nonetheless the Justice Department and the FBI wanted no part in hauling Roman Catholic priests into the dock. The Pallotine operation instead was left to the hapless Maryland State's Attorney office for investigation.

After many delays and much handwringing, the State's Attorney finally secured a sixty-one-count indictment against one—just one—Pallotine priest on a variety of criminal fraud and conspiracy charges. The short straw was drawn by the Very Reverend Guido John Carcich, one of the order's superiors and the alleged mastermind of the Pallotines' mass-mail operations.

Before the ink on the indictment had dried, however, Father Carcich had struck a plea bargaining deal with the state which resulted in sixty counts being dropped in exchange for a guilty plea on one single charge of fraud.

The good father, who incidently never uttered so much as a word of remorse to the faithful, was put on probation for eighteen months, reduced to a year, to serve as a part-time religious counselor in Baltimore's city prison. No jail time, no fine.

Rough justice, it was not. But there's more.

Father Carcich was not only permitted to remain a priest in good standing but was treated by his order as something of a martyr. Eventually he was assigned to a swank parish in North Carolina's fashionable seaside resort of Nags Head.

You might wonder what happened to the Pallotines, their mass mailing operations, and the tens of millions of dollars in ill-gotten donations.

The short answer is "nothing." The Pallotines continue to operate their mail appeals out of Baltimore and, as far as anyone knows, the money and the prayer requests still come rolling in by the bagful each day. As for the fraudulently obtained donations, the Pallotines were asked to liquidate their less-than-religious holdings, including the hotel-brothel, but were permitted to keep the proceeds. Restitution for the bilked faithful was never contemplated or offered; nor were any apologies made for all the children who might have escaped a slow, painful death from starvation and disease had the Pallotines kept their promises.

If that isn't outrageous enough, then consider this: at the same time that the whole ugly Pallotine scandal was slowly unraveling in Baltimore during 1975 and 1976 without so much as a whimper from any federal officials or the national media, just thirty-three miles away in Washington, D.C., a virtual army of federal law enforcement agencies and news organizations had already mobilized. They were mobilized behind Senator Robert Dole, who had strong suspicions that the Reverend Moon and his Unification Church might be having a negative influence on a handful of well-fed, mostly white, middle-class American youth.

Why the disparity? Why indeed.

The Pallotines, of course, weren't the only religious organization to be caught flatfooted in the pursuit of worldly goods during the 1970s.

Perhaps the most complex scandal, which also included the fleecing of poor and innocent Catholics, involved the byzantine case of the Pauline Fathers of Doylestown, Pennsylvania.

If you are not Catholic and Polish and live west of the Alleghenies, chances are you have not yet heard of the Paulines. Their scandal tied the Vatican up in knots and divided and embittered top church brass. The scandal also left two princes of the church, both of Polish origin, one American and one Polish, at dagger's point. And the affair still isn't resolved. It doesn't make Pope John Paul II look very good either.

I worked on the Pauline story for more than a year for the *Gannett News Service* in Washington, D.C. The investigation spanned seventeen states and four countries. It produced a small library of court records and reams of secret (until I broke the story) internal church documents, all relating to the Pauline scandal and the impact it had on the Vatican and a then-new pope, John Paul II.

The story dealt with a five-year effort (by the Vatican and John Paul II himself) to cover up the Pauline Fathers' misdeeds—an effort directed at containing the worst church scandal ever to occur in the United States.

The Pauline Fathers in America are a small order of monks lodged in rural northeastern Pennsylvania. They are part of a much larger Polish religious order, the seven-century-old Order of St. Paul the First Hermit.

The Polish Paulines are not without importance in their homeland. In fact, historically, they are the appointed protectors of the country's most venerated religious object, the Black Madonna, believed by the pious to have been painted by St. Luke.

It is located at the shrine on the hilltop monastary Jasna Gora near Czestochowa, Poland. Polish-born John Paul II has visited this shrine on each of his visits to Poland as Holy Father, a profoundly emotional act of veneration as well as of Polish patriotism, a gesture that the old communist authorities in Warsaw never dreamed of cutting short.

No wonder.

Through the centuries, Poles have killed to protect their Black Madonna from ravaging outsiders. Legends of miracles abound. The object was, if you believe the stories, saved by divine intervention from, among others, the Tartars, the Swedes, and the Germans (the Nazi version).

Few in Poland question the authenticity of the stories. And the communists, both Polish and Russian, who have no love for religion or show any fear of God, have never dared even to think about the ultimate act of iconoclasm.

The Paulines, in short, are not your average order of monks.

North of Philadelphia in lush Bucks County the Pauline Fathers first settled. In the mid-1970s they were not one of America's largest orders. Indeed, at their height, the fathers had attracted exactly thirty monks, most of whom came from the old country.

Their small number hardly stopped the Paulines. Especially when a Polish-born monk, the Very Reverend Michael Zembrzuski, took charge of the new American province.

Zembrzuski had big ideas. His ambition was rooted in the fact that he was a survivor. As he tells it, he had managed to escape the Gestapo in occupied Poland as well as in Hungary, and he had also outwitted the communists, who in Stalin's day knew nothing about *glasnost* and *perestroika*.

In an interview I conducted, Zembrzuski recalled one wartime experience. It happened in Budapest on October 16, 1944, during the waning days of the conflict. The Russians were pressing close and the Germans were desperate and even more dangerous. They were also looking for Zembrzuski.

"I was in a friend's apartment," said Zembrzuski, "and I was hiding in a false wardrobe. I could hear the Nazis on the staircase. They searched the three-bedroom apartment for two-and-a-half hours, but they couldn't find me."

Then the priest leaned forward and added: "When President Johnson was speaking, I couldn't help thinking back on that. I thought, 'Zembrzuski, you never would have dreamed of being here. . . .' "

His voice trailed away, but I know the look.

First, that part about Lyndon Johnson. Exactly twenty-two years after Zembrzuski spent an autumn afternoon in a Budapest closet, he was dedicating a new and beautiful, but still unfinished, shrine to Our Lady of Czestochowa (the Black Madonna) near Doylestown. The shrine was to be specifically dedicated to a millennium of Polish Christianity, and President Johnson dropped in for a photo opportunity. It was the fall of 1966 and Lyndon was still thinking about staying in the White House through January 1973. Vietnam had not yet caught up with him; Pennsylvania and the Polish vote were still important; and Eugene McCarthy was just a senator from Minnesota.

Now about that look. Men who escape near certain death are different after that. A lot different. For one thing, they rarely are content with living humdrum lives. God gave them the gift of life a second time and they intend to enjoy it.

One also feels incredibly lucky. Risk taking suddenly is not only fun—actually, it's exhilarating—but channelled in the right way, it is soon found to be immensely profitable. Ordinary rules of life somehow don't apply anymore.

So what happened to this most happy survivor? In 1951 he

traveled to France, boarded an ocean liner, and landed in New York with thirty-six bucks in his pocket. He had a mission from the Vatican to found the Pauline order in America. After the war the order had been pretty badly battered—they had been run out of communist Hungary altogether. And who knew about Poland? America would be their second chance, not just Michael Zembrzuski's.

America is a big place. Where to plant the order? Pennsylvania was a natural choice with its heavy Polish population concentrated in Philadelphia and Pittsburgh. For generations Polish Americans had mined coal and worked the blast furnaces in Pennsylvania. But the grimy inner cities and the equally gritty little coal towns where working-class Poles lived were not for Zembrzuski. He chose rural, rich, and un-Polish Bucks County instead.

Polish Americans eventually came to him by the tens of thousands. The Very Reverend Michael Zembrzuski became popular fast. He was a terrific after-dinner speaker, speaking Polish and English with a heavy but serviceable accent. The old folks especially loved him. His fiery speeches mixed American and Polish patriotism, not to mention that other potent fuel, religion. His first-hand accounts of life in Poland under the communists—and those damnable Russians—went over especially big.

Father Zembrzuski roused people's pride in being Polish like no one else had before him, and his success was soon paying handsome dividends.

In his first eighteen months, the priest from Poland netted $40,000—an absolutely unheard-of figure for the early 1950s—and from people who all their lives literally had to count the pennies.

The money was plowed into forty acres of rolling Bucks County farmland near Doylestown, Pennsylvania, a rich, boutique town just thirty miles north of Philadelphia. No coal dust here to choke the lungs.

On the property, he rebuilt an old farmhouse for himself and three other exiled Polish monks. The adjoining barn was converted into a chapel—the first Mass was celebrated on June 26, 1955.

Word of this unique chapel, with its rich allusions to the stable and manger where Jesus was born, spread like wildfire through the

Pennsylvania Catholic community of two million. Soon the faithful came.

It was Zembrzuski's genius to foresee that city and small-town Catholics would enjoy escaping their surroundings on Sunday for a nice country drive—and still go to Mass. They weren't rich, but the post-war prosperity and the tranquil Eisenhower years did allow Polish and Irish and Italian Catholics to buy a Ford or Plymouth or Chevy. With cheap gasoline, a Sunday ride in the car was enough to put the barn chapel of Father Zembrzuski on the map.

For Polish Americans the site wasn't just a quaint little chapel-in-a-barn; it was the American Czestochowa. That made the place a magnet for them. When the troubles in Poland broke out in 1956, beginning with the Poznan riots, people flocked in even greater numbers to Doylestown. They also brought their wallets with them.

In five years the Paulines were very liquid, enough so that they were able to buy another expensive 130 acres. With the new land, Zembrzuski envisioned building a church and a monastery to accommodate the flood of pilgrims anticipated for the 1960s. There would also be enough room for the forty-five priests he hoped would settle there as well.

With so much money available for the asking and his natural ambitions stirred, soon Father Zembrzuski had much bigger ideas. He decided to construct instead a huge basilica: a shrine to Polish Catholicism. The project would spark a renaissance of Polish cultural and religious feeling. Besides, why should hard-working Polish Americans go all the way to Poland to see the Black Madonna? They could come to Doylestown instead. True, there was no Madonna, but other relics could be obtained to attract them. And with the money saved by not going to Poland. . . .

Before long Father Michael was spreading the word through the Polish-language media that the Pauline Fathers were about to engage in a truly heroic task: the construction of a millennium shrine to Our Lady of Czestochowa right here in America. Doylestown, Pa.

It worked.

Before long, $1 million rolled in: enough donations to buy still more Bucks county property and hire a gaggle of professionals—

architects, engineers, lawyers, and accountants—to get the shrine started.

He also hired as general contractor Matthew H. McCloskey, a Democratic party kingpin and, even more important, a close friend of Philadelphia's Archbishop John Cardinal Krol. Since the cardinal was also of Polish descent, Father Zembrzuski soon persuaded him to act as the shrine's fundraising chairman.

It was a shrewd move. Krol wasn't just Polish; he was terrific at raising funds, especially on short notice.

As for the new shrine, the building began in early 1965 and less than two years later it was dedicated, complete with America's then First Family. Meanwhile the first money problems began to emerge. The total cost of Our Lady of Czestochowa was supposed to be $3.3 million. Zembrzuski, however, couldn't resist adding on features. Pretty soon he needed another $2 million to get what he really wanted.

At the time, it didn't seem so crazy and wild. In the last few years contributions had soared 200 percent each year. In 1965 alone, they attracted $1 million, with a net income of $200,000.

Still it wasn't enough. Not for Father Zembrzuski. A professional religious fund-raiser soon steered the monk into the curious world of the religious bond market. In a wink, the Pauline Fathers had a deal with an underwriting firm which put together a muscular bonding package that guaranteed Zembrzuski a cool $4.3 million over a four-year period. All of the bond money of course was to come from thousands of mostly elderly Polish Catholics who figured that rather than leaving their meager life's savings in bank accounts, why not let the Very Reverend Father Michael use it to promote the faith and build his shrine? They were sure they'd get their money back with interest several years later, so what could be the harm in letting the Church borrow it . . . for awhile.

All this was pretty heady stuff for a priest who had had only thirty-six dollars in his pocket just a few years before.

All he had to do to secure the bond money was not sell or mortgage any of the property the Paulines already owned. Their property was their collateral. They could not allow their total indebtedness to exceed 65 percent of the book value of the land, buildings, and equipment. Naturally they had to meet the interest payments on time, and when the bonds matured they had to repay the principal. With all that dough rolling into Doylestown, it seemed easy.

All of this taught the monk one great lesson. With hardly more than a smile and a clerical collar, he could and did get millions. Church investments were considered so secure, just about any loan officer in the land would take his word for it about his order's assets.

Having your picture taken with presidents and archbishops didn't hurt either.

Suddenly Doylestown was too small for Zembrzuski. So was Bucks County. Consequently, Zembrzuski bought more property, this time near Pittsburgh: sixty acres in Freeport, two hundred in Kittaning. Total cost: $50,000.

In Kittaning he built a second monastery for $200,000. Then it was more land in Doylestown for another $200,000. By October 1967, at celebration of the shrine's first anniversary (Vice-President Hubert Humphrey in attendance—Johnson was still after the Polish vote; so was Humphrey), Father Zembrzuski unveiled his master plan. Zembrzuski was at his apogee, the height of his influence and power. It was also megalomania time.

He called his scheme the Development Master Plan for Marian Valley. The cost was to be a mere $25 million. Included in the package were a retirement complex, an international village, a shopping mall, a Polish-American museum, an art center, a park complex that featured camping, boating, swimming, skiing, and one or two other things, like a Polish-American Arlington Cemetery.

One small problem. That hitch was a mere smudge of a cloud on the horizon. Although he had told the vice president about the plan—an appeal for federal housing funds would soon be zinging its way to Washington—Father Zembrzuski had neglected to tell anyone in Doylestown about it.

When Doylestowners caught up with the news, a lot of them weren't too happy. They were fed up with the increased traffic, the noise, and Father Zembrzuski, and not necessarily in that order. But the Pauline monk by now was too busy to bother about having a good neighbor policy.

The development, of course, was going to cost money—far more than he could get from nickel-and-dime pilgrim donations.

With all due respect, the flock was simply not thinking big. So, it was time the Pauline Fathers entered fully the secular business world.

Under the then U.S. tax laws, churches had tax advantages when they worked with worldly business partners. In short, everybody could make a buck, especially if one was not too scrupulous about how and with whom the buck was made.

To do that, Father Zembrzuski needed an associate. He found one in Howard Martin Lawn, a disbarred lawyer but one helluva money manager. For one thing, Lawn knew the tax code cold, especially the good parts about how churches can form partnerships with benefits for all.

With a "go" light from Zembrzuski, Lawn proceeded to buy a ninety-seven-acre, non-sectarian cemetery in a Philadelphia suburb. A steal for $800,000. Graveyards make money. Guaranteed demand. Next, a Los Angeles County hospital. Ninety-six beds. Another profit-maker. A bargain for $700,000.

Next, a trade school in Delaware for $170,000. Then a foundry near Pittsburgh followed by a research corporation in San Francisco. All of them, of course, were tied to the Paulines' tax-exempt religious status.

The basic Lawn scheme for riches-beyond-your-wildest-imagination-Father was a leaseback arrangement which was a thing of beauty even unto itself. The deal was also very legal.

This is how it worked. The order would buy a corporation at a much inflated price. Then the order would lease the corporation back to the original owners for about 80 percent of the year's profits. Let them deduct the rent, and beat taxes on both the income and capital gains.

With Howard Lawn's help, Zembrzuski did a leaseback deal with another hospital—this one in North Miami, Florida. The arrangement of course required obtaining new loans for the order. A hospital was one thing. How about a Long Island aircraft parts plant? Cost: $2.5 million. More loans.

There were other purchases: a New Jersey printing plant and a Florida development company. Some deals didn't go through, but they were a handy measure of the monk's ambition. One was the purchase of an entire Florida island to house yet another shrine for cold-weary Poles who would stream south to see it.

Unfortunately, these purchases were costing too much money. In fact, everything was costing too much money. By 1970, Father Zembrzuski was getting a bit desperate. The loans were coming due and he did not have the money to meet his new obligations. The old clerical collar was no longer doing the trick. So he thought fast.

Since the bankers needed some documentation for a refinancing job, he would give them documentation. Soon he began flashing financial statements demonstrating that the Doylestown shrine's assets had ballooned to $18.5 million in just four short years. Very impressive.

One problem. The reports and the figures contained therein were phony.

There were other problems. Although the shrine was taking in $1 million a year, the contributions had long since peaked. Worse, the shrine still wasn't completed. For one thing, there wasn't enough money for pews. Cheap folding chairs would have to do. The stained glass windows, well, they weren't really stained glass, just plastic imitations which kept cracking. In fact, parts of the shrine were already starting to crumble, and people were asking questions.

That last part hurt especially.

The bad news was only beginning. Interest rates were going up and the business profits from the cemetery, hospital, airplane parts, etc., conglomerate were proving to be less than expected. Even with a tax advantage, Zembrzuski was taking in a lot less money than was going out.

Then another nasty surprise. The town fathers in Doylestown turned thumbs down on his $25 million white elephant. Forget the zoning easements; forget sewer approvals, Father.

Worst of all, two notes on his original $4.3 million loan were coming due in 1972. October 1, to be exact.

So what was a good priest to do? What else? Loot the assets. Father Michael began chipping away at several of his properties, the Bala-Cynwyd cemetery being one.

Come on, you say, nobody would do that, especially a priest, even if he were in a tight spot. Besides how can you rob a graveyard?

Easy. Here's how.

Father Michael looted it in three parts. First, he illegally withdrew $500,000 from the "perpetual care" fund, the money which every cemetery is required by law to set aside for maintenance and upkeep. Second, he "borrowed" another $120,000 from current operating expenses. Third, he sold the main entrance to the cemetery for $100,000 to the Sun Oil Company for a beautiful gas station. The families of the dear departed would sure be surprised when they showed up and a row of gas pumps blocked the way into the cemetery. Which is probably just as well because the ever industrious Father Michael had yet another scheme to make a few bucks: take the artificial flowers off the graves, rearrange them, and sell them back to the bereaved loved ones, only to take them off the graves again the next day and. . . . Why not? This was not a Catholic cemetery and most of the buried weren't Polish.

It gets worse. Congress in 1969 changed the tax law, in effect outlawing the leaseback gimmick for churches on businesses that have nothing to do with worship. Then several of Father Michael's other schemes went sour for different reasons. The North Miami hospital, for example, turned out to have Mafia connections, ties that ran back to Jimmy Hoffa and misspent Teamster pension funds. And good old Howard Lawn was not only a disbarred attorney, but a convicted felon. In fact, friend Howard had done a year in a federal slammer for masterminding an organized crime scam. You guessed it, it was tax evasion. Howard Martin Lawn was also a mob lawyer.

With the walls closing in, Father Michael thought of something he hadn't for a while: Poland. Now he needed help, fast, and so he returned to his roots. Specifically, he visited the Very Reverend George Tomzinski, the superior general of the Pauline Fathers in Czestochowa.

There, Father Zembrzuski bared his soul: he was in trouble; more important, the Polish-American Pauline shrine was in very deep trouble. Through absolutely no fault of his own, money suddenly was in short supply, he told his superior. There were cost overruns for the shrine. There was an unprecedented rate of inflation in America thanks to the Vietnam War; that's the ticket, the Vietnam War was to blame.

But despite his eloquence, Father Michael got no money from his commander-in-chief. Instead, he got something better. Father

Tomzinski gave the American monk a letter, and it was a thing of beauty.

Father Michael was "to act on behalf of the order in all that concerns borrowing of money by promissory note, bond, or other evidence of debt." Incidentally, he could do so at any interest rate and in any amount the good priest from Doylestown should wish.

Even better, the letter went on to "unconditionally guarantee" any debt contracted by Father Michael and the Pauline Fathers of America. To nail down this offer, the letter from Tomzinski pledged the total assets of the entire international order, some $500 million.

For a dying man in the desert the letter was manna from heaven and an oasis filled with crystal blue water besides. Father Michael took the letter from his superior in Poland and flew back to America.

Suddenly the dismal financial picture looked distinctly brighter. Over the next eighteen months, Zembrzuski hit up at least eight banks in the Philadelphia area for $1.6 million—many of which banks never asked for collateral. One that didn't, Franklin National, now bankrupt, lent him $150,000.

As any Third World finance minister knows, however, a new loan to cover old loans just adds to the problem of indebtedness. The Pauline Fathers still needed hard cash to pay off this nightmare of escalating debt.

Father Michael was getting desperate. Truly desperate. The letter from the Very Reverend George Tomzinski had helped, but it was no panacea.

So, the troubled vicar-general of the Paulines of America became a cannibal.

He had to start selling everything the order had: that is, all the assets he had so painfully acquired in the last fifteen years. First to go was the California hospital—at a whopping loss. Then he sold the Pauline share of the Long Island aircraft parts plant. Another loss. Then the Pittsburgh foundry. Finally came complete collapse with the forced sale of nearly everything else.

Any money raised now went into the general fund, set up for the small army of creditors besieging the Paulines. And by that I mean everything from the money earned saying Masses (an estimated

$250,000; the Masses, by the way, were never said) to the offerings for bronze plaque memorials (another $400,000) that were to be hung in the shrine so Catholics could be remembered to their children and grandchildren. The plaques, incidentally, never were purchased.

About the only thing the Paulines didn't do was sell indulgences, those little pieces of paper that ticked off Martin Luther and set off the Reformation.

Zembrzuski then appealed to the original bond underwriters for fresh funds. His remaining portfolio of businesses was described in the most flattering profitmaking light. The plan didn't work. Suddenly the Paulines didn't look so reliable. Loans were only offered at a killing 11 to 15 percent rate of interest.

The good monk raged about usury. Next, with Howard Lawn's able assistance, he tried foreign banks: a British one in particular. First, he placed a modest request for $8.5 million, ostensibly to buy the mob-tainted North Miami hospital outright. But Father Michael couldn't help himself. A rush of megalomania returned and pretty soon he was building castles in the air again. Forget the $8.5 million; how about $25 million? The extra money would go for a nursing home and a retirement village at the shrine. Everything, it seems, except a skating rink.

The bank said no.

Zembrzuski was left with his last American card: John Cardinal Krol, whom he promptly touched up for $1.5 million to prevent foreclosure on the shrine. Asking for help was embarrassing. It was also humiliating. But Father Michael did it, and according to confidential church records, the archbishop of Philadelphia agreed. At least initially. Krol was under no obligation to do so, of course. Even though the Pauline shrine was within his archdiocese, Catholic law placed the Pauline order out of his control—and responsibility.

Zembrzuski, however, had made a mistake. Desperate as he was, going to Krol meant trouble. Father Michael had counted on the Polish connection. But he had also lied to the cardinal, masquerading his difficulties as only a temporary cash flow problem.

What the Pauline forgot was that he was talking to another member of the clergy, not some easily impressed layman. The Roman collar did not impress the cardinal. Krol's being Polish wasn't much help either. The archbishop of Philadelphia was a remarkably unsentimental man and, being Polish, he was hard-headed, especially on the subject of money, particularly in the million-dollar range.

Krol therefore had the archdiocesan controller look at the Pauline books. Monsignor Arthur Nace did not like what he found. Indeed, he was horrified.

The shrine was in debt up to its cracking steeple—at least $5.5 million, and that didn't take into account the millions more owed in interest and principal on the original bonds. Nace also knew that the letter from the head of the Pauline order in Poland was worthless. He dutifully reported his findings to Krol.

Nace's disclosure did not stop the indefatigable Zembrzuski, who spent the next two years on a plane flying the U.S.-Rome-Warsaw circuit in a desperate search for new funding. He raised some money, of course, but it wasn't enough. By September 1974, Father Zembrzuski was once again in federal court, receiving his second default judgment.

The courtroom was packed with bank executives and lawyers, representing scores of aged and bewildered Polish Catholic creditors.

Only then—seven years after the financial perils of the Paulines had started, plus two federal court appearances later—did the Vatican begin to suspect that something was wrong and launch its own investigation into Father Zembrzuski's very peculiar business practices.

Rome's interest began at the top this time, Pope Paul VI. The Holy Father appointed two "visitators," the Roman Catholic curia's version of an inspector-general. They were both Americans: Bishop George H. Guilfoyle of Camden, New Jersey, and the Most Reverend Paul M. Boyle, then provincial head of the Passionist Fathers of Chicago.

Both were hardboiled men of the church who had extensive experience in clerical financial shenanigans. Guilfoyle held degrees in both canon and civil law and possessed the cold heart of a bank foreclosure officer. It took the visitators several months and a small army of lawyers and accountants from Peat, Marwick and Mitchell to get at the truth.

They did, finally. But their investigation took much longer than usual, in part because Father Zembrzuski flatly refused to cooperate, and in part because the paper trail could have gone to Mars and back.

What they found in their investigation shocked even these worldly wise priests. It wasn't the huge debts piled up by the Paulines that particularly surprised them, or the fact that the order was spending annually $300,000 more than it took in.

Nor was it the string of failed businesses, or even the questionably legal sale of assets that shook them. It was rather what the Paulines themselves had become. Like Dorian Gray's picture, the order had turned into a very ugly portrait of holiness gone berserk.

Pledged to poverty, chastity, and obedience, the good monks of Doylestown, the visitators learned, had been living very well. While their sheep grazed on rocks and thorns, the good shepherds of the Order of St. Paul the First Hermit were doing somewhat better.

Item. Every monk who could drive had his own personal automobile. That meant few of them were ever in the monastery at the same time. Pastoral duties naturally were neglected. Masses? You must be kidding.

Item. Each monk, including their vicar-general, rested a lot—up to three vacations a year, usually in Europe, and, of course, the travel arrangements were first-class, all paid with funds from the faithful.

Item. Many of the monks at the Doylestown monastery lived in "cells" which were equipped with color televisions, stereos, and refrigerators for their private stock of beer, wine, and what-have-you.

Item. Most also held credit cards which were lavishly used, along with personal checking accounts. There were no controls on the spending. Those few monks who didn't go upscale were rebuked and shunned by their high-living brothers.

Item. Father Zembrzuski lived better than all of the rest. His entertaining of guests was lavish, like the gifts he bestowed on friends. In the words of the visitator report to the Vatican, "[H]is friendship with a woman, whom he supported generously with monastery funds, gave rise to many rumors and accusations."

Yes, I would guess so, to say nothing of the rumors in Doylestown that on Friday and Saturday nights the Pauline monastery was the swingingest place around.

Of course the investigators uncovered all the financial irregularities already listed plus a few more. Example: the monastery had not paid its bills, $250,000 worth, from local suppliers. By 1974 such items as food and heating oil were provided strictly on a cash basis.

The investigators at last got to the petty theft part of the operation. For example, the deducted income taxes, Social Security taxes, and union dues of shrine employees were not forwarded to the proper agencies, but pocketed by Zembrzuski.

Finally, the bottom line. Just before the adding machines overheated, the good fathers' accountants came up with a figure. The Paulines didn't owe $4.3 million or $5.5 million. The real number was closer to $7.9 million. And the red ink, like the tide, was still washing in every day. Worst of all, the order's unsequestered assets amounted to just $100,000.

If that were not enough, the Very Reverend Michael Zembrzuski, the visitators noted, was still paying a Boston law firm $75,000 a year to fight the federal court's default order.

Overall conclusion: the Paulines in general and Father Zembrzuski in particular were guilty of "serious abuses against Canon Law and Civil Law."

What to do? Any way you looked at the situation, the road back to solvency would be hard.

Somehow $5 million had to be raised fast. Fathers Boyle and Guilfoyle reported their conclusions to Cardinal Krol. Needless to say, it was not welcome news to Philadelphia's archbishop. He was damned if he did and damned if he didn't. Letting the Paulines go under—and technically they were not his responsibility—would create a scandal. And he, America's first cardinal of Polish extraction, would be humiliated.

If Krol did go out and save the shrine, its salvation would drain his resources—meant for far worthier causes. He might not succeed, getting the worst of both options. In the end, John Cardinal Krol picked up option number two; he had no choice.

Krol made two decisions immediately. First, he quietly lent $722,000 to bail out the looted Philadelphia cemetery. It was just as well. If the archbishop had not done so, civil and possibly criminal charges would have been filed against the Paulines.

Next, the archbishop "volunteered" to be the chairman of a nationwide fund-raising appeal. He did so reluctantly, especially after he received professional counsel that suggested the drive was not likely to succeed, but would have no chance at all if Krol himself were not chairman.

Faced with this Hobson's choice, he went ahead, meanwhile urging the visitators to softsoap the underwriters and the Minnesota bank left holding the bad bonds on behalf of the aged Catholic investors. The plea worked.

And why not? What would the bankers do with a quickly deteriorating Polish shrine, a monastery, and a barn chapel? The Doylestown operation was not a very liquid asset.

The fund appeal was tough. Cardinal Krol wanted the accountants to make the Pauline situation seem something less than hopeless, something that Peat, Marwick—themselves in trouble with the SEC on charges of preparing misleading financial statements—were reluctant to do.

In the end, there was a compromise. The Pauline picture was presented as less than totally bleak, but the report was shot through with so many caveats that, like ants at a picnic, it was less than welcome to the archbishop.

Nevertheless, Cardinal Krol started barnstorming the Polish parishes across the country, portraying himself as a "willing beggar" and the Paulines as a group of simple immigrant monks who had problems "coping" with strange American financial folkways. He neglected to mention, however, that he had agreed and then refused to fork over $1.5 million of his own money once he discovered the extent of Pauline chicanery.

Perhaps surprising even himself, Krol and his appeal did the trick. Five million dollars were soon raised from the faithful, many of whom had already invested in the Pauline shrine through Father Michael's ill-fated bond programs. It was a sum which kept the Paulines from falling into a pot of boiling oil.

Meanwhile, Boyle and Guilfoyle were detailed to take care of Father Zembrzuski. That they did by ordering him to hand over his credit cards, his car keys, his color TV. He was also to take the next plane to Rome.

Father Michael flatly refused. He wouldn't stand for being treated like this. He was an American citizen. He had friends, good friends in high places. How would either of them like to be the next bishop of Butte, Montana?

That off his chest, the monk cabled the Vatican and the Apostolic Delegation in Washington, D.C., with his version of events. Just to be safe, Father Zembrzuski took a powder, going into hiding with a monsignor friend of his on Staten Island. A month later he travelled to Rome and Poland—but on his own terms. He was not in disgrace; he came on his own initiative.

And he hadn't been exaggerating. He did have powerful friends. Stefan Cardinal Wyszynski, the legendary primate of Poland, and Poland's second cardinal, Karol Cardinal Wojtyla, Archbishop of Cracow, who, in a few years, became Pope John Paul II.

The trip to Poland worked wonders. Two years later, September 1976, after Father Boyle had had another go at Zembrzuski, the Pauline monk called his two best friends in Poland, and they flew to Rome to pressure the Vatican. It was an extraordinary demonstration of muscle-flexing by Poland's two cardinals, and the demonstration worked.

Rome vacated the visitators' order to expel Father Michael from the Paulines. Rome also told Boyle to withdraw the charges formally in a letter to Zembrzuski.

Father Michael was not only alive, but almost well. The rehabilitation process was completed with the ascendency to the throne of St. Peter of Karol Wojtyla who didn't waste any time. Within hours after taking office, the new pope ordered a final report on the Pauline investigation.

For their part, Boyle and Guilfoyle were happy to wind it up. The assignment had taken five years out of their lives and now they could look back on a job well done. Moreover they had kept their investigation confidential, not only from the public but from state and federal law enforcement officials as well, allowing Krol to work his fund-raising magic. The two priests had also managed to keep the bankers at bay, persuading them to write off a good chunk of the debt. In fact, they had come up with their own Zembrzuski-like plan to save money. The scheme went like this: stall paying the elderly Catholic bondholders long enough and a sufficient number would die, thus reducing the Pauline debt even further. It wasn't ethical or moral, maybe not even legal, strictly speaking. But then nobody said covering up a major religious scandal would be pretty.

Those problems solved, now all they wanted was to have Father Zembrzuski removed from his job and kept far, far away from the checkbooks at the shrine. That accomplished, they were confident that the Paulines would survive and the honor of the church would be restored.

But blood runs thicker than water, and Cardinal Wojtyla, now the newly elected Pope John Paul II, was not about to allow a brother Pole to fall in disgrace, particularly at the hands of two American clerics, Irishmen no less. Consequently the Holy Father refused to adopt any of Guilfoyle and Boyle's recommendations. There was a polite "thank you" for their work. But the point was clear. Other than a light-tap-on-the-wrist reminder that monks should observe the rules, the record of Zembrzuski and the American Paulines was to be whitewashed. To make its point emphatically clear, the Vatican announced that Father Michael would shortly accompany his pal, John Paul II, on his first papal visit to Poland.

The Pauline episode was over as far as the Roman Catholic church was concerned. Possibly its biggest and smelliest financial scandal in America had been contained though hardly resolved. But as is often the case with toxic waste containers, some leakage did occur.

It was about this time in early 1979, that I and my colleagues at *Gannett News Service* got on to the story. I had been monitoring the Pauline Fathers' financial gymnastics from a distance since 1974 when they defaulted on the second round of bonds. The press coverage given to that proceeding and the national fund-raising drive which followed was scant, and never once was there even the slightest hint of scandal as Krol and his fellow churchmen worked feverishly to keep the entire sordid affair under wraps.

With Father Michael back fully in charge and Pope John Paul II serving as his protector, the normally closed-mouth clergy, particularly those who'd spent years trying to straighten out the Paulines' financial tangle, began complaining bitterly among themselves. As so often happens, the gripes were repeated to others and eventually overheard by a reporter—in this case, yours truly.

Within weeks we were able to get a significant handle on the barest facts of the case, but it took months of digging and clandestine meetings in such far-flung places as a mountain-top monastery in Perugia, Italy, before the complete picture emerged.

The bottom line broke down into three parts.

Part One. Over a several-year period Father Michael and his cohorts had managed to squander more than $20 million in charitable donations and loans on a variety of decidedly noncharitable purposes including all those mentioned above and a long list of others, virtually bankrupting the order and the Doylestown shrine, which was still uncompleted and falling apart fast.

Part Two. In an effort to cover up what they themselves acknowledged were criminal activities on the part of Zembrzuski and Company, Cardinal Krol, Bishop Guilfoyle, Father Boyle, and a small army of American clergy engaged in activities which were not only duplicitous and immoral, but questionably legal.

Part Three. Pope John Paul II, with all the facts and the recommendations of his investigators at his fingertips, not only condoned the cover-up of the admitted crimes by the Pauline Fathers but ordered the main culprit, Father Zembrzuski, restored to his leadership role.

Those allegations were backed up by a 100,000-word twenty-one-part series, published by *Gannett News Service* in September 1979, the longest and most detailed ever by a news service, along with dozens of internal church, financial, and even Vatican documents, some signed by Pope John Paul II himself.

As they say in old movies, "the jig was up," and the *Gannett* series quite literally sent tremors throughout the American Catholic hierarchy and the Vatican.

What happened next was anticlimactic, but before I get into that, one last anecdote.

At the conclusion of our investigation of the Pauline Fathers, a couple of my *Gannett* colleagues and I decided to add up the potential criminal counts of fraud, theft, perjury, conspiracy, tax evasion, obstruction of justice, and various violations of state and federal securities laws, involving not only Father Zembrzuski, but all those connected with the scandal, clergy and laymen.

We started getting bored when we reached about five hundred criminal counts.

So what became of this explosive exposé? Not much. Certainly not enough to lead to any legal trouble for the Paulines, their business partners, or the pope, cardinals, and bishops who had a hand in the debacle. The Justice Department, the IRS, and the SEC also proved marvelously indifferent to the Paulines' high-wire act with other people's money. True, the IRS did launch an investigation of Howard Lawn; the records showed he had failed to pay more than $400,000 in back taxes, but once the feds saw that they would have to prosecute a handful of monks and maybe a bishop or two, the probe came to a screeching halt.

In the end, there were no indictments, no trials, no fines, no legal action whatsoever.

Well, that's not entirely true. Actually, my *Gannett* editors and I were investigated thoroughly by several people and we spent the next few years in court defending libel suits, all of which failed miserably.

Father Michael of course sued us, but his complaints were summarily dismissed by an irate judge.

A couple of embarrassed and demoted securities law enforcement officials didn't take kindly to my reports which indicated they had looked the other way when informed of the Paulines' less than legal activities. They sued for libel in a Philadelphia federal court, and after hearing all the evidence, a jury of our peers found that my stories were accurate and fair. Case dismissed.

Meanwhile, there was no congressman or senator or even a state legislator with courage or integrity enough to champion the cause of the hundreds of old and dying Polish Catholics who, in many cases, had lost their entire savings at the hands of the Paulines and, later, the Vatican-appointed visitators.

All was silent from the representatives of the people.

Finally, there was the press or, more accurately, there wasn't the press.

With the lone exception of the *Philadelphia Daily News*, which hit the story hard with the front-page headline, "Monkgate in Bucks," there was a near blackout on what was truly the most detailed and documented international story ever to chronicle a scandal involving the Roman Catholic Church in America; a scandal which went all the way to the Vatican and the pope himself.

Even many of the *Gannett* Corporation's own newspapers, of which there were more than ninety at the time, ran for cover when the story broke, either publishing small pieces of the series buried deep inside their papers alongside the horoscope columns, or ignoring it altogether.

As far as TV news was concerned, the story never happened—this despite or because of Pope John Paul II's surprise visit to America shortly after the series was published. Certainly the networks weren't going to touch this one with a ten-foot boom microphone. Running a U.S. president out of office for suspected misdemeanors was one thing. Asking the pope why he condoned and covered up a multi-million-dollar fraud, leaving hundreds of his own flock penniless, was something quite different.

Seven months later I was awarded the Pulitzer Prize for the Pauline series and *Gannett* became the first news service to win the Pulitzer Gold Medal.

As disappointing as the final outcome was, the *Gannett* series didn't prove to be an entirely futile exercise.

Under extreme pressure from his American counterparts and others in Rome, Pope John Paul II relented and allowed Zembrzuski to be ordered out of the Doylestown monastery. Essentially, he was retired.

As for the bondholders, Krol too was feeling some heat from his American brothers, who advised him that the best way to put an end to this unseemly and potentially damaging affair was to pay off the bondholders, at least those who were still alive.

Rather than dip into his own coffers or, worse yet, sponsor another Save the Shrine fund-raiser, Cardinal Krol put the bite on the well-heeled Knights of Columbus, who coughed up several millions to cover the Paulines' long overdue debts.

It was the third and, hopefully, the last time the contributions of the American faithful would be used to pay for the sins of the Pauline Fathers.

The Pauline debacle, however, wasn't the last scandal to rock the U.S. Catholic church during the 1970s. As the decade came to a close, and the federal government was moving full bore on its nearly ten-year effort to indict the Reverend Sun Myung Moon and his associates, another rather nasty story started emerging; this time involving the then titular head of the American Catholic church, the powerful Archbishop of Chicago, John Cardinal Cody.

As in the case of the Pauline Fathers and other church exposés, I had an early jump on the Cody scandal. However, I was eventually beaten out on my own story by the aggressive and gutsy *Chicago Sun Times* investigative team.

Whereas the Pauline Fathers and other church financial scandals were entangled in complex webs of intricate, oftentimes unfathomable corporate, banking, and legal transactions, the situation involving John Cardinal Cody was amazingly simple.

In his position as the undisputed senior prelate of the American Catholic church and the head of the largest, wealthiest archdiocese in the country, Cody set up his own personal bank accounts and transferred whatever church money he needed to those accounts, no questions asked.

Well, maybe not. By the time I arrived in Chicago in May 1980, more than a few questions were being raised, all discreetly, of course, among the clergy concerning what the good cardinal was doing with all this cash, an estimated three to ten million dollars in church funds spent over the previous several years.

As it turned out, sizeable chunks of the church money had been used by Cody on a number of very personal things: a secret and rather lavish lifestyle which included long vacations in the tropics and Europe and, as the *Sun Times* so discreetly put it, the purchase of a house for a "close woman friend" in southern Florida; a friend whom he allegedly visited frequently.

There were also reports of huge sums of cash salted away for "hush-money" bribes to avoid public scandals, and more than a little left over for so-called sweetheart deals with favored businessmen whom Cody employed.

Naturally, the cardinal had failed to pay taxes on any of the money used to fuel this less-than-holy or contemplative life, a failure which, to be blunt, left him open to criminal tax evasion charges.

Now, to be fair to Cody, such activities are not all that new, although the amounts of cash involved may be a tad unusual.

Traditionally, bishops and cardinals are considered "princes" of the church, and more than a few clerics take the title literally, meaning they are entitled to live like royalty, just keep it discreet so the common folk don't find out.

Think I exaggerate? Just check the ownerships of seven-figure, ocean-front mansions from Maine to Cape Cod, Newport to Long Island, and from the New Jersey shore to Florida.

So what Cardinal Cody did wasn't necessarily bizarre or aberrant behavior. But he had one thing going against him that most archbishops don't; namely, Cody was not beloved by his flock. In fact, he was despised by many who came in contact with him, even his own priests. So much so that a delegation of Chicago padres, Cody's own Priests' Senate, took the unprecedented step of secretly petitioning the Vatican to have him removed, not once, but twice.

By all accounts (I never met the man personally), Cody was a crude, belligerent, and unforgiving dictator who meted out punishment to friends and detractors alike with equal zeal. In fact, it was said that Cody treated his enemies better, adhering to the dictum of his dear friend, the late mayor of Chicago, the Honorable Richard Daley, who believed that the path to success relies heavily on "keeping your friends close and your enemies closer."

Much of the internal animus toward Cody spilled over into the public domain during the late 1970s when he began closing one Chicago parish after another as a cost-cutting measure. Hardest hit were the largely unprofitable inner-city ethnic parishes whose century-or-more-old churches had been the very hearts and souls of neighborhoods for generations of Catholic Poles, Hungarians, Germans, and Italians.

More often than not, Cody merely shut the old churches down with no warning, consultation, or explanation. One day a parish, the next a real estate listing.

His action broke the hearts of many Chicago Catholics, particularly the aged who could not motor to a Mass held in a suburban parish.

The worst public uproar, however, came when Cody wielded his iron fiscal mitt on some of the city's oldest and most venerable Catholic schools.

Again, no consultation, no compromise. It was emergency surgery and the patient wasn't even told that he was sick, much less asked if he wanted to be operated on.

Nor did Cody take kindly to having his decisions questioned. He scolded his flock by informing them that the schools were losing money. Collectively, the flock responded by saying, "So what? What the hell is the Catholic church anyway, a heartless, profitmaking corporation?"

Exactly.

Cody 10. Flock 0.

All of this internal, as well as public, rancor did Cody little good when a year or so later, in late 1980, word of the cost cutting cardinal's less-than-austere lifestyle found its way to the Chicago U.S. Attorney's office. The federal prosecutors, mostly Jimmy Carter appointees, knew they wouldn't be staying long in the Windy City. So as a welcome wagon present, they gave Cody to their Reagan administration replacements. Their love-gift included a criminal grand jury investigation of the cardinal archbishop, a first of its kind; an absolute original.

According to IRS officials to whom I spoke at the time, the grand jury quickly voted to indict Cody and a few business associates on a variety of criminal tax evasion, conspiracy and fraud charges. The new Reagan administration Justice Department, however, wanted no part of such a prosecution. Not in Chicago. And certainly not involving the senior churchman of the largest single religious denomination in the U.S. So the Justice Department did what comes natural in such cases: it stalled.

The *Chicago Sun Times*, fearing that it was going to get beaten out on its investigation, either by a competing news organization or by a grand jury indictment, went to press with a hastily written series on the Cody scandal, revealing for the first time that a federal grand jury had been investigating the cardinal for months.

The Justice Department began getting considerable public heat to get off the dime. That pressure was nothing compared to the political juice which cascaded from Illinois state and federal politicians who strongly urged the White House and Justice to back off and take a real hard, hard look at the political consequences of such a trial.

Meanwhile Cody checked himself into a hospital, reportedly for fatigue and exhaustion. In reality he had already been diagnosed with cancer.

Once more the Justice Department dithered while Cody appeared to be recuperating. Then, suddenly, he died.

You could almost hear the collective sighs of relief from Washington, D.C., Springfield, and then all the way to Daley Plaza in Chicago.

Everyone was off the hook: the prosecutors, the grand jury, the IRS, the Justice Department, the White House, Illinois' squeamish politicians, Republicans and Democrats, and, most of all, the Catholic church. Everyone, that is, except the *Sun Times*, which had become everyone's favorite whipping boy for its irreverent treatment of such a great and holy man. Even many of Cody's critics—and they were legion—had begun to eulogize the deceased churchman in glowing, flowery terms. It simply doesn't pay to kick around a dead prelate.

Let bygones be bygones was pretty much the way Cody's successor, Archbishop Joseph Bernardine, summed it up when he announced to the public that the book on the Cody matter had been permanently closed. Never mind that it had never been opened in the first place. No questions please. All is well in Heaven and on Earth. Pass the collection plate. *Pax vobiscum.*

As in the case of Elvis, death had proved to be a remarkably positive and timely career move for John Cardinal Cody.

Such is the luck of the Irish. But no such luck befell a minister from Korea who, a thousand miles away in New York City, had just been handed several federal indictments on charges of tax evasion, charges which would have been more justifiably served in Chicago.

So how could all this happen? How could good Catholics, often of limited means, give their money in total trust, only to be robbed by their own clergy? Not only did these good people seldom get their money back, but the malefactors often suffered no punishment, civil or ecclesiastical. At least in this life.

Jesus, according to the second chapter of St. John's gospel, drove the moneychangers from the temple. In fact, the Son of God wrecked the place. While Jesus may have been bad for business, it is hard to believe he would have handled the Cody matter in the same way the Vatican chose.

So things are done differently these days. O.K. How could all these things happen? Not just Cody but the Paulines, the Pallotines, the Salvatorians, and all the rest? Boys Town, too?

To answer that, we have to look at what the Catholic church in America—and other mainline denominations—had become.

In a word: rich.

Great wealth and the uncertain control of it does not bring out the best in human nature. Whatever else a clerical collar or ministerial robe provides, it does not guarantee people won't act like, well, people.

By the 1970s, when most of the major financial scandals had begun to surface, the American Roman Catholic church and its principal Protestant counterparts had grown wealthy. It was not always so. Not long in the past, America's churches tended to own the property and buildings of their religious institutions, and little else.

Shortly after World War I, the Vatican itself was nearly broke. In America, in 1936, the Catholic church's wealth was estimated at a paltry $891 million. The Protestants did better. They had tax-exempt wealth of more than $2.7 billion. By 1964, the figures were much, much higher. By that year, the Catholic church's wealth had grown to $44.5 billion while the Protestants had less than half that.[3]

The key stimulus to that growth came after World War II. The Depression was over, and the economic upsurge was spurred by an enormous pent-up demand. People had money and they wanted to spend it. And spend they did. By the time of the go-go years of the 1960s, sparked by the Kennedy tax cut, America was really booming. Several technological revolutions, some of them spawned by the equally important Kennedy space program, also helped. American churches were not going to miss out either. Soon many were involved in businesses only remotely—if at all—connected with the religious life. Stock and bond portfolios began to bulge as clergy learned the ropes of high finance. A doctor of divinity was still useful to the young churchman, but so was a Harvard M.B.A.

What was the rationalization? Need, of course. Churches expanded their programs even as many of them saw their memberships dwindle. The Sunday collection was not about to meet the demand for more revenue. Consequently, if the Lord's work was to get done, His representatives on earth had to do more than pass the hat.

So how rich are America's churches? That's easy to answer. Nobody, I mean nobody, knows. Certainly not the Internal Revenue Service, which cannot touch much of the wealth of America's churches for First Amendment reasons. Meanwhile, our churches tend to be shy about disclosure. For the most part, the Roman Catholic church is downright secretive. The Vatican hasn't survived 2,000 years and everything from Attila the Hun to Adolph Hitler by letting people know how much it is worth.

The truth is also, as we shall see, that the Holy Father doesn't know either. He and his financial officers can only guess. Like the rest of us. The Protestant mainline bodies aren't much better, lest you think that Rome is alone in keeping its secrets.

Thus we have only a dim idea how much America's churches are worth; in fact, we are looking through a glass darkly, in the words of the Apostle Paul.

And the concealment is quite deliberate.

We can get hints of the size of church holdings, however. Let's begin with the collection plate. Now of course the Sunday offering, once the mainstay of revenue, is probably no longer the churches' principal source of income. But that contribution can still be a considerable sum. In the early 1970s, for example, the Catholic diocese of Pittsburgh brought in $30 million a year via the weekly offering. Even in today's dollars, that's not pocket change.

That's why, although there are no official figures, one estimate suggests the total American Roman Catholic collections amounted to $4 billion a year in the early 1970s. Protestants and Jews accounted for another $7 billion, for a grand total of $11 billion annually. All tax free, of course.[4]

Naturally, some churches do far better on a per-capita giving basis than others. Those denominations that tithe, like the Seventh Day Adventists and the Latter-Day Saints, do very well indeed. The Adventists, for example, are a relatively small body, but they raked in nearly $50 million in 1974 and that did not include, as Larson and Lowell observed, "contributions to local church building funds, local church projects, the denomination's disaster aid program, and support of denominational schools."[5]

Another source of money is bequeathals by individuals in their wills. The American Catholic church alone is estimated to receive between $250 and $500 million a year from the faithful—a fountain of income that has been part of the Christian church's history since its beginning.

Now for property. That aspect of total church wealth also remains shrouded in darkness. None of our denominations likes to talk about real estate holdings. What is known and published is assessed valuation, a figure that is merely an indication of actual book value.

To give you an idea of how murky reportage about church assets is, consider the financial report of the Roman Catholic archdiocese of New York, one of the wealthiest dioceses in the world.

Its 1972 financial statement listed religious property as worth $563 million, a hefty sum even in 1990 dollars, but of course it is only a small part of the picture. One omission from the report, for example, was the worth of the archdiocese's crown jewel: St. Patrick's Cathedral—squatting as it does in mid-Manhattan.

The New York archdiocese's financial statement also did not include cemeteries, hospitals, office buildings, and recreation centers. Finally, it did not include the archdiocese's stock and bond portfolio which was estimated to be worth $29 million seventeen years ago, surely an exercise in restrained understatement if there ever was one. In fact, the old Soviet defense budgets were less opaque than the average diocesan financial statement—if one is issued at all.[6]

As sketchy as the New York diocesan report is, it's nonetheless a positive goldmine of information compared to that of other Catholic dioceses. Thirty-six of sixty-five reports were once rated by the National Association of (Catholic) Laity—a group who wish to have the temple curtain parted on this question—as being wholly inadequate in terms of reporting procedures. Which is to say more than half got the big F.

Protestant bodies, with their Reformation tradition of showing distrust toward high ecclesiastical authority, tend to make better disclosures of their holdings—the much-abused Mormons being an exception.

But even the Protestants spread their assets around in a confusing fashion that makes it difficult to figure out exactly what they do have in total. The Methodists, for example, have a long list of boards which, in fact, are semi-autonomous agencies with their own accounting procedures. Some, like the Board of Global Ministries, make their financial reserves known—in the early 1970s their assets amounted to nearly $130 million. Others, like the Methodist Board of Church and Society, refuse to do so although it is known that this agency owns some of the prime real estate in the Washington, D.C., area.[7]

That America's religious bodies possess far more than the church with the steeple should come as no surprise. Catholics, Protestants, and Jews also own schools, from one-room elementaries to major universities. They also have publishing companies, television and radio stations, hospitals, nursing homes, housing projects, and apartments. Many of these of course fall within the church's preaching, teaching, healing, and helping mission. Many, however, are merely fronts for profitable business enterprises.

But that hardly exhausts the question. In fact, church-related institutions are only a fraction of what is now owned and operated. If nothing else the sheer variety of church institutions is dazzling. They range from multi-billion-dollar operations like the Lutheran Brotherhood—an insurance company for Lutherans only—to a $12,000-a-year operation that tins turtle soup, owned by a local Catholic parish in Illinois. (The parish also engages in the manufacture of fishing lures.) In between, the St. Paul, Minnesota, Catholic diocese owns a major department store, the Lutherans own a hotel in Milwaukee, as do the Mormons in Salt Lake City. Not so long ago, the New York Catholic archdiocese owned the royalty rights to Listerine mouth wash. It sold them for $25 million.

Perhaps Jim and Tammy's Holy Roller Disneyland isn't so strange after all.

Even the posh Watergate overlooking the Potomac in Washington, D.C., an exclusive office and penthouse complex made notorious by the 1972 break-in of Democratic National Headquarters, was built and once owned by the Vatican, just one of thousands of similar properties scattered throughout the U.S.

And, of course, the Christian Brothers produce their famous wines and brandies, earning untaxed profits until their tax-exempt liquor business became the subject of a lawsuit filed by an angry competitor, a suit which the brothers lost in 1957. Other spirits-producing orders, however, have kept their non-taxable status—one of the central mysteries of American law.[8]

Speaking of Catholic orders—which are, as we have seen, independent from diocesan control—there are 539 of them operating in the United States, the majority female. How much are they worth? God alone knows, and that is no mere play on words. The only indication that can be gotten is by totalling up listed assets of twenty-four orders who have done so in prospectuses designed to gain access to the bond market. The total—again drawn from the early 1970s—is $722 million. Of course, the twenty-four are only a fraction—less than 5 percent of the total number of orders in the U.S. Interestingly, the Little Sisters of the Poor, by no means the largest, reported assets of $25 million. The Little Sisters of the Poor, in short, are not.[9]

One order, the Society of Jesus or Jesuits, is of particular interest. They are one of the oldest in North America, thanks to the French. While the early Roman Catholic church struggled to survive in the English speaking colonies, the Jesuits laid the basis of the church's future wealth by acquiring property in the wilderness as quickly as they could. Four centuries of buying can add up, and although the order's holdings are secret, one conservative estimate made in the early 1970s holds that the income generated for the Jesuits in America alone totaled $250 million a year. No corporation in the Fortune 500 would consider that a bad year for profits, especially when there never seems to be an off-year for the Jesuits.[10]

So what does this all amount to in several lump sums? Again, a warning. The estimates that exist surely err on the low side and they are also at least fifteen years out of date. Yet, church income (Protestant and Catholic) in the early 1970s was at least $20 billion a year. Accumulated assets: nearly $150 billion.[11]

This figure, it must be repeated, represents only a fraction of what America's churches own—property either religious or strictly commercial in nature.

Of course that is not quite the end of the money matter. American churches, Catholic and Protestant, are major exporters of funds to the rest of the world. So are America's Jews, in support, *inter alia*, of Israel. The total amount that is sent abroad is once again one of those figures that is unknown and quite probably unknowable.

In the case of the American Catholic church, some estimates have been made. It should be said at the outset that the Vatican considers the American church wealthy and in no need of financial assistance, no matter what. As a consequence, Rome has never, even in emergencies like natural disasters, provided any funds for the United States.

Each Roman Catholic archdiocese assesses a dollar quota from its parishes to help in its work. Included in that figure is the so-called Peter's Pence which is collected once a year in June. That money is forwarded to the Vatican. How much is contributed is also kept hidden, with the estimates ranging from a few million to hundreds of millions of dollars. One calculation in the early 1970s put the figure at $6 million—almost certainly an underestimate even for then.

In addition to the Peter's Pence, "*supplementi*" are collected by the Vatican from the American church. These *supplementi* quite probably more than equal the Peter's Pence, placing one early 1970s total estimate of contributions to Rome at $15 million a year.[12]

Any way you slice it, that's a lot of cash sloshing around, and no one knows exactly how much there is or where it is located. As for Roman Catholic wealth, even the Vatican does not know the total. The orders are secretive about what they have and so are the archdioceses. And if the Holy Father does not know, I guarantee you that the U.S. government and the IRS don't either.

One reason for this remarkable state of affairs is that the bishops and archbishops are for tax purposes considered "corporation soles." As church financial expert, Nino LoBello, explains it:

[This] allows a bishop to hold, in his own name as bishop and without paying taxes, as much real estate, stocks, bonds, mortgages, cash and other property as he can amass—there is no legal limitation.[13]

That's only for starters. LoBello continues:

The bishop may manage these assets in whatever manner he wishes, as if they were his personal wealth. Since the theory is that he is acting as an agent of the Church, there is no tax liability and he is not required to divulge any figures or other information. According to law, all the property held under corporation sole passes automatically to a bishop's successor without any need for formal transfer. Thus, as a corporation sole, the bishop is not answerable to any authority—federal, state or city—as to the management, use or disposition of whatever wealth he gains title to. Nor is he required to make any report to the priests or laymen in his jurisdiction even though the latter may have contributed the wherewithal for a corporation sole to accumulate these material things.[14]

The system, obviously, is open to abuse. Add to that the fact that the religious orders are under even less discipline. As the Pauline Fathers proved, an order can do almost as it pleases. It does not answer to the local diocesan authorities at all.

An order can only be disciplined by the Vatican. But that ancient and creaking bureaucracy can barely keep up with the most pressing problems. Rome is simply incapable of dealing with its own financial affairs, much less those of various orders tucked away in obscure parts of the world—like Doylestown, Pennsylvania. Add powerful friends in the right places, and the Pauline-like problems become almost inevitable.[15]

With all that money and only the loosest sort of controls over its acquisition and spending, financial scandals in America's churches should not surprise anyone. The only surprise in the end may be that there are not more of them. But then with the veil of secrecy being as thick as it surely is over the Lord's money, who would know?

And who would tell?

And who seems to care?

Certainly not the U.S. federal government. With the exception of the Pallotine Fathers, no matter how bad the mismanagement, no matter how criminal the dealings, nobody has gone to jail from an established church—until Jim Bakker came along. The Pallotines, remember, were hauled into court by state authorities.

Damned few even get indicted, and only a handful are investigated—usually in the most cursory fashion.

It is hard to square this kid-gloves treatment given the American mainline churches with that laid on the tiny Unification Church. While the established churches acquire hundreds of billions of dollars in assets—everything from Washington's Watergate to New York's World Trade Center—purchases which spur no interest, the Unification Church flower and ginseng-tea "empire" does.

In the 1970s and 1980s the United States had a seemingly permanent trade deficit with the rest of the world and the mainline churches were exporting hard dollars—none of which would ever yield returns on investment. The Unification Church, however, was actually bringing in money—principally from Japan, of all places—amounting to hundreds of millions of dollars.

Still, that did not stop the mighty onrush of investigation from dozens of federal and state law enforcement, tax, and security agencies, not to mention the U.S. Congress and numerous state legislatures. Why the howl and hysteria on the one hand, and the near dead silence on the other?

The hypocrisy of selective investigation and prosecution in the *Moon* case is as astonishing as it is obvious. Yet the reasons are not all that simple. But let me try to explain. We will start with the most ruthless and cynical and yet the most truthful reason.

Justice is not blind in this country, or anywhere else for that matter. We are not dealing with an impartial machine at all. The legal system is composed of human beings. That is a truism, but it is often overlooked. Men and women in the system are driven by the same desires and pressures that anyone else experiences in daily life.

In the case of the Unification Church, the reason for prosecution was quite simple. The church was disliked and feared and there was popular pressure to do something about it. Unification Church members were hardly unique, but they were a recent and vivid example of selective persecutorial prosecution. And best of all, they couldn't hit back. Or that's the way it looked in the early 1970s.

But they served another purpose too. As a religious body, they were a fat and inviting target at least to the IRS. Needless to say, while there was no enthusiasm for going after the established churches, the wealth they were accumulating, especially in non-religious enterprises, was of interest to the tax collectors. If the Unification Church members could be disciplined to the general approval of everyone, including the courts, perhaps in time the mainline churches could be chipped away at, too. At least valuable precedents would be established in court which could prove useful once the IRS went after the more established denominations.

The thought was tempting and may explain the ferocity of the war waged against the Unification Church by the federal government. But somehow other churches were never included. They were too big, too well established, and no groundswell of support emerged for rewriting the rules on tax exemption. At least not in the 1980's.

At best, America remained ambivalent about its parsons and priests and the things they did in the name of the Lord.

CHAPTER XVI

BIGOTRY: AN
HISTORICAL VIEW

*Most men, when they think they are thinking, are merely rearranging
their prejudices.*

KNUTE ROCKNE

THE city was quiet, but not at peace. Troops filtered through the
narrow, gritty streets, armed and ready for trouble. The "trouble,"
of course, was the sectarians—the Protestant majority and a Catholic minority, drawn into a cycle of hatred and violence.

The season was now springtime, but no one noticed much—
except for the heat which was greater than it should have been for
early May. Maybe the fires caused the heat.

A troop patrol picked its way carefully past the burnt-out, gut-
ted wrecks of what had been Roman Catholic churches, the fallen
timbers still smoldering, throwing off smoke and dust. The soldiers ignored the little boys who were picking their way through
the rubble looking for ecclesiastical treasure. Or just souvenirs.

Were the urchins Protestant or Catholic? Who knew? Who
cared? They did not really qualify as looters anyway, and the men
had more important things on their minds—like staying alive
during this disagreeable and unwanted duty. People had already

been killed by stray shots. The patrols were a tempting target for any hothead who had the courage of liquor in him.

So they just ignored the scores of Irish Catholics who had been left homeless while the city fathers—Protestant to a man—were still working out a plan to shelter the new homeless in the wake of the worst riots in the city's history.

The city fathers, like the troops, had other, bigger worries, too. They knew that firemen who had been called out to deal with the Protestant wave of arson had been attacked by mobs of Protestant bully boys. Even the mayor had not been spared. He had been knocked silly with a brick thrown at him while he was standing in front of St. Augustine's during a pathetic attempt to calm down his constituents.

How had this round of sectarian violence begun? As usual there were the rumors. It was clear enough that the killing of George Shiffler had started it all—at least this time. Shiffler had been young and Protestant and a bystander to a street stand-off between Catholic and Protestant toughs. Suddenly, a gunshot from who-knows-where had left Shiffler dead in the street. At least that's how the authorities eventually pieced together the story. In the meantime, Shiffler had become a martyr—at least to the Protestant majority—the city's first martyr. He would not be the last.

The inevitable procession for the dead bystander followed. Protestants displayed their flag, which they said the Catholics had trampled. Their hysteria was fed by the Protestant dominated media which reported as fact rumors that Catholic priests were stirring up their parishioners.

Then all hell broke loose.

The city's Catholic clergy were scared to death. Bishop Francis Patrick Kenrick took the unusual step of cancelling all masses until the city was safe again for the Catholic minority.

"I earnestly conjure you," Kenrick told his flock in that archaic manner that is meant to give comfort, "to practice unalterable patience under the trials to which it has pleased Divine Providence to subject you—and remember that affliction will serve to purify us, and render us acceptable to God, through Jesus Christ, who patiently suffered on the cross."[1]

As always, there were a few heroes living amidst the sectarian warfare. A few. A Protestant clergyman offered Bishop Kenrick temporary sanctuary in his home. Other Protestant leaders denounced the violence in an attempt to calm the community. Eventually the appeals, the troops, and sheer exhaustion caused the violence to sputter out—for the time being.

Belfast? Where a Protestant majority and a Catholic minority live in fear of the other? No.

It was Philadelphia in May 1844.

Conventional Fourth of July rhetoric celebrates America as a country blessed with religious freedom. Repeatedly, *ad nauseam*, we are reminded that a man or woman can worship as he or she pleases in perfect safety. He or she may even choose not to believe in anything at all. Here in America.

Not only that, but the panegyrists also suggest that such has always been the case from Plymouth Rock onward. Look at our Bill of Rights with its First Amendment, they say. It prohibits the establishment of any one religion as the state religion, and by extension it means that government cannot interfere in the free practice of one's religious beliefs. Even our British cousins don't have anything like the First Amendment. Queen Elizabeth remains the Defender of the Faith.

After all, didn't many of our ancestors flee other lands in search of religious freedom? How about the Pilgrim Fathers and the Puritans—who, it must be said, are frequently confused in this kind of panegyric? And William Penn? Not to mention Thomas Jefferson and James Madison?

Americans' zealous respect for religious freedom is understandable. But it is a child's version of history, a "Golden Book" of favorite myths and legends.

And it is wrong and misplaced in its enthusiasm. There is much to celebrate and to cherish, but propagating a myth—an unuseful one in this case—is not helpful.

The truth is that persecution of religions—especially new ones—is very much part of American history. Yes, people did come often to our shores because they themselves were persecuted religious dissenters at home. But what they sought here was not necessarily what they wanted others to have.

As Americans, we have not been a particularly tolerant people. We are not so today. The First Amendment—which was largely the work of great Virginians, especially Madison and Jefferson—was not a statement of what was, at the time, widely believed and practiced by the many. Instead, it was hammered into the body of the Constitution by a few precisely because it was needed as a wall against the prevailing religious intolerance—as those two Founders knew full well.

The story of our country's fight for religious freedom is then much more complex than the orators would have it. This does not make the achievement any the less significant. America is not, and was not, a Utopia of religious freedom. It has, however, despite our worst instincts, achieved a tolerably tolerant society, although a far from perfect one.

Unless we understand how difficult that tolerance was to achieve, we Americans will never be able to finish the work begun by a few good men.

What accounts for the lack of religious tolerance in a pluralist society?

Before our eighteenth-century Founders—Washington, Adams, Jefferson, Madison, Mason, and the rest—were our seventeenth-century forefathers. Those who exerted the greatest influence on us theologically were the men of the Massachusetts colony. The Puritans. They were Calvinists in doctrine, but Calvinism extended far beyond things of the spirit. That was so because Puritans could never make artificial divisions between body and soul, civil matters and the things of God. This understanding colored all Puritan beliefs, including, or more precisely, especially, their political and social values.

It would be as their spiritual father, John Calvin of Geneva, would have had it. Calvin was no ivory-tower man of the cloth. If right religion could deal with such weighty matters as man's relation with God, it could assuredly inform and instruct regarding man's relations with man.

The Puritans, in the wilderness of the New World, believed in fundamental tenets that deeply affected the course of our history—including our idea of religious freedom.

The Puritans sought what they could not find in England. As dissenters, they were caught between the established Anglican church and a sizeable Roman Catholic minority who returned to power (temporarily) under James II in 1685.

As Calvinists, they lived in the certainty of a universe ruled by

God under his Divine Law. Indeed, even God the Almighty, ruler of heaven and earth, was not above His own law. How then could be a mere mortal man, even a king?

That law, grounded in a close reading of the New and Old Testaments, was "fused" with natural law. Men were predestined either to heaven or hell. While on earth they were governed by holy scripture above all, and not necessarily by English common law—a belief that caused intense annoyance on the part of His Majesty's magistrates.

These basic Puritan beliefs left little room for tolerance. But Puritan rigidity had both advantages and disadvantages. The belief that law was above both man and God meant that human rulers could not be simple and arbitrary autocrats. If God was subject to divine law so were the king and his agents.

The effect on government is both obvious and staggering. It was a vast step forward. Man's relation with God was fixed. Among those who were the elect, a contract would be established, at least among those who had received God's grace. The "contract" theory naturally extended to relations between man and man. Thus, the Mayflower compact came quite naturally to our Pilgrim forefathers.[2]

But Puritan and Pilgrim belief also left little room for accepting or even respecting the beliefs of others, who quite simply were wrong—in error—in matters both small and large.

The Puritans who left England did so because they were not successful in purging the Anglican church of "Roman" influences. They were unsuccessful because they were not strong enough.

In America the situation would be different, they thought. Their Calvinist beliefs—including the one that all other beliefs were in error when they departed from their own—infused the new colonies, especially those in New England. Only Pennsylvania—founded in 1681 by William Penn, an English Quaker leader, with an ethic of tolerant pacifism—its off-shoot New Jersey, and Maryland, founded earlier in 1633 by a company of persecuted English Catholics, were greatly different from the colonies established by their English-speaking brothers.[3]

Seventeenth-century Calvinism then was the first layer of belief that would affect our attitudes on religion. But the eighteenth century had its effect, too, and in the opposite direction. The spirit of rational enlightenment which—to say the least—was skeptical of Puritan claims about man, God, and his universe added another and fundamentally important stratum to our attitudes about religion.[4]

By the 1730s Calvin had been replaced by John Locke and Isaac Newton as the intellectual guides for the colonial elite. For them, God no longer was the terrible Supreme Judge, but God the Great Architect (a favorite term, incidentally, of George Washington, a Mason) largely identified with a knowable, benign, and magnificently designed Nature and Universe, the laws of which were perfect, predictable, and not a little prosaic in their essence.

Politically the notion of "rights" changed from those given under God's grace (if they were given at all) to those given under natural law and rooted in everyday human experience. The foundation for them was a social contract worked out between men (and not between God and man) who established a government limited in its authority and unable to violate nature and man's inalienable rights without fatal consequences to that government.[5]

Two gentlemen from Virginia were crucial to this change in outlook. Unlike some of their New England brethren, Thomas Jefferson and James Madison were not rigidly religious men. In fact, they barely conformed to conventional piety at all. Virginia was not as strict with regard to religion as colonies further north.

At best, Jefferson and Madison were rational deists. There was, of course, a God somewhere. Rather remote, perhaps indifferent to human affairs. Certainly rational and orderly in His ways. Rather comfortable too, and certainly uninterested in torturing human beings in an afterlife—if indeed, there was an afterlife.

Jefferson and Madison therefore did not suffer religious fanatics gladly. Even in old age Jefferson railed against "monkish ignorance and superstition" in a letter to Roger Weightman, less than a month before he died at the age of eighty-three.[6]

For Madison, religious persecution was especially intolerable. In 1774, two years before the great Declaration and thirteen years prior to the Federal Convention, an outraged Madison wrote a friend about the "diabolical, hell-conceived principle of persecution. . . ."[7]

Madison's angst is understandable because even in relatively liberal Virginia, dissenters walked a very narrow path. But Jefferson and Madison were far more than critics of superstition and intolerance. They did something about it.

Jefferson, for one, counted the "Bill for Establishing Religious Freedom" in Virginia as one of the three greatest achievements in his life—equal to his far better known authorship of the Declaration of Independence.[8]

On a national scale, however, the fight was not that easy. The Federal Convention, held in Philadelphia in 1787, had remarkably little to say about religious freedom. That may in part be true because Jefferson was not there but in France as the new nation's minister; that is, ambassador to the court of King Louis XVI. Louis himself was about to be swept from power by the French Revolution, whose advocates had their own ideas about religion.

Madison in his "Notes on the Convention" records only one brief debate about religious tests for political office. On August 20, 1787, during that remarkably hot summer, Charles Cotesworth Pinckney of South Carolina submitted to the "Committee of Detail" the following proposition:

> No religious test or qualification shall ever be annexed to any oath of office under the authority of the U.S.[9]

That suggestion was sandwiched among many other privileges and liberties submitted by Pinckney that day: suggestions including habeas corpus, a free press, and civilian control of the military.

Ten days later the issue was debated. Pinckney again submitted that no office holder of the United States should be subject to any religious test. The mood of the convention was squarely in line with the South Carolinian's view, but Roger Sherman of Connecticut thought the clause unnecessary because of "the prevailing liberality being a sufficient security against such tests." The delegates knew better. They approved the religious test clause, which remains to this day in the last paragraph of Article VI.[10]

Such was the extent of the Philadelphia convention's work on the religious question.

After the Federal Convention was over, both Madison and Jefferson had strong second thoughts about the new Constitution. It lacked—to their mind—a clear and succinct statement of American liberties. Just what were they and how best would they be protected? Their concern was shared by others, especially their fellow Virginians.

Virginia's ratifying convention therefore stipulated that a Bill of Rights, in the form of amendments, be added to the Philadelphia charter. If not, Virginia would not accept the Constitution, and without the consent of Virginia—by far the largest and most populous of the original thirteen colonies—there would be no United States of America.

The Virginians' final suggested amendment, the twentieth, concerned religion. The amendment draft read:

> That religion or the duty which we owe to our Creator, and the manner of discharging it can be directed only by reason and conviction, not by force or violence, and therefore all men have an equal, natural and unalienable right to the free exercise of religion according to the dictates of conscience, and that no particular religious sect or society ought to be favored or established by Law in preference to others.[11]

The Virginians, if nothing else, were thorough in their statement of what they wanted. The First Amendment as finally written proved to be a somewhat truncated version that threw in everything except the proverbial kitchen sink. This catch-all change incorporated such rights as speech, press, assembly, and petition. It also included the provision that Congress shall make no law "respecting an establishment of religion, or prohibiting the free exercise thereof. . . ."[12]

We can be grateful, at least, that the author of these amendments was James Madison, no less, the man who had written the final draft of the original Constitution.

Despite such distinguished parentage, the Bill of Rights was not ratified either quickly or by unanimous consent. Like the new Constitution itself, it drew its share of critics and enemies.

More than four years after the Philadelphia convention the Bill of Rights, including the First Amendment, was finally adopted in December 1791. Some states remained holdouts for two more centuries.[13]

Still, the Bill of Rights was better than the Articles of Confederation, which made no mention of religious liberty at all. The compact that had governed the nation in the years after the War of Independence had established a pitifully weak form of government that the most ardent admirers of liberty found terribly wanting. It could not protect Americans from enemies, foreign and domestic, and it could not guarantee the rights that Americans had fought for against the English crown.

They placed their hope in the new federal Constitution—for better or worse. Neither it nor the state constitutions, each with its enumerated rights of citizens (which were not extended to slaves, of course), was sufficient to protect everyone's freedom of religion. As in the seventeenth century that freedom would be selective.

Religious bigotry in what would become the United States is as old as the first settlement. It was a product of its time and it would have a long shelf life. In no way was American religious bigotry worse than bigotry elsewhere in the world—especially Western Christendom—and as elsewhere it persists until our own day.

Those who fled persecution carried the disease within themselves. The Puritans and Pilgrims (who had first fled to tolerant Holland) were not about to exhibit any more tolerance toward others than they had experienced themselves.

After all, the question was not one of liberal feelings, but of Truth with, of course, a capital T. That contest was fiercely waged between God's elect and those who had chosen to distance themselves from the Throne. Within these tight circles of beliefs there was little quarter given or understanding extended.

The underpinnings of this religious intolerance included the fact that newly established churches in the New World were not simply prejudiced, nor did they indulge in persecution of others on the basis of whim.

These churches believed in the Law—both divine and human, and that Law was to be obeyed. Therefore, in colonial times, the instrumentalities of law had to be used against unacceptable forms of religious expression. It is a practice that is not unknown even in this enlightened age.

Punishment of religious dissenters from the local orthodoxy tended to be severe. Fines and imprisonment were supplemented by the use of stocks and exposure in a public place. A little wholesome derision, mixed with rotten eggs, was a pleasant pastime—especially in New England.

The more serious cases merited banishment and, on occasion, capital punishment. That was the case with the celebrated Salem witch trials in 1692, an hysteria which spread to the other colonies by the end of the century.[14]

In a form of punishment inspired in part by the preaching of Puritan divines, those finally found guilty of witchcraft in Salem were hanged (not burned at the stake—that was another place and another century). Most of the evidence for witchcraft was based on the testimony of two clearly hysterical adolescent girls, the "afflicted children."

The trials, however, were not drumhead affairs, but elaborate legal procedures. Far more than the twenty people who were actually executed were deemed witches by the court. The repentant were excused. Many more were accused, but the magistrates gradually became suspicious that Satan himself was part of the accusatory process. To his credit, Cotton Mather was among the first to raise suspicions regarding the girls' testimony; he recommended prayer and pastoral care for the hysterics and mercy for the accused.[15]

The trials had their grim aftermath. In one case, twelve jurors later made statements admitting that they had been mistaken in handing down guilty verdicts: the Puritan conscience, after all, was a two-edged sword.

Such admissions after the fact did little for the twenty innocent men and women who were legally executed. But they did cause the Puritan leaders to rethink their position on witchcraft, leading them to a position that if Satan was truly active in the world he could lead men wrongfully to accuse the innocent and protect the guilty.

It was an expensive lesson to learn.[16]

Salem, that great blemish on colonial America and on New England in particular, was hardly the only one to mark that City on a Hill.

Roger Williams, one of the founders of the Baptist Church in North America—though he did not remain a Baptist for long—was exiled from Massachusetts and founded what eventually became the settlement of Rhode Island.

Exiled also were Anne Hutchinson and her brother-in-law, the Reverend John Wainright. Their crime?

The latter two believed in a Lutheran-like doctrine of grace alone rather than the Calvinist belief that good works were an affirmation that God's own were truly elected by Him for everlasting life.[17]

Williams' theology was far more complex. Originally a Puritan, Williams soon became disillusioned with the Puritans in the New World. He found their government in Massachusetts dictatorial and blatantly unfair to nonbelievers in the colony. He specifically objected to the practice of making church attendance compulsory for all, while denying the sacraments to the nonelect. Williams also argued that Biblical passages were subject to a variety of interpretations, and that the Puritans had no monopoly on their meaning.

Williams therefore recommended the separation of church and state and the need for a universal tolerance in the colony. No wonder then that in 1635 he was tried and convicted of propagating "new and dangerous opinions against the authority of the magistrates."

Banished from Massachusetts, that restless soul eventually began a settlement called Providence Plantations where he could practice what he had preached. Williams, as president of the new colony, welcomed Jews and Quakers and anyone else wishing to escape the nearby Puritans.

Williams was relatively lucky, even though banishment carried with it both stigma and the questionable chance of beginning again in the raw wilderness.

He also died nine years before the Salem witch trials began.

Those in New England who were not so fortunate were beaten, whipped, fined, and put in jail, where they lived on a diet of bread and water. And on their own prayers.[18]

Baptists and other dissidents from Puritanism, most of them hardly theological radicals in our sense, were also not alone in suffering colonial legal persecution. Among the less orthodox the Society of Friends, or the Quakers as they were better known, received special and unwelcome treatment by authorities, except in Pennsylvania, Rhode Island, and New Jersey. Four were executed in Massachusetts.

William Penn traded on his connections with Kings Charles II (a Protestant) and James II (a Catholic) as well as the fact that his father was a famous admiral. This gave him the opportunity to

found a great commonwealth: an immense tract of land set aside
for all those who believed in one God, no questions asked.

Meanwhile, the Friends relied on their basic belief that within
each man a spark of the Divine could be found, even when it came
to the rather odd sort of persons who flocked to Pennsylvania after
1682 when Philadelphia was first laid out. In the early English
colonies such tolerance was singular.

The Puritan authorities, among others, could not abide a religion that cared little about doctrine and, worse, did not believe in
the corrupted nature of man.

The Roman Catholic equivalent of Pennsylvania, Maryland,
provided Catholics with religious shelter too. In the rest of the
colonies, however, they were fair game.

The Massachusetts General Court, the colony's legislature,
found in 1647, for example, that:

> [N]o Jesuit or ecclesiastical person ordained by the pope or see of
> Rome shall henceforth come into Massachusetts. Any person not
> freeing himself of suspicion shall be jailed, then banished. If taken a
> second time, he shall be put to death.[19]

Matters were no better in the Bay State forty-two years later
when a new charter was granted decreeing that "forever thereafter
there shall be liberty of conscience allowed in the worship of God
to all Christians (except papists)."[20]

Massachusetts' newfound liberty of spirit must have come as a
great comfort to Baptists—perhaps even to the Friends—but it
certainly afforded no consolation to Catholics. There and elsewhere throughout the colonies, public Mass was forbidden and
priests were routinely beaten, tarred and feathered, or even killed.
Up to and through 1850, in what is now southern New Jersey,
Jesuit missionaries headquartered in Philadelphia were hanged if
they were caught saying Mass or otherwise ministering to their few
but faithful parishioners.

Persecution of Catholics runs like a scarlet thread through our
entire history. More on this later.

The eighteenth-century's enlightenment did little beyond pene-
trating a portion of America's elite. Tolerance was never a by-word
among ordinary Americans. The new faiths that challenged old

ones were subjected to the same kind of abuse seventeenth-century pre-Americans had heaped on their unconventional brethren.

No better example of this abuse can be found than the Mormons, or as they are officially known, the Church of Jesus Christ of Latter-Day Saints.

The Mormon movement was founded by Joseph Smith, a young farmer, in 1830 in upstate New York after he published the *Book of Mormon*, the now-celebrated account of how some of the lost tribes of Israel emigrated to North America and, Mormons believe, founded an ancient civilization.

That civilization of lighter skinned Nephites, according to Smith's "golden plates," did battle with the darker-hued Lamanites.

Result? Lamanites 1; Nephites 0.

The Lamanites, incidentally, are the ancestors of the present-day American Indians, according to Mormon doctrine. Also: Jesus Christ, after his resurrection, put in an appearance in the New World.

The New World story, Smith said, was written on plates of gold that had been buried in a New York mountainside. Smith translated the plates with the aid of "divine spectacles," after the angel Moroni first appeared to him ten years earlier to reveal the exact location of the plates.

The doctrines of Joseph Smith, which included baptism of the dead and, most offensive to America's Puritans, polygamy, earned him far more than ridicule. Smith and his small band of followers were soon driven out of Fayette, New York, by his astonished and angry neighbors. Their expulsion began an extended exodus of people who would be called derisively "Mormons."

They trekked to Ohio and then Missouri. But the promising new beginning in Independence, Missouri, was soon aborted, and Smith and his followers founded a brand-new settlement in Nauvoo, Illinois, on the Mississippi River across from the dust bluffs of Iowa. The site was unpromising, being hardly more than swampland subjected to periodic flooding. Because of what would become a hallmark of Mormons—hard work—Nauvoo soon prospered, becoming in four years the largest city in the state with a population of 20,000 (although some sources claim it was a town of only 10,000).

Whatever the size, the town's sudden, even spectacular growth demonstrates yet another characteristic of American society: that is, while new religious groups are often persecuted, they also just as often flourish. Americans are hungry for the new and, more than other peoples, are willing to cast off the old. As a result, people poured into Nauvoo from as far as Europe to follow the new religion and its prophet. A huge temple was built—the Mormons' first permanent structure—and for a while the Latter-Day Saints seemed secure in their river town.

This state of affairs did not last.

In 1844, Smith, who was growing in political importance and personal arbitrariness, shut down a local newspaper that had been harshly critical of him. By twentieth-century standards the paper had probably been libelous in the extreme. But Smith was acting like an autocrat, and the local sheriff arrested him.

Under protest, he was taken to the nearby town of Carthage for trial.

Before the legal niceties began, a mob broke into the jail and murdered Smith and his brother Hyrum. The dazed and disorganized Mormons were then subjected to intense persecution and eventually driven out of Nauvoo.

The Mormons' new leader Brigham Young literally marched the decimated flock into the wilderness until they found their new home, the desolate salt flats of what would become the state of Utah, the present-day heart of the Mormon empire. As a majority the Mormons have flourished. But it was not until 1896, after the Mormon elders formally dropped the doctrine of polygamy, that the territory became a state. Congress would accept no less.

Survival for the Latter-Day Saints, in short, became a test of their skill, perseverance, and political pragmatism.

Others weren't so lucky. They could be as stubborn. And just as persecuted. The Jehovah's Witnesses come to mind. Like the Mormons, the Witnesses are an off-shoot of basic Christianity. They were founded in Pittsburgh by Charles Taze Russell in 1872, more than a generation after Smith gathered together his Latter-Day Saints. Like the Mormons, the Witnesses have a number of unconventional beliefs and practices that have earned them much persecution, a great deal from being on the wrong side of the law.

Among other things, they believe in the imminent return of

Jesus, who after the battle of Armageddon will set up God's perfect rule on an earth-turned-paradise. It is this belief that urges Witnesses to spread their beliefs, much to the annoyance of many people.

Quite probably the doctrine that has gotten the Witnesses into more trouble is their refusal to accept the rule of any government, except God's. As a result, Witnesses don't salute the flag or serve in the armed forces. That notion has gotten them into trouble with the law in regimes as diverse as Franklin Roosevelt's America and Fidel Castro's Cuba.

More than any other sect since the Mormons found safety in the Great Salt Lake Basin, the Witnesses have taken it on the chin. They also believe that all other Christians are, in fact, duped followers of the devil—especially Roman Catholics.

The Witnesses were subjected to the usual prejudice, hatred, and fear, as well as unusual anti-Witness legislation that resulted in numerous prosecutions and convictions.

As Leo Pfeffer has observed:

> New laws were enacted and old laws resurrected to supply weapons to curb their activities and, if possible, to completely destroy them. All kinds of laws were passed or were attempted to be used for that purpose—anti-peddling ordinances, traffic regulations, revenue laws, laws forbidding the use of sound trucks, and many others were invoked against them.[21]

In part because withdrawal to the safety of an unpopulated area was no longer an option, the Witnesses tried a new tactic in survival. Instead of running away like Roger Williams or the Latter-Day Saints, the Witnesses, after years of legal harassment, decided in the 1930s and 1940s to fight back.

They, like the Puritans before them, might have considered themselves God's elect—the prophetic 144,000 who would rule a new and perfect earth—but in the meantime, they would not lie down and let the unbelievers trample on what they thought were their constitutional rights.

When they fought, they fought hard—in the courts. Gritty and persistent, they took their cases through a range of local, state, and federal courts all the way to the Supreme Court—usually seeking reversals of earlier convictions and decisions handed down by hostile judges and juries. This did not occur once, but many times, in literally hundreds of cases. The Witnesses, in short, would not shut up, or dry up, or go away.

They also learned that while the courts were not friendly, judges, on balance, were fairer than juries.

After many hard and bitter lessons, the Witnesses discovered that even with *voir dire*, they could not shield themselves from the prejudice of jurors. It was a lesson that two generations later members of the Unification Church would learn all over again from the Southern Federal District of New York in a celebrated case.[22]

Because of their effort and expense, the Jehovah's Witnesses, in the opinion of many legal scholars, are more responsible than any other religious group for the formation of modern law and precedent on the treatment of America's religions.[23]

Other groups have had similar and difficult problems with American law. After the Witnesses, the Amish are probably best known for both their trials and tribulations in U.S. courts.

Only recently have they been able to receive a modicum of American justice.

The Amish are a Mennonite sect that originated in Switzerland in the seventeenth century. They are rigorously conservative, basing all of their beliefs on a literal reading of the Bible. They are the self-described "plain people" who shun nearly everything "modern"—anything developed since the end of the seventeenth century. They are thus farmers, working the land with ancient tools and methods.

Their dress, of course, makes the Amish distinctive. The men wear broadbrimmed hats and coats without lapels. No zippers, only hooks and buttons. The men never shave and women use no makeup. Women wear black bonnets, shawls—never coats—and simple long dresses. No jewelry or ornament of any kind.

The Amish, with their quaint folkways, have endeared themselves to many—especially tourists in the Pennsylvania Dutch country. Rigorously avoiding modern culture, their prosperous farms have no electricity and they refuse to accept the internal combustion engine. They therefore use buggies, not automobiles; horse-drawn plows, not tractors.

Amish attachment to the old ways does not earn them persecution—legal or otherwise—for the most part. But government, in the past at least, has taken a dim view of Amish beliefs on education.

For the Amish, preservation of their way of life—not only their religion—depends on the nurturing of the young. They do not and never have had a simple modern and utilitarian attitude toward education. Amish children are, for this reason, educated at Amish schools with an Amish curriculum suited to the Amish—not the modern—world.

American educators and regulators are distressed by Amish education. What upsets them even more is the Amish belief that by the end of the eighth grade their children have received enough learning to return to work on their farms.

For years, the American educational establishment—the great busybodies of our time, thanks largely to John Dewey and his wholly secular and utilitarian view of education—has attempted to compel the Amish to violate their most cherished convictions.

Big education's bully boys have also been secure in the knowledge that the Amish by nature are not fighters. The Amish are pacifists, not militants like the Jehovah's Witnesses. Amish toughs will never roam the streets of Lancaster, Pennsylvania, or Elkhart, Indiana, looking for a fight.

Nor do the Amish seek converts. No door-to-door pamphleteering. No radio and television appeals. No sound trucks. No circus tent evangelism. The thought of doing so would bewilder, if not shock, the Amish.

Although the Amish have gladly gone to jail for the sake of their children, they have been reluctant to go to court and fight for their rights. It seemed ungodly to do so. In time, however, the Amish saw that they had little choice. The educationist do-gooders would not leave the Plain People alone.

The Amish did begin to fight back—quietly—and strictly in the courts. In a landmark 1972 Supreme Court case, *Wisconsin v. Yoder*, the court held that the Wisconsin statute mandating compulsory school attendance until age sixteen violated the Amish's rights under the First Amendment's free exercise clause.[24]

The decision came late—the Amish had already suffered much grief for their beliefs—but it was welcome, although the educators' lobby smolders at the thought that ignorant and superstitious farmers should know more about what their children should have in life than educators do.

The Latter-Day Saints, the Jehovah's Witnesses, the Amish have all had their brushes with official and unofficial persecution during our history. That history is not especially ancient either. While in more recent years such Puritan expressions of religious intolerance as whipping and hanging have gone out of fashion, the law did not protect, for example, Joseph Smith.

American society has come a long way since the seventeenth century, but religious tolerance is still not as widely practiced as some think. The rise of new religious groups—an absolute certainty, given our history—continually tests the limits of our country's acceptance of unrestricted religious expression.

The history of religious bigotry in this country can easily create a false impression. It might appear that bias is directed only at small groups or individual dissenters like Roger Williams. After all, Quakers, Mormons, Jehovah's Witnesses, the Amish, even the Jews never have constituted a large part of the American population. The impression then arises that religious bigotry may be bad but it exists only on the fringes of our society.

That conclusion is erroneous because it leaves out one very major element in this history: the persecution of America's Roman Catholics.

Even Catholics have a hard time believing that they are a minority, much less a persecuted one. Their history in this country indicates—as the 1844 Philadelphia example and the earlier Puritan decrees readily attest—that their status has not been secure and their experience here has not been untroubled.

For much of our history we have been a Protestant-dominated nation and our institutions, even public ones, have been formed by Protestant sensibilities. This was not always recognized by Protestants, but Catholics and Jews most certainly have understood the score.

Well into the nineteenth century, anti-Catholic feeling was fed by Protestant churches and clergy—not fanatical off-shoots, but mainstream bodies.

In 1830, for example, the American Bible Society promoted the unification of all Protestant denominations in order to fight what it perceived as Rome's perfidious influence in the West. In one pamphlet the ABS charged:

> His Holiness, the Pope, has, with eager grasp, already fixed upon this fair portion of our Union (the Mississippi Valley), and knows well how to keep his hold![25]

That same year Dr. Lyman Beecher, one of America's best known clergymen, fired his opening round on behalf of his favorite cause: anti-Catholicism. Late in 1830, he preached a series of sermons that attempted to demonstrate that Catholicism and despotism worked together in opposition to the American belief in republicanism.[26]

Four years later he would break into print with *Plea for the West*, the distillation of his earlier sermons on the danger of the subject Catholic mind. A fragment of Dr. Beecher's thought is worth noting:

> If they could read the Bible and might and did, their darkened intellect would brighten, and their bowed down mind would rise. If they dared to think for themselves, the contrast of protestant independence with their thralldom, would awaken the desire of equal privileges, and put an end to an arbitrary clerical dominion over trembling superstitious minds.

His assertion raises a political question which Lyman Beecher was happy to deal with next:

> If the pope and potentates of Europe held no dominion over ecclesiastics here, we might trust to time and circumstances to mitigate their ascendance and produce assimilation. But for conscience sake and patronage, they are dependent on the powers that be across the deep, by whom they are sustained and nurtured: and receive and organize all who come, and retain all who are born, while by argument, and a Catholic education, they beguile the children of credulous unsuspecting protestants in their own communion.[27]

The simple assumption that Catholics were engaged in a dark and frightening conspiracy to subvert America probably got its clearest expression from the inventor of the telegraph, Samuel

F. B. Morse himself, in the same year that Lyman Beecher published *Plea for the West*.

Morse's "Foreign Conspiracy" informed his fellow Americans in 1834 (two years before he sent his famous message to Washington from Baltimore, "What hath God wrought?"):

> They have already sent their chains, and oh! to our shame be it spoken are fastening them upon a *sleeping* victim. Americans, you are marked for their prey, not by foreign bayonets, but by weapons surer of effecting the conquest of liberty than all the munitions of physical combat in the military or naval storehouses of Europe. Will you not awake to the apprehension of the reality and extent of your danger? Will you be longer deceived by the pensioned Jesuits, who having surrounded your press, are now using it all over the country to stifle the cries of danger, and lull your fears by attributing your alarm to a false cause? Up! Up! I beseech you. Awake! To your posts! Let the tocsin sound from Maine to Louisiana. Fly to protect the vulnerable places of your Constitution and Laws. Place your guards, you will need them and quickly too.[28]

I'd call that anti-Catholic.

Samuel Finley Breeze Morse, like Dr. Beecher, was no worse than a thousand others in America's writing class who truly believed that Protestant America was about to fall to Rome's secret legions. The more hidden they were, of course, the more frightening they became to America's Protestants.

What was said in books and tracts was repeated in easy-to-understand cartoons and illustrations. One such, circa 1855, depicts a papal figure crumpling in his right hand a copy of the American Constitution. In his left hand is a shepherd's staff pinning down a dead American eagle. Under the man's foot is a soiled American flag.[29]

Yet Catholic problems hardly ended with Protestant sermons and pamphlets, even if these public outcries were authored by some of America's leading citizens. What Catholics faced far into the nineteenth century was nothing less than a Protestant establishment, not only in politics, but in something even more important: education.

The public school system in America—until well into this

century—was in fact a Protestant, and increasingly a liberal Protestant, institution. Secular it was not.

According to one sociological historian writing in 1955:

> The King James version of the Bible was read daily, and in fact, still is in some places. Protestant hymns were sung, and still are in some public schools. Catholics quite justifiably protested, as Jews sometimes do today, particularly at Christmas and Easter. Catholic protests availed nothing, and a parochial school system was established for Catholic children. Catholics lost the battle, Protestants won it.[30]

Education was important, and until the establishment of a parochial system, Catholics could not expect religious neutrality or devise a way to teach their young their own religious beliefs and practices.

Politics was important, too. And in the nineteenth century it was rough and dirty. Especially for Roman Catholics.

It should be explained that while Catholics were not particularly accepted in most American colonies before independence, they were such a tiny minority—a sprinkling mostly of English, a few Germans and French—that they could readily seek safety in more tolerant places like Maryland and Rhode Island, thanks to Lord Baltimore and Roger Williams. They numbered only thirty thousand out of a total population of three million in 1790, the year of the nation's first census.[31]

The huge Irish immigration of the 1840s, spurred by the great potato famine, changed all that. Suddenly hordes of Catholics were washed up on the American shore, filling up the great American cities: Boston, New York, Philadelphia, and Baltimore. No one knew exactly how many Irish. No one kept count—least of all the federal government, which had less control over our borders than it does now. Only the states were involved in immigration control, and most took no interest either. The best estimate is that three million Irishmen came here between 1820 and 1880.[32]

Emigration did not just mean a better life for the Irish—it meant life, period. In most cases, the alternative to life in America was a slow death in Ireland—from hunger or hunger induced disease. Those who could go, did, rather than die after watching their children perish.

No wonder then that these Irish immigrants were poor, desperate, usually unlettered and completely unskilled: most were peasants from the southern counties of their home country, now forced to live in the unfamiliar cities of booming America.[33]

When they were lucky, the men could find work as day laborers. Although they spoke English, albeit a dialect that sometimes was unintelligible to native Americans, the Irish were not popular—with anyone. Nor welcome.

Sometimes with reason. Sociologist Joseph Kane explains:

> The poverty of immigrant Irishmen made them seek living quarters in the poorer if not slum sections of American cities. Their lack of occupational skills kept them at a low economic level. Herded together in what amounted to Irish ghettoes, they created a health problem, and this was the time when periodic plagues threatened American cities. They also had a high crime rate, although discriminations against them undoubtedly explained some of it. A grand jury investigation in Philadelphia claimed that in one Irish area four or five thousand people lived by begging and stealing, their babies were hired out for begging purposes, and sick infants were at a premium. Gambling was common, junk shops were fences for stolen goods, and baskets of garbage, collected by beggars, were exchanged for rum.[34]

Yet they survived. The two institutions that helped the Irish survive in this New and sometimes not so wonderful World were the Democratic party and the Roman Catholic church, particularly the tough, combative Irish clergy who replaced—after a short, sharp struggle—the more refined French hierarchy. Their loyalty to both have stood the test of time, with good reason.[35]

But the Irish and, by extension, all Roman Catholics faced more than general prejudice—and yes, the signs did say "no Irish need apply"—or even angry mobs such as stalked the streets of Philadelphia in 1844. There were organized political movements directed against them as well. These movements were sinister—not at all the conspiracy hobgoblin of papal power with which Protestant preachers delighted in frightening their flocks on Sunday morn. They were, in fact, scary.

The best-known of these groups—and in some ways the least-known—is the Know-Nothing movement. The Know-Nothings as popularly portrayed were a group of ignorant and xenophobic native Americans who wished to keep the United States free of foreigners. They were not very effective or powerful.

Actually, the Know-Nothings were a good deal worse than the popular portrayal. The Know-Nothings were a highly secretive, and at one time powerful political force in this country. Because they were powerful, Catholics in this country suffered more at the hands of the Know-Nothings than from any other group.

The origins of the Know-Nothings are clear enough. In reaction to the tide of immigrants arriving in the 1840s, the American Republican party was formed in New York in 1843. The party was the outgrowth of numerous local societies which advocated nativism: the rights and privileges of native-born Americans.

The American Republican party grew quickly, and in two years it could afford to have a national convention in Philadelphia. By then the party had changed its name to the Native American party. Its beliefs remained the same. That great gathering of bigots took place one year after the Philadelphia anti-Irish riots mentioned earlier.

The Native American party stalled thereafter and nativism became inactive for four years until the formation of a secret society, the Order of the Star Spangled Banner, founded in New York. Once again the order of nativists grew slowly until 1852, when the movement began to spread nationwide.

The order initiated new members with great secrecy and ritualistic rigamarole: meetings were announced by bits of white paper in the shape of a heart; in times of danger, the heart was red. The inductees swore an oath never to reveal "the mysteries" of the order—including its name. There were secret hand grips, gestures, and a cry for help to which every good Know-Nothing was pledged to respond. Schoolboy stuff, but sinister as well. If members were asked about the movement, its members and motives, they were to reply: "I know nothing about it," hence the name.

Although their ostensible aim was to restrict immigration by slapping on a twenty-five-year residence requirement for citizenship, the Know-Nothings' real purpose was to fight Catholicism any way they saw fit. Keeping the Irish out or driving them back home was only one goal.

Naturally, no dirty, ring-kissing Catholics could be members of the order; even Protestants married to Catholics were excluded. Catholics, they believed, voted as ordered by their priests. Moreover, there was a papal plot to seize the whole of the United States, not just the Louisiana Purchase.

The screed which the Know-Nothings wrote for themselves said that they supported "Anti-Romanism, Anti-Bedinism, Anti-Pope's Toeism, Anti-Nunnerism, Anti-Winking Virginism, Anti-Jesuitism, and Anti-the Whole-Sacredotal-Hierarchism with all its humbugging mummeries."[36]

Know-Nothing congressmen trumpeted their biases routinely from the safety of Capitol Hill. A favorite target: the Jesuits. Members of the Know-Nothing movement were required to vote for "their" congressmen and against any Catholic or pro-Catholic politician. Where possible, Know-Nothings were supposed to remove Catholics from office legally.

The high tide of Know-Nothingism came in the 1854 election, when the movement sent no fewer than seventy-five men to Congress, all of them no doubt clutching each other with the secret grip. Their greatest success was in ever-liberal Massachusetts, where the movement held majorities in the legislature and took control of the bureaucracy.

That triumph, however, led to the Know-Nothings' first fiasco. Their Massachusetts legislators established a committee to investigate the state's Catholic seminaries, convents, and academies. According to Joseph Kane:

> It visited Holy Cross College, a Jesuit institution at Worcester, Massachusetts, where, as Professor Billington states, "it reported favorably not only on that Jesuit institution, but also on the local wines that were consumed freely at state expense." It then went on to a convent school in Roxbury where it terrified the children, treated the nuns disrespectfully and poked into closets looking for evidence of Popery. Its zealous activities were cut short when it submitted a bill to the state for expenses involved in its relationships with a lady of notoriously easy virtue.[37]

As so often happens, the Know-Nothings, emboldened by their 1854 success, decided to go public in an attempt to win it all—the presidency in 1856—under the banner of the American party.

Although united on the dangers of Catholicism, the members

who gathered at the 1855 convention soon quarrelled over another topic: slavery. Southern delegates lobbied for a pro-slavery plank in the platform. Their Northern brothers refused, and the nascent American party split into two parts. The Know-Nothings became hopelessly divided, and their candidate Millard Fillmore managed to carry only Maryland. James Buchanan of Pennsylvania, a northern Democrat with Southern sympathies, won the election—ironically with the help of Irish-American voters.

After the 1856 election the Know-Nothings declined rapidly. Northern partisans joined the new Republican party, the Southerners drifted back to the Democrats. Only in the border states did the Know-Nothing movement continue to exist until the Civil War. The movement could still produce ugly results, however. In St. Louis shortly before the Civil War, pitched battles were fought between Protestants and German Catholics.

The Irish, of course, were not entirely defenseless or free from deep-seated prejudice themselves. Even though they were a minority, they could and did fight back. The Know-Nothings or any of their kind were not about to drive the sons of St. Patrick back to the Emerald Isle, a place which meant little to them except a slow and unpleasant death—and continued British rule.

The British had long nurtured the Irish distaste for Protestantism. Whether the Protestants in question were the Anglican cavaliers that served Charles I or the harsh Puritan followers of Oliver Cromwell, the Irish, for good reason, had had their fill of Protestants before they arrived in America.

The American experience, however, had its own peculiar twists, different from anything experienced in the British Isles.

One twist was American "public" education.

In the nineteenth century, public education was far different from what we have now. Sentimentalists do go on about its quality—compared to now—extolling the virtues of the McGuffey Readers, but there is, in fact, little good to say about public schools of that time, especially when it came to religious questions.

Catholic children avoided the schools like the plague when they could.

The reason? Public schools were then, in fact, Protestant schools administered by Protestants and taught by Protestants. In New York by 1840 the Protestant Orphan Society had a near monopoly over public education. In Philadelphia, it was the Protestant Northern Home for Friendless Children that supervised the public schools. The mainline Protestant denominations therefore found no need to establish an expensive parochial school system.[38]

Catholics did.

They did so to avoid, among other things, Protestant prayers and hymns that began each school day along with readings from the Bible, the King James version. Catholic parents' requests to read from the Douay version were rudely rejected—except in Baltimore.[39]

When Catholic bishops asked for funds from city councils for Catholic schools, they were refused.

That was not all. School textbooks were written invariably from a Protestant point of view. Here is a choice excerpt from *Parley's Common School History* in wide use during the last century:

> From this time forward the Popes rapidly acquired power. . . . Their pride was equal to their power, and neither seemed to have any bounds. . . . No other tyranny had even been like theirs, for they tyrannized over the souls of men. . . . If any person denied the Pope's authority he was burned alive.

So much for the benevolence of the Holy Father. Abbeys and monasteries "became seats of voluptuousness." Convents, and even Catholic orphanages, were equally suspect and frequently targeted for investigations into reports of sexual abuse, brainwashing, and kidnapping. And as far as the Irish are concerned, America's school children learned from Dr. Parley that they "consider Saint Patrick as in Heaven watching over the interest of Ireland."[40]

Worse, "they pray to him, and to do him honor, set apart one day in the year for going to Church, drinking whiskey and breaking each other's heads with clubs."

Partly as a result, the growth of Catholic schools accelerated by the middle of the nineteenth century, although some schools had been founded in late colonial times: St. Mary's of Philadelphia is more than two hundred years old. The Franciscans had opened schools in Spanish Florida in the sixteenth century, before the events of Jamestown and Plymouth Rock.[41]

Catholic children in Catholic schools hardly solved the problem.

The schools were not numerous and could not accommodate the school-aged Catholic population. Parochial schools were sometimes attacked in the last century. In 1834, in Charlestown, Massachusetts, the Ursuline convent and the school attached to it were burnt to the ground by a mob of Protestants. They feared that the convent school was attracting too many Protestant daughters of wealthy merchants. A decade later, in Philadelphia, the parochial school of St. Michael's was also destroyed by fire—arson.[42]

Sometimes the hostility toward Catholic education took less extreme forms. Schoolteaching nuns, of course, were targets for years of obscene rumors—perhaps a form of Protestant sexual fantasizing. In 1850, 3,000 women signed a petition to the Pennsylvania legislature requesting that it control the establishment of convents in the commonwealth. The legislators referred the ladies' cry of distress to the Committee on Vice and Immorality.[43]

The state of Oregon passed a law in the early 1920s to require public school attendance. The rule would no doubt still be on the books except the Supreme Court ruled the legislation unconstitutional in 1925, much to the disappointment of the National Education Association, big education's most powerful and vociferous lobby.[44]

Anti-Catholic feeling never has disappeared in this country, but its worst forms weakened as America entered the twentieth century. Perhaps the feeling weakened because the Catholic population kept growing. After the Irish came the Italians, Germans, Poles, and others. In northern New England French-Canadian Catholics filtered in and became part of local life. Later Hispanic Catholics moved into the American Southwest and, after Fidel Castro took power in Cuba, into southern Florida as well.

With so many to pick on, the numbers perhaps became too large, especially in big cities like Boston, Chicago, New York City, and Philadelphia—at least for casual bigots. In the rural areas, things could be different, as the spiritual heirs of the Know-Nothings, the Ku Klux Klan, became important after the Civil War. Although their chief target was blacks, with the revival of the Klan after World War I other targets such as Jews and Catholics became important. In 1923, the Klan had three million members.

A handbill that the Klan distributed in the 1920s throughout the country—not just the South—read:

The Ku Klux Klan holds that any man who kneels before his fellow-man kissing hand or ring will do the bidding of that fellow-man.[45]

It's subtle, but Catholics got the message. For the most part, however, anti-Catholic feelings had become more effete. That meant they would remain alive and well into the twentieth century.

The 1928 presidential election throws some revealing light on how far we have come from the ashes of St. Augustine's of Philadelphia in that spring of 1844.

Alfred E. (Al) Smith, governor of New York, was the Democratic party candidate. He was also a Roman Catholic—the first to be nominated by any party—and far closer to the church than his political heir John Fitzgerald Kennedy ever was.

If Smith had been a Protestant, it is likely he would still have lost in 1928 to the Republicans and the formidable Herbert Hoover. That year the Republican machine would win forty of forty-eight states and outvote the Democrats by more than a four to three ratio.

The Democrats since the Civil War had been in eclipse, winning only on occasion: Grover Cleveland and Woodrow Wilson were the great exceptions. The party's time came four years later after the Great Depression had hit the world, and, incidentally, ruined Republican fortunes for two decades.

Al Smith and his campaign were definitely hurt by anti-Catholic feelings that were once more stirred up. Some reached back to the nineteenth century.

The attack on Smith as a Catholic came from high and low. Bishop James Cannon, Jr., of the Methodist Episcopal Church led the charge among respectable clergymen—as distinct from the redneck, tub-thumping yahoos that proliferated in the rural backwaters of America. Cannon printed and circulated a pamphlet titled *Is Southern Protestantism More Intolerant Than Romanism?*

According to Bishop Cannon, the Catholic church taught that no Protestant could be saved; that all non-Catholic marriages were adulterous affairs and the children illegitimate; and that public schools were a damnable heresy.[46]

The archly sedate mainline Protestant publication, the *Christian Century*, warned its genteel readers:

[We] cannot look with unconcern upon the seating of a representative of an alien culture, of a medieval Latin mentality, of an undemocratic hierarchy and of a foreign potentate in the great office of President of the United States.[47]

Meanwhile, at the ultra-respectable Trinity Methodist Church in Los Angeles, sermon topics during the election season covered such stimulating subjects as: "Was Abraham Lincoln Assassinated by a Roman Catholic?" and "Is the Roman Machine Directly Connected with the Policy of Assassination?" and "May We Expect Assassinations During the Present Political Campaign?"[48]

The sermons, of course, were the "good news" for the Smith campaign. The down-and-dirty stuff was put on display at the Democratic National Headquarters.

Included were such jewels of Protestant bigotry as a pamphlet entitled *Convent Horrors, Illustrating What Will Happen to American Womanhood if Smith is Elected.* Nothing like it had been available since the confessions of Maria Monk, a pseudo-autobiography that pornographically thrilled a generation of nineteenth-century Protestants with a taste for improving literature.

There were other 1928 bestsellers on display: *Traffic in Nuns; Three Keys to Hell;* and *Rum, Romanism and Ruin,* the temperance movement's swan song.

Smith's candidacy gave some of his supporters trouble as well. The liberal *New Republic* in the end endorsed the New York governor. But its editors were not pleased about his religion.

They told their readers in 1927:

The Catholic Church will remain an alien guest in the American body politic as long as it tries to form the minds of American Catholics by educational methods different from those which are used to form the minds of other American citizens.

The editors concluded:

[C]onsidering the special nature of their tradition, education and organization, it is not unreasonable to watch Catholic candidates for President with unusual care.[49]

The defeat of Al Smith was not the end of anti-Catholicism in this country, but in the thirty-two years that separated Smith from Kennedy enormous changes took place. Catholics by 1960 were no longer a minority.

The Kennedy campaign managers did understand one thing. The film of the famous encounter of John Kennedy with the Protestant ministers in Houston (the city, ironically, where Al Smith was nominated) was shown repeatedly as a Democratic campaign commercial in the fall of 1960—in areas with heavy concentrations of Roman Catholics.

So America is not an unspotted lamb when it comes to religious, or for that matter, racial prejudice. Yet this country is no ravenous wolf on the prowl. There is nothing in our history, for example, that compares to the systematic persecution of all religions in the Soviet Union or in the People's Republic of China.

In fact, there is nothing quite like the persecution of minority religions in supposedly civilized European countries of years past. Examples: the Puritan persecution of Anglicans and Catholics during the ill-starred Cromwellian commonwealth, or the destruction of the Huguenots by his Catholic Majesty Louis XIV.

Nor is there anything that approaches Chancellor Otto von Bismarck's unsuccessful *Kulturkampf* in which Europe's craftiest, if not greatest, statesman engaged the Prussian state machinery in a systematic struggle with the Roman Catholic Church and the German Catholic Center party.

Bismarck probably would have felt at home with the Know-Nothings on the subject of a Catholic conspiracy, but the difference between the chancellor and the American nativists is that he ran one of the most powerful countries in the world for decades, and the Know-Nothing candidate Millard Fillmore captured only the state of Maryland.

A final thought: America's history of racial bigotry is a long one. Sometimes the bigotry has been displayed by individual groups like the Klan. Sometimes, such groups have been able to use the machinery of government to pursue their goals.

There is much in our culture that suggests that the past, no matter how dark, is just that: the past. In this optimism, there is the sense that we as a people are evolving into something better—as if it were some law of nature that we are following.

Unfortunately, that is not the case. Yes, many barriers to religious discrimination have been built over the years. But they hardly guarantee that bigotry won't find other victims.

Now and in the future.

APPENDIX

When, if ever, can a church be taxed legally by the IRS?

The Service tried—at least on one occasion—to sort the business out. The results, however, were something less than satisfactory.

To a constitutional lawyer, IRS efforts were close to ludicrous. Yet the IRS was struggling with what is not only a very fundamental question, but one that common sense would indicate is tough to answer.

The real question was (and still is): What is a church? It is not easy to define. In one case, *United States v. Kuch*, the court had to balance the narcotics laws against the "Neo-American Church" which, to a man of common sense, was little more than a semi-organized attempt to get stoned legally. The "church's" own leader, the Chief BooHoo priest, described the movement as "a bunch of filthy, drunken bums whose motto was 'Victory over Horseshit'."

Despite the adolescent nihilism of this quaint group, the court went through an exhaustive and exhausting legal exercise before deciding that the Neo-Americans were not a religion.[1]

So what is a church? The simple truth is, nobody really knows. A close examination of the Internal Revenue Code and case law conducted by Justice Department lawyers in 1979 shows no authoritative, or even persuasive, definition of what constitutes a "church."[2]

The Service, keenly interested in getting out of this definitional bog, released in early 1978 a set of fourteen criteria to be used to determine whether a church was really a church or not.

The standards, bearing the signature of the Internal Revenue Service's commissioner, were the following:

1. A distinct legal existence;
2. A recognized creed and form of worship;
3. A definite and distinct ecclesiastical government;
4. A formal code of doctrine and discipline;
5. Distinct religious history;
6. A membership not associated with any other church or denomination;
7. A complete organization of ordained ministers ministering to their congregation;
8. Ordained ministers selected after completing prescribed courses of study;
9. A literature of its own;
10. Established places of worship;
11. Regular congregations;
12. Regular religious services;
13. Sunday schools for the religious instruction of the young;
14. Schools for the preparation of ministers.[3]

Very obviously the list was not really a litmus test. It was, in effect, a guideline. But a guideline for whom?

The Service's news release admitted problems with the whole exercise. They conceded right off that few, if any, established religions could fulfill all fourteen demands. As a result, the IRS commissioner said:

> For that reason, we do not give controlling weight to any single factor. This is obviously the place in the decisional process requiring the most sensitive and discriminatory consideration.[4]

Several of the criteria have already been held invalid. For example, the Eighth Circuit Court of Appeals has ruled that a church can be legitimate even if its members belong to other religious bodies—point six.[5]

But that's only a beginning. The provision that a judgment must be made about what is and what is not a "recognized creed"— among other things, who does the recognizing?—itself suggests that the government would have to make the judgment and, in doing so, would most likely violate the First Amendment's free exercise clause. Point two, in short, opens up another Pandora's box that few, if any, courts in this country would allow to remain open.

Finally, on this particular question, putting the government in the position of acting as arbiter of what is and is not legitimate, radically bends the rules against new and unpopular religions, and is unconstitutional.[6]

That is only the beginning of the commissioner's little list. According to a Justice Department Memorandum of Law:

> The concept of a distinct religious history [point five] is not particularly helpful, as this would also discriminate between religions on the basis of age, which would appear to be also inappropriate under the Establishment Clause.[7]

That clause forbids government from favoring one religion over the other, and its interpretation has become quite broad and comprehensive over the years.

But this hardly exhausted the constitutional problems for the IRS attempt to define a church.

As the memorandum put it:

> The requirement of having an established place of worship [point ten] would also seem to violate the Free Exercise Clause of the First Amendment, as it is doubtful whether the Government could require religions to establish a particular place in which all religious services will occur.[8]

Points seven and eight suggest that the government is in a position to decide who qualifies as clergy and what course of study is acceptable. This, too, is a pretty clear violation of the First Amendment's free exercise clause—especially against religions that do not have a specially trained priesthood.

In summary, Justice's Memorandum of Law found:

> [T]he entire set of criteria is probably violative of the First Amendment for the reasons already outlined in the First Amendment analysis.[9]

To make matters worse for the Service's attempt to get a handle on what constitutes a church, a court instruction to the jury in the

Colorado district (*United States v. Piester*) said flatly that the terms
"church" or "religious order" had no legal definition. Period.

Consequently, the Justice Memorandum of Law found:

> [D]ue to the lack of specificity or accepted meaning for the terms,
> the Government is virtually forced to accept taxpayers' organiza-
> tions as churches and the designated heads of these churches as
> ministers.[10]

What is also important about the 1979 Memorandum of Law
from the Justice Department is that it did not address new and
unpopular religions like the Unification Church or Hare Krishna.
Their legitimacy was not and never has been under discussion by
the Department of Justice, or even the Internal Revenue Service,
after an initial inquiry regarding tax exemption.

NOTES

I The Secret Tapes

1. Sealed transcript, U.S. District Court Southern District of New York, *United States of America v. Sun Myung Moon, et al.*, October 1, 1982, p. 63.
2. These facts are drawn from the prosecution's "Memorandum of Law in Opposition to Defendants' Motion for an Inquiry Relating to Jury Conduct," which was submitted *in camera* pursuant to court order, pp. 11–12. The prosecution, predictably enough, attempted to discredit the evidence on jury tainting by discrediting one of the men who turned up the evidence, in this case, Bruce Romanoff. In a footnote, the government's memorandum also cited a book on the Mafia which described Romanoff as close to New York's Gallo family. Next the government contradicted itself by saying in the same footnote that FBI evidence (presumably raw files) showed that Romanoff was an associate of the Colombo family. If that were so, Mr. Romanoff led a most dangerous life. See *ibid.*, p. 12(n).
3. Found in the October 1, 1982, sealed transcript previously cited, p. 29.
4. All quotes found in the *Prospect Press* (Brooklyn, New York), May 27–June 9, 1982, p. 7.
5. See John Curry's testimony, for example, in the previously cited sealed transcript of October 1, 1982, pp. 29–43.
6. *Ibid.*, p. 41.
7. *Ibid.*, p. 63.
8. See the government's previously cited "Memorandum of Law," p. 8.
9. See *ibid.*, pp. 10–11, and the sealed transcript of September 30, 1982, containing the testimony of Bruce Romanoff. Note especially, pp. 13–45.
10. Transcript of the sealed record of the telephone conversation between Virginia Steward and John Curry, July 26, 1982, p. 2.
11. *Ibid.* Later in the conversation Steward added: "I mean I felt so sorry for him the day, in fact I didn't even look at them [the defendants] when they turned around and read off, you know when they told the jury, yes, you know I couldn't look at him." *Ibid.*, p. 5.
12. *Ibid.*, p. 2. Evidently, Nimmo's bullying was not confined to Mrs. Steward. Steward related at one point in the July 26 tape that another juror, Esperanza Torres, was talked to repeatedly "until she was almost crying." *Ibid.*, p. 3. Steward also disclosed at the end of the phone conversation with Curry that

Esperanza had a difficult time believing that Moon had done anything wrong "because he's a religious man." On the other hand, "she wanted to go home." *Ibid.*, p. 8.

13. *Ibid.*, p. 3. Later Steward recalled that "[T]hey were saying, oh see he keeps his children from their families and he tells them that the families, their parents are devils you know, and they're, they have to . . . everything over to him and all this stuff, you know, so I don't know, like with the stuff, like I said I never heard about him, my kids weren't involved. Like I told them I don't know why they even picked me, I really don't." *Ibid.*, p. 7.

14. *Ibid.*, p. 2.

15. *Ibid.*, pp. 3–4.

16. *Ibid.*, p. 6.

17. *Ibid.*

18. See the government's previously cited "Memorandum of Law," p. 4.

19. Transcript of the sealed record of the telephone conversation between Virginia Steward and John Curry, July 26, 1982, p. 8.

III WITCH HUNT

1. See the *Washington Post*, "IRS Probes Evangelists' Operations," December 10, 1988. According to the *Post*, some thirty-four teleministries were under scrutiny by the nation's publicans, representing about 10 percent of the industry. Jim Bakker has since been indicted and convicted on twenty-four counts of fraud and conspiracy.

2. Letter from Clarence M. Kelley, Director of the FBI to Mrs. Alma Clark, January 24, 1975. The letter from Mrs. Clark is dated January 16.

3. *Ibid.*

4. *Ibid.*

5. Memorandum from Special Agent in Charge, Albany, New York, to Director, FBI, December 8, 1975.

6. Letter from Clarence M. Kelley, Director of the FBI, to Senator Walter Mondale, October 21, 1974.

7. What Senator Mondale's constituent wanted to know—his name has been deleted from the FOIA-released document—was whether CARP was "legit or subversive." Mondale's correspondent complained that the local FBI office would tell him nothing and said that he should write Washington, D.C. But as he put it: "Now what the hell good is it having a local FBI office when you go to them for help . . . ?"

8. Letter from FBI Director Clarence M. Kelley to Hamilton Fish, Jr., April 15, 1975, and letter from Director Kelley to Philip J. Hart, February 5, 1973.

9. FBI internal memorandum to the director from the Washington Field Office, September 17, 1973.

10. *Ibid.* Still, the memorandum recommended considering an active investigation of the matter if (name deleted) returned to the United States. It is not clear from the memo whether it was the informant or someone in the Unification Church he had fingered that could trigger a possible investigation.

11. Sheeran may have been led astray by his eldest daughter Josette, now a deputy managing editor for the church-owned *Washington Times*. Earlier, Sheeran had asked his daughter to "rescue" the two younger women, Jamie and Vickie, from the "Moonies." Instead, Josette also joined the Unification

Church. The immediate event that tripped off the raid on Tarrytown was the previous night's phone call from Josette to her parents. Although she had placed the call from New York City, Sheeran was led to believe she had been phoning from Tarrytown. When he told her to come home, she refused, thus setting in motion the next morning's events. See FBI Memorandum to the Director, FBI from ADIC, New York, February 2, 1976, pp. 2–3.

12. *Ibid.*, p. 2.
13. *Ibid.* As the reader might guess, Sheeran was no shrinking violet. When the state troopers arrived, the ex-SA told them he was a friend of the governors of New York and New Jersey as well as the current commissioner of insurance for the state of New Jersey. He was also, he said, a former member of the FBI.
14. *Ibid.*, p. 4. Even then Sheeran would not give up. In October 1975 he asked his congressman, Joseph Minish of New Jersey, to launch an investigation of the church. He annoyed Minish by prematurely announcing to the press that such an investigation would be carried out. Minish forwarded the complaint to the FBI and agreed with the bureau that the whole thing was a family dispute. FBI memorandum from Legal Counsel to J.B. Adams, December 8, 1975.
15. U.S. Department of Justice memorandum to Director, FBI, January 8, 1976, p. 1. The memo also mentions in passing two other "limited investigations" of the bureau in relation to Unification Church activities in Dutchess County.
16. Memorandum from LEGAT, Tokyo to Director, FBI, February 14, 1967, p. 1. The KCFF is the Korean Cultural Freedom Foundation.
17. *Ibid.*, p. 2.
18. Memorandum from Director, FBI to SAC, Newark, March 3, 1967.
19. Memorandum from SAC WFO to Director, FBI, May 5, 1967, p. 2.
20. Contained in *ibid.*, p. 2. Again, through the haze of censorship, it appears the WFO also checked out a man named "Jong Pil Kim" who, after retiring from the KCIA, attempted to raise funds for the KCFF. The bureau found nothing irregular about this.
21. Attached memorandum entitled "The God-Inspired Korean Unification Association (GIKUN) *Nankuk T'ongi Sin yong Nyophoe* (also known as the Unification Church)," p. 1.
22. *Ibid.*, pp. 1–2.
23. *Ibid.*, p. 2.
24. *Ibid.*
25. *Ibid.*
26. Under this grading system, used once by both the CIA and the DIA until abandoned in the 1970s, A-1 was the best grade a source could get. And, according to friends of CIA Director Allen Dulles, who liked the system, there were no A-1 sources except himself.
27. Department of Defense Intelligence Information Report, November 29, 1967. Report Number 2 221 2576 67.
28. *Ibid.*
29. Department of Defense Intelligence Information Report, December 1, 1967. Report Number 2 221 0102 68. This source, too, would be a casual informant who would receive a C-6. Quite probably it is the same source for the previous and all subsequent DIA cables from Seoul in 1967 and 1968.
30. *Ibid.*
31. *Ibid.*

32. *Ibid.* Some of the information on recruiting appears to be based on a more sparsely detailed Army G-2 report that also found its way into the FBI memorandum referred to earlier.

33. *Ibid.*

34. *Ibid.*

35. Department of Defense Intelligence Information Report, December 4, 1967. Report Number 2 221 0104 68.

36. *Ibid.*

37. *Ibid.*

38. *Ibid.*

39. Department of Defense Information Intelligence Report, December 21, 1967. Report Number 2 221 0161 68.

40. Department of Defense Information Intelligence Report, April 25, 1968. Report Number 2 221 1166 68.

41. An undated CIA memorandum released April 24, 1974, after a FOIA request. The memo concludes: "Although he is known to [deletion] it has not been established that he is a direct recipient of [deletion] funds. It is more likely that [deletion] or other Korean backers would channel funds through MUN's industrial empire in South Korea. [Deletion]." The deletions almost certainly refer to the rumored Korean Central Intelligence Agency's alleged funding of Moon—at least in the early years of the church.

42. CIA Memorandum for the Record with date and other identifying tags removed. The approval for release date under a FOIA request is April 24, 1979.

43. CIA Outgoing Message dated September 1975. All other identifying tags have been removed. It was approved for release on April 4, 1979, under the FOIA.

44. *Ibid.*

45. CIA Intelligence Information Cable TDFIRDB-315/05810-76, June 10, 1976, and released under FOIA on April 6, 1979. All that remains of the summary is the following: "A connection between the Unification Church and the domestic defense industry through Church-owned businesses producing weapons under defense contracts." *Ibid.*, pp. 2–3.

46. *Ibid.*, p. 5.

47. *Ibid.*, pp. 5–6.

48. *Ibid.*, pp. 6–7.

49. *Ibid.*, p. 7.

50. *Ibid.*

51. *Ibid.*, p. 8.

52. *Ibid.*

53. *Ibid.*, p. 9.

54. CIA biography of Sun Myung MOON. All tags have been removed and no date indicated, including the FOIA date of release.

55. See the *Chicago Tribune*, "Moon Church Traced From Sex Cult," March 27, 1978.

56. See the affidavit of Sue Tuttle describing her kidnapping at the hands of Ted Patrick. (Undated).

57. Letter from Bob Dole, United States Senator, to Donald Alexander, Commissioner, Internal Revenue Service, January 9, 1976.

58. *Ibid.*

59. *Ibid.*
60. *Ibid.*
61. *Ibid.*
62. *Ibid.*
63. *Ibid.*
64. *Ibid.*
65. *Ibid.*
66. Aside from lack of evidence, there is a rather basic flaw in the senator's logic. If the church were really endangering America's young, dropping its tax-exempt status seems a ludicrously inappropriate response.
67. News from U.S. Senator Bob Dole, "Dole Asks for Unification Church Audit," January 12, 1976. In a concluding paragraph not included in the Alexander letter was the notice that a petition circulating in Kansas demanding a government investigation of the church had been signed by 7,000 people. When completed (another 7,000 names nationwide would be added), the press release said, Dole promised to call it to the attention of President Gerald Ford.
68. Incidentally, getting 14,000 people to sign a petition is child's play as any political professional knows. People will sign virtually anything that sounds good. Often they are just relieved that they are not being sold anything like a Fuller brush or a ticket to the policemen's ball.
69. In fact, exactly one of more than thirty organizers, panelists, experts, and other assorted ranking poobahs connected with their Dole-sponsored Day of Affirmation and Protest was a resident of Kansas. Nor were those 14,000 signatories all from Kansas either—as Bob Dole admitted during the non-hearings—although CERF would pretend otherwise. *Part One: A Special Report. The Unification Church: Its Activities and Practices, compiled by the National Ad Hoc Committee, A Day of Affirmation and Protest.* For Dole's version of who signed the petition, see p. 5. CERF's version is found on p. 1.
70. *Ibid.*, p. 6. The all-important steering group of this particular Ad Hoc Committee was CERF or, more accurately, Citizens Engaged in Freeing Minds (CEFM). CEFM was a nationwide coalition of state and regional anti-cult groups. Davis founded CERF in 1975 and Dr. Swope took it over a year later. The Ad Hoc leadership was provided by Messrs. Swope, who was chairman of the committee, and Davis. The committee's general attitude can be gathered by its report on the result of the Dole non-hearings: "Our government is the only power large enough to stop Moon now. We incur whatever risks there are as responsible citizens who value our American Freedoms above all else and who know beyond doubt that unless the growth of pseudo-religious political cults is stopped, those very same freedoms will be destroyed." *Ibid.*, p. 2.
71. Despite Dole's cautious caveats, the Ad Hoc Committee thought it was an investigation or that it would lead to subsequent government investigations. After all, why shouldn't the organizers of this event think so? There were no fewer than ten members of the executive branch—all invited by Dole—present at the proceedings. It was at least an investigation and probably a Star Chamber proceeding. But more on that later. See *ibid.*, pp. 1–2.
72. *Ibid.*, p. 6.
73. *Ibid.*
74. *Ibid.*

75. *Ibid.*, p. 7.
76. Letter from Senator Bob Dole to his colleagues, February 11, 1976.
77. The two who managed to show up were Senator James Buckley of New York and Representative George O'Brien of Illinois. Representative Richardson Preyer of North Carolina left before the meeting started. Dole later asserted, however, that thirty-one senators had made inquiries—their character carefully not disclosed—as had forty-four House members.
78. *A Day of Affirmation and Protest*, p. 8.
79. *Ibid.*
80. *Ibid.*, p. 15. Actually, she was relatively restrained. Another "witness," a Mrs. James Goldsmith, said, among other things, that "[p]arents in this country and countries around the world are fearful of the rise of another Hitler-like power." *Ibid.*, p. 18.
81. *Ibid.*, pp. 15–16. Senator Buckley, incidentally, was the young Greene's godfather.
82. *Ibid.*, p. 16.
83. *Ibid.*, p. 19. Some months after Ms. Slaughter's appearance before the cameras, she relapsed back into the Unification Church. She then gave lectures denouncing the deprogramming movement.
84. *Ibid.*, p. 20.
85. *Ibid.*
86. *Ibid.*
87. *Ibid.*, p. 22.
88. *Ibid.*
89. *Ibid.*
90. *Ibid.*
91. *Ibid.*, p. 13.
92. *Ibid.*, p. 15.
93. *Ibid.*, p. 27.
94. *Ibid.*, p. 28.
95. *Ibid.*, p. 23.
96. *Ibid.*, p. 28.
97. *Ibid.*, p. 30. In keeping with the family theme on A Day of Affirmation and Protest, married female participants do not have first names of their own.
98. *Ibid.*, p. 32.
99. *Ibid.*, p. 30.
100. *Ibid.*, p. 31.
101. *Ibid.*, p. 39.
102. *Ibid.*, p. 40.
103. Patrick, in fact, made an appearance before the Dole non-hearing and offered his own by then well-known views on the cult menace. Curiously, Patrick's presence at the February 18 event is nowhere recorded in CERF's transcript of the meeting. Patrick had suddenly become an unperson, perhaps reflecting the fact that the California deprogrammer was by early 1976 in deep legal trouble, arising from indictments on multiple counts of kidnapping and false imprisonment. It had also become known that he had been a convicted felon. See also a letter from Bob Dole to Unification Church official Cynthia Tarryne Shea, February 26, 1976.
104. Telegram sent to Senator Bob Dole from 177 U.S. clergymen, February 17, 1976.

105. Letter from Senator Bob Dole to Office of Congressional Liaison, Immigration and Naturalization Service, August 6, 1976.

106. See Michael Isikoff, "New Moon" in the *New Republic*, August 26, 1985, p. 15. Isikoff is a *Washington Post* reporter who has specialized in once-yearly attack pieces on the church. The *Post*, of course, has a self-interest in doing so since its crosstown rival, the *Washington Times*, is owned by the church.

107. See, for example, the *New York Daily News*, June 3, 1976. An Associated Press report dated June 4, 1976, said that the IRS review had begun several months earlier, placing the start date sometime around January.

108. See the *Daily News*, the Gannett newspaper serving Tarrytown and Irvington, New York, February 4, 1976.

109. See the *Washington Post*, September 4, 1976; the *New York Post*, September 4, 1976; the *Wall Street Journal*, September 20, 1976.

110. The exact quote is: "Hegel remarks somewhere that all the great events and characters of world history occur, so to speak, twice. He forgot to add: 'the first time as tragedy, the second as farce.'" Scholars agree that great philosopher of history Georg Hegel is unlikely to have said anything as dumb as that. Marx picked it from his friend Friedrich Engels and used it for his own polemical purpose. It worked. See Karl Marx, "The Eighteenth Brumaire of Louis Bonaparte," and republished in *Karl Marx: Surveys from Exile*, ed. David Fernback (New York: Vintage Books, 1974), p. 146.

111. Quoted from a newsletter published by the Bureau of National Affairs, Washington, D.C., December 4, 1978.

112. *Ibid.* Actually no one, not even the IRS, has ever alleged the church members were taking cash out of the United States, only in.

113. Senator Long, a wise and savvy man, did not share Dole's zeal for stomping on the First Amendment. He denied the request for the hearings. But then the Louisianan was not running for the presidency.

114. Letter from Neil Salonen to Senator Bob Dole, January 24, 1979. For those who are interested, Salonen's note was sent by certified mail. It is not clear who first opened Bob Dole's letter from the UC president.

115. *News World*, February 1, 1979. The United Church of Christ's legislative counsel Barry Lynn drafted the letter which said in part: "America has always been the champion of the rights of minority religious groups. No strong advocates of religious liberty are represented . . . yet vital First Amendment concerns are at the heart of the debate about so-called cults." Quoted in *ibid.* Also see the *Washington Post* of the same day.

116. *Ibid.* "A witch hunt," he grumbled to the *Washington Post*, February 1, 1979.

117. *News World*, February 6, 1979. Others were kept out. Cynthia Slaughter, who had a starring role in the 1976 Day of Affirmation and Protest, wanted to reprise her part, only this time as a witness against the deprogrammers. She had, after the first Day of Affirmation and Protest, rejoined the Unification Church. Her request was denied. See *Time*, February 19, 1979, p. 54. *Time* decided she was a "suggestible sort." Perhaps Henry Luce's old publication was miffed that it had published a personal essay by Slaughter on the "Moonie menace" in 1976, shortly before her reconversion.

118. Quoted in the *Washington Post*, February 1, 1979.

119. See *News World*, February 6, 1979.

120. The *New York Times*, February 6, 1979.

121. Quoted in *ibid.*

122. *Ibid.* Speier, incidentally, did not explain how she got the ten million figure for cult membership—a number at least double that of any previously known estimate. Also *Time*, February 19, 1979, p. 54.

123. *Ibid.*

124. Quoted in *Time*.

125. Quoted in the *Washington Post*, February 6, 1979. Next to Speier, Patrick got the most attention from the media. Some of it unintended. His interview in *Playboy* accusing the president's sister, Ruth Carter Stapleton, of being a cult leader who needed to be watched did not go down well. The *Washington Post's* "Style" section, February 6, did a slightly caustic interview with the nation's first deprogrammer, depicting Patrick as more of a street hustler than a humanitarian.

126. Quoted in the *New York Times*, February 6, 1979.

127. The *Washington Post*, February 6, 1979. *Time*, February 19, 1979, p. 54.

128. Quoted in the *Washington Post*. Also the *New York Daily News*, February 6, 1979.

129. Quoted in *News World*, February 11, 1979.

130. Quoted in *News World*, February 6, 1979.

131. *Ibid.*

132. Richardson and Guttman were quoted in *News World*, February 6, 1979.

133. See *Time*, February 19, 1979.

134. *News World*, February 6, 1979. The one issue of tax exemption with which no one quarrelled was, oddly enough, almost completely neglected in the February 5, 1979, meeting. Not one of Dole's twenty-four guest speakers was an expert on tax law and religious exemptions. Despite the Kansan's concern about this matter, professed to his Finance Committee chairman in December 1978 and to the IRS Commissioner three years earlier, there was no follow-up in February 1979.

135. *Time*, February 19, 1979.

136. *Dallas Times Herald*, May 12, 1977.

137. *Ibid.*

138. *Dayton Daily News*, May 19, 1977.

139. A Justice Department spokesman, Robert Havel, told the *New York Times* in early 1979 that the department had received four hundred letters of complaint about cult brainwashing in the previous three years. Only thirty investigations were ever made and no prosecutions were carried out. See the *New York Times*, January 22, 1979.

140. Quoted in *ibid.*

141. Quoted in *ibid.*

142. Letter from FBI Director Clarence Kelley to Joseph D. Early, May 9, 1977.

143. Special Agent report from Kansas City, Missouri field office re: Rev. Sun Myung Moon: The Unification Church, January 18, 1976.

144. Memorandum to Director, CIA from Commissioner, INS, May 26, 1978.

IV   MISCARRIAGE AT JUSTICE

1. See *Teterud v. Burns* 522 F. 2nd 357 (C.A. 8, 1975), and cited in S.L. Snyder, "Memorandum of Law for Assistant Attorney General Ferguson," U.S. Dept. of Justice, Washington, D.C., November 26, 1979, pp. 1–2.

2. *Ibid.*, p. 2. The advertisement appeared in the *Fairfax Journal*, August 10, 1979.
3. Cited in *ibid.*, p. 1.
4. Letter from IRS District Director Charles Brennan to Sun Myung and Hak Ja Han Moon, October 12, 1976.
5. "Information Relative to the Prosecution Memorandum in the Rev. Moon Tax Case," p. 2.
6. *Ibid.*, p. 3.
7. *Ibid.*
8. *Ibid.*, p. 4.
9. *Ibid.*
10. *Ibid.*, p. 1.
11. Letter from John F. Murray, U.S. Department of Justice, to Bernard S. Bailor, Esquire, Caplin and Drysdale, September 21, 1981.
12. Allisa Rubin, "Bull Dog Prosecutor Returns to Paul, Weiss," *The American Lawyer*, November 1982.
13. Letter from Robert C. McConnell, assistant attorney general for legislative and intergovernmental affairs, to Senator Orrin G. Hatch, August 9, 1984, p. 1.
14. *Ibid.*, pp. 1–2.
15. *Ibid.*, p. 2.
16. *Ibid.*, p. 3.
17. *Ibid.*, p. 4.
18. Letter from Attorney General William French Smith to Mortimer M. Kaplan, October 22, 1981. Smith's letter also dryly notes that the Kaplan letter was received the same day that the Moon indictment was returned.
19. "Memorandum: Analysis of the Department of Justice Letter of August 9, 1984," Caplin and Drysdale, August 31, 1984, pp. 4–5.
20. *Ibid.*, p. 6.
21. *Ibid.*, p. 8.
22. The McConnell letter, p. 2.
23. *Ibid.*

v THE CASE OF THE MISSING TRANSLATOR

1. "Prosecutorial Misconduct in the Indictment and Trial of Reverend Moon and Takeru Kamiyama," unpublished manuscript prepared by the Association for the Advancement of Human Rights, Tokyo, Japan, pp. 7–8.
2. *Congressional Record*, 146 at S16310, Column 2 (October 14, 1981), and quoted in *ibid.*, p. 4.
3. See *United States v. Chapin*, 515 F.2d 1274 (D.C. Cir. 1975), *cert. denied*, 423 U.S. 1015 (1976).
4. *United States v. Tonelli*, 577 F.2d 194 (3d Cir. 1978), and quoted in "Prosecutorial Misconduct," p. 1. *Tonelli* also forbade constructing a perjury charge by lifting a statement of the accused out of context and then giving it a meaning completely different from what was originally intended. As we shall see that ruling applies to Kamiyama with a vengeance.
5. Record of the Proceedings at the Beginnings of Grand Jury Sessions on July 9, 16, and 21, 1981, in *Court Interpreters Improvement Act of 1985*, Hearing

before the Subcommittee on the Constitution, Committee on the Judiciary, United States Senate: Ninety-Ninth Congress: Second Session, February 25, 1986 (Washington, D.C.: Government Printing Office, 1986), p. 176.

6. *Ibid.*, p. 178.
7. "Analysis of the Interpretation Services Provided in the Grand Jury Proceedings Against Takeru Kamiyama," p. 440 and p. 306.
8. Quoted from the Grand Jury transcript and cited in *Court Interpreters Improvement Act of 1985*, p. 179.
9. *Ibid.*, p. 183.
10. *Ibid.*
11. Kinko S. Sato, "On the Grand Jury Investigation of Mr. Kamiyama's Conduct in Connection with Suspected Violation of Tax Laws," in *Issues in Religious Liberty*, Hearing before the Subcommittee on the Constitution of the Committee on the Judiciary, United States Senate, Ninety-Eighth Congress, Second Session, June 26, 1984 (Washington, D.C.: U.S. Government Printing Office, 1985), p. 571.
12. "Statement of John Mochizuki," and quoted in *Court Interpreters Improvement Act of 1985*, p. 196.
13. "Declaration of John Mochizuki," and quoted in *ibid.*, p. 197.
14. "Responses of John Mochizuki to Written Questions from Senator Hatch," in *ibid.*, p. 240.
15. "Declaration of Takeru Kamiyama," August 9, 1985, and quoted in *ibid.*, p. 130.
16. Quoted in *ibid.*, p. 109.
17. The letter dated June 18, 1985, can be found in *ibid.*, pp. 109–114. The quote is found on p. 109.
18. Quoted in *ibid.*, p. 110.
19. "Affidavit" of John Hinds, and quoted in *ibid.*, p. 184.
20. Quoted in *ibid.*
21. The translation was not only wrong in a vital way, it was also garbled. Here is an exact translation of the interpreter's Japanese into English: "So at [or in] Tong Il, that is . . . er . . . did [he] know that there are stocks in the Reverend's name, under his title?" See redacted Indictment S81 Cr. 705, Exhibit B, in *ibid.*, p. 149.
22. Again the interpreter: "So then . . . er . . . have you ever spoken about there being stocks worth five hundred . . . er . . . fifty thousand dollars in the Reverend's name?" Quoted in *ibid.*, p. 150.
23. Again the interpreter: "Er . . . as for Reverend Moon . . . the checkbook . . . is he carrying this together with [him or you]." In addition to everything else, the interpreter's use of *issho ni* to modify the verb might mean joint activity with something or someone else—an element that was not in the prosecutor's question at all. Quoted in *ibid.*, p. 154.
24. Quoted from Kinko S. Sato's *amicus* brief, reprinted in *Issues in Religious Liberty*, p. 600.
25. Quoted in *ibid.*, p. 601.
26. Quoted in *ibid.*
27. "Prosecutorial Misconduct," p. 10.
28. "Interview of Mr. Eisuke Sasagawa on His Re-translation of the Grand Jury Hearing of Mr. Takeru Kamiyama by Kinko Sato," August 25, 1984, in

Tokyo, Japan. Quoted in *Issues in Religious Liberty*, p. 545. The text of the entire interview is found between pp. 528–563.

29. Sasagawa translation, p. 420.
30. *Ibid.*, p. 23.
31. *Ibid.*, p. 18.
32. *Ibid.*, p. 253 and p. 148.
33. *Ibid.*, p. 149.
34. *Ibid.*, p. 446.
35. *Ibid.*, p. 447.
36. *Ibid.*
37. *Ibid.*
38. *Ibid.*, p. 448.
39. *Ibid.*
40. "Prosecutorial Misconduct," pp. 41–42. For the actual Sasagawa analysis, p. 87.
41. *Ibid.*, p. 233.
42. "The Prejudicial Effect of the Joint Prosecution and Trial of Reverend Sun Myung Moon and Takeru Kamiyama," a brief prepared by Casey, Scott and Canfield, attorneys at law, and quoted in *Issues in Religious Liberty*, p. 423. The quotation originally appeared in *American Lawyer*, November, 1982.
43. "Prosecutorial Misconduct," p. 141.
44. *Ibid.*, p. 57.
45. *Ibid.*, p. 67.
46. Grand Jury transcript, December 15, 1981, pp. 9–10 and quoted in "Prosecutorial Misconduct," p. 11.
47. *Ibid.*, p. 12.
48. *Ibid.*, p. 13.
49. *Ibid.*, p. 15. See also "Issues in Religious Liberty: Hearing before the Subcommittee on the Constitution of the Committee on the Judiciary," United States Senate, 98th Congress, Second Session on Oversight on the State of Religious Liberty in America Today, June 26, 1984, p. 535.
50. "Prosecutorial Misconduct," pp. 15–16.
51. "S.1853," p. 3.
52. *Ibid.*, p. 4.
53. *Ibid.*, p. 5.
54. *Ibid.*, p. 8.
55. "Prepared Statement of Judge Kevin Thomas Duffy," and quoted in *Court Interpreters Improvement Act of 1985*, pp. 65–66.
56. Duffy in *ibid.*, p. 66.
57. *Brady v. Maryland*, 337 U.S. 83, 87, 1963.
58. *United States v. Phillips Petroleum Co.*, 435 F. Supp. 610, 618 N.D. Oklahoma 1977, and cited in "Prosecutorial Misconduct," pp. 19–20.
59. See *United States v. Ciambrone*, 601 F.2d 616 623 (2nd Cir. 1979), and cited in "Prosecutorial Misconduct," p. 20.
60. As outlined in *United States v. Agura*, 427 U.S. 97, 110, 1976.
61. Sasagawa translation, pp. 1–6.
62. See *United States v. Provenzano, supra*, 440 F.Supp. at 564 citing *United States v. Estepa*, 471 F.2d 1132 (2d Cir. 1972), *cert.denied*, 439 U.S. 1115 l(1973). Also *United States v. Tonelli, supra*, 577 F.2d at 198, and *Van Liew v. United States, supra* 321 F.2d at 678.

63. And there is even more. Flumenbaum justified the calling of the second grand jury because such was requested by the grand jury foreman. Later, under oath and questioned by Kamiyama's lawyer during the trial, Flumenbaum changed his story. In fact, it was Flumenbaum who instructed the grand jury foreman to have a second grand jury take Kamiyama's testimony. See "Prosecutorial Misconduct," pp. 70–71.

64. See *United States v. Bagley*, 473 U.S. 667 (1985).

65. "Prosecutorial Misconduct," p. 63(n).

VI   THE TRIAL BEGINS

1. Quoted in Larry Witham, *Pyongyang to Danbury: The Tax Trial of Reverend Sun Myung Moon*, October 1988, p. 221.

2. Quoted from the trial transcript of *The United States v. Sun Myung Moon and Takeru Kamiyama*, April 15, 1982, p. 3713.

3. *Ibid.*, April 1, 1982, p. 2194.

4. *Ibid.*, March 30, 1982, pp. 1759–1760.

5. *Ibid.*, p. 1760.

6. *Ibid.*, April 1, 1982, p. 2156–2157.

7. *Ibid.*, April 1, 1982, p. 2159.

8. *Ibid.*, p. 2160.

9. *Ibid.*, pp. 2164–2165.

10. *Ibid.*, p. 2167.

11. *Ibid.*, pp. 2175–2176.

12. *Ibid.*, pp. 2178–2182.

13. *Ibid.*, p. 2195.

14. *Ibid.*, April 1, 1982, p. 2197.

15. *Ibid.*

16. *Ibid.*, p. 2198.

17. *Ibid.*, p. 2202.

18. *Ibid.*

19. *Ibid.*, p. 2203–2204.

20. *Ibid.*, p. 2205.

21. *Ibid.*

22. *Ibid.*, p. 2208.

23. *Ibid.*, p. 2210.

24. *Ibid.*, pp. 2212–2213.

25. *Ibid.*, pp. 2213–2214.

26. *Ibid.*, p. 2214.

27. *Ibid.*, pp. 2215–2216.

28. *Ibid.*, p. 2216.

29. *Ibid.*, p. 2218.

30. *Ibid.*, pp. 2218–2219.

31. *Ibid.*, p. 2222.

32. *Ibid.*, p. 2223.

33. *Ibid.*, pp. 2223–2224.

34. *Ibid.*, pp. 2224–2225.

35. *Ibid.*, p. 2225.

36. *Ibid.*, p. 2230. Lawler briefly touched upon Kamiyama's perjury charges,

taking only a few seconds to mention them at the very end of his opening statement. See *ibid.*, pp. 2230–2231.

37. *Ibid.*, p. 2231.
38. For an explanation, see the testimony of Charles Richard Brinkerhoff, a Chase Manhattan Bank official at the time, in *ibid.*, pp. 2237–2241.
39. *Ibid.*, p. 2270. On cross-examination, the witness suggested that they were handbags instead of pocketbooks. See *ibid.*, p. 2305.
40. *Ibid.*, p. 2243.
41. *Ibid.*, p. 2302.
42. Mrs. Maddux was a "team manager" of the International Private Banking Group at the Park Avenue branch of Chase Manhattan. She had specific responsibility for Asia and two other geographical areas. See *ibid.*, p. 2307.
43. *Ibid.*, pp. 2313–2314.
44. *Ibid.*, p. 2316.
45. Trial transcript, April 2, 1982, p. 2474.
46. Trial transcript, April 1, 1982, p. 2337.
47. Trial transcript, April 2, 1982, pp. 2461–2462.
48. Trial transcript, April 5, 1982, p. 2553.
49. Trial transcript, April 2, 1982, p. 2487.
50. Trial transcript, May 3, 1982, p. 5677.
51. *Ibid.*, p. 5724.
52. Trial transcript, April 27, 1982, pp. 5036–5037.
53. Trial transcript, April 15, 1982, pp. 3725–3736.
54. Trial transcript, April 8, 1982, p. 3006. A week later the prosecution was at it again, same questions, different witness. On this next occasion the repetitious questioning netted thirteen objections in nine pages of testimony, six of which were sustained. Trial transcript, April 13, 1982, pp. 3332–3341.
55. Trial transcript, April 13, 1982, pp. 3366–3367.
56. *Ibid.*, pp. 3370–3371.
57. Trial transcript, April 22, 1982, p. 4627.
58. Trial transcript, April 13, 1982, pp. 3330–3332.
59. Trial transcript, April 29, 1982, pp. 5315–5316.
60. *Ibid.*, pp. 5317–5322.
61. Trial transcript, April 26, 1982, p. 4878.
62. Trial transcript, April 29, 1982, p. 5348.
63. See *ibid.*, p. 5348, p. 5363, and p. 5366.
64. Trial transcript, May 5, 1982, p. 6015.
65. Trial transcript, May 3, 1982, p. 5615.
66. *Ibid.*, pp. 5617–5621.
67. *Ibid.*, pp. 5683–5688.
68. Trial transcript, April 13, 1982, pp. 3473–3474.
69. Trial transcript, May 3, 1982, pp. 5691–5695.
70. Trial transcript, May 4, 1982, p. 5771.
71. *Ibid.*, p. 5772.
72. Trial transcript, May 10, 1982, p. 6174.
73. Trial transcript, April 2, 1982, p. 2497.
74. *Ibid.*
75. *Ibid.*, p. 2498.
76. Trial transcript, April 5, 1982, pp. 2545–2554.

77. Trial transcript, April 28, 1982, p. 5256.
78. See Martin Flumenbaum's *in camera* statement: ". . . we have not tried to meet this issue head on and we don't think we have to meet this issue head on." Trial transcript, April 30, 1982, p. 5520.
79. *Ibid.*, p. 5521.
80. *Ibid.*, pp. 5525–5526.
81. Trial transcript, May 3, 1982, p. 5632 and p. 5646.
82. Trial transcript, May 6, 1982, p. 6116.
83. Trial transcript, April 14, 1982, p. 3615.
84. *Ibid.*
85. Trial transcript, April 16, 1982, pp. 3798–3799, and April 19, 1982, p. 4108.
86. Trial transcript, April 20, 1982, p. 4197.
87. Trial transcript, April 6, 1982, p. 2650.
88. Trial transcript, April 21, 1982, p. 4428.
89. *Ibid.*, pp. 4430–4431.
90. *Ibid.*, pp. 4514–4515.
91. *Ibid.*, p. 4515 and p. 4522.
92. Trial transcript, April 22, 1982, pp. 4592–4605.
93. *Ibid.*, pp. 4636–4637. Later, a professional accountant, Margaret DeBoe, would, under oath, find the church records "very rudimentary." See trial transcript, May 4, 1982, p. 5879.
94. Trial transcript, April 26, 1982, p. 4868.
95. Trial transcript, April 30, 1982, p. 5463.
96. Trial transcript, May 10, 1982, pp. 6208–6209.
97. *Ibid.*, p. 6212.
98. Trial transcript, May 11, 1982, p. 6410–6411.
99. *Ibid.*, p. 6413.
100. *Ibid.*, p. 6412.
101. *Ibid.*
102. Trial transcript, April 19, 1982, p. 4055.
103. Trial transcript, April 20, 1982, p. 4216.
104. Trial transcript, April 27, 1982, pp. 5040–5044. One witness, a former church member who worked at East Garden and was in charge of the grounds, lived in a basement. But was this taxable income? The government clearly wanted it to be such to add to their "proof" that Moon was a common tax cheat. The tenancy was yet another example of a tax-related gray area. Also, for certain items related to the account, the tax liability was zero.

VII THE TRIAL ENDS

1. Trial transcript, April 7, 1982, pp. 2924–2925.
2. Trial transcript, April 15, 1982, pp. 3709–3710.
3. Trial transcript, April 21, 1982, pp. 4359–4364.
4. See the trial transcript for April 12, 1982, pp. 3142–3155.
5. Trial transcript, April 16, 1982, pp. 3904–3906.
6. Trial transcript, April 19, 1982, p. 4001.
7. Trial transcript, April 20, 1982, pp. 4307–4308.
8. *Ibid.*, pp. 4311–4325.
9. Trial transcript, April 16, 1982, p. 3954.

10. Trial transcript, April 22, 1982, p. 4686. Nor, of course, did Runyon have total recall. When pressed about documents and the dates he saw them, Runyon's memory gradually sharpened, but understandably he had a hard time pinpointing the date he first saw them—a frequent demand by Flumenbaum. "I have seen literally trillions in the last five years," Runyon told the court. *Ibid.*, p. 4689.
11. Trial transcript, April 23, 1982, pp. 4745–4746.
12. *Ibid.*, pp. 4733–4734.
13. *Ibid.*, pp. 4771–4772.
14. *Ibid.*, p. 4837.
15. *Ibid.*
16. *Ibid.*, p. 4838.
17. Trial transcript, April 27, 1982, pp. 5039–5040.
18. *Ibid.*, p. 5042.
19. *Ibid.*, pp. 5048–5049.
20. *Ibid.*, p. 5055.
21. *Ibid.*
22. *Ibid.*, pp. 5055–5056.
23. *Ibid.*, p. 5064.
24. Trial transcript, April 28, 1982, pp. 5087–5099.
25. Grand jury proceedings, October 13, 1981, p. 66.
26. *Ibid.*, pp. 68–69. Also p. 83 where Warder claims that in speaking to numerous Japanese missionaries, the question of their bringing in funds from abroad was never mentioned.
27. *Ibid.*, pp. 69–70.
28. *Ibid.*, pp. 73–74.
29. *Ibid.*, pp. 75–76.
30. *Ibid.*, p. 78.
31. Trial transcript, May 4, 1982, pp. 5754–5761.
32. Trial transcript, May 11, 1982, p. 6433.
33. Trial transcript, April 28, 1982, p. 5117.
34. *Ibid.*, p. 5129. The prosecution seems to have missed the point—which is that Moon was very interested in lectures; less in the cash flow.
35. *Ibid.*, p. 5138. Selling the Korean delicacy ginseng tea was a major business item for the Tong-Il company, of which Warder was the nominal president. The real decisions regarding the ginseng, however, were made among the Asian senior command, with or without Warder present. Flumenbaum introduced into evidence, with great flourish, an inscribed ginseng tea box, one of several that Moon had passed out to members of the Tong-Il board. The relevance of the box was never quite explained when the prosecutor offered it in evidence—"with the hot water or without," Stillman sarcastically observed—but it was typical of the government's case to offer minutiae to the jury without making clear why. Even the court was unimpressed, allowing the questioning to go on while the jury examined the box. See *ibid.*, p. 5136 and pp. 5145–5146.
36. And a hundred bucks in their pockets for walking around money. The Europeans had even less, according to Warder. See *ibid.*, p. 5181.
37. *Ibid.*, pp. 5182–5183.
38. *Ibid.*, p. 5183. On the face of it, Warder's request was an odd one and most unbusiness-like. Would the publisher of a failing Catholic newspaper go to

the Vatican and ask for money from the Holy Father's personal fund? Not likely.

39. *Ibid.*, p. 5186.
40. *Ibid.*, p. 5192.
41. *Ibid.*, p. 5193.
42. *Ibid.*, p. 5196.
43. *Ibid.*, pp. 5202–5205.
44. *Ibid.*, p. 5213.
45. *Ibid.*, p. 5214.
46. *Ibid.*, pp. 5224–5226.
47. *Ibid.*, p. 5218.
48. *Ibid.*, p. 5219.
49. *Ibid.*, p. 5220.
50. *Ibid.*, p. 5222.
51. *Ibid.*, p. 5223.
52. *Ibid.*, p. 5255.
53. *Ibid.*, pp. 5252–5254.
54. Quoted in *ibid.*, p. 5259.
55. *Ibid.*, p. 5258.
56. *Ibid.*, p. 5260.
57. *Ibid.*, p. 5261.
58. *Ibid.*, p. 5262.
59. *Ibid.*, pp. 5263–5266.
60. *Ibid.*, pp. 5278–5283.
61. *Ibid.*, pp. 5288–5289.
62. *Ibid.*, pp. 5294–5295.
63. *Ibid.*, p. 5302.
64. Trial transcript, April 29, 1982, pp. 5353–5555.
65. *Ibid.*, pp. 5372–5390.
66. *Ibid.*, pp. 5349–5350.
67. *Ibid.*, p. 5395.
68. *Ibid.*, p. 5398.
69. *Ibid.*, pp. 5399–5304.
70. *Ibid.*, p. 5404.
71. *Ibid.*, pp. 5407–5409.
72. *Ibid.*, pp. 5412–5415.
73. *Ibid.*, pp. 5419–5420.
74. *Ibid.*, p. 5420.
75. *Ibid.*, pp. 5420–5421.
76. *Ibid.*, p. 5421.
77. *Ibid.*
78. *Ibid.*, p. 5422.
79. *Ibid.*, pp. 5425–5426.
80. *Ibid.*, p. 5426.
81. Trial transcript, May 3, 1982, pp. 5587–5596.
82. *Ibid.*, pp. 5596–5603.
83. *Ibid.*, p. 5603.
84. *Ibid.*, p. 5607.
85. *Ibid.*, pp. 5712–5713.
86. *Ibid.*, pp. 5713–5714.

87. *Ibid.*, p. 5719.
88. *Ibid.*, p. 5720.
89. *Ibid.*
90. *Ibid.*, p. 5721.
91. *Ibid.*
92. *Ibid.*, p. 5722.
93. *Ibid.*, p. 5723.
94. *Ibid.*, p. 5724.
95. *Ibid.*, p. 5726.
96. *Ibid.*, p. 5727.
97. *Ibid.*, p. 5728.
98. *Ibid.*, p. 5732.
99. *Ibid.*, p. 5733.
100. *Ibid.*, pp. 5735–5736. In fact, Flumenbaum never took no for an answer. With defense witness David Kim, for example, the prosecutor again asked questions about Moon as Master and Father. Did Kim consider him that? Yes, Kim, patiently explained. And Master meant Teacher. As for Father, "any organization even Catholic as a father, priest, he is a Father, nothing wrong with it." But Flumenbaum wanted more from Kim. "You believe he is a prophet?" he asked. The question got no answer. Andy Lawler's objection was sustained. Trial transcript, May 4, 1982, pp. 5784–5785.
101. Trial transcript, May 3, 1982, pp. 5740–5748.
102. Trial transcript, May 4, 1982, p. 5834.
103. *Ibid.*, pp. 5836–5838.
104. *Ibid.*, pp. 5843–5844.
105. *Ibid.*, p. 5848.
106. *Ibid.*, p. 5863. That attitude, of course, is typical of men and women bent on a mission. Their focus is on the last days, not the bottom line. Case in point: first century Christianity. If the Romans had had an IRS, St. Paul could have been jailed as a tax cheat. Instead, of course, he was beheaded. See Acts, chapter 28 and F.W. Farrar, *The Life and Work of St. Paul* (New York: E.P. Dutton and Company, 1880), pp. 685–686, for an account of The End.
107. *Ibid.*, pp. 5874–5875.
108. *Ibid.*, p. 5878.
109. Trial transcript, May 5, 1982, p. 5971.
110. *Ibid.*, p. 5970.
111. See trial transcript, May 4, 1982, p. 5903 and p. 5906 for samples of Flumenbaum's technique.
112. Trial transcript, May 4, 1982, p. 5916.
113. *Ibid.*
114. *Ibid.*, 5917.
115. *Ibid.*, 5918.
116. *Ibid.*
117. Trial transcript, May 5, 1982, pp. 5981–5982.
118. *Ibid.*, p. 5983.
119. *Ibid.*
120. Trial transcript, April 5, 1982, pp. 2576–2577.
121. Trial transcript, April 7, 1982, pp. 2842–2845.
122. Trial transcript, April 19, 1982, p. 3979.
123. Trial transcript, May 10, 1982, p. 6172.

124. *Ibid.*, p. 6173. Harris failed to mention that the documents in question were largely and willingly—even eagerly—supplied by the church itself, a rather strange way of going about a cover-up.
125. *Ibid.*, p. 6177.
126. *Ibid.*, p. 6297.
127. *Ibid.*, p. 6300.
128. *Ibid.*, p. 6301.
129. *Ibid.*, p. 6305.
130. *Ibid.*, p. 6306.
131. *Ibid.*, pp. 6306–6307.
132. *Ibid.*, p. 6313.
133. *Ibid.*
134. *Ibid.*, p. 6335.
135. Trial transcript, May 11, 1982, p. 6344.
136. *Ibid.*, pp. 6353–6354.
137. *Ibid.*, p. 6356.
138. *Ibid.*, p. 6370.
139. *Ibid.*, pp. 6362–6363.
140. *Ibid.*, p. 6385.
141. *Ibid.*, p. 6388.
142. *Ibid.*, p. 6389.
143. *Ibid.*, p. 6395.
144. *Ibid.*, p. 6399.
145. *Ibid.*, p. 6400–6401.
146. *Ibid.*, p. 6401.
147. *Ibid.*, p. 6416.
148. *Ibid.*, p. 6418.
149. *Ibid.*, pp. 6420–6421.
150. *Ibid.*, p. 6421.
151. *Ibid.*, pp. 6437–6441.
152. *Ibid.*, p. 6443.
153. *Ibid.*, pp. 6477–6478.
154. *Ibid.*, p. 6496.
155. *Ibid.*, p. 6497.
156. *Ibid.*, p. 6514.
157. *Ibid.*
158. *Ibid.*, pp. 6514–6515.
159. Trial transcript, May 5, 1982, p. 6011.
160. *Ibid.*, p. 6015.
161. *Ibid.*, p. 6020.
162. *Ibid.*, pp. 6021–6022.
163. *Ibid.*, p. 6035.
164. Trial transcript, March 17, 1982, pp. 28–29.
165. *Ibid.*, p. 30.
166. Trial transcript, April 21, 1982, pp. 4439–4440.
167. *Ibid.*, p. 4440.
168. *Ibid.*, pp. 4440–4441.
169. *Ibid.*, p. 4460.
170. Trial transcript, April 26, 1982, p. 4878.
171. Trial transcript, April 30, 1982, p. 5527.

172. Trial transcript, May 12, 1982, p. 6538.
173. *Ibid.*
174. *Ibid.*, p. 6541.
175. *Ibid.*, pp. 6586–6588.
176. *Ibid.*, p. 6587.
177. *Ibid.*, pp. 6587–6588.
178. *Ibid.*, p. 6588.
179. *Ibid.*, pp. 6645–6646.
180. Trial transcript, April 20, 1982, pp. 4285–4286.
181. Trial transcript, April 15, 1982, p. 3713.
182. Trial transcript, April 7, 1982, pp. 2813–2814.
183. Trial transcript, May 14, 1982, pp. 6706–6708, and pp. 6712–6713.
184. Trial transcript, May 17, 1982, pp. 6719–6720.
185. Trial transcript, May 18, 1982, pp. 6722–6724.

VIII THE JURY

1. "Memorandum of Law in Support of Defendant Moon's Rule 23 Motion," p. 6(n). The memo written after the trial was authored by Professor Laurence H. Tribe of Harvard University.
2. Pollster hyperbole? Two businesses in New York nearly went broke after rumors (false ones) began circulating that they were "Moonie" connected. See *ibid.*
3. "Affidavit of Stephen Roth," and "Affidavit of Charles A. Stillman," quoted in "Memorandum of Law," p. 4(n).
4. Stephen Roth, "Comparison of Those Who Would Throw Reverend Sun Myung Moon in Jail and Those Who Wouldn't," Table I, p. 1. Still, all was not shadow. Among those who wanted Moon locked up now, 1.1 percent still had a positive reaction to Moon. *Ibid.*
5. Memo to Charles Stillman from Steve Roth, February 9, 1982, p. 1.
6. *Ibid.*
7. Roth, "Comparison," Table I, p. 3.
8. Memorandum of Law," p. 4(n).
9. Affidavit of Stephen Roth, paragraphs 16–19. Quoted in "Memorandum of Law," p. 5(n).
10. The Sixth states: "In all criminal prosecutions, the accused shall enjoy the right to a speedy and public trial, by an impartial jury of the State and district wherein the crime shall have been committed, which district shall have been previously ascertained by law, and to be informed of the nature and cause of the accusation; to be confronted with the witnesses against him; to have compulsory process for obtaining witnesses in his favor, and to have the Assistance of Counsel for his defense." The "put it in writing" restriction has not always been observed. In *United States v. McCurdy* the defendant waived his right in open court with the consent of both counsels and after close questioning by the court. *United States v. McCurdy*, 450 F 2nd 282–283 (9th Circuit 1971). See also John Peter Friedrich, III, "*United States v. Sun Myung Moon:* The Right of an Unpopular Defendant to a Bench Trial," University of Texas Law Review, Vol. 8:445, 1985, p. 447(n).
11. *Ibid.*, p. 448.
12. *Ibid.*, pp. 449–450.

13. On the courthouse steps Moon had said: "I would not be standing here today if my skin were white and my religion were Presbyterian. I am here today only because my skin is yellow and my religion is Unification Church. The ugliest things in this beautiful country of America are religious bigotry and racism. . . . Why are we singled out? Simply because our name is Unification Church and the founder happens to be a Korean, a yellow man." Quoted in *ibid.*, p. 446(n). What the prosecution in its *aide memoire* left out was another passage in Moon's statement: "I have respect and confidence in the United States judicial system. . . . America is still the best country in the whole world to let justice be done." Quoted in the "Memorandum of Law," p. 6(n).

14. Quoted in the *Texas Law Review*, p. 446.

15. The government's concern for the pressures that would be placed on the court was wholly outside the rule. Moreover, it was a spurious concern. Judges—federal judges in particular—are supposed to take the heat, or in the more elegant terms framed by Justice Felix Frankfurter—surely no drooping Dora himself—are "to be made of sterner stuff." Frankfurter's opinion is found in *Maryland v. Baltimore Radio Show*, 388 U.S. 912–14 (1950). Quoted in "Memorandum of Law," p. 18(n).

16. *Ibid.*

17. The citation is from *Rosenblatt v. Baer*, 383 U.S. 75, 85 (1966) and quoted in "Memorandum of Law," p. 19.

18. The prosecutors, incidentally, did not have to give a reason for denying waiver, but having done so, their argument was subject to review for constitutionality. See *ibid.*, p. 22.

19. *Texas Law Review*, p. 448.

20. *Patton v. United States*, 281 U.S. 276, 50 S. Ct. 253, 74 L.Ed. 85 (1930) and cited in *Texas Law Review*, pp. 448–449.

21. *Ibid.*, p. 449.

22. *Singer v. United States*, cited in *Texas Law Review*, p. 449.

23. *Ibid.*, pp. 449–450.

24. *Ibid.*, p. 452. The Supreme Court has not considered the issue since it took up *Singer* a quarter century ago.

25. *United States v. Schipani*, 44 F.R.D. 461 (E.D.N.Y. 1968) and cited in *Texas Law Review*, p. 453.

26. *United States v. Panteleakis*, 422 F. Supp. 247 (D.R.I. 1976), and cited in *Texas Law Review*, pp. 453–454.

27. Rule 2 states: "These rules are intended to provide for the just determination of every criminal proceeding. They shall be construed to secure simplicity in procedure, fairness in administration and the elimination of unjustifiable expense and delay." Quoted in *ibid.*, p. 454(n).

28. *United States v. Braunstein*, 474 F. Supp. 1 (D.N.J. 1979), and cited in *Texas Law Review*, pp. 454–455.

29. "Memorandum of Law," p. 28.

30. *Ibid.*, p. 29. By the way, he was not impaneled.

31. *Ibid.* And as Roth predicted, the "don't knows" were the less educated and sophisticated members of the jury pool.

32. See trial transcript, March 30, 1982, pp. 1759–1760.

33. *Ibid.*, p. 1760.

34. *Ibid.*

35. *Ibid.*

36. *Ibid.*
37. *Ibid.*, p. 1761.
38. *Ibid.*, p. 1703.
39. *Ibid.*
40. *Ibid.*, pp. 1705–1707. The 97 percent either hung up right away or during the preliminary questioning eliciting the basic demographic data, long before the sensitive questions about Moon and his movement were asked.
41. *Ibid.*, p. 1720.
42. *Ibid.*
43. *Ibid.*, pp. 1720–1721.
44. *Ibid.*, p. 1722.
45. *Ibid.*, p. 1723.
46. *Ibid.*, p. 1730.
47. *Ibid.*, p. 1731.
48. *Ibid.*
49. *Ibid.*, pp. 1733–1734. What Ms. Harris forgot to mention regarding the relevant cases, including *Irwin*, was that none of them dealt with the subject at hand, namely, a defendant asking for a bench trial. See *ibid.*, p. 1737.
50. *Ibid.*, pp. 1735–1736. Goettel was wrong as we have seen on what *Singer* and subsequent cases did allow.
51. *Ibid.*, p. 1736.
52. *Ibid.*, p. 1743.
53. *Ibid.*, p. 1744.
54. *Ibid.*
55. *Ibid.*, p. 1752.
56. *Ibid.*
57. *Ibid.*, pp. 1752–1753. Nor did the prosecution's tactic of dismissing jurors because they appeared to be intelligent and fair-minded bother Goettel much either. See *ibid.*, p. 1754.
58. *Ibid.*, p. 1755.
59. *Ibid.*
60. *Ibid.*, p. 1757.
61. *Ibid.*
62. *Ibid.*, p. 1759.
63. *Ibid.*, pp. 1760–1761.
64. *Ibid.*, p. 1761.
65. *Ibid.*
66. For Judge Goettel's remarks on these instructions, see trial transcript, March 22, 1982, p. 7.
67. *Ibid.*, p. 15.
68. *Ibid.*, p. 31.
69. *Ibid.*, pp. 35–36.
70. *Ibid.*, pp. 36–37.
71. *Ibid.*, p. 41.
72. *Ibid.*, pp. 43–44. It was a position Judge Goettel would not retreat from even after reviewing a written analysis prepared by defense attorneys and citing case precedents. See trial transcript for March 23, 1982, p. 240.
73. *Ibid.*, p. 43.
74. *Ibid.*, p. 69.
75. *Ibid.*

76. *Ibid.*, pp. 69–70.
77. It was important. The day before the formal *voir dire* proceedings began, New York radio station WYNY, a popular rock station, had a disk jockey read the news about Moon. The disk jockey concluded his report with the words: "Hang the sucker." The incident was reported to Judge Goettel by defense counsel. See trial transcript March 23, 1983, p. 256. The court instructed all potential jurors once more on what they must do to insulate themselves from trial publicity. "If you are in a living room," he warned, "and the television set suddenly comes on with a comment on the case, you either leave the room or turn it off. When you are reading the newspaper and come across some mention of the case, you have to skip over it." *Ibid.*, p. 261.
78. Case in point: Mary Nimmo. She eventually became the jury foreman. Nimmo also demonstrated a streak of prejudice a mile wide, as the post-trial inquiry shows. Ironically, she had asked to be excused on the basis of hardship. Her aging in-laws were coming in from Florida and she didn't think anyone else could take care of them. The court refused to believe it and kept her on. See trial transcript, March 22, 1982, pp. 153–154.
79. This enlightening episode appears in *ibid.*, pp. 86–88.
80. *Ibid.*, p. 93. One other potential juror, Eleanor Stappers, was even more vehement about her anti-church prejudice. Did she mean it, asked the court? "I mean it." Was she serious? "Very serious." She was dismissed. Stappers, Hill, and Zilkowski (interestingly, all women) were very much in the minority in terms of open disclosure of prejudice. One male, however, joined these ladies. Nicholas Visalli thought that Moon ran a "pseudo-religious organization that makes millions of dollars and they don't pay taxes." In the case of Visalli, however, part of his observation was made in open court, arousing some laughter from the other potential jurors, a fact that disturbed defense lawyers, but apparently not the court or the prosecution. See *ibid.*, p. 193 and trial transcript, March 23, 1982, pp. 275–276.
81. *Ibid.*, p. 304.
82. *Ibid.*, p. 305.
83. *Ibid.*, p. 306.
84. *Ibid.*, p. 307. When pressed for a church name, Mr. Llenza came up with the Catholic church. As for the Unification Church, he did not know anything about it, except later, on further questioning, he identified it as "mostly they're South Koreans. Mostly white, you know, Koreans, you know." *Ibid.*, p. 308.
85. *Ibid.*, pp. 321–322.
86. *Ibid.*, pp. 322–323. Nevertheless, lawyer Stillman tried to show the importance of the issue. Flowers were sold by the Unification Church members. The prosecution raised the matter in its context as a source of funds for the church and Moon. Judge Goettel brushed the question aside. *Ibid.*, p. 324.
87. The quotes can be found in *ibid.*, p. 349.
88. *Ibid.*, p. 350.
89. *Ibid.*, pp. 351–352.
90. The quotes can be found in *ibid.*, pp. 353–354.
91. *Ibid.*, p. 354.
92. *Ibid.*, p. 357.
93. *Ibid.*, p. 358.
94. *Ibid.*, pp. 360–361.
95. *Ibid.*, pp. 375–377.

96. *Ibid.*, p. 377.
97. *Ibid.*, p. 379.
98. *Ibid.*, pp. 380–381.
99. *Ibid.*, p. 387 and p. 440.
100. *Ibid.*, p. 442.
101. *Ibid.*, p. 451.
102. *Ibid.*, pp. 451–452.
103. *Ibid.*, p. 480.
104. *Ibid.*, pp. 480–481.
105. *Ibid.*, p. 514.
106. *Ibid.*, p. 516.
107. *Ibid.*, p. 527.
108. *Ibid.*, pp. 528–529.
109. *Ibid.*, p. 540.
110. *Ibid.*, p. 789 and p. 791.
111. *Ibid.*, p. 793.
112. A Mrs. Kramer was almost a textbook example of the problem. A college-educated librarian, the woman attempted to appear fairminded. Asked about what she thought of Unification Church members, Mrs. Kramer said: "Well, they seem to be fanatical about their religion, and they seem to go no ends to enhance it or to get more converts into their religion." Do cults exploit people? She saw two sides to the question—a technique she used often in her *voir dire*: "I feel that it is—young people with an insecure background, with a personality problem are usually prime prospects for this kind of what you might call exploitation." Yes, but was it brainwashing? "There again, I feel—I don't know enough about brainwashing. I think it is really—I can see the logic in young people who have personality problems, you know, who—that kind of thing." *Ibid.*, p. 581 and p. 644.
113. The drawbacks to the *voir dire* process have been discussed by the courts. The Federal Second Circuit in 1950 said that "any examination on the *voir dire* is a clumsy and imperfect way of detecting suppressed emotional commitments to which all of us are to some extent subject, unconsciously or subconsciously. . . ." See *United States v. Dennis*, and quoted in the "Memorandum of Law," p. 34(n).
114. Trial transcript, March 24, 1982, p. 592. Professional pollsters wrestle with a similar problem. As pollster Richard Morin observed recently: "People tend to give socially acceptable answers to pollsters. Ask people if they are registered to vote or not and the results will be higher than more reliable estimates of voter registration. Then ask those self-described registered voters if they plan to vote, and more than nine out of ten dutifully say they will." See Richard Morin, in the *Washington Post*, October 16, 1988.
115. Trial transcript, March 23, 1982, p. 593.
116. *Ibid.*, pp. 593–594.
117. Even well-known national telephone surveys are having problems in which fully one-third of people contacted will not finish the interview. See Morin, *Washington Post*.
118. Trial transcript, March 24, 1982, p. 720. Not surprisingly prosecutor Jo Ann Harris agreed. "Strongly held religious views are things that people are going to have. It is information that counsel now have to exercise their peremptories from, but not the basis for cause." *Ibid.*, pp. 720–721.

119. *Ibid.*, p. 721.
120. Paul Lazarsfeld, *Two Step Flow of Communication* (The Free Press: Glencoe, Illinois, 1954.) His thesis relied on the two-step process used by local opinion makers who would shape the media's message for others. In small groups "opinion-makers," because of their personal contact with others, wield enormous influence. Juries, of course, are the ideal small group, held together for a prolonged period of time, who provide fertile soil for the growth of shared views. That is precisely what happened in the Moon-Kamiyama jury.
121. "Memorandum of Law," p. 28. Also the trial transcript, March 25, 1982, p. 804, and p. 851. Trial transcript March 29, 1983, pp. 1396–1397 and pp. 1521–1522.
122. Trial transcript, March 26, 1982, p. 1195. Also quoted in the "Memorandum of Law," p. 29.
123. *Ibid.*, p. 38. Also the trial transcript, March 23, 1982, p. 473.
124. Trial transcript, March 25, 1982, p. 862–863, and p. 857.
125. Trial transcript, March 31, 1982, p. 2052.

IX THE TAINTING OF A JURY

1. Sealed transcript of September 30, 1982, previously cited. See especially p. 18 and p. 25.
2. *Ibid.*, pp. 27–28.
3. *Ibid.*, p. 29.
4. *Ibid.*, p. 46. Romanoff's answer, curiously enough, came in response to a direct question from prosecution about a fee for Curry.
5. This strange contradiction can be found in *ibid.*, p. 47. Compare lines 3–4 and lines 19–21.
6. Previously cited "Memorandum of Law," p. 2.
7. *Ibid.*, p. 3. The government's outrage at the surreptitious taping of jurors' views of the trial did not extend to those jurors who, despite being warned against giving post-trial comments, did so to the press. In fact, juror Freddie Bryant's comments to the *New York Daily News* on May 19, 1982, and the previously cited Virginia Steward's interview with the *Prospect Press* are actually commented upon favorably in the "Memorandum." See *ibid.*, pp. 4–5.
8. *Ibid.*
9. *Ibid.*, p. 14. At the time John Curry's identity was not known by the government.
10. *Ibid.*, p. 13(n).
11. See the previously cited sealed telephone conversation between Steward and Curry, July 26, 1982, pp. 4–5, and p. 7.
12. *Ibid.*, pp. 14–15.
13. *Ibid.*, p. 22.
14. Cited in *ibid.*, p. 23.
15. Cited in *ibid.*, p. 24.
16. *Ibid.*, pp. 25–26.
17. Quoted from the sealed "Defendants' Reply to Government's Opposition to an Inquiry Relating to Jury Conduct," p. 2.
18. *Ibid.*, pp. 2–7.

19. *Ibid.*, pp. 9–11.
20. *Ibid.*, p. 7(n). Other cases cited by the government, such as *United States v. Hockridge* and *United States v. Mulligan*, in fact had resulted in a jury inquiry. That they did so went unmentioned in the government's memorandum. See *ibid.*, p. 9(n).
21. See the previously cited "Memorandum of Law," p. 2(n).
22. Sealed transcript of the September 3, 1982, proceedings, p. 2.
23. Or were opaque and patronizing, as was Professor Laurence H. Tribe of Harvard University, who was Moon's third attorney. In an early offering on September 3, Tribe observed to Judge Goettel: "It seems to us that Moten is really a fortiori and if you look at McMahon [*sic*], Remmer and other cases, the threshold predicate for factual inquiry by this Court is overwhelmingly established, and although it is entirely possible that nothing will happen in the next week, what we cannot control is [Bruce] Romanoff. He may try to reach any of us since he has had a recent meeting with Mr. Hager." *Ibid.*, p. 7. Needless to say, Tribe was overruled and the proceedings were delayed.
24. *Ibid.*, p. 9. Goettel, for example, refers to "Mr. Romanoff's seedy background" and while expressing a "gut reaction" that collusion did not take place, "I shouldn't attempt to foreclose you from making a showing in that regard." *Ibid.*, p. 10. He did not. Ms. Harris continued to press the collusion argument (without evidence) for the balance of the September 3 hearing. See especially *ibid.*, pp. 12–13.
25. *Ibid.*, pp. 18–19.
26. *Ibid.*, p. 20.
27. *Ibid.*, p. 21.
28. *Ibid.*, pp. 21–22. In other words, Judge Goettel placed the onus of proving the existence of a biased jury on the defense rather than on himself, the man who denied the defense a bench trial in the first place. It was an argument Goettel repeatedly employed before, during, and after the trial.
29. *Ibid.*, p. 22.
30. *Ibid.*, p. 23. Judge Goettel estimated in September that the appeal would not be argued before January. Defense counsel seemed to agree—in any case, they let it go by without challenge as well.
31. See discussion of this point in *ibid.*, pp. 24–27.
32. From the sealed transcript, September 30, 1982, pp. 9–10.
33. *Ibid.*, p. 16.
34. *Ibid.*
35. *Ibid.*
36. *Ibid.*, pp. 17–19. Romanoff's inconsistency was not picked up by the prosecution, although later slips of other witnesses were to be pounced upon as significant.
37. *Ibid.*, p. 35.
38. *Ibid.*
39. *Ibid.*, p. 38.
40. *Ibid.*, p. 42 and p. 44.
41. Sample question for Bruce Romanoff from Jo Ann Harris: "Have you ever been involved in any way with contacting jurors in cases after verdicts?" *Ibid.*, p. 52. Once again Kamiyama's lawyer, Andrew Lawler, objected. The court overruled him, but confined Romanoff's answer to a yes or no. The answer was no. *Ibid.*, p. 53.

42. Quoted in the sealed transcript of October 1, 1982, p. 10.
43. *Ibid.*, p. 11.
44. *Ibid.*, pp. 13–16.
45. *Ibid.*, p. 23.
46. *Ibid.*, pp. 23–24.
47. *Ibid.*, pp. 25–43.
48. *Ibid.*, p. 50.
49. *Ibid.*, p. 52.
50. *Ibid.*, p. 53.
51. *Ibid.*, p. 54.
52. *Ibid.*
53. *Ibid.*, p. 56 and p. 63.
54. *Ibid.*, p. 63.
55. From the sealed transcript of the October 4, 1982, proceedings, pp. 17–19.
56. *Ibid.*, p. 23.
57. *Ibid.*, p. 24.
58. Details of the subpoena escapade were supplied by prosecutor Jo Ann Harris in the sealed transcript of October 6, 1982, pp. 7–11.
59. *Ibid.*, p. 13.
60. *Ibid.*, pp. 13 and p. 17.
61. *Ibid.*, p. 14.
62. *Ibid.*, pp. 18–19.
63. *Ibid.*, p. 20.
64. *Ibid.*, pp. 23–28.
65. *Ibid.*, p. 43. At another point, Virginia Steward told the court: "In fact, I wish you had a tape where I told him [Curry] that I thought it all over and I did do the right thing and I didn't want no part of it." *Ibid.*, pp. 49–50. As for Curry, Steward later stated on October 6: "I mean, to figure a person that I have known most of my life can manipulate—to twist a friendship into something to do wrong, I cannot condone it, and as far as I am concerned, I never want to see him again." *Ibid.*, p. 94.
66. *Ibid.*, pp. 44–46.
67. See *ibid.*, pp. 66, 68–69, 91.
68. *Ibid.*, pp. 74–75. Later, however, through extensive questioning Virginia Steward said that Torres might have meant the Unification Church was the source of the pressure. *Ibid.*, p. 76.
69. *Ibid.*, pp. 95–98.
70. *Ibid.*, p. 102.
71. *Ibid.*, p. 116.
72. *Ibid.*, p. 118.
73. *Ibid.*
74. From the sealed transcript of the proceedings on October 7, 1982, p. 4.
75. *Ibid.*, p. 7.
76. *Ibid.*, pp. 8–28.
77. *Ibid.*, p. 12. The other direct denials are found on pp. 8–12.
78. *Ibid.*, p. 12.
79. *Ibid.*, p. 13.
80. *Ibid.*, p. 14.
81. *Ibid.*, p. 17.
82. *Ibid.*, pp. 17–21.

83. *Ibid.*, p. 22.
84. *Ibid.*, p. 24.
85. *Ibid.*, p. 25.
86. *Ibid.*, p. 30.
87. *Ibid.*, p. 33.
88. *Ibid.*, pp. 38–42.
89. *Ibid.*, p. 42.
90. Sealed transcript of October 13, 1982, pp. 8–11 and pp. 14–15 and p. 19.
91. *Ibid.*, p. 20.
92. *Ibid.*, p. 12.
93. *Ibid.*, pp. 37–38.
94. *Ibid.*, p. 44.

X AMICI, APPEALS, AND PRISON

1. American Civil Liberties Union and the New York Civil Liberties Union, Motion for Leave to File Brief *Amici Curiae*, quoted in "Constitutional Issues in the Case of Reverend Moon," Herbert Richardson, ed. (New York: 1984), pp. 362–363.
2. *Ibid.*, p. 596.
3. Brief *Amicus Curiae* for the Institute for the Study of American Religion in Support of Petition for Certiorari, and quoted in *ibid.*, p. 528.
4. The American Civil Liberties Union and the New York Civil Liberties Union, quoted in Petition for Certiorari in *ibid.*, p. 368.
5. Brief *Amici Curiae* for Bishop Ernest L. Unterkoefler, Clare Boothe Luce, Eugene McCarthy, Robert Destro, and a Coalition of Catholic Laymen, found in *ibid.*, p. 383.
6. Brief of Catholic Laymen, quoted in *ibid.*, p. 385.
7. *Ibid.*, p. 384.
8. Brief of the National Council of Churches in *ibid.*, p. 565.
9. *Ibid.*, p. 560. This same brief notes that the Presbyterian Church (U.S.A.) has $357.9 million invested in securities in some 175 corporations. The American Baptist Churches in the U.S.A. have $370 million worth of securities in more than 100 corporations. *Ibid.*, p. 56(n).
10. Brief of Catholic Laymen, in *ibid.*, p. 390.
11. Brief for the Catholic League for Religious and Civil Rights as *Amicus Curiae* in *ibid.*, p. 415.
12. Brief of Catholic Laymen, quoted in *ibid.*, p. 398.
13. Brief of the National Council of Churches, in *ibid.*, p. 571.
14. Brief for the Church of Jesus Christ of Latter-Day Saints, in *ibid.*, p. 462.
15. Transcript of *U.S. v. Sun Myung Moon and Takeru Kamiyama*, 81 Cr. 0705, July 14, 1982, pp. 32–33. For a full explanation of the thirteenth juror concept, see *ibid.*, pp. 38–39. As we shall see Judge Goettel wanted no part in playing number thirteen.
16. *Ibid.*, p. 3.
17. *Ibid.*
18. *Ibid.*, p. 4.
19. *Ibid.*, pp. 5–7, and p. 13.
20. *Ibid.*, pp. 9–10.
21. *Ibid.*, pp. 11–12 and pp. 31–32.
22. *Ibid.*, p. 12.

23. *Ibid.*, p. 14.
24. *Ibid.*, pp. 14–15.
25. *Ibid.*, pp. 23–25.
26. *Ibid.*, p. 26. See also *ibid.*, p. 19.
27. *Ibid.*, p. 39.
28. *Ibid.*, p. 43.
29. *Ibid.*, p. 45.
30. *Ibid.*, p. 48.
31. *Ibid.*, p. 49.
32. *Ibid.*, p. 56.
33. *Ibid.*, p. 57.
34. *Ibid.*, p. 59.
35. *Ibid.*, p. 92.
36. Transcript of *United States v. Sun Myung Moon and Takeru Kamiyama*, 81 Cr. 0705 (GLG), July 16, 1982, p. 12.
37. *Ibid.*, pp. 16–17.
38. *Ibid.*, p. 18.
39. *Ibid.*, p. 20–21.
40. *Ibid.*, p. 23, and p. 32.
41. *Ibid.*, p. 28.
42. *Ibid.*, p. 30.
43. *Ibid.*, p. 35.
44. *Ibid.*, pp. 35–36. Goettel, of course, offered no proof of that. He did not deal with the available evidence that suggested otherwise. But such is the discretion of a federal judge.
45. *Ibid.*, p. 36.
46. *Ibid.*, p. 37.
47. *Ibid.*, p. 40.
48. *Ibid.*, p. 41.
49. *Ibid.*, p. 50.
50. *Ibid.*, pp. 52–53.
51. *Ibid.*, p. 53.
52. Quoted in Larry Witham, *Pyongyang to Danbury: The Tax Trial of Reverend Sun Myung Moon*, (n.p., 1988), pp. 251–252.
53. Transcript, *United States v. Sun Myung Moon and Takeru Kamiyama*, U.S. Court of Appeals for the Second Circuit, Docket Nos. 82–1275, 82–1277, 82–1279, 82–1357, March 23, 1983, p. 6.
54. *Ibid.*, pp. 7–8.
55. *Ibid.*, p. 8.
56. *Ibid.*, p. 9.
57. *Ibid.*
58. *Ibid.*, pp. 11–13.
59. *Ibid.*, p. 24.
60. *Ibid.*, p. 29.
61. *Ibid.*, pp. 29–30.
62. *Ibid.*, p. 32, and p. 37. Martin Flumenbaum though present in court made no oral arguments to the appeals court.
63. *Ibid.*, pp. 47–48.
64. *Ibid.*, p. 64.
65. *Ibid.*, p. 69.

66. Quoted in Witham, p. 259.
67. David M. O'Brien, *Storm Center: The Supreme Court in American Politics* (New York: W. W. Norton and Company, 1986), pp. 129–133.
68. *Los Angeles Times*, Editorial: "Church and State," March 2, 1984.
69. Colman McCarthy, "The Real Issue in the Case of Rev. Moon," *Washington Post*, February 5, 1984.
70. William Raspberry, "A Fair Trial for Rev. Moon," *Washington Post*, April 18, 1984.
71. *Ibid.*
72. James J. Kilpatrick, "Moon Conviction Imperils Religious Freedom," *Star-Ledger* (Newark, New Jersey), November 4, 1973. Kilpatrick's column appeared in some 700 newspapers in the United States.
73. *Ibid.*
74. Quoted in Witham, p. 281.
75. Letter from Justin Ignizio to *Hustler* magazine, undated, and reprinted in *Victory for Freedom: Portrait of a Movement for Freedom*, James M. Gavin, ed., (Washington, D.C., Committee to Defend the U.S. Constitution, 1985), p. 38.
76. George Rush, "Club Fed," *Manhattan, Inc. Magazine*, and reprinted in *Eastern Review*, October 1985, p. 84.
77. *Ibid.*

XI THE DEPROGRAMMING CULT

1. Ted Patrick with Tom Dulack, *Let Our Children Go!* (New York: E.P. Dutton and Co., Inc., 1976), p. 231.
2. *Ibid.*, p. 235.
3. *Ibid.*, p. 38.
4. *Ibid.*, p. 39.
5. *Ibid.*, p. 44.
6. *Ibid.*, p. 46.
7. *Ibid.*, p. 47.
8. *Ibid.*, p. 48.
9. *Ibid.*
10. *Ibid.*, p. 50.
11. *Ibid.*
12. *Ibid.*, p. 53. For the menu, see p. 55.
13. *Ibid.*, p. 63.
14. *Ibid.*, p. 64.
15. *Ibid.*, p. 65.
16. *Ibid.* As we shall see, hiding behind the parents was critical to Patrick's legal defense as the civil and criminal charges would pile up.
17. Details can be found in *ibid.*, pp. 65–67.
18. *Ibid.*, p. 67.
19. *Ibid.*
20. *Ibid.*
21. *Ibid.*, p. 68.
22. *Ibid.*, p. 96.
23. *Ibid.*, p. 104.
24. *Ibid.*, p. 105.
25. *Ibid.*, p. 106.

26. *Ibid.*, p. 165.
27. *Ibid.*, p. 236.
28. *Ibid.*, p. 149. In the case of Kathy Crampton, she later escaped from one of Patrick's parties and returned to Seattle. See *ibid.*, p. 151.
29. *Ibid.*, pp. 221–222.
30. Affidavit of Sherrill Anne Westerlage, taken June 6, 1978, State and County of New York, p. 2.
31. *Ibid.*
32. *Ibid.*
33. *Ibid.*, p. 4.
34. *Ibid.*, p. 3.
35. Testimony of Sue Tuttle, undated, pp. 2–3.
36. *Ibid.*, p. 3.
37. Affidavit of Laura Jean Wilson, September 18, 1978, taken by notary public Bruce A. Brown, State and County of New York, p. 4.
38. *Ibid.*, p. 3.
39. *Ibid.*, p. 6.
40. *Ibid.*, pp. 7–8.
41. Affidavit of Maree Patricia Ryan, August 18, 1983 taken before Johnston, Pritchard, Fee and Partners, Auckland, New Zealand, p. 4.
42. *Ibid.*
43. Affidavit of Krzysztof Hempowicz, January 1982, State and County of New York, p. 1.
44. *Ibid.*, p. 2.
45. *Guardian*, (London), October 4, 1976.
46. Robert J. Lifton, *Thought Reform and the Psychology of Totalism* (New York: Norton and Co., 1961), pp. 420–437.
47. See Patrick, pp. 43–60.
48. The essay can be found in Thomas Robbins, William C. Shepherd and James McBride, eds., *Cults, Culture and the Law* (Chico, Calif.: Scholars Press, 1985), p. 59.
49. See John T. Biermans, *The Odyssey of New Religions Today: A Case Study of the Unification Church* (Lewiston, New York: The Edwin Mellen Press, 1988), p. 31 and pp. 44–45.
50. Lee Coleman, *Psychiatry the Faithbreaker: How Psychiatry is Promoting Bigotry in America* (Sacramento: Printing Dynamics, 1982), p. 7.
51. *Ibid.*
52. There would be another connection with the Shapiro case for Clark, as we shall see.
53. Biermans, p. 47.
54. Coleman, p. 26.
55. *Ibid.*, p. 10. Coleman, however, suggests what may have slipped Singer's mind. He notes: "She did not mention the fact that the five had all been taken into custody by force and were ordered by a court to take such tests. She did not acknowledge that resentment and lack of cooperation from the five could easily explain a rather hasty and withholding performance on such tests." *Ibid.*, pp. 10–11.
56. *Ibid.*, p. 11.
57. Biermans, p. 47 and pp. 200–201.
58. Quoted in Eric Alterman, "In Moon's Orbit," *New Republic*, October 27,

1986, p. 22. But it was not a grand slam with the media—even in that glorious first decade, 1971–1981. There were skeptics, even on television. CBS's Steve Young (now with CNN) filed a report that positively enraged Ted Patrick, although by any other account it was evenly balanced: the targeted religions certainly got little comfort from the report. But then neither did Patrick. It was the First Deprogrammer's great misfortune that Young persuaded him to allow Young to observe a deprogramming that didn't work, Kathy Crampton's. Patrick complained that Young made "all of us look like villains, kidnappers, violators of Kathy's civil rights." Young concluded his segment: "I feel very strongly about what Patrick is doing. I think he makes broadbrush, unfounded charges against whole religious groups. Some of what he says may very well be true, but my own feeling is that he is a flimflam man, that he is manipulative and that he preys upon desperate parents." Quoted in Patrick, p. 151 and p. 153.

59. Quoted in Robert W. Dellinger, *Cults and Kids: A Study in Coercion* (Boys Town, Nebraska: The Boys Town Center, n.d.), p. 12.

60. *Ibid.*, p. 19.

61. Flo Conway and Jim Siegelman, *Snapping: America's Epidemic of Sudden Personality Change* (New York: Delta Books, 1979). *Snapping* was the first anti-cult book that received critical review, if not a demolishing, from social scientists. Lowell Streiker, a theologian and no friend of the new religions, dismissed Conway and Siegelman's notion of "information disease." He wrote: "Anything which reaches above the threshold of boredom is suspect. . . . Obviously there is a whole lot of brainwashing going on, and very little of it by the handful of religious sects routinely lambasted by the ACN [Anti-Cult Network]." See Lowell Streiker, *Mind-Bending* (New York: Doubleday and Co., 1984), p. 166. Brock K. Kilbourne, a social psychologist at the University of Nevada, Reno, reviewed the Conway and Siegelman data and found it woefully wanting. In his view, the actual evidence ran against the thesis on information disease. See Brock K. Kilbourne, "The Conway and Siegelman Claims against Religious Cults: An Assessment of the Data," *Journal for the Scientific Study of Religion*, December 1983, pp. 380–385. There were other professional critics as well. Perhaps Conway and Siegelman got the message. In any case, they soon went from the menace of the cults to what they believe is the greater menace of fundamentalist religions. See their *Holy Terror* (New York: Doubleday and Co., 1982).

62. Christopher Edwards, *Crazy for God* (Englewood Cliffs, New Jersey: Prentice-Hall, Inc., 1979).

63. *Ibid.*, p. 51.

64. *Ibid.*, p. 201.

65. *Ibid.* Others, however, have not been so kind in the judgment of the book. Sociologists David Bromley and Anson Shupe pronounced: "Aside from demonstrating a remarkable memory for details and events that allegedly occurred while his brain was being washed, Edwards' account of his indoctrination at the hands of the Unification Church's Oakland, California, family is a modern illustration of a literary genre as old as the anti-Mormon and anti-Catholic movements of the early nineteenth century. . . . With a literary style and deliberate melodramatic construction reminiscent of the script for a made-for-TV movie, *Crazy for God* makes one feel as if the ghost of Maria Monk, that self-proclaimed ex-nun from a nineteenth century Mon-

treal convent, had reappeared to promote another potboiler tract, this time substituting the Unification Church for the 'Papist' Roman Catholics." See their *Strange Gods* (Boston: Beacon Press, 1981), pp. 200–201.

66. William Shakespeare, *The Tragedy of Hamlet: Prince of Denmark* (New Haven, Connecticut: Yale University Press, 1947) Tucker Brooke and Jack Randall Crawford, eds., Act IV, scene 1, pp. 128–136.

67. Thomas Robbins and Dick Anthony, "New Religions, Families and Brain-washing," in Robbins and Anthony, eds. *In Gods We Trust* (New Brunswick, N.J.: Transaction Books, 1981), pp. 264–265. One study of thirty-five ex-members from three controversial religious groups showed that volunteer defectors rarely raised the question of brainwashing, and most claimed they felt "wiser for the experience."

68. Thomas McGowan, "Conversion: A Theological View," in Herbert Rich-ardson, ed., *New Religions and Mental Health* (New York: Edwin Mellen, 1980), p. 167. According to my research, McGowan is the first to have actually talked to members of the Unification Church and published his results—eight years after Patrick went on his snatching spree.

69. See, for example, the ACLU's resolution from its Church-State Committee condemning the persecution of religions on the basis of allegations of brainwashing—a resolution which was passed at its national board meeting in March 1977. Cited in *Deprogramming: documenting the issue* (unpublished manuscript), p. 181.

70. See Dean M. Kelley, "Deprogramming and Religious Liberty," *The Civil Liber-ties Review, July/August 1977*, pp. 23–32. The article is a stinging attack on the deprogramming movement. The author is Director for Religious and Civil Liberties for the National Council of Churches. See also Biermans, p. 70.

71. Quoted in Coleman, p. 18.

72. Louis H. Gann, "Dr. Margaret Singer: An Evaluation of Her Work," Hoover Institution, Stanford University (unpublished manuscript), p. 8, and quoted in Biermans, p. 50.

73. Memorandum from the APA Board of Social and Ethical Responsibility for Psychology to Members of the Task Force on Deceptive and Indirect Methods of Persuasion and Control, May 11, 1987, and quoted in Biermans, p. 145.

74. Quoted in *ibid.*, pp. 144–145.

75. Quoted in Lee Boothby, "Government as an Instrument of Retribution for Private Resentments," in Dean Kelley, ed. *Government Intervention in Religious Affairs* (New York: Pilgrim Press, 1986). Boothby is the General Counsel for Americans United for Separation of Church and State.

76. Regarding the Episcopalians, see the *Houston Chronicle*, May 7, 1977. Patrick told the *Chronicle* that he had deprogrammed several members of Redeemer Episcopal Church of Houston including Peter Willis, twenty-two years old. Bishop J. Miller Richardson, head of the diocese of Texas, made clear that Redeemer "is a bonafide Episcopal Church in good standing in the diocese of Texas." For the experience of Debbie Dudgeon, see the *Catholic Register*, March 22, 1975, pp. 2–3.

77. See the unpublished manuscript, "The Facts on Deprogramming," February 1982, p. 46. No author is cited.

78. See, for example, Roberta J. Moore, "Terror in Denver," *Liberty*, March/April 1975, pp. 9–13.

79. "The Facts on Deprogramming," p. 46.
80. The letter dated January 11, 1977, is found in *Deprogramming: documenting the issue*, p. 36.
81. For details on the Reithmiller case, see the *Cincinnati Post*, October 17, 1981. For the rest, see "The Facts on Deprogramming," p. 103. Also Biermans, p. 284(n).
82. Cited in Boothby, p. 11.
83. Biermans, p. 282(n).
84. "The Facts on Deprogramming," p. 103, and Bierman, p. 282(n).
85. Robert H. Greene, "People v. Religious Cults: Legal Guidelines for Criminal Activities, Tort Liability, and Parental Remedies," *Suffolk University Law Review*, Vol. XI, 1977, p. 1048. Also Patrick, pp. 268–275.
86. John E. LeMoult, "Deprogramming Members of Religious Sects," *Fordham Law Review*, Vol. XLVI, 1977–1978, pp. 626–628. Also Patrick, pp. 167–180.
87. LeMoult, pp. 626–627.
88. *Ibid.*, p. 628. Unfortunately, the court ignored the fact that the federal law on kidnapping does not allow for motive or intent. *LeMoult*, p. 628.
89. *People v. Patrick*, 541 F.2d 320 (Colo. App. 1975) and cited in LeMoult, p. 629.
90. See *ibid.*
91. Cited in LeMoult, p. 621.
92. *Ibid.*, p. 622.
93. Boothby, p. 14.
94. Terri Siegel, "Deprogramming Religious Cultists," in the *Loyola of Los Angeles Law Review*, Volume II, 1978, pp. 874–876.
95. Coleman, p. 10.
96. *Ibid.* See also Siegel, pp. 816–817.
97. LeMoult, p. 603.
98. Siegel, pp. 817–818.
99. LeMoult, p. 631.
100. *Katz v. Superior Court*, 73 Cal. App. 3d 952 (1977) and cited in Biermans, pp. 203–205. Also Siegel, pp. 818–821.
101. Quoted in "Conservatorships and Religious Cults: Divining a Theory of Free Exercise," a Note from the *New York University Law Review*, December 1978, p. 1255.
102. *Ibid.*, p. 1256.
103. Boothby, p. 12.
104. *Ibid.*, pp. 13–14.
105. *Molko and Leal v. The Holy Spirit Association*, 179 Cal. App. 3d 450 (1986), and cited in Biermans, p. 201.
106. *Molko and Leal*, and cited in Biermans, p. 202.
107. *Reynolds* established the principle that religious belief was absolutely protected by the Constitution. Religious practice, however, such as polygamy, could and would be regulated by the state. See Greene, p. 1031.
108. *Molko and Leal*, and cited in Biermans, pp. 202–203.
109. Quoted in the *New York Times*, October 19, 1988. Also *Molko and Leal v. Holy Spirit Association, et al.*, October 17, 1988, pp. 31–32.
110. Quoted in the *Washington Post*, October 22, 1988. Also *Molko and Leal v. HSA*, p. 33.

111. *Ibid.*, p. 34.
112. *Ibid.*, p. 53.
113. *Ibid.*, pp. 47–51 and p. 44.
114. "Concurring and Dissenting Opinion" in *Molko and Leal v. Holy Spirit Association*, p. 24 and p. 34.

XII THE REVEREND SUN MYUNG MOON

1. From *People Serving People*, a booklet published by the Unification Church in New York, 1985, p. 6.
2. Larry Witham, *Pyongyang to Danbury: The Tax Trial of Reverend Sun Myung Moon*, (n.p., 1988), p. 25.
3. *Ibid.*, p. 31.
4. *Ibid.*
5. That comes to a modest 36.6 parishioners per "church." See Ch'oi Sun-dak, "Korea's Tong-Il Movement," *Transactions of the Korea Branch of the Royal Asiatic Society*, October 1967, p. 169.
6. Quoted from *ibid.* McCabe was describing the Unification Church's most recent acquisition, the first it would own outright, a fixed-up Buddhist temple that is still used today by the church.
7. *Ibid.*
8. His bride was much younger—eighteen at the time—and the marriage eventually produced thirteen children. Moon had been married once before, but that marriage ended in divorce. See Ch'oi Sun-dak, "Korea's Tong-Il Movement," p. 167.
9. *People Serving People*, p. 6.
10. *Ibid.*
11. This particular twist to the Fall of Man doctrine may well have been the seed that sprouted later into the sex cult scandal which first hit the Seoul newspapers in the mid-1950s, repeated by the *Chicago Tribune* twenty years later.

XIII THE PRESS

1. "Head of Unification Church to Talk at Lisner Auditorium," *Washington Post*, February 19, 1972.
2. See, for example, the *Frederick* (Maryland) *Post*, February 24, 1972, and the *Morning Herald* (Hagerstown, Maryland), March 2, 1972.
3. See, for example, the *Raleigh Times*, July 4, 1972, and the *Florida Alligator* (Gainesville), July 31, 1973.
4. "A Korean Seeking to Establish New Religion Starts U.S. Tour," *New York Times*, October 7, 1973. The tour began in Manhattan at Carnegie Hall.
5. "Moon-Struck," *Time*, October 15, 1973, and "One, Big, Happy Family," *Newsweek*, October 15, 1973.
6. "Moon-Struck."
7. "One, Big, Happy Family."
8. *Ibid.*
9. "Rev. Moon Imports Gospel to Tampa," *Tampa Tribune*, November 3, 1973; Ray Ruppert, "Rev. Moon Appears Here Tomorrow," *Seattle Times*, January 12, 1974; and the *Dundee Sun* (Omaha, Nebraska), November 15, 1973 which

ran a column by the Reverend Lester Kinsolving titled "Unification Church Seems to Feel It Doesn't Have to Explain Anything." Also Tony Lang, "The Gospel According to Sun Moon," *Inquirer Sunday Magazine* (Philadelphia, Pennsylvania), January 4, 1974, and " 'God' with an Ulcer," *Christian Crusade Weekly* (Tulsa, Oklahoma) December 9, 1973.

10. Tom Basham, "West: Rev. Moon," *Performance*, October 26–November 1, 1973. As for the term "Moonie," that too was invented by the bully press. "Moonie" rhymes with "loony." Perfect.

11. *Ibid.*

12. *Ibid.*

13. *Ibid.*

14. *Ibid.*

15. Ellen Ellick, "Zeal Attracted Man: Now 'Illusion' Is Gone," *Omaha World-Herald*, November 27, 1973.

16. *Ibid.*

17. Stryker McGuire, "Moon 'Child' Returned," *San Antonio Light*, August 31, 1975.

18. For a full-length exploration of these themes see John D. Marks, "From Korea with Love," *Washington Monthly*, February 1974.

19. Lawrence Stern and William R. MacKaye, "Rev. Moon: Nixon Backer," *Washington Post*, February 15, 1974. For a similar line of thought, see "The Word from Reverend Moon" in *Rolling Stone*, February 28, 1974, a near-perfect thematic pickup from the earlier *Post* piece. Sample: "[T]he Reverend Sun Myung Moon has gone back to Seoul after a four-month crusade to save Richard Nixon from the Americans."

20. *Ibid.* One paragraph beautifully illustrates the point. It is a work of art: "The established, mainline Christian churches in the United States and Korea generally take a less admiring view. In these ecclesiastical circles Mr. Moon is regarded as a quack, a Korean-style Elmer Gantry who enjoys a warm and privileged relationship with the military-backed dictatorship headed by President Park." *Ibid.*

21. See, for example, the *Evening Express* (Portland, Maine), February 20, 1974. Newspapers reprinted the *Post* story or quoted from it extensively in their own stories as Moon proceeded on his 32-city tour following the Watergate rallies.

22. See the *Morning News* (Wilmington, Delaware), March 1, 1974, which details a parent's charges of the brainwashing of her twenty-one-year-old daughter by the Unification Church.

23. Roger King, "Moon Skeptics Include Ministers," *Montana Kaimin*, April 16, 1974, and Kathy Helms, "The Rev. Moon—Is He a Danger or a Savior?" *Desert News* (Salt Lake City), April 20, 1974.

24. Ann Crittenden, "Moon's Sect Seeks to Build Support in the U.S. for the South Korean Regime," *New York Times*, May 25, 1976.

25. *Ibid.*

26. *Ibid.*

27. *Ibid.* Kim now serves in South Korea's National Assembly.

28. *Ibid.*

29. *Ibid.* But the *Times* had just warmed up. Five days later, Moon was on the front cover of the paper's Sunday magazine. The article, written by the senior editor of *Psychology Today*, served several purposes. It reaffirmed the legit-

imacy of the upcoming Fraser hearings—something must be wrong, there is going to be a congressional investigation—and then rehashed all the "Moonie Menace" stories it could, including the theme of the regimentation of the young. "An exhausting and rigid schedule leaves little time for sleep and none for private reflection." Church members have a "glassy, spaced-out look." Apparently, the writer had not actually observed any church members but was only reporting what others (read: the clip file) had observed. Why not cover all of this with the patina of psychology that so impresses the upper-middle-class who read the magazine and which is to be expected from one of the princes of contemporary psycho-babble? See Berkeley Rice, "The Pull of Sun Moon," *New York Times Sunday Magazine*, May 30, 1976.

30. Barbara Ross, "Moon Stadium Rally Seen as Effort to Get Numbers," *Daily News*, May 27, 1976.
31. Paula Bernstein, "Rabbi Sheds Light on the Moon-Struck," *Daily News*, June 1, 1976. Interestingly enough, beyond the *Times* and the *Daily News*, another popular journal, the Sunday magazine newspaper insert, *Parade*, also ran a similar piece on Moon and his followers. Sample quote: "Former members of the cult insist they never got more than five hours of sleep a night. Moonies, they report, are kept busy with a regimen of exercise, group discussion, lectures, songs and prayers, games like tag and, of course, long stretches of recruiting and peddling in the outside world." That, I suppose, is the ultimate horror of the white middle class—to be deprived of eight hours of sleep a night. They could take acid trips, wear crazy clothes, live in communes featuring non-stop orgies, but sleep only five hours per night? Never. See L.H. Whittemore, "Sun Myung Moon: Prophet for Profit," *Parade*, May 30, 1976.
32. Pete was played by *Newsweek* in its "Life with Father Moon," June 14, 1976. Repete was *Time* in "The Darker Side of Sun Moon," June 14, 1976.
33. James Coates, "Moon Church Traced from Sex Cult," *Chicago Tribune*, March 27, 1978.
34. *Ibid.* Pak urged Fraser to call Chung from the hearing room and verify the quote. Even-handed Don Fraser declined.
35. *Ibid.*
36. See Jim Adams, "Cheers, Chants—a Retreat with the Moonies," *Minneapolis Star*, September 1, 1978; Jim Adams, "Loyalty to Moon Unites Disciples," *Minneapolis Star*, September 1, 1978, and Jim Adams, "Moon Church is Object of U.S. Scrutiny," *Minneapolis Star*, September 1, 1978.
37. Adams, "Loyalty to Moon."
38. Adams, "Moon Church is Object."
39. *Ibid.*
40. *Time*, "Sun Myung Moon's Goodwill Blitz," April 22, 1985. The boys on Sixth Avenue could not resist one more punch to the kidneys. After ridiculing church members' attempts to polish the image of their founder (who was then still in jail) with American clergymen, *Time* let a vociferous church critic have the last word—in other words the zinger. Quoting Anson Shupe of the University of Texas at Arlington: "What the Moonies do is ludicrous. Most people who go through that experience with them walk away later." *Ibid.* With *Time* the church had come full circle. From object of mirth to menace back to mirth again. All in a single decade.
41. Thomas J. Leuck and Paul A. Gigot, "Moon's Orbit: Unification Church and

Businesses Prosper Despite Controversies," *Wall Street Journal*, February 3, 1982.
42. *Ibid*. Boettcher, in fact, was the driving force behind the Fraser investigation and maintained his anti-church animus long after Fraser grew tired of the issue. Boettcher later committed suicide.
43. *Ibid*.
  44. *Ibid*. How much of this is moonshine, megalomania, or misrepresentation by the notetaker is impossible to tell. But whatever it was, it was enough to be taken seriously by the *Journal* reporters.
45. *Ibid*.
46. *Ibid*. For an account of the fishing fleet flop, see Ben A. Franklin, "Moon Church's Flotilla Strikes a Reef," *New York Times*, July 4, 1984.

XIV KOREAGATE

1. The first of the Unification Church's Korean "Family" members arrived in 1960 and settled quietly in Washington State.
2. Again, skeptics believe these figures are much exaggerated.
3. Quoted in the *Washington Post*, May 17, 1978.
4. *Korean Influence Investigation, Part I*, Hearings before the Committee on Standards of Official Conduct, House of Representatives, 95th Congress: First Session, October 19, 20, and 21, 1977 (U.S. Government Printing Office: Washington, D.C, 1977). Summary statement of Deputy Special Counsel, Peter J. White, p. 209.
5. *Ibid.*, p. 207.
6. *Ibid.*, p. 115. General Kim's testimony was translated from the Korean by Hong K. An. In the Korean language there is no definite article equivalent of "the," hence, the sometimes awkward translation.
7. *Ibid*.
8. *Ibid*.
9. Testimony of William Wurster, President, Woodward and Dickerson, Philadelphia, Pennsylvania, in *Korean Influence Investigation, Part I*, pp. 123–132.
10. *Ibid.*, p. 12.
11. See the testimony of Mrs. de la Garza and Mrs. Myers in *ibid.*, pp. 90–100.
12. Quoted from *ibid.*, p. 161.
13. *Ibid.*, p. 29.
14. President Park's letter was reprinted by the Ad Hoc Committee of Members of the Unification Church, *Our Response* (New York: January 15, 1979), p. 264.
15. *Korean Influence Investigation*, Part I, p. 29.
16. *Ibid.*, p. 166.
17. Cited in *Our Response*, pp. 13–14. The only country that did not clearly fit into one camp or the other was that non-aligned but then pro-Soviet favorite, India.
18. *Ibid.*, p. 16.
19. The Derwinski letter to Chairman Zablocki was dated February 10, 1977. It is found in *ibid.*, p. 153.
20. From *ibid.*, p. 154.
21. From *ibid*.

22. "Statement of the Honorable Edward J. Derwinski before Subcommittee of Accounts, House Administration Committee, March 2, 1977." Quoted in *ibid.*, p. 157.
23. Quoted in *ibid.*, p. 158.
24. "Committee Resolution," quoted in *ibid.*, pp. 159–160.
25. *Ibid.*, p. 160.
26. See the Final Report, p. iii, and quoted in *ibid.*, p. 7.
27. *Korean Influence Investigation*, Statement of the House Ethics Committee, John J. Flynt, p. 6.
28. *Ibid.*
29. *Ibid.*
30. "Investigation on Korean-American Relations," April 4, 1977, and quoted in *ibid.*, p. 162.
31. *Ibid.*, p. 163.
32. *Ibid.*, p. 162.
33. *Ibid.*, p. 165.
34. Quoted in a letter of Charles A. Stillman to Clement Zablocki, Chairman, Committee on International Relations, in *ibid.*, p. 177.
35. *Ibid.*, pp. 14–15.
36. The Fraser Final Report, pp. 321–322, and quoted in *ibid.*, p. 55.
37. Quoted in *ibid.*, p. 111.
38. *Ibid.*, p. 11.
39. Quoted in *ibid.*, p. 112.
40. *Ibid.*, p. 113.
41. *Ibid.*, p. 114.
42. From the Fraser Final Report, p. 334, and quoted in *ibid.*, p. 67.
43. *Ibid.*, p. 67.
44. The passage from John in the King James Version reads: "He that rejecteth me, and receiveth not my words, hath one that judgeth him: the word that I have spoken, the same shall judge him in the last day."
45. *Ibid.*, pp. 61–63.
46. *Ibid.*, pp. 63–64.
47. For the church account of the bank question see *ibid.*, pp. 105–108.
48. *Ibid.*, pp. 50–52.
49. Quoted from the Final Report, p. 360 and found in *ibid.*, pp. 95–96.
50. *Ibid.*, pp. 92–99.
51. *Ibid.*, pp. 78–79.
52. *Ibid.*, pp. 79–80.
53. *Ibid.*, pp. 82–83.
54. These points are discussed in Charles A. Stillman's memorandum to the subcommittee, and can be found in *ibid.*, pp. 178–179.
55. Fraser Final Report, p. 354. Cited in *ibid.*, p. 5.
56. Fraser Final Report, p. 389. Cited in *ibid.*
57. *Ibid.*, p. 91.
58. See the Fraser Final Report, p. 392, and cited in *ibid.*, p. 122.
59. Dr. Pak's testimony is reprinted in *Day of Hope In Review*, part III, Vol. 1, printed by the International One World Crusade (New York: 1981) p. 1152.
60. *Ibid.*, p. 1174.
61. *Ibid.*, p. 1188.
62. *Our Response*, pp. 29–30.

63. Quoted in the subcommittee report, Part 4, Hearings of March 15, 16, 21, 22, April 11, 20, and June 20, 1978, pp. 5–6, and cited in *ibid.*, p. 27.
64. Rules of the Investigation of Korean-American Relations by the Subcommittee on International Organizations of the Committee on International Relations. House of Representatives. Adopted June 7, 1977, p. 4, and cited in *ibid.*, p. 27.
65. Cited in *ibid.*, p. 28.
66. *Chicago Tribune*, March 27, 1978. See also *Our Response*, pp. 24–25.
67. Notarized statement of Nina Lopez, April 28, 1978, and in *ibid.*, pp. 139–140.
68. A copy of the flyer is reprinted in *ibid.*, p. 146.

xv   A Matter of Selective Persecution

1. See Nathaniel Hawthorne, *The Scarlet Letter* in *The Complete Novels and Selected Tales of Nathaniel Hawthorne* (New York: Modern Library, 1937), pp. 81–240.
2. Another order, the LaSalette Fathers, also got into big trouble with a high-flying investment advisor. In this case, the stockbroker was a priest, the Reverend Mr. Rene Sauve, who figured that he could beat Wall Street with a legally dubious scheme to sell stock in a failing electronics firm. He didn't. Sauve's dealings on the Boston stock exchange resulted in the loss of $20 million, collected mostly from his brother clergy, including several orders of priests and nuns and the Reno, Nevada, diocese, all of which went bankrupt. Federal law enforcement officials, including the Securities and Exchange Commission, could have prosecuted Father Sauve for numerous counts of stock fraud and securities violations but chose instead to look the other way. Father Sauve was sternly reprimanded by his superiors and then sent in exile to a posh parish on the golden shores of Cape Cod.
3. Martin A. Larson and C. Stanley Lowell, *The Religious Empire* (New York: Robert B. Luce Co., Inc., 1976) p. 257. The figures are apparently not in constant dollars. Nevertheless the growth in wealth in less than thirty years is astounding.
4. *Ibid.*, p. 179.
5. *Ibid.*, p. 180.
6. *Ibid.*, p. 182.
7. *Ibid.*, p. 184.
8. *Ibid.*, pp. 186–194.
9. *Ibid.*, pp. 197–199.
10. Nino LoBello, *Vatican, U.S.A.* (New York: Trident Press, 1972), pp. 41–42.
11. Larson and Lowell, p. 204. That is so because the U.S. tax code permits profits from church-related businesses to be exempt. Those that are not essential to the integral part of a church's mission are not. Distinguishing between the two in the real world, however, is often very difficult and a matter of judgment. And judgments differ. See LoBello, p. 88.
12. LoBello, pp. 202–203.
13. *Ibid.*, p. 119.
14. *Ibid.*, pp. 119–120.
15. The ongoing Vatican bank scandal which has rocked the church for nearly a decade illustrates a number of these points. The failure of the Milan-based Banco Ambrosiano, partly owned by the Vatican, has resulted in indictments of thirty-five employees who bilked stockholders of $1.3 billion. One of those

not indicted—to the disappointment of Italian prosecutors—was American Archbishop Paul C. Marcinkus of Cicero, Illinois. The churchman who headed the Vatican body with the responsibility to oversee the bank's operation has been extended papal protection by John Paul II. In the meantime, as Vatican auditors reconstruct what went wrong, the balance sheets remain for papal eyes only. The College of Cardinals, which has long sought to look at them, has been steadily denied access. See the *New York Times*, April 30, 1989.

XVI BIGOTRY: AN HISTORICAL VIEW

1. Bishop Kenrick's proclamation can be found in John J. Kane, *Catholic-Protestant Conflicts in America* (Chicago: Henry Regnery Company, 1955), p. 1. The bishop signed his appeal on May 12, 1844.
2. For a discussion of the Puritans and their double effect on us, see Winton U. Solberg, ed., *The Federal Convention and the Formation of the Union* (Indianapolis, Bobbs-Merrill Company, 1958), pp. lv-lvi.
3. In a curious reversal of roles, the Maryland colony was founded by George Calvert (later Lord Baltimore), his son, and his fellow Catholic gentlemen (about twenty in number), plus a band of two hundred Protestant laborers who did all the work. More important, the new colony's charter did not expressly forbid the establishment of religions other than the Church of England. That was enough for English Catholics to live and prosper in the new Maryland.
4. And yet these two would be linked. As historian Winton Solberg observed: "The free individual, voluntary association, and consent were postulates of Puritanism. New England clergymen early discussed all of the rights later asserted in the Declaration of Independence, and these ministers form the one unbroken line of descent between the political philosophy of the seventeenth century and the constituent assembly of 1787 [in Philadelphia]." See Solberg, p. lvi.
5. See *ibid.*, pp. lvi-lvii.
6. Quoted in *The Portable Thomas Jefferson*, Merrill D. Peterson, ed. (New York: The Viking Press, 1975), p. 585. Jefferson was referring to other lands—principally the struggling South American republics—but it was his view that ignorance was rooted in the wrong belief and practice of religion.
7. Quoted in *The Complete Madison: His Basic Writings*, Saul K. Padover, ed. (New York: Harper and Brothers, 1973), p. 298. Madison's mature views on the need to separate church and state were written in his "Memorial and Remonstrance against Religious Assessments, 1785," submitted to the General Assembly of the Commonwealth of Virginia and found in *ibid.*, pp. 299–306.
8. See Richard John Neuhaus, *The Naked Public Square: Religion and Democracy in America* (Grand Rapids, Michigan: William B. Eerdmans Publishing Company, 1984), pp. 99–100.
9. *James Madison, The Debates in the Federal Convention of 1787 which Framed the Constitution of the United States of America*, Gaillard Hunt and James Brown Scott, eds. (Buffalo, New York: Prometheus Books, 1987), Volume Two, p. 428.
10. *Ibid.*, p. 495.
11. Quoted in Solberg, ed., p. 370.

12. Found in *ibid.*, p. 377.
13. It was not until 1941 that Connecticut, Georgia, and Massachusetts got around to formally ratifying these first ten amendments. See *ibid.*, p. 376.
14. The Salem trials, bad as they were, have become infamous but taken out of historical context. New England of the seventeenth century was not an extraordinary example of a place afflicted with religious hysteria. Only a dozen witches had been executed before 1692—five thousand were burned to death in tiny Alsace alone in the seventeenth century. See *Eerdmans' Handbook to Christianity in America*, Mark A. Noll, et al., eds. (Grand Rapids, Michigan: William B. Eerdmans Publishing Company, 1983), p. 68.
15. Although Cotton Mather is usually blamed for the whole mess, he had deep misgivings about the events in Salem, and eventually stressed the need for scrupulously lawful procedures. His concern did not save the twenty, however. See Richard Lovelace, "The Salem Witch Trials," in *ibid.*, pp. 68–71.
16. See Leo Pfeffer, "Brief Amicus Curiae for the Institute for the Study of American Religion in Support of Petition for Certiorari," in the case of *Sun Myung Moon and Takeru Kamiyama v. United States of America*, p. 4.
17. *Eerdmans' Handbook*, pp. 46–47. In 1637 the stubborn and very brave Ann Hutchinson was driven from the Massachusetts colony after she informed the General Court of her latest revelations. After ten years of wandering with her many children, she and they (with one exception) were murdered by Indians in Westchester County, New York.
18. Pfeffer, pp. 4–5.
19. Quoted in S. Cobb, *The Rise of Religious Liberty in America* (1902), p. 177, and cited in Pfeffer, p. 6.
20. Quoted in Cobb, p. 233, and cited in Pfeffer, p. 6.
21. Pfeffer, p. 7.
22. Witness feistiness played its part in the trouble the Witnesses often found themselves in. Failing to salute the flag was finally tolerated in America (in Cuba, Witnesses are still sent to concentration camps for this offense) after the Witnesses took that one on during World War II. Another problem: Witness theology is notably anti-Catholic, a hostility that was more than reciprocated in Catholic neighborhoods where Witnesses would engage in door-to-door missionary work. When it came to trying to avoid facing Catholic jurors, insurmountable legal obstacles presented themselves. Not only could the Witness lawyers not constitutionally exclude Catholic jurors automatically, it is doubtful that a prospective juror under *voir dire* would have to respond to questions regarding his religious beliefs and practices. See *ibid.*, p. 8.
23. See *ibid.*
24. *Ibid.*, pp. 12–13.
25. Quoted in Roy Allen Billington, *The Protestant Crusade* (New York: Rinehart and Company, 1952), p. 120, and cited in Kane, p. 3. The thought that Pius VIII (1829–30) or his successor Gregory XVI (1831–46), amidst the chaos of revolutionary, post-Napoleonic Europe and shrinking Papal States to boot, had time for plots against the Mississippi Valley is ludicrous. But wide-eyed Americans believed it.
26. Cited in Billington, p. 70, and found in Kane, p. 4.
27. Quoted from Lyman Beecher, *Plea for the West* and cited in *Eerdmans' Handbook*, p. 236.

28. Quoted in Billington, p. 125, and cited in Kane, p. 11. Morse's solution was the formation of an "Anti-Popery Union."
29. Reproduced in *Eerdmans' Handbook*, p. 237.
30. Kane, p. 19.
31. *Ibid.*, p. 35. Maryland's Anglo-Catholics, the bulk of the Catholic population in America at that time, were doubly protected: by their class (which was upper) and by their state's tradition. The Catholic hierarchy at that time, however, was mostly French. In 1855 there were an estimated 3.3 million Catholics. In 1930, 14.5 million. See *Eerdmans' Handbook*, p. 355.
32. Why did they come here and not somewhere else? First, travel was cheaper from Sligo to the U.S. East Coast—cheaper than to Canada and far cheaper than to Australia. Second, travel conditions were better on American ships. Third, the Irish community established earlier in the U.S. sent passage money back home to their relatives. Remittances in 1851 alone totalled nearly a million pounds sterling. Fourth, wages were higher in the United States: even unskilled laborers could get fifty cents a day—sometimes a dollar— more than twice the going rate in Ireland when there was employment. Kane, p. 36. Also p. 127.
33. Why didn't they go West where the prairie was opening? Too poor and ignorant are two reasons. The most important factor was that the Catholic hierarchy discouraged any thoughts of moving West in fear that their flock would lose their religion or, worse yet, that the well-heeled city churches would lose parishioners and donations. In short, some of the Irish misery was brought on by their own religious leaders who exploited them. See *ibid.*, p. 36.
34. *Ibid.*, pp. 36–37.
35. The Democrats' motive, of course, was hardly altruistic. They were looking for voters, and they got them—right away—by arranging to have false naturalization papers written—Cradles of Liberty, they were called. In exchange, Irish ward heelers rounded up their countrymen on voting day to endorse the whole ticket. See *ibid.*, p. 37.
36. *Ibid.*, p. 126. For the quote from the Know-Nothing world view see Anson P. Stokes and Leo Pfeffer, *Church and State in the United States* (New York: Harper and Row, 1964), p. 236.
37. Kane, pp. 128–129.
38. *Ibid.*, p. 41. Except the Lutherans. These stubborn German and Scandinavian immigrants arrived at about the same time as the Irish. Like the Irish, they were locked into their own culture and religion. Schools were founded to protect the children from the English-speaking world and to teach pure Lutheranism; that is, the original Reformation movement, and not some adulterated "Protestant" product with its Calvinist or Arminian errors shot throughout. The schools could also preserve the native tongue: German, Swedish, Norwegian. Unlike the Irish most of these Lutherans were farmers, leaving them less exposed to the prejudices of local native Americans, or to hostile urban mobs. Only in World War I were German Lutherans to get a taste of what the Irish had experienced in America.
39. *Ibid.*, pp. 107–108. See also Rockne McCarthy, "Protestants and the Parochial School," in *Eerdmans' Handbook*, pp. 298–299. McCarthy adds: "Protestants were in the majority and they took advantage of the fact to make policy by legally defining such terms as sectarian and nonsectarian education and

public and private schools in a self-serving way. The result was the creation of a public school system where everyone's taxes were used to support schools which reinforced the world view of the majority."

40. Kane, pp. 40–41.
41. *Ibid.*, p. 115.
42. *Ibid.*, pp. 115–116.
43. *Ibid.*, p. 43.
44. *Ibid.*, p. 116.
45. Quoted in *Eerdmans' Handbook*, p. 414.
46. Kane, pp. 135–136. On the other hand, Bishop Cannon also praised candidate Hoover for segregating the races at the Department of Commerce. *Ibid.*, p. 137.
47. *Ibid.*, p. 136.
48. *Ibid.*
49. *New Republic*, Vol. L, p. 315, and quoted in Kane, p. 31.

APPENDIX

1. *United States v. Kuch*, 288 F. Supp. 439 (D.C. 1968), and cited in S.L. Snyder, "Memorandum of Law for Assistant Attorney General Ferguson," U.S. Department of Justice, Washington, D.C., November 26, 1979, p. 11.
2. *Ibid.*, p. 21.
3. *Ibid.*, pp. 21–22.
4. Quoted in *ibid.*, p. 22.
5. See *Teterud v. Burns* 522 F. 2d 357 (C.A. 8, 1975), and cited in Snyder, p. 22.
6. *Ibid.*
7. *Ibid.*
8. *Ibid.*
9. *Ibid.*, p. 23.
10. *Ibid.*

INDEX